The Total GERMAN SHEPHERD DOG

The Total GERMAN SHEPHERD DOG

Fred L. Lanting

Alpine Publications Inc.
214 S.E. 19th St., Loveland, CO 80537

The Total German Shepherd Dog

Copyright © 1990 by Fred L. Lanting

Library of Congress Cataloging-in-Publication Data

Lanting, Fred L., 1936-
    The Total German Shepherd Dog/Fred L. Lanting
      p. 386 cm.
    ISBN 0-931866-43-X
    1. German shepherd dogs.   I. Title.
SF429.G37L36 1990
636.7'37—dc20   89-18386
                                            CIP

Printed in the United States of America

DEDICATION

This work is dedicated to the memory of all men (and women) with fire in their bellies, but especially to three worthy heroes. To men who knew (and those who now know) that to take off and soar among the eagles, one must fly into the wind, not with or away from it.

To Max von Stephanitz, whose love of the species and the breed, coupled with an insatiable curiosity, and then combined with a desire to share what he had learned, gave the world a wealth of knowledge. He understood dogs, and they understood him.

To Billy Mitchell, the father of military aviation. He was a man of vision, seeing truth that was beyond the sight and imagination of his colleagues. Time proved him right, and the majority (as it usually happens) to be wrong.

To Rudyard Kipling, who also observed much of the physical world but saw further than most. A man among men, known for his humor and immense literary talent.

All three had strength of character, conviction, and courage, virtues I admire and desire. All three died the year I was born, and while I don't want to sound superstitious, I feel the weight of at least a few threads of their mantles upon my shoulders. I claim an inheritance of sorts because they represented ideals that I hold dear, and they said and did many things I have seen unwitting mimicry of in my life.

CONTENTS

FOREWORD

I have known and admired Fred Lanting for many years. I am impressed by his tireless effort to *find out* as much as possible about the German Shepherd and to *speak up* on its behalf. He is also an excellent writer.

With this book, the author has exceeded even the high expectations I had of him. Much research added to his own experience has enabled him to put together the most current and complete book on the German Shepherd Dog. It will appeal not only to breed fanciers but to all dog lovers. He gives the reader a historically accurate and updated picture of the breed and presents its metamorphosis in the U.S. He has especially impressed me with his correct, unbiased presentation of the German lines. Naturally, I applaud his goal, which mirrors my own, to help return the German Shepherd Dog in America to equal status with the breed in other countries.

Fred has studied the German Shepherd in Germany and elsewhere, judging it in Japan as well as in the U.S. and Canada. He has been particularly enamored of some of the great Shepherds of the 1960s, including my German and World Sieger and U.S. Champion Bodo vom Lierberg (Schutzhund-3, FH, ROM). He has trained several Shepherds to obedience titles, owned Schutzhund-trained dogs, and has been instrumental in establishing obedience trial rules for the SKC. He has been an officer and member of noteworthy dog and kennel clubs, including the Shaferhund Verein (SV) and the Japan Kennel Club. He was chairman of the Orthopedics Committee of the GSD Club of America, Inc.

With a Bachelor of Science degree in chemistry and minors in English and physics, Fred has written a wide variety of columns, articles and essays for the dog-owning public. His acquaintance with veterinary specialists and practitioners complements his extensive personal observations as both breeder and student.

I know that his book will be read and re-read for many years to come; it should be part of any personal library on the canine.

Erich Renner

PREFACE

Among other things, a preface is supposed to tell why a book was written, but authors traditionally sneak in a few tidbits they want to share with readers but which don't seem to fit in the main body of the work.

It probably began with my first German Shepherd Dog in 1947. Lance was both enormous and beautiful and had all the characteristics one could hope for in the breed. He gave me a love and admiration for his race that has never diminished. In the mid 1960s, I finally acquired the land to raise dogs seriously, and eventually became an AKC licensed professional handler. This multiplied my contacts with and study of the German Shepherd Dog.

I started on the breed book with bits and pieces in the 1970s, then stopped to expand one chapter on hip dysplasia into a book on orthopedic disorders which was published by Alpine in 1981. After the HD book was well on its way, I returned to the GSD breed book. The work took an extra six years to gestate; meanwhile, I was privileged to judge the breed at innumerable specialty and all-breed shows, and watch the German Shepherd Dog under other circumstances.

Like the mountain which is climbed simply because it is there, this book wrote itself because it already existed in my mind and needed to get out. I had no choice!

ACKNOWLEDGEMENTS

I am grateful to the people of the breed who lent precious photographs and answered various inquiries, to the people of the sport who taught me about other breeds, and to the people of the veterinary profession who let me wander through their operating rooms and libraries.

While this book was a one-man effort, it could not have had any depth at all without the many enrichments afforded by others. I listened and discoursed; the interplay of ideas and exchange of experiences became this book.

Above all, I give God the glory and thank Him.

INTRODUCTION

While the title of this book indicates that the main subject is the German Shepherd Dog, the book is also about the canine in general and should be useful to fanciers of other breeds. More than half of the chapters would be at home in a book on another breed, and much of each of the remaining chapters would likewise apply.

Detailed instruction on obedience training would have added too many pages on a subject that is better covered by other authors. The Appendix will lead you to such books and more. Much more could have been said on diseases of the German Shepherd Dog, immunology, and other topics, and a great number of personal anecdotes and illustrations have likewise been omitted for the purpose of producing a book of manageable size.

What are the goals of this book, when there are already several others concerned with the breed? The first goal is to inform, educate, and entertain from a fresh perspective. The second is to help, to give practical assistance in dealing with the dog's needs in training, care, and breeding. Obviously, I wanted to share my own experience and knowledge, some of which may be unique. I have double checked the structures of living dogs, examined slow-motion films of dogs gaiting, performed artificial insemination, and learned just about every medical procedure I've described, including assisting in surgery. Training tips have also come from personal experience, not textbooks alone.

I rejoice in these blessings God has given me and in the opportunity to share some of them with you.

HISTORY AND ORIGINS OF THE BREED

NATURAL HISTORY

While the American and Canadian Kennel Clubs recognize some 130 dog breeds, adding a few every several years, worldwide there are about 500 distinct breeds of domesticated dogs varying greatly from the tiny Chihuahua to the massive Saint Bernard. Genetic plasticity is not as apparent in the domesticated dog's cousins, that have been molded more by nature than by human whim. Where did all these breeds and varieties come from?

All dogs—wild or domesticated—have devolved from a common ancestor, but I assume that Noah's dog looked more like a wolf than a bulldog. (I prefer the use of the word *devolve* rather than *evolve* because the latter often has an implication of upward change—from simple to more complex—while just the opposite is true in nature.)

The dog's original progenitor had all the genes present in modern canids (barring any rare true mutants which may have survived), but today's canids do *not* have all the genes possessed by those original animals. Some have been lost to subspecies in the devolution of the dog family through the ages. Take color, for example. Within Canis familiaris the merle factor, which gene has been identified and located on a specific place on a chromosome, is now found only in certain breeds and varieties. The same is true with other color patterns such as ticking, and with many other physical qualities presumably owned by the original canine pair.

No fancier with a pen and notebook was around to witness devolutionary changes between Creation and the Flood, and later observers apparently were not inclined to record the changes within species of plants and animals until relatively recent days, so most of what we now know about the early dog we have deduced both from fossil records and extant life. Perhaps because of the sketchiness of early evidence, taxonomists and other scientists involved in the various disciplines within natural history differ slightly in their classifications of dog types. Zeuner believed present types descended from the original canid through these ancient breed groupings: (1) *Canis familiaris inostranzewi*—wolves and arctic breeds; (2) *C. familiaris palustris* and *C. familiaris spolleti*—toys and spitz types; (3) *C. familiaris poutiantini*—wolf-dingo types. Another classification preferred by many is: (1) *C. familiaris matris-optimae* (Latin for *best mother*)—herding breeds; (2) *C. familiaris intermedius*—many hunting, toy, and working breeds; (3) *C. familiaris laineri*—terriers and cursorial dogs (sighthounds, for example); and (4) *C. familiaris inostranzewi*—the mastiff group and some water dogs.

Richard and Alice Fiennes classify modern dogs into another four major categories, noting the wild-dog or wolf type they each most resemble: (1) *Canis lupus*, the Northern or Gray Wolf—German Shepherd Dog, Corgis, Collie, and probably most of the spitz types, sheepdogs, and terriers; (2) *C. lupus pallipes*, a pale-footed Asian wolf now extinct—probably gave rise to the dingo group which includes the Australian Cattle Dog and, in part, the Basenji; (3) *C. lupus arabs*, a subspecies with racing ability—the Greyhound group; (4) *C. lupus chanco*, also called *C. lupus laniger*, commonly known as the

Tibetan wolf—the mastiff group, scenthounds and gun dogs.

As ancient dogs and wolves wandered and spread over the continents, they were shaped by various environments and, in most cases, natural boundaries and pack territories allowed groups of dogs to change in relative isolation from other packs. Isolation on the Australian continent has allowed the dingo to remain pretty much unchanged from the days in which its human wards brought it there in canoes possibly in the last Pleistocene era, about a million years ago, according to some estimates.

The Eastern Timber wolf is an endangered species as are most wolves. Does he look like any Malamutes you have known? Photo by L.D. Mech, U.S. Fish & Wildlife Service

Even a Greyhound is no match for the coyote. This is a good seasonal coat. The coyote rarely interbreeds with either wolf or domestic dog cousins, preferring its own pack members.   Photo by E.P. Haddon, U.S. Fish & Wildlife Service.

MAN MEETS DOG—EARLY DEVELOPMENT

Scavenger dog undoubtedly learned that man was an efficient hunter and an easy source of food. In turn, man found he could train dogs to help in herding, hunting, and for protection. Characteristics were gradually selected which gave rise to hounds and control dogs, including protective and herding types. Both of the latter were incorporated into the forerunners of the German Shepherd Dog two or three thousand years before von Stephanitz, the developer of the breed, in the nineteenth and twentieth centuries. Nehring and others have given evidence of *C. familiaris decumanus* in use as a companion and coworker about 2500 B.C. This variety was a link between *C. familiaris inostranzewi* and the herdsman's dog called *Rude* by the old Germans. In fact, as early as 60 A.D. the Roman writer Columella drew a distinction between the heavy yard and perimeter guard dogs and the fast-moving dogs that worked cattle and sheep. Petrus in 1494 A.D. advocated the farmer keep three types of dogs: watchdogs, herd protectors, and hunting dogs.

In the Middle Ages, dogs accompanying the keepers of livestock were of various size and appearance, but most were fairly large, usually rough-coated, and with hanging or lopped ears. As sheepherding grew in organization, specialization of the *Rude's* skills became desirable. The large, powerful dogs of mastiff type remained as sentries and fearsome protectors of the yard and the flock, while the lithe trotting dogs with herding instincts were selected for more training along *those* lines.

Descendants of *C. familiaris poutiatini* probably contributed (through the Bronze-Age dog, the dingo, and the Serbian type) smooth-coated and smooth-moving dogs that we would recognize as being very similar to the modern German Shepherd Dog. But there occurred some interbreeding of these with the large, shaggy descendants of *C. familiaris inostranzewi*. Thus, even as more and more land was put into cultivation by growing human populations, thereby increasing the need for dogs that could keep the flocks together, the two types continued to cross paths and chromosomes.

The dingo-sized *C. familiaris matris-optimae* lacked the size and strength to satisfy the shepherds of the Bronze Age. Three alternatives must have been open to them: They could try to train larger breeds to herd as well as protect, they could cross the small

with the large and hope for an intermediate-size dog with the best qualities of each, or they could bring in wolf "blood." All three tactics have continued up to the present era and were being employed during the time the German Shepherd Dog breed was being refined at the end of the nineteenth century.

By the time the term *Rude* was coined (in the thirteenth century), breeds further specialized into dogs for hunting wild boar, and dogs for herding sheep and other domesticated stock. The protective dogs that were also used in swine hunting were sometimes called sheep dogs, but never shepherd dogs, the latter term being reserved for dogs that kept the flocks from wandering into the tilled fields en route to other destinations. As European civilization progressed, the need for the heavy herdsman's dog diminished and that for the driving and tending dogs increased.

Around the end of the seventeenth century in Germany, pasture land had become progressively more rare, in contrast to the burgeoning of tilled land. The bear had been pushed back to Poland and other distant reaches. The necessity of protecting flocks from wild beasts was largely a thing of the past, and so was the *Rude* in most of Germany. The need for large shaggy-coated protectors continued only in the colder elevations, and the "Old German" type of dog performed the dual service of tending and guarding flocks in the upland areas. From Wurtemberg and Upper Bavaria in the South came characteristics we see in many of our modern German Shepherd Dogs: heavier bone, longer coat (sometimes shaggy, sometimes curly), ears semi-erect, and mild temperament. In the northern, central and western parts of Germany, the ancestral type similar to the Gray Wolf remained and contributed its characteristics to the breed: sharpness (related to wolf shyness), light frame, shorter coat, and perhaps a longer stride in relation to its height. Both heritages are obvious in the breed today, though one might expect the regional differences to have been wiped out in more than a century of mixing. This is evidence that characteristics are often inherited in "bundles."

When shepherds looked for the lighter-weight driving/herding dogs, they selected for the same type as had previously been dispersed over most of Europe, known as the Bronze-Age dog or *C. familiaris matris-optimae*. We know this from the skulls

Ch. Kountry Music of Billo, ROM working cattle on the ranch, 1982. Note his excellent gait, which highlights von Stephanitz' emphasis on utility being the measure of beauty.
Photo courtesy Bill & Lois Greene.

and other remains of these dogs, which compare closely with the structure of modern shepherd-type dogs, including the German Shepherd Dog. The shepherds went full circle back to the original shepherd dog, giving us some claim to at least a 1600 year history for the German Shepherd Dog and similar breeds.

The best workers were developed in those areas with the most land under cultivation. The inherited nature of the shepherd dog in patrolling the perimeter of the flock while moving or grazing was put to many related uses. The early yard dog, the *Hovawart*, knew his master's property and generally kept within its borders, warning of the approach of strangers. This ability was transmitted to the shepherd dog in such intensity that these dogs were purchased by many nonshepherds. City dwellers valued the territory awareness as well as the protectiveness. In later years, police found these dogs of value in their work, and in World War I many were used to carry messages and medical supplies to and from the front. Albertus Magnus, who died in 1280 A.D., mentioned the use of the yard dog of his time in tracking thieves, so we see that police work by the German Shepherd Dog's similar ancestor goes back at least 700 years. This dog was also known as a "wolf dog," a term that later was applied especially to the modern German Shepherd.

DEVELOPMENT OF THE MODERN TYPE

Around 1890 an alliance of shepherd dog fanciers, the *Phylax*, was formed. It fell to internecine

squabbling because too much emphasis was placed on beautiful rather than useful dogs. Out of the ashes of this attempt, one man with great authority and vision rose to inspire followers. This man, an officer in Bismarck's cavalry, had great knowledge of, and an innate feel for animals, as well as mastery of organizational skills. He was Captain Max von Stephanitz, who, with Artur Meyer and others, founded the parent club of the breed, the *Verein für Deutsche Shäferhunde* (SV) on April 22, 1899.

By this time, two specific types of shepherd dog had developed. In the central German state of Thuringia, many dogs of a wolf gray color with erect ears were bred to meet a growing demand. This color was probably similar to the sables we see today, both the gray and tan hues. Many of these Thuringian dogs had a high-set curled tail, many were small, wiry, coarse, and stocky. They were generally vivacious and vigorous, in contrast to the dogs of Wurtemberg which had better hindquarters, size, and gait. The best of these two types were purchased by breeders in the North, and the overall quality there improved by this combination of bloodlines.

Foundation Dogs—The First Quarter-Century

Though the German Shepherd Dog's roots went much farther back than the formation of the SV, the breed was refined under the firm and capable leadership of von Stephanitz from the 1890s to World War I. During this time, a few major strains were developed, three of them built on Pollux and his Thuringian background: the Horand/Dewet line, the Horand/Beowulf line, and the Horand/Starkenburg line. A fourth brought in Swabian bloodlines, and some from the Krone kennel.

Horand—Near Frankfort, in the town of Hanau, a breeder named Wachsmuth was known as one of the best. A Mr. Sparwasser, who was partial to the show type, bought his first pair of shepherds from Wachsmuth and from them bred a dog called Hektor Linksrhein. After passing through the hands of a couple of owners, the dog was procurred by von Stephanitz, renamed Horand von Grafrath (Grafrath was von Stephanitz's kennel name) and given the SV registration number SZ-1. Horand was considered very large at twenty-four inches at the shoulders, and his personality of unbounded joy and energy was the epitome of the Thuringian type. Horand was fearless, alert, active, tolerant of harmless people, and crazy about children, and he passed his traits to his offspring. His genetic value had been proven by the time von Stephanitz acquired him.

Roland—A dog many German Shepherd Dog fanciers like to call attention to as the first solid black German Shepherd Dog is Roland von Starkenburg. One pair of writers called him a mutant, but this is not accurate, as there had been plenty of black dogs and black wolves prior to Roland. His color was simply a matter of inheriting black and bi-color genes from each parent. Roland was an ideal blend of the southern (Wurttemberg) and north-central (Thuringia) lines. He probably is in the pedigree of every present—and therefore every future—German Shepherd Dog in the world. His son Hettel was Sieger in 1909, his grandson Tell v d Kriminalpolizei was Sieger* in 1910, and Tell's sister Flora was Siegerin the same year. Roland himself won the title in 1906 and 1907.

Others—A much used, important stud in the early days was the sable Thuringian dog, Dewet Barbarossa. Closely related was Geraf Eberhard Hohen-Esp, sire of the 1908 Sieger Luchs v. Kalsmunt, who in turn sired the 1910 winners. From the Horand-Dewet line also came a dog von Stephanitz called "remarkable," the first (in 1906) to hold the title of Field Trial "Champion," (Sieger), Siegfried v. Jena-Paradies. Siegfried was smaller in build to the modern American style, and a little longer in body than most of his peers.

Sieger: literally "winner." Used most frequently to refer to the top dog of the year, i.e. there is a herding Sieger, Schutzhund Sieger, etc., as well as a conformation Sieger. Feminine: Siegerin.

1906-07 Sieger Roland v. Starkenburg.

Hektor Linksrhein (Horand v. Grafrath), the first SV-registered dog.

IN THE EARLY DAYS OF THE BREED

Rough or Wire-Coated German Shepherd Dog from Wurtemberg.

Max von Stephanitz
"He cannot be a gentleman which loveth not a dog."
John Northbrook

Blue Merle German Shepherd Dog from Wurtemberg.

F.D.R. with his German Shepherd Dog
at Campobello.

Beowulf—A daughter of Horand was bred to Hektor and produced one of the true cornerstones of the breed, Wolf, later renamed Beowulf and given the registration number SZ-10. Most of the good qualities we see today have been attributed to the line-up of Pollux/Horand/Beowulf. The "Beowulf flecking gene" may have been inherited by the 1904 Siegerin, Regina v Schwaben, as she was sired by Beowulf and whelped by Elsa v Schwaben, the 1901 Siegerin. Beowulf produced many excellent bitches through whom his greatest contributions were passed to posterity; these included the 1902/03, 1905, and 1906 Siegerins. The first of these was the dam of Siegfried and the 1909 Siegerin. All were closely linebred on Horand.

Audifax—Around 1900 von Stephanitz saw the need for adding "fresh blood" to his lines and introduced his latest acquisition, a big, strong male of Swabian stock, Audifax v Grafrath, SZ-368.

Swabia, a region in southern Germany, was comprised of Baden-Wurttemberg and Bavaria.

Beowulf (SZ-10)

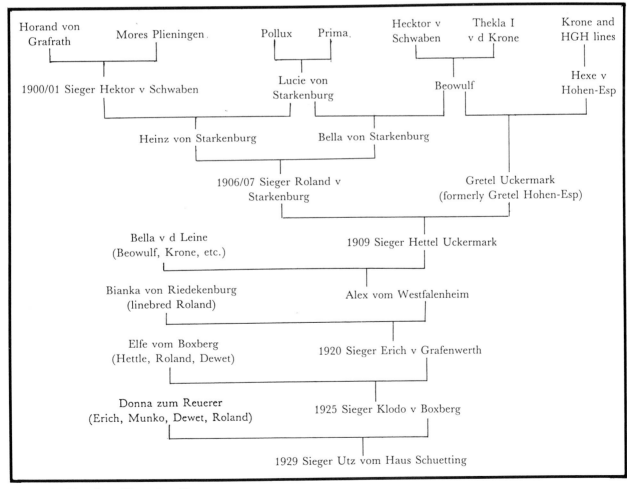

Fig. 1 The Line from Horand to Utz.

Audifax was known for his very strong back and excellent gait, as well as his head, which was proportionately larger than those of most other dogs in his day. He sired the 1904 Sieger Aribert v Grafrath.

Early German Shepherd Dogs in Service

The ancestor known as *Hovawart* followed in the guard work footsteps of his own antecedent, the Bronze-Age dog, but even before that many writers as far back as Sophocles, between 500 and 400 B.C., spoke of dogs used to track thieves. So it was natural for the utility of the German Shepherd Dog to be demonstrated in police and military work. In 1901 the SV had arranged trials with the Belgian police, and before long police all over central Europe were raising and training dogs. Not a few of these were German Shepherd Dogs.

The police or service dog, able to track criminals, find lost children, alert the policeman to unconscious drunks in the dark, and do dozens of other tasks, was naturally suited for war duties. Suspicion, alertness, energy, speed, devotion, intelligence—all these and more were apparent in such service. The SV, urged by von Stephanitz and other leaders, gave help and guidance in this area, but it was the German Shepherd Dog itself that was most responsible for the service-dog movement. During World War I there were about 28,000 dogs used on the German side alone, many of them German Shepherd Dogs. They were primarily dispatch dogs, transport dogs to carry ammunition and rations to the front, and ambulance dogs to seek out wounded.

Those qualities that made the breed so well adapted to service as sheep herder, flock protector, home guardian, babysitter, and police and war dog, have prepared the German Shepherd Dog for nearly any work and association with humans. The Ambulance Dog Association in Germany, for example, directed its considerable resources after World War I to training dogs as guides for the blind. This lifted the blind person's dog (usually a Poodle) from the status of beggar's assistant, to valuable worker. It also opened a world of freedom and independence to veterans who otherwise might have been doomed to degrading existences.

One exceptional story of service during the First World War is that of Romeo v Schlossgarten

SZ-23781, PDH, SH. Born in 1908, this dog worked as a railway guard for a police department, and transferred to the military as an ambulance dog in 1914. He served on many fronts, saved dozens of lives, and was wounded himself, but survived to re-enter his first occupation with his handler, that of railway official. Many dogs distinguished themselves in such cases, but what made Romeo remarkable in addition to his work in those prevaccine, prewormer days was the fact that he lived to be twenty years old!

The Second Quarter-Century

Many of the dogs highlighted in this book are show dogs because these figure most prominently in pedigrees. But the origin and development of the breed are based on the central quality of *utility*, and we must not forget that most of the early Siegers and Siegerins earned their titles in competition designed to demonstrate their abilities, and many were working shepherd or service dogs. The German Shepherd Dog, with the the guidance of the SV, distinguished itself as a true working breed in the nineteenth century, and continued to be so in the twentieth, even though sheepherding diminished and different tasks developed.

At the same time, the German Shepherd Dog was becoming extremely popular as a companion or pet in the cities as well as in the country. However, as always happens when a breed rises quickly in popularity and thus occurs in greater numbers, the average quality seemed to slip as more and more unsuitable dogs were allowed to procreate. Before and during the First World War, the SV members did not pay special attention to faults because nobody had the foresight to realize what damage could—and would—be done by amateurs indiscriminately breeding unworthy animals. Breed warnings became, in the postwar years, a way to improve and correct the breed, though they were not always heeded in the beginning.

Constant attention to working ability and structure in the 1920s and early 1930s gave the breed many beautiful, sound winners in both areas of competition. Titles such as ZPr (*Zuchtpruefung*, roughly comparable to our CDX degree); PH (advanced guard or police dog); and SchH (*Schutzhund*, basic guard and protection dog) became as common as had the HGH (herding) and SuchH (tracking) suffixes in the previous era. The 1920 Sieger Erich von Grafenwerth PH was an excellent example of a well-built dog with great courage and trainability, characteristics he passed along to his descendants. His son Klodo v Boxberg won the Sieger title in 1925 and Klodo's son Utz v Haus Schuetting ZPr earned it in 1929. Klodo, and to a slightly lesser extent, Erich and Utz, were longer than most of their competition. However, some readers and commentators go overboard in implying Klodo was almost a mutant in this regard but Sieger Norbert, Sieger Siegfried, and others were long dogs of the same general build, and many a later dog was even longer.

Between the shows at which Klodo and Utz were chosen as typifying the desirable build and character of the breed, Erich v Glockenbrink SchH was awarded the top title in 1926 and again in 1928. This Erich was of a quite different type than the 1925 and 1929 winners, being more square than they, yet not as square as today's Belgian and other sheepdogs. His smaller prosternum and shorter body gave an impression of legginess. He appar-

ently didn't produce as well as the other two, so the return to the Utz type came about.

Utz was whelped in 1926 by a sable bitch, somewhat faded in color, of excellent structure and producing ability. She was linebred on Roland and Munko v Boll, but also carried lines to Erich v Grafenwerth, Dewet, and Audifax. In today's American show ring, Utz would look small, measuring 24 inches at the withers, 28-3/4 inches from forechest to "buttocks bone", and weighing 72 pounds. But this was a good medium size in those days. The bigger dogs of Swabian type often brought with them poor gait and lack of speed and agility.

The German Shepherd Dog had grown in popularity in many parts of the world in the prewar days, but rocketed to universal fame and commerce after World War I. Eager buyers drove prices up and German breeders easily found markets for even their poor-quality dogs. (Sounds like today, doesn't it?) Among the better ones shipped to the US was Utz. One of Klodo's grandsons named Odin v Stolzenfels ZPr was Sieger in 1933 and was then sold to owners in Japan, where he earned the title of Japan Sieger in 1935.

The most versatile breed.

1925 Sieger Klodo v. Boxberg.

The Influence of the Second World War

The dark shadow of World War II fell on man and dog even before hostilities became widespread. National socialism promised glory, an end to inflation, and equality (for Aryans), but delivered persecution, and ever-tightening control, and the death of freedom for most of Germany's citizens. Normal life became difficult. Dog shows suddenly declined in national importance, and concurrent with the nation's focus on a military buildup, Nazi leaders devised ways of confiscating the dogs of private citizens in case they ran out of "volunteers" supplied by Schutzhund and other activities.

About the time Germany got deeper into its own brand of imperialism, the Sieger title was dropped for a while, due to the feeling of some that too much emphasis was placed on the number one dog instead of on a group of select animals. Also, the disruption following the invasion of Poland in 1939 had to have had a bad effect on the total numbers and quality at the shows. Yet the Germans did not desert their favorite breed entirely.

Due to the anti-German sentiment in England, the dog Americans first knew as "Shepherd Dog" was originally registered as "foreign sheepdog" in England before World War I. Later the British looked for a name that would not inflame the populace or detract from the acceptance of the breed. They noted that the French called it *Chien de Berger Allemand*, later *Chien de Berger d'Alsace*, after a French province on the border with Germany. The newly

formed club in Britain in 1919 chose to call it the Alsatian Wolf-dog. In 1924 a new club known as the Alsatian League joined with the Wolf-dog Club. In 1936, shortly after Hitler came to power, the British, still bearing an anti-German grudge, named the dog *Alsatian (German Shepherd Dog)*. At least they retained the true name in parentheses. Even today we find some Americans confused about the differences between police dogs, Shepherds, and Alsatians. Some think the Alsatian is a white German Shepherd Dog, though this is without basis and has very little support even among breeders of whites. In the 1970s the British finally decided to call the dog by its legitimate name, as the Americans had done since the 1930s—the German Shepherd Dog.

Returning American servicemen brought with them the stories of the noble, intelligent, heroic dog they encountered during "The Big War," much as their World War I doughboy counterparts had done a quarter of a century earlier. They also brought home a few specimens of the breed, unfortunately not good ones. The film industry was quick to latch onto another good thing, and what had been good for Strongheart before the war became even better for Rin-Tin-Tin afterward. The German Shepherd again became America's idol, and almost everybody wanted one. The market was easily supplied by quick-acting hustlers who bred anything and everything that had prick ears and a bushy tail, and called the pups German Shepherds. Some considerable number of Germans who still had dogs but little else got in on the game too, and imports became big business after the smoke of war had cleared. The general quality of the breed was hurt and its image tarnished by the overabundance of sharp-shy, small, faded, and generally poorly built examples found in thousands of American homes.

Yet the serious breeder and competitor did not flee from the scene. The United States National Specialty Show was held throughout the war years, and the VA Group (equivalent to the Siegerschau but without the naming of Sieger or Siegerin as such) was held in Germany in 1938, 1941, and 1942. The German shows resumed in 1946 and 1947 and were doubled in number, one show each year being held in both the British-occupied and American-occupied zones. In 1948 things began to return to normal, and in 1955 the Sieger title was resumed.

A list of German (actually World) Siegers and Siergerins is given in chapter 7, with a description of leading individuals for the years in which the titles were not awarded.

ANCIENT CUSTOMS SURVIVE

Archeologists, in examining the refuse heaps of primitive North European peoples, have found dog and wolf bones only very rarely, an indicaton that they were buried elsewhere or not buried at all. Fox bones, on the other hand, some of them split open to extract marrow, are evidence that these animals were eaten quite regularly. This evidence points to recognition of the dog's usefulness other than as a meal, and possibly is a result of a belief that the dog had supernatural powers to sense and warn of spirits undetected by humans.

However, at one time or another, all over the world, the dog has found his way into the human belly. Even today's dog flesh is considered a delicacy. A large number of trained service dogs left poorly guarded during the recent war in Indochina were stolen and eaten by Vietnamese who euphemistically call it "fragrant meat." In 1980, in one of America's western states, police were called to investigate a complaint that a Samoan family was preparing to consume a large shaggy dog which neighbors earlier that morning had seen playing with the immigrants' children. When the police arrived, they found the dog's carcass hanging from the eaves of the house, and the islanders dressing it out. In spite of the horror it brought to others, it was not an act punishable in the courts since there was no law prohibiting the eating of dogs, and no evidence the animal had been inhumanely killed.

A Basenji-like dog, probably of mixed dingo-spitz heritage is native to the islands between Australia and China, varying slightly in breed characteristics from the Philippines to Indonesia. The cannibal Batta tribe of western and central Sumatra had welcomed this dog as a companion, watch dog, hunting partner, mouser, and when fattened up a bit, as a meal.

Von Stephanitz reported that at the dog-flesh market on Samosir Island, Sumatra, the preferred meat is that of black dogs having a black palate. I wonder if there is any connection between that preference and the false belief among some people in the United States that the best German Shepherds have black palates? I have even heard these "experts" claim that the way one can tell if a dog is "a purebred" dog is to look at the roof of his mouth! Most, but by no means all, dark-pigmented Shepherds (and other breeds) have very dark palates.

The German Shepherd Dog in Stamps

2

MODERN BLOODLINES

In the war years and shortly afterwards, the appearance of German Shepherd Dogs around the world reflected regional breeding trends and isolational forces. We often speak of the ''German look'' or the ''American look,'' and while there should not be any great differences between German Shepherd Dogs around the world, there are minor distinctions within the Standards. In the United States, some of these differences are largely due to little or no attention to training and an overemphasis on prettiness and a fast-trot side view of the moving dog.

Uniformity of judging and the practice of outcrossing results in less variation dog-to-dog in Germany than elsewhere, especially in America. German males tend to be more masculine in head appearance, though they are slighter in body build than many United States dogs. Temperament in both sexes is generally better than in the United States and Britain, though much is a result of the training nearly every German dog undergoes. On the other hand, many German winners and exports have less than pleasing toplines and proportions.

Some British dogs are generally longer in body, lighter in color, full of coat, and more angulated at the stifle/hock area than the average German or American dog. Much of this stems from a couple of widely used studs such as Avon Prince, and much of its persistence is due to the isolation imposed by the inconvenient 6-month quarantine which has served well to keep rabies out of the British Isles, but has also kept out some genetic interchange. Males are often a little too bitchy in head and body,

though bitches are feminine and pretty. Many are pinched at the elbows and turned out at the feet. Thanks largely to Bernd v Lierberg and Busecker-Schloss genes, pigment and working-dog qualities have improved since the mid-1960s. Other German lines were introduced into England, but as was the case with Odin v Busecker-Schloss in America, the genes were ''lost'' by spreading them out among large numbers of unrelated bitches. Had there been more linebreeding on the imports, the face of the breed in Britain would have been somewhat different over the past decades. Today the German-style dogs outnumber the old Alsatian-style ones, and only the United States remains mostly out of fashion, in regards to appearance, with the rest of the world.

A dichotomy exists in America, with one growing group based on recent German imports because of the advantages, real or fancied, for Schutzhund work. The other group is largely made up of show types, a great many of which are lacking in such qualities as good health, longevity, and tough, stable temperament. Deficiency in secondary sex characteristics (doggy bitches and, more common, bitchy dogs) exists in most show lines, as do relatively inadequate front assembly and weakness in the rear. Rear Angulation is more severe than is seen in the average German dog, and its handmaiden, Loose Hocks, is also brassy and audacious. Pigment spans the spectrum, with faded color seldom penalized. Poor feet and pasterns are common in some popular lines. Nevertheless, there is much more variation in America, thus more to choose from, than in Britain or Germany.

THE BREED IN AMERICA

The first two decades of the German Shepherd Dog in the United States were almost totally dominated by imports. By the time of our involvement in World War II, some American-bred bitches were being bred to recent German imports such as Utz v Haus Schuetting, Pfeffer v Bern and his half-brother Odin v Busecker-Schloss. Marie Leary's Cosalta Kennel was among the first with high-quality show winners in the late 1930s, though many less famous bitches were bred in the 1920s to both German and American males. Utz did as much to revolutionize type in the US in the 1930s as did Klodo in Germany in the late 1920s. Had Utz remained in Europe with Klodo, a different type probably would have emerged in Germany during and after World War II. Dewet v Starrenburg, Erich v Grafenwerth, Klodo, Utz, Pfeffer, Odin, Geri v Oberklamm, Cito Bergerslust, and others all came to the United States in exchange for much-wanted American dollars in inflation-plagued Germany.

The Ruthland and Hoheluft lines, the latter being John Gans's, were the best known during the war years, with James and Eleanor Cole's Dornwald another notable effort. By the close of the war, Grant Mann had produced some excellence in his Liebestraum kennel, including the 1946, 1947, and 1951 Grand Victrixes, and the dam of the 1964 Grand Victor. His was the "breed type-to-type regardless of blood relationship" approach that worked at least as well as any inbreeding program. Many other wealthy Americans imported famous dogs to show and offer at stud but did little or no breeding themselves. Anton Korbel's acquisition of Chlodulf v Pelztierhof is an example. In those days the sport of dogs was only for the rich. If you want a really big winner, that's still true.

Early Lines

San Miguel and Rocky Reach kennels—One of Marie Leary's bitches, Ramona of Cosalta, became the foundation of the San Miguel line owned and operated by Joan Michler and Lois Brundred.

1931 Grand Victrix Ch. Gisa v. Koenigsbruch.

1937, 1938 Gr. V. Ch. Pfeffer von Bern (Sieger, 1937).

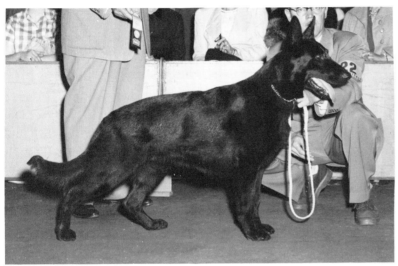

Ch. Tor v. Liebestraum - late 1950's. Another of Grant Mann's many champions, this black had a very deep chest, long body, but short back as described in the Standard. Photo courtesy Chum Porter

Ramona made breed history by producing five champions in her A (first) litter sired by Chlodulf, including Arno of San Miguel. For several years the western breeders and fanciers showed their dogs in regional competition similar to the Landesgruppen in Germany, and named a Pacific Coast Victor and Victrix. The Rancho San Miguel dogs frequently trotted off with the titles: 1946 Canadian Grand Victor/1946 and 1948 Pacific Coast Victor Ch San Miguel's Baron of Afbor UD, ROM is one example. From his titles it is obvious that he was both an important producer and obedience trained. In fact all the San Miguel dogs were trained in obedience, refuting the persistent belief that such training dampens a dog's spirit for the conformation ring. The 1947 and 1949 P.C. Victrix was Ch Christel of San Miguel CD, ROM; the 1949/50 P.C. Victor was Ch Lorian of San Miguel and his daughter Ch Solo Nina of Rushagen CD (linebred on D litter von Bern) became US Grand Victrix

in 1955. The black 1949/50 Gr. V. Ch Kirk of San Miguel was a son of Baron of Afbor, as was the 1953 Gr.V. Ch Alert of Mi-Noah's, ROM.

Margaret Pooley's Rocky Reach kennel was also established on the West Coast during the formative years of the breed, and she collaborated with San Miguel in producing a number of winners. The lighter-pigmented Ch Orex of Rocky Reach (Arno son) was a successful outcross that was used with several bitches including the sable daughter of Ch San Miguel's Ilo of Rocky Reach UD, ROM, the 1950 P.C. Victrix San Miguel's Chula of Afbor, ROM. Several of the dogs by Orex out of Chula inherited the tendency toward paling pigmentation: 1950 Canadian Gr. Victrix Ch Minx of San Miguel, Ch Rogue of San Miguel, and Christel. Several of Christel's offspring showed and transmitted this light coloration, though other Orex/Chula get such as Ch Rodan of San Miguel CD, had Chula's more desirable pigmentation.

1946 Grand Victrix Ch. Leda v. Liebestraum.

The Benlore kennel and a sampling of the Liebestraum lines were used in the San Miguel/Rocky Reach programs to good effect. The 1946 US and Canadian Grand Victrix Ch Leda v Liebestraum, ROM was an outcross daughter of Odin grandson Ch Garry of Benlore and when bred to Ilo, Leda produced Lorian and other good dogs. Another Liebestraum dog, Judo, was bred to Christel and produced the 1953 Gr.V. Ch Ulla of San Miguel, a magnificent example of German Shepherd femininity and type. Other studs used in the San Miguel program included Ch Cosalta's Ace of Wyliewood CDX, ROM, and the 1940 GR.V. Ch Cotswold of Cosalta. Linebreeding on Chlodulf was probably the key to much of the success, and helped establish a type on the West Coast that Odin did not accomplish because of less linebreeding and more outcrossing of his offspring.

LongWorth—Another famous program of the late 1940s was the LongWorth line of Lloyd Brackett. Noah Bloomer's GR.V. Ch Alert of Mi-Noah's dam was Mi-Noah's Ophelia of LongWorth sired in turn by Alert of LongWorth (Odin/Orla v Liebestraum). Ophelia's dam was a Pfeffer daughter, so it can be seen that the Grand Victor's LongWorth genes come largely from Dachs v Bern, the Utz grandson.

The LongWorth dogs did a lot of winning and producing in the late 1940s and 1950s, and their genealogical branches intertwined with those of Browvale, Edgetowne, Dornwald, and Rocky Reach. Many of the LongWorth dogs were richly pigmented with much of their coloration coming down through Pfeffer. Vol of LongWorth ROM, for example, was strongly pigmented with a great amount of black. His sire Derry, of the famous 6-champion D-litter LongWorth, had typical black and tan markings but nothing outstanding. Derry was by a Pfeffer son and a Garry of Benlore daughter. Vol's dam was by Pfeffer out of a Dolch v Bern daughter. Lloyd Brackett had innumerable dogs of high quality go out all over the US, but mainly in the central and eastern parts of the country. By the 1950s and early 1960s, many experienced dog watchers could guess at the LongWorth background by simply looking at a dog's markings and build.

In 1951 a long, low-stationed, well-angulated dog of dark pigmentation owned by Mrs. Betty Ford (not the wife of the later US president) won the National Specialty show. His style and appearance gave a hint of LongWorth and Pfeffer, and this indeed was the case. Gr.V. Ch Jory of Edgetowne, ROM was a son of Vol and Ch Orpha of Edgetowne, ROM. Orpha's dam was from San Miguel, Rocky Reach, and Pfeffer breeding, and she had the same sire as did Vol. Jory's brother Jolly Arno CDX, ROM was of slightly lighter build, a little leggier, and of the same mostly-black coloration. These two brothers formed the foundation that much subsequent West Coast breeding was built on, as witness the example of Ch Bismark v Graustein owned by the Cowleys. Bismark's sire was Nordraak of Matterhorn, a great dog on which to linebreed. Nordraak's sire was Jory and his dam was Charm of Dornwald, a product of mostly recent German imports. When Nordraak's genes teamed up with those of Rocky Reach and Jolly Arno through Ch Ulla, the result was the B-litter v Graustein which was very influential on the coast. Grant Mann did much the same thing in establishing his Liebestraum kennel; he bred popular American winners to various American and imported dogs.

Hessian—Gr.V. Alert figured in the pedigrees of a few dogs owned by Art and Helen Hess of Ohio, who also used the formula of linebreeding followed by outcrossing. Alert's daughter Gale of Stevens Rancho, ROM was bred to the tremen-

dous, once-in-a-lifetime German import Quell v Fredeholz, ROM (VA-5 in 1948) to produce Kern Delta's Exakta, ROM. Exakta was bred back to Ch Alert and yielded Hessian's Quella who was outcrossed to the Gr.V. Troll son, Kurt v Bid-Scono, of all-German breeding. The exciting result was the beautiful 1963 Grand Victrix Ch Hessian's Vogue, ROM. When Exakta was later bred to the Grimm v d Fahrmuhle/Lexa v OsnabruckerLand import son Ch Atlas v Elfenhain, she gave Ch Hessian's Baldur. Baldur was a medium-sized, somewhat low-stationed dog that typified Hessian's claim to fame with the ideal shoulder layback that made for a beautifully balanced, ground-covering stride. As this foreassembly was much needed at the time, Hessian's dogs made an important contribution to the breed. Bel-Vista's kennel used a healthy dose of Hessians, certain amounts of Lance of Fran-Jo and Bernd v Kallengarten, and a dash of Caralon's Hein to build a fine reputation from their midwestern base.

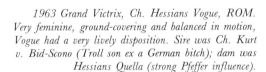
1963 Grand Victrix, Ch. Hessians Vogue, ROM. Very feminine, ground-covering and balanced in motion, Vogue had a very lively disposition. Sire was Ch. Kurt v. Bid-Scono (Troll son ex a German bitch); dam was Hessians Quella (strong Pfeffer influence).

Ch. Erko v. Dinkelland Sch HIII, CACIB, 12 times Landesgruppen Sieger. Before coming to the U.S., Erko was shown 56 times in Germany; he placed 2nd in four of those, and V-1 (1st) in 52 of these shows! He returned to compete in 1971 Siegerschan and was VA-3 in a tight race. Seldom defeated in the U.S., Erko left his mark in both countries.
Photo courtesy Jane Lightner, Valleybrook Kennels.

1962 Grand Victor Ch. Yorkdom's Pak.
Photo courtesy M. Schuetzler

1962 Grand Victrix Ch. Bonnie Bergere
of Ken-Rose, UD, ROM

A New Trend in America

During the war and the post-war occupation of Germany, US Grand Victors and Victrixes were almost all American-bred, a departure from the 1920s and 1930s when most were imports. Beginning roughly around 1955, the German dogs came again into our rings and breeding kennels, and some of their better dogs again won top honors at the German Shepherd Dog Club of America National Speciality Shows on a fairly regular basis. In the fourteen years from 1952 through 1965, excluding 1964 when there was no competition, only two Grand Victors were American, bred out of American parents (Alert and 1959 Gr.V. Ch Red Rock's Gino CD, ROM) and one, Yorkdom's Pak, was born here but from two imported parents, Ch Lido v Johanneshauch and Jutta v Colonia-Agrippina.

The bitches, however, had a different story to tell. Only two of the titled thirteen were imports, though five of them had a least one imported par-

ent. Could it be that the American male dogs during and after the war years were too feminine, and that the Teutonic invasion of dogs with the recommended strong secondary sex characteristics was refreshingly overpowering? I think that may have been part of the reason for the imports' success during this time span.

Recent Lines

In the late 1960s another turnaround developed regarding the winners of Grand Victor awards; there was at the same time a reversal of the breeding situation with many independent kennels returning to a few famous and sometimes overused breeding/showing homes. Although a great deal of good breeding had been going on in the past decade, now the better dogs were increasingly surfacing at Llano Estacado, Hessian, Nanhall, Kenbriar, Ginny McCoy's continuation of the LongWorth name, Bundespolizei, Ireton, Maur-Ray, Grafmar, Lahngold, Von Nassau, Arbywood, Beckgold,

Von Schrief, Eko-Lan, Elwillo, Waldenmark, Waldeslust, Wilva-Don, and others.

Some of these kennel names were quickly rising to places of considerable prominence. Using the great studs of the mid-1960s and the 1970s, breeders with good bitches were again beginning to produce homegrown Grand Victors. The Freeny family in California put Bernd v Kallengarten to good use in linebreeding which hit a peak in the late 1960s with 1966/68 Gr.V. Ch Yoncalla's Mike and his brother Ch Wilhelm aus der Winterzeit. Harry Schneider's Wilva-Don's Schatz was bred to Wilva-Don's Faust to give the 1966/67 Grand Victrix Ch Hanarob's Touche. Faust was linebred on Hein v Richterbach through two of his sons, and on the 1955 Can. Gr.V. Ch Alfa v Wormserweg, a not-long, not very angulated but good moving bitch owned by G. W. "Bill" Collins. When Faust, a bicolor black and tan, was bred to Jeenellyn's Jubliee (a dark sable) the result was Ch Jeenellyn's UFO, a solid black that covered the ground with a long, easy stride but loafed around the ring. This lack of interest, plus his color, which not every judge appreciates, made it difficult for him to finish his championship; he finally did so at age nine. UFO remains an important name in blacks. Jubilee was linebred on Ch Quellason of Ridgewood, a Quell v Fredeholz grandson, with one line to Maur-Ray thrown in. All three of these kennels, Jeenellyn, Ridgewood, and Maur-Ray, more or less specialized in breeding blacks.

Arbywood—The 1957 Gr.V. Ch Troll v Richterbach, an Axel v Deininghauserheide son, came on the American scene about the time so many Rolf OsnabruckerLand descendants were being imported. When a daughter of Gus Schindler's import Ch Cito v d Hermannschleuse was bred to Troll, another valuable combination occurred, and the record set by the D litter LongWorth was matched by the 6-champion F litter Arbywood, bred by Lucy Woodard. Fortune of Arbywood, a large sable Troll-type stallion of a male, became the most famous of the brothers of this litter when he produced the 1967 Gr.V. Ch Lance of Fran-Jo.

Troll had a tendency to produce good rears, high withers, a little less than ideal shoulder layback, a noble head and expression, and great size. Lance and others of similar breeding had very powerful rear drive and follow-through, and partly because of this the fads of excessive gaiting and fast flying trots became a way of life in the US specialty shows. This was by no means a totally new development, however; the SV in von Stephanitz's time had the same problem of handlers racing their dogs around the ring in an effort to show off the flying trot and what they believed was a superior reach. Von Stephanitz said it was done "to fascinate and deceive the judge's eyes."

Waldesruh—An excellent import, VA Brix v Grafenkrone, became Grand Victor in 1965. His grandfather Caesar v d Malmannsheide as well as Caesar's sire Hein v Richterbach had been sold to US fanciers and had become ROM champions here. Brix also had lines to Lido v Johanneshauch and Lido v Friedlichenheim. This latter Lido was VA-1 in both 1952 and 1954, which is equivalent to being Sieger, but in those days the title was not used.

Meanwhile, Ch Biff of Ken-Rose, a half brother to the 1962 Grand Victrix through Ginger Girl of LongWorth, was bred to Waldesruh granddaughter of the great Troll, producing the D litter Waldesruh. One of these, Del Dena, was bred to Brix, and an important line was established with the K litter Waldesruh. Korporal, Korry, Kaiser, and others were well-known for their sable coat patterns, considerable rear angulation, and beautiful side-gait. Many if not most of their offspring were mild-tempered, somewhat loose in ligamenture, and slow to mature. Some of the most successful descendants of this family were produced by blending the line with those of Lance of Fran-Jo. In fact, the chances are greater than 50 percent that any good-looking sable (and most of the mediocre ones too) are out of Waldesruh breeding, and probably also from Lance.

Fran-Jo—The Fran-Jo kennel, operated by Fran and Joan Ford of central Ohio, was the most notable American program of the post-war years. This was due to their own breeding successes as well as Lance's wins and production for other kennels. Although Covy-Tucker Hill was more famous for winning bitches and Mary Roberts better known for show wins with a lot of great studs, Lance was the most popular and accessible dog for most Americans. The Fords used many of their own bitches and arranged co-ownerships on others, then linebred on Lance until it seemed one could not turn around without tripping over Lance's descendants.

1967 G. V. Ch. Lance of Fran-Jo, ROM, OFA GS-401.

His domination continued into the 1980s when Lance-free lines once again began to be seen, thanks largely to an increase in interest in Schutzhund and imports. By 1985, Lance figured in the pedigrees of more than 90 percent of American German Shepherd Dogs. Fran-Jo has contributed much in the way of style, but as in any close linebreeding, one must exercise care and judgment to escape the unwanted recessives that inevitably come with such a practice.

Cobert—One of the most successful "clicks" in American German Shepherd Dog history was the combination of Lance of Fran-Jo's genes with those of Ch Bernd v Kallengarten, ROM. Ted and Connie Beckhardt have turned out probably the most famous and fabulous Lance/Bernd dogs. Beginning with their Bernd/Cobert's Amber daughter Ernestine, named in honor of Ernest Loeb who imported Bernd, they bred her to Falk of Bihari Wonder and came up with Cobert's Melissa of Lakeside. (Lakeside was the kennel name of Danny and Sharon Dwier, friends of the Beckhardts and collaborators with them in some breedings.) Melissa

in turn was bred to Lance and produced the fantastic G litter: Lakeside's Gilligan's Island, Golly Gee, and others. It was a breeding that *had* to be repeated, and in the H litter the future (1972) Grand Victor Lakeside's Harrigan appeared, later to be sold to long-time breeder Ann Mesdag of Von Nassau kennel fame. If "Gillie" had lived longer than his few short years, he probably would have become Grand Victor, since he was about the most handsome specimen the breed had seen in a long time. So once more it was decided to employ the magic Lance/Melissa cross, and the resulting R litter contained Cobert's Reno of Lakeside, who turned out to be a prolific and valuable producer as well as a multiple-Select winner. I held the 2-day-old Reno (and littermates) in my hands, but couldn't put him in my pocket—Connie and Melissa were counting, and all were spoken for.

Combined with the Beckhardt's great German dog, Ch Treu v Wolfsstock, Ernestine produced a bold male, Cobert's Jet Ace, who in turn was bred to a bitch from some old Hobby House/San Miguel lines to give Ch Dot-Wall's Vance, an important ingredient in East Coast breeding for many years.

Multiple Working Group Winner. Ch. Caralon's Hein v.d. Lockenheim, C.D. The great Caralon's Hein was known for his over-all soundness in movement and temperament, quiet disposition, black recessive, and probably unsurpassed U.S. record for producing such a huge percentage of x-rayed normal hips. Linebred Harald v. Haus Tigges 3-2; Axel 5,5,5-4; R-OsnabrueckerLand 5-4,4. Hein contributed a great deal to the show world, and his influence will last. He "blended" well with Bernd, Lance, Hessians, and nearly every other known line. He reigned in the late 1960's and early 1970's. Photo courtesy Caralon Kennels.

Eko-Lan—Another very successful use of Lance was by Fred Migliore who multiplied Axel v Deininghauserheide's genes through Troll son Ch Eko-Lan's Aragon and through Gr.V. Axel v Poldihaus's son Ch Llano Estacado's Gengis. He then brought in Harry v Donauki on the bitch tail line and bred this combination to Lance. This clicked and gave Ch Eko-Lan's Morgan, one of the top ROM producers in the breed. The blend was repeated with several variations and gave us a great number of sturdy bitches and large, good-looking males, including Eko-Lan's Paladen, Shiloh, and Quasar, among others.

Celler-Schloss—The 6-champion I litter von Celler Schloss was sired by Cliff and Judy Haigler's most illustrious product, Ch Falko v Celler-Schloss, a Bismark son out of a bitch of Rocky Reach breeding. Falko and his pups were transition dogs, bridging the gap between the old and the new and representing, perhaps, Pfeffer's last "pfling."

Caralon—Back in the Midwest, a couple of ladies hit black gold when Hella v d Spessartheide became a foundation bitch for Helen "Scootie" Sherlock and Dr. Pat Parsons. Hella, dark and beautiful, was a daughter of Ch Harald v Haus Tigges, the fantastic Hein v Richterbach/Axel combination later imported by Erich Renner. Her dam was a Rolf OsnabruckerLand granddaughter, and when Hella was bred to the Joll aus der Eremitenklause son Bodo v Katzenkopf, the result was linebreeding on Harald through Bodo's dam. It was also linebreeding on Axel, so once again that beneficial blend of OsnabruckerLand and Axel was proven and the result was the great Caralon's Hein von der Lockenheim. Hein became famous for a high percentage of normal hips in his offspring, partly because of his own genes and partly because of his owners' early adherence to a strict regimen of selection of pups by palpation and radiography. The most promising pups were placed in breeding homes where the same attention to good hips and other qualities would be given priority.

Caralon's Hein was an easy-going dog with a gentle manner and strong, effortless gait. He passed along good coloring including the black factor, his own moderate yet balanced angulation and deep chest. Unfortunately, he also produced a number of doggy bitches and a few more high-in-the-rear than most other popular studs of his time. One product of Hein was Ch Amber a d Edelheim, a beautiful yet not over-refined foundation bitch for the Pinebeach kennel in Wisconsin.

Hein was principally responsible for upgrading the image of the solid black through his sons Icon and Phantom and several black beauties of the opposite sex. For too long, many blacks in the US had been spindly and of poor general quality, usually bred by the outcasts of the breed who specialized in white dogs and pedigrees with Rin-Tin-Tin, or some other gimmick. Thanks to Hein, Bernd, Maur-Ray dogs, and a few others, the picture changed and black became beautiful once again.

Others—Space would not permit a chronicle of all the good breeding kennels in the US and Canada, nor would time allow the *status quo* of names and emphasis to remain unchanged.

The Golden Age

To this sometimes lone observer, the golden years of the German Shepherd Dog in America was the decade of the 1960s, for it was then that the best blends of Axel, Rolf/Rosel, Pfeffer/Odin, and Haus Schutting blood were combined anew with the more recent strains from Germany. Naturally, some of this fresh influx was rich in OsnabruckerLand, such as the Wienerau, ZollgrenzschutzHaus, and Lierberg lines. Lines to Axel came through Bernd v Kallengarten, Troll, Veus Starrenberg, Mutz Pelztierfarm, and others. But the Germans had wisely or luckily kept a few lines open and separate, with Ajax v Haus Dexel, Treu Wolffstock, and others going back directly to such early dogs as Alex Westfalenheim and Hettel Uckermark. Ajax, Treu, and others with such open lines were to figure in American bloodlines more in the 1970s and 1980s although they were present in the 1960s.

The 1960s included such terrific combinations of Eremitenklause, Piastendamm, Bernd v K., Vello, Liebestraum, early Wienerau, and others already named. In the 1970s, especially toward the end, too many dogs of the same American line-breeding were winning top honors at the National Specialty and thus getting most of the stud services. United States dogs began to be characterized not only as high in the withers but also high-stepping and somewhat faulty in front, just as described by von Stephanitz in the 1930s. Our top dogs also became more extreme and sloppy in the hocks, and questionable or at least not very hard in temperament.

Those dogs in the 1970s and early 1980s had strong rearthrust, good femininity in bitches (and unfortunately in males, too) and less pigment than had been the rule in the previous decades. Meanwhile, too many German imports were showing a break in the topline such that the second part fell away before the croup was reached—the hyena dogs that von Stephanitz talked about were being resurrected! Among the good points furnished by the imports in the 1970s and 1980s (besides non-Troll lines so breeders can take advantage and breed into those for outcrossing), are masculinity, stronger ligaments, tough working-dog temperament, good pigment, balanced gait, and better over-all health and longevity, much of this being a natural result of outcrossing. Combined with the growing interest in Schutzhund training, these qualities should give much improvement before the end of the century. We are entering a time of exciting and promising upturn, a new golden age, if we would but have the wisdom to nourish and culture it.

THE IMPORT

Other than a minor adjustment to a new language, the purchase of an imported dog should be hardly any different from buying an American-bred adult. The dog will know certain routines such as leash work, heeling at your left, and basic manners, which are not language related. Your supplier will have filled you in on a few key words and procedures and will have given you whatever advice you need to start. From there, it's a matter of the dog getting used to what you do and expect, and that happens rapidly. The Schutzhund-trained dog is a bit more of a responsibility, and most dogs imported from Germany will have had some of this protection and obedience training, so read up on Schutzhund and try to attend some trials before you get the dog, if possible, but certainly as soon as he arrives. If you're not as well schooled as your dog, say so; people you meet at the trials will be happy to give you help and encouragement.

Reading the German Pedigree and Other Documents

Even if you don't buy an import, you may have a copy of an SV pedigree in your files. If not, use the accompanying example to refer to while reading this portion of this chapter. You may find that such a pedigree is pretty and impressive, but in a language you don't understand! You may even have bought a paperback German-English dictionary, but still can't find the dog terms that appear in the pedigree. What follows are tips on how to read such documents, followed by a translation of most of the words commonly used in them.

Almost all of the original SV pedigrees you will see are pink, which means that the parents of that dog have been examined by SV officials and found suitable for breeding. Years ago there were a few pale green pedigrees around, but they are now quite rare in Canada and the United States. The *Ahnentafel* (ancestor listing) is folded in half to the metric European letter size, roughly equivalent to our 8½ by 11-inch stationery, so that it has 4 sides. All the necessary breeding information in on these, and this official pedigree must accompany the dog if he is sold, with ownership transfers recorded in a block on the back page.

The inside pages give information on the dog's ancestors, with the first two generations described in detail. The *Eltern* (parents) are listed with *Vater* (father) on the top and *Mutter* (mother) on the bottom. There, now—your first German lesson wasn't too hard, was it? The example given of the copy of the pedigree of Otti von der Erlalohe may be too small for you to read, so I'll describe the portion dealing with her sire, Gin vom Lierberg, one of Germany's best Shepherd Dogs. Under Gin's name is his SV registration number and Schutzhund III title; below that is "+1967-68," which means he was *Angekoert* (surveyed or examined) and recommended for breeding in 1967 for the customary 2-year period. This particular pedigree was issued in 1968, before Gin's producing record was well known and before his *Angekoert* could be updated. When a good dog has had those first two years of approval and has given enough offspring so the SV can assess his producing ability, he may be given a lifetime approval rating, *Lebenszeit*, but most may have to be reevaluated by a *Koermaster* every year after reaching eight years of age.

On the same or another line one might find an abbreviation such as "*a*" *zuerk.*, which means that the dog's hips were radiographed and found good enough for breeding. This started appearing in the German pedigrees in the 1970s and thus is not seen in this particular illustration. The ZB stands for *Zuchtbewertung*, which is the best rating earned in conformation shows to date (open class) and in this case it is followed by the V, standing for *Vorzueglich* (excellent), the highest rating in non-Sieger shows. The year this survey was run, two of Gin's older brothers won VA (*vorzueglich auslese*, excellent select): Bernd VA-3 and Bodo VA-1 (Sieger). Incidentally, I wish to remind you here that almost any time you see *ue, ae,* or *oe* in a German word set in American type, it is probably an Anglicized spelling to replace a single German vowel that has an umlaut (two dots) above it. Thus, *Kör* becomes *Koer, Bär* becomes *Baer*, and *vorzüglich* becomes *vorzueglich*.

Next in order is Gin's base color and markings (*Farbe und Abzeichen*): sbA, the s standing for *schwartz* (black), and the bA for *braun Abzeichen* (brown markings). Other color abbreviations and translations include s (all black); sgrbA (black saddle with *grau* [gray] and brown markings); sgrgA (black with gray and *gelbe*). *Gelbe* means "yellow," but is equivalent to what we call tan, as compared to *braun*, which Americans love to call "deep red."

Here's an easy exercise: figure out what coloring this dog has: sgbA. If b precedes g, then there is more dark tan (*braun*) than light tan (*gelbe*) in the coat. Sometimes M follows the subcase letters and the A, to designate a mask, and sometimes the colors of the legs (L), feet (Pf), saddle (S), or muzzle (F) are designated. Besides Otti, an sgrgA bitch, the front page of her pedigree shows that her littermates included three blacks (s), two with gray and tan (sgrbA and sgrgA), and the color sgbA. Gin himself was a "bicolor," mostly black with *braun* on the lower legs and some other areas, as was Bodo. Otti's dam was a black and tan with gray markings probably mixed in the saddle at the withers and shoulder areas like so many others of that coloration, and she apparently carried the black recessives in order to produce solid blacks in Otti's litter. Otti had much of her dam's coloration, which some people call a salt-and-pepper effect, on parts of her back.

Back to the inside pages now. A description of Gin follows—his *Koer* report summary (*Koerbericht*). Roughly translated, it reads: Over middlesized, with strong "bone" and very good proportions. The forequarters are well developed, with very good shoulder and upper arm. The back is firm, the croup well positioned or laid on (proper angle), the legs broad and substantial (strong). Motion is floating, covering much ground with very good firmness. With a steady temperament, he has an outstanding fighting spirit for his friends (a way of saying he is protective under the test conditons of the examination).

Below that survey is a listing of his siblings (*Geschwister*) and their coloring: Gero and Gabi are the only ones, though farther below you will notice that Eris, to whom Gin was bred, had seven brothers and sisters.

Vello's *Koer* description is not given on this pedigree, his breeding recommendation having been withdrawn because he was producing too many oversized dogs, but we know that he was a very large dog that had the misfortune of being shown and surveyed around the time that the head of the SV decreed that the current trend toward greater size must be reversed. Vello otherwise might possibly have been named Sieger because of the other qualities he had. His son Bodo became Sieger in 1967, and others out of Betty v Eningsfeld gained fame around the world. Dogs from the B, D, F, and G litters vom Lierberg are found in some of the finest working-dog pedigrees as well as those of many top show dogs.

The third and fourth generations shown on the pedigree with their names, SV numbers, and titles, also show a plus mark (+) before the name. This, or an asterisk sometimes substituted for it, shows the dog was recommended for breeding. (*Approved* might be a better word.) On the far right margin of the inside page is a listing of abbreviations and marks including titles and rankings. An interesting item on the lower right of this example is a continuation of Betty's siblings' names, showing there were twelve in that litter that were allowed to live, many gaining titles or show ratings by the time this pedigree was issued. The general rule in Germany is that only six pups would be allowed to live unless a foster mother can be found, which is what must have happened here.

Look to page one of the German pedigree. This front page gives more information on the dog or bitch itself. Again using Otti's as an example, we see the words *Koerzucht-Leiftungszucht-Ahnentafel* (Breeding and Production Pedigree). In some years just the last word of the three is used. To the right of *Ahnentafel* is room for breed book and evalution remarks. Here we see the "a" stamp, always in subcase type with quotation marks when referred to in print, while the actual stamp is the letter in a double concentric triangle. This signifies acceptability of hip radiographs. In more recent years further categorizing has been implemented, but in Otti's day all that passed certain radiographic requirements were given the same "a" stamp. We radiographed her again at six years and found her hips to be excellent. Even today, the "a" stamp can be given to dogs with slight dysplasia, called near-normal or *fast-normal*, as well as *noch zugelassen* (still permissible). As in the game of pitching horseshoes, "almost" may be sufficient for you, especially if the dog's other qualities outweigh a slight case, and other hip-pedigree information is better (for instance, that of siblings and parents). For breeding purposes, however, the better the hips of both the relatives and the dog himself, the safer you'll be.

Also appearing on some pedigrees may be the *Koerklasse* rating, applied after a breed survey when the dog is old enough. Otti was imported just before she was eighteen months old, when she could have been surveyed or entered in a Schutzhund trial, so no remarks are found on her pedigree. Others in my files show such remarks as *"Angekoert 1975-76/ Koerklasse 1a,"* which means that besides having the "a" stamp the dog has been found to be of the highest quality and especially recommended for breeding—to the right partners, of course. *Koerklasse-II* dogs are still suitable for breeding, but may have some fault in structure or movement that is partially compensated for by performance or other redeeming qualities deemed valuable by the SV.

The next line to which I call your attention reads "for the German Shepherd Dog _____" and has a space for her name on line 2, *Geschlecht* (gender) appears, which in this case is *Huendin*. If

Körzucht-Leistungszucht-Ahnentafel

für den deutschen Schäferhund ___Otti von der Erlalohe___

Geschlecht: __Hündin__   Haarart: __stockhaarig__

Farbe und Abzeichen: __schwarz, grau-gelbe Abzeichen__

Besondere Kennzeichen: _____

Wurftag: __11. April 1968__   Wurfjahr: __Neunzehnhundertachtund-sechzig__

Züchter: __Werner Narr__

Anschrift: __Hof/Saale, Neutauperlitzer Weg 16__

Inzucht auf:	Geschwister:	
Lex Preußenblut (5-5)	Odin s	Odo sgbA
Maja Osnabrücker Land (5-5)	Olf s	Olymp sgrgA
(Osnabrücker Land, Ina, Rosel-Rolf	Orff sgrbA	Ossie sgrgA
(4,5-4,5)	Otta s	

Erläuterung über Wurfstärke:

Wurfstärke 5,3   Aufzucht 1,1

Die Ahnentafel hat nur Gültigkeit, wenn sie vom Züchter eigenhändig unterschrieben ist; sie gilt als Urkunde im juristischen Sinne! Wer Ahnentafeln fälscht oder mit solchen Mißbrauch treibt, wird vom SV strafrechtlich verfolgt. Die Ahnentafel ist der schriftliche Nachweis über Rassereinheit, Name und Abstammung des Hundes, sie gehört somit zum Hund und ist beim Verkauf dem neuen Eigentümer unbedingt auszuhändigen. Beim Eingehen des Hundes ist sie an das Zuchtbuchamt einzusenden.

Bemerkungen: _____

Für die Richtigkeit vorstehender Angaben: (Unterschrift des Züchters) *W. Werner Narr*

Eintragungs- und Prüfungsbestätigung: Der oben bezeichnete deutsche Schäferhund ist am ___27.5.68___ in das Zuchtbuch für deutsche Schäferhunde (SZ) Bd. __67__ unter Nr. __1156099__ eingetragen worden. Die Ahnentafel wurde ausgefertigt am ___27.5.68___ vom Verein für deutsche Schäferhunde (SV), Mitglied des Verbandes für das deutsche Hundewesen (VDH) in der Fédération Cynologique Internationale (F.C.I.). Die Abstammungsangaben sind nachgeprüft, und ihre Richtigkeit wird hiermit bestätigt.

Das Zuchtbuchamt des SV
I. A.:

I. Eltern	II. Groß-Eltern	III. Urgroß-Eltern	IV. Ururgroß-Eltern	Abkürzungen und Zeichen
Vater: Gin vom Lierberg 1077060 SchHIII +1967-68 zb: V Farbe und Abz.: sbA Körbericht: Übermittelgroß, mit kräftigen Knochen und sehr guten Verhältnis. Die Vorhand ist gut entwickelt, mit sehr guter Schulter und Oberarmlage. Der Rücken ist fest, die Kruppe gut gelagert, die Keulen breit und kräftig. Die Gänge sind flott und viel bodenschaffend bei sehr guter Festigkeit. Mit sicherem Wesen ist ausgeprägter Kampftrieb verbunden. Geschwister: Gero sbA/Gabi sbgA	Vello zu den Sieben-Faulen 935874 SchHIII FH sb zb: V Körbericht: Geschwister: Vagant shb SchHI,SG/Valett s/Valto s/Vasall shb/Valsa sb/Valta s/Veta sb SchHI,SG	+Lex vom Drei-Kinder-Haus 890773 SchHI +Grille zu den Sieben-Faulen 899660 SchHII	+Yasko von der Tido 822235 SchHIII +Frikka von der schwarzen Perle 697668 SchHI FH +Held zu den Sieben-Faulen 752521 SchHIII +Ina vom Osnabrücker Land 693527 SchHIII	Zb zuchttauglich Zb2 Zuchtverwendet Farbe und Abzeichen: [abbreviation key] Ausbildungs-Kennzeichen: [list] Bewertungsnoten: V-A Vorzüglich-Auslese V Vorzüglich SG Sehr gut G Gut A Ausreichend M Mangelhaft U Ungenügend
	Betty vom Eningsfeld 971660 SchHII +1962-67 sgA zb: V Körbericht: Mittelgroß, mittelschwer, gestreckt, gute Brusttiefe, normale Vorbrust, sattes Pigment, gut gewinkelte Gliedmaßen, hinten etwas besser als vorn. Fesselung nicht ganz straff. Leichtfüßig ausgreifender Gang auc nicht ganz vollendet straffem Rücken mit Vortritt übertreffenden Nachschub. SG-gewecktes, gutartiges Wesen, Kampftrieb ausgeprägt. WA 62: Rücken sehr fest. und Mut Geschwister: +Baldur sgA SchHIII,SG/Ben sgA/Bill sgA/Bodo sgA/Brando s,SG/Erix sgA/+Bella sgA SchHIII,FH,SG/P.s V.	+Arko von Riedersknapp 90592 SchHIII FH +Delfi vom Kleistweg 903137 SchHII	+Heiko von Böhmershof 834412 SchHI Burga von Cinkushof 840006 SchHI ZHI +Hain von Richterbach 700070 SchHII +Adda von Reiffeck 763052 SchHI	
Mutter: Eris von der Erlalohe 1044575 SchHII +1967-68 zb: V Farbe und Abz.: sggrA Körbericht: Etwas übermittelgroß, gutes Verhältnis, schöne Rückenlinie gute Brustanlagen, Oberarm dürfte etwas schräger sein, Gliedmaßen gerade, Gänge korrekt, Wesen gutartig und sicher, Kampftrieb ausgeprägt. Geschwister: Ex sggrA SchHIII,V/Edda SG/Elke sggrA SchHII,V/Erle sggrA SchHII,V/Estra sggrA SchHI,SG/Evi sggrA	Zibu vom Haus Schütting (1964 Sieger) 971574 SchHIII +1962-67 sgA zb: V-A Körbericht: Mittelgroß, vorbildlich aufgebaut, ausgezeichnete Vorhand und recht gute Hinterhand, wunderbarer Linienfluß, mit voller Gebäudeharmonie, trockene, saubere Knochen, gute Fesselung und gut gewölbte Pfoten, gutes Verhältnis, bei recht guten Gängen geht er hinten etwas eng. Bei gutem Wesen und Temperament ausgeprägter Kampftrieb. Geschwister:	+Donar von der Pirnskuppe 809666 SchHIII FH +Niobe vom Haus Schütting 850715 SchHIII FH	+Rolf vom Osnabrücker Land 640721 SchHIII FH +Mirja von Holzheimer Eichwald 623034 SchHII +Burache von Pfingsthügel 787577 SchHI +Wonne von Maschtor 612017 SchHI	Raum für Vermerke Forts. zu Spalte II/4 Geschwister: Britta sgA Burga sgA Bürgel sgA Dirk s 2x zuerkannt W. Weyer SV-Zuchtbuchamt
	Cisa vom Schloß Schachen 998957 SchHII +1963-68 sgAKBrL zb: V Körbericht: Mittelgroß, gut proportioniert, guter Ausdruck, festes Gefüge, gute Vor- und Unterbrust, gute Vor- und Hinterhandwinkelung, leicht abfallende Kruppe, raumschaffendo Gänge, sicheres Wesen Kampftrieb vorhanden. WA 1964: Sehr schön angelegt, mittelgroß, ausgeprägter Kampftrieb. Geschwister: Carlo sgAKBrL/Cherry sgAKBrL SG/+Conny sgAKBrL SchHII,SG/Cita sgAKBrL/Cora sgAKBrL,G	+Donar vom Elforhain 922501 SchHIII FH +Vessi vom Zollgrenzschutz-Haus 935477 SchHII	+Alf vom Nordfelsen 739163 SchHIII +Ansel vom Elfenhain 870263 SchHII +Harry vom Donaukai 684xxx SchHI +Perle von Zollgrenzschutz-Haus 904216 SchHII	

a male, it would have read *Rüde* with the umlaut, Ruede in the Anglicized spelling. Hair is almost always *stockhaarig* (stiff- or coarse-haired) rather than long. Line 3 gives the coloring, and line 4 has space for *Besondere Kennzeichen* (special identification marks), which may include a tattoo number. On line 5 are the *Wurftag* (birthdate) and *Wurfjahr* (year of birth). The breeder *(Zuechter)* is named next, and on line 7 is his address.

The center section of this front page is divided left and right, with linebreeding on the left, *Inzucht auf*, literally translated as 'inbreeding on'. The 5-5 after *Lex Preussenblut* means she had Lex in the fifth generation on both Gin's and Eris's sides of the pedigree, and the same is indicated for *Maja OsnabrueckerLand*. Otti was linebred on Ina/Rosel/Rolf, these three being treated here as one dog for the purposes of reporting ancestry, because two were littermates, and the other from the same parents but a different litter. Since subsequent litters by Lex and Maja did not result in dogs of equal quality to the R litter, there may be truth in the report that Maja chose fence-jumping Falk in the still of the night during her betrothal to Lex. In any event, Lex is listed as the legal sire of both R and I litters, and Otti's linebreeding is given as 4,5-4,5 I?R, meaning these combinations appear in the fourth and fifth generations on each side.

To the right of the dividing line are listed Otti's siblings. The next section, "Explanations about litter size," shows *Wurfstaerke 5,3*, which indicates the quantity in the litter as five males and three females. *Amme nauf zucht* (brought up by wet nurse or foster mother) were one male and one female, showing that Eris nursed her maximum of six.

The rest of the front page includes some regulations, warnings about falsifying information, and certification by the breeder and the keeper of the stud book *(das Zuchtbuchamt des SV)* that the information is correct and has been recorded.

Other Records for German Imports

Shows—Besides the pedigree, show cards, and official records of his ranking or evaluation in German competition may also accompany your imported dog. Rather than simply giving out four ribbons in each of several classes as we do in the US, the Germans have fewer classes and may be more fair and equitable in their rankings and ratings. For instance, if we had a dozen of the best dogs in the world shown together in one AKC or CKC show's open class, only four would receive ribbons. In Germany, the dogs are rated *vorzueglich* (excellent), *sehr gut* (very good), *gut* (good), *ausreichend* (sufficient), *mangelhaft* (defective), or *ungenuegend* (unsatisfactory), and every dog is rated. It's unlikely that all dogs in a given class would receive the same high rating, but it is possible. In some shows, only the dogs whose owners are certain they have a chance at winning are entered, due to the expenses involved, so the lowest ratings are seldom seen in the ring.

German shows do not have puppy classes or intersex competition. Within each sex, the three main classes are *Gebrauchshundklasse* (open) for dogs two years or older, with training degrees and previous V or SG ratings (*vorzueglich* or *sehr gut*) earned at previous, perhaps smaller, shows; *Junghundklasse* (young dog class), eighteen to twenty-four months; and *Jugendklasse*, translatable as 'youth' or 'teenager' class, twelve to eighteen months old. There may also be a veterans class called *Altersklasse, alt* meaning 'old'.

On the left top of the sample *Bewertungsausweis* (show competition) card is Otti's entry number, corresponding to armband number in US shows. Following that is information on parents and their training titles, then the breeder's name. You can see what a difference exists in Germany where a dog's parentage can influence its rating by the judge. In AKC events the catalogue must be kept from the judge's eyes and he must pretend not to recognize exhibitors or dogs in the ring.

The right side of the card tells where the *Sonderschau* (particular show) was held and when, and the class in which the bitch was entered. Below that the judge had circled the *sehr gut* rating, the highest attainable at her age. He then signed it and it became the property of the owner after the information was recorded in the SV report.

The reverse of this card gives information that there is only one breed club in this breed, with around 41,000 members (at that time) in fifteen regional groups and 1,400 local groups (we would call them clubs and the British would call them societies). The SV have their own *Zeitung* (magazine) and the number of dogs registered in the SV records is over 1,100,000. They have their own specialty shows (*Sonderschauen*) and their own performance trials (*Leistungspruefungen*) as well as sales contracts and purchase agreements. Prices are then quoted for the publications. Announcements, inquiries, information, and advertisements can only be arranged through the *Verein* (club) for German Shepherd Dogs, and the address of this SV is given.

Verein für deutsche Schäferhunde (SV) e.V.
Hauptgeschäftsstelle Augsburg – Telefon (08 21) 2 50 35
Rechtssitz Hamburg · Gegründet am 22. April 1899
Postscheck: Amt München 167 47

Einziger Zuchtverein der Rasse
Rund 41 000 Mitglieder in 15 Landesgruppen
und 1400 Ortsgruppen
Eigene Zeitung am 20. jeden Monats
Maßgebendes Zuchtbuch der Rasse (SZ) mit über
1 100 000 Eintragungen
Eigene Sonderschauen
Eigene Leistungsprüfungen
Verkaufsberatung, Kaufpreishinterlegungsstelle

Jahresbeitrag einschließlich Nebensteuer. Zeitungsbezugs-
gebühr DM 17.–, für Diensthundeführer DM 14.–, für Schä-
fer und Schwerbeschädigte DM 11.–
Eintrittsgeld DM 3.–, bei Beitragsermäßigung DM 1.50

Anmeldungen, Anfragen, Auskünfte, Werbesachen,
verlange man bzw. richte man nur an den

Verein für deutsche Schäferhunde (SV) e.V.
89 Augsburg 5, Postfach 63

Selbstverlag des Vereins für deutsche Schäferhunde (SV) e. V. im VDH
Rechtssitz Hamburg   Nachdruck verboten

30 000 / 8 / 68

BEWERTUNGSAUSWEIS

Der deutsche Schäferhund Nr. *51*	**Wurde auf der Sonderschau**
~~Rüde~~/Hündin	in Tirschenreuth
	am 13. April 1969
O t t i v.d.Erlalohe	geführt in der
SZ 1156099 Ausbild.-Kennz. —	**Gebrauchshundklasse** **Junghundklasse**
Wurftag 11.4.1968 196	**Altersklasse** ~~Jugendklasse~~
angekört Ja / Nein für 196	wurde vom Preisrichter mit
Vater Gin v.Lierberg	**Vorzüglich** **Ausreichend**
SZ 1077060 Ausbild.-Kennz. Sch.H.3	~~Sehr gut~~ **Mangelhaft**
Mutter Eris v.d.Erlalohe	**Gut** **Ungenügend**
SZ 1044575 Ausbild.-Kennz. Sch.H.2	bewertet.
	Das Zutreffende ist mit Blaustift einzufassen. Nichtzutreffendes ist durchzustreichen.
Züchter Werner Narr in Hof / Saale	Unterschrift des Richters:
Eigentümer Werner Narr ,	
in Hof / Saale	

Official evaluation—The full *Koer* report is a 2-page compilation (both sides of a sheet) of data on the dog and his characteristics as determined by an official representative of the SV. As you can see from Herby Merkel's translation (which first appeared in *K-9 Kapers*, the bulletin of the Northern New Jersey German Shepherd Dog Club) of Sieger Marko v Cellerland's *Koer* report, it includes registration numbers, breeder identification, training degrees, a full description of the dog (in this case as judged by Dr. Rummel, head of the SV), and advice on breeding. A summary or excerpts are used in the official pedigree. Marko produced good pigment, bone, gait, and harmony. Disadvantages included some poor upper arms and croups, longhairs, oversize, and lower jaw problems.

Besides the conformation show ratings, there is one more, *VA*, which is only awarded at the international Sieger Show held in a different city in Germany each year. It is given to the top half-dozen or more dogs (and the same for bitches) considered by the SV's top officials to be the most desirable breeding animals. In 1980, there were fourteen VA dogs and ten VA bitches. The VA-1 male is called the *Sieger* (literal translation: 'winner' or 'champion'), and the VA-1 female is the *Siegerin*. Most of the Siegers/Siegerins and VA dogs and bitches are German, but the awards are sometimes given to a dog from another country. The VA dogs must have a Schutzhund II title or better, and their parents must have training degrees, too. They must be *Angekoert* and have the "a" stamp (since 1968) and the Sieger/Siegerin in addition must be *Koerklasse-I*. A dog cannot attain such a high placement without having proven himself in his progeny as well, and such details are known to the judge at the time of decision.

Sieger

You may see the word *Sieger* used in other contexts, too, because it is literally translated 'winner'. For example, it is used to designate the winner of any of the fifteen hundred or so regional shows, as in *Landesgruppen Sieger*, abbreviated LG. Some dogs have the title of Czech Sieger, Holland Sieger, or Canadian Sieger, but the value of these titles in each case depends on the competition, as does the value of any championship title or even a blue ribbon. Nowhere is the competition close to that of the Sieger Show in Germany. Some other

examples: *Leistungssieger* means a field trial, (working dog) competition winner, *Preishueten Sieger* is the herding champion, and the meaning of *Klubsieger* is obvious.

International Champion

You have seen the C.A.C.I.B. title, often used without the periods. This stands for the French term, Certificate of Aptitude for International Champions of Beauty, and is awarded at certain FCI-approved shows. The FCI is the International Cynologic Federation, of which the SV is a member, and a CACIB international championship can be earned if the dog is given winner's cards (tops in its breed and sex) in three different countries. In addition, the dog must have done well in tracking, obedience, and temperament tests. When you see a dog advertised as being an international champion, make sure it's really CACIB instead of a dog that has won a championship in the US and Canada or a couple of other countries. It is far from being the same thing.

Other Training Titles

On some stud service advertisements and pedigrees, you will see additional titles or abbreviations beyond the SchH degree. One that used to appear more often was the herding title, but these days sheepherding and its trials are hard to find. Around 1970, a super dog with the HGH degree lived in Michigan and greatly impressed fanciers in middle America. He was Ch Axel v Kirschental, from a German kennel that still trains for this skill. Following are some more titles and German words you may come across:

AD: Ausdauerpruefung—passed an endurance test, gaiting for nine miles, followed by an obedience test and a physical exam.

BLH or BFH: Blindenfuehrer Hund—blind leader dog.

DH: Dienst Hund—service dog.

FH: Faehrten Hund—trailing dog.

GrH: Grenzen Hund—border patrol dog.

HGH: Herdengebrauchshund—herding dog.

LawH: Lawinen Hund—avalanche rescue dog.

MH: Meldehund—message dog (mostly in wartime).

KOER REPORT

**1972 Sieger
Marko v Cellerland**

Marko v Cellerland, 1169323, SchH III, Fh, whelped 5/3/68, angekoert for 1971/72/Ia, Lambertheim 7/25/70 by Dr. Rummel, Koerzucht, Leistungszucht. Sire: Kondor vom Golmakauer Krug, 1109329, HGH (Cyrus vom Baltikum, 1014049, SchH FH. - Forma vom Piastendamm, 1039364, SchH I.) Dam: Cilla v Huenenfeuer, 1112613, SchH I. (Lork v Eningsfeld, 1048410, SchH II. - Baerbel v d Pferde Heide, 1027152, SchH I.) Linebreeding: Hein Richterbach (5-5). Breeder: Ernst Lindhorst, Winsen/Aller. Owner: Erwin Bork, Niederkleen, Hilzweg.

Overall Evaluation: Medium large expressive male, very good angulation, good standing, strong bones, very good withers and back, very good croup, strong joints, strong hindquarters, correct, very good ground-covering gait, good drive, steady temperament, distinctive courage and fighting ability.

Temperament Including State Of Nerves: Lively, alert, good natured, fearless, audacious, strong nerves.

Analysis Of Structure While Posed: Trotter built, medium substantial, good posing.

Height of withers	64 cm	26"
Depth of chest	29 cm	12"
Chest circumferance	81 cm	32"
Weight	40 kg/	88 lbs.

Color And Marking: Black and tan marking, head strong, muzzle good, scissor bite, teeth healthy and strong.

Evaluation Of Gait And Walk: Trotter, feathery much ground covering and transitory gait, gaits straight, back tight and very good, elbows very good, good tight pastern, good hocks, effective drive, very good reach.

Analysis Of Temperament Characteristics: Expressive male, strong natural temperament, alert and brisk, strong nerves unaffected in traffic, gun steady and courageous.

Passed The Following Working Dog Trials: SchH I, good; SchH II, very good, SchH III and FH.

Breed Advice: For all loose bitches with less angulation than recommended.

Translated by Herby Merkel from the November 1972 K-9 Kapers.

PH: Polizei Hund—police dog.

PDH or DPH: Polizei Dienst Hund—police dog currently in service.

PFP-I, PFP-II: Polizei-Faehrtenhund-pruefung—two occupational titles, degrees given to dogs expert in police trailing work.

PSP-I, PSP-II—Schutzhund titles given to working police dogs expert in man-work.

SH: Sanitats Hund—Used for Red Cross dogs or ambulance dogs, particularly during wartime.

SuchH: Such Hund—search dog, tracking dog; earned in sports competition.

ZH-I, ZH-II: Zollhund—customs dog; two occupational titles available to dogs involved in customs work, and expert in narcotics and explosives.

Zpr: Zucht Pruefung—passed breed survey and is suitable for breeding. Like AD, this is not really a title, but you'll find it alongside actual titles.

MODERN GERMAN LINES

Other writers have built a case for a dividing line in time between the early days of German Shepherd Dog history and the "new era" by pointing to the 1925 Sieger Klodo von Boxberg that was chosen by von Stephanitz to signal an end to the overuse of large, square dogs. But I am unable to find a dramatic demarcation and therefore the only distinction I have made has been an arbitrary one of terms of roughly quarter-centuries.

The famous kennel names of the old era in Germany have largely and gradually been replaced (more slowly than in America) but are not to be forgotten: Blasienberg (no direct relation to the present Canadian kennel of that name), Riedekenberg, Grafenwerth, Bergerslust, Starkenburg, Starrenburg, Krone, Hohen Esp, Grafrath, Westfalenheim, Schwaben, Memmingen, and Kriminalpolizei.

Haus Schütting—One of the first kennels to arise out of the fertile soil of Klodo v Boxberg and the distant past was the Haus Schütting dynasty which reached far ahead into the post-World War II days. These were the highly respected lines of Dr. Werner Funk, and their glory and genes spread around the globe. Witz v Haus Schütting, for example, was exported to Japan, other dogs went to various European countries, and several were sent to America. A small sampling of Witz's worth is seen in his son

Hanko that became the 1965 Sieger, and in the G and H litters by von Sixtberg out of Caret v Elfenhain.

The 1929 Sieger Utz was the first luminary in a Haus Schütting galaxy of stars, with Sonja in the early 1930s, 1933 Siegerin Jamba, and 1935/36 Siegerin Stella (a befitting name). An Utz son in Dr. Funk's kennel, 1932 Sieger Hussan, also drew world-wide attention to his program. In 1964 Haus Schütting made the top spot again with Sieger Zibu, a Donar v d Firnskuppe son out of Niobe v Haus Schütting. On Utz were based Pfeffer and Gockel v Bern, Odin v Busecker-Schloss, some of the Piastendamm dogs, Lex Pruessenblut, R litter OsnabruckerLand, and their descendants.

Piastendamm—The Piastendamm name is another that has continued from the post-Klodo days to the present in both Germany and the Western Hemisphere. Gockel's son Ingo, linebred on Utz, was the grandsire of Lex Preussenblut that in turn sired the R litter OsnabruckerLand, and Ina v OsnabruckerLand, a bitch found in almost as many German and American pedigrees as are Rolf and Rosel. Dr. Simon's breeding expertise has given the world a large number of great individuals and families, especially through Ingo and his son Harras who were described as ideal specimens of the breed, a compliment not lightly tossed about. Beowulf, the massive dark gray sable, Ch Atlas, Atlas's sire, Ulbert, and son Raps were all links in a mighty chain that spanned the Atlantic Ocean.

As with the Pelztierfarm kennel, the Piastendamm dogs were generally known as much for their beauty as for their working ability. Atlas, son of Ulbert, produced Raps v Piastendamm. Both Atlas and Raps were sent to America and easily earned their championships, after leaving their imprints on German breeding. Raps' dam was a daughter of Lido v Friedlichenheim, a great Sieger-level dog that also left his mark on German dogs before being sent to the US where he earned his championship but was under-used by American breeders.

Dr. Simon was one of the early fans of a Klodo Eremitenklause son, Jupp v d Murrenhutte, who fulfilled his promise by becoming an excellent producer in the early 1970s. Jupp's dam was a Raps daughter and linebred 3-2 on Ulbert. By combining the Rolf-free, Axel-free lines of this Klodo with the Piastendamm lines (Axel/OsnabruckerLand in background), Jupp proved the value of outcrossing again. Jupp's son, Hero v Lauerhof, VA-2 in 1972 and 1973, has been used extensively in breeding programs. He is found in many American pedigrees, especially in those with Schutzhund titles and in many of those with black recessives or solid black, characteristics he was chosen for. Jupp was the sire of the VA-2, 3, and 5 bitches at the 1972 Sieger Show as well as many SG (very good) offspring shown in the younger classes.

Elfenhain/Sixtberg—These were two separate kennels but one Elfenhain bitch, Caret, was used to form the basis of the Sixtberg line. Bred to Witz, she gave the G and H litters; bred to Sieger Volker Zollgrenzschutzhaus she produced the C and D litters von Sixtberg. This tremendous producer was sired by Axel son Alf v Nordfelsen and her dam Anka was a member of the famous A litter which included Atlas v Elfenhain. Atlas was by Grimm v d Fahrmuhle out of Lexa v OsnabruckerLand.

The combination used by the crafty breeder of the Sixtbergs in this case was well planned to outcross from the very heavy OsnabruckerLand concentration which in Germany had often become *too* much, yielding some faults that could well have been repressed, if not eliminated, for the good of the breed. For example, Lexa's pedigree demonstrates the number of times the R litter and consequently Maja appeared. Heavy linebreeding is common in the US, but the Germans have generally frowned on the practice—especially closer than the fourth generation.

```
                          Trutz Schwanenstadt (Ingo Piastendamm)
              Lex P.*
                          Esta Preussenblut
        Rolf v OsnabruckerLand
                          Achilles (ex a Haus Schütting bitch)
              Maja v Osna.
                          Xanda Preussenblut
Lexa v OsnabruckerLand
                          Lex Preussenblut*
              Racker v OsnabruckerLand
                          Maja v OsnabruckerLand
        Vena v OsnabruckerLand
                          Falk OsnabruckerLand (Lex P. son)
              Blanka Fortunastolz
```

Caret was not the only accomplishment of Willi Sufke, the man who engineered the introduction of Grimm and then followed that with another outcross the next generation to Alf to yield that fantastic bitch. Besides her and Atlas, there were Grief and Dux, not to mention many other examples of this man's foresight and adherence to well-researched principles and data.

Can. Ch. Otti v d Erlalohe, CD, ''a''-normal. This excellent daughter of Gin v Lierberg and granddaughter of Sieger Zibu was imported by Ernie Loeb and owned by Fred Lanting. Temperament was both loving and ''tough as nails'', gait was floating and true, and Otti was the world's best mother.
Photo courtesy of E. Loeb, about 1970

OsnabrückerLand—The Axel/R litter combination again surfaces—this time in the Osnabrücker-Land lines. Axel daughter bred to a Rolf son gave Sieger Condor v Hohenstamm; Rosel daughter bred to Axel yielded Troll v Richterbach; a Rolf daughter bred to Grimm produced Frack v d Burg Arkenstede. R litter outcrossed to Sieger Arno v Haus Gersie, Volker, Eremitenklause and other lines seemed to bring a bit of magic to many breeders' attempts. And this magic spilled over into US breeding.

As you are no doubt beginning to suspect, there is a tendency for all roads to lead to Osnabrücker-Land. Almost all the great dogs in Germany and the rest of the world go back to Rolf, Racker, Rosel, Ina, or a combination of these. Ina was a Lex/Maja daughter and was also a valuable producer. Many of these great dogs are descendants of the super Rosel son, Hein v Richterbach, and some are from Hein's son Caesar v d Malmannsheide, but there are so many others that listing them all would require a separate chapter.

Sieben-Faulen—Another notable German breeding program of the middle years was conducted in Heinz Roeper's Sieben-Faulen kennel. Careful outcrossing from the Dettmar brothers' Preussenblut and OsnabrückerLand lines produced many fine animals. Drusus zu den Sieben-Faulen sired Amor v Haus Hoheide of Wikingerblut fame (Ulk's grandsire). Held bred to Ina v OsnabrückerLand gave Grille, the dam of Vello z d Sieben-Faulen, Roeper's most famous dog. Fred bred to a Colonia-Agrippina bitch produced the dam of Ute Grubenstolz that in turn was bred to a Mutz a d Kuckstrasse son to give a leading producing bitch of modern times, V-1 Renata de la Louve Romaine. She became famous for producing working dogs, some of whom also did quite well in German conformation shows. Ursus was a top show dog with an excellent front, but his moderate rear angulation would not have been appreciated by many US judges, hence he appears in few American pedigrees. Fix bred to Aja v Haus Solms gave Hein vom Koenigsbruch, the sire of the famous Canto v d Wienerau. Fix also was the sire of Mecky v Klammle and his full sister Ina v Klammle.

Vello and the Lierbergs—None of Roeper's many successes had as great an impact as Grille's son by Lex v Drei-Kinder-Haus, Vello zu den Sieben-Faulen, a controversial dog because he was born at the wrong time when large size was being heavily penalized. Vello nevertheless was an excellent specimen that really clicked when bred to Betty v Eningsfeld, a tough, V-rated bitch whose sire Arko v Riedersknapp was three times declared the best police dog in Germany.

The first Vello/Betty production was the B litter Lierberg whose members were so good looking, true moving, hard biting, courageous, and intelligent that they stunned the German Shepherd Dog world. Bodo, after becoming Sieger, was bought by Erich Renner of California, where he continued producing good dogs of great working ability. Bandit established himself in Denmark where he carried on the family tradition of producing a high percentage of good hips. Bernd stayed in Germany to represent the family there and become almost a necessity in Schutzhund pedigrees in future years. They were soon joined by repeat breedings, the D litter, F litter, and G litter von Lierberg. Most of the well-known members carried the black factor and were mostly black themselves. All were known for pronounced fighting spirit and great temperament as well as for very good body structure and gait.

Vello also demonstrated his worth when bred to the Hein v Richterbach daughter Gunda v Fohlenbrunnen by producing Jalk v Fohlenbrunnen. In one of those fortuitous combinations similar to the Vello/Betty, Lance/Bernd clicks, Jalk was outcrossed with Dixie v d Wienerau to produce many great offspring. Roon z d Sieben-Faulen is another Vello son found in some American pedigrees.

Pelztierfarm—The Pelztierfarm lines are also noted for a combination of conformation and working ability. The bitch that produced my N litter von Salix had as her grandsires VA-3 Erko v Dinkelland and VA-2 Mutz v d Pelztierfarm, a son of Axel v d Pelztierfarm. I feel a lot of boldness and working-dog qualities in some of my litters of the 1970s and 1980s have come down from the Lierberg, Eningsfeld, and Pelztierfarm dogs with a little help from the Spessartheide line (Hein).

Dr. Rummel, head of the SV, owned Mutz and regarded him very highly, but decided to sell him to an Italian breeder. Mutz was entered in the 1970 Sieger Show and took VA-2 under Rummel. Had the judge been someone else, Mutz may have become Sieger, but Rummel avoided controversy by not putting up a dog he had owned shortly before. Mutz had good hips, earned top scores in man-work (the attack/protection part of Schutzhund), and was V-rated (excellent) in spirit and courage.

Busecker Schloss—One of the oldest and most respected kennels in the world is and has been Alfred Hahn's Busecker Schloss. Early in the breed's history, a large sable male of sometimes overly-aggressive temperament was sent to America to take up the task of improving the breed on the West Coast. Odin v Busecker Schloss took the West and soon the whole country by storm. In the years following, many other Busecker Schloss dogs became famous for their working abilities, and the kennel began to have a strictly utilitarian reputation in the beauty-conscious United States. However, most of the Busecker Schloss dogs were as good in Europe's conformation rings as in the Schutzhund and other working-dog trials.

The 1957 Sieger Arno v Haus Gersie sired innumerable good dogs including the V litter von Busecker Schloss (Valet, Veit, etc.). V-rated Valet was bred to Zita v Busecker Schloss, a daughter of VA Jonny v d Riedperle, to give the excellent Issel who earned the HGH title in sheepherding trials. This title is fairly common among Busecker Schloss dogs, as are many others such as the FH

for tracking. Issel bred to Bernd v Lierberg produced the VA bitch Seffe v Busecker Schloss in a proven combination of Herr Hahn's lines with those of the Lierbergs.

Wienerau—A breeding program which may go down in history as one of the most successful is that of Walter Martin. Rarely does the SV allow very close linebreeding, requiring that dogs of quality and ability not have hidden or obvious faults in common before agreeing to close-up breeding. It is to Martin's credit that SV officials have given him such permission a number of times. He seems to have been very successful in linebreeding on dogs carefully researched, then outcrossing when the qualities of the linebred ones were optimal, predictable, and beneficial.

Martin used the Vello son, Jalk v Fohlenbrunnen to great advantage as a stud for Dixie v d Wienerau. Dixie was a product of VA Arno v Haus Schwingel and Berta v Lorscher Sand, an excellent daughter of 1955 Sieger Alf v Nordfelsen, and was linebred 3-3 on Axel. The outcross to Jalk was a gold mine, giving him the great L litter von Wienerau which included the 1965 Siegerin, Landa. V-1 Lido was a littermate and he was bred to his half-sister out of Dixie, Frigga vom Asterplatz, to give Yoga v d Wienerau. Then Yoga was bred to 1965 VA-4 Condor v Zollgrenzschutzhaus—one of Joseph Wasserman's later successes—a son of Condor v

Alfred Hahn, owner of Busecker Schloss Kennel since 1925, shows a photo of Sagus, one of his famous sables.

Quanto Wiernerau son, VA Herzog v. Adeloga celebrates his 13th birthday with breeder/owner Albert Platz.

Can. G. V. Ch. Harry vom Donaukai, owned by Bill Ford. This import had a significant influence on German breeding, siring Volker v. Zollgrenz-Schutzhaus among other famous and important dogs, before coming to work his magic in the U.S. and Canada. Photo by Norton of Kent, courtesy Chum Porter.

Schnapp and V Carmen v Sixtberg. This fortunate blend produced the great VA dog Quanto v Wienerau, sire of the 1973 Sieger Dick v Adeloga and his brother Quinn.

Quanto's Koer report described him as medium sized, full of expression, very strong, very well angulated both front and rear, with good wrists, tight pasterns, broad legs, and good "bone" (substance). His back, croup, and ligaments were good and he covered much ground as a result of his strong and powerful drive. He had steady nerves and pronounced fighting spirit in Schutzhund and other temperament tests. Quanto, V-2 in 1971, was ultimately exported to Italy, but not before he left many promising progeny in Germany. After his move he continued to be available to many Europeans and has left his mark in many countries. He was known for passing along good fronts, size, bone, pigment, and generally good type and structure. Disadvantages include short croups, long coats, and an undesirable amount of hip dysplasia, but much has to be laid at the feet of the bitches bred to him.

Liane, a sister of Lido and Landa, was bred to Hein v Koenigsbruch to yield Canto v Wienerau, a V-1 rated dog that proved to be one of the more valuable studs in recent history. His sire, Hein, was a large dog, long and very angulated, with harmonious and balanced far-reaching movement and an "ideal" topline. He exhibited a confident temperament, friendly composure with pronounced protective instinct and courage. Hein went to England but was possibly underused there.

Canto was of medium size like his mother, showed beautiful and balanced proportions and movement, with the same good back and croup possessed by both parents. He had very good chest development, good angulation fore and aft, and substantial "bone." He stood slightly cowhocked and tended to throw his hocks out when moving, which often happens in the case of much angulation such as he and his sire had. Although considered a little loose the first time he was breed-surveyed, he was said to have tightened up for his second Koer evaluation. Canto had only two siblings, though his dam was from a litter of ten and his sire one of seven. Canto produced both blue pigment and hemophilia, but only his daughters inherited and passed the blood disorder. He was also faulted for producing poor "strength of nerves" in some pups, as well as poor pigment. He passed good croups, great stride, and considerable rear angulation.

The combination of Quanto and Canto lines in many variations has produced and will probably continue to produce an abundance of good dogs, though the breeder must beware of heavy linebreeding. Other Wienerau dogs and their descendants will, I predict, make news for many generations to come. VA Nick v Dreimarkenstein, a Lido son and the sire of the 1971 Siegerin, is one to watch for in the pedigrees, but there are plenty more.

Conclusion

History is the present looked at from the longer viewpoint of the future. Therefore, what remains to be said of the history of the German Shepherd Dog will best be condensed in later years from the voluminous records of today, but with the advantage of perspective of time.

3

The Standard

The Standard for German Shepherd Dogs in the United States has undergone several changes over the years. The first edition was published in 1929; in 1943 and 1958 revised versions were adopted. The Standard as we know it today was accepted in 1978. For the purpose of comparison, the complete present-day version and part of the 1929 Standard are included.

1929 STANDARD

(From: *Pure-Bred Dogs,* 1929 edition; Courtesy, American Kennel Club.)

Shepherd Dogs are regarded as suitable for a great variety of purposes. Sheepherding is an instinct, although it is perfected by training, while they are also suitable for any kind of work requiring strict obedience to commands, speed, and some strength. They are largely used for police work.

Description and Standard of Points

(Courtesy of Shepherd Dog Club of America, Inc.)

General Appearance—(a) Structure—The Shepherd Dog is a dog above the middle size. He is long, strong and well muscled, full of life and at attention; nothing escapes his sharp senses.

The average height for dogs is 60 centimeters (24 inches) and for bitches between 55 and 58 centimeters (22 to 23½ inches). This height is established by taking a perpendicular line from the top of the shoulder-blade to the ground with the coat parted or so pushed down that the measurement

will show only the actual height of the frame or structure of the dog.

The most desirable height for the Shepherd Dog as a working dog, is between 55 to 64 or 65 centimeters (22 to 26 inches). The working value of dogs above or below these heights is lessened.

Note—Height above the average should not be considered a fault, however, provided the proportion of length to height is correct, and the weight of bone is also in proportion and not so great as to make the dog clumsy or readily fatigued. In all cases the proportion of length to height should not be less than as ten is to nine, preferably as ten is to eight.

(b) Characteristics—The traits and special characteristics of the Shepherd are watchfulness, loyalty, honesty, and an aristocratic bearing, forming a combination which makes the purebred Shepherd Dog an ideal guard and companion. It is desirable to try to improve his appearance, but nothing must be done which in any way detracts from his usefulness.

Head—The size of the head should be in proportion to the body, without being clumsy. It should be clean cut and of medium width between the ears. The forehead, seen from the front, only moderately arched, lacking or with very slight, center furrow. The skull slopes in a slanting line without abrupt stop, continuing into the wedge-shaped long muzzle; the muzzle is strong, the lips tight and dry, firmly fitting together; the cheeks slightly rounded toward the front, but without undue prominence as seen from the front. The bridge of the nose is straight and in parallel line with an imaginary elongation of the line of the forehead. Jaws and teeth are very strong, teeth meeting in a scissors grip, but not overshot.

OFFICIAL STANDARD FOR THE GERMAN SHEPHERD DOG
(Approved February 11, 1978.)

General Appearance—The first impression of a good German Shepherd Dog is that of a strong, agile, well-muscled animal, alert and full of life. It is well balanced, with harmonious development of the forequarter and hindquarter. The dog is longer than tall, deep-bodied, and presents an outline of smooth curves rather than angles. It looks substantial and not spindly, giving the impression, both at rest and in motion, of muscular fitness and nimbleness without any look of clumsiness or soft living. The ideal dog is stamped with a look of quality and nobility—difficult to define, but unmistakable when present. Secondary sex characteristics are strongly marked, and every animal gives a definite impression of masculinity or femininity, according to its sex.

Character—The breed has a distinct personality marked by direct and fearless, but not hostile, expression, self-confidence and a certain aloofness that does not lend itself to immediate and indiscriminate friendships. The dog must be approachable, quietly standing its ground and showing confidence and willingness to meet overtures without itself making them. It is poised, but when the occasion demands, eager and alert; both fit and willing to serve in its capacity as companion, watchdog, blind leader, herding dog, or guardian, whichever the circumstances may demand. The dog must not be timid, shrinking behind its master or handler; it should not be nervous, looking about or upward with anxious expression or showing nervous reactions, such as tucking of tail, to strange sounds or sights. Lack of confidence under any surroundings is not typical of good character. Any of the above deficiencies in character which indicate shyness must be penalized as very serious faults and any dog exhibiting pronounced indications of these must be excused from the ring. It must be possible for the judge to observe the teeth and to deter-

mine that both testicles are descended. Any dog that attempts to bite the judge must be disqualified. The ideal dog is a working animal with an incorruptible character combined with body and gait suitable for the arduous work that constitutes its primary purpose.

Head—The head is noble, cleanly chiseled, strong without coarseness, but above all not fine, and in proportion to the body. The head of the male is distinctly masculine, and that of the bitch distinctly feminine. The muzzle is long and strong with the lips firmly fitted, and its topline is parallel to the topline of the skull. Seen from the front, the forehead is only moderately arched, and the skull slopes into the long, wedge-shaped muzzle without abrupt stop. Jaws are strongly developed. *Ears*—Ears are moderately pointed, in proportion to the skull, open toward the front, and carried erect when at attention, the ideal carriage being one in which the center lines of the ears, viewed from the front, are parallel to each other and perpendicular to the ground. A dog with cropped or hanging ears must be disqualified. *Eyes*—Of medium size, almond shaped, set a little obliquely and not protruding. The color is as dark as possible. The expression keen, intelligent and composed. *Teeth*—42 in number—20 upper and 22 lower—are strongly developed and meet in a scissors bite in which part of the inner surface of the upper incisors meet and engage part of the outer surface of the lower incisors. An overshot jaw or a level bite is undesirable. An undershot jaw is a disqualifying fault. Complete dentition is to be preferred. Any missing teeth other than first premolars is a serious fault.

Neck—The neck is strong and muscular, clean-cut and relatively long, proportionate in size to the head and without loose folds of skin. When the dog is at attention or excited, the head is raised and the neck carried high; otherwise typical carriage of the head is forward rather than up and but little higher than the top of the shoulders, particularly in motion.

Forequarters—The shoulder blades are long and obliquely angled, laid on flat and not placed forward. The upper arm joins the shoulder blade at about a right angle. Both the upper arm and the shoulder blade are well muscled. The forelegs, viewed from all sides, are straight and the bone oval rather than round. The pasterns are strong and

Femininity Personified
Am. & Can. Ch. Hexe's Bella of Highland Hills, C.D.
(1967) This bitch was an excellent example of the desired "secondary sex characteristics" called for in the Standard. Bella won her first major at 14 months, later amassed over 20 BOB's and BOS's in both specialty and all-breed shows, including Group wins in Canada. A granddaughter of Ch. Ulk Wikingerblut, she more resembled the Longworth and Edgetown dogs on whom she was linebred. *Photo courtesy Elli Matlin*

Select Ch. Rex Edlu-Mibach. One of the last of the great Bernd vom Kallengarten's sons, born 1964, Rex resembled his sire most in this photo (courtesy Louise & Ed Ryske, owners). Linebred Axel 3-4 and R-OsnabrukerLand 4,5-5,5,5, Rex exemplified the magic of this genetic combination, possessing and passing along the size, rear angulation, length, and masculine head of Axel's genes as well as the great shoulder layback, balance, pigmentation, and nobility of the OsnabruckerLand lines.

springy and angulated at approximately a 25-degree angle from the vertical.

Feet—The feet are short, compact, with toes well arched, pads thick and firm, nails short and dark. The dewclaws, if any, should be removed from the hind legs. Dewclaws on the forelegs may be removed, but are normally left on.

Proportion—The German Shepherd Dog is longer than tall, with the most desirable proportion as 10 to 8½. The desired height for males at the top of the highest point of the shoulder blade is 24 to 26 inches; and for bitches, 22 to 24 inches. The length is measured from the point of the prosternum or breastbone to the rear edge of the pelvis, the ischial tuberosity.

Body—The whole structure of the body gives an impression of depth and solidity without bulkiness. *Chest*—Commencing at the prosternum, it is well filled and carried well down between the legs. It is deep and capacious, never shallow, with ample room for lungs and heart, carried well forward, with the prosternum showing ahead of the shoulder in profile. *Ribs*—Well sprung and long, neither barrel-shaped nor too flat, and carried down to a sternum which reaches to the elbows. Correct ribbing allows the elbows to move back freely when the dog is at a trot. Too round causes interference and throws the elbows out; too flat or short causes pinched elbows. Ribbing is carried well back so that the loin is relatively short. *Abdomen*—Firmly held and not paunchy. The bottom line is only moderately tucked up in the loin.

Topline—*Withers*—The withers are higher than and sloping into the level back. *Back*—The back is straight, very strongly developed without sag or roach, and relatively short. The desirable long proportion is not derived from a long back, but from over-all length with relation to height, which is achieved by length of forequarter and length of withers and hindquarter, viewed from the side. *Loin*—Viewed from the top, broad and strong. Undue length between the last rib and the thigh, when viewed from the side, is undesirable. *Croup*—Long and gradually sloping.

Tail—Bushy, with the last vertebra extended at least to the hock joint. It is set smoothly into the croup and low rather than high. At rest, the tail hangs in a slight curve like a saber. A slight hook—sometimes carried to one side—is faulty only to the extent that it mars general appearance. When the dog is excited or in motion, the curve is accentuated and the tail raised, but it should never be curled forward beyond a vertical line. Tails too short, or with clumpy ends due to ankylosis, are serious faults. A dog with a docked tail must be disqualified.

Hindquarters—The whole assembly of the thigh, viewed from the side, is broad, with both upper and lower thigh well muscled, forming as nearly as possible a right angle. The upper thigh bone parallels the shoulder blade while the lower thigh bone parallels the upper arm. The metatarsus (the unit between the hock joint and the foot) is short, strong and tightly articulated.

Gait—A German Shepherd Dog is a trotting dog, and its structure has been developed to meet the requirements of its work. *General Impression*—The gait is outreaching, elastic, seemingly without effort, smooth and rhythmic, covering the maximum amount of ground with the minimum number of steps. At a walk it covers a great deal of ground, with long stride of both hind legs and forelegs. At a trot the dog covers still more ground with even longer stride, and moves powerfully but easily, with coordination and balance so that the gait appears to be the steady motion of a well-lubricated machine. The feet travel close to the ground on both forward reach and backward push. In order to achieve ideal movement of this kind, there must be good muscular development and ligamentation. The hindquarters deliver, through the back, a powerful forward thrust which slightly lifts the whole animal and drives the body forward. Reaching far under, and passing the imprint left by the front foot, the hind foot takes hold of the ground; then hock, stifle and upper thigh come into play and sweep back, the stroke of the hind leg finishing with the foot still close to the ground in a smooth follow-through. The over-reach of the hindquarter usually necessitates one hind foot passing outside and the other hind foot passing inside the track of the forefeet, and such action is not faulty unless the locomotion is crabwise with the dog's body sideways out of the normal straight line.

Transmission—The typical smooth, flowing gait is maintained with great strength and firmness of back. The whole effort of the hindquarter is transmitted to the forequarter through the loin, back and withers. At full trot, the back must remain firm and level without sway, roll, whip or roach. Unlevel topline with withers lower than the hip is a fault. To compensate for the forward motion imparted by the hindquarters, the shoulder should open to its full extent. The forelegs should reach out close to the ground in a long stride in harmony with that of the hindquarters. The dog does not track on widely separated parallel lines, but brings the feet inward toward the middle line of the body when trotting in order to maintain balance. The feet track closely but do not strike or cross over. Viewed from the front, the front legs function from the shoulder joint to the pad in a straight line. Viewed from the rear, the hind legs function from the hip joint to the pad in a straight line. Faults of gait, whether from front, rear or side, are to be considered very serious faults.

Color—The German Shepherd Dog varies in color, and most colors are permissible. Strong rich colors are preferred. Nose black. Pale, washed-out colors and blues or livers are serious faults. A white dog or a dog with a nose that is not predominantly black, must be disqualified.

Coat—The ideal dog has a double coat of medium length. The outer coat should be as dense as possible, hair straight, harsh and lying close to the body. A slightly wavy outer coat, often of wiry texture, is permissible. The head, including the inner ear and foreface, and the legs and paws are covered with short hair, and the neck with longer and thicker hair. The rear of the forelegs and hind legs has somewhat longer hair extending to the pastern and hock, respectively. Faults in coat include soft, silky, too long outer coat, woolly, curly, and open coat.

DISQUALIFICATIONS

Cropped or hanging ears.
Undershot jaw.
Docked tail.
White dogs.
Dogs with noses not predominantly black.
Any dog that attempts to bite the judge.

Changes to the Standard over the Years

Coat—Of special interest in the 1929 edition is the emphasis on utility as ''an ideal guard dog and companion'' in preference over superficial beauty.

Also at that time three coat varieties were recognized: smooth, long, and wire-haired or rough-coated. Quite a few long-coated dogs are still around, though not often in the show ring. American fanciers and too many judges react with much more violence to long coats than any of the versions of the Standard would indicate is needed.

The 1929 Standard reads, ''Too short a coat is a fault,'' but by the time the 1943 revision was adopted, discrimination in coat resulted in the statement: ''Faults in coat include … too long outer coat and curly … coat.'' There is no mention of a separate rough-coated variety except as can be inferred from the statement: ''A slightly wavy coat, often of wiry texture, is equally permissible.''

Size—Measurements to the top of the highest point of the shoulder blade have increased over the years. In 1929 the Standard was 24 inches (60 cm) for males and 22 to 23½ inches (55 to 58 cm) for bitches. Today, both the American and German Standards list the correct or desired height for males at 24 to 26 inches (60 to 65 cm) and for females 22 to 24 inches (55 to 60 cm). Actually, the tendency for judges and breeders to give preference to those on the upper end of the height range continues, though some control by the SV is exercised whenever the trend gets too strong in that direction (see figures 3.1 and 3.2). Also regarding size, most early specimens were a little lighter in weight than were the breed-surveyed German dogs in 1973 (or today's dogs). They were less uniform, as would be expected in a newly organized breed, and included taller, leggier dogs than have been seen in recent decades. In short, today's dogs fall within more narrow ranges of both height and weight.

Character—Nothing explicit or detailed regarding temperament appeared in the 1929 Standard, but those were still the days when it was understood that the dog *must* possess the strength of character suiting it for ''an ideal guard and companion.'' Popularity of the breed in the years between the big wars necessitated adding, in 1943, the first sentence under the heading of *Character* as it now appears in the 1978 Standard, and in a later paragraph, some wording similar to the rest of the present description of its personality. The 1978 revision added one phrase designed to impress upon judges the importance of tightening up where they had become lax. This sentence directed the judge to excuse from the ring any dog exhibiting pronounced deficiencies in character, or temperament faults. It will take some time before this is adequately enforced, as many judges have no vested interest in the betterment of the breed, and many are unable to recognize, by the look in a dog's eyes, the indications of a lack of confidence. Only experience enables one to distinguish between the watchfulness unfortunately described in 1929 as: "Eyes ... expression should ... show distrust of strangers," and the frightened-but-trained-to-stand appearance of a dog with a faulty temperament. The 1978 Standard uses "...certain aloofness ..." to replace the 1929 sentence on distrust—a good choice, I might add.

Head—Missing teeth had become a problem worthy of corrective measures by 1943 when a short statement was added: "While missing premolars are frequently observed, complete dentition is decidedly to be preferred." Slightly stronger wording was introduced with the 1978 version: "Any missing teeth other than first premolars is a serious fault."

The mention of ear carriage, "... center lines ... parallel ... and perpendicular to the ground," has remained untouched, even though no one has yet described a satisfactory way to determine where the center lines *are*; best to look at good dogs and use them for comparison. The outer (lateral) edges of the ears start out almost vertical at the base and curve inward (medially) just before the tips. It appears that even more clarification is needed in this area.

Gait—Twenty-three percent of the present version covers the topic of gait, which is only briefly mentioned in the German Standard and in the 1929 American Standard. Von Stephanitz tried to de-emphasize a lot of gaiting during judging in the show ring, because a lot of faults can be hidden by a skilled handler moving his dog, especially at a fast gait.

Feet—Pasterns have been described in all versions as having a combination of springiness and strength, but it was not until the 1978 revision that the ideal angle was said to be 25 degrees from the vertical. Yet this was not a recently determined angle. Von Stephanitz said two things of interest in this context: The length of the metacarpus "must not be excessive," and the pastern should have "an

angle of from 25 to 30 degrees." Very interesting that it took nearly half a century for that latter specification to be put into our Standard. Could it be that weak pasterns had become a serious and widespread problem? Undoubtedly, for they are still prevalent in the 1980s. Perhaps a stronger warning is needed in either the next revision or in announcements made in the *Gazette*. The 1929 Standard seemed to reverse von Stephanitz and called for long pasterns. This was changed in 1943 to "of medium length," but reference to length was dropped in 1958 and subsequent revisions.

Regarding what was translated as the "rear pasterns," von Stephanitz said that the hock itself should be long, this length coming from the fibular tarsal bone, mostly—the one which juts upward from the other tarsal bones to serve as a point of attachment for the Achilles tendon. It would be natural to assume that if this one bone were long, others in the limb, especially those nearby, would also be relatively long. Speaking of the rear feet, von Stephanitz said, "They must be proportionately stronger and longer" than the front feet, and I feel sure he meant to include the metatarsus itself as well. The 1929 AKC Standard called for great strength in the metatarsus, and a considerable angle with the "stifle," used inaccurately to refer to the shank or lower thigh. The 1943 Standard referred to the metatarsus (commonly called the *hock*) as the metacarpus, which typographical or typesetting error was corrected in the 1958 revision. But in both it was called "the fulcrum upon which much of the forward movement of the dog depends" and required to be short. This contributed to the confusion between the tarsus and metatarsus. I prefer the 1929 wording best: "comparatively short."

Cowhocks were listed as a serious fault in 1929, but the 1943 and 1958 revisions cautioned that this "decided fault" be evaluated in motion to ascertain if the condition truly exists. Later versions say nothing about cowhocks except by implications when describing the transmission "going away." Faults of gait are there shown to be very serious.

Tail—In 1943, the tail's slight hook to the side (which has been present in the breed since long before registration) was suddenly and subtly claimed as being somewhat faulty. This statement underwent modification until the 1978 Standard declares the slight hook to be faulty "... only to the extent that it mars general appearance."

Disqualifications—The 1943 Standard disqualified dogs that did not have both testicles descended into the scrotum, and in 1956 the AKC ruled that such a condition would bar *any* breed from show competition. In addition, effective April 1986, the AKC added a disqualification for *all* breeds, in the case of a dog which "attacks any person," and directs the judge to excuse any that appear unsafe to approach or examine.

In addition to the specific disqualifications for each breed, the American Kennel Club has made the following apply to all breeds:

A dog which is blind, deaf, castrated, spayed, or which has been changed in appearance by artificial means except as specified in the standard for its breed, or a male which does not have two normal testicles normally located in the scrotum, may not compete at any show and will be disqualified except that a castrated male may be entered as Stud Dog in the Stud Dog Class and a spayed bitch may be entered as Brood Bitch in the Brood Bitch Class. A dog will not be considered to have been changed by artificial means because of removal of dewclaws or docking of a tail, if it is of a breed in which such removal or docking is a regularly approved practice which is not contrary to the standard. (Note: Spayed bitches and monorchid or cryptorchid dogs may compete in obedience trials.)

A dog that is lame at any show may not compete and shall not receive any award at the show. It shall be the judge's responsibility to determine whether the dog is lame.

No dog shall be eligible to compete at any show, and no dog shall receive any award at any show in the event the natural color or shade of natural color or the natural markings of the dog have been altered or changed by the use of any substance, whether such substance has been used for cleaning purposes or for any other reason. Such cleaning substances are to be removed before the dog enters the ring.

Any dog whose ears have been cropped or cut in any way shall be ineligible to compete at any show in any state where the laws prohibit the same, except subject to the provisions of such laws.

A dog that in the opinion of the judge menaces or threatens or exhibits any sign that it may not be safely approached by the judge or examined by the judge in the normal manner shall be excused from the ring. When the judge excuses the dog, he shall mark the dog "Excused," stating the reason in the judge's book. A dog so excused shall not be counted as having competed.

A dog that in the opinion of the judge attacks any person in the ring shall be disqualified. When the judge disqualifies the dog, he shall mark the dog "Disqualified," stating the reason in the judge's book. When a dog has been disqualified under this section, any awards at that show shall be canceled by the American Kennel Club, and the dog may not again compete unless and until following application by the owner to The American Kennel Club, the owner has received official notification from The American Kennel Club that the dog's show eligibility has been reinstated.[1]

Future Changes

Although the Standard is only half of what is needed to evaluate German Shepherd Dogs—the other half being competent judging—most revisions need only be modifications designed to clarify rather than greatly change. For one thing, a better knowledge of color genetics can rectify the confusion between blues and livers as being "serious faults" and the next sentence disqualifying them, since such dogs will be among those whose noses are "not predominately black." In addition, we might consider copying the British Standard regarding eyes: "... as nearly as possible matching the surrounding coat but darker rather than lighter in shade" if we wish to reflect the situation, or simply state that dark eye pigment is to be preferred. Light eyes have nothing to do with anything except aesthetics. Also, perhaps someday the first digit on the forelegs will no longer be called a "dewclaw," which word refers properly to that structure on the rear legs only. "Oval bone" also is anatomically incorrect, though people know what is meant and desired in the foreleg shape. Hopefully, the reference to testicles will be moved from the paragraph on *Character* to the one on *Body*, or the statement might just say that the dog should willingly submit to a judge's examination. But all of these suggestions are minor compared to the more important revisions that will eventually come about as a result of better understanding of gait and structure.

The Standard's present wording on overreach appears to conflict with the description in the next paragraph of feet being brought "... inward toward the middle line of the body when trotting." When

---

[1] *Rules Applying to Registration and Dog Shows,* American Kennel Club, 1989.

slow-motion cinematographs of a dog moving away from the camera and circling around the observer are compared with footprints left on wet sand or on paper, it is clear that the dog randomly alternates or changes which hind leg is placed under the body and which is outside the plane of the front leg on the same side. A dog that circles to his left as in a show ring will most of the time overreach with his left rear foot passing the left front paw on the inside of the circle. A dog moving relatively straight shows a variable pattern, sometimes bringing the left rear foot in closer to the midline than where the left front foot is leaving or will leave, and sometimes several steps are taken with the other foot in that position. The dog may vary this placement based on his perception of a crack in the sidewalk or anticipation of turning. This variation can be seen if you roadwork your dog by letting him trot ahead of you on at least a 6-foot leash. While following him, concentrate on the placement of one of his rear feet in relation to the front one on the same side. The proper tendency to single-track will someday be addressed in the Standard, with parallel metatarsi in motion added as a fault in some future revision.

The nonsense of expecting the upper and lower thigh to form a right angle will be eliminated when radiographic studies are brought to the attention of a revision committee. Such structure simply is not realistic, and those dogs that are posed in such a way as to suggest such a build are made grotesque in their appearance. Actually, X rays are not needed; by simply feeling the joints, bones, and angles, one can easily determine the angle that *does* exist. Nor does the upper thigh bone parallel the shoulder blade except for a fleeting instant in each full stride. The femur is vertical in a normal stance, and the shoulder is not (hopefully!). Numerous errors, possibly inserted by members of the Flat Earth Society, are made regarding structure and angles, and thanks to Rachel Page Elliot's work and the preaching of others including this author, these will someday be changed.

The phrase concerning the shoulder assembly being "... about a right angle," leads too many to feel that the range from 89 to 91 degrees is "about" enough, but the famous *Fortunate Fields* work by Humphrey and Warner in the 1930s concluded that the ideal angle for the trotter-built working dog was 102 degrees. The real angle in most excellent specimens is closer to the range of 100 to 110 degrees than the fanciful 90 degrees mentioned in so many texts. The next major revision of the Standard could well address this problem as well as make reference to exactly how the angle is measured or estimated. (See the chapter on anatomy for details.)

Ideal proportions (body length: height at withers) are 10:9, and have been described as such by no less than von Stephanitz, Humphrey and Warner, and other utilitarians. In the future when we finally realize that the modern, stretched-out dog with loose ligaments is *not* the working dog that the founders envisioned, the Standard will abandon the 10:8½ or 10:8 proportions now in vogue and return to the original and best ratio. I join with Goldbecker and Hart, Pickett, and other authorities in looking hopefully toward that day.

While we're on the topic of proportions, which figured tremendously in von Stephanitz's mind, let's address body weight. The breed is supposed to be of *medium* size, yet most of even the German *auslese* or *vorzüglich* dogs are described as *over-medium* size. I feel the "weights of dogs of desirable size in proper flesh and condition" should reappear in a future revision, as it was in the 1943 edition: 75 to 85 pounds for males, 60 to 70 pounds for females. Most Shepherds over these weights are ungainly, non-athletic in appearance, and would probably be found to be inefficient if true tests were possible.

While this Standard is in need of some change, it is still the best concise description of the ideal German Shepherd Dog in the English language, and it is one of the best Standards of all breeds of dogs. It's well worth reading and rereading.

4

ANATOMY

Anatomy is not simply the study of the separate parts of the dog, but is also an attempt to understand how all the organs and systems function. This chapter is an abbreviated survey of the anatomy of the dog, with a look at the structures in roughly the same order followed in the Standard. The sensory and musculo-skeletal systems are discussed in this chapter and the next, which deals with gait. Internal organs are dealt with in the chapter on diseases.

The Standard attempts to describe the ideal German Shepherd Dog mostly in terms that are difficult or impossible to quantify. Instead of mathematical ratios, points, measurements, and other specifics, the dog is described in vague terms such as: moderately, in proportion, noble, medium, strong, and relatively. In order to evaluate dogs of any breed, a person needs at least a basic knowledge of anatomy, utility, gait, and dog psychology. Judges should be familiar with the similarities and differences between breeds, and so should you.

Most people first notice the German Shepherd Dog's longer-than-tall appearance and the typical pose of one rear leg positioned partly under the body. This stance differs from that of most other breeds in that it is less "square." Actually, the breed standards of half the old working group (now working and herding groups) call for a dog with more length than height, with the others calling for a square dog. This squareness is measured from the prosternum (forechest) to the ischiatic tuberosities (rump) and is approximately equal to the height from the top of the scapula or withers to the

ground. In contrast, the German Shepherd Dog Standard calls for a length to height ratio of 10:8½, though many authorities think 10:9 is better.

PROPORTIONS AND SIZE

The matter of proportion is one of harmony, and in the German Shepherd Dog harmony of form must be based on utility. Understanding canine anatomy helps one develop an eye for the merits and proportions of the individual dog.

Some thirty years after the SV was organized, the breed Standard height range was 21¾ inches to 25¾ inches. Some people look at this and think the modern Shepherd Dog is larger than in the early days—not so. The average dog today is *heavier*, but the range of heights is now less than it was then, thanks to selection for a longer, lower-stationed dog since 1925. Americans in particular tend to think that bigger is better, and we must be continuously reminded that, as Gershwin put it: It ain't necessarily so!

All working dogs (I use the word *working* deliberately, in spite of the show classification of the Shepherd as a herding breed) whether used for herding, hunting, police duty, or similar activities, must be untiring, strong, capable of turning quickly, and agile enough to overcome obstacles by climbing or jumping. A breed which is supposed to be about 75 to 80 pounds and around 25 to 26 inches (males) is done a disservice when 30-inch dogs of nearly twice the serviceable weight are admired.

These are not comments based simply on aesthetic preference, but proven by time and test. "Giants are never nimble," said von Stephanitz. According to all physiological evidence, with an increase in size, the weight increases more than does the strength needed for movement equivalent to that of an agile dog. A dog that is 75 percent heavier does *not* have 75 percent greater length of its striated muscle fibers and it consequently can do less work of the type for which the German Shepherd Dog has been developed. Giant breeds do well at power-lifting and pulling, but cannot hope to match the smaller ones in endurance, speed, or agility. However, a dog that is too small lacks the bearing and strength for much of the work expected of the German Shepherd Dog, but undersized dogs are seldom as saleable and therefore not as threatening to type preservation as are the oversized ones.

HEAD

A "noble" head is a combination of structure and voluntary expression. The blunt wedge of the skull and muzzle should not be as long and narrow as the Collie's head, nor as short as a Rottweiler's. In the German Shepherd Dog, the skull from the stop to the occiput should be approximately as long as, but no shorter than, the foreface from stop to tip of the nose. We generally think of the face as being that portion of the head including the eyebrows and everything forward, but the foreface is properly applied to the area from the middle of the stop to the nose tip although the terms are often interchangeably used.

Although the cranium is not truly flat, but rather is steadily curved in a long arch from stop to occiput, it should give the impression of a fairly flat plane which further appears to parallel the nasal ridge atop the muzzle. There is no such thing as a perfectly straight line in the skeletal structure of the dog, for all bones curve, taper, or otherwise change from one end to the other. Erect ears effectively block one's view of the most curved part of the backskull, so a profile of an excellent German Shepherd Dog head will give the impression of those two "parallel" toplines.

Besides ear carriage, nobility of expression is most fully presented by the eyes and their setting. The greater the stop, the more forward-looking the eyes appear to be and therefore, they tend to give a somewhat more alert, intense expression than do the "kinder, milder" eyes of Collies, Borzois, and similar dogs with little or no stop. Less stop gives the impression (or actual condition) of the eyes being set more on the sides of the head, while a sharp break between those two planes places the eyes more on the "front" of the face. Of course it follows that a too-pronounced stop may give the impression of a coarse, ugly, bug-eyed head with too-round eyes.

Seen from the side, the head should not be "snipey" (excessively pointed). Such a head on a male is an outrage, but even bitches can have substance to the lower jawbones and sufficient width to the forward limit of the muzzle without losing their femininity. American breeders must continually be on guard against the problem of bitchy males—those which lack obvious masculinity—and the head is a good place to start evaluating these secondary sex characteristics. A less frequent problem in the US is the doggy bitch although they too

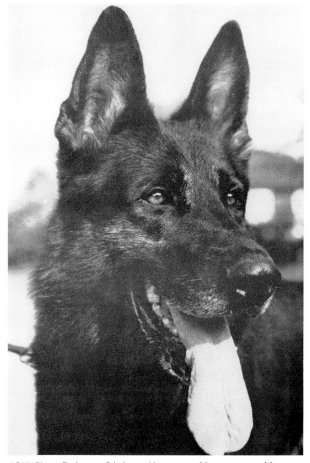

1967 Sieger Bodo vom Lierberg. Almost everything anyone could want in a dog.

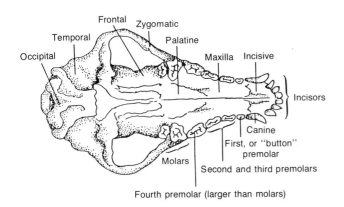

a. Skull and upper jaw, ventral view.

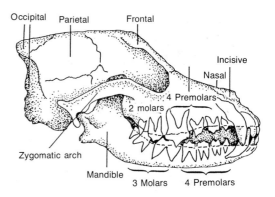

b. Skull bones and teeth, lateral view.

may be on the increase. The great Caralon's Hein produced many such bitches, but lately I've seen some from lines unconnected with his. Calipers to measure the width of a dog's head and relate it to the size of the rest of the dog are cumbersome and don't necessarily work. Best to rely on experience and the willingness of veterans to point out the qualities that constitute a proper male or female head.

Teeth

The twenty-two lower teeth in the adult dog are imbedded in the lower jawbone called the mandible; of the twenty upper teeth, fourteen are in the maxillary bones with the other six in the incisive bones which in the adult have fused with the maxilla. It's easier to count the teeth in bunches rather than try to remember which are molars, which are premolars, and then try to count all forty-two choppers. From the centerline of the front, count three little ones on top, one big canine, three little ones again, then the one big carnassial (cheek) tooth, then two smaller ones. On the bottom, it's the same story, except that between the canine and the carnassial giant, there are *four* little ones. Not exactly a scientific description, but so much faster to judge and count accurately!

The incisors (front six teeth on top and bottom) should meet in a scissors bite in which the top front edge of the bottom teeth rest against the inside surface of the top teeth when the mouth is closed and the rear teeth are meshed. Of course, the mandible is movable so the dog can thrust its lower jaw out

at will in order to pinch something between the leading edges of each set. The truly level bite—in which four top incisors meet directly with their opposing teeth on the bottom when the mouth is in a fully closed position—is undesirable but not a serious fault. Sometimes the middle two on top and the middle two on bottom are level, and the immediately adjacent teeth are nearly in a scissors position; and sometimes lower teeth are so crowded and out of line that it is a toss-up whether to call the bite level or scissors or something else. I use this guideline: the more abnormal the bite, the more it should be penalized. It appears the wolf doesn't have the overcrowding that is common to his second-cousin, the German Shepherd Dog.

An overshot mouth has upper incisors far enough ahead of the lower ones to leave a space. The greater the space, the more serious the problem for that individual, especially if he is to have a show career. (Yet the beautiful Select Champion Ravenhaus Noah's overshot condition didn't keep him from much winning.) When a dog's teeth are described as undershot, it means that his lower jaw has "shot" out further than the upper one—the mandible has outgrown the maxillary bones—not as far as a Boxer's, but to whatever extent, this condition is a disqualification in Shepherds.

Classification—Teeth are classified as belonging to one of four groups: incisors, canines, premolars, and molars (the latter two groups sometimes simply are called cheek teeth). The technical difference between molars and premolars is that the molars which lie furthest back in the jaws erupt without following any "puppy" or "milk" teeth, *not* that molars are big and premolars small. In fact, that biggest one on top has been preceded by a baby tooth, so is really a premolar. Thus, behind each canine fang there are four premolars before the molars. To make it even more confusing, the "button" premolars just behind the canines are not shed, but remain in place just as do the molars.

Function—The largest of the premolars and molars, called carnassials, shear through tough tissue such as tendons and muscles in pieces of meat too large to gulp down after a perfunctory grinding action. These are also the scissors used by the bitch to crush and cut the umbilical cords of her newborn pups. If there were not this grinding action, there might be too much bleeding from the cord, and that's why you should be prepared to tie the cord if you have to use a sharp instrument to cut it.

The major functions of the other teeth are fairly obvious. Incisors are used to pull, scrape, pinch, and pick up; canine teeth are designed to puncture, tear, and secure a hold; small premolars protect the gums while great force is applied to hold and crush. Molars are primarily used for grinding and gnawing, which are seldom-seen activities in the domesticated dog raised on commercial dog food.

Eruption—Puppy teeth are more accurately called deciduous since they are shed at the proper times to make room for the new, permanent ones. Eruption of each permanent tooth usually precedes the loss of its corresponding deciduous tooth, the latter often hanging by a thread for many days. These old puppy teeth should be helped out, for

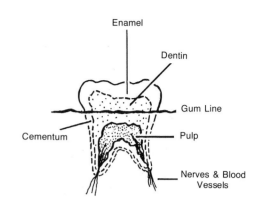

Tooth Structure

malocclusion can result if they remain in too long and crowd their replacements.

Puppies are born with deciduous teeth already in place, but these do not erupt through the gums until the pups are almost ready for solid food. You'll notice the gums getting rougher and sharp at around three weeks of age. Table 1 shows a typical pattern of eruption for breeds of medium size such as the German Shepherd Dog. Generally, the larger the breed, the shorter the average life span, and the earlier the eruption of permanent teeth; something you may want to bear in mind when speaking of teething to a fancier of another breed.

Structure—A tooth is composed of three parts: crown, roots, and neck. The crown is the visible part covered with white enamel down to the neck, just under the gum line. There we find a very slight constriction before the roots or tubercles begin. These roots are imbedded in the jaw bones and are longer than the crown. In the center is a soft tissue called pulp, which is enclosed by a bonelike yellowish or ivory-colored dentin which in turn is covered by cementum at the roots and enamel at the crown.

There are no blood vessels in dentin, and very few nerves in the roots. What few nerve fibers are present recede with age and are replaced by calcified deposits so there is no pain associated with such erosion. Dentin can be repaired if a tooth is accidentally chipped, but not if it has been severely fractured. Biting edges of incisors and canine teeth are the most likely to be chipped in such minor ways, and as a rule they easily repair themselves. A major fracture of a tooth may be left alone in the case of

---

TABLE 1. TYPICAL ERUPTION TIMETABLE OF PERMANENT TEETH

14-15 weeks:	Central incisors, top jaw
15-17 weeks:	Central incisors, bottom jaw; Second incisors, top jaw
16-18 weeks:	Third incisors, top and bottom; First premolars, fourth premolars
5 months:	Canines; Rest of fourth premolars; First molars
6 months:	Second and third premolars
6-7 months:	Remaining molars: second and third on bottom; Second on top

While more likely to occur in heads of breeds that man has changed over the years by intentional genetic selection for head shape, tooth abnormalities are found commonly enough in the "ancestral type" dog such as the German Shepherd Dog, shown here. Rotation, an abnormal position of a tooth in relation to others or to dental arch, may promote periodontal (gum) disease, and may require extraction or trimming with a grinding disc. This is an example of a slight, harmless rotation in one plane, but teeth can also rotate laterally and erupt or grow "sideways", horizontally.

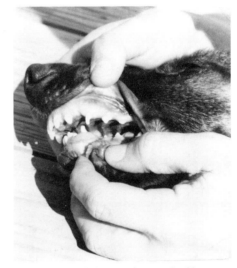

Overshot mouth. A little over four months old.

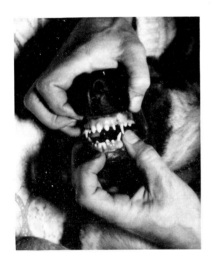

Four-month old puppy has three incisors erupted on top, middle two bottom have replaced deciduous teeth, but #2 bottom incisors are coming in before the "baby teeth" are loose, and behind the line of the other lower teeth. German Shepherd Dogs seldom have a "perfect bite", but most are acceptable.

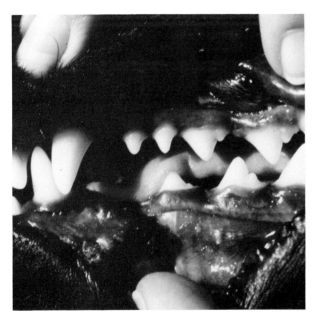

She has 42 teeth, but not in the right places! One extra premolar on top, one missing on bottom. 5½ month old female.

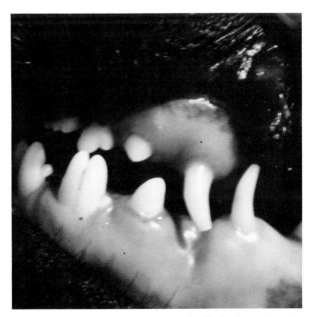

An example of a split incisor, seen occasionally by the author when judging and examining various breeds. 4 month old female.

"clean" breaks, but fissures into the roots require surgery.

Hereditary anomalies—The growth rate of the upper jaw appears to be genetically controlled independent of the growth of the lower jaw; therefore a pup may inherit an upper jaw growth rate from one parent and a lower jaw growth rate from the other, and the two will not be matched. It may be that both parents carried recessive factors for unequal growth rates or completion codes in their genes. Whatever the mode, the inheritance of unequal or mismatched genes appears to be the cause for overshot, level, and undershot conditions. Because of the wide range of expression, I lean toward the idea that such inheritance may be polygenic.

The most usual pattern in the abnormal mouth is for the upper jaw to grow faster or the lower jaw's

development to be retarded during the earliest stages of life. Most of the time, the lower jaw plays catch-up to some extent, and the overbite improves to a degree. For this reason slight overbites in early puppyhood are seldom cause for alarm. On the other hand, I've never seen a truly level bite correct itself, nor an undershot condition improve.

The tendency to have a full set of teeth is genetically dominant over incomplete dentition, and seems to be determined by more than one gene. Occasionally a German Shepherd Dog will have less than a full complement, but even less frequent is the incidence of extra teeth.

Other dentition faults appear in smaller numbers of dogs than do bite and missing teeth problems. Once in awhile a dog will have a wry mouth—one that is twisted because of an interrupted growth rate on one side or in one portion so that the bottom jaw does not meet the top one along the cheeks, and is pointed in a different direction. The rotated tooth is rarely noticed and barely obvious since it is placed properly and apparently growing toward the opposite jaw in normal fashion, but is turned up to 90 degrees on its vertical axis. The Standard doesn't cover such an anomaly, nor other different but not necessarily abnormal conditions. One dog I saw in Georgia had fantastically long canine teeth, as if he had saber-tooth tigers in his family tree. Wolves have for the most part retained this characteristic.

The bottom two central incisors often do not meet the inside of the top ones, and are sometimes slightly forward as seen from the side, but I do not consider this a disqualifying undershot mouth since the others are still in a scissors bite. The two central ones may simply be too short to reach the top teeth. As dogs mature, these two bottom teeth are the first to wear down, then the top two, then the other incisors; at some point, it may be difficult to define a normal bite in an aging dog.

Jaws—The muscles inserted into the mandibles are among the strongest, inch-for-inch or ounce-for-ounce, in the body. It has been claimed by some that the bite of the average male German Shepherd Dog exerts close to 1,000 pounds per square inch, though confirmed measurements with which I am familiar give a figure of around 700. Either way, that's enough pressure to break an arm bone or separate the bones in a man's wrist, not to men-

HOW TO ESTIMATE AN ADULT DOG'S AGE

By looking at the teeth, you might make a pretty close guess as to a dog's age, but remember that wear will also vary as a result of diet, habits, and malocclusions. The following points are given strictly as approximations, but they are typical and may help:

1½ years: cusps (rounded or pointed surfaces) are worn off the lower middle incisors.
2½ years: cusps worn off lower intermediate incisors.
3½ years: cusps worn off upper middle incisors.
4½ years: cusps worn off upper intermediate incisors.
5 years: cusps of canines and corner incisors show some wear.
6 years: corner incisors show more wear; canines are blunt.
7 years: wear continues with great variation between individuals; estimation is unreliable.

The teeth that show wear earlier continue to wear down, until the lower middle incisors are all but gone in most old dogs, and gradually more tooth is seen as one examines those further away from the centerline. If no wear is apparent, the dog may be an exception or may be between six months and two years.

5-month-old pup with genetic ear weakness. Note that there is no support at the base of the right ear and almost none on the left. Despite a surgical muscle/ligament "tuck" at ten months, the ears never came up. This pup was the largest of the litter, fitting a pattern—big dogs more often have ear carriage problems, or are later in getting their ears up.

von Salix's Justice, 11 weeks old. Some pups have ears fully erect by this time, others only after teething (5-6 months), a few not until 8 months.

tion the effect on muscles, blood vessels, nerves, and psyche.

While the bite is considerable, the dog risks losing teeth when exerting near-maximum power. I recently witnessed a Schutzhund trial in which one energetic dog that tried to shake the sleeve off an agitator actually broke off one of his canine teeth.

Ears

The first thing a person notices about a dog is his face or expression, but most people are unaware of the large part the ears play in creating the dog's "look." When the Standard calls for "moderately pointed," it means that ears should be longer and more gradually tapered than those of an Alaskan Malamute or wolf. A cropped ear has had a portion cut off so the remaining cartilage will stand erect, and a hanging ear is completely down like that of a spaniel. Both deviations are disqualifications in the German Shepherd breed rings. Neither the semi-prick ear characteristic of the Collie nor the button ear exemplified by the Fox Terrier is a disqualification, but these *would* tend to spoil the image and are consequently penalized more severely than the Standard requires.

Many large, stocky German Shepherd Dogs that have inherited many genes from their upland-Germany ancestors, and are a bit closer to the herd-guardian type, have heavy ear leather and therefore cannot carry the ears fully erect as a result of the combination of weight and weakness. Some of the

Relaxed　　　　　　*Attention!*

LEFT: Can. Ch. von Salix's Frolic v. Guengerich at 9 years of age. She had the ear set typical of a lot of her sire Lance's kids, shown by her left ear. Her right ear was infected at the time, and she carried it down to the side as a result.

RIGHT: Left ear carriage ideal; right one is o.k. but turned very slightly, perhaps in response to a sound behind her. von Salix's Ginny, OFA.

Ear carriage is largely a matter of how a dog feels. Providing stimulating environments during teething and ear erection can help train ears the same way a serviceman can learn good posture: practice.
Photos of v. Salix's Felicia of Rebelhaus, OFA.

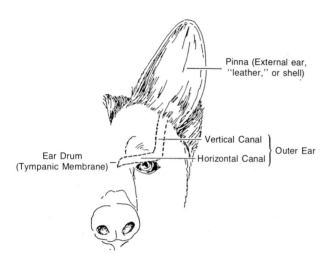

Ear Canal and Structure

greatest winners and producers have been known or alleged to produce weak ears of one sort or another. For example, Bernd v Kallengarten has been blamed for passing on ears so heavy that they may require taping to train them upright. Lance of Fran-Jo and many others have been pointed out as the sources of wide ear sets which, in combination with heavy leather, make it difficult to get a good expression or sometimes even an erect ear. Doppelt-Tay's H-litter's descendants often have ear tips touching or leaning toward each other in what we call a "bonnet." K-Waldesruh offspring often had wide, weak ears. These examples are far from alone—weak ears are an increasing problem. Generally such show dogs do better at specialty shows where a judge may emphasize side-gait over anything else.

Structure—The outer ear is also referred to as the pinna, shell, or concha, and is composed of hair, skin, blood vessels, nerves, muscles, and tendons covering and attaching to cartilage. Since the outer ear is *not* bone, feeding calcium tablets to the dog in vain hopes that this will help the ears come up is useless. However, the muscles *can* be affected by sore gums during teething, and some people report success in getting and keeping the ears up by massaging the ears and surrounding muscles at this time. Next time you have a 5-month-old pup whose ears drop during teething the canines and molars, try rubbing his forehead and cheek in the directions those muscles lie, and pulling his ears in firm but gentle strokes.

Hearing—Second only to the dog's sense of smell is his sense of hearing, but where scenting usually operates alone, hearing is used in conjunction with other senses. Association (what we erroneously call "memory") is strong in regard to voice sounds, but not so much to scent. Von Stephanitz recounts the story of a pup that was given away when eight weeks old, but recognized his former owner when next they met, even though nine months had elapsed. Von Stephanitz credited scent, though I believe a combination of senses, with heavy reliance on hearing, probably played the major part in that recognition. I've owned dogs with equal scent and sound "memory."

The erect shell of the German Shepherd Dog's ear, as compared with the fur-covered pendulous ears of an Afghan Hound or setter, probably enables them to hear sounds at much greater distances, and "noiseless" things nearby. Over fifty years ago Katz and Engelmann demonstrated that a faint noise that could be heard by humans three to six yards away could be picked up by a German Shepherd Dog from twenty-five yards off. While we humans lose the ability to hear sound when the frequency climbs above 30,000 cycles per second, Pavlov showed that the dog could hear tones at 75,000 cycles, and later research indicates our canine friends can hear 100,000 cycles per second! The German Shepherd Dog is also very good at pin-pointing the direction from which the sound has come.

Old dogs tend to lose much of their hearing, especially at the higher frequencies. Gunshots, thunder, and such low-frequency noises may make an old dog uncharacteristically fearful or uncomfortable because they are the only loud sounds he hears on an occasional basis, or because the sound is different. Age deafness is not normally a matter of the external ear nor of the middle ear, but usually is caused by a nervous system failure somewhere between the inner ear and brain.

Why do dogs howl at the sound of a siren, violin, or wailing instrument? Forget all that nonsense about such noises "hurting the dog's ears." If pain were the reason, gun dogs would stop to howl instead of retrieve. Even the faintest mournful or "midnight call," while far from painful, evokes a like sound from the listener, full moon or not. I believe the answer to the question is simply that dogs like to be part of the pack; just as coyotes and wolves sing to identify themselves and their groups, dogs feel the ancestral need to participate in the ritual.

Vibrissae—While as far from the ears as they can be and still be on the head, whiskers may play a part in hearing, according to some recent evidence. Cats and other animals of prey have been photographed with the vibrissae (scientific name for the sensory whiskers on the muzzle) brought forward at the very instant before the prey is grasped in the mouth, or at the end of a lunge. It may be that some sort of sonar is employed with the ears and vibrissae working together. Since sound is composed of waves of vibrating air, it's quite possible the vibrissae transmit these vibrations to the brain which then computes and compares their message with that of the ears. This new evidence may be part of the reason for exhibitors showing their dogs with these sensory whiskers intact, even though their breeds have traditionally been shown with the muzzle trimmed. The German Shepherd has never gone through that artificial phase, though I once caught a Sheltie owner trimming the whiskers of a German Shepherd puppy I had sold her for show, just before entering the ring.

Eyes

The eyeball is almost spherical, so when the Standard speaks of "almond-shaped" and set "obliquely," it is not referring to the organ of sight but to its surrounding tissues, especially the eyelids and eyebrows, and to the angles of the bones in the area. Because of the taper of the Shepherd head, the eyes appear to be set a little bit on the sides of

the skull. A darker colored triangular or spear-shaped patch (like Cleopatra's make-up), exists at the outside or rearward edge of the eye opening giving it even more of an oval or almond-shaped appearance.

The nictitating membrane ("third eyelid") can be seen in tranquilized German Shepherd Dogs, but should not otherwise be obvious. Behind the eye lies the lacrimal gland, and its secretion of salty liquid is carried by the tear duct not only to the eyes, but also to the nasal cavity so any excess should not stain the muzzle. This is why eye irritation can cause mucous secretions in the nose as well as sneezing.

Structure—The figure below shows a three-quarter section view of the eyeball. Light reflected from viewed objects enters the front via the cornea, a clear, 5-layered, fibrous tissue containing many nerve endings. The canine cornea is much tougher than that of the human, but still the site of intense pain if damaged. Behind it lies the aqueous humor, a chamber of fluid that is in a constant state of replacement. It covers the iris and the pupil, which latter is not so much a structure as a hole in the iris. The amount of light passing through is governed in part by muscle action causing the iris to open or close the pupil, just as in the mechanical controls of the aperture of a camera.

Behind the iris is a double-convex clear structure called the lens which because of its shape tends to focus light rays. Actually, the dog is myopic, which means that focusing takes place before the rays reach the back of the eye. If this happened in your camera, the developed photograph would be

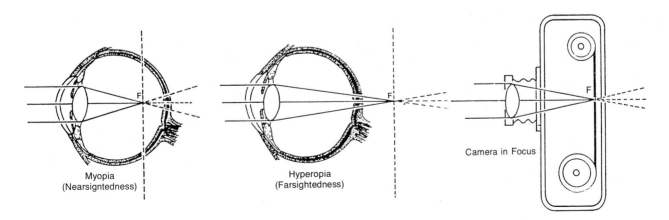

| Myopia (Nearsightedness) | Hyperopia (Farsightedness) | Camera in Focus |

Function of the lens.

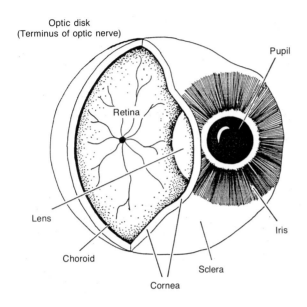

Structure of the eye.

out of focus and in fact everything *is* slightly out of focus to the dog. The poor focusing ability in the canine explains why your dog may not recognize you if you put on a wig, change clothes, or walk toward him without speaking.

In the eye, what corresponds to photographic film is the light-sensitive retina, fed by a network of blood vessels and containing specialized nerve endings. As the lens-refracted light passes through the main chamber of the globe known as the vitreous body, it strikes the retina and excites the nerve endings, sending electrical impulses along the optic nerve to the brain.

An intriguing part of the choroid (the layer behind the retina) is a patch of iridescent tissue called the tapetum. This is what you see when making eye contact with an animal at night. It is also the cause of eyes that look like little, round, bright lights in photographs taken with a flash.

Function—Dogs, like other domestic animals, are color-blind to the visible spectrum.[1] However, they are very able to distinguish between articles with extremely slight differences in brightness/

[1]There are some reports that dogs may be able to distinguish some shades of red light, which may lead one to wonder whether they can also see a little into the infrared spectrum which is invisible to humans.

darkness. Man and other color-sensitive animals have cone-shaped structures in the focusing part of the retina, which enable them to see colors.

Perhaps the most notable realm in which canine sight is known or believed to be "better" than man's is night vision. The iris is capable of much more variation in inside diameter, reducing to a very thin ring around a consequently enlarged pupil. The prismatic or rod-shaped structures in the retina are much more light-sensitive than are the cones, and dogs have 95 percent rods. Man's abundance of cones enables him to see colors but only with the help of plenty of light. On a night when we would be afraid to take one slow step after another without a lamp, dogs rush fearlessly and easily through the woods and over broken ground.

Pigment—Eye color is determined mainly in the iris. In the German Shepherd Dog, the Standard calls for the darker eye strictly as a matter of arbitrary preference, since a light eye is quite acceptable in many other breeds. Often, two dogs with the same eye pigmentation but different facial hair color or markings will give the illusion of two different eye colorations. The setting or background also has a lot to do with the impression. I tend to disbelieve the old claim that light eye color is related to greater intelligence or excitability in the German Shepherd Dog.

The Mouth

Taste—Taste is one of the less acute senses in the dog. This may be hard to believe as our dogs continue to surprise us with the relish they evidence in consuming goods other than their regular dog food. One producer of a vitamin/mineral supplement discovered that dogs would "really eat up" raspberry-flavored tablets.

The tongue—The organ of taste is the tongue, which is composed of several types of tissues. It is very mobile and in addition to serving to transmit information on taste, it assists in mastication and overall temperature control. Just as people perspire through the skin, dogs "perspire" through only two surfaces: the pads of their feet, and their tongues. Most of the metabolic heat exits via the rapid exchange of air during panting, but a good bit drips off in water and dissipates in evaporation.

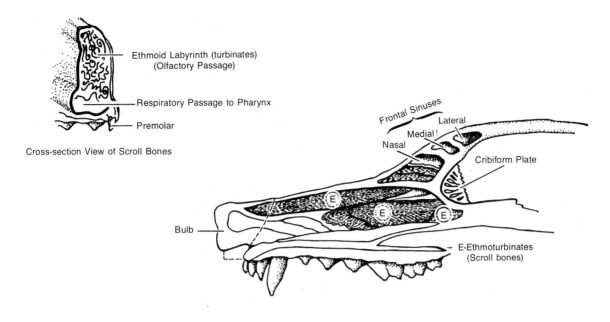

Ethmoid Labyrinth (turbinates)
(Olfactory Passage)

Respiratory Passage to Pharynx

Premolar

Cross-section View of Scroll Bones

Frontal Sinuses

Lateral

Medial

Nasal

Cribiform Plate

Bulb

E-Ethmoturbinates
(Scroll bones)

Medial view of nasal turbinates. Olfactory nerves most abundent nearest cribiform plate, extending into scrolls.

There is one other major function of the tongue—drinking. Without this valuable organ the dog would die of thirst.

The Nose

"The brain of the dog is in his nose."

It may not be anatomically correct, but that phrase accurately describes what dog psychologists, trainers, and others have known almost from the beginning of the man-dog association. It is through the nose, and related olfactory (scent) structures in the muzzle, that most of the dog's world reaches him. It is with the nose that the dog confirms what his eyes or ears have indicated, and with the nose that a multitude of stimuli find their only passage to his brain. (When I use the word *nose*, I am referring to *all* those sensory surfaces of the foreskull which play a part in smelling, not just the black bulb on the end which is more accurately called the external nose.)

In tracking, the dog utilizes other messages in addition to the scent of the individual being tracked. He associates a disturbance of the dirt with the scent of whoever trampled that ground or crushed the tiny plants along the track. However, if the person being followed gets into an open conveyance such as a trolley or even a golf cart on pavement, there is no disturbance of ground, and most dogs will lose the track.

How is it that the dog, especially the German Shepherd Dog, has such a highly developed sense? How can it be that dogs have been so successful in finding uranium and other ores by scent, and in discovering narcotics even when samples were completely encapsulated inside a wax-sealed candle? The answer lies in the study of canine anatomy.

Structure—A cross section view of a dog's muzzle at about its third and fourth premolars reveals in the upper jaw a maze of bony folds shaped like scrolls. The surfaces of these tiny scrolls are covered with mucous membranes very rich in nerve endings. The interior chambers of man's nose are about 80 percent occupied by scroll bones. But because our olfactory receptors are at the extreme distant reaches, close to the pituitary gland, with a volume of about 1.5 cubic inches in that part, they contribute nearly nothing to our sense of scent. The German Shepherd Dog's organ containing the olfactory, ethmoidal cells is about six cubic inches. Almost half of a dog's folds of bone and *all* of the mucosal folds close to the brain are olfactory with the remainder serving his respiratory needs. Sensory nerve impulses are recorded in the convolutions of the brain in roughly a similar way that vibrations are pressed into the walls of grooves in a phonograph record. Further, the olfactory nerves are larger and more numerous in the dog than in most other animals, including man. It has been said

Ch. Schaferhaus Kazam Ringo Star. Sire: Can Ch. Cempiem's Ziro; Dam: Schaferhaus Fenya, R.O.M., a black daughter of Ch. Von Nassau's Hussan. He was a bicolor of extensive black, and structure decribed by the Standard. Judge Don Jones pictured. Owner/breeder: Dr. Charles Kruger of Seattle.   Photo courtesy Lucas (about 1970).

that the actual surface area of the olfactory mucous membranes is approximately equal to the apparent entire exterior surface of the dog's body. Man's 5 million olfactory cells are a paltry sum compared to the Dachshund's 125 million and the German Shepherd Dog's 200 million cells. An instrument called the olfactometer has been used to show that the dog's sense is a million times better than ours.

Relaying the message—Some materials release into the air many more particles than do others. For example, gaseous substances and liquids with high vapor pressure or low boiling point will disperse rapidly and to great distances compared to the molecules of wood, leather, and other solids. Even metals emit some of their molecules, although in infinitesimally small numbers. Whatever the substance, molecules drifting through the air are inhaled by the dog, pass through the labyrinth of moist convolutions, and excite the olfactory nerve endings. Some of these molecules are absorbed into the bloodstream through the mucous membranes from the nasal passage to the lobes of the lungs.

For this reason care should be exercised when scenting in toxic environments.

Causes for reduced efficiency—In order to function properly, the nasal linings must be moist enough to facilitate absorption. If the cells around the nerve endings do not "capture" and hold some of those odor molecules, no message can be relayed to the brain. Certain circumstances may cause the nose to temporarily lose most of its powers—illness, work in an extremely dry climate, life in a house without humidifiers, or certain stress conditions are some of the more common causes. The beginning of a bitch's season can considerably reduce her sensitivity to odors, perhaps partly by decreasing the moisture in her nose.

In addition, strenuous exercise will lower scenting ability, perhaps by changing the acidity in the blood, perhaps by raising body temperature and thus decreasing moisture in the nasal passages. A dog that follows a number of tracks in succession will lose efficiency and become uncertain after the third or fourth exercise. Kahn found that both pulse rate and body temperature had increased by the time tracking dogs lost some of their ability after a few such trials.

The nature and amount of what has been recently eaten also affects ability. Newhaus found that two hours after he had fed dogs one gram (⅛ ounce), the sense of smell had greatly diminished. When a wild canid has not eaten for a few days, its ability to track its prey is honed to a sharp edge. With this in mind, it follows that hunters get much better results if they withhold food from their dogs the day before the opening of hunting season. It's not a bad idea to follow suit with the show dog as he will be more alert and aware of his surroundings due to the lack of interference from some recently ingested food.

Nose memory—"Nose memory" is a remarkable faculty of the dog. In *The Odyssey*, Homer was generally reliable in his descriptions of animals, but may have been exaggerating when he wrote that Ulysses' dog recognized him after he had been gone twenty years. There are innumerable stores of how German Shepherds have found long-lost items. The odor of those articles may have been part of so great an impression in their brains that they associated the found article with some olfactory experiences in their distant pasts. Dogs seem to possess a better storage system for odors than we do. It suits their needs.

NECK

The neck of the German Shepherd Dog should be pleasingly long and blend well into the head and torso. The Standard reads "without loose folds of skin," and while this defect is uncommon, there is a minor amount of dewlap or throatiness in many of the US German Shepherds. The slight fullness of skin on the neck between the chin and brisket or prosternum is seen in those dogs of fuller coats and looser ligamenture, whereas the "dry," short-coated, tight dogs are not observed to have any noticeable dewlap.

In motion the head is thrust forward and approaches the level of the back as the dog picks up speed. At rest the head is held relatively high even when not at attention, in contrast with many sighthounds that hold their heads low when nothing special is going on around them. Head carriage is effected by a number of muscles primarily attached to and overlying the neck and withers, especially the splenius which origin is on the third thoracic vertebra and insertion on the back of the skull. Assisted by parts of the longissimus muscle group which are attached to the first cervical vertebrae, it raises the head and helps turn it to the side. Unless there is the seldom seen bone disorder or trauma, carriage is only affected by the dog's attitude.

SKIN AND HAIRCOAT

The haircoat and skin account for 10 to 15 percent of the total weight of the adult dog. The purposes of hair are obvious: protection from sun, insects, briars, and cold temperatures; as well as mate attraction, camouflage, and the tactile sense (touch). The skin also has many functions. It covers and protects the fluid-filled body from its environment; forms an effective barrier against bacteria and other malevolent organisms, toxins, and irritants; synthesizes vitamin D; secretes oils for the hair; contains fat for insulation; and is the site of nerve endings which react specifically to cold, heat, pain, and pressure stimuli.

If one follows the skin over the lips and other border areas into the orifices, it will be seen that there is no sharp division between the tissues. Considered together, the skin, lungs, conjunctivae, alimentary canal, and genital tracts form what is called the integument. To pass through this continuous yet varied covering/lining, materials must either puncture it or permeate it in solution or by osmosis. Specialized variations on the dermis-epidermis theme are found in the external nose, pads, nipples, and umbilical scar, all of which are hairless.

The German Shepherd Dog has the same type of intermediate coat as is found in wild canids (wolves, jackals, etc.). The other two major types are exemplified by the Boxer's short coat and the Chow Chow's long coat. However, there is much variation among breeds and bloodlines within each classification so the three basic types of coat overlap. Texture also varies between breeds and between pups of different ages. There are also several types of hair on each individual, depending on age and location on the dog.

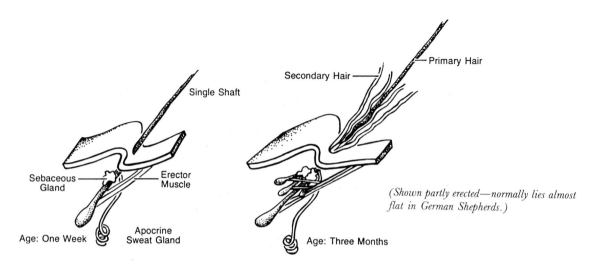

Hair Follicles. Accessory hairs develop as the puppy gets close to 3 months old, at which time there are two to five secondary hairs around each primary hair. At six months there are five to fifteen in each follicle bundle, and bundles further are grouped in clusters of three in irregular rows, 100 to 300 bundles per square centimeter.

Structure—Each root is imbedded in a sheathlike follicle extending down to a bulb at the bottom. Around the bulb is a generous network of capillaries and nerve endings.

At birth, pups have a single hair implanted in each follicle opening, but by about six months there may be about ten hairs emerging from the same follicle, with the original hair the longest. The primary hair is somewhat stiffer than these satellite hairs, although it started out velvety smooth in the newborn pup. As he grows, the longer hairs change from soft to coarse, beginning at a spot on the upper surface of the tail an inch or two from the croup, then spreading along the tail and up the spinal line, later down the flanks and legs.

Although the dog perspires through his feet and tongue, there is what is known as an apocrine "sweat" gland at the hair root which moisturizes the hair with the considerable assistance of the fatty sebaceous glands closer to the surface. These glands keep the coat glossy and the skin supple unless the hair dies, parasites in the intestine affect nutrition, the diet lacks fat, the dog get sick, or certain stress conditions such as estrus occur.

An area especially rich in sebaceous glands is on the top side of the tail, a few inches from the sacrum, where hairs emerge singly from the follicles instead of in bunches. This oval area of a couple inches' length identifies the sex, species, and possibly the breed, age, and personality of the individual. Dogs get a lot of information by sniffing this

area and the surrounding coat which broadcasts the chemicals produced in those glands.

As the growing German Shepherd pup's primary hairs become coarser, they are joined by the softer, wavy or curved secondaries, known as the undercoat. If a dog is slow to change the texture of those primary hairs, he is said to still have his puppy coat. I have seen many bitches with more soft fur on their sides than coarse topcoat, yet they all seem to lose most of the fuzzy appearance when they "shed out" during or just prior to their first real season.

Hair loss—Finally, when a dog "bristles for a fight," erector muscles at the roots cause the shafts to stand up, making the dog look bigger. These muscles also squeeze the apocrine and sebaceous glands which then emit an aroma of warning and assertion. Shedding dead hair is common to all breeds, but more obvious in some. Typically, the German Shepherd Dog has a major change of coat twice a year, though not all the hairs are lost that often nor at the same time. The process is gradual enough to insure the dog *some* protective coat, even though it sometimes appears as though the dog will resemble a billiard ball before returning to normal coat.

Bitches shed more conspicuously if not more often than do males, but both are affected by one condition—the environment. The length of daylight triggers hormone activity which arrests the growth of many hairs. Any time growth is stopped, the hair

Lori Maier, SZ-183773, HGH, Rough-coated German Shepherd bitch from the 1920s. The wire coat is no longer in the breed.

dies and when it falls out, growth of a replacement begins. If the dead hair isn't pulled out, the cells at the root will go through a resting stage and finally start producing a new hair that will push the old one out. For this reason, groomed dogs have a shorter resting period because the removal of dead hairs both "awaken" the dormant cells and stimulate the glands. This also is why daily brushing produces a sheen that impresses dog show judges and non-doggy people alike.

Climatic conditions have some effect on coat, though not as much as is generally believed. In fact, coat type is mostly due to genetics, but there *is* a slightly greater amount of shedding in warm weather. In winter, the outside dog's average number of hairs per bundle increases, but no new bundles form. As dogs age, the coat gets thinner as some bundles cease production completely and others reduce their output of hairs.

Coloration—Pigment granules are formed in the base of the follicle and placed into the cortex (which accounts for most of the hair's bulk), and in the medulla as the shaft is developed and pushed upward. If the deposition of pigment is not uniform, the dog may have bands of different colors on individual hairs, as in the sable German Shepherd

Dog. This agouti type marking has lighter tan on the two-thirds of the shaft lying closer to the skin. The longer the portion containing the lighter granules, the more it will appear that the canid's underwear is showing. Some of the light color *is* undercoat, but some is on the proximal end of the guard hairs. Some hairs have an absence of granules, or nearly so, and the air in the medulla makes the hair look white at that spot, while the pigment granules are confined to other bands on the same hair. Usually, black will be in the tip, but not always.

SKELETAL SYSTEM

The most obvious functions of the skeleton are support and protection. But there are other important jobs for bones, such as manufacture of blood cells and storage of both fat (marrow) and minerals. Bone is living tissue, with blood vessels, nerves, and organic components besides calcium and phosphorus compounds.

The Topline

A dog's back is only one part of its topline although the two terms are often used interchangeably. Let me describe and define the various segments of the dog's topline. (Please have a copy of the Standard handy as you read this.) The topline runs from nose, muzzle, stop, ears, and skull, down the neck to an area known as the withers.

Withers—Used in the plural, this term denotes the section where the neck blends into the back. It gives the impression of a second line or angle, the first being the neck, the third being the back itself. The withers should be long and gradual, with a well-laid-back and long scapula. "A" shows no separate withers at all, while "B" indicates a wide area of transition between neck and back. Part of the correctness of the withers is obtained by a correct "layback" of the shoulder blade.

Back—The next section is the true back. It begins where the withers end, at about where the fifth rib attaches to the spine, and includes all that portion posterior toward the last rib and beyond to the hip bones which can be easily felt. The latter section of the back from the last rib to the hip prominence is known as the loin.

The Standard calls for a straight and level back. The pictures of dogs posed so that their backs seem to rush downhill like Rasputin heading for hell are caricatures, but it's amazing how many people look at them with a straight face. A *slightly* sloping back on a free-standing dog is fine, but no better than a level one. Any slope should come at the withers and at the croup.

At full trot on a loose lead or running free, the whole topline appears more level than when standing, for the dog will thrust his head forward and hold his tail more or less horizontally. When standing *or* moving, the withers should be higher than the back, but not at the expense of proper shoulder angulation; too many high-withers dogs have no breadth or good shoulder layback.

Loin—The loin is almost as misunderstood as the rest of the back. Dogs with long necks and backs overall are not likely to have truly short loins. A loin which appears long is most often the result of poor conditioning, lusterless coat, lack of exercise, or being underweight. I have seen dogs that looked poor in this area improve so much with roadwork that one would never suspect they ever had such a problem. Unfortunately, when exercise is again neglected, those beautifully muscled, powerful loins again waste away to slimness. Some dogs will retain their weight and not require activity for conditioning, but many dogs, especially sables and lighter colored ones, will *seem* to evidence a greater loss in the loins when the total loss may only be a couple of pounds. A little more food or exercise could put them into winning condition again.

Spinal column—The so-called backbone is made up of approximately fifty segments called vertebrae.

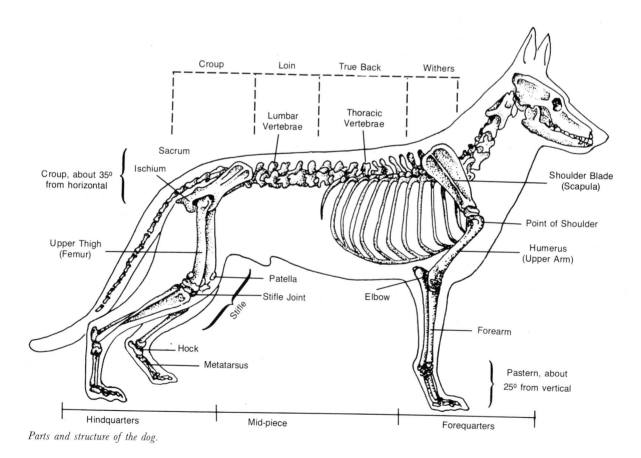

Parts and structure of the dog.

Each vertebra is slightly different in shape than the ones adjacent to it, but all perform basically the same functions: they protect the spinal cord and its branches, support the head and body, and provide for the origin and attachment of various muscles used to move the limbs and other parts.

The vertebrae are classified into seven cervical (neck), thirteen thoracic (ribs attached), seven lumbar (loin), three sacral bones fused together between the hip bones, and a variable number of tail vertebrae (German Shepherds have about twenty). The chain is quite flexible, although each link does not make a great angle with the very next in line when flexed. Between the vertebrae are laminated fibrous cushions with a gelatinous "filling." These disks are shock absorbers and flexible connectors holding the spine together and the parts thereof separate. Several other ligaments assist in bracing and being supported by the vertebrae.

The croup—Only four words, "long and gradually sloping," describe the croup in the Standard, yet this portion of the topline is very important to the appearance and gait of the German Shepherd Dog. The croup consists of several types of tissues: bone, tendon, fat, muscles, and the skin with its hair. One of the bony structures is the pelvic girdle. You can feel the top of the iliac crests with the spinous processes of the sacral vertebrae between them. Extending from the back of the sacrum are the coccygeal (tail) vertebrae, and just below and to each side you can feel the back end of the pelvic bone—these are the "bones" astride the anus and upon which the dog sits, with support from the tail and hocks.

If a dog has been worked hard or lived in extreme cold and has not had a sufficiently high calorie diet to compensate, it will have used up some of the stored energy (fat) and may show a bony croup. All dogs lose this fat over the sacrum as they age. Roadwork and adequate food will round off the contours of the croup, if age and genetic inheritance allow.

A pelvic bone approximately 7 inches long should lie at about an angle of 30 to 35 degrees from the horizontal. Measure by feeling the top and back as described above, then estimate what angle an imaginary line between them would make. This angle seems to facilitate fluid movement with adequate thrust to the rear as well as a good reach

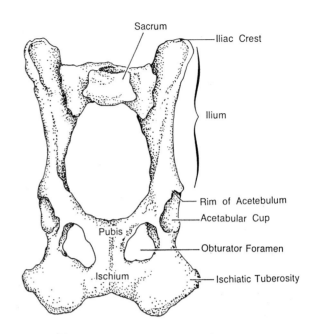

Lateral view, Pelvis four bones (ilium, ischium, pubis, and acetabulum bone) fuse into a box when right and left halves join.

under the body. This structure and movement are best noticed during a slow trot or walk, when one leg is extended and the other flexed.

Since croup slope almost surely results from polygenic influences, there are many intermediate angles. The steep croup is quite common in the German Shepherd. For an extreme example, an angle of 50 degrees from the horizontal would produce more of an upward thrust than a forward one, or at least a greater upward vector than would occur

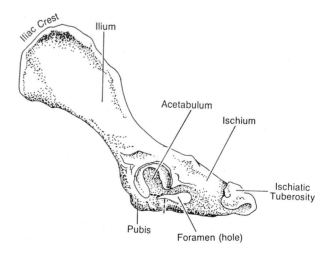

Ventral view pelvic girdle.

At rest, this puppy's tail hung straight down, but as soon as she started trotting, she hooked it up (thanks to linebreeding on Caralon's Hein?) and over to one side (thanks to linebreeding on the Lierbergs?). She passed this tail on to many of her offspring, some of whom had a ring tail when excited.

"Ring Tail" apparent when excited, probably only a slight hook when moving calmly.

with the ideal croup. Such a dog typically does not reach both far *and* low under his torso, has less than ideal transmission, and often can be found to have a shorter pelvic bone. Even one inch shorter in a comparably-sized dog amounts to 16 to 17 percent less room to accommodate some of the muscles providing thrust to the rear legs. The great Caralon's Hein had a slightly steep croup, but not so much that it prevented him from being judged one of the top specimens of the breed. It was noticeable only to the seasoned observer, and was not objectionable in motion. Since he produced a number of dogs "high in the rear" by popular standards, the impression those progeny gave may have been partly due to sacral angle, by which I mean the angle at which the sacrum fastens to the pelvis.

The flat croup likewise can vary in degree. A beautiful champion of a few years ago named El Malachi had a relatively flat croup which obviously was not a great detriment to his career. He made a nice picture standing, and a firm back with strong ligaments compensated to produce a nice enough side gait. A much flatter croup, say for example one with only about a 25-degree slope can give an awkward standing image in the hindquarter area. Such a dog's gait will be restricted with poor under-reach, and he may tend to lift his back foot too high at the rear-most instant of his step. Otto Matthei, in a 1973 issue of the SV *Zeitung* magazine, expressed the thought that the pelvis was too short in both the flat croup and most steep croups, but I don't know on what he based his conclusion.

Because of the variety in croup length, angle, and padding, this portion of the topline should be examined in motion as well as standing naturally, and with the hand as well as the eye. Though the croup constitutes a minor percentage of a dog's length, it is a vitally important structure in a trotting dog. Also, the width of the hindquarter as viewed from the side is partly the result of croup angle and length.

Tail—Another contributor to croup appearance is what is referred to as "tail set." The tail emerges from the caudal end of the sacrum and extends from between the halves of the pelvic bones in a manner greatly determined by mental attitude and its effects on the nerves enervating the coccygeal muscles. But there *are* differences in tail carriage that can be attributed to structural angles. It appears that the sacrum may be attached at a sharper angle in most of the sighthounds. The spine, descending from a higher relative position in the lumbar region, seems to enter the sacroiliac area with a less horizontal approach than it does in the typical German Shepherd Dog. Consequently, leaving that area it continues with a more downward angle creating a low tail set. There are some German Shepherds with this problem but a more common one is a tail set that is too high. This is also known as a "gay" tail if it is held curved too high or too far over the back.

The impression of a tail being set too high can be given by a flat croup, or by the angle at which the tail leaves the sacrum. As important to the impression, however, are the effects of fat and coat over the croup. Many dogs have a "dip" in the hair at approximately the sacro-coccygeal juncture, which is the base of the movable tail. This should not deter an observer from feeling the croup to confirm or expose it. If the dog has a normal croup and a gay tail, feel for the ''exit angle'' at which the tail leaves the sacrum and croup, comparing this dog against another with the same croup angle but different tail carriage.

The tail should at least reach the tarsus or hock joint, and be carried down or slightly curved toward the horizontal near its tip. It has been described as saberlike, though many more closely resemble a scimitar. It is normal for an animated dog to carry his tail high, but it should not curl over the back as do the tails of arctic breeds or spitz types; neither should it be as high and vertical as those of the Foxhound or Beagle.

A slight hook, which is a change in direction to either side, sometimes is seen in the last half-dozen vertebrae of the tail, and to most people it is of very little importance. Von Stephanitz gave as a possible (but unlikely) reason that the dog learns to carry an over-long tail up and over so it doesn't drag on the ground. I believe there is a definite gene for the upward curl and another one for the sideways curve. An accompanying photo shows a hook in a bitch's tail, which appeared as soon as she started moving, but was not evident at rest. On an extremely angulated dog in an exaggerated show pose, such a tail would appear to be excessively long.

The Front

Variously called the front assembly, forequarters, or shoulder, the whole combination made by the shoulder blade (scapula), upper arm (humerus), breastbone (sternum), and their related soft tissues is at the heart of much poor movement in German Shepherd Dogs the world over.

Shoulder assembly—The least understood and most controversial portions of the Standard as well as of the dog relate to the angles proscribed for the forequarters and hindquarters. I disagree with the angles commonly reported to be ideal in the shoulder area, though much of the discrepancy may be a matter of *how* that angle is usually measured. To specify angles is useless unless exact points of reference are not only agreed upon but also easily determined. Since the bones forming these angles are curved, such ''landmarks'' as (1) the highest point of the scapula, (2) the foremost point of the upper arm where it meets the shoulder, and (3) the topmost point of the elbow should be used as well

as a detailed illustration decided upon. None of the German Shepherd Dog Standards have been so explicit, nor have any in other breeds. Some years ago I radiographed standing dogs and found that what I had been reading in books and seeing in artists' drawings was not so. The call for a 45-degree shoulder layback plus another supposed 45-degree angle to the ''line'' of the upper arm, equalling a 90-degree shoulder angle, is inaccurate and misleading. If lines are drawn along the scapular spine and down the center of the humerus, as they usually are, a 90-degree angle in the real, live dog standing there before you will never be realized. Since the time I started challenging this notion, there have been noted authorities who have corroborated my claims with independent research, but it will be a long time before the old books are all revised and longer still before writers do their own investigatory work instead of copying sketches from each other. Probably the best drawing of the ideal German Shepherd Dog ever published in this country is Lloyd Fanning's which appeared in the *Review* and in a small booklet on the breed published by the German Shepherd Dog Club of America. Strange that so many have used incorrect representations instead of this accurate sketch.

Sketches in this chapter represent the typical German Shepherd with a good shoulder. Dogs with better reach and a floating gait have close to the same angles and layback. I suspect much more credit for such gait lies in the muscles and ligaments than has been imagined, measured, or hinted at in the past.

In actuality, the ideal shoulder with a 90-degree (approximate) angle from point of elbow to point of shoulder to highest point on scapula has about a 35-degree layback, not 45 degrees (see page 62). Additionally, factors such as the relative lengths of scapula and humerus, and the angle at which the humerus inclines, play parts in the standing appearance and in the reach in motion. While they didn't have all the answers, Humphrey and Warner had most of them, and they determined that 102 degrees was ideal for the working German Shepherd Dog.

The scapula does not articulate with any bones at its top, but is attached by four muscles to the spinal column at a number of places from the first cervical to the ninth thoracic vertebra and to the first seven or eight ribs. This is the case whether the dog is steep-shouldered or well-laid back, so differences between the two types *must* be due to dif-

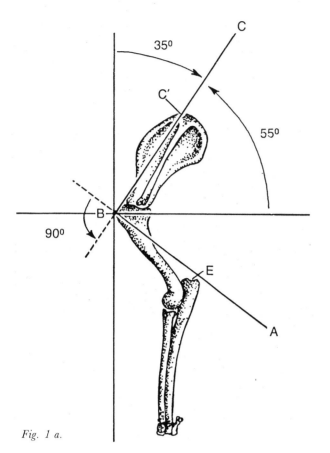

Fig. 1 a.

*The most accurate way to estimate shoulder angle. Angle ABC is 90°
and is that formed by imaginary lines from elbow E to forward point
of shoulder joint B, and from B through cranial angle C, the highest
point on the scapula.*

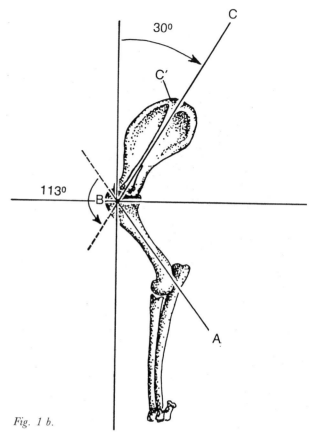

Fig. 1 b.

*This method of estimating angle is almost impossible to duplicate as
the centers of the humerus shaft and the articulating joint must be guessed
at. This gives various apparent angles, all over 90°. Fig. 1 a. is of
a tracing of Fig. 1 b., so the true angle is the same in each sketch.
In this one, angle ABC was used, with line BC running along the spine
of the scapula.*

ferences in scapula and humerus lengths and ratios;
perhaps the lengths of the vertebrae; and possibly
the tightness and condition of the ligaments and
muscles which hold the bones in their positions.

In examining the standing dog, the good layback
of 35 or 30 degrees can be determined either by
feeling the slope of the scapular spine or by
palpating the highest point of the scapula and the
most forward point of the upper arm (point b in
Fig. 1. a.) and imagining a line between these
points. The two lines will be essentially parallel,
so take your choice—in either case, you will have
approached the question scientifically. By observing the facts for yourself you will be able to arrive
at a conclusion or hypothesis. The sooner we
understand what *is* as opposed to what we *imagine*,
the sooner we'll understand how to get the most
out of our dogs.

Another problem in reporting a 45-degree or
greater layback, is that while it doesn't occur in the
standing dog,* it *does* happen when the dog is trotting or running. The reason for this is that the
scapula is not fixed or stationary; its lower end is
pulled back by the trapezius and forward by the
omotransversarius and serratus, with many other
muscles being involved to a lesser extent. These
angles can be visualized by watching slow-motion
movies or the frames taken from those, and
superimposing (technically, *infra*imposing) the
skeleton or lines representing the bones. Examining many dogs of varying qualities, hopefully with
the guidance of a knowledgeable veteran, will

---

*I am excluding achondroplastic dwarfs such as the
Corgi.

enable you to see these proper angles in motion and in standing.

The foreleg—The front (thoracic) limb is comprised of three major sections: upper arm (humerus), forearm, and foot. The largest bone is the humerus, a long, slightly S-shaped bone whose oval head fits into the shallow socket at the base of the scapula and whose distal end articulates with the lower arm at the elbow.

A fascinating design is found in the two bones of the lower arm: the radius is the major weight-bearing bone, and the longer ulna has more and larger muscle attachments to facilitate movement in relation to the humerus. The radius and ulna are slightly bowed and slightly entwined as if beginning a long, gradual, double spiral. The top of the ulna is the olecranon, that process (bump) which is the most obvious point of the elbow, and right

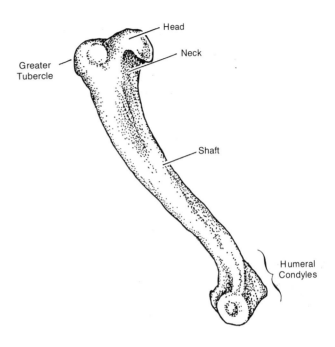

Humerus (upper arm), lateral view.
The greater tubercle, narrowed and like the prow of a ship, can be felt easily, being the foremost extremity of the limb. It is referred to as the point of the shoulder.

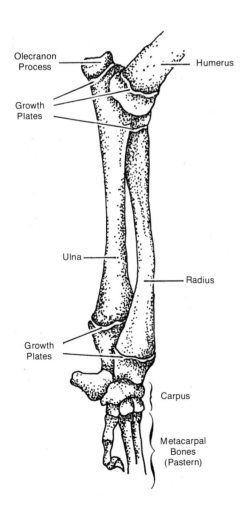

Medial view of left lower foreleg of a young dog, showing growth plates, where cartilage-bone transformation is still taking place.

below it, fitting into a depression in the end of the humerus is another bump called the anconeal process. This latter process is the site of the most common elbow disorder in German Shepherd Dogs.

Many top dogs and bitches have shorter legs than other dogs, possibly both in humerus and radius/ulna, though apparently more so in the latter. Such dogs are said to be "low-stationed," strictly a relative characteristic, and the overall impression can often be attributed to a deep or deep-appearing chest in the underline at the elbow area. An example of a beautiful low-stationed bitch is the Lance granddaughter linebred on Bernd Kallengarten (see photo on page 64). Another excellent low-standing dog of the early 1970s was Ch Bar v Weirturchen owned by the Schermerhorns and handled by Denny Kodner. The Germans apparently like to see a little more daylight under their dogs.

The pastern—Strong, springy pasterns, normally at about a 25-degree angle with the vertical, mark the beginnings of the feet. Dog people frequently consider the word *wrist* to be synonymous with the word *pastern*, but veterinary surgeons may be a little more specific using the worlds *carpus* for the actual wrist, and *metacarpus* for the pastern. That part of the forepaw that would correspond to your palm, the hand without the fingers, is the metacarpus.

One short and four long metacarpal bones are bound together by ligaments and fibrocartilage, all bundled with tendons, muscles, nerves, and blood vessels inside one skin-covered unit called the pastern. The reason the Standard calls for a strong pastern when the dog is standing is because the greater the angle, the weaker the action. A working dog whose job requires much trotting, running, and turning will either tire too easily or break down at the pastern if the ligaments and muscles are not firm enough to keep the dog "on his toes."

Since the pastern is flat on the ground during part of the gallop, the muscles and ligaments must be very extensible and elastic, able to return quickly to their former lengths and shapes. A breed such as the Shepherd, selected for stock work and jumping, cannot afford many representatives with weakness in such a key area. Yet few breeders give the pasterns much thought, as can be seen by perusing a few pages of advertisements in dog magazines.

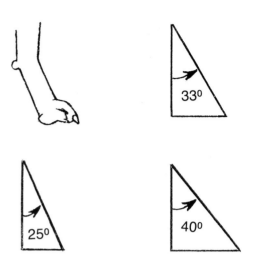

Fig. 2. Which is best for strength and endurance?

Neither do we want a terrier front on our dogs, which is to say both a steep shoulder and a very "straight" (vertical) pastern. Such a pastern may be strong and good for digging, but it's not very flexible. Much of the fluidity and spring of the trotting dog came from the correct combination of

Winning from the Novice class, Lieb'n lusts Kallen-Gal V. Salix. Sire: Ch Rex Edlu-Mibach (Bernd K. son). Dam: Can Ch. von Salix's Frolic v. Guengerich. (Gr. V. Lance daughter; lines to Bernd K.) bred by the author, owned by Shirley Folkema, an example of a low-stationed bitch.   *Photo by Martin Booth*

elasticity and strength in the metacarpal area. Since photos may mislead by camera angles and other factors, the image of a 25-degree angle must be kept in mind (see Figure 2) in order to judge living dogs' pasterns. When breeding, avoid doubling up on faults or recessives such as poor pasterns, and your obedience dog, rescue dog, sheep dog, or show dog will have the equipment and appearance of a true working breed.

Feet

The correct German Shepherd Dog foot is compact and well-arched, and almost as tight as a cat's foot in front. Feet to a working dog should be as important as crawler tracks to a bulldozer, for they are his foundation. The ideal foot, like the pastern, was chosen and developed after many years of observing good, working sheep dogs. Unfortunately, faults in feet are quite common because they are not held to be of great importance by breeders of show dogs whose working lives consist of running up and down a vinyl mat in a 20 by 30-foot ring.

An example of excellent feet and pasterns.

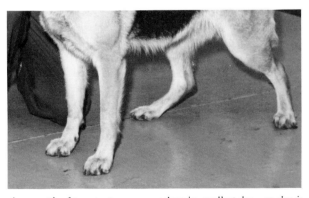

An example of poor pasterns on an otherwise excellent dog...no dog is perfect.

The longer the toes, the more likely the foot will spread out when gaiting, though a true splay-foot probably is genetically determined separately. A sable male dog I handled for a short time was linebred on K-Waldesruh dogs known for loose ligaments. He in turn had "paper feet," a condition which is a combination of splay-foot *and* too-long toes. Such a dog is usually also loose in hocks, pasterns, and elsewhere.

An intermediate between cat foot and the long-appearing foot is sometimes called "hare foot," and is a perfectly serviceable type. Probably the greatest number of good German Shepherd Dogs have this type. It should not be heavily penalized in the ring.

Nail color is of inconsequential importance, but may be used by the breeder as part of the total data bank used to choose breeding partners when pigment is important to him or his buyers. One of the most beautiful examples of the breed I've seen, Gilligan's Island, had pale, straw-colored nails. Some dogs have longer nails than do others, and may present a problem in trimming to give the appearance of shorter toes.

Hindquarters

The thigh—What is meant by "the whole assembly of the thigh" in the wording of the Standard? Viewed from the side, it includes the croup, upper thigh (femur and associated soft tissues), and lower thigh (tibia and fibula). If these three skeletal sections are too "vertical" or steep, the hindquarters will not present the broad picture called for by the Standard. Obviously, if the croup and lower thigh are slanted downward toward the rear, the femur will not also be so. Nor is it angled forward when the dog stands in a normal pose, in spite of the Standard's inaccurate statement about it paralleling the scapula. Many books on many other breeds have made the same error, even some written by well-known judges who should have known better than to report on something they did not experience in real life.

From experience, both in radiographing live, standing dogs and in feeling for the bones in the hindquarters, I have found that the femur is vertical when the metatarsus (hock) is vertical. The natural stance for German Shepherd Dogs is with one rear leg placed a little under the torso for added support of a long, substantial body. In this leg, the

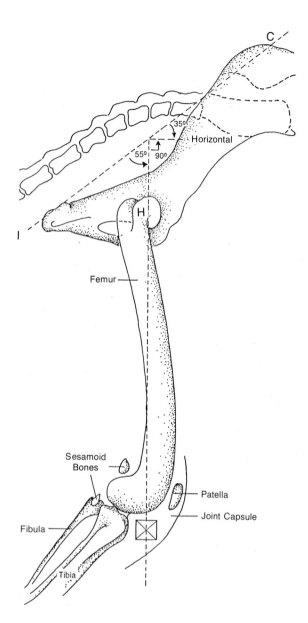

Tracing of an actual radiograph made of a German Shepherd Dog standing with hocks vertical. H represents pivotal center of hip, X is where stifle joint can be palpated; don't try to feel the patella, as it's movable and hard to identify with fingers. Line HX is vertical, as are hocks (not in picture). Line IC from rearmost part of ischium to topmost part of hip (crest of ilium) is at approximately 35° from horizontal, which is a good croup angle.
Tracing has been reduced to fit in this book.

femur is not vertical, but neither is the hock. Lift the dog's rear leg while you feel with your fingers for the acetabular (hip) joint capsule, and make a chalk mark there. Then feel the depression between the upper and lower leg bones. This is some distance below the patella which is too hidden in cartilage to be accurately palpated. You can now

see that the femur is quite straight and vertical between these two easily-located points.

The slant of the lower thigh roughly approximates that of both the croup and the humerus, and although there is considerable variation, it probably comes closest when the metatarsus is vertical, but even then not in all dogs. The angle the lower thigh bones make with the femur in a natural stance is *not* a right angle. Here again I am forced to contradict a poorly worded line in the Standard which is more fancy than fact, and probably harks back to the days before radiography was used much.

Even von Stephanitz may have understated conditions a little when he said this angle should be "90 to 100 degrees, sometimes even a bit more." He was talking about the angle made between the pelvis (croup) and femur, which I have shown is not possible. But one of the axioms of geometry indicates that if the croup is parallel with the tibia, the angle between the femur and tibia equals that between the femur and croup. Remembering that this premise of parallel lines is approximate at best, consider the fact that most excellent, moderately, or even very-angulated dogs have 120 degrees or more between lower thigh and femur, however one measures it.

The angle between pelvis and femur is *not* a right angle. With a slope of 35 degrees to the croup, and a nearly vertical femur, that angle will be around 125 degrees in the ideal dog (90 + 35). To have a right angle would necessitate a horizontal croup or a forward-slanting femur, neither of which are found. The angle between a vertical line running through the stifle and approximating the femur, and the line from stifle to point of hock varies from 95 degrees in an extreme dog to about 130 or 140 degrees in a less-angulated, straighter-stifled dog. This means the angle from the horizontal varies from 5 to 50 degrees in the lower thigh.

The hindquarters of the German Shepherd should never be so steep that both hocks are found directly under any part of the croup or pelvis when the dog is standing in a natural pose. An imaginary line dropped from the ischiatic tuberosity should either pass through the foot (in a fairly straight-legged dog) or meet the ground ahead of it, assuming the metatarsus to be vertical.

If the "sweep of stifle" (the underline of the thigh from flank to hock) is very long in appearance and the lower thigh's angle from horizontal is very small, the dog is commonly spoken of as having "extreme" rear angulation. While this word is used with ungrounded and unbridled admiration by many, it is a good description, for the condition of extremity is neither correct nor desirable in a working dog. Once called a "backward position" by those trying to translate the German description, the rear feet stand too far behind the center of gravity and the legs consequently cannot give as much stability to the movement. Coupled with weak ligaments, this condition can produce a wobbly or "eggbeater" gait, a cow-hocked stance, a breaking down of the back after hard work, and general lack of endurance. It can be caused by or compounded by the lower thigh bones being disproportionately long in relation to the femurs. With weak ligaments, the dog may crouch and exaggerate this condition, and a fearful disposition

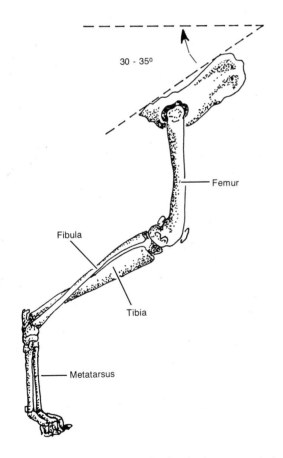

Contrary to innumerable drawings based on imagination or unquestioning acceptance, the femur does not make a 90° angle with the slope of the pelvis, unless the dog crouches or stands with his foot beneath his body. When metatarsus ("hock") is vertical, the femur is also vertical, and makes an angle of about 55-60° with the pelvic slope. The drawings are based on both palpation of the reference points and radiographs (X-rays don't lie).

can have the same effect. A "slightly backward" rear angulation, one of strength and moderation, is natural for a well-proportioned German Shepherd Dog.

Hock—The true hock, or tarsus, contains seven bones and is analogous to the carpus (wrist) of the foreleg, but the word *hock* is often applied to the metatarsus which is analogous to the pastern. The hock corresponds to the heel and ankle in the human, but what is usually *meant* when the word is used corresponds to the *whole* ankle and *most* of the foot.

Should the metatarsus really be relatively short, as the current wording of the Standard requires? Actually, the metatarsus usually is in proportion to the rest of the leg, and an over-all leggy dog will have long-appearing "hocks" as well. Select for short legs, and the "hocks" will take care of themselves.

Ligaments of the tarsal and metatarsal bones seldom cause problems, so these bones stay firmly knit together. However, "loose hocks" do occur. A dog that stands or moves cowhocked (points of hocks closer together than the rest of the legs) does so because the muscles and tendons of the thigh are relatively weak and their attachments may be too far apart. The weakness mostly arises from their stretched or too-long condition. The weakness of ligaments, tendons, and muscles in the whole area of the hocks and stifles is found most often in dogs of extreme angulation. It is a condition not conducive to improvement of the breed nor to working ability of the individual.

Hind feet—As with the front feet, the structure of the rear feet should also be short and compact. But nature dictates and von Stephanitz echoes, "They must be proportionately stronger and longer because their function is to impart a forward push to the body." This notion is confirmed by the fact that the fibular tarsal bone to which the Achilles tendon is attached is larger than the corresponding bone in the carpus of the foreleg.

Minor Skeletal Features

Just a few words are sufficient to describe a few minor bones not previously mentioned. The clavicle is almost non-existent in the canine. The prosternum is that collection of hair, skin, fat, muscle, tendon, cartilage, and sternal bone which normally protrudes ahead of and between the shoulder joints, and often gives a false impression of shoulder layback. Reason enough to use the fingers to feel the joints and angles.

The subject of ribbing is self-explanatory in the Standard, and I have already stated that the appearance of the loins is usually more a matter of fat and muscle tone than actual distance between the last rib and hip. The depth of chest is important and should be around 45 to 50 percent of the height at the withers. Looking at a mounted skeleton would be misleading because of the lack of soft tissue and coat, but a living dog should appear to have very little, if any, space between the point of the elbow and the bottom line of the chest. In full-coated dogs, there may be no visible space, while in short-coated dogs of equal body build this space may *appear* excessive.

The penile bone, known also as the baculum or *os penis*, is the only constant heterotopic bone in the dog (all others have a corresponding right or left half).

Ch. Kuhler Wald's Dotterblume, 1973. A Midwestern favorite, this bitch had excellent gait and temperament. Owners: Dick and Diana Riedel.
Morrissette photo.

5

THE GERMAN SHEPHERD DOG IN MOTION

NATURE OF SKELETAL MUSCLES

According to studies carried out early in this century, skeletal muscle tissue accounts for over half, 53 percent on the average, of the total weight of a well-conditioned German Shepherd Dog. The bones comprise about 14 percent of the working dog, coat 12 percent, internal organs and viscera 13 percent, and blood the remaining 7 or 8 percent. Interestingly, the wild dog (wolf, primarily) is about 60 percent muscle. All this means that light weight, agility, speed, and efficiency are matters of survival not only for the individual competing in the wild, but survival of the species as well. All the more reason to keep our breed within sensible size limits.

Muscles serve all animals in a variety of ways: locomotion, circulation, digestion, excretion, secretion, and respiration among other things. Concerning gait, of course, movement of the bones and propulsion of the body are the specific functions addressed in this chapter. The British dog expert R. H. Smythe, in his 1957 book *Conformation Of The Dog*, said, "Practically the whole propelling force of the hind limb is dependent ... upon the muscle power of a well-developed second thigh." Some of this thrust is derived from the hamstring muscles running from the pelvis to the femur and lower bones, including the biceps femoris, semitendinosus, and semimembranosus muscles. While it is not necessary to remember or even pronounce these, they can be easily felt in the caudal (rear) area of your dog's haunches, below the buttocks.

The German Shepherd Dog has been designed and developed for speed and endurance, not for lifting or pulling great loads. The emphasis on judging and breeding, therefore, must be on length of bones and muscles more than on thickness. Picture the difference between a weightlifter and a swimmer—both are athletes, but our athlete-dog should resemble the latter more than the former, with movement providing the ultimate proof. Greater size is associated with a greater ratio of bone to body weight, restricting endurance and agility, and making the gait slower and more ponderous as exemplified by the very heavy breeds.

GAITS

The German Shepherd Dog uses a variety of gaits at different times and for various reasons, though the one most frequently utilized is the trot. Galloping, loping, walking, and pacing are other gaits often seen in the dog at work.

Pace

The pace is characterized by both front and rear limbs on the same side (right or left) being moved forward at about the same time. You may see the pace if a dog is moved from a walk into a slightly faster motion, or when a dog is tired or out of condition. Pacing, frequently called ambling, has also been attributed to a straight front or a weak back. Off-lead and free, the German Shepherd Dog will almost never pace, which makes me think it is often less a structural problem than an environmental one, though I have seen a familial tendency to pace. If tired, the dog will lie down if he has a choice. Whether one can draw the conclusion, as some have, that pacing is an energy saver because high-endurance animals such as the elephant and camel do it, is questionable.

The pace is not desired in the show ring because it causes the body to lean first to one side, then the other, creating a rolling movement which does not contribute to a smooth impression. Also, it should not be considered a natural gait for the German Shepherd. To correct a pace, give the leash a sharp jerk forward and suddenly increase your speed, causing the dog to momentarily break into a gallop, then slow down just enough for the dog to settle into a trot. Another alternative is to stop and start again, with a faster take-off than previously.

Canter

In order for a dog to cover ground a little faster, but not with the full exertion of a gallop, he will canter. This gait is easily identified by a rocking progression in which the dog leads out with one front limb. The canter is characteristic of Arctic sled dogs such as the Siberian Husky and Samoyed, but it is also frequently used by others in play, for short distances, or for faster movement than a leash allows. The canter is sometimes mistakenly called a lope, which term should be reserved for a relative speed instead of a gait type.

Gallop

A faster gait than the canter, the gallop is used for greatest speed during pursuit, play, and at other times. In order to fully examine this very fast gait, it is useful to view the gallop in slow-motion cinematography. Upon so doing you will see one rear leg touch down first, then the other very quickly thereafter. Similarly, the front feet meet the ground one right after the other. This is to smooth out the motion and prevent the greater impact that would occur if both forelegs had to take the force of the landing at the same time. Thus the four-beat gait has a built-in shock absorbing nature to serve the endurance needs of the hard-working dog.

Trot

The gait that comes most easily to the German Shepherd Dog is the trot, in which the diagonally-opposed limbs move together, or nearly so. The right front leg and the left rear leg advance at the same time, while the left front and right rear also work together. As your dog runs ahead of you on the end of a 6-foot or longer leash, watch his feet. After you get used to seeing how he puts his feet down, cut across a dew-wet lawn then onto dry pavement such as concrete and study the pawprints. At a slow trot, the dog's rear feet will land in the same place as the front feet, perhaps overlapping a fraction of an inch. At a faster trot, the rear legs overreach the front feet placement, and you will be able to see the marks of a progressively longer stride by running across snow or wet sand.

The next stage in increased speed is called the flying trot. The dog not only reaches to his fullest extent, but moves so quickly and covers so much ground that for a short time the dog is completely free of contact with the ground. We must remember that this "long period of suspension" is an infrequent, somewhat unnatural gait in the movement of a working animal although at dog shows, there are often some handlers who will try to impress and deceive the judge by using the flying trot. If the judge doesn't immediately put a halt to it, all the other handlers will feel compelled to copy, and no one will be able to tell much at all about the dog's structure and true gait.

STRUCTURE AND MOTION

Even the natural speeds and gaits of the dog in the ring do not tell us all we need to know about construction or endurance, more information being obtainable by examining the standing dog. In fact, only a quarter of the Standard deals with the dog in motion and this is perhaps a good rule of thumb to use in determining proportionately how much time need be spent on gait when evaluating a dog, whether for purchase, stud use, or show awards. However, at times the inverse will be seen, with dogs being run around and around the ring while the judge tries to determine minute and inconsequential differences between the side gaits of a couple of dogs at a time. Although the time allotted for gaiting in the show ring is *usually* quite short, it is necessary either to confirm or change the judge's opinion of the dog's structure.

Front Assembly

During the trot, a dog will normally hold his head almost on the same level with his back. A timid or uncertain dog may carry his head higher as if on the lookout for danger, and a dog with an upright front assembly will also tend to hold the head higher than will a well-built dog moving at the same speed. In a trotter-built dog (one with correct structure), the top of the head will be slightly higher than the back while trotting, with the eyes approximately on the same horizontal plane as the back. Ears are usually carried folded back close to the neck or turned slightly, unless there is something specific the dog is looking for, in which case the ears will be more erect and the head held higher.

A dog that is "strung up" at the neck with a high, tight leash, will demonstrate inhibited movement since a higher head carriage does not allow for maximum utilization of the brachiocephalicus muscle which, with others, moves the front limb forward. Therefore, a dog that is busy looking for "Mommy," or is nervously attentive to the ring exit, or is being handled improperly as described above, cannot extend his shoulder and forearm as far as he otherwise would, and will appear to have a slightly stilted gait. In short, a confident, at-ease dog whose mind is fixed on moving rather than searching will make the most out of his structure, as will one that is allowed to move in the ring as if free in an open field.

Extension—When the trotting dog extends his front leg forward, the spine of the scapula falls back at the top end (the withers area) because the point

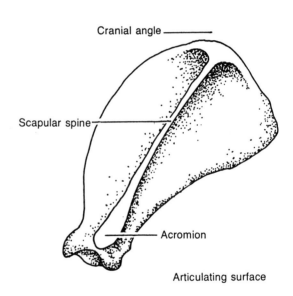

Left scapula, lateral view.

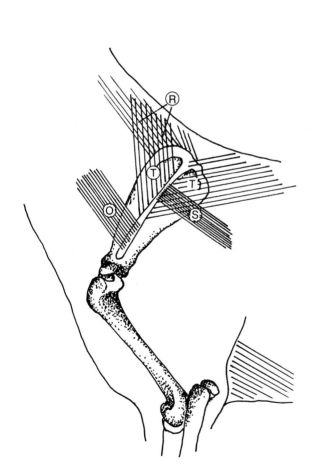

Placement of muscles attaching scapula to trunk. Ⓡ *Rhomboid runs from vertebrae to top edge of scapula.* Ⓢ *Serratus fans out from upper medial (reverse) side of scapula to last five neck vertebrae and first seven or eight ribs.* Ⓣ *Trapesius runs from scapular spine to last five neck vertebrae and first nine thoracic vertebrae.* Ⓞ *Omotransversarius runs from the first neck vertebrae to near the acromion.*

of the shoulder at the bottom end is being pulled forward by muscles attached to the humerus as well as to the lower end of the scapula. The shoulder blade sort of pivots in the middle, and this is when the much-touted 45-degree angle of layback actually occurs. It probably exceeds 45 degrees a bit during a fully extended trot, but the amount of reach is equally dependent on other factors.

The humerus, meanwhile, changes inclination from a backward angle to approximately vertical. The lower foreleg is roughly parallel to the spine of the scapula, with the most efficient reach allowing for about a 45-degree angle at the instant the pad hits the ground at the most forward portion of the stride. At this point the foot pad is under the head, and much ado is made by novices as to whether it reaches an imaginary vertical line dropped from the tip of the nose or from somewhere further back on the head. It makes for silly, senseless arguments, since a great deal depends on carriage of the head, and whether or not the dog lifts his front feet too high.

The flying trot—What is the effect on angulation when a dog is moving faster—in a flying trot, compared to a slower trot? There is probably not very much difference, though undoubtedly maximum effort yields maximum reach. I would suppose the shoulder angle changes just a little, and that efficiency therefore is not appreciably increased with speed. Were the efficiency greatly improved, the flying trot would be the most natural gait in the sheep-tending dog's repertoire, and it isn't, nor is it so in any other occupation of the working dog. Greater is the change in the angle made by the *lower* foreleg.

The great fascination with the flying trot comes about because of what we call the ''period of suspension.'' During the flying trot the whole dog is clear of the ground each time right foreleg and

Great front reach, but note hock nearest you is turned in (cowhocked) and the other rear foot is flat on the ground. This dog is too extreme and sloppy in hock action, as more easily seen going away.

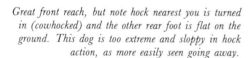

Ch. Trommel's Jasmin of Ryandale, exhibiting perfect balance a split second before reaching maximum extension.

"The Shadow Knows!" Atrice vom Klammle illustrating the flying trot, in which you can see that all four feet are off the ground at once, and the left rear foot will land far ahead of where the front paw had been. Photo courtesy M. Goldfarb, M.D.

left hindleg are thrust forward while the opposite legs leave their ground-points of departure behind. On the next step when left and right legs alternate position, the dog again leaves the ground.

The great thrust of the muscles in the hindlegs with an important assist from those in the forequarters gives the dog sufficient forward motion and speed that the trajectory he makes while thus "leaping" is very flat. When this leap is made, the dog remains "suspended" in the air; actually he is moving in relation to the ground, but the parts of his body are motionless in relation to each other. One foreleg is stretched forward at about an angle of 35 to 40 degrees from the horizontal, and the hind leg on the same side is extended rearward at about the same angle but only if one uses an imaginary line from the acetabulum or ischiatic tuberosity to the rear foot pad as the foot leaves the ground. The angles of the *individual* bones in the rear limb are not quite the same as those in the foreleg during trotting.

During this period of suspension in the flying trot, the shoulder layback is probably 35 to 45 degrees from the vertical, exceeded by that which the lower leg makes, which I estimate to be close

to 55 degrees from the vertical. These estimates are based on photographs of well-built dogs in suspended gait, using draftsman's tools. But while one can easily find the pad, elbow, even the point of the shoulder with some ease, the exact slope and location of the scapular spine remains as elusive in photographs as it does in reality. Since the coat and flesh overlying the scapula do not move exactly with or as far as the bone beneath, what we see isn't what we are looking for.

Movement Faults

Many are impressed by the dog that actually reaches further than his nose, thinking this to be the ultimate in movement perfection. In fact, it is in most cases *faulty* movement, for the paw is lifted too far from the ground, approaching the horizontal in both scapular spine and lower leg. The shoulder joint also is lifted higher than is necessary and the elbow is either flexed a little or at least not fully extended. So, in studying the side gait of a German Shepherd Dog, look to see how high he steps when his foreleg is at its foremost position. If you can see a lot of daylight under the pad, the dog is

German Landesgruppen Sieger. INT "V", Ch. FAX vom Diersheim, SchH 111, AD, CD, OFA.

wasting motion and since waste is the opposite of efficiency it has no place in the correct working dog.

Lifting—Why does one dog *lift* his feet high, and another swing his feet "close to the ground on both forward reach and backward push," to quote the Standard? "Good muscular development and ligamentation" are given the credit for proper movement, though the shoulder layback and relative lengths of the bones have at least as much to do with it. If a dog has better angulation in the hindquarters than it does in the front, as is very common, the rear legs will have a slightly longer stride than the front legs. Since the dog can't run faster (take more steps) in front than he can in the rear, he must do something with those front legs (lift them) which will take up that tiny amount of time required to wait for the rear legs to complete their full stride. Don't confuse the prancing of a puppy that has not yet learned to settle down and trot in a businesslike manner with this fault. Give such a pup a chance to get rid of some energy before making a judgment.

Flipping the wrist—This is another movement fault that can be attributed to this lack of front/rear balance. At the forward end of his reach, a dog may *flip* his wrist outward, rotating the pastern and pad as if to shake a bug off the top of his foot.

Padding—A little bit of a flip, like a little bit of an east-west or turned-out stance, is natural to nearly every breed, and the fancier has to learn from experience how much is normal and how much is *too* much. A variation of this flip has been called padding, and involves the front foot landing far back on the metacarpal (largest) pad. This should not be confused with a fault of a similar-sounding name, "paddling." The latter is a wide-in-front gait that reminds one of the action of someone propelling a kayak or a canoe, turning the pad outward as the leg is brought fully *under* the body.

Pounding—Pounding, like padding, is another result of poor front angulation compared with a more correct rear. In pounding, the front feet visibly hit the ground harder than normal, and jar the whole front end of the dog. This isn't often seen in German Shepherds, because it is associated more with steep pasterns which are not much of a problem in the breed. Pasterns that are angled too sharply (over 30 degrees) produce a "mushy" gait, not a level and strong impression. The dog lacks spring and endurance and generally has a slightly excessive up-and-down motion at the withers. This movement is wasteful and therefore contributes to inefficiency, especially in the working dog breeds.

Toeing out—Many dogs will at times stand with the front feet somewhat turned out. This ungainly stance is variously called "east-west," "Frenching," or "toeing out." Many dogs that stand this way also exhibit this while in motion, and then it is definitely a fault. Although a slight turning out at the pasterns is perfectly normal for the Shepherd, this acceptable variation should diminish or disappear when the dog gaits.

I have seen toeing out at the pasterns mostly in dogs that have other structural faults and believe it often may be an effect of those, rather than a genetically separate, independent problem. It seems not to be related to pastern angle, though a greater angle caused by weaker ligaments can magnify the impression. Most east-west dogs are also somewhat pinched at the elbows, with flatter ribbing than desired. Whether standing or moving toward the observer, this relatively narrower chest may be difficult to identify and the dog may be incorrectly faulted for toeing out.

Throwing the elbows out—Besides ribbing, another cause for such a toeing out stance and gait may be an orthopedic disorder in the elbow joint. In the Shepherd, the most common problem lies in the ununited anconeal process of the front assembly. The elbows are thus abnormally positioned slightly out from the body, and the dog may compensate for the lower limbs being pointed toward each other at the feet by turning his feet outward to gain stability. The combination of out-at-the-elbows and turned-out pasterns is most easily seen when the dog approaches the viewer, although it is not exactly difficult to discern as he trots away.

Being out-at-the-elbows can also be a matter of non-disease-related structural faults such as barrel ribbing wherein the dog turns his elbows out as he draws the foreleg back, in order to avoid jabbing himself in the ribs. It may also be related to a straight front, short scapula, or bulkier and thicker than normal shoulder muscles which deviate the rather flat attachment of the scapula. Some breeders refer to this as "loaded shoulders." If the ribbing does not look abnormal, a dog that moves with elbows thrown out on the backstroke and feet swung around in a wide arc on the forward stroke should be carefully radiographed by a veterinarian instructed to look for a "joint mouse" and other evidence of an orthopedic disorder. The combination of out-at-the-elbows and east-west feet is frequently seen, and some of these dogs cross over or weave in front, though weaving also occurs in a few dogs without these particular problems.

Toeing in—Toeing-in at the front, or "pigeon toes," is the opposite of toeing out and is not a

Ch. Von Freya's Aeric, CDX, three times Select, showing full extension during the trot.
Photo courtesy of breeder/owners Manuel and Diane Garcia.

major problem in German Shepherd Dogs; one almost never sees it in the breed.

Crabbing—An excellent book that appeared in the 1970s, *Dogsteps*, maintains that pacing and crabbing can result from an attempt to avoid interference (stepping on the front feet with the rear feet). Crabbing is a slightly sideways motion in which the rear feet hit the ground to one side of the line set by the front feet. Sometimes one rear leg will reach under the body, but in worse cases both rear legs regularly track to the left or right of the placement of the front feet.

It may well be that the reason some dogs crab or pace or exhibit some other gait anomaly is that they are trying to avoid interference, but attributing motives to actions has always been a pitfall for experts in every field from dog watching to politics. In the case of the above-mentioned faults, it is quite possible that avoidance of interference has absolutely nothing to do with the results, and that such movement is simply more comfortable for a dog with certain ribbing, angulation, length, topline, or what-have-you. It could even be attributed to simple fatigue. I have handled dogs that crabbed until they were taught to run straight, after which their trotting was perfectly normal. I have handled others that paced until speeded up or restarted, at which time they trotted with no awkwardness at all.

If it is important to make a good guess as to the reason for these faults, in order to better select breeding partners, I wish you luck in identifying those causes. Otherwise, just eliminate poor gait of whatever type without regard to the source, and you'll be just as far ahead if not farther.

The Back—Back action is much misunderstood. There is a lot to be said for the goal of movement so smooth that one could envision a full tumbler of water balanced on the trotting dog's back, not spilling a drop. But let's be realistic. The dog does not have a motionless back attached to moving legs riding on a perfectly laid rail track. Muscles and bones turn and stretch, lean and contract, no part being absolutely motionless relative to another. Even the spinal column stretches and bends during gaiting. The entire body is lifted up and forward except for that part of the foot which at that moment is pressed against the ground for propulsion. The beauty of fluid gait and hence the imaginary nonspilling glass of water is a result of the body

moving forward so fast that the up and down movements are carried out over a long distance and thus appear flattened. A well-angulated, tightly ligamented dog will show a minimum of undulation and if you haven't done so already, you will soon observe that most moderately angulated and balanced dogs move with firmer backs than the ones with extreme angulation and balance.

Good angulation in the rear is not sufficient to produce good movement unless it is coupled with correct angulation in front and complemented by a good topline and correct proportions. Two-piece dogs whose forequarters are larger than their hindquarters, may look good to some at first glance, but observation of such a dog in motion will bring to light a rear that seems weak, a front that seems to be loafing, and an impression that the dog is running up a hill or out of a hole.

Some back faults cannot easily be seen from the side, yet this is usually the position from which dogs are viewed. An abnormally pronounced roll, such as frequently seen in Bulldogs, Saints, and Old English Sheepdogs, is best seen from the top, either coming or going. I feel that if show judges were to gait the dogs themselves, as has been done in other areas, they would see a great deal more of certain characteristics than they do from their long-distance position.

A fault sometimes known as a "whip" is most easily seen by looking down on the back while the dog is moving away. The back and croup areas curve from side to side like a snake as the result of weakness in muscles and ligaments, possibly associated with excessive length.

Undulating backs also result from weak, soft tissues, but can have other causes as well. A poor front assembly, for example, which is manifested by high-stepping action, may cause the withers and head to move up and down too much. This bouncing may continue down the back, and is quite noticeable when viewed from a distance or from a low viewpoint. With a little practice, anyone can spot the high step, but envisioning the scapula and humerus beneath the coat and tissues covering those bones is difficult, if not impossible. The angle between the humerous and scapula is a little more than the reputed 90 degrees in the standing dog, and a lot more when the foreleg is in its rearmost position at the rear end of its cycle. At the farthest forward end, the angle should again be very

Sieger, Ch. Bodo vom Lierberg SchH 111 FH CACIB. Read the Standard's wording on topline as you study this photo of Bodo gaiting.

obtuse (open) and approximately equivalent to that between the humerus and the lower leg. Until recently, there have been no accurate means of identifying or demonstrating such an open angle in the live, moving dog, but I believe it to be in the proximity of 135 degrees if the structure is good. It is common to hear fanciers talk of ''a good shoulder opening,'' yet some do so without realizing which angle is being opened.

Even with proper angulation in the forequarters, a dog can exhibit poor back action if it is not balanced. Some dogs stand considerably higher in the rear and when gaiting appear to be always running downhill. If it is just a matter of being a little ''overbuilt'' (higher at the croup than at the withers), then the problem is usually not very serious; but when it is accompanied by looseness, the combination is quite unattractive.

Other examples of non-level backs are the swayback or hollow back, and its opposite, the roach back. The former is almost always very weak and does not allow the full transfer of power from the muscles of the rear legs. Inertial resistance of a front leg in contact with the ground meets with the force from the rear, but the spinal column con-

nection is a fairly weak, slightly valley-shaped spring. A rigid bar would completely transfer the force, but such a flexible spring will bend even further in the direction of its curvature, absorbing some of that force instead of delivering it to the body as forward movement. An extreme simile of a swayback would be the attempt to push a dead snake forward by the tail.

The reason a roached back is not as objectionable, regardless of whether the arch begins immediately behind the withers or over the last ribs, is that it is much stronger than the swayback. Its strength is probably equal to that of the ideal nearly-level back, though it is not as attractive to many observers. In addition, a roach back does not interfere with strenuous movement such as galloping or trotting, to any noticeable degree.

Another poor topline, frequently called ''banana-back,'' shows an obvious break in the backline, making for *two* lines rather than one from withers to pelvis. The slope begins far ahead of where it should, at the croup.

Hindquarters—In a normally moving dog, regardless of what gait is being used, the rear leg reaching far under the body becomes partially straightened from the femoral head to the toenails. After the foot touches down and the dog moves forward, the leg becomes more bent. Then, as it extends behind the rest of the body which is still moving forward, it is again straightened out, this time much more so than before. Just before pushing off to resume forward motion, the bones of the limb are closest to being all pointed in the same direction, especially the lower thigh and the metatarsus. In a very few German Shepherds (more commonly in Afghan Hounds), the lower leg remains quite flexed at that moment, and instead of a good straight follow-through, the stride seems suddenly cut short and the bent *hock* area (flexed joint) is brought forward without any appreciable straightening. Dogs with these *sickle hocks* have shorter strides and the loins tend to bounce up and down excessively.

There are a number of other faults associated with the hocks, most of them in the German Shepherd Dog being attributable to *over-angulation* in the rear. This is a result of fad-breeding, since the more one selects for greatly angulated dogs, the more their offspring will appear like them, including some with more extreme angulation than either parent. As angulation increases, so do speed and length of stride, but past a certain point decreasing strength and stability arise. The longer the muscles and ligaments, the less can they control the hock and keep it in line with the lower thigh and metatarsus. There is a loss in balance of power between abductor and adductor muscles which assist in flexing and extending the metatarsus. The result is a twisting motion at the hock as thrust is delivered through and to it.

A dog that stands slightly *cowhocked* and has overlong or otherwise weak ligaments may push his hindquarters sideways away from the rear foot he pushes off with, causing a slight side-to-side motion in the rear. Even without this obvious waste of motion, cowhocked dogs cannot transmit as much of their muscular contraction energy into forward motion; the sideways springiness is inefficient in the same way as a swayback. Many loose, extreme German Shepherds will, when they lift the rear foot they've just pushed off with, twist that hock outward for an instant before straightening it out in time to put it down under the body. This wasteful motion is probably the most common rear movement fault in the breed. If you suspect a dog of being cowhocked, move him from a standing position several times; some dogs appear to stand a little "hocky" but don't move that way.

Toeing-out of the rear feet is usually accompanied by cowhocks and/or very weak ligaments and is

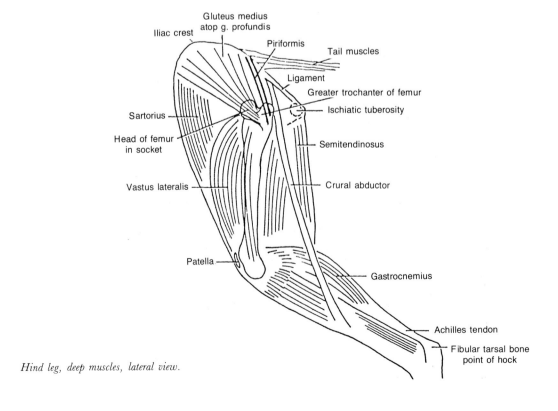

Hind leg, deep muscles, lateral view.

almost never seen as the only evidence of a faulty rear. On the other hand, *toeing-in of the rear feet* is fairly common, especially in dogs linebred on Lance of Fran-Jo. I don't know where he got this tendency, but it may go back to the early progenitors of many related working breeds, as it is still common in many of these today. Although toeing-in can be one of the clinical signs of hip dysplasia, that alone should not be cause for alarm, as there are any number of normal-hipped descendants of Lance that toe in. I've handled many of his sons and daughters with that characteristic and have noticed no adverse effect on gait; it is certainly preferable to toeing-out. It has been claimed that human runners whose feet point almost straight ahead or even a little bit pigeon-toed outperform those whose feet turn out; the same may be true for dogs.

Going-away—Another rear movement sometimes associated with dysplasia, but as often due to other inherited factors, is what we call *moving close behind*. Metatarsal areas, erroneously referred to as hocks or rear pasterns, pass each other so closely that sometimes they rub together. In order for such a dog to single-track at a brisk trot, he must swing his feet inward a little after passing and outward a bit before doing so. Therefore, this dog easily falls into the habit of crossing over in the rear, the right foot landing on a line to the left of the one the left foot is tracking on, and vice versa.

Moving wide in the rear is seldom a real problem in the German Shepherd Dog. Almost always, a dog that seems wide going away will change to a more normal appearance if he is speeded up.

For the German Shepherd Dog, single tracking (the rear legs tilted inward so a V can be visualized between where the feet hit the ground and the hip sockets) is the norm in a moderate to fairly rapid gait. A dog that is wide tracking yet still brings his feet closer together at the pads than at the hocks may simply need to be speeded up, and should not be faulted unless he still fails to single-track.

On the other hand, *parallel tracking* is a fault that will not clear up by changing speed. This is when the hocks are no further apart than are the foot pads when the feet hit the ground. I used to think the problem was mainly one of the chunky, dwarf breeds, but have seen a lot of German Shepherd Dogs parallel-track. The dog may move "close,"

i.e., with the hocks (metatarsi) nearly rubbing each other, or wide, and parallel-track in either case. It is usually the cowhocked, weaker-ligamented dog that will parallel-track, though I've seen dogs of less extreme angulation and with tight ligaments also move this way.

Side view—Just as a high step in front is wasteful, so too is the less frequently seen high *kick-up* in the rear, after the dog has extended the rear limb as far as he can. This kick-up indicates that the dog is not able to extend the leg as far back as he should and therefore cannot utilize all of the power available in the leg muscles. Seen from the side, both the overstepping and lack of extension will be more readily apparent than they are from the rear, going away. It is not uncommon to see the kick-up in a dog with sickle hocks, but most cases are independent of that condition. Often, it is a result of a croup that is too flat. Occasionally poor angulation in the rear legs compared to the front has been blamed, but that would be rare.

A few dogs will lift the knee (stifle) abnormally when bringing the leg forward under the body, perhaps because of a short femur and/or a short, steep pelvis (croup). This tends to make the dog raise the femur toward the horizontal instead of the more efficient 45-degree angle, wasting motion and spoiling what should be a smooth, fairly level side gait.

Croup—Even assuming the femur and lower leg are of proper lengths, a steep croup can interfere with length of stride by causing a slightly shorter extension rearward and a somewhat forward movement of the limb. As stated earlier, a flat croup will also restrict underreach, and it may contribute to

Sickle Hocks

Ch. Abraxas Gable of Langenau. Owners: Ken and Pat Downing. Breeder: Dave Rinke.
Photo by Morrissette

rear kick-up. A good moderate croup angle of about 35 degrees from the horizontal not only makes for a broad thigh section as seen from the side, but also facilitates the maximum reach and efficiency of the rear limbs. The width is easier to see in the standing dog while its effect is manifested in motion.

If the highest point of the croup is as high or higher than the withers, the dog is said to be "high in the rear," or as von Stephanitz's translators put it, "overbuilt." If this condition appears in the skeletally mature dog, it is often the result of "straight stifles" (steep hindquarters). But if the dog has decent angulation, "a moderate amount of overbuiltness cannot be considered a severe defect," to quote von Stephanitz again. The more pronounced the condition, the more the dog will seem to be running downhill, marring the appearance, and he should be penalized when it is severe. The form is quite acceptable in many breeds, and is actually called for in the Standard of the Chesapeake Bay Retriever. I once got group placings with a top Chessie I handled for awhile, and he moved beautifully, with strength and length of stride, though he was very obviously and typically high in the rear.

SUMMARY

The ideal type for the German Shepherd (working) Dog has been described in regard to its body structure and how that structure relates to gait. Gait is the proof of structure, and an important facet of utility. To maximize utility and therefore efficiency, all of these body parts must be correct in their individual *and* relative proportions, whether it be tight feet for traction, strong pasterns for endurance, proper length and angulation of bones for speed and stride, good muscle development and attachment for power, or the most suitable shape, size, and strength of a myriad of organs.

The breed Standard has been written as a set of specifications based on observable qualities of good specimens, and descriptions of faults have been made in this and other chapters in order to better define what is correct. If only one lesson would be learned from all this, it should be Louis Sullivan's well-known phrase, "Form follows function." This means that natural and human selection forces will mold a breed to fit the requirements of its work. It also means that the most beautiful examples of the breed should be those that are structurally and temperamentally best suited for herding livestock, protecting people and property, and being hearty, strong, willing companions to man.

Many a dog with steep shoulder and neck, highly held head, and high-stepping front reach has finished his championship title because of a lack of understanding of the true definition of beauty: utility. May we all strive to evaluate our own dogs as well as we do others', with an unbiased eye and a mind set on protecting and improving the breed to whatever extent we can. The German Shepherd Dog will be faithful to us; let us be faithful to the German Shepherd Dog.

6

SHOWS AND SHOWING

To an all-breed professional handler, the "big" shows in North America would include Westminster, Chicago International, Montreal, Detroit, Santa Barbara, and others with notable entry size or tradition. In addition, specialty clubs hold annual national and regional specialty shows which can be quite large. In foreign competition, the list would start with Crufts, an enormous and prestigious British show. Entries there total around 9,000 dogs, with German Shepherd Dogs contributing a large portion of that number.

> "Heaven goes by favor; if it went by merit, you would stay out and your dog would go in."
> *Mark Twain*

However, in most shows, large or small, the German Shepherd entry is very low, unless there is a German Shepherd Dog specialty the day before or after in the same city or nearby. Even winning Best of Breed at Westminster, unless the dog goes on to place in the Group, is a shallow victory since there is usually very little competition against which to compare him. Why do Shepherd folk not turn out for all-breed shows, as a rule? As a judge, a German Shepherd Dog breeder, and former handler, I believe I understand at least part of the reason.

The popularity of the breed, the largest in registration worldwide, has brought into the ranks a host of new people, not all of whom stay with the breed for long or learn very much. These I call "perpetual novices." Because of their numbers, many are elected to office in local clubs, do a lot of breeding to flashy winners, and produce a lot of pups, some of whom win championships. Thus they have some credentials, although of dubious value, to present to the American Kennel Club in order to become judges.

THE JUDGES

Too many specialty judges have not been adequately educated as to what makes up a good dog, much less as to what it is that makes a good *Shepherd* Dog. Too few have studied von Stephanitz or the history of the breed; too few have any appreciation of anatomy, structure, and soundness; and too many ignore the purposes this noble breed has been developed to meet.

The kind of poor specialty judge I've been describing overlooks what the Standard describes as *very* serious faults. Part of the problem lies in the manner of choosing the National Specialty judges: by popularity contest (vote of those members interested enough to return ballots). The ones whose names have been seen most often shortly before the vote are likely to be in the running if nominated by others like him or her who are on the board or nominating committee. Certainly not all specialty judges overlook serious faults, nor do all multi-breed judges understand the German Shepherd Dog. But enough of the popular but less-demanding specialists continue to get assignments to make it a noticeable problem.

In Germany, popularity carries no weight. Instead, judges are selected according to their knowledge and experience that have been tested for many, many years by other judges. They have worked their way through a difficult apprenticeship conforming to the Standard all the way, and are well-grounded in anatomy, training skills, and other details necessary to the complete understanding of the breed.

THE EXHIBITOR

Given this trend, what does the fancier who has puppies sired by a specialty-type dog do when it comes time to show them? Many try a few all-breed shows and come home disappointed when their flashy, side-gaiting beauties are defeated by a sounder, perhaps more moderately-angulated dog. They then may, if they haven't given up entirely, try a specialty show and have better luck. Of course, what the exhibitor *should* do is question the judge to find out his opinion of the dog. However, even this can be a problem since the AKC has a policy of discouraging judges from commenting on the dogs being shown under them. They are supposed to say something presumably safe such as, "Maybe he just wasn't using what he has today as well as the winning dog," rather than give any criticism which might be overheard by others. Even private discussions with the handler are supposed to be

Fig. 6-1. Ch. Lakeside's Gilligan's Island, R.O.M., OFA-normal. Gillie was one of the most beautiful and most admired German Shepherds ever shown. He died early, otherwise he would have set unbeatable records. He won his first major at six and one half months of age, beat over 500 entrants in getting BOW at the National Specialty, was National Futurity Victor, chosen "Select" twice before two years old, and in six months after that amassed 25 Working Group Firsts and 12 BIS awards. From the famous Lance/Melissa combination. Kim Knoblauch, handler; D. Dwier, owner/breeder.
                                                                                                                                Photo courtesy D. Dwier, owner/breeder.

Fig. 6-2 "Hatter," the top winning GSD of all time. Ch. Covy Tucker Hill's Manhattan, owned by Jane Firestone and Shirlee Braunstein.
Photo by Alverson Photographers.

postponed until after the judging assignment so as not to interfere with the AKC requirement to judge at a rate of 25 to 30 dogs per hour. This delay means that the judge tries to answer a question long after he has forgotten who was in which class with whom.

Another problem could be that the exhibitor often is too disgruntled or intimidated to ask a quick question. Frankly, I have known many judges who would risk offending the AKC and answer the brief question before the exhibitor leaves the ring. It doesn't take much time to answer a simple question, and the judge may feel an obligation to the breed and to the people who spent their entry fee money for his evaluation. Quite frequently the reason a dog doesn't place higher is because of sloppy hock action or poor shoulder layback and front action; just as often it is a lack of confidence denoting a temperament fault. Since these two problem areas (movement and character) are where we find the worst plagues upon the house of breed, the breeder/exhibitor has as much right to know about them as the judge has an obligation to point them out.

In conclusion, the only way to find out which judges know their stuff and which do not is to *show*. Enter multi-breed competitions and stay for Group judging whether or not you have won Best of Breed. By staying to see the best compete, you'll learn much about movement in the canine and you can apply that knowledge to a greater understanding of your favorite breed.

THE SHOWS

US Specialty Shows

Having now given sufficient warnings, let me encourage you to attend and compete in the specialty shows, for it is here you can see the development of the breed and enough specimens to observe the range of quality. In the United States there is one German Shepherd Dog Club which is a member of the American Kennel Club. It is recognized as the official voice of the breed, and is known as "the parent club." In addition, there are over 100 "regional" clubs affiliated with the

GSDCofA. Some serve fanciers in and around a major city, such as the GSDC of Long Island, and others try to serve the needs of a larger area, perhaps even a whole state, such as the GSDC of Alaska. Each one puts on one or two shows annually.

Often, a good-sized specialty show will have, in addition to its regular and non-regular AKC classes, a pre-show event called a Sweepstakes or "Puppy Sweeps." The Sweepstakes is judged by a different person than the one(s) doing the point show, and classes are offered for puppies up to 18 months of age. The Sweeps judge can be anyone chosen by the club, and is usually a handler or a breeder, but seldom an AKC-licensed judge.

To find out where and when the specialty shows are held, look through issues of the AKC's magazine, *Pure-Bred Dogs* ("The Gazette"), available by subscription, or in *Dog World*, which can usually be found on magazine stands and is also available by subscription. The GSDC of America magazine, the *Review*, is sent to members and also lists most of the specialty shows and all of the futurities, with dates, show secretaries, and judges.

Canadian Specialty Shows

Canada's specialty shows are run about the same way, but they are organized a bit differently. Since individuals, not clubs, are members of the Canadian Kennel Club (CKC), there is not one universally-recognized German Shepherd Dog Club of Canada which can speak for all German Shepherd Dog fanciers in the country. However, there is one club in Ontario moving in that direction, trying to tie all Shepherd people in that vast land together. This club holds an annual show at which a Canadian Grand Victor and Victrix are chosen. There is in addition, a separate show at which the Canadian Sieger and Siegerin are picked, and there is a fledgling magazine called the *Journal*. Notice of the Canadian shows is found in the newspaper-style magazine *Dogs In Canada* published by the CKC.

US Futurity/Maturity Shows

These shows, often simply called "the Futurities," are held in various parts of the country, one in each of about eight or nine regions (the number has changed a little over the years), and each is hosted by one or two clubs in the region. These are not point shows, so they may not be listed in *Dog World* or the *Gazette*, but can be found in the *Review*.

The parent club Futurities are designed to give area breeders a chance to "show their wares" and compare their efforts with those of their colleagues. But because of the practice of hiring professional handlers to show these youngsters, and the practice of handlers flying to several Futurities, the flavor of these events has changed somewhat from the breeders' showcase they were envisioned to be. Because of this mobility, breeders now have an opportunity to see how one stud's genetic stuff works with that of several bitches from different lines.

The Futurities are held in late spring, usually late May to mid-June. Judges are frequently chosen from the ranks of popular breeders or professional handlers, though some AKC judges are used even though their license status is not required. It used to be standard practice to have one judge for each sex, and use both regardless of size of entry.

In effect, the Futurity/Maturity is one BIG fun match. The number of entries is generally much higher than at most specialty shows, and these shows are often held in conjunction with one to three specialty shows over a long weekend. Nearby clubs, one of which is a Futurity host club, stage these specialties back-to-back, sometimes at just one location, at least within easy driving distance of each other, to capitalize on the large number of people and dogs in the area.

Futurity classes are a little different than those at an AKC show; there are four in number: Junior, Teen-age, Intermediate, and Senior Puppy. The Junior classes are open to all dogs born in September, October, or November of the previous year. The Teen-age class is for those born in June, July, or August, and the Intermediate dogs were born in March, April, or May of last year. The Seniors are those that were born in January or February of last year or December of the year before.

The Maturity is for dogs that had been entered (whether shown or not) in last year's Futurity. Naturally, the Maturity entry is much lower than that of the Futurity with many of these dogs having earned points and some of them having even become champions.

Futurity entries are made in two steps. First, before the pup is 3 months old, the breeder of a litter or the owner of the puppy must fill out and send in a litter nomination form bearing the breeder's signature, plus the litter entry fee. Then, sometime after the first of February, the second forms will be mailed to the breeder for distribution to his puppy buyers. These can then be sent in, with individual entry fees, to the chairman of the regional Futurity of the owner's choice. No dog can be entered in more than one Futurity or Maturity. Only members of GSDCA may "nominate" (pre-enter) puppies, and can get forms from the Futurity Chairman who is listed in the *Review*.

A puppy that wins his class and goes on to capture Best in Futurity or Best of Opposite Sex in Futurity, would be eligible to compete in the Best in Futurity Sweepstakes at the National Specialty Show the following autumn. The same is true for the Maturity winners, and ROM points are thereby earned for the dog's parents. Winning a placing in the Futurity Sweepstakes carries the added benefit of a share of the entry fees, something which is a rarity in point shows, where cash prizes, if any, are mostly limited to the Best In Show.

Futurities are fun, but there may be some imbalance in the amount of importance given a win in such a match, especially with regard to the ROM points. I haven't seen any hard evidence that

Futurity winners do any better in attaining championships than other good pups. However, some recognition is certainly called for when a dog's or a bitch's offspring wins in a sizeable-entry competition such as a Futurity.

The US National Specialty

The biggest US German Shepherd Dog specialty point show is the National, held in a different city each year. In addition to the classes at other AKC shows, the National features a Veterans class in which a few dear old bitches and dogs revive many pleasant memories for onlookers. All dogs seven years and older are eligible, and it's a shame more are not entered for there is something majestic and special about the old ones—they project a certain dignity. Stud Dog and Brood Bitch classes give the audience a chance to see dogs with several of their progeny in the same ring at the same time. The National also features a passing parade of Shepherd Greats that includes past Select winners, UD dogs with another title, Obedience Victors or Victrixes, and ROM sires and dams.

From the Specials Class are chosen roughly the top 10 to 15 percent which are called Select. The #1 Select dog is given the title Grand Victor, and the #1 Select bitch is called the Grand Victrix. The

Fig. 6-3. "The Incomparable One." 1962 Can. Gr. V., Ch. Ulk Wikingerblut, SchH III, FH, CACIB, ROM. Ulk was bred by E. Sander of Germany and imported in 1960 at three and one half years of age. By the end of 1962 he had become the number one GSD winner of all time, a distinction held for eight years. He also produced 48 champions to earn the title of number one producer, replacing his sire Troll as the highest ROM point winner of all time. Linebred Rolf Osnabruckerland 3-3,4. He contributed most toward Ralph and Mary Roberts' list of over 80 champions.
Photo courtesy owner/handler M. Roberts.

dog that scores the highest in combined Open and Utility obedience trial points is named Obedience Victor (or Victrix). The requirement that a dog earn a ribbon in conformation competition was added years ago in order to prevent dogs with disqualifying faults (especially white dogs) from winning this honor.

The winners of the past spring's regional Futurity/Maturity shows are eligible to compete in special classes at the National. The winners of these Finals are named Futurity Victor and Victrix, and Maturity Victor and Victrix. Tracking tests and obedience trials are also held in conjunction with the conformation show, though tracking competition is held at a location out of town. Many other special events or demonstrations may be sponsored by the parent club, including relay hurdle races, police dog exhibitions, or whatever they think will interest the spectators and show off the breed's versatility.

The entry at a National is so huge that judging and other events are spread out over three days, with judging duties divided between three judges elected by popular vote from a nominated list prepared by the GSDC of A's Board of Directors. The Specials (champions) Class alone runs around 70 to 100 dogs and takes half a day to judge. However, quantity does not necessarily guarantee quality and, therefore, the National Specialty is only one more dog show, with no more than five points awarded to Winners Dog and Winners Bitch each. The judge may or may not be good, since he is chosen by a popularity context rather than by acclamation of knowledgeable judges and other experts. Indeed, if the judges at the National were the very best available, the same ones would undoubtedly be used every year, as is done in Germany.

Nor are the best dogs always shown. Because of location, economics, choice of judge, discourage-

---

Titles Awarded to German Shepherd Dogs

AKC, CKC, and SKC

Ch (Champion): In AKC (American Kennel Club) shows, 15 points including at least two "majors" of 3 or more points from two different judges, and any number of minor or major wins. In CKC (Canadian Kennel Club) shows, 10 points under different judges (5 points maximum per show for either AKC or CKC). In SKC (States Kennel Club) shows, four certificates of merit, two of which must be earned after 15 months of age.

CD, CDX, UD: Progressively more difficult, these are obedience titles awarded by AKC, CKC, and SKC. These registration organizations also offer TD and TDX degrees for tracking.

SV (Shaferhund Verein)

Sieger, Siegerin: most often used for the top dog and bitch at the Siegershau held annually in Germany. Also used by other countries and to denote "Winner" of regional and local shows, herding trials, etc.

VA, V, SG, etc: rankings used at SV shows (see text). Other countries have adopted this method as well.

FH, AD, etc: Many titles or designations are given for tracking, endurance tests, and other evaluations (see text).

SchH (Schutzhund) In three levels, but literal translation is "Protection Dog." Similar requirements for IPO (other than German) and Ring Sport.

Others

FCI, the international association of dozens of national and breed clubs, awards the CACIB, an award loosely translated as International Champion. Dogs must win under FCI judges in or from several countries.

United Schutzhund Clubs of America (USA) awards the same training titles as does the SV and cooperates with the SV in many ways, including having the SV handle their breed registration.

GSDC of America: ROM (Register of Merit) is given to dogs meeting certain requirements regarding production of winning offspring. *Grand Victor* and *Grand Victrix* are the top dog and bitch in the Specials Class at the annual National Specialty. *Select* means the dog placed in the top 8 to 15, depending on the judges' choice. The German Shepherd Dog Club of Canada has the same or similar titles.

ment, an unwillingness to face steep odds, or some other reason, many owners and handlers keep their worthy dogs at home. Yet, with all this in mind, there is still nowhere else where the average American has the chance to see as many of the best dogs in the country under one roof during one time period. If there is one held near you, don't miss it!

The Sieger Show

There are a number of differences between the way the US National Specialty is run and the methods employed in conducting the World Sieger Show in Germany. Besides being international in scope, the Sieger Show is completely controlled by the SV, not some supra-organization such as the

1987 Grand Victrix Howard's Magic Moment
Photo courtesy Jane Firestone

1970 Grand Victor Ch. Hollamor's Judd, ROM, being handled by Jim Norris at a GSDC of Wisconsin show in 1974.
Morrissette Photo

AKC. They therefore can set requirements that would not be allowed here in the US.

To begin with, all entrants in the Open Class (the *Gebrauchshundklasse*) are pre-screened the day before and are admitted into the ring in order based on records compiled in the preliminary judging. These dogs must have been surveyed, passed a temperament test, be gun-sure, have a Schutzhund title, and have earned at least an SG (*sehr gut*) ranking at some previous competition such as one of the *Landesgruppen* 'regional' shows. So, by the time the males enter the ring to be judged by the president of the SV (females are customarily judged by the vice-president), their pedigrees and past records are *known* to the judge. Conversely, in AKC and CKC shows, the judge is not supposed to base his decision on anything other than what he sees in the ring on that day. This directive puts a terrible burden of dilemma on a judge who knows a certain dog is dysplastic, or of poor temperament, or produces very poorly, yet is under control and shows none of his problems on the day of the show.

On the day prior to being judged in the "show" ring, the adults must pass the courage tests in a different field or arena. (Meanwhile, the younger dogs are being judged in the conformation ring.) Elements of Schutzhund training are used to test the dog's temperament and willingness to protect his handler. While the two walk down the field, an agitator jumps out from behind a blind making threatening gestures. The dog must attack, bite hard, and hold on until commanded by his handler to release. The villain also goes through the escape-turn-threaten routine and the dog must pursue and again attack the stick-wielding agitator. The dog must work well in spite of the cheers and other noises made by the enthusiastic crowd, something he is probably not used to.

Double-handling is less controlled, especially in the preliminary judging, at the Sieger Show than at the GSDCofA National Specialty. Family members and handler's assistants are allowed to run into and out of the ring to give the dogs water, get their attention, take snapshots, etc., as long as they don't interfere with the judging. Also, there is a great deal more gaiting than is seen at the National. In the Sieger Show, handlers can be relieved by an assistant, and this happens often; very few are what we would call professional handlers.

The judge, sometimes in a tent, sometimes seated in the middle of the very large ring, makes notes and comments to the secretaries rather than rely on his memory, since the entry is usually well over 100 in the Open Class, perhaps some 30 percent greater than a typical American National Specialty Specials class. As has been mentioned, judges are the same year after year, and no one is allowed to judge at any show until he has passed extensive testing and apprenticeship.

Some of the judging is done off-leash at a fast trot in order for the judge to be sure he sees the movement free of any outside influence. In the US, show dogs are almost never trained to run or walk off-leash on a heel command and some are never seen in any posture other than straining against the leash, which can cover up or magnify faults, especially in back and front assembly. In Germany, the off-leash trotting is often taken over by the one who trained the dog for his Schutzhund titles, while another may do the on-leash work.

1933 Sieger Odin v. Stolzenfels

In US shows, the National included, "coming and going" are usually evaluated somewhere in the middle of the judging procedure, then apparently forgotten by the time the finalists are gaited around and around. It is at this point, when the specialty judges have all those terrific side-views to watch, that most make their decisions.

In the Sieger show, which also sets the style for smaller shows, "coming and going" is evaluated more toward the end of the class. Notes made at that time are compared with notes on everything else that day plus the past days and previous records, and finally the dogs are placed.

The Open Class at the Sieger Show is something like a combination of the Open plus Specials classes at the American National, but instead of placings only for the top four in each class (plus top ten or so in Intersex competition), *all* of the dogs in the Sieger Show's classes are ranked, from first place to last place. The Siegerschau Open Class does not have dogs and bitches in the same ring, as we do in our Specials Class, but somewhat analogous to our Select ranking is the naming of the best half-dozen to a dozen or so as *Auslese*. These are designated VA-1 (*vorzueglich auslese*) 'excellent select' number one, VA-2, etc. After the VA dogs, the V dogs are similarly ranked, beginning with V-1 to the end of however many the judge considers to be excellent. In an important show like the Sieger, there may be many V dogs, as owners who have consistently placed lower in preliminary shows wouldn't want to take the chance of looking bad in the company of even stiffer competition. After the V-rated dogs come the SG (*sehr gut*) dogs, also ranked from SG-1 on.

1929 Sieger Utz v Haus Schuetting.

There is only *one* winner or *Sieger* in any one German competition, but many champions may be in the ring in a US, Canadian, or British show. The same competition exists for bitches as described above, with the VA-1 named *Siegerin* for that year. There have been years when the Sieger title was not used, but dogs were ranked VA-1,2, etc., anyway. This happened during some of the years during and immediately following the war, then again from 1974 through 1977.

1968 Grand Victrix Ch. Valtara's Image. Owned by the Engelmanns, East Coast breeders of note. *GSDCA photo.*

Younger dogs and bitches are judged in their respective age groups and classes, but puppies under twelve months of age are not shown at the Sieger Show or many other preliminary events during the year. Compare this with American shows where many puppy entries at specialties would raise the number of points awarded there were it not for the AKC reaction of making the requirements tougher for "majors." At the Sieger Show, the winner of the 18- to 24-month-old male class is named *Junghündsieger* (young dog winner) and the female winner is *Junghündinsiegerin*. The popular translation as Youth Sieger and Siegerin is confusing to most non-German-speaking people at first, since both *Jung* and *Jugend* can be translated as 'youth'. The *Junghundklasse* winner is awarded SG-1, since the V rating is not given it other than the *Gebrauchshundklasse* (Open or Adult Class). The SG rankings are also made in the 12- to 18-month-old *Jugendklasse*, but no similar title is given.

Similar to our Stud Dog/Brood Bitch classes are the *Nachkommengruppen* with (*Nachkommen* meaning 'descendants' or 'progeny'). Another is the Breeders' Class (*Zuchtgruppen*) which is judged on excellence and uniformity of each breeder's or kennel's dogs shown in the ring together. I think we would do well to hold such a contest in the US, *if* we could be assured of truly qualified judges every time.

OBEDIENCE AND OTHER TRAINING COMPETITIONS

Both the American Kennel Club and the Canadian Kennel Club (plus the new States Kennel

Four-Continent, Ten Ch. Clayfield's Mon Ami CACIB, by Am/Can Ch. Lakeside's Harrigan ROM; out of Clayfield's Bonnelle. Owned by the Neal Leas family, and bred by Ann Mesdag, Sharon Earl and Alice Likens.
    On April 24, 1986, the lovely Mon Ami was inducted into "The Guinness Book of World Records," for her ten world wide championships: American, Portuguese, South African, Venezuelan, Mexican, Colombian, Canadian, Bermudan, Dominican, and FCI International. In addition, her record embodies worldwide competition wins in eleven countries on four continents, multiple Group wins in eight countries and Best In Show on 4 Continents, always owner-handled. She flew in excess of 100,000 miles during her globe-trotting career. The Leas family was presented with a "Special Achievement" award honor for Mon Ami's achievements by the GSDC of America, Inc. on November 17, 1988, at the National Specialty Show in Houston, Texas.
    She is pictured going Best in Show over more than 1000 dogs in Johannesburg, South Africa, with owner Neal Leas under the Premier Judge of Holland, Mr. T. Van Dijk.

Club) offer titles in obedience training. A CD
(Companion Dog) title is awarded for passing scores
in three trials; the dog must heel, sit, come, and
stay during prescribed exercises. Additional and
more difficult exercises such as jumping, retrieving, following hand signals, and scent discrimination are required for CDX (Companion Dog Excellent) and UD (Utility Dog). The AKC awards
an OTCH (Obedience Trial Champion) title for
consistently high scores in the advanced classes.

Tracking degrees (TD and TDX) are given
when a dog successfully follows an aged track laid
by the handler walking across a field, and finds articles left there. In addition, there are a variety of
tests and competitions, some primary for fun and
some more utilitarian: Versatility, Herding Instinct, Flyball, Relay-hurdle races, and more. Some
are sponsored by specialty clubs or obedience clubs.

*Obedience trials evaluate the dog's reliability and his responsiveness to
his handler. Obedience work also increases the bond between dog and
owner and increases the pleasure of dog ownership.*

Photo by Betsy Duffner.

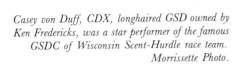

*Broad jump, an Open obedience exercise.
Handler pivots 90° right as dog leaves the
ground.   Morrissette Photo.*

*Casey von Duff, CDX, longhaired GSD owned by
Ken Fredericks, was a star performer of the famous
GSDC of Wisconsin Scent-Hurdle race team.
Morrissette Photo.*

1968 Obedience Victrix Heidi von Zook, UD. Owned and trained by Ron and Ann Roberts, Heidi was the GSDCA's first to hold this title. No dog qualified in 1969, but there have been Obedience Victors (or Victrixes) named at National Specialties since. The title involves the highest combined qualifying scores in Open and Utility. Heidi had 199½ in each, out of a possible maximum of 200.

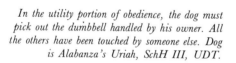

In the utility portion of obedience, the dog must pick out the dumbbell handled by his owner. All the others have been touched by someone else. Dog is Alabanza's Uriah, SchH III, UDT.

The High Jump: an exercise in advanced obedience training. Von Salix's Hein, a son of Ch. Caralon's Hein, clears the 3-foot barrier with ease.

Photo by Lee Merkle, Toledo Times.

SCHUTZHUND

Clubs

There are today three main clubs in the US for Schutzhund enthusiasts, with a fourth in the wings. At this writing, one American-based club is the North American Working Dog Association, which began in 1970 as the North American Schutzhund Association and even today retains the initials from its earlier name, NASA. The organization spread from California into well over a dozen countries, and developed an independent program of certification of judges, trainers, and decoys (agitators or "bad guys"). Dogs of any breed win NASA SchH-I, II, and III titles, as well as a few other titles at NASA-sponsored events.

The United Schutzhund Clubs of America, also known as Schutzhund USA, is German Shepherd Dog oriented, affiliated with the SV, and much more demanding of dogs in regard to hardness and eagerness to bite. Also started in 1970 in the United States, Schutzhund USA stresses German rules, German judges, (although they have been working to certify American judges), and competition in Germany to fulfill all the requirements for their titles and *Koerklasse* (breed quality) ratings. In this country, other breeds are allowed to compete, and a mixed-breed dog from Canada won USA's 1980 National Championship. USA has recently begun registration and breed survey activities, drawing the wrath of AKC and GSDCofA.

The third club is the all-breed German Alliance of Utility Dog Sports Clubs (DVG) founded in 1902 in Europe but which has been in the United States only since the mid-1970s. This club's big attraction for Americans is the lack of a monolithic, central governing body. Less expensive, less extreme on the bite work, and more tolerant of a range of hardness than is USA, the DVG does not stress obedience work as much as does NASA, yet it is growing rapidly.

All three organizations mentioned are similar in their degrees, registrations, and rules, at least in regard to competition in this country. The fourth, the WDA, is sponsored by the GSDCofA. It has sent teams to Europe to compete in the annual Schutzhund "finals." The parent club had done nearly nothing for so many years that the WDA is seen by some to be a jealous reaction to the success that Schutzhund USA has had. However,

at this writing it seems quite strong. Time will tell whether the growth in interest in this sport will be sustained and be enough to warrant four such organizations in the US and Canada.

Trials

Growing rapidly in popularity, even in low population density areas of North America, protection dog training also utilizes the natural abilities of the German Shepherd and prepares the individual for service as home and personal guardian as well as for law enforcement. Indeed, many of the participants in Schutzhund competition are police officers, and there is quite a bit of friendly rivalry between departments. Basic Schutzhund work involves some of the exercises seen in obedience trials such as heeling, the down-stay, and recall. Not only are jumping and retrieving added, but elements of tracking also form part of the work.

The exercises and requirements in Schutzhund trials have remained, for many years, a means of screening out dogs that do not have the vigor,

During the obedience phase of a Schutzhund trial, the dog must demonstrate control, reliability, and willingness. Here the dog is returning a 5 pound dumbbell to his owner. He is at the highest level of training—returning the dumbbell over a six foot scaling wall.

Photo courtesy of Betsy Duffner

stability, and mental agility desired for their breeds' purposes. Ideally, every German Shepherd Dog should have the ability and desire to protect his family or handler. Indeed, in Germany a dog must have Schutzhund titles in order to win top awards in conformation or be in demand as a breeding animal.

There are three divisions in each level of Schutzhund competition: tracking, obedience, and protection. A maximum of 100 points is possible in each division. Each level is more involved than the preceding, and more demanding of both dog and trainer.

SchH-I tracking—With his dog parked somewhere out of sight, the handler walks about 400 to 500 paces, making a few turns as predetermined by the judge. He drops two small, approved articles carrying his scent (a billfold, keycase, etc.), one somewhere along the track and the other at the end of the track, then continues some distance past the end of the track before returning to the starting point. At least twenty minutes after laying a track,

the handler puts his dog in a tracking harness which includes a very long leash, and gives him a chance to sniff around at the starting point. Then, he follows the dog at the end of the 30-foot leash and hopes the dog will stay on the track. The dog must not weave back and forth or otherwise lose either interest or the scent. Some dogs are trained to pick up the article and stay at that point until the handler comes to get it. Others are trained to return to the handler with it, and still others are to stay with the article without touching it. The judge must know in advance which each dog should do.

SchH-II and III tracking—Strangers are employed to lay the tracks, which are progressively longer and older, with up to three of the stranger's articles being dropped. Points are deducted for less than perfect performance.

SchH-I obedience—Heeling is similar to that found in AKC obedience trials, except that the loose leash is held in the left hand, and instead of a figure-eight around two stationary ring stewards, the dog

On the trail.
Photo courtesy of Rudy Drexler's School for Dogs, Elkhart, Indiana

A tracking dog works intensely with his nose deep into the ground cover. He must locate the article dropped by the tracklayer. Tracking assesses the dog's perserverance, his natural capacity and his willingness to work. Shown here is Alabanzas Uriah, SchH III, UDT, owned and trained by Susan Barwig.
Photo courtesy of Betsy Duffner

In the protection portion of a Schutzhund trial the dog must protect his handler. However as soon as the "bad guy" stops the attack, the dog must sit and guard him. Shown here is Cello vom Markenfeld owned and trained by Susan Barwig.
Photo by Amy Jordheim

During a Shutzhund trial the dog must protect his handler from attack. In this picture the "bad guy" has been captured and is being escorted back to the judge.
A Schutzhund dog is a friendly, good natured family member, an alert courageous protector and an obedient, reliable companion. Shown here is American-bred Alabanzas Uriah, SchH III, UDT owned and trained by Susan Barwig.
Photo by Betsy Duffner

is walked through a milling crowd. Off-leash heeling includes a gun being fired some distance behind the dog; this should not distract or worry him. A second shot is fired ten seconds later, and additional shots may be used if the judge suspects the dog is unsure. The obviously very gun-shy dogs are dismissed immediately from the rest of the examination. Possible point accumulation is 15 on-lead, 15 off-lead.

The sit exercise requires the handler to walk his dog forward off-leash at least ten paces, and give him the sit command at which the dog must sit *immediately* while the handler continues at his normal pace without looking back. Thirty paces later, the handler turns and faces the dog for a few seconds, then returns to the dog's right side. Ten points are possible. Next, the dog is "dropped" during heeling, and when the handler is thirty paces past where he told his dog "Down!", he turns and calls his dog. The rest is just like the AKC drop-on-recall exercise and is worth 10 points.

Retrieving on flat is worth 10 points and is executed as is the AKC version. Retrieval over the one meter (39+ inches) high jump is also done as it is in AKC Open obedience trials and is worth 20 points.

Similar to one of the AKC Utility Class routines is the "Away and Down" exercise worth 10 points. While heeling, the handler gives his dog the command to leave him and run forward, "Away!" at which the dog runs out until told to drop: "Down!" at which point he should turn to face the handler and lie down immediately. In the "Away and Down," the handler may call to his dog and then use the upraised hand signal to drop him. The dog must then remain down while the handler returns to his right side and is told by the judge that the exercise is over.

Before the next dog is put through his paces, the first dog is taken off to one side and made to lie down while his handler walks about fifty paces away and stands with his back to his dog while the next team is evaluated in the first six exercises. During this, the judge has another opportunity to see if dog #1 is nervous about gunshots when the handler is not at his side, for he is in a position to see him as well as dog #2 when the gun is fired. After dog #2 completes his sixth exercise, the handler of dog #1 may return to his dog and take him off the field. Up to 10 points can be earned for this exercise.

SchH-II and III obedience—Advanced Schutzhund obedience requires performance with heavier dumbbells, higher jumps, and a stand-stay while walking and running.

SchH-I protection—This division's points are divided as follows. Search: 5 points, Attack on handler (by agitator): 30 points, Pursuit and capture: 55 points, and another possible 10 points reflecting the degree of courage the dog displays in the above exercises.

Search: An agitator is hidden in a blind and when the handler brings his dog out onto the trial field, he is told to search. When he finds the hiding, suspicious stranger, the dog should bark (some like to take a little nip although they're not supposed to) and stay there barking until his handler arrives and leads him away. Because of the possibility of bites, the agitator should always wear protective padding and, in the Search exercise, stand quietly with arms at his side and hands hidden. He should not stare at the dog or make threatening or quick moves, otherwise, the dog will be all the harder to teach not to bite under such circumstances.

Attack on handler: The handler heels his dog off-leash in a direction that leads to a hidden agitator who jumps out to attack the handler but doesn't actually touch him. Most SchH-I dogs will instinctively go for an arm or leg and even when struck lightly with a stick should not let go until commanded to by his handler, and the agitator stands still.

Pursuit and capture: The captured "prisoner" will suddenly flee after the handler has a grip on his dog's collar, and when the dog is released and told to get him, the agitator stops running, turns, and comes at the approaching dog. The dog should not waiver in his attack for his duty is to subdue the agitator and prevent further escape, whether by actual biting or not. When the handler catches up to them, he'll be told by the judge to pull the dog off or simply command him to let go. The dog is told to lie down while the agitator is "frisked." Following that, they escort the agitator to the judge, the dog between the two and watching the agitator. This exercise is judged on the dog's courage and obedience to commands.

SchH-II and III protection—The same elements, with greater difficulty and vehemence, are found in advanced protection or "man-work," as it is also known. More searching and barking are required, more escapes, more attacks on the handler, and more light hits to the dog with the stick. The agitator must be sensible and well-versed in Schutzhund procedures and must know where and how hard he can hit the dog without doing any damage. If a dog, especially in early training, is hurt and intimidated, all the work that he had been through can be ruined and retraining and confidence-building can be an almost interminable task.

Temperament Testing

In Germany, dogs must pass a temperament test before entering Schutzhund trials. In the US, a separate temperament-testing procedure has been developed in recent years by the German Shepherd Dog Club of America, which awards a temperament certificate. It is not a very demanding test but still is of possible value to the breed.

Training for Schutzhund

I would recommend that any dog you wish to train for Schutzhund titles be thoroughly educated in obedience and tracking long before you start man-work. This pre-education will give him a chance to build confidence in himself and reliance on you. Also, don't join any organization that advocates or uses harsh, cruel methods in man-work, and make sure the dogs owned by the instructors are happy, stable, and trustworthy in non-threatening surroundings. In short, these dogs should act in such a way that strangers would never suspect that they are "attack dogs." If they don't measure up to these criteria, look elsewhere for your training, for a protection dog is a *defensive* weapon, not a hair-trigger bomb ready to go off with the slightest hint of provocation. The Schutzhund dog should use his talents *only* when required, and not be on edge and overly excitable when conditions are normal.

O.V. OT, OTCH,CM. Scotswd New Wave T.D.X. SchH III, FH, HC. "Cam" owned, trained, and shown by Lee Pulis, has had many record-making wins:

1987 & 1988 - *Obedience Victrix* at the GSDC of America Nationals. This has never been done before in the history of the German Shepherd Club. She is the first.

1988 - *Schutzhund Victrix* at the German Shepherd Nationals. She is the first dog to have taken the obedience and Schutzhund Victrix ever in any year.

O.T.C.H. - Earned her obedience Trial Championship in 7 months, with two perfect 200 scores and numerous High in Trials. Based on the Delancy System she was the highest scoring German Shepherd in Open and Utility divisions for 1988.

Placings in the U.S. Gaines Obedience Competitions:

1986 - Gaines Western Regional Novice Division 2nd place;
1986 - U.S. Dog Obedience Classic, Novice Division 5th place;
1987 - U.S. Obedience Classic 10th place Open Division;
1988 - Western Regional, Super Dog Division 5th place.

Schutzhund III - She has earned this title again through active competition in the protection, tracking, and obedience. Won the Schutzhund III competition at the German Shepherd Nationals in 1988; eligible to be on the U.S. team to Yugoslavia for the World series in Schutzhund competition in September 1989.

FH - Earned the FH, the highest form of Schutzhund tracking degree.

HC - Herding Instinct test for sheep.

1988 Highest Living Register of Merit Sire, Am/Can. Sel. Ch. Stuttgart's Sundance Kid ROM, ROMC.

German commands often used in Schutzhund training

Achtung! (Ahk-toong´): Watch! Attention!
Aus! (Ows): Out! Drop it! Let go!
Bleib! (Blibe or blipe): Stay!
Bringen!: Bring! Fetch!
Fass! (Fahs): Attack! Take hold!
Fuss! (Foos): Heel!
Gib laut!: Bark!
Hier!: Here! Come!
Hopp!: Up! Jump!
Komm!: Come!
Nein! (Nine): No!
Pass auf! (Pahs owf): Pay attention! Heads up!
Pfui! (foo´-ey): Shame! Stop that! Drop that!
Platz! (Plots): Down! (place)
Setz!, Setzen! (Zetz´n): Sit!
Such! (Zook): Search!
Voran! (For-ahn´): Go forward! Take the lead!
Voraus! (For-ows´): Go forward! Run out!

SHOWING

Once you have accurately assessed the breeding and show quality of your dog and have decided to seriously compete, you must decide who is to handle the dog. Will you hire a professional handler or do the job yourself?

Professional Handlers

There are many reasons to hire a handler, but the most obvious is that this is their vocation—many do it full time. Because of this, they simply have more experience and, in turn, have a little edge with judges in a number of ways. They see the judges more often (in the year before I moved south and quit handling, I went to seventy shows) and this very fact tends to make a judge certain he doesn't overlook a dog being handled by a professional. Of course, a good judge will not intentionally favor a handler but his subconscious may be saying: "That's a handler … I'd better make sure I don't ignore a good dog, so I'll take a little harder look." Thus, the handler will accentuate his dog's "good points" and try to hide the faults which he

believes or knows the particular judge won't appreciate. If these are minor, he can often get away with it. Handlers will also know a judge's habit of looking back at the line while examining one dog up front, and so will have their dogs correctly posed at all the crucial moments.

Another reason for hiring a handler could be economic: A handler with a van full of dogs can split his expenses six or eight ways, while a one-dog owner/handler will probably have to bear the entire cost of showing. This can include gasoline, wear and tear on the family wagon, motel and restaurant bills, and more. Even after paying the handler's fee and your dog's share of expenses, it may be less expensive to send the dog alone rather than go with him, *especially* if the whole family is involved.

Finally, there is the time element. Most shows are held on weekends so those who work during the week can attend. For others, however, weekends are not convenient for them to leave home—they may even be weekend workers. In short, potential owner/handlers who do not have control over most of their weekends, should use a professional handler.

How to choose a handler—Since handlers are no longer licensed by the AKC, how do you distinguish between competency and incompetency? First, steer clear of those who brag about their "in" with certain judges; they're likely to be

A great dog, Ch. Bär vom Weirturchen, with handler Denny Kodner, one of the nicest people in the breed

dishonest about other things as well. Knowing judges and having an ''in'' are two different things (as are a lake and a mirage), though the one describing them may think they are the same.

Second, look for a person who demonstrates a knowledge of anatomy, movement, breed characteristics, and those qualities that make for soundness regardless of breed. In order to fully understand breed type, a good handler should have seen a lot of examples of the breed, and therefore should have been to shows in a fairly large segment of the country. Although a handler need not memorize *every* breed standard, if he more or less specializes in handling German Shepherds (most Shepherd handlers do), he'd best know that Standard inside and out. He should know how the breed is supposed to look and move, both from the standpoint of the written Standard, and from common sense which comes partly through experience and knowledge of other breeds. A handler, conversant with many breeders and judges, is likely to have picked up some of their knowledge, too.

Third is the ability to handle. This sounds obvious, but go ahead and ask him what accomplishments he's had and what experience he offers. Some handlers are really introverts, having been drawn to dogs instead of (other types of) politics, and may not readily brag about themselves. You may have to pry this information out of him, in a friendly way, of course. Also, be sure to watch him in the ring and ask his clients and fellow handlers for their opinions.

The fourth requirement for a good handler is a love of dogs. I've seen professional handlers who've gotten so far from their original reasons for involvement with dogs that they have abused them, kicked them in the tails, left them in the crate all day, or roughly handled them if the dogs didn't perform in a desired way. Try to watch the handler when he isn't in the ring. Is he busy with cocktail parties or tailgate socializing when the dogs in his ''care'' need water or exercise? Does he express love and communication in his interactions with the dog he has at the moment? Also, you can ask others what they've seen.

Fifth, weigh the chances of your dog winning when he's happy to be with you in the ring against those existing when he's in the ring with his ears up and nose twitching, trying to pick his hiding master out of the ringside crowd. Is the handler a lot smoother than you, or just slightly better? Are you able to adequately present your dog's best features to the judge, or can your teenage kid do as well as anyone you could afford? Maybe a friend has the talent if not the inclination to take a whole string of dogs on a show circuit.

At shows, watch for exhibitors who look professional, don't call undue attention to themselves, and take several dogs or breeds into the ring. Perhaps a PHA lapel pin will be the first thing to look for, as the Professional Handlers Association and similar groups can help you find just the right person.

Do-it-yourself

As with any other endeavor, handling your dog involves learning certain basic steps in order to build upon whatever level of innate ability you have. First, observe those who have perfected the art. Go to dog shows and watch the professional handlers, especially the older ones with the quiet demeanor. They may be hard to identify at first, because their job is to be inconspicuous and draw attention to the dog. Also, you could ask the chief ring steward for his opinion as he is one of the most likely at most shows to know who the better handlers are.

Another way to learn about handling is to attend classes. Sometimes a professional handler who is a member of a local club will volunteer his services to help fellow members pick up some pointers for a few weeks before the local show. In recent years, several well-known and proficient handlers have been holding seminars and one- to three-day sessions in various cities. You are almost certain to learn something from these, maybe even enough to make the difference between the purple ribbon and the ''also-rans.''

Practice. Enter your pup or adult in matches and shows. There's an old maxim in the field of education: ''We learn by doing,'' and handling is no exception. At ringside, note how the judge conducts his classes so you will be ready, when your turn comes, to run through the same routine without additional explanation from the judge. Anticipate what the judge wants and follow his gestures as well as his words. Having practiced setting up your dog in the ''show pose'' at home, you should be able to do it in the ring with the least amount of resetting, moving around, and other physical activity.

The pose—To start with, you will need a chain collar, either the martingale type or a choke collar with the leash snap attached to both rings so the choking action does not work. The collar should be held fairly high on the neck as you enter the ring, hold the dog in a pose, or take him away and back. As the dog gets used to being shown, he will move in a straight line even if the collar is loose and low, but in the beginning, hold it just behind the ears for best control. The leash should be bunched up and in your left hand. As you reach the spot where your dog is to stand in a pose, turn into his path and take a couple of steps backwards until his left rear leg is extended and his right rear leg has just been placed under his body in the act of taking a step forward. By now you have one hand on the collar and the other on his muzzle, and at this instant, stop his forward progress with a little push backwards, lifting up slightly on the collar. You could also use both hands on the collar, one on each side of the head near the ears.

When the dog has stopped, quickly move to his right side, keeping a light upward tension on the collar with your left hand (the one holding the bunched-up leash) so that the dog continues to get the signal that he is still under control and should not move. With your fingertips and thumb you may want to press forward on the base of the ears so they get up and stay in an "alert" position; as he gets used to this, he'll keep them up himself. With your right hand adjust the dog's front legs so the feet both point forward, are a few inches apart at the wrists, and are in an apparently vertical position. This is accomplished by grasping the point of the elbow (the olecranon process) in the palm of the hand, thereby lifting the forearm, and repositioning the foot if need be. Do not make the common beginner's mistake of lifting the dog's feet too near the wrists; this causes any dog to lift the foot even higher and try to get out of that hold. Also, once the feet are set in a fairly decent placement— let them be. By practicing backing and stopping,

Select Ch. Stormhaven's Dolf, ROM. An important producer of the 1960s, Dolf was a son of the unforgettable Ch. Bernd v Kallengarten and a grandson of Ch. Harald vom Haus Tigges, that great dog who also figured in the pedigree of Caralon's Hein.

Ch. Luxi v. Liebestraum with Chum Porter in a handling style fashionable in 1957 and before, and brought back by Jim Moses and Hatter in the 80's.

eventually the right front leg and both rear legs will stop in place almost every time, and even the left front leg might not be in need of being moved.

Transfer the collar from left to right hand, but keep the tension exactly the same, and the dog's head in the same place, or he will move his feet and break the pose. At this time, with the collar, your knuckles, or your thumb and little finger keeping the ears forward, look down over your dog's left shoulder to see if his left foot needs to be turned.

Now check the rear legs. The characteristic stance of the German Shepherd Dog has first been standardized, then stylized, then exaggerated by the ignorant lover of fads. The left rear leg should be placed so that the ''hock'' (metatarsus) is vertical, *not* at an exaggerated backward angle. In most cases it won't be necessary to adjust that leg unless the dog feels off balance and brings it beneath his body along with the right one. The right foot should be anywhere ahead of the left but *not* so far under the body as to look unnatural and awkward. An ideal set-up would be for the pad to be directly below the stifle (knee). This looks best because it looks *natural*, not because of any arbitrary artistic preference. If your dog is well-angulated, he will probably often walk into a pose, when simply out loose in the yard or on a loose leash. (See the photo of ''Kallie'' on page 64.)

Looking down on the dog from various positions above him, the legs should appear to be in fairly vertical planes, neither straddling the ground beneath in a wide A-shape stance, nor too close together in a narrow stance. However, it is customary to give the beginner dog a feeling of more stability by spreading the rear feet wider than the front feet; this also tends to drop the topline a bit, which helps if the dog is high in the rear or the judge has expressed a liking for an unnatural topline. Too far apart, though, and the dog will look cowhocked. If he *is* cowhocked, stretching the left rear foot too far back and the right foot too far forward, or placing the feet in a wide stance, will accentuate the problem. With such a dog, allow his right rear foot to be placed only a *little* further forward than the other one. This is also the rule for a dog that is a little longer in body than he should be. Seen from the front, the front legs should appear parallel and vertical, with the toes pointing straight ahead or very slightly outward, *never* inward (pigeon-toed).

If your dog is a little less angulated than the other dogs in the ring, position him as you would the long dog, with both rear feet fairly well back. With such a dog, putting his right front foot far under him will only make him look cobby and leggy.

Finally, when and if you position the rear feet with your hands, grasp the metatarsus near the foot, not high on the shank. Pull it back at the curve just opposite the hock.

Baiting—Erect carriage of the ears is characteristic of the breed and helps give the impression of nobility, alertness, and responsiveness called for in the Standard. In order to get the dog's ears up it is usually necessary to do more than simply push forward on the base of the ears. Once you have taught your dog to hold the pose, you might want to alert him to raise his ears by baiting.

The bait most handlers use is baked, dry liver, as this is any dog's favorite treat, though Liv-A-Snaps® or a similar biscuit treat can be as effective and is cleaner in your pocket. A little piece waved before his nose and then tossed out onto the floor will draw his eager attention at the crucial time when the judge shifts his glance to your dog. An older style of baiting German Shepherds, just as valid today, but less in fashion is to walk the dog into a natural pose, tell him to stay, back away a few feet facing him, and toss the piece of liver in your hand at the right moment. Some judges are offended by a handler's constant baiting and littering of the ring, so keep this practice to the minimum necessary to alert your dog.

Gaiting—If you have practiced well at home, you may be able to run your dog at the very end of the 6-foot leather lead. If you master this technique there is almost no way anybody behind you can ''cover up'' your dog (put his on the inside of yours so the judge doesn't get a look at yours). A light flip of the leash can steer the dog, though he'll probably naturally follow the course because of other dogs ahead and because of the ropes or fence around the ring. As you approach the exit gate, the dog will have a tendency to head out, so anticipate this by running faster while you reel in the leash. By the time you reach the exit, you'll have caught up with him and will be between him and the way out of the ring. Don't change his speed if you can help it, and keep the light tension on the leash again. Until your pup is used to turning in

The Dog Show Game. Photographer Tom Morrissette, also GSD breeder, captures the range of emotion and intensity of exhibitors and spectators. The dog is Von Mibach's Flint, known for his iron back and hard, dry (muscular) condition. Photo courtesy Louise Ryske

the ring, you may have to catch up at the other three corners as well.

The trot, whether fast or slow, is the gait by which dogs' movements are evaluated in the show ring, so it is important to prevent any other gait, however normal, while the judge is looking at you. If the dog begins to canter or gallop, give a quick jerk back on the leash to settle him down into an easy trot. If he starts pacing, jerk forward to speed him up.

A slight tension on the leash during trotting is okay but if the dog is dragging you around the ring, his rear is doing all the work and consequently his front action will not be as smooth or as extended as it should be. Sometimes an experienced handler will "string up" a dog to disguise a poor front action to some extent and intimidate a rushed judge enough so he doesn't ask to see the dog run again a second or third time. But if the judge insists on seeing each dog trot properly before making his decision, this little trick can backfire.

Down and back—Part of each dog's individual examination in the conformation ring is the trot from the judge down to the designated corner or across the ring, then back in the same straight line. In order to do this exercise at home, stretch a string on the ground, and go back and forth over it until you will be able to visualize that line in the ring when you are asked to move your dog. Weaving prevents the judge from correctly assessing the soundness of your dog and may prevent you from being considered for a placement. Of course, if your dog is faulty in this regard, you may want to move

him in a slight arc to try to fool the judge, as many handlers do.

Probably the greatest difficulty in keeping the dog in a straight line is his learned tendency to turn left and go into the counter-clockwise pattern. A few light tugs on the collar while running alongside the dog's head may be sufficient, but if the dog is a real puller or insists on either leaning hard or crabbing, you *could* use the somewhat strange but effective approach of taking the leash in your right hand and taking the dog down the mat on your right side. This way he won't turn in toward you, and you can switch sides when you get to the far end. Watch others maneuver in this way to decide if you want to try this unorthodox technique. If you do opt for it, make sure the dog has run on your right in practice sessions before you try it in the ring.

Occasionally, (*often* in some shows) a dog will start off very poorly by crabbing, pacing, galloping, or what-have-you, and the handler wants to start over. When this happens to you, don't ask the judge, for asking takes up time itself, and so does the rerun, which will cause most judges to deny the request for a fresh start. Make up your mind before you get to the show that if you get off to a poor start you'll quickly turn around, return to the starting position, and begin again. Don't hesitate, and don't even make eye contact with the judge; that way he'll have no choice but to let you go ahead with your restart, since you will be well into the motion before he can say anything to get your attention.

7

U.S. AND GERMAN WINNERS

US GRAND VICTORS AND GRAND VICTRIXES, 1960-1987

Because very few of my readers will possess pedigrees that go back very far, and because lists are of doubtful value when one doesn't remember the dogs on them, I will describe Grand Victors/Victrixes beginning in 1960, except for Troll who *must* be included. Titles have been omitted; Grand Victor is named first, then Grand Victrix.

1957

Troll v Richterbach: Son of Axel v d Deininghauserheide, and Lance of Fran-Jo's grandfather, was a tremendous influence on the breed through Ulk Wikingerblut and many others. His shoulder was

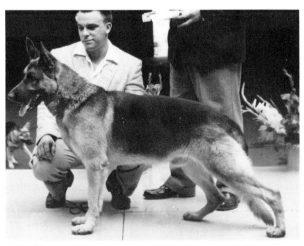

1957 Grand Victor, Ch. Troll v Richterbach, SchH III. Probably the most influential stud dog ever to be imported into the U.S., Troll sired Ulk, the "F" litter Arbywood, and many other famous animals in the breed.

not ideal, and some of his descendants have better rear angulation than foreassembly, as is also found in other lines. A fearless and lively dog, Troll was substantial (93 pounds) yet not overly tall (just over 25 inches). His deep chest and ground-covering gait is seen in many of his descendants. Troll, like his sire, was the result of another successful outcross.

1960

Axel v Poldihaus: Sable son of the great Axel v d Deininghauserheide and thus half-brother to 1955 Sieger Alf v Nordfelsen as well as to Troll.

Robin of Kingscroft: Sired by the great 1956 Gr.V. Bill v Kleistweg that in turn was a son of the "immortal" Hein v Richterbach, one of Germany's favorite dogs on which to linebreed.

1961

Lido v MellerLand: His dam was Jola v Richterbach.

Nanhall's Donna: Classy, beautiful daughter of Field Marshall of Arbywood (from the famous 5-champion litter by Troll) out of Bonnie Bergere of Ken-Rose.

1962

Yorkdom's Pak: Sable son of the outstanding dark, dark-gray sable Lido v Johanneshauch and a bitch from the Colonia-Agrippina kennel.

Bonnie Bergere of Ken-Rose: Not only a conformation winner, but also earned her obedience titles through UD, her tracking degree, and her ROM. A winner in every sense.

1963

Condor v Stoerstrudel: German import whose genetic value was obvious for many generations. British geneticist Dr. M. B. Willis reports he had 44 teeth, but does not say where; probably they were molars.

Hessian's Vogue: Homebred by Art and Helen Hess; sired by Kurt v Bid-Scono, from the same kennel that produced the 1971 Grand Victrix.

1964

No competition, because the GSDCofA failed to get an AKC-approved date in time.

1965

Brix v Grafenkrone: A SchH-III import of great substance and gait. Probably has been responsible for the color pattern of the majority of the sable winners in the US and Canada since, largely through the Waldesruh line which did so well with Lance ''blood'' and other ''clicks.''

Mar-Sa's Velvet of Malabar: Not very angulated (in rear) but smooth-gaiting daughter of ''the incomparable one,'' Ulk Wikingerblut. As mentioned earlier, Ulk was the top-producing son of Troll.

Velvet's dam was from the famous old-time Rocky Reach kennel.

1966

Yoncalla's Mike: Linebred on the great Bernd v Kallengarten through the Freenys' own breeding program, Mike's influence will be seen for a long time, rivalling those of Lance and Ulk.

Hanarob's Touche: Daughter of Wilva-Don's Faust, who also sired the very popular black of the 1970s, Jeenellyn's UFO.

1966 and 1968 Grand Victor Ch. Yoncalla's Mike, OFA

1922 Grand Victor Ch. Erich v Grafenwerth (Sieger, 1920) imported by Hamilton Farms, after which he went by his AKC name, Ch. Hamilton Erich v Grafenwerth. In later years he was purchased by Mrs. Dodge's Giralda Kennels. This photo was taken when he was quite old but still at stud. The most important sire of his time, he was not as ''hard'' in temperament as was required of later top Sieger show winners; this was one reason he was made available to the U.S., the other being money.

1965 Grand Victrix, Ch. Mar-Sa's Velvet of Malabar, owned by Sam and Marie Stall.

1967

Lance of Fran-Jo: Unforgettable son of Fortune of Arbywood and Frohlich's Elsa v Grunestahl. Lance has been the most-used and linebred-on dog in modern German Shepherd Dog history, winning hearts and ribbons because of his rear angulation and drive, his high withers which helped give him the stallion, stand-up alert and ready-for-action look, his size, and his noble, expressive head. A lot of Troll was obvious in Lance.

Hanarob's Touche: Repeated her 1966 win again this year.

1968

Yoncalla's Mike: Repeated his spectacular win of 1966.

Valtara's Image: A sizeable daughter of Bernd v Kallengarten, Image inherited his great angulation and many other qualities.

1969

Arno v d Kurpfalzhalle: Moderate angulation, which generally is accompanied by beautiful suspension and balance, certainly is true in this case. Like other German imports of the era, he either didn't reproduce himself or was lost in the shadow of Lance.

De Cloudt's Heidi: A very substantial sable homebred. I didn't get to know her or observe her up close.

1969 Gr. V. Ch. Arno v d Kurpfalzhalle Correct size, proportions, and movement helped this handsome import win his titles quickly. Owned by Sam Lawrnce, shown here early in 1969 with handler Jimmy Moses. Graham photo courtesy Mary Southcott

1970

Hollamor's Judd: Mike son of correct balance, he was not as extreme as some others of the day, but truer moving than most. Contributed good pigment, and perhaps some weak ears which may have come from Bernd and elsewhere. Good producer.

Bel-Vista's Solid Sender: Daughter of the excellent but underused Treu v Wolfsstock and a Hessian bitch. A very good example of the Poeppings' fine breeding based partly on Hessian's and Mike which produced several notable dogs. Besides Hessian's, Caralon's Hein, and Bernd Kallengarten lines, Bel-Vista made good use of Lance's genes and built a very good line of their own.

1971

Mannix of Fran-Jo: An "extreme" son of Lance whose extra angulation and slightly loose hocks probably came as much from Bernd on his dam's side. One of many examples of the famous Lance/Bernd "click." Flashy sidegait dazzled many judges into giving him the nod. Mannix passed on Lance's noble looks and size to his progeny.

Aloha v Bid-Scono: A low-stationed, exquisitely beautiful bitch, a daughter of two Bid-Scono dogs. Aloha's story is like Cinderella's: sold as a pet, repurchased when the princess in her became obvious, she floated on her crystal slippers to win the title and the hearts of many thousands.

1967 Grand Victrix Ch. Hanarob's Touche. Owners: Wilva Don Kennels. Pictured with Touche is handler, Mrs. Bill Collins and Judge Mr. James Norris.

1972

Lakeside's Harrigan: Bred by Danny Dwier and bought by Ann Mesdag, he was a product of one of the most famous Lance/Bernd combinations. Harrigan was a son of Cobert's Melissa, a super bitch linebred on Bernd and owned by the Beckhardts. Gilligan's Island was from a previous combination, Reno from a later repeat.

Cathwar's Lisa v Rob: Sired by Lakeside's Gilligan's Island. A bitch of great beauty and femininity.

1973

Scorpio of Shiloh Gardens: Followed in the footsteps of his sire, Mannix, and produced many fleet-moving sons and daughters. A handsome link in a long chain of winners. Linebreeding on Scorpio has uncovered the recessive blue dilute gene so seldom seen—in public, anyway.

Ro-San's First Love: A welcome relief from the trend of over-angulated dogs, this bitch's structure and movement was as near-Standard as one could get. Sired by the almost-forgotten but excellent producer Elwillo's Rand (also the sire of Ro-San's El Sabre of Charay, a multiple Best-In-Show winner and Select #7 dog at the 1974 National).

1974

Tellaheide's Gallo: Dam was Baroness Bella v Friden, a bitch of flashy red pigmentation on the head and other tan parts, typical of several of her breeding. Gallo's sire was Tellaheide's Enoch, linebred by Bernd v Kallengarten through Yoncalla's Mr. America, and on Ch Fritz of Maryden, a Ch Nordraak of Matterhorn son. Enoch was a son of a Grand Victor (Mike) as well as the sire of one.

Lor-Locke's Tatta of Fran-Jo: A pale sable that was frequently out of coat, a common problem in campaigning bitches. Sire: Eko-Lan's Paladen; dam: Bess of Fran-Jo, sister of Beau and Bridget, both extreme sables from the Lance/K-Waldesruh "click."

1975

Caesar von Carahaus: Son of Mannix; a sensibly-angulated dog of considerable reach and balance. Finally won over very, very tough competition at the 1975 National; the top three males that year were so close in quality that I feel I should describe the other two here. Select-2 went to Shaft of Del-Shire, a Zeto/Pam of Fran-Jo son that was built like and looked very much the same as Caesar. Shaft was also Maturity Victor this year, Can. Gr. V. in 1975, US Select-2 in 1977 also, and Select-3 in 1978. Select-3 in 1975 was Asslan v Klammle, Junghund Sieger at Munich in 1973 (sister Atrice was Junghund Siegerin) and for awhile the crowd thought judge Julius Due would continue moving Asslan up to #1 spot. While he had not as flashy a side gait or apparent reach, he was perfectly balanced, perfectly masculine, perfectly noble, and worthy of any top award. Asslan also placed Select-3 in 1976.

Langenau's Tango: This well-pigmented bitch of considerable angulation and femininity was also Maturity Victrix this year. She was a daughter of Mannix and Langenau's Etude.

1976

Padechma's Persuasion: This Zeus of Fran-Jo son out of a Lance/Bernd bitch did a lot of early winning. He reflected most of the extreme rear angulation of his sire, and the early maturing of his dam's side. He was also Maturity Victor this year.

Covy's Rosemary of Tucker Hill: For the second year in a row, Cappy Pottle and Gloria Birch engineered a spectacular showing with the help of associates such as J. Stevens. Rosemary, a fantastically pretty bitch with extreme angulation, femininity, and outreaching gait, was a daughter of Lakeside's Harrigan and Tucker Hill's Angelique. Full sisters this year were also in the Select Class (Tarragon: Select-4, Tartar: Select-7). Angelique herself went Select-3, and the Maturity Victrix, Jo-San's Charisma (Reno/Covy's Bonita of Tucker Hill), placed Select-2. The previous year in Louisville, Tarragon was Select-3, Rosemary Select-6, and Angelique Select-8. The following year (1977) Angelique was Select-6. This beautiful producing bitch was a daughter of Ch Gauss v Stauderpark and Jodi of Tucker Hill; was 1970 Maturity Victrix, and Select in 1970 and 1972 through 1977. Truly unquestionable was her beauty and worth.

1977

Langenau's Watson: Bred by Dave Rinke who also bred 1975's Grand Victrix, Watson was one of

1971 Grand Victrix Aloha v Bid-Scono. Breeder, Luke Geraghty. Handler, Terry Hower   *Photo by Martin Booth*

1973 Grand Victor Ch. Scorpio of Shiloh Gardens getting BOB two months before earning the Grand Victor title. Handler, Jimmy Moses. Owners, Tom and Carol McPheron.   *Morrissette photo*

1973 Grand Victrix Ch. Ro-San's First Love.   *Bennett Photo*

1974 Grand Victor Ch. Tellaheide's Gallo ROM. Owner/breeder/handler, Angelo Latella.

Photo courtesy M. Schuetzler

1974 Grand Victrix Ch. Lor-Locke's Tatta of Fran-Jo. Breeders, Fran and Joan Ford. Photo courtesy of Mary Schuetzler.

a few good-looking champions in this litter by Gr. V. Scorpio and Langenau's Quessa. Watson carried the blue recessive. Brother Windsor was usually close behind, or sometimes ahead, and not far off were Winchester and Wyatt. Like Scorpio, he showed nobility of expression and reaching gait. Another nice Scorpio son, Haydelhaus Augie v Zahnarzt, was Select 6, and Scorpio daughters were Select 1 and 3.

Charo of Shiloh Gardens: Sable daughter of Scorpio and Waldesruh's Pia of Shiloh Gardens. The Waldesruh lines included many showy sables in the 1960s and 1970s.

1978

Baobab's Chaz: Early-maturing and unfortunately early to die, this handsome son of Doppelt-Tay's Hammer (also from a short-lived litter) was Maturity Victor this year as well. One of many successes of Larraine and Jesse Clifford, Chaz's dam was Pinebeach's Darlin, one of a multiple-champion litter by Ch Cobert's Reno of Lakeside out of Ch

Amber aus der Edelheim, a super daughter of the great Caralon's Hein. Hammer's brother Hawkeye was Select-4 and a Hawkeye son Winners Dog and Select-8. The Doppelt-Tay's H litter was by Ekolan's Paladen out of Doppelt-Tay's Jessette. Chaz was much appreciated and bred to before he left the scene.

Jo-San's Charisma: The Reno daughter who went Select-2 in 1976 returned to take the highest honors at this year's National. She was a smaller bitch than most, but had true and floating gait with a strong back and drive. Very feminine and pretty.

1979

Schokrest On Parade: Half-brother to Covy-Tucker Hill's Finnegan, both sons of Covy's Oregano of Tucker Hill. "Harry" was Select-9 in 1978.

Anton's Jesse: Like her sire, Zeus of Fran-Jo, this bitch exhibited extreme rear angulation, but was well-balanced with a good shoulder layback. Medium-large but still feminine. A litter sister was Select-4 in 1980, and Grand Victrix in 1981.

1976 Grand Victrix Ch. Covy's Rosemary of Tucker Hill ROM, OFA. Sire, GV Ch. Lakeside's Harrigan ROM, OFA. Dam, Sel. Ch. Tucker Hill's Angelique CD ROM, OFA. Owners, Cappy Pottle and Gloria Birch. Breeders, C. Pottle and J. Stevens. Dam of: Ch. Covy's Mazarati of Tucker Hill, OFA; Sel. Ch. Covey's Mercedes of Tucker Hill; Ch. Covy-Tucker Hill's Triumph; Ch. Covy's Starwars of Tucker Hill; Am/Can Ch. Covy-Tucker Hill's Manhattan.
                                                                                                Photo courtesy of Covy-Tucker Hill Kennels.

1977 Grand Victor Ch. Langenau's Watson. Watson was known for his powerful drive and deep stride. Breeder/owners, Dave and Marty Rinke. Morressette photo.

1987 Grand Victor Ch. Rio Valle's Nestle's Crunch, ROMC, OFA shown in the most commonly used "stack" or hand-set pose, though stretched out in the rear too much.   Photo courtesy F.J. Williamson.

1979 Grand Victrix Ch. Anton's Jesse.   Thacker photo

1980

Aspen of Fran-Jo: By Quint of Shiloh Gardens out of Elfie of Fran-Jo; this medium-sized sable with considerable rear angulation, less in front, and not especially deep-bodied, had minor ear weakness, but this problem comes through several well-used stud dogs and will be deeply imbedded in many bloodlines for some time to come. A better "trend," if it continues, is the recognition of sables for top placings—too many have had less of a chance at some shows because of color prejudice. This year's intersex (BOB) judge was reportedly leaning toward sables. Aspen's larger sable son, Destino's Serge, was built the same way as Aspen, and also inherited the ear problem. Along with Hammer and Hawkeye offspring, and a few from other lines, overset "bonnet" ears are being produced fairly frequently now.

Lacy Britches of Billo: Another Zeus daughter of extreme rear angulation with consequent looseness; a very light sable, feminine and lively, always alert, not always in the best of coat, but that seems to be a problem with most bitches and shows up more in sables than black-and-tans that hide the loss of coat and weight better. Britches was Select-2 in 1979.

1981

Sabra Dennis of Gan Edan: A medium-sized dog as to height, but with a massive body, deep-chested, with good ribbing and loins finished off with a pleasing croup and good angulation. Other than height,

he showed a lot of his Lance heritage. His type and linebreeding predict a bright producing future.

Anton's Jenne: Litter sister to 1979 Grand Victrix; with the same structure and movement.

1982

Kismet's Impulse v Bismark: A 7-year-old dog of excellent proportions, properly level topline, great shoulder layback and prosternum, and beautifully balanced and sound. Upper-middlesized, he is a son of the medium sized Marty v Bid-Scono. Ear set a trifle wide.

Merkel's Vendetta: This large bitch nevertheless has good secondary sex characteristics. Considerably angulated in the rear, with enough at the front to balance it well, she displayed a stronger back than do many dogs of such body length.

1983

Sukee's Mannix: Very large, he produced many likewise oversized offspring. In spite of his size, he and a good percentage of his get showed good balance and very pleasing gait.

Von Ivo's Blithe Spirit: A Hawkeye daughter. A very feminine, fleet-moving bitch, and a crowd pleaser.

1984

Cobert's Trollstigen: A Hawkeye son of quite large size but good proportions, Trollie proved to be a good producer, though many of his offspring are too large and many have somewhat wiry, open coat on the saddle area.

Jeanden's L'Erin of Langenau: A fairly extreme but pleasingly-moving, nicely pigmented daughter of Doppett-Tay's Hammer (Hawkeye litter brother).

1985

Ossipee Ceasar v Clover Acres: Another large dog, Ceasar had a good front assembly, sensible rear angulation, and good balance. Select-4 in 1984.

Lynrick's Kristal: She was the big hit of the National and went on to be an exciting all-breed Best-In-Show winner all over the country. She had an extremely long, ground-covering stride with an excellent shoulder and front end, though her rear hock action was a mite loose and too extreme in stifle-hock angulation. She was pretty and always excited.

1986

Sequal's Senator v Merivern: Select-4 the year before, Senator was a medium-sized dark dog with excellent gait. He was overweight when he won, and was beginning to fade when the judge made his decision. (Only bitches of strong temperament should be bred to him.)

Dawnhill's Carli: A beautifully balanced, medium-sized bitch that looked as if she could go all day. Not flashy, not heavily campaigned or advertised, she was a very deserving Grand Victrix of correct proportions.

1987

Rio Valle's Nestle's Crunch: Select-2 in 1984. Mature, well-angulated dog of medium pigmentation, Crunch is a son of one of the decade's best producers, Stuttgart's Sundance Kid that was Select-5 in 1985.

Howard's Magic Moment: A Howard's Snakemaster daughter, she is a medium-sized bitch of very nice gait.

1988

Piper Hill's Polo: A somewhat oversized son of Gr. V. Crunch and Piper Hill's Kodachrome, he moved with power and vigor. In winning, he carried on the tradition set by so many of the "Bear" (Sundance Kid) progeny and grandchildren. Bear sons placed Select 2 and 9, and another Crunch son was Select 8 this year.

Sea Lair's Ciera: A very beautiful, well-proportioned, richly-pigmented sable of correct size and ground-covering gait. She stood out as soon as she entered the ring and sparkled all the way to the title.

1988 Grand Victrix Ch. Sea Lair's Ciera.

1988 Grand Victor Ch. Piper Hill's Polo.

U.S. GRAND VICTORS AND VICTRIXES, 1918-1959

Grand Victor		Grand Victrix
Komet v Hoheluft	1918	Lotte v Edelweiss
Apollo v Huenenstein	1919	Vanhall's Herta
Rex Buckel	1920	Boda v Fuerstenburg
Grimm v d Mainkur	1921	Dora v Rheinwald
Erich v Grafenwerth	1922	Debora v Weimar
Dolf v Duesternbrook	1923	Boda v Fuerstenburg
Cito Bergerslust	1924	Irma v Doernerhof
Cito Bergerslust	1925	Irma v Doernerhof
Donar v Overstolzen	1926	Asta v Kaltenweide
Arko v Sadowaberg	1927	Inky of Willowgate
Arko v Sadowaberg	1928	Erich's Merceda of Shereston
Arko v Sadowaberg	1929	Katja v Blaisenberg
Bimbo v Stolzenfels	1930	Christel v Stimmerberg
Arko v Sadowaberg	1931	Gisa v Koenigsbruch
	(no awards in 1932)*	
Golf v Hooptal	1933	Dora of Shereston
Erikind of Shereston	1934	Dora of Shereston
Nox of Glenmar	1935	Nanka v Schwyn
(not awarded)*	1936	Frigga v Kannenbaeckerland
Pfeffer v Bern	1937	Perchta v Bern
Pfeffer v Bern	1938	Giralda's Geisha
Hugo of Cosalta	1939	Thora v Bern of Giralda
Cotswald of Cosalta	1940	Lady of Ruthland
Nox of Ruthland	1941	Hexe of Rotundina
Noble of Ruthland	1942	Bella v Haus Hagen
Major of Northmere	1943	Bella v Haus Hagen
Nox of Ruthland	1944	Frigga v Hoheluft
Adam of Veralda	1945	Olga of Ruthland
Dex of Talladega	1946	Lega v Liebestraum
Dorian v Beckgold	1947	Jola v Liebestraum
Valiant of Draham	1948	Duchess of Browvale
Kirk of San Miguel	1949	Doris v Vogtlandshof
Kirk of San Miguel	1950	Yola of Longworth
Jory of Edgetowne	1951	Tawnee v Liebestraum
Ingo Wunschelrute	1952	Afra v Heilholtkamp
Alert of Mi-Noah's	1953	Ulla of San Miguel
Brando v Aichtal	1954	Jem of Penllyn
Rasant v Holzheimer Eichwald	1955	Solo Nina of Rushagen
Bill v Kleistweg	1956	Kobeil's Barda
Troll v Richterbach	1957	Jeff-Lynne's Bella
Yasko v Zenntal	1958	Tan-Zar Desiree
Red Rocks Gino	1959	Alice v d Guten Fee

This was one of those years a judge from Germany officiated; he didn't like what he saw.

GERMAN SIEGERS AND SIEGERINS, 1899-1937

Sieger		Siegerin
Joerg v d Krone	1899	Lisie v Schwenningen
Hektor v Schwaben	1900 & 1901	Canna
Peter v Pritschen	1902	Elsa v Schwaben
Roland v Park	1903	Hella v Memmingen
Aribert v Grafrath	1904	Regina v Schwaben
Beowulf v Nahegau	1905	Vefi v Niedersachsen
Roland v Starkenburg	1906 & 1907	Gretel Uckermark
Luchs v Kalsmunt Wetzlar	1908	Flora v d Warthe
Hettel Uckermark	1909	Ella v Erlenbrunnen
Tell v d Kriminalpolizei	1910	Flora v d Kriminalpolizei
Norbert v Kohlwald	1911 & 1912	Hella v d Kriminalpolizei
Arno v d Eichenburg	1913	Frigga v Scharenstetten
	No titles awarded (WW-I)—1914-1918	
Dolf v Duesternbrook	1919	Anna v Humboldtpark
Erich v Grafenwerth	1920	Anna v Humboldtpark
Herras v d Juech	1921	Nanthild v Riedekenburg
Cito Bergerslust	1922 & 1923	Asta v d Kaltenweide
Donar v Overstolzen	1924	Asta v d Kaltenweide
Klodo v Boxberg	1925	Seffe v Blasienberg
Erich v Glockenbrink	1926	Arna a d Ehrenzelle
Arko v Sadowaberg	1927	Elli v Fuerstensteg
Erich v Glockenbrink	1928	Katja v Blasienberg
Utz v Haus Schutting	1929	Katja v Blasienberg
Herald a d Niederlausitz	1930	Bella v Klosterbrunn
Herald a d Niederlausitz	1931	Illa v Helmholtz
Hussan v Haus Schutting	1932	Birke v Blasienberg
Odin v Stolzenfels	1933	Jamba v Haus Schutting
Cuno v Georgentor	1934	Grete v d Raumannskaule
Jalk v Pagensgrueb	1935	Stella v Haus Schutting
Arras a d Stadt Velbert	1936	Stella v Haus Schutting
Pfeffer v Bern	1937	Traute v Bern

1947 Grand Victor, Ch. Dorian v Beckgold, also became Canadian Gr. V.

1948 Grand Victor and '48, '49, and '50 Can. G.V. Ch. Valiant of Draham.

1946 Grand Victrix Ch. Leda v Liebestraum, owned by Grant Mann.

1963 Grand Victor Ch. Condor v Stoerstrudel imported for and owned by Tom Bennett and Fred Becker.   Photo courtesy M. Schuetzler

GERMAN AUSLESE WINNERS, 1938-1954

1938

Eight dogs were named VA (excellent select) this year, but were not ranked. Two of them were sired by Dux, the father of the 1934 Siegerin. Ruth v Stolzenfels was dam of two and Dolfi v Bern was dam of one. The best known even today was Ferdl v Secretainerie, a son of Sieger Odin v Stolzenfels. Ferdl and his dam were owned by Joseph

Schwabacher who fled Nazi Germany and settled in England, where he was recognized as one of the foremost authorities on the breed and its history. Schwabacher translated von Stephanitz's last edition into English. Ferdl left a deep mark on German, British, and some Western dogs of later years, especially through his important daughter Ch Carol of Ruthland, the dam of Grand Victor Nox.

Seven bitches were VA: Two Starrenburg bitches, one sired by Curt v Herzog Hedan, the other by Gockel v Bern; a Ferdl sister, a Haus

Schuetting bitch, and a Friedlichenheim bitch were also in the list.

1941

Although 1939 and 1940 were busy years of conquest, dog lovers managed to gather enough dogs and people together to spit in hardship's face and hold a show in 1941 and another in 1942. The 1938 VA Onyx v Forellenbach sired two VA dogs, and the 1936 Sieger sired one. Thora v Bern also had a son in the top few. The most famous 1941 VA dog was Baldur v Befreiungsplatz, a sire that figures in many US pedigrees. The translation of his kennel name is ironic, bittersweet, and hopeful in the light of the time: "Place of Freedom." Among the 1941 VA bitches were another Haus Schuetting bitch, the same Gockel daughter that was VA in 1938, and a daughter of Ingo Piastendamm out of Ferdl's dam.

1942

VA males included a littermate of one of 1941's Onyx sons, Baldur again, the Ingo Piastendamm son Rodrigo v Haus Schuetting, Faust v Busecker Schloss, and others. VA bitches in 1942 were not numerous, but Ingo Piastendamm had one daughter there, as did Ferdl Secretainerie/Seffe v Aichtal.

1943-1947

The early years, 1943-1945, were full of grief and bombs in Germany—no room for dog shows. By the time the country had been split up into zones controlled by the Russians, British, and Americans for more than a year, the fanciers who survived gathered together what dogs had also survived and held two VA shows in both 1946 and 1947, one in the British zone (B) and the other in the American zone (A). Unfortunately VA Faust was shot by US troops, and thus lost to the breed before his time.

The great dog Pirol v d Buchenhohe, son of Baldur-from-the-place-of-liberation, was VA-1 in the A zone and VA-2 in B in 1947. Another Baldur son, Arry v d Gassenquelle, was VA-1 (B) 1946, which he repeated in 1947. Nora v Aichtal's son, Carlo v Haunstetten, was VA-2 (A) both in 1946 and 1947; more of him later. Claus v Haus Werle was VA-1 in 1946 (A), VA-3 in 1947 (A). A dog that has been mentioned earlier in this book, Harras v Piastendamm, son of Ingo, was VA-2 (B) in 1946,

placing barely ahead of Lex Preussenblut (VA-3, B) that year. Lex was only 5 years old when he died by poisoning in 1949, but no other dog of the time had as remarkable a producing record. In my opinion he would have overshadowed Rolf had he lived. Another Preussenblut dog was VA-3 (B) in 1947. A bitch from a combination of Haus Schuetting/Aichtal lines became VA in 1946 (A) and another Haus Schuetting bitch was VA (B) in 1946. A daughter of Faust v Busecker Schloss was VA-1 (A) in 1947, and the famous Maja v OsnabrueckerLand was VA-1 (B) in 1947; her sire was Achilles v d Hollenquelle, and her dam was Xanda Preussenblut. Other Preussenblut bitches also did quite well: Lex's sister Lende and 1938 VA Dewet Preussenblut's daughter Fusca were both VA in the British zone in 1946. A couple of Stuveschacht bitches went VA-2 and 3 (B) in 1947. After those two years the SV was able to hold the single VA show, though they still didn't name Siegers and Siegerins for a few years.

1948

VA-1 was *Carlo v Haunstetten*, mentioned earlier; he was also VA-3 in 1949. Claus, the 1946 VA-1 dog, was VA-2 in both 1948 and 1949 and then went to the United States. Harras v Piastendamm continued to show well with VA-3.

Among bitches you will recognize the Preussenblut name, with one whose dam was a Lex litter sister (Lerche), plus a Kattenstroth bitch and a daughter of an Aichtal bitch. There were not many to choose from in those lean years, but a few good lines were preserved. A son of Pirol and Nella v Fredeholz was VA-4 and a half-brother (Pirol/Nixie Fredeholz), the famous Quell v Fredeholz, was VA-5.

1949

This was the year the stupendous producer *Axel v d Deininghauserheide* was awarded VA-1. Some ear problems (large and/or weak) came from Axel, but good body structure also was his legacy. Carlo was mentioned above, and between the two was Claus again.

VA-1 in bitches was *Reina v OsnabrueckerLand* from the noted R litter by Lex out of Maja. Sister Rena was VA in 1950 and Ina from a repeat litter was VA-3 in 1951. The Preussenbluts were coming into their own.

1950

Munko v d Hohen Fichte was VA-1; his dam was a VA bitch (1947 VA-1, A) out of Faust v Busecker Schloss. Hard on Munko's heels was Axel with VA-2, and other famous competitors that year were Rolf (VA-4) and the Pirol/Nella son Asso (VA-5).

Werra z d Sieben-Faulen was VA-1 for the bitches; she was VA in 1949, too.

1951

Rolf v OsnabruckerLand: Having proven himself in both competition and production, he came into his own this year as VA-1. Right behind him was Arno v d Pfaffenau VA-2 and a Rolf/Wally z d Sieben-Faulen son, Drussus Sieben-Faulen, VA-3.

Bora Preussenblut: VA-1, she was out of two Preussenblut parents.

1952

Lido v Friedlichenheim: VA-1, later made a big hit in the United States. A Rolf/Hella Kattenstroth son was VA-2.

Linda v d Rehbockswiese: VA-1. Lex, Pirol, and Axel also had daughters in this year's VA rankings.

1953

Edo v Gehredner: VA-1, other than being the sire of 1957 Sieger Arno, never became as well known as his sire Claudius v Hain, used extensively in Germany and found in American pedigrees. His dam was a Haus Schuetting bitch. Drusus Sieben-Faulen was VA-4 and a Rolf/Werra Sieben-Faulen son, Gero v Stuhri-Gau, was VA-2. Edo was a gray sable.

Fee v Stuhri-Gau: VA-1 and was a daughter of the same VA dogs mentioned above, Rolf and Werra. Werra was later to be used again with VA Brando v Tappenort to give the 1958 Siegerin.

1954

Lido v Friedlichenheim: Again became VA-1 this year. His competition included sons of Claudius v Hain and VA Munko, but the dog pressing him hardest for the win was a beautiful Axel son, VA-2 Alf v Nordfelsen. (More about him later.)

Frigga v Bombergschen Park: Named VA-1 she had a litter sister that was VA-7 in 1952. They were Axel daughters ex Bella v Haus Trippe. With her in this class was a beautiful bitch, Lore v

Tempelblick, VA-3 this year, VA-2 in 1955, and VA-3 in 1956. Lore was purchased by Dr. Otto Schales, a transplanted German-American. It was my pleasure to meet Dr. Schales early in my handling years, and to see him judge the breed he knew so well.

SIEGERS AND SIEGERINS, 1955-1986

Following is a list of the Sieger Show winners since 1955 with comments. Just as Sieger awards were not given from 1938 through 1954, neither were there any from 1974 through 1977. Siegers are listed first, then Siegerins.

1955

Alf v Nordfelsen: Son of Axel v Deininghauserheide who was a tremendous advertisement for outcrossing, since he was an outcross yet one of the greatest producers the breed has ever seen. Regardless of what bloodlines he was bred into, he produced innumerable dogs of highest quality, though a few had a somewhat straighter front and insufficient forechest and depth of breast. Some have said these were faults noticed in Alf. Alf was known to produce many slowly-maturing dogs, which in part may have given rise to the reputation of deficient fronts, but gave more rear angulation than most others of the time, and thus was good for Rolf/Rosel lines. Alf himself was only slightly linebred (Gockel v Bern in the fifth generation), was larger than Axel (nearly 90 pounds) and could really only be faulted by the official judges for a slightly bouncy back (according to his Koer report).

Muschka v Tempelblick: From a very successful kennel of that day, she was the daughter of VA-2 Arno v d Pfaffenau and Nandl v d Hohen Fichte.

1956

Hardt v Stuveschacht: Son of the famous Rolf v OsnabrueckerLand, who with Rosel and Ina probably appear in more pedigrees than any other dog in recent times except perhaps Lance in America. Hardt is in the background of a number of great Canadian dogs and in several US ones as well. Italian-owned, he inherited and passed along Rolf's moderate rear angulation and good shoulder. He was VA three times.

Lore v Tempelblick: Kennelmate of 1955 Siegerin and VA-1 in 1956, after rising from VA placings in 1954 and 1955. She was later moved to America.

1957

Arno v Haus Gersie: Popular in many American as well as German pedigrees, he was the sire of the famous V-litter v Busecker Schloss, from a kennel known far and wide for excellent working stock. Arno produced good foreassemblies and some long bodies.

Wilma v Richterbach: Axel v Deininghauserheide daughter out of a sister of the famous Hein v Richterbach. Also VA in 1958 and 1960.

1958

Condor v Hohenstamm: Yet another successful out-cross, Condor had the low-stationed, deep chest look that fortunately was becoming so much appreciated during the 1950s. He had a very good front and a short, tight back, weighed a little over 90 pounds and measured about 25 inches at the shoulders. Condor's outstanding temperament and courage have been described as perfect, though he had a slight tendency to stand with his less-than-fully-arched front paws in a turned-out, "east-west" position. However, this did not affect his light-footed, reaching gait. His moderate rear angulation was certainly no hindrance to his excellent movement, though it wasn't enough for most American tastes. In this he more resembled his grandsire Rolf than his maternal grandsire Axel.

Mashca v Stuhri-Gau: Her dam was a VA Sieben-Faulen bitch, mentioned earlier, and her sire Brando was a Rolf son.

"Buffalo Bill and His Dog." A bronze from the collection at Gilcrease Museum, Tulsa, shows a Shepherd Dog type was used in America before the breed was defined in Germany.

1959

Volker v Zollgrenzschutzhaus: This excellent son of an excellent sire, Harry vom Donaukai, was gentle, good-natured, and quiet, yet had a confident and fearless temperament which became very protective in a defensive situation. Volker had a very slight bounce to his back, good angulation, and good pigment. Some of his most illustrious get include the C and D litters vom Sixtberg out of Caret v Elfenhain later bred to Witz v Haus Schuetting. Volker was noted for transmitting the nobility, majesty, and masculinity he himself had in abundance. He went to America for awhile in 1963, long enough to lay the groundwork for his ROM title.

Assja v Geigerklause: Daughter of Caesar v d Malmannsheide, another great Hein v Richterbach son. Caesar's Koer reports for 1955 and 1956 contradicted each other, but agreed that his defensive reaction could have been stronger. His line was quite popular in the US, but not as much as Volker's and Harry's. Caesar inherited and passed on the rich, deep pigment for which the R-OsnabrueckerLand dogs were known.

1960

Volker v Zollgrenzschutzhaus: Again he won the Sieger title for the second consecutive year.

Mascha v Stuhri-Gau: The 1958 Siegerin, she was again chosen this year as best bitch.

1961

Veus v d Starrenburg: A son of Alf v Nordfelsen, Veus carried on the tradition and qualities of Axel.

Assie v Hexenkolk: A daughter of Sieger Caesar's sister, Cora v d Malmannsheide.

1962

Mutz aus der Kuckstrasse: A son of Condor v Hohenstamm, Mutz made the financial pages of the Shepherd press by being sold for a princely sum to a Pakistani rajah. He was the same size as Condor, had the same good rear angulation and outstanding gait, and took after his sire in temperament and courage. Although it was said his shoulder was less than perfect, Mutz produced many excellent sons and especially daughters, including the 1964 Siegerin. His descendants in America got here only through his early progeny in Germany, and in both countries are known for flashy markings and "showy" expression and carriage although some had ear weakness and some were long-coated.

Rike v Colonia Agrippina: From another now-famous and respected kennel, she was VA-3 the previous year and probably needed maturing in order to win this year.

1963

Ajax v Haus Dexel: Linebred on the R litter OsnabrueckerLand, Ajax became well known for a very high percentage of normal hips in his offspring. He had a very good "trotter" build and gait, with excellent shoulder and moderate but balanced rear, and possessed a very good temperament.

Maja v Stolperland: By Marko v Boxhochburg out of Werra v OsnabrueckerLand.

1964

Zibu v Haus Schuetting: A fantastically handsome dog from one of the oldest, most respected kennels of the modern era (post-1925). Zibu's qualities of balance, reach, temperament, and correct structure kept popping up in dogs many generations later but so did a few flat croups and over-long backs. He sired four VA dogs, including 1966 Sieger and the 1967 VA-2 dog, Quax v Haus Beck.

Blanka v Kisskamp: A fine daughter of Sieger Mutz a d Kuckstrasse.

1965

Hanko v Hetschmuhle: Son of SV president Dr. Funk's Witz v Haus Schuetting. Witz was sold to some Japanese after leaving his mark with Hanko and such others as the G and H litters vom Sixtberg. Hanko himself was later sold to an American.

Landa v d Wienerau: From a kennel whose fame has spanned several decades, Landa's dam was the great producer Dixie v d Wienerau. Her sire was the popular Vello zu den Sieben Faulen son, VA Jalk v Fohlenbrunnen, who was linebred on those OsnabrueckerLands. Jalk, who is possibly the most repeated name in linebreeding of the dogs of the 1970s and the 1980s, had plenty of pigment, which might be expected considering his own linebreeding. Landa inherited the same characteristics.

1966

Basko v d Kahler Heide: Son of Sieger Zibu and Nixie aus der Eremitenklause, Basko is not as well known in America as other Zibu offspring. His croup was better than Zibu's, but his foreassembly not quite as good. Nixie was a product of that successful and oft-repeated "click" of Arras v Adam Rieseswinger and Halla a d Eremitenklause. Another well-known Arras/Halla son was Klodo a d Eremitenklause, a somewhat long dog with great chest, moderately sloping topline, somewhat long and narrow head, and plenty of black pigment. Though long and well-angulated, he had a strong back and good movement, weighed over 90 pounds and had beautiful proportions. Klodo passed on a number of dentition problems, a few weak ears, and a few less-angulated shoulders, though not all should be laid at his doorstep. The presence of Klodo in a dog's pedigree should be considered fortunate.

Cita v Gruchental: As is the case with many bitches, Cita is almost unknown in the Western Hemisphere.

1967

Bodo v Lierberg: One of the many excellent dogs from the Vello z d Sieben-Faulen/Betty v Eningsfeld breedings. Bernd v Lierberg was VA-3 this year. The Lierberg line is known for great working ability and health, enthusiastic and hard biting, dark pigment, and other fine qualities such as balanced gait; sound coming and going; strong back, feet and pasterns; masculine head, etc. Willis calls it possibly one of the best matings of all time, and I heartily agree. Bodo was imported to the US and owned by Erich Renner, guide dog trainer on the West Coast. At the 1971 National Specialty in Detroit, Bodo appeared in the Parade of Greats carrying two flags in his mouth: one US, denoting his championship and new citizenship, and the other German, showing his origin and Sieger title. He brought down the house with tears and the well-deserved greatest applause of the day.

Betty v Glockenland: Her sire, Black v Lambertzeck, was a dark, richly pigmented dog that won Junghund Sieger in 1964 and found his way into a lot of U.S. dogs' pedigrees. Black was a son of Jalk v Fohlenbrunnen, that other important Vello son.

1968

Dido v d Werther Koenigsalle: Another great Zibu son. The VA-2 dog, Caro v Schaafgarten, produced many dysplastics, was re-x-rayed and found to be not up to "a" stamp requirements. His owner was disciplined, but Caro had already left his mark. He was maternal grandsire to 1973 Sieger Dick v Adeloga. Caro did have a good head and balance.

Rommy v Driland: A great producing bitch; sired by Kay v Hexenkolk, a dog that also sired Erko v Dinkelland. He had an almost unbeaten string of wins on his way to an AKC championship before returning to Germany to be placed VA-3 in a near tie for Sieger, after which he returned again to his US home.

1969

Heiko v Oranien Nassau: Popular and a sire prepotent, Heiko was produced by Alf v Convent and Cilly v Oranien Nassau, a Klodo Eremitenklause daughter.

Connie v Klosterbogen: Daughter of 1968 Sieger Dido and Farah v d Starrenburg, she became a very important force in producing top dogs in Germany over the next ten years.

1970

Heiko v Oranien Nassau: Deservedly repeated his 1969 victory. The SV leadership felt he exhibited and produced what the breed needed at the time. Mutz Pelztierfarm, VA-2, was Italian Sieger the next year; he was faulted for only a slightly steep upper arm.

Diane v d Firnskuppe: From one of Germany's top kennels, Diane was a daughter of the great Ajax v Haus Dexel.

1971

Arras v Haus Helms: Best known on our side of the pond as another fine example of the producing ability of Tom v Haus Solms.

Katia v d Rheiliese: Daughter of Nick v Dreimarkenstein, a popular sire of American imports in the 1970s. Nick was linebred Hein Richterbach, R- and I- OsnabrueckerLand, and Axel, was lively and of excellent temperament, as was Katia. He had strong ligaments in back, hocks, pasterns, and elsewhere. Nick's sire was Lido v d Wienerau from one of Germany's top kennels, that of

Walter Martin. Lido weighed 97 pounds and stood 25½ inches, and inherited his good gait, strong back, and bold temperament from *his* sire, Jalk v Fohlenbrunnen. (One begins to see the strong influence of Vello and Jalk. This is only the tip of the modern iceberg in German waters.) Celly v d Wienerau, Canto Wienerau's sister, was VA-7 in 1971; Canto himself did not make VA, and died early, yet had more "V" progeny at the 1973 and 1974 Sieger Shows than did any other sire.

1972

Marko v Cellerland: Marko was much favored by American breeders who wanted to improve pigment and perhaps breed black dogs. Linebred 5-5 on Hein Richterbach (a Rosel v OsnabrueckerLand son), Marko was destined to be used often and to good advantage for both black pigment and good hips. Many US blacks today have Marko as a contributor of those genes, especially those dogs owned by Schutzhund enthusiasts. This medium-large (26 inches, 90 pounds), very expressive and masculine dog had an extended saddle, perhaps indicating his black recessives. He had a strong head and muzzle, good scissors bite, and very good angulation and topline. Willis considered him lacking in upper arm, but well-balanced in motion. Marko's strong drive and rear contributed to a good, ground-covering gait with correct movement. His back was firm, as were all other joints and ligaments, with pasterns we would do well to emulate in the United States. Temperament was lively, alert, stable, and befitting his SchH-III title. He was recommended as a stud that could improve tightness and angulation.

When compared to the wording in the American (AKC) Standard, his topline in photos appears a bit more sloping than it should be, but this was about the time that the trend began in Germany toward smaller rears and higher withers. Incidentally, the German Standard can be translated as "straight" in reference to the back, while the US Standard says both straight *and* level. Either we do not understand the definition of the word "level" or have poorly understood the original German intention when our Standard was built on theirs. I tend to think the former is true, and the Germans are now deviating from the ideal, original, and literal meaning. Too bad von Stephanitz didn't foresee the confusion and clarify this to reduce future arguments.

Hero was VA-2 this year, and Quanto Wienerau VA-7. The Junghung Sieger was Dick v Adeloga. All three were destined for greatness, though Hero went to Japan, and Quanto moved south to Italy where he was able to continue to contribute to German breeding.

Katinka v d Netten Ecke: Was Siegerin in 1972.

1973

Dick v Adeloga: Son of Quanto, he was to become a future leader in producing top-winning dogs, although his maternal grandsire (VA-2, 1968) was dysplastic. Quanto led in the stud dog (progeny) class this year, along with Canto Wienerau and Mutz v d Pelztierfarm. The progeny group of Hero did very well, also, as did those of Marko and the black dog Frei v d Gugge. (Black dogs were more frequently seen in the top echelons after 1972.) Hero was a very dark son of Jupp v d Murrenhutte, a Klodo Eremitenklause son, and produced many good blacks, as did Marko and, of course, Frei. Canto's sire, Hein v Koenigsbruch, was surveyed "V" in 1968 as being in good condition with pronounced fighting spirit, but at the 1969 Sieger Show Dr. Rummel rated him only as "G" (good), commenting on his excellent construction but deducting for his lack of toughness which can be taken to mean lacking in hardness in his pre-show man-work (attack) testing. Hein was sold to England in 1970 where he won a Challenge Certificate, but did little more of significance there, though he arrived in the prime of life at 5 years of age. In his first four years in the UK, he sired 447 progeny in 73 litters, an indication that the breeders thought highly of him.

Erka v Fiemereck: Daughter of Canto Wienerau (also the sire of this year's Junghund Siegerin and Sieger littermates, Atrice and Asslan v Klammle). Atrice was bought by Dr. Mort Goldfarb of Birmingham, Alabama, and Asslan entered the record books as going for the highest price ever (in non-inflation-adjusted US dollars) to Greg Peters of Connecticut. (See remarks under 1975 Gr.V.)

Also in 1973, the Marko son, Kai v Silberbrand, was VA-6. Kai's genes were much used by Canadian and northern US fanciers and importers. VA-8 Gundo v Klosterbogen, a son of 1969 Siegerin Connie, was to be much heard of in later years.

A Quanto daughter was VA-3, and Marko himself was VA-4

1974

Beginning this year, the 75th SV World Show, the words *Sieger, Siegerin,* and *Sieger Show* would not be used, because the SV leadership felt that too much emphasis was being placed on the *one* VA-1 dog for stud service, while the next eight or ten might be as good (or even better for certain bitches). To encourage outcrossing and less dependence on just one stud dog per year, the VA dogs and bitches would be listed in kennel alphabetical order, and the show would be referred to as the *Hauptzuchtschau* (chief breed show). Additional requirements regarding training titles, hip status, and Koer (survey) were added to dogs aspiring to VA ranking.

Among those nine males receiving VA were Dick v Adeloga, Canto v Arminius, Gundo v Klosterbogen, and Kai v Silberbrand. Seven VA bitches were named, including Xanta v Kirschental, from a highly respected kennel with many HGH dogs (a daughter of Hero and an Altanbachtal bitch), and Zilga Grubenstolz, whose kennel name is familiar to many Americans.

Canto v d Wienerau, a dog that had more V offspring in the 1973 and 1974 shows than any other dog, was tops in the progeny (stud dog) class in 1974, with Marko, Quanto, and Xanto v Coburger Rosengarten not far behind. Busecker Schloss won the kennel group competition. I believe the Busecker Schloss kennel, begun in 1925 by A. Hahn, is one of the oldest continuously operating kennels in the world. Herr Hahn is still an active breeder!

1975

Although referred to as the *Bundeshauptzuchtschau* (National Main Breed Show) this year's event was again international in scope, as it had always been, and again no ranking was given to the VA dogs.

In the males, Canto v d Wienerau (sire line: Hein v Koenigsbruch - Fix z d Sieben-Faulen) was sire of two: Canto Arminius and Datscha v Patersweg, both of whom were VA also in 1974. Mutz v d Pelztierfarm had three sons, and the Quanto son Gundo v Klosterbogen again appeared among the top twelve. Marko and Canto Wienerau each had a daughter named VA among seven so chosen, and Gundo's dam Connie was also represented by her daughter sired by Cliff v Haus Beck. Zibu v Haus Niermann also was the sire of a VA bitch, and another Grubenstolz bitch was in the select group.

1976

Marko v Cellerland sired two of this year's VA dogs, and Canto Wienerau also sired two, one of which was Canto Arminius. Quanto had one VA son (Lasso) and Dick v Adeloga had a son and a daughter in the VA ranks. Hero v Lauerhof, Mutz v d Pelztierfarm, Gundo Klosterbogen, Zibu v Haus Niermann, and others were represented as well. Asslan v Klammle, a dog that had wisely been used at stud before being sold, sired two of the eight VA bitches. A couple of Marko/Eri Steinbockfelsen sons placed in the V category. Gundo Klosterbogen's progeny class of 30(!), all similar, attest to his value in a pedigree.

1977

The *Siegerhauptzuchtschau* this year had a VA class designation but to encourage breeders to use dogs other than just the Sieger, and offspring of bitches other than just the Siegerin, again they were not placed in order.

Some of the dogs were: Sieger Dick v Adeloga's son, Grando v Patersweg (VA-2 in 1979), Eros v d Malvenburg (1979 Sieger), Sieger Dick v Adeloga's son Herzog, the Quanto v d Wienerau son Lasso di Val Sole (VA in a couple of other shows in the late 1970s), and Argus v Aducht, a son of Argus v Klammle.

Among the VA bitches were Canto Wienerau daughter Diana v Patersweg, Asslan v Klammle daughter Ninni v Kirschental, and Gundo v Klosterbogen's daughter Romona v Kai-Ro. Walter Martin (Wienerau) won the kennel (breeder's) *Zuchtgruppe* competition.

1978

For the first time in four years, the *Welteshauptzuchtschau* (World's Main Breed Show), was again a Sieger Show with rankings in the VA and other wins because of popular demand. The people had been choosing their own Siegers, anyway, with considerable agreement among themselves. Herman Martin's Canto Wienerau son, *Canto v Arminius,*

at last was given the recognition he deserved: Sieger. Of the fourteen VA males and ten VA females, some old names reappeared as parents that had been winners or well-known kennel names in years past: Rheinhalle, Wienerau, Pelztierfarm, Marko, Adeloga, Murrenhutte, Grubenstolz, Gundo Klosterbogen, and Arminius.

Ute v Trienzbachtal: This year's Siegerin was a Hero Lauerhof daughter.

1979

Eros v d Malvenberg: A Canto Wienerau son ex a Bodo Lierberg granddaughter, later went to the Japanese and little was heard of his lines after (in Europe). His descendants have been little used in Germany.

Ute v Trienzbachtal: A beautiful bitch whose breeder, L. Bucher, won the *Zuchtgruppe*. She was sired by VA Hero v Lauerhof, out of Otti v Trienzbachtal. In my 1984 trip to the Japan Sieger Show near Tokyo, I saw many Trienzbachtal dogs, all of them very nice.

1980

The Canto/Quanto Wienerau lines had been coming to the fore more and more, taking over the prominence held in the past by Marko v Cellerland, Klodo Eremitenklause, and Lierberg lines. Quanto son, Lasso di Val Sole, Canto Arminius and Caesar Arminius, and a couple of others were current leaders in production.

Axel v d Hainsterbach: A well-pigmented son of Lasso di Val Sole unfortunately had a hip status of "fast-normal" (almost normal, but not quite), a possible warning to Americans who are concerned with this disease of genetic origin. There's not too much difference between normal and near-normal as long as other relatives' hips are equivalent and the dog with "fast-normal" is from a family with a good record. Axel was characterized as a middle-sized, substantial dog with much expression and "image" coming partly through harmonious proportions and firmness. To good pasterns and firm back was added a good, long, sloping croup. The breast structure gave good forechest (prosternum) and a long underchest. In addition, a good course of long bones was obvious. He had a normal shoulder blade layback and the upper arm was long, contributing to his very good front angulation. Very good hindquarter angulation with strong, firm ligaments at the joints, and good, tightly arched feet continued his impression of dryness. In motion he was also dry and muscular. No doubt his owners capitalized on this physical toughness in roadworking him prior to the 1980 show, for Axel was still fresh and in great condition after almost grueling gaiting which began to tire or at least relax his competition.

Ten of the fifteen VA dogs were linebred on Jalk v Fohlenbrunnen, many of these through L litter v d Wienerau (Lido, Liane, Landa). Jalk was a Vello son, and twelve of the fifteen were linebred on Vello z d Sieben-Faulen! Not bad for a dog that was refused a breed survey report because he was a little too big! The VA-4 dog, Apoll v Haus Tigges was 1980 Italian Sieger. The line from Vello also extended to the 1980 Sieger, though only on his sire's side (Lasso), I believe. All ten VA bitches are Vello descendants, mostly through Jalk and L-Wienerau, and some through Quanto and Lasso.

Dixie v Natoplatz: This year's Siegerin was a 4-year-old middle-size bitch; dry, strong, and firm, with good pasterns and topline. The croup was on a good angle but could have been somewhat longer. With good front and rear angulation and breast development, she had a free and easy stride, yet her drive was powerful. The judge mentioned her improved development into fuller maturity since last year when she was VA-2, and praised her for being three times successful. He said she was deserving of the title, and was good for her descendants and the breed.

1981

Natan v d Pelztierfarm: This dog was also exported, and again, relatively few people in Germany used him, especially considering that he was Sieger twice in succession.

Anusch v Trienzbachtal: Her dam was Otti v Trienzbachtal, so she was half-sister to the 1979 Siegerin. Argus Aducht sired two of the VA bitches, as did Lasso di Val Sole. Otti also was the dam of 1983 Siegerin Tannie.

1982

Natan v d Pelztierfarm: Natan repeated his victory this year, then was VA-3 in 1983.

Perle v WildsteigerLand: She was VA-5 in 1981 and took the Siegerin title this year. Her sister produced the terrific 1984-85 Sieger. Argus this year sired two VA bitches and the Junghundklasse Ruden (18- to 24-month-old males) winner. Ola v Arminius (Argus dam) was VA-3 this year, VA-4 in 1981.

1983

Dingo v Haus Gero: This dog has excellent character and type, and a better shoulder assembly than most. His sire was Casar v Arminius that was also the sire of 1981 VA-4 Apoll v Haus Tigges. Casar's brother, Sieger Canto v Arminius, sired the 1983 VA-9 and 1984-85 VA-6 dog, Valk v Michelstadter Rathaus. Dingo's descendants include some very nice dogs with good fronts and toplines. He supposedly was not the best in production of good hips, but Willis has not seen that notoriety showing up in his British data (the English use a lot of German-imported genes). Dingo was still in great shape when seen at the 1986 Sieger Show.

Tannie v Trienzbachtal: By taking Siegerin, she helped Herr Bucher to win the *Zuchtgruppe* again this year. Her dam, Otti, was obviously a good producer. Tannie's sire, Irk v d Wienerau, also sired Ch Vax v d Wienerau that in turn produced many good dogs in Germany before George Collins in the US bought him.

1984

Uran v WildsteigerLand: He won the title in both 1984 and 1985. His sire was Irk v Arminius and his dam was Perle's sister, Palme v Wildsteiger-Land. Although Uran was an exceedingly handsome dog, he carried some unwanted characteristics, and line breeding, if any, should be done with caution and forewarning. These include dwarfism, weak ear carriage, and poor pigment.

Tina v Grossen Sand: She was a worthy winner and had impressed judges and the public when, in 1983, she placed VA-6. Uran's sister, Ulme, placed VA-8 in 1984.

1983 Siegerin, Tannie v. Trienzbachtal

1983 Sieger, Dingo v. Haus Gero

VA in Germany in 1982, Ora v. Adeloga. We saw her in 1984 in Japan.

1984 Siegerin, Tina v. Grossen Sand

1985

Uran v WildsteigerLand: Repeated his 1984 win.

Tina v Grossen Sand: She was given the title again this year as was Uran. Her brother, Tell, was VA-2 dog followed by Onex v Batu at VA-3. Onex was disappointing in the area of hip dysplasia. Quando Arminius, the VA-5 dog, was bred by the judge, Hermann Martin, and is a half-brother to Uran through their dam. Dingo, Vax, and Canto Arminius (Quando's sire) contributed sons to 1985's VA dog list.

A VA Jupp HallerFarm son, Putz v Arjakjo was VA-8 this year and VA-5 the year before. He was sold to people in the US, though his "noch zugelassen" hip X ray status may or may not have had much to do with his departure from Germany (they seldom let their best leave while still fairly young), yet Lasso, with the similar quality of hips, remained and was used considerably. But then,

Lasso was a VA Quanto Wienerau son, and there is much emphasis (too much) on Quanto and on Canto Wienerau and Mutz Pelztierfarm.

VA-2 and VA-3 bitches were Irk Arminius daughters, and VA-4 was a Lasso daughter. The genetics were becoming very concentrated by 1985.

1986

Quando v Arminius: This Sieger was a good-looking dog, but disappointing to many spectators because of the way he was placed in 1986 and 1987 by his breeder and judge. Taking third place was a dog I had predicted would eventually be Sieger when he won the Junghundklasse in 1985, Eiko v Kirschental. Eiko is a Uran son out of Xitta v Kirschental, and is a beautiful animal.

Pischa v Bad-Boll: An Irk Arminius daughter, this Siegerin moved up from VA-3 taken in the previous year. Palme v Bad-Boll, her half-sister by Uran, was VA-3 this year.

1986 and '87 Sieger, Quando v. Arminius

1986 Siegerin, Pischa v. Bad-Boll

1987

Quando v Arminius: While Quando again took Sieger, Eiko was VA-2, getting closer while his offspring racked up their own records. The SV doesn't want to give the Sieger title to dogs that have been disappointing producers. Dingo son, Rambo v Reststrauch, VA-4 in 1986, was VA-5 this year.

Senta v Basilisk: A Quando daughter, she had been VA-9 in 1986 under Herr Beck who has been doing the adult bitches since Dr. Rummel died and Herr Martin vacated that position to judge dogs which Rummel had been doing previous to 1983. Palme v Bad-Boll was VA-2 this year.

I suspect that the breed in Germany may have needed a show of more vigor, since the VA-1 dog and bitch were both singled out for their spirit, indefatigable natures, conditioning, and foreassemblies.

I'm sure the emphasis will be noted by German breeders and exhibitors in the years to come.

1988

Eiko v Kirschental. An outstanding son of Uran, whose progeny group at this year's show was almost endless. With dogs like Eiko as proof, Uran will prove to be at least as influential in the breed as Canto and Quanto Wienerau. Eiko is a brightly colored dog, but not as light as many Uran offspring. Bitches of good pigment should be bred to him and other Uran sons.

Ronda v Haus Beck. Uran daughter with not the most pleasing topline, at least to American eyes. Uran also sired the VA-3 and VA-4 bitches and the VA-4 dog as well as innumerable V-rated Sieger show dogs and bitches.

Eiko v. Kirschental Junghundbester (Junghundsieger) in 1985, VA-3 in 1986, VA-2 in 1987, and Sieger in 1988. Great example of Uran's value, and a great producer himself.

1984 and '85 Sieger, Uran v. Wildsteiger Land destined to be one of Modern Shepherdom's most valuable producers.

British Champions

British Champion Amulrees Heiko. Sire: Dorvaak Jarro; dam: Robuna's Black Diamond. Bred and owned by Mr. and Mrs. H. Anderson, Fife, Scotland. This British-bred dog, who has much "presence" in the ring, is linebred on Rossfort Premonition. He held the record for CC's (Champion Certificates) in the U.K. Photo by Jack Oliver.

International (British, New Zealand, and Australian) Champion Rossfort Premonition. Born 1969, one of the best and most important dogs England has ever produced. "Lex" was the son of an "English type" bitch and a British-born police dog of German parentage. His superb movement brought him numerous big wins, including the Gold Medal at the B.A.A. under Dr. Rummel, and the 1973 Crufts Best Of Breed. Pictured at nine years of age. Photo courtesy of Mr. and Mrs. Bryne (owners) and Mrs. S.M. Hunter (breeder).

German Influence In England

1981 British Champion Fairycross Salina. Sire: Ch. Delridge Erhardt; dam: Ch. Fairycross High Society. Both parents British bred. Breeder Ann Adams. A pretty bitch with rather small hindquarters, reflecting recent German trend in type which is being emulated in England.

British Champion Fanto vom Bayrischen Wald 1981. German import bred by E. Seibold, owned by Mrs. Y. James. Sire: Caesar von Arminius; dam Beggi v. Bayrischen Wald.

British Champion Dunmonaidth Gythe. This bitch earned her title in 1981. Bred and owned by Miss Moncrieff. Sire: Int. Ch. Chicko vom Gut Friedburg; dam: Dunmonaidth Oak Beauty. In spite of quarantine, British breeders continued to draw heavily on German imports, more so in recent years than since the 1960's.

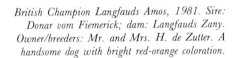

British Champion Langfauds Amos, 1981. Sire: Donar vom Fiemerick; dam: Langfauds Zany. Owner/breeders: Mr. and Mrs. H. de Zutter. A handsome dog with bright red-orange coloration.

Tadellos Hein vom Koningsbruch, SchH-II in 1971 (October 1965 - October 1976). V-rated 16 times in Germany before being exported to England. Sire of the famous Canto v. Wienerau who died young but not before producing a great percentage of top winners. Consequently, it was reported by one Britain that Germany tried to get Hein back for stud services, even offering to pay all expenses for his owner, Mrs. V. Egger. She declined the offer because of Hein's age and England's long re-entry quarantine. Hein had rich color, a somewhat steep croup, very angulated hindquarters, and an excellent shoulder. The Tadellos prefix is seldom seen on U.S. and German pedigrees, since it was added after importation to England.

8

NUTRITION AND FEEDING

Many dog owners pick up an article or book on nutrition in hopes of learning how to feed their dogs for best results in health, coat, condition, and economy. All too often they are confronted with a confusing plethora of kilocalories, amino acids, enzymes, grams, nutrient indexes, and other terms. Some simply give up and feed what the breeder or the TV commercial recommended. However, the subject need not be confusing if approached one step at time.

A dog is worthy of his food.
Erasmus, 1908

NUTRIENTS

Chemically, nutrients are primarily combinations of carbon, hydrogen, and oxygen with other atoms in smaller amounts. Besides these "combustible" carbon-hydrogen organic compounds, the animal requires a variety of inorganic (mineral) elements for such uses as nerve impulses, enzyme production, and fluid control. Some foods are richer in trace elements and inorganic compounds than others.

The three classifications of nutrients are proteins, carbohydrates, and fats. Not only does your dog need approximately forty-five different nutrients within these three groups, but they should be present in certain proportions for optimum nutrition. Some of these are synthesized by the body, but others must be found in the food in ready-to-use

forms, and so are called "essential" nutrients. Most commercial dog foods today are balanced, except for an overabundance of calcium. In a dog food grains supply most of the carbohydrates, meat provides a high percentage of the protein, and both animal and vegetable fats are present. To these are added important chemicals such as vitamins and minerals. Some fiber for bulk and varying amounts of water make up the rest.

Fats

Fat as a class is about 94 to 98 percent digestible by the dog, a very different situation than with human digestive systems. Besides producing more than twice the number of calories (heat energy) than either carbohydrates or protein, dietary fat contains some of the building blocks of the body, the fatty acids. Linoleic acid, the sole essential fatty acid, must be added to dog food, and is found in abundance in pork fat. Corn oil is also an excellent source of linoleic acid as well as being the equal of lard in energy value. Certain vitamins and enzymes rely on fatty acids for use by the body.

Carbohydrates

While the most commonly known carbohydrates are sugars and starches, many vitamins and minerals are supplied through other elements in this nutrient class—cereal grains for one. The major carbohydrate component of grains is starch, which the dog digests into sugars. Second only to starch in bulk is cellulose, an indigestible carbohydrate.

Many of the starches and sugars as well as the minerals they contain can be physically locked up in the cellulosic fragments of leaves and stalks or the fruit pulp of the specific plants eaten. Since the dog does not masticate his food, grinding and/or cooking makes these simpler carbohydrates available for the dog's digestion and assimilation.

Protein

The major purpose of protein in the diet is to provide amino acids for the repair of wounds, manufacture of antibodies, replacement of worn tissues such as hair and pads, and to serve in other maintenance and growth functions. When there is insufficient caloric content to food, the dog will use some amino acids as fuel that should have been kept available for those other uses. High protein diets are safe for most healthy dogs because the excess can be metabolized into fat after the nitrogen is split off and discarded into the urine.

A healthy, well-nourished dog. Ch. Robynmar's Joshua, OFA, owned by Margie Jones.   *Robins photo.*

Most amino acids can be synthesized by the body, but some nine in the adult and ten in the growing pup cannot thus be manufactured, or at least not at the rate and quantity necessary for good health. These ten are called essential amino acids.

arginine	lysine	threonine
histidine	phenylalanine	tryptophan
leucine	methionine	valine
isoleucine		

The measure of amino acid availability is known as biological value (BV). As a standard of reference, whole egg protein has been given an index of 100. Meat proteins have a biological value index between 70 and 99, while cereal grain proteins have a BV of around 50 to 65. The soybean's BV of 68 is pretty good for a nonmeat, but corn is quite a bit lower and serves better as a carbohydrate source rather than an amino acid source. Some amino acids such as lysine, tryptophan, and methionine are not generally found in foods other than animal tissue, so the carnivorous canine is best given meat as part of his diet.

VITAMINS

Vitamins are dietary chemicals essential for good health. The absence of vitamins over time results in deficiency diseases and interferes with normal growth and optimum function, although it is not entirely clear just how. Vitamins appear to be activators containing certain structures and elements that cause or allow two or more chemicals in the body to properly operate together. They are widely available, and standard dog foods usually contain enough of all types of vitamins in the food ingredients themselves to prevent a vitamin deficiency. In addition, a commercial diet often contains added concentrates, extracts, or synthetic vitamin supplements. However, methods of storage and preparation can destroy or remove vitamins; for example, boiling water may extract some B vitamins. In order to salvage these vitamins and get them into the dog, it is a good practice to use vegetable-cooking water to moisten the dog's food.

Vitamin A and Vitamin D

Used to excess, these two vitamins can cause a syndrome known as hypervitaminosis. In the extreme, an excess of vitamin D can kill, usually by helping calcium to be deposited in soft body tissues such as heart, lungs, muscle, and blood vessels. Since it is often found in calcium supplement tablets, it can be especially dangerous when given this way. A typical succession of events took place when a woman I know asked me to take a look at her litter, all of whom were acting drunk, stumbling and tripping, nervous yet lethargic, and showing diarrhea. Upon questioning, my suspicions were confirmed: they had been given liberal helpings of a vitamin-mineral-powder supplement, and when the woman noticed a slight falling off of activity she increased the dosage. Still they worsened, and she upped the additive level again. When she eliminated the supplement at my suggestion, the pups quickly recovered from a classic case of hypervitaminosis.

Vitamin E

This vitamin is composed of a group of chemicals called tocopherols and is recognized as having antioxidant functions, "stretching" the effect of vitamins A, D, and C. Especially when combined or alternated with vitamin A, but remarkable all by itself, vitamin E has curative powers when applied topically to burns and cuts—ulcerative sores that refuse to heal with other treatments very often are quickly transformed into healthy tissue. Taken internally, vitamin E has been reported to help reduce pain of arthritic joints and to help coat condition as well as general wellbeing. Wheat germ oil is a good natural source, but synthetic tocopherol in capsules is less expensive. Capsules also avoid the problem of oil-soaked food getting rancid by standing around until the dog is hungry.

The B Complex Group

A fairly large group of related water-soluble vitamins are commonly identified by their chemical names. These are thiamine (B_1), riboflavin (B_2), niacin, pyridoxin (B_6), pantothenic acid, biotin, folic acid, choline, inositol, and vitamin B_{12}.

Thiamine—Seldom does a cared-for adult dog exhibit vitamin B_1 deficiency disease, but puppies with poor appetites will often respond dramatically with a dosage of iron/vitamin tonic containing thiamine. Good sources include brewer's yeast, pork, and eggs. If you feed your dog raw fish in large amounts, do so at a time of day other than when you give him his regular dry meal, for minnows or other fish contain thiaminase, an enzyme that destroys thiamine. Cooking gets rid of thiaminase, but also loosens fish bones from the meat and presents a potential problem in swallowing and digestion.

Riboflavin—While thiamine primarily helps metabolize carbohydrates, riboflavin's main action is in the metabolism of proteins, and hence growth. Until recently, it would have been hard to find German Shepherd Dogs that were not getting a good bit of soybean (a major source of B_2) in their diet, but no-soy meals have developed as a result of suspicions about soy's unproven connection with bloat. Other sources of B_2 include liver, yeast, milk, eggs, kidney, heart, and cheese. All have high BVs and would be excellent food supplements for nursing mothers and growing pups that need extra food and riboflavin without too much extra bulk.

Niacin—Niacin has a number of names, one of which is nicotinic acid. Its amide (organic salt) called niacinamide has the same vitamin value as niacin but does not dilate blood vessels, so it is in this form that you'll most likely see it on food labels. Sources are brewer's yeast, muscle and glandular meats, fish, and poultry.

Pyridoxine—This vitamin, plentiful in commercial dog foods, helps metabolize carbohydrates, fats, and proteins, and is important for blood production. It is abundant in chicken and its organs, liver, fish, and eggs, as well as grains.

Pantothenic acid—Only choline and niacin are needed in larger quantities than are the pantothenates, and synthetic production is big business because of its demand in the cattle business. The best natural sources of pantothenic acid are liver, kidney, eggs, and yeast.

Biotin—This vitamin is synthesized in the digestive tract with the help of beneficial bacteria, so a deficiency would be rare except for one thing: raw egg whites. Not many dogs would be fed several egg whites without the yolks, but a protein called avidin in raw whites can render unavailable the biotin in other foods. Either cook the whites or make sure the yolks are not withheld. Liver, kidney, and milk are good sources, but biotin is found in almost all foods.

Folic acid—Found in liver, and to a lesser extent in muscle meats and grains, folic acid is added to dry foods to insure that enough is eaten to take care of the need for blood formation, growth, and protein metabolism.

Choline—Needed for fat as well as protein metabolism, choline is apparently a precursor of acetylcholine, a chemical necessary for the transmission of nerve impulses. A dog cannot synthesize it, but it is readily available in soybean and wheat germ oils, glandular meats, eggs, and yeast, most of which may be common ingredients in high-BV commercial dog foods. It is added as a synthetic, as well. Rarely will a dog get enough to cause diarrhea, but that is a possibility.

Inositol—This is another essential for growth and is found in the same foods that provide the other B vitamins.

Vitamin B$_{12}$—When anemia occurs, the body has lowered resistance to infections and other stresses. Quick improvement in appetite, growth, and vitality usually follow injection or dietary addition of B$_{12}$. Food supplementation of B$_{12}$ seems to help a dog reach the peak of his alertness, and many exhibitors feel that administration a few hours before a show gives their dogs an edge. Also called cyanocobalamin, this vitamin is abundant in animal organ meats, especially kidney and liver. Vitamin B$_{12}$ is said to help in cases of coprophagia (stool eating).

Vitamin C

In recent years, this vitamin has caused great controversy. What claims abound! Are most or any of them valid? There are many things we know or think we know about vitamin C, especially its role in human nutrition, but man is not able to synthesize his own ascorbates while the dog and most other animals are. So, for canines, it has been considered a nonessential vitamin and the basis for its prescription is the belief that in certain stress conditions the natural synthesis is insufficient to take care of peaks and elevations in demand.

Because of a few ads and articles by people marketing vitamin C, scores of dog owners have placed unwarranted faith in the vitamin to cure or prevent hip dysplasia, jaundice, distemper, heart disease, and an almost endless list of viral and bacterial disorders. A few of these *may* be helped but most are extremely unlikely to be affected much if at all by the vitamin therapy. In fact, a study at Cornell University showed that vitamin-C-treated dogs actually had less vitamin C in their adrenals than did the control dogs that had not been fed any extra. The more the vitamin was given, the faster the dogs seemed to expel it through the urine. In short, it won't hurt for you to share your vitamin C with your dog, especially under stressful conditions, but don't expect miracles. It has absolutely no effect on hip dysplasia.

MINERALS

A mineral is often thought of as something that is mined or dug from the earth. For our purposes, it refers to certain metals and elements of nonmetallic nature, such as chlorine and sulfur, which play important parts in nutrition. Some have extremely vital roles, as seen by the abundance of calcium and phosphorus in bone tissue, iron in red blood cells, sodium in nerves, and chlorine in stomach acid. These elements, incidentally, are not in free form but are combined chemically with others or balanced in solution, lest they range from useless to dangerous.

Calcium and Phosphorus

Bone is the chief repository for both of these most plentiful minerals in the body, and bones and joints suffer most from unwise attempts to "fortify" the diet with them. Unlikely though it may seem, deficiency disease can be caused by adding them and upsetting the balance in relation to each other or to other minerals.

The domesticated dog gets more than he needs for growing bones and teeth from the bone meal, beet pulp, meat, and other ingredients in commercial dog foods. Supplementation with calcium tablets or bone meal is definitely not a good idea for German Shepherd Dogs, regardless of age. Unless directed by a veterinarian with recent, thorough experience or study in nutrition, the dog owner should avoid such supplements. The one exception would be in the lactating bitch with a large, late-weaning litter. Calcium excess can cause deposits in joints, and is a contributing factor to bloat and gastric torsion.

Ch Tucker Hill's Angelique CD, ROM, OFA. Seven times "Select"; U.S. Maturity Victrix. Sire, Gauss vom Stauderpark, SchH III, AD, OFA. Dam, Jodi of Tucker Hill. Owners, Cappy Pottle, Jean Stevens, and Gloria F. Birch.

Salt

A broad definition of a salt would be the reaction product of an acid and a base, but when we speak of salt, we usually refer to common table salt (sodium chloride), found in our bodies as well as in the shaker on the table. A great excess of salt can be harmful. It is known to exacerbate high blood pressure, promote fluid accumulation in various cavities and tissues, and cause heart trouble and kidney disease. It never needs to be added to a dog's diet. Some commercial foods contain added salt, possibly to make up for not enough meat (blood is quite salty).

Iron

Iron is required to make hemoglobin, a complex protein compound that gives red blood cells their color. Iron deficiency can be mild or severe, especially in puppies that have been weakened by coccidiae and intestinal worms that cause blood loss. A vitamin/iron tonic or addition of liver to the diet will usually supply enough iron to build new blood cells while you attack the cause of the anemia. Symptoms include a paling of gums and tongue, and perhaps the appearance of blood in stools and vomit. After the pup is cured, drop the supplementation of iron tablets, because too much can disrupt the balance of zinc and other minerals.

Zinc

A healthy prostate gland can practically be assured if a male dog has sufficient zinc in his system. If your dog has prostatitis, poor digestion, or poor growth, zinc tablets from the drug store can be given. But be aware that excess calcium in the diet can cause zinc deficiency in which case extra zinc probably won't help. Again, the best rules for supplementation are caution and veterinary supervision.

Other Minerals

Potassium is found in many foods, and is not likely to be needed as a supplement by your dog, unless he has been on a high-sodium diet. Various trace elements (substances in extremely small amounts) are seldom missing from balanced commercial foods. Some of these are copper and cobalt for iron uptake, magnesium for normal ligament development, manganese for good enzyme production and temperament, iodine for normal thyroid function, selenium to facilitate use of vitamin E, and molybdenum for interactions with copper, phosphorus, and other minerals. Flourine, chromium, silicon, sulfur, and others are needed but easily provided in almost all foods. Generally, it's unwise to supplement with minerals except to overcome a specific disorder under your veterinarian's supervision.

WATER

While technically not a nutrient, water is truly the elixir of life. It serves to transport chemicals in the dog's circulatory system, softens the contents of his digestive tract, eliminates toxins and other waste products through urine, dissolves and makes available nutrients, gives turgidity to tissues, lubricates the joints, cleanses and protects the eyes and nose, and by evaporation from the tongue, regulates body temperature to a small, critical range. If the dog loses 10 percent of the water in his tissues, he will die. If deprived of water, he will not continue to eat, for food processing takes great quantities of water. Typically, he will become lethargic in an attempt to conserve energy (which is made available by metabolism with water). Finally, urine production ceases, and when this happens, the dog is near death.

Water trough, country style. A board caulked with lead-free caulk and nailed onto one or both ends of a hollow log will keep the water in. Wood keeps water cooler than does a metal trough.

"Now this is what I call an ice bucket!" Six-month-old pup enjoying the last (for now, anyway) of the water in an ice container made when a bucket of water froze. Later, the pups chewed up and ate the "container."

Keep plenty of fresh water on hand at all times. If you have to restrict water in the evening to help a puppy through a night of housebreaking, make sure you restrict the evening meal as well.

Does your dog drink a lot of water? This is probably normal, unless you have reason to suspect kidney disease or diabetes. Puppies seem to enjoy drinking water as a pastime as well as a necessity, and some German Shepherd Dogs never seem to grow out of puppyhood. Canned or moistened food will reduce the need for as much water. Most of my dogs will eat about a pound of dry food a day, depending on climate and activity. Such rations typically have about 10 percent moisture content, and a minimum of one quart of water for each pound of such food should be available at feeding time. Some of this water is used in digestion and softening right away, but some goes quickly to the bladder, and the dog will require more water later to finish the job of metabolism. If he has eaten any salty food such as bacon grease, cured meats, soft, moist dog food, or high-sugar treats, he will need additional water to "flush out" the system. Rather than rely on calculations, however, keep fresh, clean water in abundance. Any excess will easily pass through the body, there being practically no danger in too much drinking.

FEEDING

All normal diets for healthy dogs serve two major purposes: (1) provide energy for activity, and (2) supply nutrients for growth, repair, and replacement. All three energy providers (fats, carbohydrates, and proteins) will also furnish nutrients (fatty acids, sugars, amino acids, vitamins, and minerals). The question is: How much of what will give a balanced diet?

Fat

Fat is the highest-calorie food of the three types. Some 25 percent or more of the calories required by the dog are supplied by fat in most optimum diets. However, since dry foods generally contain only about 10 percent fat, additional fats or oils should be given in the dog's rations. Bacon drippings, lard, pork fat scraps and meat scraps or a small amount of corn oil will raise the fat level.

A gross imbalance in fat content can cause problems. Too little and the dog may not produce enough energy for temperature control, adequate activity, lactation, reproduction, and growth. Too much fat in the diet can result in obesity although a large excess may actually cause a dog to *lose* weight and condition because as he gets more than enough energy from the fat, he will reduce his total intake, thus depriving himself of non-fat-related nutrients, including vitamins and minerals. Loose stools can be a sign of too much fat, if exercise is minimal.

Carbohydrate

The proportion of carbohydrate should be limited to 50 or 60 percent of the dry weight of the diet, otherwise there may not be enough fat and protein. Most good dry foods have 23 to 27 percent protein, 9 to 12 percent fat, and often around 5 percent moisture. The remainder is made up of carbohydrate and "ash" (the mineral portion left when a sample of food is burned completely), that consists of salts and metallic oxides such as calcium compounds.

Protein

The lower-protein dog foods are generally considered lower quality as well, but some may be better for old dogs with kidney problems. The key is BV, or digestibility. For most, 20 percent protein just isn't enough for good nutrition. I saw a generic brand with only 18 percent protein, yet with all that carbohydrate, there wasn't any evidence of added thiamine on the analysis to handle it. If you have the money, or can prove it gives you more "mileage," a 31 percent protein content might be acceptable. However, recently it has been indicated that high protein diets can give other problems such as browning of black coat pigment, carpal ligament weakness and other reactions which need to be studied.

Vitamin/Mineral Balance

Although an excess of one vitamin does not seem to reduce the effect of another, excessive amounts of A and D can be toxic. I know of a very few humans who have mild to moderate reactions to a specific vitamin and I have not seen the same reaction in dogs except for very minor reaction to a great abundance of choline or niacin. There are many positive synergistic effects between vitamins C, A, and E, with some enhancing of the B vitamins also reported.

Minerals, on the other hand, can be very touchy regarding their absolute quantities as well as rations; the most striking is the calcium/phosphorus relationship. We may well add vitamin D to this triangle because this vitamin, which is synthesized or activated by the influence of sunlight, is needed for the body to assimilate calcium. If the ratio is upset, the more prevalent mineral tends to prevent the other one from being used by the body, and in some doses the body seems to react negatively to an excess, refusing almost *all* of whatever it is, not just the excess.

If the diet contains significantly more than about one percent of each of these two minerals, they may effect additional nutrients. Zinc, for example, may have its benefits blocked by too much calcium, and the same effect on manganese and iron has been identified as a cause of lethargy and drowsiness. Too much calcium and phosphorus in the diet, whether by supplementation or overeating a balanced food, seems to cause hypertrophic osteodystrophy (HOD) symptoms and other forms of osteochondrosis, and contributes to torsion. This is treated in more detail in my 1981 book published by Alpine Publications, Inc., *Canine Hip Dysplasia*.

In one study on joint and bone disease as related to nutrition, it was found that pups fed as much as they wanted exhibited abnormal bumps and knobs on some joints, and had weak pasterns, backs, and hocks compared to those pups on restricted amounts of food with the same ideal ratios of calcium to phosphorus. Likewise, the tendency toward hip dysplasia increases when pups genetically prone to it have been fed too much. Calcium supplementation is definitely not indicated for growing dogs and is possibly harmful to most adults as well, even if phosphorus is increased in proportion.

Most dog food ingredients, as well as most table scraps, are richer in phosphorus than calcium. Red meat is especially high, with Ca/P ratios running from 1:12 for well-marbled chuck roast to 1:44 for liver. To compensate for the meat in high-BV dog foods, mills may add bone meal (2:1) and beet pulp (7:1). A fast-growing German Shepherd puppy needs the same ratio of phosphorus to calcium as does a toy-breed adult, and the same percentage in the analysis, or less. Growing pups of large breeds do *not* need more per pound of food, although they will eat more food and thus get more per pound of body weight than a sedentary lap dog. If the dog eats the proper amount of food, he will not only get enough of these minerals, he will probably get too much, but most of them will be excreted as long as they aren't over-supplemented.

YOUR DOG'S DIET

The dogge waggeth his tayle, not for you, but for your bread.
Thomas Draxe's version of a seventeenth century English proverb.

Foods

Dry—Among kennel operators and owners of more than one dog, dry dog foods are preferred for a variety of reasons: no refrigeration is required, it is most economical, and it is convenient. Whether as meal, nuggets, kibbles, or combinations of these, the grains are ground and cooked to make nutrients available. All you need to add is fat and love.

Soft-moist—This alternative is a compromise between the economy of dry foods and the palatability and high biological value of canned and frozen foods. The biggest advantage is convenience, but

Stainless steel baking pans may be hard to find, but are often more economical and sturdier than what you might find in pet stores. Even in this pan, you can see tooth marks.

major disadvantages besides cost are related to the high level of sugars used as preservative/humectants and hence a non-nutritive source of energy. In addition, sugar has been identified as a culprit in some loose stool problems, reason enough to avoid the regular use of this type of commercial food.

Canned—With quality varying greatly from nearly worthless offal to highly digestible, one still pays for the weight and freight of water and steel in canned foods. But, since extra-high levels of protein and other nutrients are beneficial to convalescing dogs, a supply of very good canned dog food is good to have on hand in case of sickness or injury.

Frozen—With the highest BV of all types and high palatability, frozen foods offer a concentrated source of fresh nutrients and appetite stimulants. However, they are seldom nutritionally complete, contain up to 50 percent water, and require freezer space.

Choosing a Dry Dog Food

The first thing to examine in shopping for a good food is the label. This should tell you two things: what nutrients and energy (calories) the food contains, and what ingredients comprise the food. In the guaranteed analysis, printed on the package, look for ash content, fiber, water, and certain minerals. If the product has a high-fat ratio (over

10 or 12 percent), the chances are good that it will go rancid; so store it in a cool place, and don't buy a lot at a time.

Next, check the ingredients list; they are supposed to be listed in descending order of percentage by weight. If the first on the list isn't meat, the second one surely should be, since there is a higher BV to meat than to grains and beans. Soybeans have higher protein than corn, but some breeders prefer to have minimal amounts, if any, of soy; so some foods now have wheat as a prime ingredient. Corn is there mostly for energy, bulk, and to provide many vitamins.

After you have determined that the protein is high and the fiber is low, and are satisfied with the digestibility of the ingredients, try one brand for a couple of months, then another one, and see if the dogs did any better on one than the other. The proof lies in how well the dog is nourished and how well he likes it. The amount required to maintain desired condition is also important, because you are paying by the pound. Make sure the dog is worm-free before and during the test, and remember that colder weather will necessitate more food for energy. There are many variables, so you may want to try one dog on one food, a second dog on another, and switch after two months or more.

Supplementation with "People Food"

Fruits and vegetables have most of their nutrients locked away behind cellulose-cell walls of the plant's fibers. However, anything that people eat is often of interest of a people-oriented dog, and raw vegetables and fruits can be considered fun foods. What nutrition the dog gets from them is a bonus in addition to their enjoyment and taste.

The greatest supplementation by volume is in the category of animal tissue: meat, bone, and fat. When treating your dog with hamburger, make it the cheapest available since it will contain more fat. The more expensive hamburger contains a higher proportion of muscle meat which would tend to unbalance his diet.

Liver is truly a miracle food for dogs, contributing many minerals and vitamins in concentrations other foods cannot match. Whether chicken, fish, pork, or beef liver, this organ yields many as-yet unidentified nutrients in addition to the better known ones such as iron and vitamin A. Liver

seems to promote virility in stud dogs, easier delivery in pregnant bitches, and vitality in sick puppies and nursing mothers. Wound healing is accelerated, possibly due in part to the vitamin C content. It may cause loose stools, but simply cut back on the amount fed if this is a problem. Most adult German Shepherd Dogs can easily take between a heaping tablespoon's equivalent and about three ounces without developing stool problems. Pork liver, especially, should be cooked.

There is some disagreement as to the benefits of milk to the canine, but given the expense, the argument may not matter much—milk simply isn't widely used as a food supplement. Some authorities have taught that the adult dog does not produce the enzymes to digest the starches and fats in milk and that is why it causes diarrhea or loose stools. However, recent work shows that if milk is introduced gradually to such an adult, the ability to digest it is developed. Milk is a good enough source of protein and vitamin D, and when soured with a culture to produce yogurt, buttermilk, or sour cream, may be used to counteract the side effects of antibiotics on stomach and intestinal bacteria after ten or fourteen days of treatment. The lactobacillus in such foods is a "friendly" bacterium needed by the dog to help digestion and prevent the growth of "unfriendly" bacteria. Puppies on a regimen of sulfa to combat coccidiosis should be fed cultured buttermilk (not the acid-coagulated kind), yogurt, or another source of lactobacillus about a week or two after antibiotic therapy has begun.

Another frequent addition, especially to the show dog's diet, is an expensive preparation containing certain fatty acids, especially linoleic acid. This can easily be replaced be relatively inexpensive corn oil. A tablespoonful or two should be enough to give better condition to the coat of most German Shepherd Dogs. In addition, the same ingredients are found in lard or bacon drippings.

SPECIALIZED DIETS

While the standard commercially available dry, soft, and canned rations are suitable for most dogs under most conditions, there are times in the life of almost any dog when he needs something different. The bitch may be nursing pups; the dog may be working extremely hard, subjected to cold weather; or they may be sick. Each of these conditions may require a tailored diet.

Illness

German Shepherd Dogs can be prey to a host of microorganisms and genetic disorders that affect their digestion and utilization of nutrients. Diet changes can aid control and/or recuperation.

Anemia is commonly caused by coccidiae and worms. A liquid tonic containing vitamins A and the B complex can help, but if it strikes when you don't have this on hand, a little liver will do until you can get some. About 5 to 10 percent of the anemic pup's total diet by weight can safely be replaced by liver, chopped or pureed, and mixed well with his food. Quantities should be small, so as not to overwork the inflamed stomach or intestines.

Kidney disease historically has been supposed to require a low-protein diet, but recent evidence suggests that the opposite is true, that a high-protein, very digestible food is best. *Hills-Riviana* makes several specialized foods for disease conditions, and since they are sold by veterinarians under the name P/D® (Prescription Diet), you can get both the food and proper medicine from the same source: your local vet.

Pancreatitis in its chronic, subclinical, or often undiagnosed mode, is fairly common in German Shepherd Dogs of certain bloodlines. Signs of pancreatic insufficiency may resemble vitamin-A deficiency and may indeed be related to it, because vitamin A is fat soluble and the pancreas helps in digestion of fats. Supplementation with vitamin A and pancreatic enzymes should be supervised by a veterinarian who is knowledgeable in this area

Ch. Only A Rose Of Billo having a romp in the shallow water.   Photo courtesy Mary Schuetzler, GSDC of A.

''Come on, horse—let's work off some of those calories!''   *Photo courtesy of Margie B. Jones.*

and has been made aware of the genetic nature of the problem in certain lines of our breed.

A dog with the subacute form of pancreatitis may exhibit *coprophagy*, which means he eats his own (or others') stools. It may be that he smells the undigested fats and carbohydrates and instinctively consumes it as food to give those nutrients ''another chance.'' Often, the addition of liver to a low-fat diet and daily administration of enzyme powder or capsules will bring the condition under control or at least improve it. Researchers at Tulane University found that a commercially available enzyme supplement improved blood analysis, neonatal vitality, digestion, and generally better health. The manufacturers of Viokase®, a dried raw pancreatic enzyme brand, have shown that supplement/medicine to be effective in combating nonspecific diarrhea as well as German Shepherd Dog subclinical pancreatitis.

The Pregnant Bitch

It is a mistake to think you need to start supplementing your bitch's diet with minerals as soon as she's been bred. The fetuses don't get over the size of walnuts until the last couple of weeks of gestation and consequently don't need a lot of extra nutrients, being only a tiny fraction of the total bitch-fetus weight most of that time. As the weight of bitch plus pups *in utero* increases, she'll eat more of her normal balanced diet or a higher-BV one, either of which contains adequate calcium in the correct ratio to other ingredients. Don't add more! Even during lactation a bitch will normally wean pups before she ''runs low'' on calcium.

Stress Foods

Working dogs in high-stress situations may require more energy than is found even in high-fat commercial dry foods. These dogs may need a very highly concentrated source of both energy (fats, primarily) and nutrients, and you might not be able to formulate that yourself. A commercial offering called Maximum Stress Diet® is available for racing hounds, military dogs, and those in strenuous all-day work or competition. There are now several such rations on the market.

Broker of Crystaridge CD

9

GENERAL CARE AND INFORMATION

HOUSING

Regardless of your location, one of your dog's basic needs is shelter. This should be a place with shade and a breeze for warm, sunny days, as well as a snug, draft-free place to combat severe weather conditions.

Kennels

Starting with the kennel building, decide whether it will be elaborate or simply a storage/shelter facility. If there are to be many indoor runs, a large, powerful fan on the leeward end of the building will be required for positive air replacement so odors and airborne microbes can be removed. Doors should be constructed of a nonchewable substance, because puppies love to remodel their abodes, and edges or corners should not be made of wood, aluminum, or vinyl. Angle iron, brick, or some other durable material will withstand the test of time.

If you are contemplating the construction of a kennel facility, it is a good idea to visit several boarding, breeding, and training kennels that have different designs. Ask the owner and employees what they like and don't like about every feature and then apply this information to your particular needs.

Surfacing for runs—There are four or five types of outdoor surfaces for housing or exercising dogs. Plain dirt, such as your lawn, is the least satisfactory: the dog will dig holes, will always be filthy and muddy in wet weather, and will likely pick up hookworms. Stools may be difficult to clean up without scalping your lawn in the process, and impossible if your dog has diarrhea. Sand runs have been used by some who believe it greatly improves the compactness of their dog's feet, but that is more an old wives' tale than truth. Sand harbors as many little creatures as does dirt: fleas, mites, chiggers, worm larvae, coccidia spores, and vermin carriers of disease. Every time you scrape up stools, you lose some flooring you will have to replace with manual labor. Gravel is another, more popular surface; if small enough it won't hurt the feet, but if too fine, it can cake up like dirt. Whatever the size, it will be eaten by some dogs. Gravel is picked up by the feet, especially in freezing weather, and tracked into living quarters.

By far the best surface is concrete. Impervious, easy to keep clean, difficult for eggs and larvae to get established unless it is badly cracked, concrete dries quickly in the disinfecting sun and needs no replacement for a lifetime if properly installed. A shovel/scraper combination tool will pick up 99 percent of even the sloppy stools, and the residue, along with pine needles, hair, urine, and whatever is easily brushed or hosed off. Concrete gives the feet a chance to develop normally as long as the pups have a variety of footing for part of their day. The area surrounded by a security fence, or upon which it stands, should be concrete with a slope sufficient to encourage rapid run off of water. This water can drain in a larger gravel apron or be carried off by irrigation pipe.

Although most breeders blame poor feet and pasterns on the surface the dog is raised, heredity is far and away the leading factor. However, a 3-year research program at the Purina Dog Care Center used dogs with no known hereditary pastern or foot defects, and varied the footing, exercise, and food. It was found that heavy puppies of large breeds often lost good tight conformation in their feet during the time they were teething if they were kenneled solely on concrete. Some went from a well-knuckled to a straighter toe joint, with the toes spreading out to some degree as well. Once the dogs had passed the active growing stage (at about 7 or 8 months of age), the danger of smooth, hard floors affecting them had subsided. Varying the surface textures the young dog was allowed to run on before he was seven months old gave a better foot, and if a pup that was raised for a time on smooth hard floors that were spreading his feet was moved to rough-textured flooring, it was found the spreading problem could be halted, but not reversed.

A little cluttered, but convenient. The crates on top are in storage but can be put on the floor if they must be temporarily occupied by an adult, or left where they are to hold a pup until you can move him. The 4 X 4 foot enclosures with 2 x 4 foot door each open to the outdoor concrete runs. Plastic cans to keep mice and insects out of dog food remain uncovered to prevent mold and mildew spoilage.

Shelter in kennel building (see openings in brick lower portion). Primary enclosure with six-foot chain-link provides security, for sanitation concrete floor, food/water area, and shelter from bad weather. Aluminum panels over part of the runs gives additional shade, and rain protection.

Indoor surfacing—I do not recommend any of the waterproof indoor/outdoor carpetings for dog-house use, because of the danger that pups or even some adults will chew, pull, or otherwise damage it, perhaps developing dangerous intestinal obstructions as a result. It is harder to clean than smooth flooring and may take quite a while to dry out. It will also harbor fleas and other vermin.

If your dog sleeps in the house at night or takes occasional snoozes there, provide some throw rugs for him or put a couple of carpet samples at the end of a hallway where he can curl up out of the way. You may find it infinitely better to use vinyl flooring throughout the house and add a couple of such small rugs here and there that can be picked up and washed when they get gritty, or combed and rubbed when hair accumulates. Our dogs prefer the cooler vinyl floor when warm, and the throw rugs keep them from eyeing the furniture when they want a softer surface.

Fences

Fences should be constructed to effectively keep kids and strays out while keeping your dogs in. A first, inner, fence should be a maximum-security one, and chain link is best, since it is extremely difficult to climb, chew, or pull from the posts. You might consider some sort of top for at least one of these 6-foot-high enclosures, to give bitches in season the greatest protection or to contain an escape artist. Corrugated aluminum or reinforced plastic sheets commonly used in construction as roof or wall panels can be laid atop the fence. Heavy aluminum wire or insulated copper wire can then be inserted in holes drilled near the edges and twisted to secure the sheets to the fencing. Copper and most other metals in direct contact with aluminum set up galvanic corrosion that can eat away at the wire or fence, though galvanized fence wire is pretty safe to rest on the aluminum. These tops also provide some shade and limited rain protection, but may sag under a heavy snow load if they have to span more than a 4-foot-wide run without support. Tops made of fence wire often collect twigs and leaves and are a little harder to clean off.

A second outer fence, sometimes called a perimeter fence, encloses the first fence, the building, and whatever free-exercise space you can provide for your dogs. Many people use affordable "hog wire" to construct a 4-foot-high fence with openings approximately 4 to 6 inches square at the top and additional horizontal wires at the bottom to prevent piglets from slipping through. The fence can be stapled to cedar or treated-pine posts sunk at least 2 feet into the ground, or can be secured to steel fence posts with wire. You may be tempted to add poultry fencing to the bottom, but it rusts and gets clogged with weeds, and pups can fairly easily push or pull it aside or climb on it.

Be sure to never leave a dog unsupervised with a choke collar on. One of the best dogs I ever sold, known as "The Wonder Dog of Louisiana" because of his apprehension record, hung himself when his policeman handler left him alone overnight...the "live ring" of such collars can easily be caught on a nail, part of a fence, or other object. Even without the live ring, another dog's jaw can get caught during play, and resultant twisting can strangulate.

An electric fence is the most economical and effective way to prevent puppy escapes and deter adult fence climbers. A single strand of galvanized wire about 6 or 8 inches from ground level, and another closer to the fence top, will keep your perimeter fence intact. You may have to invest in a rotary-whip grass cutter or a chemical weed-killing spray, for if weeds make contact with the wire, they "ground it out," cutting the voltage to below what is needed. The transformer should be mounted in the kennel building, and its ground wire attached to a 10-foot-long iron rod driven deeply into the soil. The soil is one giant electrode, and the "hot" wire the other, and when a dog makes contact with both at once, he completes the circuit. The sensation of electrons running over the surface of his body gives him second thoughts about future contact but does not harm him.

EXERCISE

Whether your dog is a serious competitor or a companion, he must have exercise to release his emotional and physical energy, stimulate intelligence growth, and help keep him in good health in order to ward off diseases and other stresses. To get and keep a dog in this condition, feed him properly and run him often. Road work is a most popular and successful means of conditioning. If you or a friend is a runner or jogger, take the dog along but be careful to choose the running surface with his bare feet in mind. Also, don't expect a new dog or a pup to go twenty miles with you the first time out. At least one company makes a treadmill for dogs, so owners who live in the city or in areas

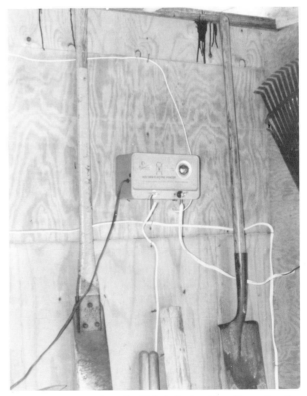

Housing/kenneling plans should include electricity. Shown here is a transformer used to put a charge to a wire around the exercise area; It is called a fence charger, but the charge does not go anywhere until a dog standing on the ground or in touch with the ground by the fence makes contact with the wire. Harmless but effective.

of frequent bad weather can still build up a dog's muscles and endurance.

Whether you run your dog inside or out, be sure to examine his pads before and after each trip to insure there aren't any cuts, and that the pads are not being abraded by too rough a surface. Choose grassy routes free of aluminum-can rings or such dangerous debris as broken glass. Don't run on hot asphalt or macadam (running in the evening or early morning is best), and scout the neighborhood for strays and traffic patterns before choosing your route. Bring along a switch to discourage other dogs and keep *your* dog on-leash for maximum control.

While strenuous exercise that raises the pulse and respiration rates is best for the heart, less demanding activities such as walking and climbing will help build up your dog's muscles and endurance. Ordinary play is also good exercise. A fenced-in yard in which it is possible to build up to full running speed is ideal, and a play partner will keep both dogs in fairly good shape.

Swimming is also excellent therapy for dogs that can't run, and is very good for building up muscles and endurance if properly handled. The main thing to remember is that dogs are not as buoyant as you are and cannot do the backstroke to relax; therefore, swimming is much more strenuous for canines than it is for humans. The dog has to paddle constantly and hard in order to keep his nose above water.

GROOMING

Although it is a characteristic of the German Shepherd Dog, the double coat is not unique to this breed, and the grooming techniques I have found to be best are applicable to many breeds. The soft, fluffy undercoat is very light and somewhat flyaway, while the topcoat is coarse, heavier, usually straight, and imbeds itself like a whipworm into woven fabric, snaking in and out of the warp to defy your best efforts in brushing. Classifying haircoat types on the basis of length, the German Shepherd Dog's is considered to be "normal" or intermediate, compared to the short hair of the Boxer and the long hair of the Chow Chow.

There are a number of reasons for hair loss and the undercoat is often affected at a different time than the topcoat. In bitches about two months away from an estrus cycle, the undercoat typically is released in great hunks if the bitch is not regularly combed, and is very easily drawn out with the comb if she is groomed. This is followed by a considerable loss of topcoat a month later, and is perfectly normal as part of the preparation for the heat and possible litter. In males, the same hormone-initiated change takes place, though on a less dramatic scale, most often in early spring and late summer as a result of the seasonal change. If you see undercoat loss one month, then topcoat loss the next month while the undercoat is growing back, it's probably the

The "Jog-A-Dog," a treadmill designed to exercise dogs inside, avoiding road hazards, tailgaiting, and climate problems.
Photo courtesy H.O. McClure Co.

semiannual molting process. If topcoat is lost first or at the same time and in the same quantities as undercoat, worms are more likely the cause. Look for hot spots, excessive dandruff, or other signs of dermatitis, then check your calendar to see when the dog was last wormed and for what type of worms he was treated. He may have become reinfested or picked up some different larvae. Good grooming begins with good nutrition, and worms inhibit the assimilation of nutrients in the inflamed intestines.

Undercoat

These hairs of the undercoat vary from short, fine, and wavy (described by some as fuzz or down), to thick, slightly longer, fine and wavy with a small bristle on the tip, to even longer, soft with a slightly more visible bristle and waves in the bottom two-thirds. All three types are best groomed with a good undercoat comb. These combs are either brass, steel, or a combination, but all are generally chrome plated. They have rounded teeth for lowered friction and do not scratch skin with normal use. The label may recommend the comb for toy breeds, but

as long as it's sturdy and comfortable to hold, it can be used on your German Shepherd Dog.

Hold the comb so the teeth are perpendicular to the dog's skin, or, if the coat is a real mess, slanted a little so the teeth may be dragged over the coat, but not stuck into it. Comb one small section at a time, in the direction of hair growth, using very short stokes no longer than six inches. You will usually build up a "bank" of fuzz, fur, and some guard hairs at the end of the 6-inch section. Working from one side of the bank, lift it with the comb and pick up the mass of soft hairs with your other hand. When there is no more fuzz coming up and no drag at all on the comb, even if slightly slanted, move on to the next section and repeat the procedure, combing toward the just-finished section. I find it best to start at the tail and work toward the head, so you won't comb into the thick, uncombed areas.

After the entire coat has been combed and you have a hefty pile of wool, go over the dog again combing backwards, against the direction of hair growth, being sure the comb is perpendicular to the skin. Back-combing catches stray undercoat hairs you will miss even with the most fastidious

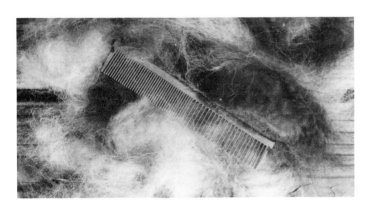

The undercoat comb and the fuzz it removes.

Using the undercoat comb.

first combing. As long as the combing is not too vigorous, only the dead undercoat will come out unless there is a serious skin problem or intestinal parasite infestation.

By removing the dead undercoat, you will also be cleaning your dog because a lot of dirt and debris is loosened and removed in the grooming process. The remaining flakes of dust and dandruff will disappear in a week or two of toweling or brushing with a soft-bristle brush, depending on how dirty the coat was before grooming. Frequent combing will generally prevent this dirt from accumulating, and a regularly groomed dog may never have to be bathed in his lifetime, barring a run through a sewer, skunk's nest, or herd of goats.

Topcoat

Whether you have to remove topcoat because of internal worms or normal seasonal changes, you will need different equipment than you used on the undercoat. The hard, straight (some are slightly wavy toward the roots) guard hairs which are long enough to extend through the crinkly undercoat, defy combing. The teeth of the comb slide between these hairs, which are held in place not only by the skin, but also by static electricity with the adjacent hairs, and catch only the wavy undercoat. The dead topcoat hairs lie side by side with the live coat, but because they are not receiving oil from the follicles, are microscopically ragged, and have different resistance to friction.

During my employment in the rubber polymer industry, I discovered that certain blends of natural and synthetic rubbers have the proper hardness, resilience, and frictional properties to draw out those dead hairs with no pull at all on the live hairs. What rubbing of the live hairs occurs stimulates oil flow, as does bristle brushing. At that time I marketed a molded rubber item shaped like a doughnut, but thicker, which was used for grooming, but you can do as well with the toe of a sneaker, or a piece of shoe sole made from natural crepe rubber. Vinyl and other rubber substitutes are not satisfactory, so if your kid doesn't want to give up his tattered tennis shoe, ask your shoe repair shop for a piece of crepe of the size and thickness used in soling.

Holding this "groomer," stroke the dog firmly in the direction the hair lies. Working from the head

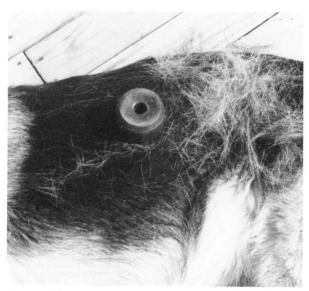

Topcoat. The use of a rubber toy, sneaker, etc. can do a great job in removing dead topcoat. Notice these hairs are straighter, coarser, and of more than one color each, as compared to the undercoat. The white or gray appearance is partly from the hair over the shoulders (left edge of photo) but mostly because the black saddle hairs are not pigmented much further down than the part that shows before pulling them out. A solid black dog will not show this banded feature.

toward the tail, once again, work one section at a time, moving on to the next patch only when no more straight topcoat comes out. Unlike combing, use of the groomer does not build up a bank of fuzz unless the dog has not been combed at all and is losing his undercoat. Rather, the dead topcoat collects in a pile at the end of each stroke, and falls off onto the floor. The groomer is also very effective on the throat and other areas where the soft intermediate type hair (neither hard and long nor wavy and long) grows. Use gentle, upward strokes so you don't make the dog uncomfortable with too much pressure over the trachea.

After combing and grooming, clean the dog by wiping him off with a damp towel to remove any remaining dust and dandruff. If you have a show coming up right away, a lanolin spray might be used, but wipe it all off before entering the ring.

Ear Taping

One of the reasons for the popularity of German Shepherd Dogs with non-dog people is the erect ear which gives the face an alert, appealing look. The head and expression are what sell a dog when a novice is buying. The German Shepherd Dog is one of the relatively few breeds whose standards call for naturally erect ears. With such a demand for the expressive prick-ear look, it is no wonder that both responsible breeders and puppy mills alike have a hard time placing pups whose ears aren't on the way up.

How is the problem of weak ears minimized? Knowing the phenotype of as many of a dog's ancestors as possible will help, especially if the weak-eared ones are close up or the dog is heavily linebred on them. Of course, some will not show the fault themselves, but will pass on the trait to their progeny, so breeding to a weak-eared dog's sire may be almost as dangerous as using that dog himself in your breeding program. Siblings likewise are suspect.

Generally speaking, if the ear base is up by three or four months of age, and the tips are dropped like a Collie's or an Airedale's, don't worry about it for the next six weeks or so. But if the ear carriage resembles that of a Saint Bernard, with the center of the base low and weak, there is a problem, and it's time to get out the erector sets.

I use tape and empty cardboard toilet paper rolls. The best tape is wide tan plastic carton-sealing tape—it is lightweight, waterproof, has good adhesive strength, and a single loop is sufficient. Clean the ears and insert the cardboard half core,

Two methods of training "slow" ears. A piece of "moleskin" (a Dr. Scholls product) is cut to fit into right ear; it has its own adhesive backing. The left ear contains a cardboard core with plastic lightweight tape wrapped around the ear and the form.

cut at a 45-degree angle (see photo this page) taking care not to let it rub against the tubercle of anthelix, which is the large "bump" of cartilage inside the ear. Wrap a precut length of tape, starting at the cardboard form, around the pinna of the ear—without folding any of the ear leather over double on itself—and continue until the tape circle is complete. Do the same on the other ear. If the ears are pointing too far outward, cut a long, narrow strip of tape and loop it around the base of the ears, then pinch it together to form a figure eight. This will draw the ears together toward the center of the head as far as you wish. Check every few days for irritation.

Depending on how much the pup's kennelmates pull at the new apparatus and how much rain the cardboard is exposed to, the arrangement should last anywhere from a couple of days to a couple of weeks. I would rather redo the job than separate a pup from his littermates and deprive him of important peer socialization, but sleeping alone may be required if the others are too curious when you're not there to supervise their behavior. If the ears appeared extremely soft and weak at the base, it's best to keep the forms in (or replaced) and the ears taped longer than you would for ears that are only tipped and lazy.

If the cores need replacing, or irritation occurs, you can cut them out and leave the tape on the back of the ear—it may give enough stiffness so that you might not have to replace the core at all. If so, leave the tape on, or add some for additional stiffness, for a week or more. After removing the core and tape, allow the ears to stand freely, and perhaps after a day without a core or tape they will stand up on their own. If they don't do so in twenty-four hours, give the ear a thorough cleaning and examination for inflammation before putting in a new core. If, instead of flopping over to the front or side, the ears flop over the head and touch or even cross, watch them for three or four days before retaping, as this type of weakness is less serious and less permanent.

At the approximate age of five to six months, most puppies have sore jaws because the large canines and molars begin to cut through (see Chapter 4). This ache will reach clear back to the muscles affecting ear carriage and is why erect ears often "go down" when teething. Sometimes exercising those sore muscles will help. Provide the pup with a chewy toy such as a tough rubber ball to give those muscles extra work. An interesting life will also help, as the pup that is confined within four blank walls or only sees the world through one end of a kennel run will not have his head (and ears) up as much, and thus will do no self training. Massage is also helpful. Pull gently at the base of the ears, rub the muscles of the jaw and top of the head, and play tug of war with an old piece of burlap or rope.

If the ears don't come up and stay up after most of the large teeth have emerged to over 50 percent of their visibility, the prognosis for erect ear carriage is poor. Few are improved after 5½ to 6 months. We had one dog whose right ear was still questionable at eight months, sometimes lying flat on his cranium, but at least it wasn't hanging to the side of his head. We really worked his ears, massaging until our fingers had biceps and retaping until our pharmacist thought we were reselling the stuff (those were the days before we discovered the plastic tape, and bought white surgical adhesive tape). At last we worried them both up, though the right one leaned a little all his life and he had less control of it.

SHIPPING

A dog traveling any distance over a few hundred miles almost has to go by air. If the bitch is to be sent to a stud, if a dog is to join a handler at some show, or a puppy is to be united with his new owner, flying is about the only way to go. Air has proven to be the quickest, surest, safest, and, once upon a time, the most economical means for a dog to get from here to there, but all is not sweetness and light in those usually friendly skies—the requirements for shipping a dog are becoming almost unbearable in some locations. Airline executives, wary of lawsuits, set ridiculous and arbitrary limits on when, how, and where you can ship your dog, over and above the regulations set by the USDA.

In preparation for shipping a dog, call the air freight office and ask detailed questions. What are the airline's ground temperature requirements? How far ahead do you really have to get the dog there if you already have a crate? Do you need to make reservations? What is the weather forecast for the destination city for the time of arrival? How recent does the date of rabies vaccination and health

certificate have to be? Can they include the price of the crate in a C.O.D. shipment?

Contact different airlines, for their rates vary widely. Besides a surcharge for live animals, there are other charges. One is the requirement of a larger crate than is adequate for your pup's comfort. After you've measured the length, width, and height of your crate, phone the air cargo office and ask how much it will be to ship that size crate with dog from point A to point B.

Always try to ship the fastest way. A nonstop flight is best, but a direct flight that may include one or more stops but no change of planes is not bad. A distant third choice is the one-airline schedule with connecting segments using two different planes (because of the long layover required when a dog changes planes, I would not advise a three-plane trip).

Using more than one airline is not advisable, though in some international shipments one might have to accept it as the only way to get the dog there. Transferring air cargo to other lines involves more handling, more people, more chance of error or neglect. It also involves more money, for each will bill you for at least their minimum rate. Dogs don't benefit from joint-fare arrangements, so you could pay more than double. Perhaps some day soon the decreasing costs of frozen semen will make much of the business of shipping bitches unnecessary.

SHIPPING TIPS

Some of the following tips may seem obvious, but are often overlooked:

- Shop around for the best connections, prices, and airports.
- Avoid plane changes at high-traffic airports.
- Look for a line that has a flight that will arrive at the same destination as the one you chose, to use as a backup.
- Ask all the questions listed earlier, and more if you wish.
- Ask about insurance costs. Keep a record of freight cost even if shipped collect.
- Be ready to answer questions such as consignee's name, address, and phone number; the model or dimensions of the crate, if you have one, or

the size of dog if you don't. Make sure a crate will be on hand if you want to buy one.

- Don't feed the dog the day of shipment. Exercise him before putting him in the crate, and give him only a little water before leaving for the airport.

- Try to hustle the dog from car to crate before the agent sees how big he is and tries to move you up to a larger crate.

- Instruct your consignee to have a choke collar or noose leash ready to forestall escape at the destination airport—it happens!

- Be sure to call the consignee and give him the Bill of Lading #.

- Tape a sturdy envelope to the top of the crate with the following information: consignor (that's you) in upper left corner, with address and phone number, consignee name, address, and phone followed by "HOLD FOR PICK-UP AT ____" (use the airport code if you know it, or the name of the airport or city). Inside you can put the pedigree, feeding instructions, letter, worming history, last-minute instructions, and anything else you want. See if the airline wants you to enclose the health certificate or if they want to put it in a separate envelope with the weigh bill.

HOW TO CHOOSE A VETERINARIAN

These days it's difficult to find anyone who has lived in the same town all his life, and as we move from place to place we must start all over with banking, medical, and commercial contacts. This includes finding a new veterinarian. *Don't wait* until you have an emergency to do so; put "find a vet" on your list of "things to do," and don't cross it off until you have found one that will suit your needs.

One method of choosing a veterinarian is to ask breeders for their recommendations. You'll probably get the best advise from those who have been raising pups for the show ring for several years. Go to some kennel club meetings and corner the breeders. If you hear the same reports from two or three who have different breeds, you'll have a good idea of which veterinarians to call for introductory meetings, and possibly which few to avoid. Not all are as nearly perfect as you or they might fantasize, but nearly all have been well-trained and have entered the profession because they have the same compassion for animals that motivated you to get a dog.

Your initial contact will be with the veterinarian's receptionist who can tell you the fees charged, the office hours, whether the doctor is available for emergencies, and other details such as his specialty. Tell the receptionist that you are new in the area and arrange a time to meet with the veterinarian to ask him some questions and to get to know each other.

When you meet with the veterinarian ask enough questions to enable you to make your final decision. In what professional activities and continuing education does he participate? Is he willing to handle breeders differently, such as selling medication without an office visit (after he's assured of your competence), or give a volume rate for litters or several dogs? Are other veterinarians associated with this clinic? Will you be able to make appointments with one or another of the professional staff exclusive of the others? Are there special interests among them that you might draw upon? Finally, do you think you will get along? If you don't like your veterinarian (for whatever reason), it may affect how well you respect him, and eventually you'll be unhappy with him or his work.

Also, don't overlook the facilities. Note how new or adequate the equipment is—*and* how clean. Is the waiting room comfortably arranged—*and* clean? Does this clinic stock "special diets" foods? All these "extras" may be important to you later on, if not at the time of your meeting, and the more thorough you are in your initial examination, the more accurate your choice will be.

THE WORLD AROUND YOU

Your Dog and the Neighbors

There is a very uncivil civil war currently in progress in at least the United States and Canada, and its skirmishes draw relatively minor journalistic coverage. This is not a war of republicans verses democrats or welfare militants against taxpayers, it is the conflict between people who do not own dogs and dog owners. Our civilization is polarized into these two factions in hundreds, perhaps thousands of large or medium cities and smaller towns and villages. Most of the battles, by far, are over dogs that are running loose.

Loose dogs—Nondog people are either neutral or antidog to some extent, sometimes vacillating between the two positions, depending on how often or how recently they've been exposed to loose dogs. There are a lot of folks with or without a dog in their lives who feel a dog should have the "right" to run free. But free-roaming dogs are exposed to many more parasites and diseases than are those that stay home.

Leptospirosis is picked up from urine deposited by other dogs or wildlife, and can be transmitted to humans even if the dog himself has been vaccinated and recently immunized. The principal mode of transmission of parvovirus seems to be infected feces, and other diseases afflicting dogs are spread more rapidly by and among the liberated canines than the protected ones. There is also a minor though real public health hazard involving infected dogs and the people with whom they come into contact. Besides the occasional cases of leptospirosis, humans can pick up scabies, red mange, ringworm fungi, rabies, pinworms, *Echinococcus* tapeworm, hookworm and roundworm larvae, spotted fever ticks, and *giardia lamblia* from dogs and their excreta.

A loose bitch in season attracts dogs from enormous distances and often leads them on a binge lasting many days and leaving a trail of worm eggs, overturned garbage cans, trampled petunias, frightened toddlers, and indignant neighbors along the way. Her roaming romancers are so frenzied and preoccupied that they lose not only weight but sense of direction, and expose themselves to traffic, fights, and irate property owners. Provide your bitch with maximum security for three weeks each time she comes into season, and support intelligent leash/confinement legislation.

In some areas, free-roaming dogs become part-time wild or semiferal animals, often joining in packs to go on nightly expeditions of maiming and killing domestic animals, livestock, and wildlife. Come morning, they're found on the porch, all tuckered out despite what the negligent owner believes was an innocent, restful night of sleep. The western range lands of the US and Canada are not alone in the incidents of sheep, pigs, cattle, and poultry killed or injured by dogs, and attempts to blame the massacre on coyotes won't wash, for wild canids take only what they can eat. Feral dogs can wreak havoc any place they are allowed to roam, and when pet dogs join them, a dangerous pack

is formed. The sweet and lovable farm, rural, or suburban dog on the loose can instantly turn into a killer carnivore.

Dogs ride quieter and safer when in a crate. Some find the crate a great place to nap without fear of getting underfoot.
Photo courtesy Kennel-Aire Mfg. Co., St. Paul, MN.

Property damage—Even dogs that wander no farther than down to the corner cause nondog people to turn into active antidog crusaders. They also irritate responsible dog owners who confine their animals to the leash or a fenced yard. Once or twice a week in nearly every town in the country, many sidewalks, lawns, and driveways are strewn with garbage. The owners come home from work to find the litter that the garbage man naturally refused to rake up. Not only are they obligated to pick up every dime-sized scrap of paper and other trash, but they may have to take their own dog to the veterinarian if it survived a chicken bone splinter through the esophagus or aluminum foil blockage in the intestines.

I've known many irate people who've had their lovely lawns burned yellow in spots and their bushes killed by dog urine. Flower and vegetable gardens and family pets have been damaged or destroyed. Plants, pots, vases, and other items have been knocked off porches and broken, and other personal property has been carried off, never to be found again.

The stool problem—You may have seen the statistics, mostly blown out of proportion, but fuel for the antidog engines nonetheless, on the tonnage of feces and urine dropped by dogs. If you calculate that America's 65 million owned dogs (⅔ of Humane Society of the United States's pet population estimate) leave an average of ½-pound of feces every day, the total amounts to over 16,000 *tons*! The same dogs would in a 24-hour period pour over 167 *million* gallons of urine into our ecosystem without benefit of septic tank or sewage disposal plant's chemical treatment. Fortunately, the vast majority of these pounds and gallons are neutralized by nature before getting into our water supply.

With these statistics in mind, it is simple to understand the irritation felt by many nondog people. But responsible dog owners are able to somewhat combat the problem. First, they make themselves aware of their community's ordinances affecting the disposal of feces. Next, they follow those recommendations or, if their community offers no guidelines, they responsibly clean up after their dogs. The one-dog owner may carry plastic bags with him to scoop feces, or he may use a devise called a scooper to facilitate the process.

However, kennel owners have a bigger problem due to the greater number of dogs in his care. The responsible owner may deposit stools in vacant fields and turn the ground there once a year (or more often). Most well-planned kennels actually have a septic tank to handle the problem. This is the cleanest, easiest, and safest method of disposal, although not entirely labor-free. Others construct a simple trench along the back of the property and fill it in as necessary.

In short, responsible owners are aware of the stool problem and the resultant irritation—and they *do* something about it! Not only do they keep their own place neatly picked up, but they police other areas where their dogs may deposit their wares—places such as picnic grounds and rest stops along the highway. These people do much in the way of removing a great deal of ammunition from the guns of the antidog population.

Noise—Barking dogs may be the greatest stimulus for people to call the police, hire a lawyer to sue you, stir up the neighbors against you, or take any combination of these actions. Getting back to sleep when one is angry is extremely difficult, and anger easily forms at the sound of a barking dog.

You must teach your dogs to bark at night only when truly necessary. If it requires you running out to the kennel in your robe, even in winter, do so. It'll cost you some sleep, but better stop the habit before it gets stronger. Use the muzzle-squeeze (see Chapter 20) and let the miscreant know you are displeased. Be firm, and you will have to get out of bed less frequently as the dog learns. If you don't know which one of several barked, scold and squeeze them all.

Crating the dog works, but keeps him from performing the guard duties for which the breed is known. Most of us who breed have outdoor kennel runs or yards for most of our dogs. Electronic collars that shock when the dog barks are very expensive and may teach the dog *not* to alert you when there is an intruder. Training is the best solution.

Dognapping

The theft of dogs is a practice that is practically impossible to stop. Part of the reason may be the high success rate of amateurs and professionals alike; hence the large number of people active in the trade.

But what else motivates these people to steal dogs? One reason is the big money paid by research labs for stolen dogs. In reality, this is a *very small* market for the dognapper as most labs raise their own dogs or obtain them through known suppliers who breed specifically for that market and can regularly deliver dogs of a given age, size, and medical and genetic background. Nevertheless, a black market does exist for stolen dogs—usually a second-rate company willing to take fewer precautions when it comes to the reputation and reliability of their suppliers. The dogs usually get there because somewhere between your back yard and the final middleman, a con artist has told a convincing lie about the dog's origin. Occasionally, crime syndicate figures are involved.

More often these days, a junkie needing money for a "fix" will steal dogs and dispose of them in one of at least a couple of ways. German Shepherd

Dogs, Doberman Pinschers, Rottweilers, and similar breeds are sold to guard dog training schools. These schools are not necessarily reputable, and few will probe deeply when there's a bargain to be had. Perhaps your club could get a state legislator to sponsor a bill requiring such buyers to get positive identification from their suppliers, which would inhibit many stolen dog sales.

Some thieves have the patience to run ads and sell dogs through the newspapers, but the more frequent alternative is the classical dognapping-for-ransom idea. In this scam, the thief may run an ad in the Lost and Found column, describing the dog and noting that he would accept a reward for taking care of it. Or he may watch the Lost column and answer the ads most closely resembling his hot property. This alternative is less risky since the dognapper need not give a phone number or identification to the newspaper. Should you find yourself on the receiving end of an extortion attempt, enlist the help of specialists at your police department.

Less patient thieves will unload the stolen dog as fast as they can, often to a semi-conscious bar patron who will fall for the hard-luck story and pay $20 or $50 for a good-looking dog. Or, just as "hot" watches, TVs, and appliances find their way to bargain hunters, so do "hot" dogs. These buyers, of course, risk being accessories to the crime just as they do when receiving any stolen item.

Prevention—A tattooed dog is a well-protected dog. Tattoos, if noticed by professional dog thieves, will cause them to drop dogs as if they were hot potatoes. A tattoo may not be noticed by the amateur, but the "fence," the laboratory, or the guard dog school may spot it and turn the dog away or turn the dognapper in.

Many clubs hold tattoo clinics for public benefit; an organization called National Dog Registry (NDR) is in the forefront of this effort, and can give the details of organizing such a project. For a fee, your information is kept on file and when someone finds a dog with a tattoo number he can call NDR and track down the owner. NDR advertises frequently, and most veterinarians and some police departments have their phone number. In some cities, similar groups operate lost dog services; if your town does not have such an organization, consider starting one. The Society of St. Francis, a "hotline" operation for stolen or lost pets in Chicago, was started in 1975 by one concerned citizen.

I recommend the use of AKC registration numbers for tattooing since dogs will normally change ownership at least once, but will never change registration numbers. If the dog is not (yet) registered, a litter number can be used: K-5, for example, would be the fifth pup from the K litter. If the dog is not to be registered, the owner's social security number would be the best choice.

Several exhibitors with tattooed dogs put window or bumper stickers on their vans, and signs on their fences stating that the dogs are tattooed, thus hoping to discourage thefts. This undoubtedly works, as identification of stolen goods is something a thief must avoid. The most modern method of positive identification involves a microchip injected under the skin. It can be "read" by a scanner connected to a computer.

Public Relations

In order to foster a better image for dog owners and dogs, join with action organizations such as the American Dog Owners Association or local ad hoc committees. You may need to form your own breeders' or dog owners' rights group, but your fight for your rights to enjoy dogs will be enhanced if you serve the community or hold a public benefit function.

One place to start would be the nearest animal shelter or humane society. You may choose to

Your dog is your only philosopher.

Plato, 375 B.C.

volunteer to work there or you may persuade your club to donate a portion of their show proceeds. Some clubs rent the humane society's meeting rooms to hold obedience classes, a few show HSUS films at school assemblies to educate people on proper care, humane treatment, and the dangers of overpopulation. The Humane Society of the United States is located at 2100 "L" Street, Washington, D.C. 20037, and they'd be happy to send you sample flyers and a list of available films. On the whole, humane societies need your support and leadership, and there are more than one thousand animal protection organizations in North America. The vast majority are local groups, and at least one of them could use your help.

On your own, or in the company of other club members, take your cuddly puppies and pettable pets to visit folks who may like dogs but can't keep them. Take your friendliest dogs, not just your show winners. The majority of the public does not know the difference, and what they need is not bragging about pedigrees but the sheer joy of getting an affectionate response from a dog. "The worst dog waggeth his tayl," said the British writer J. Florio around 1578. So bring your tail-waggers to the orphanages, rest homes, retarded children's schools, and you'll derive the added benefit of making friends for the breed and neutralizing the anti-dog forces.

At your next show, your club could set aside one ring to be designated in the judging program, as a "petting ring." You could invite a group from a school for retarded persons to be special guests of your club, and ask for volunteer "petters" when the premium list is sent out.

Contact your nearest Public TV station and see if they'd like to do an educational program about dogs. If there's a "talk show" on one of the radio stations, maybe you could persuade a couple of your more experienced club members (perhaps a judge and a handler or long-time breeder), to be guests and answer questions phoned in by listeners with real concerns or problems. Our club used to arrange for veterinarians to be occasional guests so dog fanciers would not get drawn into giving medical advice on the air.

Hold a charity "Walk-A-Thon" on behalf of the Animal Welfare League or the Children's Hospital or whatever group needs some help. With the local government's blessing, you could solicit funds from businesses and individuals with the assistance of man's best friend at your side. Most people are curious enough, seeing someone with a dog at his door, to ask and listen.

Is there a crafts program at the Senior Citizens Center? If so, perhaps you could commission these craftsmen to make special trophy awards, thereby putting your trophy money to more beneficial use once in awhile. Don't worry about affecting entries—people don't enter shows for trophies, they want the purple or blue ribbon.

Tax your fertile imagination for more ideas, and get together for a brainstorming session where each idea will stimulate even more. Be of service to your community, and sooner or later the public will repay you; even if they don't, your very acts will be reward enough.

The New Skete monks at supper, with their dogs on down-stay, learning patience and compatability.

Photo courtesy M. Schuetzler, GSDCA.

The author happily awards Best Puppy (all-breed) to a GSD bred by Margie and Gail Jones. Gail handling, while Boots Rogers of States Kennel Club awards trophy.

10

HOME HEALTH CARE AND FIRST AID

Veterinary medicine evolved from the practice of animal husbandry which was the art of healing, breeding, feeding, and caring for domestic animals. Today breeders could as well be called practitioners of animal husbandry since the rising costs of veterinary care have induced many to revert to "doing it themselves." In this chapter I offer practical tips that will save you money and spare your veterinarian for the jobs that require his or her special skills. However, if you have the slightest question about any of this medical information *do* consult your veterinarian. Also, if you doubt your ability to perform any of the procedures outlined, let your veterinarian handle them for you.

ROUTINE CARE

Body Temperature

A rectal thermometer with a little *Vaseline®* or *Panalog®* on it will easily slip three inches or more into the rectum. Lie the dog on his side to lessen the danger of his running off or sitting. Dogs have a normal body temperature of around 101 to 102.5 degrees F. The farther off the reading is, and the longer it stays abnormal, the more likely it is that the dog has a fever—or in the other direction, hypothermia—and should be treated. If you take a temperature right after the dog has been lying in the sun or exercising, take it again twenty minutes later after cooling him off in the shade.

Body temperatures of new puppies can be lower than that of a normal adult. The importance of supplying heat in the first several days of life is

discussed in Chapter 19. It is also not unusual for bitches in the last days of gestation to show a temporary drop in temperature.

Pulse

You probably won't be able to tell much by taking the pulse, unless there isn't one or it's racing for no reason, but you might be interested in learning how to take it and what is normal for your dog. The heartbeat can be felt on the chest wall just behind the elbow, but an accurate count at that location may not be possible because of breathing motions. A more accurate spot is inside the thigh where it meets the groin where the femoral artery runs close to the surface.

The dog's normal heartbeat is somewhat erratic, but the pulse will probably be similar to or lower than your own. Generally speaking, if your German Shepherd Dog has less than 45 or more than 100 beats per minute after resting for at least 10 minutes, it may be abnormal yet not an emergency unless other signs indicate poor health or distress. If the beat is irregular, don't worry—that's quite common. Under anesthesia, the dog's heartbeats typically even out to a very regular rhythm.

Hematomas

When a dog receives a crushing or shearing blow, the attachment between the skin and its underlying tissues can be disrupted, with small broken lymph vessels and capillaries discharging serum and blood into the area beneath the skin. The swelling

A length of folded rubber tubing used to drain a seratoma, when draining by hypodermic syringe a few times doesn't work. This is surgery only your vet can perform.

due to that fluid accumulation is called a hematoma, and is similar to a big blister, but contains blood. If it is mostly lymphatic fluid and very little blood, it is usually called a seratoma.

To drain a hematoma with a hypodermic syringe, insert the needle at a shallow angle so that fluid flows easily into the syringe, then remove the plastic part, leaving the needle alone in the hematoma. Very slight pressure with your fingers may help, and you may have to do it again several hours later but don't leave the needle in during the meantime.

Ear-flap hematomas occasionally occur in the German Shepherd Dog, and other hematomas can happen over a flat bone, such as the skull. If drainage with a hypodermic needle does not allow the skin to reattach itself to the muscles and connecting tissue, a small incision may have to be made by the vet to allow drainage. If the swelling keeps returning, take your dog to the veterinarian for surgery, bandaging, and an antibiotic.

Anal Glands

Much needless work and worry is generated over the topic of anal gland impaction, but you should know how to express the sacs yourself if this does become necessary. The sacs are supposed to have *some* fluid in them, but if there is obvious discomfort squeeze them out and check for an obstruction.

On each side of the anal sphincter, in the 4- and 8-o'clock positions are the tiny, sometimes invis-

ible openings to the anal sacs. Use plenty of paper towel to cover the spot and gently but firmly squeeze the outside of these openings simultaneously, applying pressure to force out the contents. A strong-smelling fluid should come out but if it doesn't, put your finger inside the rectum and squeeze one side at a time between this finger and your thumb which is opposite the anal sac being expressed. If the fluid is very dark and you need to repeat the procedure, insert the tip of a *Panalog* tube and flush out the sac with the ointment. Tubes with a long narrow tip—like a blunt needle— are available from your veterinarian. (The same type of tube is used in flushing out the swollen area under the eyelids of neonatal pups with conjunctivitis. Because the tube is made of tin, it will not allow anything back into it, and cleaning the tip prepares it for further use in eyes, anal sacs, or puncture wounds.)

Mouth Bleeding

Active dogs frequently will present with blood running from the mouth, although the amount being lost is usually magnified by the owner's imagination. Blood spread throughout the mouth is a sight that panics many dog owners, but it is not always a situation demanding emergency care.

The cause of bleeding may be the tongue which is sometimes sliced or nicked on any of a variety of things, but the cut is seldom deep enough to warrant sutures. Rinse out the mouth with cold water and examine the wound. During your examination, check the inside of the cheeks and lips, especially around the carnassials and canine teeth since sometimes these areas will be pierced by a tooth. Look for wood splinters between teeth, abrasions and punctures in the gums, and examine both the top and bottom of the tongue. Once you have found the location of bleeding, watch the area and in a day or two you should notice a lump or scab which indicates healing. However, if the area swells, oozes pus, and continues to do so, a visit to the veterinarian is in order. Naturally, if on your initial examination you find that bleeding is profuse and the wound is large, you will contact your veterinarian.

Dental Hygiene

Dogs seldom develop cavities but they do experience a normal pattern of wear beginning at the lower middle incisors and gradually extending to blunt canines and premolars in old age. Build-up of tartar should be cleaned off periodically. The frequency depends on how rapid the accumulation and how interested you are in your dog's appearance. Dry food, hard dog biscuits and rawhide chewies are helpful in slowing tartar deposit formation, but none of these is a cure-all.

Most of the tartar builds up on the biggest cheek teeth where they touch the cheek lining, and on the upper canines; the tongue seems to keep the inside surfaces "wiped off." There are a couple of ways to remove the hard tartar shell—one being the use of regular dental picks. However, with a patient that is not very patient, there is the danger of puncturing or lacerating gums and lips with those sharp instruments. What I have found much easier and safer is a very short-bladed screwdriver. With one of my thumbs or fingers over the opposing teeth and gums, a sudden loosening of the plaque or wiggling of the dog is harmless to both of us. Push the gum back and exert a strong scraping motion toward the point of the tooth (see below). Press hard.

Distemper Teeth

Yellowish, grayish, or unevenly stained teeth may result from either the virus itself or from the vaccine, though the latter is uncommon. If your dog has such a tooth condition, it may be that he had been given a tetracycline antibiotic at some point. Dog show judges should lay no importance to such stains; however, if it's obvious that tartar is the cause of discoloration, the judge is not going to get a good overall impression. Most veterinarians recommend brushing the dog's teeth with bicarbonate of soda, or a nonfoaming, slightly abrasive cleanser.

Laryngitis

German Shepherd Dogs that are not properly trained may bark excessively and develop a sore larynx if allowed to persist. If you come home from work some night to find your dog greeting you with a whisper and a wag, find out if he had been bark-

Scraping tarter off teeth the easy way. When your dog gets used to lying still for this, you can graduate to a dental scaler.

ing a lot. If so, rest from barking will cure him. If not, look at his tonsils and take his temperature. If he has been kenneled in the past couple of weeks he may have picked up kennel cough, in which case he'll probably be wheezing, coughing, or gagging, and may show discomfort when swallowing.

Inspecting the Skin

Get into the habit of petting your dog and scratching him on various parts of his body. You thereby can find ticks, tumors, cysts, and other skin problems before they get serious. Often a thorn will be found imbedded in a cyst or sac of pus under the skin. Sometimes you'll find flea excrement or signs of other problems that are easiest to correct when detected early.

SPECIFIC SITUATIONS

Eye Treatment

Removing foreign objects such as seeds, lashes, or grit from the eyes is not difficult unless you're doing it on a struggling puppy. With your thumb, pull down the lower lid, exposing the conjunctiva—you'll almost always find the offender there. With your other hand, touch a dry, lint free piece of cloth or paper towel to the matter with a gentle sweeping motion. Your fingertip will do as well most of the time, but it must be clean and dry. Sometimes a thorn or splinter will stick in some tissue around the eye, and blunt-nosed tweezers may be needed. *If you are not absolutely sure of your control over your dog, leave this up to a veterinary surgeon.*

Applying medicine to the eye is easy, once you've taught your dog the sit-stay. Pull the lower lid down with your thumb, squeeze the tube of ointment, and lay the "worm" of medicine in the pouch you have created with the eyelid. Your veterinarian can sell or prescribe an ophthalmic preparation—*never* use anything that has not been approved for use on the eyes. If you have stored the tube in the refrigerator to prolong its shelf life, let it warm up before using. If the expiration date on the label has expired, or if the label has fallen off and the box has been lost, throw the tube away and get a fresh one.

After applying the ointment or dropping liquid medicine directly onto the eyeball, close the lid and gently, briefly, massage the closed eye. If the eye

is abraded, don't massage, just wait for blinking motions to spread the medication.

Removing sutures from or close to eyelids is a little trickier. If you are capable of doing fine, close work and can talk your pup into relaxing, you may want to remove the sutures yourself in the quiet and comfort of your own home. Because some hair may have grown that is the same color as the suture material, count the stitches as you remove them, comparing the number with your records to determine that you got them all. Some sutures can be removed in ten days, but those on the head and those that are holding a long incision, such as on the belly, should stay in longer, usually about two weeks.

Oral Medication

Medicines given by mouth can be in liquid or solid form, but must reach the back of the mouth in order to trigger a swallowing reflex. It will help greatly if you have taught your dog the sit-stay, as it's quite difficult to administer medicine to a dog that is wiggling on his back, and when he's standing it's next to impossible to tilt the head back far enough for positive results. The dog is likely to walk backwards if he's standing.

Sit the dog and put one foot behind his tail (which you've curved around close to his haunches) or put him in a corner so he cannot back up or stand. To open the mouth, bridge the top of the muzzle with the thumb and press inward with one or two fingers behind the "eye teeth" (upper canines). Until the dog gets used to this, you may want to use the other hand in the same manner from beneath the jaw in order to prevent squirming. Teach your dog to open up and hold his head still so you can push the pill to the back of the tongue. Before *Heartgard®*, my adult dogs had enough daily *Caracide®* that they all knew the command "Sit. Open."

With your free hand, hold the pill between thumb and finger or between two fingertips and place it far back on the center of the tongue, quickly closing of the mouth. Hold the muzzle shut loosely until your dog licks his nose, which is an almost infallible sign that he has swallowed.

When giving solid medicine to very small puppies you must push it down the throat farther than you might for an adult or larger pup. To ensure a swallow, you may want to splash a little water onto his nose to make a reluctant little one lick his nose before you release his muzzle and look into his mouth to see if he fooled you or not. We teach our pups to give us a little ''kiss'' on the cheek or ear, thus starting the lick-swallow action.

Liquid medicine can be given in a variety of ways. When pups are three to eight weeks old use an eyedropper, or a small syringe (without the needle, of course). As the pups grow older, a spoon may be handier and hold more, but it may also be harder to maneuver. Use a larger syringe, but make sure you clean it by rinsing well, or take it apart and put it in the dishwasher with the forks and knives. In either case, get the liquid onto the back of the tongue where it will elicit that swallowing response.

Injections

If you are comfortable with the idea of giving your dog injections, your veterinarian can teach you how and where to safely use the needle. Some people recommend swabbing the injection site with alcohol to sterilize it, but I never bother, nor do most of the veterinarians I know. One veterinarian told me he thought it bad procedure to rub the site with alcohol because it did nothing more than stir up the dirt, but follow your own veterinarian's suggestions.

Two types of injections are used: intramuscular and subcutaneous. Both are easily learned, simple to perform, and you are much better off if you get your veterinarian to teach you. The intramuscular injections (i.e., steroids, rabies vaccine) can go into any muscle, but the thickest and safest to use are the thigh muscles. Subcutaneous injections are perhaps the easiest to perform, and include parvo, DHL, DNP, and many other types of vaccines and medications. Another method of injecting medicine is in the vein, but this is more difficult and should not be done at home unless you have been thoroughly instructed by your veterinarian.

Suppositories and Enemas

When a dog cannot take oral medication, and the medicine is not suitable for injection, you may find it in suppository form. These torpedo- or cylinder-shaped items are made with a wax base and may be formulated or coated with petroleum jelly. The suppository and coating melt at body temperature and allow the medication to spread throughout the rectum and lower colon where it is absorbed into the blood capillaries in the lining.

Suppositories are often given to treat constipation. Sometimes just the presence of something in the rectum will stimulate defecation, particularly if the substance is irritating. This is why many show exhibitors will put a couple of paper matches in a dog's rectum to stimulate elimination before entering the ring. If a suppository doesn't relieve constipation, the next step is the enema. The most commonly used is made with a mild soap in a dilute solution. Also used are dilute salt or baking soda solutions.

Use an infant-size enema nozzle, a hot water bottle or enema bag and tube. About one ounce of solution for every ten pounds of body weight is a good rule of thumb. After the nozzle has been inserted, the dog lying on his side, hold the container of solution about two feet or less above the dog so the pressure won't be too great and let gravity drain the solution into the dog.

Dips

A dog with a skin condition or external parasites may need to be ''dipped,'' a term which is a holdover from the days when cattle and sheep were driven through a ditch filled with insecticide. The farmer usually tossed the dogs in afterwards. Now, it also includes sponging or spraying the dog with the pesticide emulsion.

Mix the medicine with water according to directions, then soak a small towel in it. Lift the towel out and squeeze the excess liquid back into the jar or bowl. With the dog lying on his side, rub him briskly with the towel, squeezing more liquid out and soaking the hair down to the skin. If practical, perform this operation in the area in which the dog is accustomed to lying so that whatever spills may attack the pests there. Sprays are less efficient, so push the coat backward while spraying in order to reach the skin, then massage it in.

Most dips are pesticides, and depending on what kind is used and frequency of application, you may want to wear waterproof gloves, especially if you have cuts or scratches on your hands. Comb your dog thoroughly before treatment or you'll waste a lot of the substance on dead hair which will quickly be shed. A shampoo first will also improve application by removing hair oils and dirt that might decrease effectiveness.

Ear Medication

In German Shepherd Dogs, possibly the most common ear problem other than genetic weakness is fly-bite dermatitis which, if not prevented or arrested, can cause the loss of part of the ear leather. A fly repellent made by the Ralston Purina Company for use on horses does an excellent job of keeping all sorts of flies off my dogs. It comes in a plastic container with a flip-top spout which is very convenient for putting a drop or two on the front and back surfaces of the ear tips. If your dogs are bothered by deer flies or similar pests, also put a drop on the muzzle and on the stop since these are favorite spots for bloodsucking deer flies. Daily application of the repellent should be sufficient, but in humid weather you may need to increase the frequency of application. Also apply some whenever there's a prediction of rain, for this is the time flies are most annoying.

Mites are the next most common ear malady. They require an insecticide to get rid of them, and such preparations are available from your veterinarian.

Before applying the insecticide clean the bulk of the debris out of the ears by using a commercial wax softener (about 10 drops) for about a 3-minute soak, then wrap a paper towel around your finger and vigorously "ream" the ears out. Finally, remove the rest with a cotton-tipped swab. The waxy black substance you see is digested blood and wax—fecal matter from mites—and may contain mites even though you can't see them without a magnifying glass. Dispose of the used swabs and paper towels in fire or drop some insecticide on

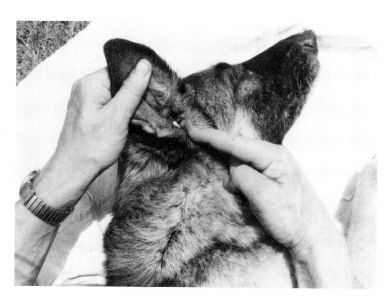

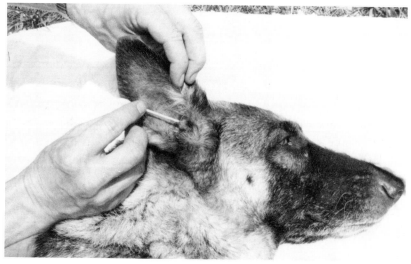

Illustrating how far you can actually insert a "Q-Tip." This one's lower end is resting against the eardrum. By pulling strongly on the pinna (see left hand) the angle between the horizontal canal and vertical canal becomes straight enough to allow passage of the cotton swab stick. Don't push the swab further than shown here (upper tip just below tubercle of anthelix) or force it hard against the drum. Keep turning the swab in only one direction both in and coming out.

Old bitch with chronic inflammation of ear and pinna. A "Q-Tip" is used as a pointer to indicate the tubercle of anthelix, the largest "bump" in the ear. The white hairs nearly an inch forward of her eye resulted from scar tissue formation following being bitten by a kennelmate.

them before putting them into the garbage. When the ear is clean and the cotton gets only slightly stained after wiping all the little corners, put a few drops of the ear-mite insecticide (according to directions) into the ear. If the ear has been cracked, add a few drops of neomycin sulfate ointment.

Ear mites are sometimes found even on the tip of the tail and, if left untreated, will eventually work their way up to the head. In order to assure the destruction of *all* mites, use a mange dip on the dog when you treat the ears. Your veterinarian will be able to provide you with an effective preparation, or ask him about using ivermectin.

Local Sores

Burns, cuts, and wounds that tend to form dry scabs respond best to greasy ointments such as *Panalog®* , a brand of neomycin sulfate in a petroleum-jelly base. Extended use of antibiotics such as this can promote fungus growth, so a fungistat or fungicide may be one of the ingredients added by the manufacturer. As they are greasy, these preparations may pick up dirt and necessitate washing and reapplication.

Vaseline® or vitamin E are alternative treatments. Puncture a vitamin E capsule with a needle, squeeze some of the oil onto your fingertip, and massage it onto the burn or cut. Pop the rest of the capsule(s) into the dog's mouth.

A moist or oozing sore may respond better to a dry preparation such as sulfa powder or neomycin sulfate in dry form. Hold the little plastic jar upside down, point the tip at the wound, and tap the bottom lightly to drop some powder onto the lesion. Squeezing the bottle will cause the powder to go everywhere *except* onto the sore.

FIRST AID

First aid is a matter of knowing what to do until professional help is available. One who administers initial emergency treatment should be able to recognize some symptoms of serious disorders. The troubleshooting guide(See Appendix) has been designed to educate and partially fill that need.

Although certain specific recommendations must be made, one general principle applies to most emergencies: Do whatever is opposed to what happened. For overheating, lower the temperature; for extreme cold, warm the dog; for bleeding, apply pressure to stop the flow.

Restraint

A dog in pain may snap wildly and unintentionally bite and/or scratch the person attempting to help him. A quick muzzle can be fashioned from a roll of gauze, surgical tape, or a strip of rag. Make sure the dog's tongue is in his mouth before closing the teeth and tightening the knot. Of course, the muzzle will not be needed if the dog is unconscious, having trouble breathing, or injured in the area of the mouth.

If you have quick reflexes and are stronger than the dog, grasp him with the thumb and first or second finger of one hand just behind the skull and in front of the winged first vertebra. With the other hand or arm lift the dog by the chest or belly, as getting the dog's feet off the ground gives you a much greater advantage. Once the dog is restrained, you can proceed to give him the necessary treatment.

Cuts and Contusions

If a dog is bleeding, try to stop the flow by pressing a wad of cloth against the wound. If it's a serious cut, hold the cloth in place until you can get someone to drive you to the veterinarian. If it is less serious, you might be able to bandage it and do your own driving. Tape should not directly touch the wound, but should be long enough to pull flesh from both sides of the cut toward the center, closing the bandage around the wound and promoting clotting. This will also help stanch the blood flow and keep out dirt.

A tourniquet applied between the cut and the heart may help if an artery has been severed, but in many cases is not possible or effective. For instance, most cuts involving the femoral artery are so high in the groin that nothing can be done, and it isn't a good idea to put a tourniquet on the neck, yet these are the two places where arteries of significant size are closest to the skin; most others are well protected under deep muscles. Because of the danger of gangrene, some people advise not leaving a tourniquet in place for more than twenty minutes, but loss of blood may be far more dangerous than any risk of infection. Best concentrate on getting to the clinic fast, and, if possible, alert the staff that you're on your way.

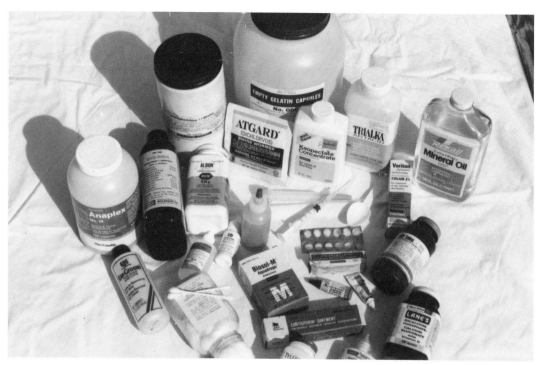

A typical medicine box's contents. Starting at lower right and spiraling inward: calcium diphosphate for nursing bitches; sulfa powder for wounds; Tylenol (do not use—recently found to be unsafe); cotton and swab sticks; ear wax softener; Anaplex (dichlorophene and toluene) for tape, round, and hookworms; Oto-derm or Panalog neomycin sulfate, two jars of sulfa tablets (Albon and sulfaguanadine) for coccidiosis and other infections; dichlorvos (Atgard sold for pigs, but can be used in place of Task if your vet approves) for round, hook and whipworm; empty gelatin capsules for Atgard and other bitter or distasteful medicines; Kaopectate concentrate; antacid; mineral oil for constipation or poisoning; Variton cream for moist ecsema and other skin lesions; jar of Difil (Caracide equivalent) for heartworm prevention; Dramamine; chloromycetin ointment for eyes (conjunctivitis); two other tubes of eye salves (erythromycin and zinc/neomycin); cortisone cream for hot spots and other skin inflammation; Biosol-M for diarrhea; Confite anti-fungal ear lotion; Otocide (rotenone) for ear mites; applicator bottle for neomycin sulfate lotion; hypodermic needle and syringe. Anything with an expiration date I keep refrigerated unless I'm sure to use it up well before that date, but follow label and veterinarian's directions. Add to this collection whatever you need and are capable of administering, but always check with your veterinarian if you want to use something for an extended period or something out of the usual routine.

Flush less serious wounds with water, as it is likely there will be dirt in them. Follow this washing with a good cleansing, using hydrogen peroxide, Merthiolate, tincture of iodine, or rubbing alcohol. Get the dog sutured within twelve hours if possible, or the borders of the wound may have to be sliced off to provide fresh surfaces that can knit together.

One fairly common cut which can vary greatly in extent is the sliced foot pad. Running, swimming, or playing in strange or littered areas often results in such unexpected injury from glass or metal scraps, and it seems this usually happens when you are far away from your regular veterinary clinic. Rinse with water (and peroxide if available), follow with an antibiotic such as neomycin sulfate or an antiseptic such as iodine, then place the foot on several layers of gauze or clean cloth in a wad that is then folded over the foot. Secure with tape

but leave some cloth exposed for air circulation, since the foot pad is the main place where dogs perspire, and moisture building up inside a tight envelope can interfere with healing and promote bacterial growth. A sock covering over the bandage will prevent the dog from loosening the tape. The dressing should be inspected frequently and changed when necessary. Keep the dog from walking too much or better yet, rig up a sling to keep the affected limb flexed so the dog cannot touch the ground with the foot. Keep in mind that a really nasty cut may need sutures.

If you get bleeding from trimming a nail too closely, keep the dog off the carpeting until it stops. If you insist on a quick stop, dip the bleeding nail in a little styptic powder or all-purpose flour.

Punctures (from sharp sticks, cat claws, etc.) easily become infected, so look carefully for such holes and point them out to your veterinarian. Usually they will be found where there is some swelling, so use your fingers in the search. Once located, you might want to cut hair from around such wounds, but try not to let much fall into them. First aid for puncture wounds involves vigorous rubbing of the area with peroxide or rubbing alcohol on a clean rag or piece of cotton.

Shock

Most injuries result from dog fights or from encounters with automobiles. Often the scrapes and external bleeding may appear minor, but a more serious internal injury may lie hidden. If you notice paling gums and tongue, a weak pulse or very fast heartbeat, depression, and lowered body temperature, the dog is most likely in shock. Keep the dog warm and calm while you determine whether there are broken bones or abdominal swelling which may indicate internal bleeding or a ruptured bladder. Don't take a long time with your examination as you should call or have someone else immediately call the veterinarian.

If a long-muzzled dog has stopped breathing, mouth-to-nose resuscitation may be very difficult, but artificial respiration by rhythmic pressure over and just behind the last rib can be dangerous if there is a chest puncture or abdominal injury. Make sure the mouth and nasal passageways are clear for breathing, and try to keep the head level with the body until you reach the animal hospital.

Broken Bones

Fractures are not usually emergencies unless there is a lung puncture, or the bone is protruding through the skin. Your veterinarian may want to see the dog right away, but will seldom want to set the bone until the swelling goes down in a day or two. In the meantime ask about splinting, though dogs are smart enough not to put weight on a broken leg unless on strong pain killers.

Heatstroke

I've seen a number of dogs succumb to overheating, a couple of them collapsing after running around in an outdoor show ring on a hot day after waiting in the sun for their classes. Dogs on their own in even the largest enclosures will not exert themselves in such a way, and unfortunately,

human encouragement is often to blame for such attacks.

The most frequent circumstance in bringing on heatstroke is leaving a dog in a car in the sun, whether or not the windows are partly or fully closed—it doesn't even have to be a hot day. Confinement without shade, and exercise in the sun and heat are the next most frequent factors.

Quickly bring the heatstroke victim's temperature down. Some recommended methods are: cold water hosing or covering with cold wet towels, air conditioning and cold-water enemas. If you don't have a rectal thermometer handy, watch for symptoms, such as rapid panting, to subside. Keep your veterinarian advised; he may ask you to bring the dog in right away, because it is easy to confuse the symptoms of torsion with those of heatstroke.

Throat Obstructions

If your dog has a stick, chicken bone, or similar object lodged in the throat, you *may* be able to get it out with your fingers if he'll hold still. If you have a pair of kitchen tongs—the kind that operate like forceps—see if you can reach the object and remove it while you hold the mouth open with the other hand using the technique you've learned for ''pilling.'' If the object doesn't easily come out, get professional help, for if you try too hard, you may force it farther back damaging the throat or esophagus.

A word of advice: Don't let your dog play with small solid rubber balls since dogs characteristically toss such things to the back of the mouth while playing. We learned this lesson the hard way when one day the breeder of a dog we bought called to tell us she had lost the sire—he had choked to death on a rubber ball. Coincidentally, two days earlier the son that we had purchased nearly died when a similar ball got stuck in his throat. With much effort I managed to get a thumb behind it and flipped it out just in time, receiving only a cut thumb in the process. From then on we have always been careful about the size of the toys we gave to our dogs.

Poisons

Most poisons your dog might be exposed to fall into these categories: rat poisons, insecticides, herbicides, chemicals not intended to poison yet still toxic, and food toxins.

Insecticides commonly contain ingredients which adversely affect the nervous system. Rat and slug bait contain ingredients such as arsenic, strychnine, and others that either attack the central nervous system or cause internal bleeding. Whatever the poison, it should be eliminated from the body as quickly as possible—this means inducing vomiting (except for swallowed gasoline and solvents) and giving warm-water enemas. Two tablespoons of syrup of ipecac likely will be enough to make a 60-pound German Shepherd Dog vomit, or a heaping teaspoon of salt at the base of the tongue may do the job. If the dog seems already to have vomited, administer some *Milk of Magnesia*® (about half the adult human dose for an adult dog) to promote bowel movement, then *Pepto-Bismol*® or vegetable oil to coat the digestive tract.

After you have taken these steps, collect a sample of the *initial* vomitus and/or the poison if you know what caused the episode, and bring these along with the dog to the clinic. If the dog has swallowed solvent, induce excretion by giving three or four tablespoons of mineral oil or vegetable oil, then *Milk of Magnesia*® about a quarter of an hour later. Make sure the dog has fresh air and be ready to stimulate breathing with artificial respiration.

Snakebites—If you have seen a snake bite your dog and are not sure if it is poisonous, try to kill it without crushing its skull, and take it to the veterinarian with you. Caution: It may still bite even after the head is severed, so throw the snake into the trunk, and not into the back seat with the dog.

The best first aid for snakebite is speed: *rush* to the clinic. By all means start therapy in less than four hours, or the prognosis will be very poor. Treatment within an hour will generally result in complete recovery. Of course, if it were a non-venomous snake, there's no need for concern.

Ch. Odo vom Hodingerhof, SchH-I, HGH, ''a''. This terrific import made a great many admirers and friends along the East Coast and Canada during the early 1970's.
Owner: M. Pierce; handler: Gerlinda Hockla.

German Shepherd Dogs at Work

Dog is scaling the wall during SchH III Obedience phase. Alabanzas Uriah, SchH III, UDT.

"The Right Stuff" von Salix's Azzi a d Sudenstadt. "Azzi" shows correct full-mouth bite, leaping to reach arm instead of being "fed" the sleeve at her level. Owned by author.

Red Cross dog in South Africa.

Photo courtesy The Seeing Eye, Morristown, N.J.

"ROCK HOUND"

The German Shepherd Dog as a prospector. It began in Finland, where geologist Dr. Aarno Kahma reasoned that a dog's superior sense of smell should be able to locate weathering (disintegrating) sulfide rocks much further away than a human could. Many metals are found in the form of sulfide ores, including zinc, lead, and copper. In a 1964 test, a Finnish dog found 1330 such rocks on a test field, while an experienced human prospector found only 270. The trainer was awarded $2,000 for his invaluable work, and the dog was paid four frankfurters.

In 1970, the University of British Columbia and the Vancouver Police Dog Detail cooperated in a training program that proved the dog's value, and subsequent tests rated the canine as five times better than experienced prospectors in finding soil covered outer croppings, plus the dog could cover five times the area including ground too rough for normal human traverse.

Today, companies producing zinc, nickel, copper, lead and other metals are using German Shepherd Dogs in some areas and conditions where they have advantages. Precious metals (silver, etc.) are often found as "contaminates" in other ores. Dogs generally locate ore "floats" from a couple inches to a couple feet beneath the surface, with one very good Finnish dog found boulders ten feet below the surface.

The photos show "Jai" in 1972, one of two dogs involved in the pilot program. He was rented by St. Joe Minerals and other firms.
Photos courtesy John Brock, president, Welcome North Mines, Ltd.

"The German Shepherd Dog is first a working dog"—von Stephanitz. This tremendous example of the breed founder's emphasis on utility had a very good pedigree but was shown only twice in conformation, once winning Best Canadian Bred Puppy and later a 4th place in a U.S. open class. His forte was training: starting in obedience training at one year of age, he earned his U.S. UDT and Canadian UDTX within two years, then retired. At 6½ years, he came out of retirement to train for and compete in Schutzhund which was becoming available and popular. Within a year he had progressed all the way to SchH-III and FH, placing highest in trial every time but one, in which he was second highest, and scoring 96 in FH.

Avenger ("Sam") also demonstrated the breed's value to man in working a 94-mile-long buried pipeline to find more than 150 leaks, was used to detect supposedly inert and odorless gasses leaking from cable systems, and was the first dog ever to track an insect, searching and finding egg masses of the destructive Gypsy Moth in 1975. Glen and Sam worked with the Windsor police department to develop their K-9 Police training units and programs.

Sam died at 10½, a victim of gastric torsion; Glen wrote the book on tracking and is still active in that field.

Avenger 1968-1979 with owner, trainer, handler, Glen Johnson, Oldcastle, Ontario, Canada.

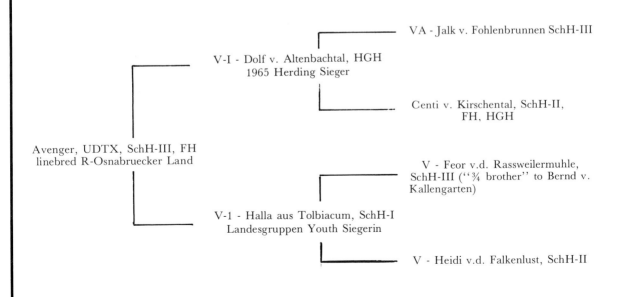

Avenger, UDTX, SchH-III, FH
linebred R-Osnabruecker Land

V-I - Dolf v. Altenbachtal, HGH
1965 Herding Sieger

VA - Jalk v. Fohlenbrunnen SchH-III

Centi v. Kirschental, SchH-II, FH, HGH

V-1 - Halla aus Tolbiacum, SchH-I
Landesgruppen Youth Siegerin

V - Feor v.d. Rassweilermuhle, SchH-III ("¾ brother" to Bernd v. Kallengarten)

V - Heidi v.d. Falkenlust, SchH-II

Drop in for a bite? When the place is closed, that's exactly what you may get! An 18th Century English proverb, still honored by some civil judges in some cases, is "Every dog is entitled to one bite".   Photo courtesy Rudy Drexler's School For Dogs.

Dreamweaver's Henry Winehard CDX TC OFA CERT. Owned by Mary Adelman who calls him "Zorro".

Keelain's Kid Kaila CD ATD, STD. owned by Kay Lorrain doing his job with sheep.

Fri., August 7, 1981   ST. LOUIS POST-DISPATCH

Bait Shop Puppy Puts Bite On Would-Be Robber

By Martha Shirk
Of the Post-Dispatch Staff

Marcia Hadley's 8-month-old German Shepherd puppy, Sarge, hasn't even finished obedience school. But early today, Sarge came to Mrs. Hadley's rescue, biting a robber as he throttled her and rifled the cash drawer at an Imperial, Mo., bait shop.

The robber dropped the cash and fled, leaving a trail of blood. Sarge's action earned him a steak dinner, Mrs. Hadley said.

"I'm so proud of him," she said this morning. "That man could have really hurt me."

The attempted robbery occurred about 1 a.m. in the bait shop at Lambrich Brothers' Shady Valley fishing lake on Missouri Highway 21 in Imperial, about 25 miles south of St. Louis. Mrs. Hadley, who lives in Arnold, was working the night shift. Her children, J.J. and Gina, both 6,

were asleep in a room above the office.

"About 1:10, a man walked in off Highway 21 and asked me if he could use the phone," Mrs. Hadley said. " I said sure, figuring he had had car trouble. He acted like he was using the phone, but I saw him reach over the cash drawer and grab money.

"I said, 'Hey, you can't do that.' He slapped me in the face, real hard, and knocked my glasses off, and then he grabbed me by the throat with one hand. I didn't hear Sarge come down the stairs, but the next thing I knew he was there. He clamped his teeth around the hand that was holding the money. The robber dropped it and kicked at Sarge and finally got free and ran out."

Mrs. Hadley said the man fled in a waiting automobile. The Jefferson County sheriff's office is investigating.

"Sarge," a grandson of Ch. Bel-Vista's Joey Baby, at 8 months and 75 lbs. "Self-taught" protection dog, later entered an obedence school, he was named by the Humane Society of Missouri as Most Heroic Dog of 1981. Good evidence of the innate characteristics of the breed.

Photo courtesy M. Hadley

"Let dogs delight to bark and bite, for God hath made them so." (Isaac Watts) Photo courtesy Rudy Drexler's School For Dogs

"A team surveys the territory".   *Photo courtesy Royal Canadian Mounted Police*

11

PARASITES AND IMMUNITY

A parasite is an organism that lives on or in another organism and derives its nourishment from that "host." Two broad categories involving the canine are the *endoparasites*, inside the dog, and the *ectoparasites*, on the outer surface.

ENDOPARASITES

Worms

Most worms (nematodes) settle and grow in the small intestine, though some species are found in the cecum, heart, lung, and other tissues in various stages of development. The intestinal nematodes produce eggs which are carried with the digestive products to exit in the feces. But since the egg laying does not always coincide with the dog's bowel movements, stool samples may not show the presence of worms. A 5-day sampling will probably reveal some eggs if hookworms or roundworms are present, but tapeworms or whipworms may still escape detection. For this reason, many breeders rely instead on outward signs of poor coat, flatulence and/or diarrhea, loss of weight, and an abnormal look or smell to the stool.

The German Shepherd Dog's topcoat should lie flat, straight, and smooth, giving a water-resistant thatch over the softer undercoat and skin. If these coarse, straight guard hairs stand up and out, or if the ends curl out away from the body, it may be a temporarily "open" condition due to worms. Lustre and texture also is gone, and the feel is rough and dry, the natural lubrications being lost when worms take their tariff from the intestinal lining's rich supply of blood vessels, or otherwise interfere with normal absorption of nutrients.

Roundworm—This is the most widespread of parasitic worms in dogs, cats, and many other animals. They are present in almost all newborn pups, having passed in larval stage through the placenta into the fetus's liver. After birth, these larvae are carried by the blood to the heart, then to the lungs. Irritation of the bronchial passages causes the dog to gag and cough the larvae up, then swallow them. This enables the larvae to reach the intestines where they latch onto the walls with lampreylike tenacity, and in as few as ten days can be found to have matured into identifiable roundworms of egg-laying capacity.

So the lone Taenia, as he grows, prolongs
His flatten'd form with young adherent throngs.
—Erasmus Darwin, in *The Temple of Nature*

Older pups that get worms a second time usually do so by ingesting worm eggs from stool or stool-contaminated surfaces. Pups (and adults) may also pick up roundworms from cat stools which present a tremendous attraction. Larvae have also been detected in bitch's milk. Swallowed roundworm eggs hatch in the intestine where the liberated larvae penetrate the wall and are carried in the lymph system to the veins. They, too, take the liver-heart-lungs route, molt, and start laying eggs of their own four weeks after being ingested. So, it's a good idea

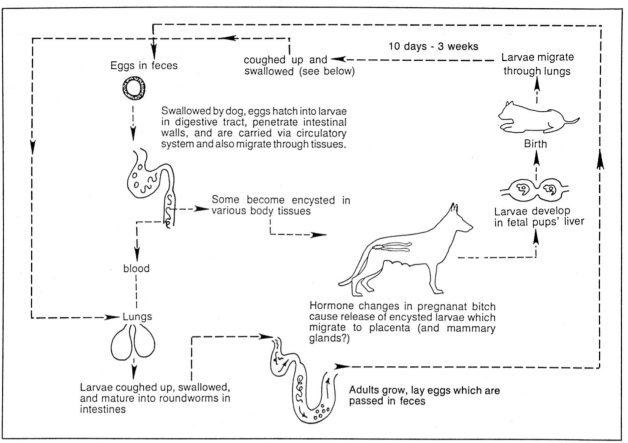

Life Cycles - Roundworm

to repeat worming a couple of times at 2-week intervals.

Adults and half-grown dogs tend to trap some roundworm larvae in body tissues in an encapsulated or encysted condition, where they do no further harm. Pregnant bitches, however, undergo a hormone change about three weeks before whelping that releases the encysted larvae, freeing them to migrate to the placenta and affect the fetuses as the bitch herself was affected when she was a growing embryo. This dormant stage of roundworm larvae can also exist in transient or intermediate hosts such as rodents, and if mice are eaten, the process of digestion will release the larvae in the dog's intestine, where they will not migrate (because they are in a different form), but develop into roundworms. Dogs that catch and eat beetles, cockroaches, mice, even earthworms, all of which may be hosts for roundworms, should periodically be given anthelmintics (wormers) as a routine control measure.

Hookworm—Hookworms are much smaller than roundworms and cannot be seen outside the dog, but as in the case of roundworms, eggs can be detected in fecal matter under the microscope. Hook, as dog fanciers often call it, is a debilitating disease in adults and a frequent killer of pups. It is probably the leading cause of death in puppies over two or three weeks of age. In chewing their way to blood vessels serving the intestinal walls, hookworms inflame the lining and make the organ less efficient. As a result, the dog becomes malnourished as well as anemic. Bloody stool, diarrhea, anemia, weakness, and dehydration are symptoms of hookworm infestation, in addition to the signs of poor coat condition.

There are a number of good anthelmintics, but one I find convenient and effective is *Task*® (dichlorvos). Since all wormers are dangerous to debilitated pups, follow your veterinarian's orders when worming sick or very weak pups.

Hook is commonly picked up at dog shows, veterinarians' lawns and lobbies, city sidewalks, and parks where dogs defecate. The eggs can live a long time in the soil, but sunlight helps to kill them, and full-strength chlorine bleach can force them to hatch and be susceptible to attack by products available from your veterinarian.

Whipworm—Whipworm infestation is usually less of a problem since it is not so widespread, but it's harder to detect and eradicate. Eggs are extremely resistant to the environment, and larvae can exist for several years in the soil or cracks in basement floors. Whipworms don't lay as many eggs, or as often, as other worms. Symptoms are similar to those of hook, and repeated doses with *Task*® or specific whipcides are quite effective when strict sanitation is an adjunct. Generally, anything that will kill hookworms or whipworms will also kill roundworms.

Tapeworm—A variety of tapeworms infest dogs and all of these flatworm parasites rely on an intermediate host in order to be transmitted from one direct host to another. Depending on the genus and species, some require an insect, others a crustacean, still others a different mammal in which they exist in a nonworm stage such as a larva, usually encysted. Eggs are seldom detected in flotation slides, but the owner may see little white crawling things on the surface of some stools. These are called proglottids, segments of the tapeworm that contain the

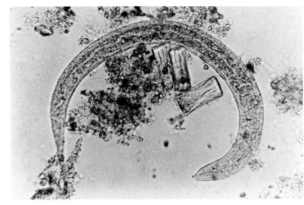

Hookworm larva. Mouth parts at right (thicker end). Photomicrograph courtesy of Center for Disease Control, Department of Health and Human Services, Atlanta, GA.

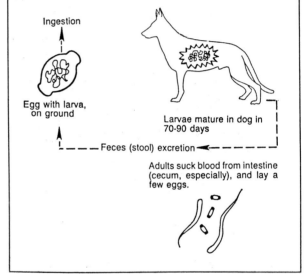

Life Cycle, Whipworm (Trichuris vulpis)

Life Cycles, Hookworm.

eggs and are shed by the worm in order to propagate itself while the head and younger segments remain attached to the inside of the dog. The shed segments have been likened to rice grains, cucumber seeds, and tiny blunt arrowheads and can vary in size from those of cucumber seed dimensions down to nearly microscopic particles that can be mistaken for frost if seen on a cold morning.

The stool is not necessarily soft, unless the infestation is so bad that diarrhea is around the corner. However, tapeworms should be suspected when the dog has been wormed for hook yet still has flatulence and poor coat. He must then have the specific tapeworm anthelmintic.

Dipylidium caninum, a member of one of the most common flatworm parasite groups in dogs, is trans-

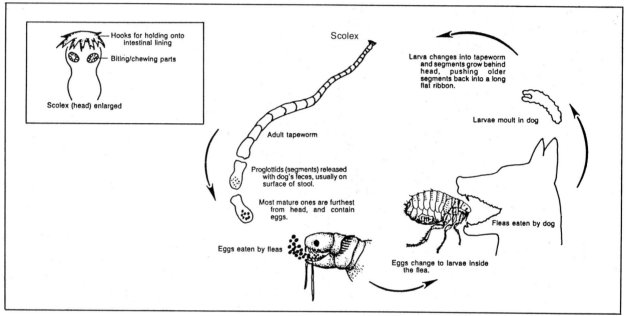

Life Cycle, Dipylidium caninum (tapeworm).

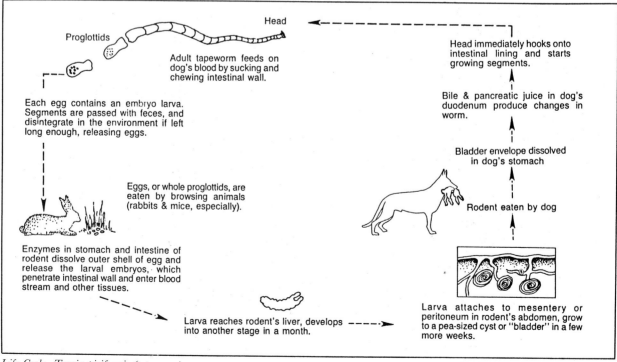

Life Cycle, Taenia pisiformis (tapeworm).

mitted by the dog flea and the cat flea. When the dog bites and eats the flea, the tapeworm larva is given access to the canine intestine where the cycle starts again. The flea's relatives, meanwhile, are waiting in the grass to feed on the eggs in the proglottids shed by earlier tapeworms. The genus *Taenia* includes several species of tapeworm, the most common of which is *T. pisiformis*. Most cases of infestation come about when the dog eats a rabbit or mouse in whose intestines can be found encysted *Taenia* larvae.

Prevention of infection with *Taenia* includes not allowing your dog to eat raw wildlife, particularly the internal organs, and especially rodents. The best preventive measure against *Dipylidium* is to keep your dog from socializing with cats or visiting places where cats hang out, for our feline friends are typical intermediate hosts even though they are seldom bothered by the bites.

A greatly improved wormer called praziquantel (trade name *Droncit*®), is nearly 100 percent effective against both types of tapeworm. *Task*® and other anthelmintics for hookworms, roundworms, and whipworms don't affect either of these tapeworms. *Vermiplex*® and similar wormers may kill a fairly high percentage of hookworms, roundworms, and considerable numbers of tapeworms, but not enough to completely eradicate an infestation.

A few minor flatworms are transmitted by the eating of raw fish. Another species, *Echinococcus granulosus*, is a danger to man, its intermediate host. It is found mostly in Alaska and parts of Canada.

Heartworm—Once a southern problem, heartworm has spread rapidly since the 1960s, due to increased travel around the United States. Only mosquitos apparently can incubate the heartworm nematode, and only certain species of mosquito seem willing to do the job; unfortunately, they seem to be everywhere.

Prevention can be obtained through daily administration of diethylcarbamazine citrate, sold under various tradenames, the best known of which is *Caracide*®. Most German Shepherd Dog adults need 200 mg. per day. Another major form is *Styrid-Caracide*®, which also contains a factor that inhibits the development of hookworm larvae. This is available in liquid form, and both are sold as tablets, so take your pick after conferring with your veterinarian. *Warning*: Do not give your dog either form

of the medicine if he might have adult heartworm, because this can be fatal. A good blood test should uncover microfilariae, but if you happen to skip testing and start administering *Caracide*® at the beginning of the mosquito season and your dog gets sick after a few pills, stop the dosage and wait a few days before having the blood tested.

Another control measure, followed in some parts of the deep South where the mosquito season never ends, is the twice-yearly treatment with "arsenic" (thiacetarsamide), which is used to kill adult heartworm. Thus, if any develop in the six months' time between treatments, they'll be knocked off before they can do appreciable damage.

A newer, and in many ways superior, preventative is ivermectin (tradename *Heartgard*®) which prevents heartworm with once-a-month doses. Long used by farmers as a cattle wormer, they found ivermectin got rid of all worms (except tapeworms) in their dogs, too. Ivermectin has been used in Australia as a public health measure because it kills fleas and ticks which infest the crossbred dingoes and their Aborigine owners.

The lifecycle of the heartworm begins with the mosquito feeding on an infested dog. It picks up, with the blood, some tiny heartworm embryos called microfilariae. Within minutes, the microfilariae begin to migrate from the gut to another part of the mosquito, changing into an infective form called larvae. In a couple of weeks these larvae move to the mosquito's mouth and when the insect bites the dog they escape into the blood, fat, and mucous tissues of that victim. There they continue to develop in the fatty tissue under the dog's skin and undergo more molts. In a few weeks they enter the veins as immature worms and reach the heart three months after entering the dog. Growing to a length of some seven inches for males and almost twice that for females, they lodge in the heart, copulate, and produce eggs that then hatch into microfilariae, and the cycle is complete.

The danger to the dog is in the worms' interference with flow of blood, proper opening and closing of the heart valves, effective oxygenation of cells, and proper blood flow to the lungs, especially when the worms die and clog up the pulmonary arteries. The principal danger to the dog with an adult heartworm population being treated with arsenic is when the dead worms let go and obstruct the pulmonary arterial flow; pneumonia is then the

Table 11.1 RECOMMENDED ROUTINE WORMING SCHEDULE. (modify as needed)

Age	Anthelmintic	Worms Affected
Two weeks	*Nemex* or *Strongid*	Roundworms
Four weeks	same as above, or dichlorvos	Roundworms, hookworms
Six weeks and quarterly thereafter	dichlorvos	Roundworms, hookworms, whipworms
Monthly	ivermectin	Heartworm, roundworm, whipworm, hookworm*

Different dosages are required for heartworm prevention than for the intestinal worms. Ivermectin also useful in killing mange mites and other ectoparasites.

For a house dog, sanitation is a good preventative...for a farm dog, forget it! Most dogs live in "in-between" conditions/environments. Vets may not promote routine worming, but cost-conscious and knowledgeable owners often find it to be better than taking samples to the clinic every month. Especially true when it's an "outside" dog or a dog exposed to show grounds..

Table 11.2 EFFECTIVE WORMERS (ANTHELMINTICS)

Drug	Mode of Action	Efficacy				Comments
		HOOK	ROUND	WHIP	TAPE	
Diclorvos (*Task®*)	Cholinesterase inhibitor.	95%	95%	90%	-	Do not give to dogs with liver or kidney damage or heartworm. Avoid other cholinesterase inhibitors (some flea killers, etc.).
Mebendazole (*Telmin®*)	Interferes with the worms' metabolism.	over 95%	96-99%	over 95%	100%	(note:) Excellent; no contraindications. This is only effective against *Taenia* (not *Dipylidium*). Must be given for 3-5 days.
Pyrantel pamoate (*Strongid®*, *Nemex®*)	Affects neuromuscular system of parasite, produces asphyxiation.	95%	95%	-	-	Excellent, pleasant taste, safe for the youngest pups. Probably the best first wormer.
Praziquantel (*Droncit®*)	Loss of parasite's resistance to digestion by the host.	-	-	-	over 95%	Most tapeworms disintegrate and are not found in feces. Best wormer for both *Taenia* and *Dipylidium* species.
Bunamidine (*Scoloban®*)	Destroys all parts of the tapeworm	-	-	-	90%	Most effective on an empty stomach.
Ivermectin	Affects neuromuscular system of parasite, paralyzing them.	(very high %)			-	Very safe, though when packaged for cattle, package inserts caution against use in dogs. Maybe fatal to Collies and Shelties in dosages greater than that for heartworm.

Others: *Injectable DNP is 95 percent effective against hookworm, but overdoses can be fatal. Piperazine®* is 85 percent effective against roundworm, but overdose can be a problem. *Caracide®* is 80 percent effective against roundworm, but should not be used unless heartworm is ruled out. *Vermiplex®* , etc. are 90 to 95 percent effective against round and hook, 70 percent against tape, but require fasting. Consult package, insert, or veterinarian for instructions regarding repeat doses. *Styquin®* injectable is easy to administer, effective against whipworm, and safe for heartworm-positive dogs. Liver and kidney disease should be ruled out before dog owner administers *any* wormer.

most likely cause of death, so the dog must be kept from exercise or exertion during this treatment period.

Other worms—There is insufficient room to describe the other, much more minor, worms that can bother dogs, but if your dog exhibits typical "wormy" symptoms and a couple of routine wormings a few weeks apart don't improve his condition, take a 5-day stool sample into the veterinarian for a complete study.

Protozoa

Although not related to worms except in the sense that they are also members of the animal kingdom, one-celled protozoa often give signs similar to those of worms. Several types afflict dogs, their eggs varying slightly in appearance, but all of them are considerably smaller than worm eggs, which are also microscopic.

Coccidia—Coccidiosis is a fast-acting killer of puppies around the ages of four to nine weeks, and especially if other parasites, such as hookworm, are present. Adult dogs seem capable of tolerating these protozoa, but may be carriers if stressed by worms or other conditions. Puppies wormed early and often seldom get coccidiosis, but those that do will typically go suddenly off their feed and in a few hours begin the most foul-smelling diarrhea you're likely ever to encounter. The stool is usually a grayish color, very loose, containing much mucus, and smells like blood even before you notice specks or streaks of red. Dehydration and loss of nutrition combine to weaken the pup, and blood loss with secondary bacterial infection and perhaps worms in the intestines can easily complete the fatal process.

A dog and cat owner from Natchez
Wore clothing just covered with patchez.
When asked reason why,
He replied with a sigh,
"Because when I itchez, I scratchez!"

Prompt identification and about ten days of treatment with sulfa drugs is needed. The sulfa combats the secondary bacterial attack and the veterinarian may also prescribe something he thinks may kill the protozoa (often the dog will overcome them on his own). Nitrofurazone has been used in the past, and amprolium (tradename *Corid®*) has been found effective in recent years. Thiamine to help control diarrhea is also recommended, and I give it both in injections and orally in vitamin-iron tonic. Use of sulfa requires that an abundance of drinking water be on hand at all times. Although something like immunity is acquired by the adult dog, puppies have an excellent chance of getting coccidiosis again. Such return engagements may be touched off by the weakened condition resulting from worm reinfestations.

Giardia—Another protozoan parasite that is normally well tolerated by most dogs except in times of stress is *Giardia*. If *Giardia* is specifically looked for, it appears in as much as 50 percent of dogs, but most of the time it is overlooked. Perhaps this is because a different magnification is needed than is used for worms, and there are fewer oocysts. Treating the symptoms of mucus in stools, diarrhea, loss of weight, and poor coat by giving *Kaopectate®* , corn oil, and vitamins may be enough until the dog shrugs off the attack, but if worms are present (they usually are) this treatment will probably be ineffective. Instead of using these stopgap measures, try to *kill* the organism because it can be spread to humans as well as other dogs. Treatment is quite effective with something like metronidazole.

Toxoplasmosis—This is another protozoan disease, but while widespread, it is not as serious except in pregnant bitches. Dogs can pick it up in the kitty-litter box or by eating raw meat, such as wild game, that has been contaminated by flies or cockroaches.

ECTOPARASITES

Ticks

Ticks are a frequent problem for dogs, and also pose a public health danger to humans in that they can serve as carriers of diseases such as the frequently fatal Rocky Mountain Spotted Fever. This disease is most prevalent in the Southeast and parts of the Northeast, and is not as common in the Rockies. There are two tick varieties, *Dermacentor variabilis* and *D. andersoni* that spread this disease to man and dog, but other ticks may carry bacterial diseases including anthrax, as well as cause tick paralysis, which subsides when the tick is removed.

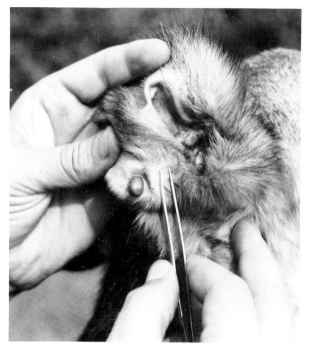

Brown dog tick

Ticks suck blood, copulate, and lay eggs while on their host. The eggs fall to the ground to undergo a series of molts, and when the larva matures it generally climbs a blade of grass or hangs on the end of a shrub leaf with hooked, clawlike legs extended. When it catches on a dog brushing by, it slowly makes its way to a sheltered spot where blood vessels close to the skin give off radiant heat. If numerous, ticks can weaken a dog simply through loss of blood.

In the late 1980's, the fastest spreading disease in the U.S., other than AIDS, was Lyme disease. This is spread mostly via ticks, but other vectors are now being identified. It is another zoonosis, a disease both humans and other animals can get.

If you have only a few dogs, you can go over each one at a time, and manually pull off the ticks. I sit in a well-lighted area (outdoors is best) with the dog lying between my legs or over my lap. Pointed tweezers are used to pull the tick close to its head, and drop it into a bowl containing a few tablespoons of soapy water. They drown or asphyxiate in a few minutes.

If the infestation is severe and/or you have too many dogs to treat, you may have to fill a large plastic garbage can with a lindane solution and dip the dogs, soaking them up to their faces. Every two weeks should be frequent enough, or you can alternate with the pick-and-drown method to minimize contact with pesticides. I put a drop of a pyrethrin/citrus extract mixture on individual ticks found between toes and in armpits, by using a plastic bottle with applicator tip. This way the whole dog doesn't have to be soaked in pesticide as often. When pulling ticks, forget all that nonsense about putting a drop of mineral oil or petrolatum on the tick till it loosens its grip, unless you have one dog and only a few ticks. Infections are almost non-existent and scabs minor where a little skin is retained by the stubborn tick.

Mites

Much smaller but similar in structure, with foreleg claws for grasping hairs, parasitic mites are abundant on some individuals. The nonburrow-

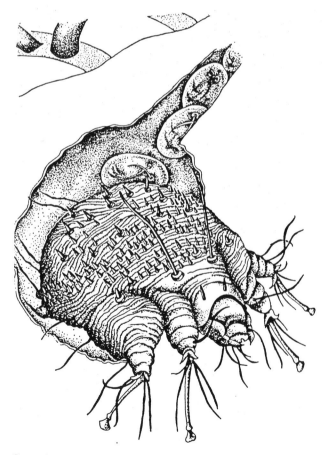

Sarcoptic mange mite.

ing types are called scab mites, and the disorder is called scabies. The burrowing species such as sarcoptic mites, tunnel through the skin and lay eggs along the way or at the base of hairs.

Sarcoptic mange—An infestation of *Sarcoptes scabiei* causes the dog to scratch and bite, and open the skin to secondary infections. The cause is difficult to detect; even skin scrapings are less than 50 percent effective in diagnosis. Sarcoptic mites usually prefer the skin areas on the belly, inside legs, and face. Symptoms often include crusty eruptions on elbows and around the base of the ears. If not treated, the dog will experience much hair loss, pus formation, and thickened skin. The disease can easily be transmitted to humans.

Demodectic mange—When one speaks of ''mange,'' it is usually this type, once called ''red mange.'' It is very difficult to treat because many of the mites that cause it are in a dormant stage in well-protected hair follicles until the animal becomes sick from other causes. This illness seems to ''awaken'' the mites that then come out of hibernation to do their dirty work. Combatting demodecosis is largely a matter of curing the dog's other ills, both physical and psychological. Years ago it was thought the only cure was euthanasia, but today a series of varying treatments in succession can have good results, if patience is part of the prescription. There is a definite and considerable genetic factor involved which determines how

Demodex folliculorum mite.

STRESS AND THE DEMODEX MANGE MITE

It is widely believed that stress of various kinds, whether of a genetic origin such as a very nervous temperament, or either a genetic *or* acquired immunodeficiency disease which suppresses T-cell function in the immune defense system, may be the major factor in an outbreak of demodicosis in a dog. With lowered cell-mediated immunity, the individual reacts adversely not only to the mite and its toxins, but also to the presence of other microbes and antigens.

If your dog exhibits demodectic mange symptoms, look for another disease or condition that should be treated at the same time. Is there a history of subclinical pancreatitis? Has there been recent surgery or other physical or emotional trauma? Any exposure to debilitating diseases? Even the minor stress of teething may be sufficient to tip the balance and encourage sudden proliferation of mites and their symptoms. Very healthy dogs rarely show symptoms even when intentionally exposed to clinical transmission of demodectic mites.

---

susceptible he will be to *Demodex* attack. The rapid growth months of a pup's life are stressful enough to contribute to susceptibility. Classic signs of infestation are hair loss just below the ears, around elbows, and over the croup and base of the tail, plus itching and scratching. Insecticides used on the major portion of the dog by means of rag or sponge baths may contain chlordane and lindane in water emulsions, and benzyl benzoate cream is good to apply around the lips and eyes.

Ear mites—A relative of the mange mite, *Otodectes cynotis* is responsible for most irritations in dogs' ears. This mite is combatted with selected insecticides and cleansing agents that help remove the old wax as well as the mite and its waste products.

After cleaning the ears, put several drops of the insecticide into the ears and let it coat the surfaces for awhile before removing most of it with a cotton swab. If normal, clear wax production doesn't start in a couple of days, repeat the process of cleaning and applying insecticide. If the ear makes a squishing sound, get the swab all the way to the drum and dry out the ear canal. Since mites may accumulate outside the outer ears, sponge the hair around them with mange remedy. Make inspection a regular habit. Some veterinarians prescribe ivermectin for mange and ear mites, administered orally or by injection.

Fleas

Fleas are the most widespread ectoparasite on dogs. Of the more than 13 thousand species discovered so far, two are most common: the cat flea, *Ctenocephalides felix*, is by far the most abundant, and the dog flea, *C. canis*, is the next most likely to be found. Because they spend less than 10 percent of their lives on the dog (or other host) it sometimes seems to be an endless or at least difficult and frustrating battle to eradicate fleas.

As mentioned before, a dog's worst enemy (flea-wise) is the cat. After practicing cat-avoidance techniques, use the various poisons available to attack the fleas themselves, on the dog and in the carpets. While brewers yeast is a nice tasty treat and a good source of B-complex vitamins, there is no scientific basis to its use as a flea repellent. Flea collars are not effective on medium-to-large dogs.

Who sleepeth with dogges, shal rise with fleas
—John Florio

Powders containing carbamates, organophosphates, rotenone, or pyrethrins are probably among the most effective, especially if you can work them down to the skin. If I have a flea problem, I first try a spray or shampoo containing non-toxic citrus extract (limonene) and then resort to fenthion (available only from your vet) if the problem persists. Most dogs that get plenty of fresh air and exercise can handle the occasional flea with ease.

Flea-bite allergy—This is probably the most commonly recognized allergic reaction in dogs.

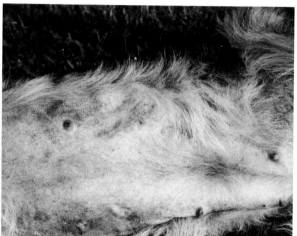

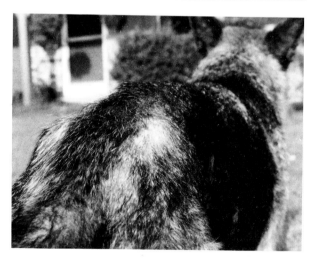

Flea-bite dermatitis. Most of the redness is due to injury inflicted by the dog, in scratching and biting; even the elbow callus is scratched raw. The toxin in the dog's blood not only produces an allergic itch reaction, it also causes loss of hair; note especially on base of tail and over hip bones, while loss on belly, behind elbow, and on forearm is partly due to biting and scratching. Itch may continue for weeks after flea saliva enters bloodstream, and it may only take one flea to make some dogs react, though most bad cases like this are simply neglect in fighting fleas. This dog lived with cats.

Long after the flea bites and its saliva has infected the dog's blood system and skin cells, the area will itch. This irritation will lead to worse trauma than the bite itself since if the dog scratches too much and bites too long, he can mutilate himself and open the skin to bacterial action. A shot of a steroid may be needed to give the dog a rest. Hair loss seems to occur in hypersensitive dogs whether or not the biting and scratching is controlled. The most difficult part of handling the flea/allergy problem is convincing the owner that it exists. Most owners who see few or no fleas seem unwilling to believe the explanation that the symptoms are related to the parasite.

Female Ctenocephalides (flea).
Photo courtesy of Center for Disease Control.

IMMUNOLOGY

Immunology, the study of reactive resistance to infection, is at once an old and new field of study. In the past thirty years the use of vaccines in human and veterinary medicine has grown enormously. In the past twenty years we've learned much about antibodies, and in the past ten years dynamic growth of knowledge about immune response has been noted. In the future we may well see the development of vaccines for a multitude of problems now afflicting the German Shepherd Dog.

While humans acquire most of their initial immunity *in utero*, dogs get 90 percent of their maternal antibodies in the colostrum; the importance of nursing, and the dangers of bottle-feeding pups are

Little buggies, little buggies,
Swimming 'round inside my vein,
I don't understand your actions,
But there's one thing you make plain:
If I'm good and take my vaccines,
My immunity will soar,
And those nasty bigger buggies
Just won't bug me anymore.

obvious. After the maternal antibodies dissipate, the pup must be exposed directly to the virus (or whatever antigen is involved), or preferably, be given a vaccination to stimulate its own cells to produce immunoglobulins or antibodies. It is not easy to tell when the dam's protection wears off in the pups and when they are ready for vaccines, and if you vaccinate too early, those maternal antibodies will keep the vaccine from producing the desired reaction. This is why so many puppies have died from parvovirus even though they were vaccinated; in between the time the dam's protection wore off and the date of the next vaccination, they were exposed to live virus that then took a couple of weeks in incubate. Thus, some puppies die days after being vaccinated, and the owner tends to blame the vaccine. By blood tests to determine the dam's titer (level of antibodies), this risk can be reduced considerably.

Vaccination

Immunization is the process of becoming resistant to disease. A dog can become immune upon exposure to a virulent antigen, such as a virus or bacteria, or by the introduction of a less dangerous yet similar agent that is intended to either prevent infection or limit it. The way to provide such protection and safety is through a good vaccination program.

The major diseases most dogs should be vaccinated against are rabies, distemper, hepatitis or adenovirus (CAV), and parvovirus. If pups are exposed to wildlife or show dogs, it would be a good idea to include shots for leptospirosis. If dogs are kenneled close to one another indoors, parainfluenza vaccination may be indicated. How often depends on vaccine type, exposure, and other factors. Your veterinarian is your best ally for advice and administration of necessary vaccinations.

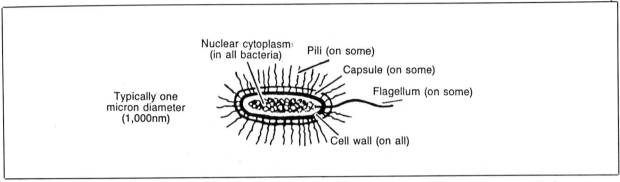

a) Composite representation of a bacillus-type bacterial cell: rod-shaped, elongated. Many variations, each with its own peculiar features.

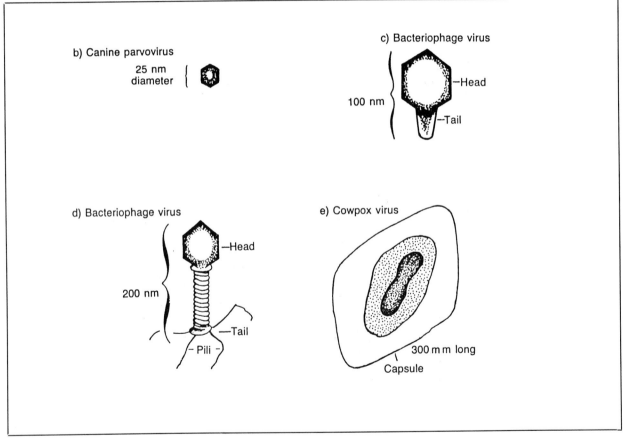

b) Viruses (drawn to a much larger scale than bacterium above).

12

DISEASES AND DISORDERS OF THE GERMAN SHEPHERD DOG

The German Shepherd Dog is subject to a multitude of problems, partly because of indiscriminate breeding practices of the past and present. The problems are often no more than the average in some lines, somewhat more in others, but all are more noticeable because of the great number of Shepherd Dogs in the world. (You may see more Chevies with dented fenders simply because there are more Chevies on the road.)

PART ONE

Birth Defects

Midline closure defects are expressed in a variety of ways; in German Shepherd Dogs, I have seen incomplete closure to the midline of the scalp, incompletely formed tails, and cleft palates. I believe all of them to be related in most cases. Sometimes other midline abnormalities are found in pups with or without cleft palate; these may include umbilical hernias, skull defects, spinal disorders, and others. Cleft lip (harelip) is sometimes found, though this is caused at a different time during gestation.

Cleft palate is a condition in which, for genetic or environmental reasons, the hard surface of the roof of the mouth and the softer palate behind it fail to close. The first sign something is wrong (if you don't examine your pups immediately after delivery) is usually milk bubbling out the nose when the newborn attempts to nurse. In addition to genetics, there are numerous other causes for cleft palate. It is a frequent defect found in offspring of diabetics. It has been produced experimentally by

vitamin A imbalance whether too much or too little, and is often a result of poisons and steroids taken or produced by bitches in the first three weeks of gestation. In canines, a deficiency of vitamin B_{12} has been identified as a cause. Antihistamines given early in pregnancy, at least in some doses, are also suspect. Viral infections at that stage, or certain other chemicals have also been determined to have caused cleft palate.

Eyes

Diseases of the eyes and surrounding tissues are sometimes confused with disorders elsewhere in the body that manifest themselves in the eyes. In some cases, only your veterinarian will be able to tell the difference, but by comparing the following information, that in the Troubleshooting Guide (Chapter 13), and that in Chapter 4, you may be able to diagnose many ailments.

Eversion—Eversion is an outward rolling or sagging of the lower lid, also known as ectropion. It is mostly an inherited and probably recessive condition. It appears mostly in other breeds,but a few cases in Shepherds have been serious enough to warrant surgery.

Entropion—It's usually the bottom lid which produces this condition also known as inversion. The lower lashes roll inward, irritating the conjunctiva and the cornea. This problem is occasionally found in the Shepherd.

"Third eyelid"—A syndrome known as nictitating membrane eversion (or inversion) is seen in several of the large breeds. It is not rare in the German Shepherd Dog, although many have never seen it. Using statistical methods information from T.M. Fisher's article, "Genetic Counseling for Veterinarians," in *Modern Veterinary Practice*, the hybrid carrier population in German Shepherd Dogs is about 22 to 23 percent. Most cases are congenital and hereditary, though a few are acquired.

Hypertrophy—Excessive growth of the nictitating membrane in the lower inside corner, can also be either inherited or acquired. In German Shepherd Dogs, it often occurs along with another condition called pannus.

Epiphora—Chronic tear spillage can be caused by irritation, though a genetic origin is suspected in some cases. In this syndrome, allergies frequently are the villains.

Myositis—Eosinophilic myositis, often fatal, is marked by an elevated white blood cell count with swelling of the muscles around the eyes and cheeks, edema (fluid-filled condition) of the eyelids, discomfort or inability in closing the mouth, or some, if not all, of these symptoms. German Shepherds are affected in varying degrees of severity. Also known as masticatory myositis-myopathy, it is actually a nervous system disorder, but is mentioned here because of its effects on the eyes.

Conjunctivitis—Inflammation of the conjunctiva (the mucous membrane that lines the front of the eyeball and the inside of the lids), is usually caused by injury, bacteria, virus, or other foreign material. However, on the West Coast a parasite in the form of tiny worms in the corner of the eye is often mistaken for simpler conjunctivitis. The condition clears up when the parasitic larvae are scraped out.

Neonatal conjunctivitis—In some pups under ten days of age, pus forms beneath the lids causing a swelling and weeping of some of the purulent exudate. When you see this, take the pup to the veterinarian since the lid may have to be cut open. But, in most cases, a simple treatment can be demonstrated; thereafter you can do it at home. Force the long applicator tip of the ointment tube into the hole that the pus leaks out of, and widen the opening enough to get the rest of the matter out and bathe the globe in the medication. Do this twice a day, and the lids soon open naturally, although perhaps earlier than normal.

Glaucoma—This condition of excessive pressure within the eyeball is very rare in the German Shepherd Dog. However, if the dog exhibits pain or lightly rubs his eyes on you or the furniture, all possibilities should be examined.

Corneal disorders—"Blue-eye" is an opacity of the cornea which affects the apparent color of the iris; it can be a result of active hepatitis, distemper, or administration of modified live vaccine called A_1. This reaction can be avoided by using DA_2L instead of DHL or DA_1L vaccines.

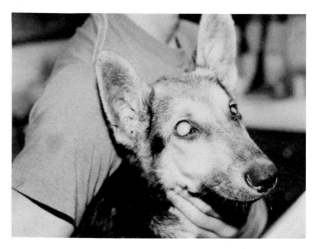

"Blue-Eye". This ocular condition occasionally results from vaccination with CAV-1 in "DHL" combination vaccines. CAV-2 vaccine has become widely used instead, and does not produce this blindness.

Pannus—About 6 percent of German Shepherd Dogs have a chronic keratitis (inflammation of the cornea) which is peculiar to our breed. It usually begins as a grayish, hazy, semi-opacity; the advancing film is sometimes preceded by melanin pigmentation and by blood vessels becoming more apparent. Treatment is both surgical and chemical—steroids are used to prevent recurrence.

Cataracts—The word *cataract* is used for any opacity of the lens and in some dogs it occurs secondary to Progressive Retinal Atrophy (PRA). Although rare, cataract in German Shepherds is believed to be due to a dominant gene. True cataracts may not be detected simply because a dog doesn't need reading ability vision to get around, and doesn't complain about things looking dim or fuzzy. If you suspect cataracts in an old dog you are probably wrong; the bluish color beyond the pupil and lens is seldom a true cataract, but rather the normal result of old age.

Other opacities may appear on the cornea over the pupil. For example, an allergic reaction or some other cause may show up as a small spot, the opacity varying from slightly translucent to white. The size is usually less than 5mm. Most eye specialists refer to this type of opacity as ''corneal dystrophy.'' Most of the spots are somewhat horseshoe-shaped and do not interfere with vision. In my experience the spots have faded away in a few years after reaching maximum size. Corneal dystrophy appears to be genetic, but is not serious. Probably less than one percent of the breed is affected.

As with cataracts, there is another opacity that is occasionally found on the lens. Therefore, fibrillar nuclear opacity may be diagnosed as a cataract by a non-ophthalmologist.

PRA—There may not be a breed extant which is not affected by PRA, a simple Mendelian recessive disorder of extremely variable expression. Night blindness and dilated pupils may be the first symptoms. Eye examinations can reveal only the homozygous individuals, but taking advantage of an eye clinic is recommended, especially if there has been a history of eye disorders in the dog's family tree. Your veterinarian can put you in touch with a national eye registry called Canine Eye Registration Foundation, Inc. (CERF).

Ears

Fungus—Sometimes a chronic swelling and uncleanliness of the external ear canal is blamed on mites, when the actual cause may be a fungus. Whether picked up from straw bedding or simply the air currents, the fungus attack is often fought on two fronts: dogs with this infection in their ears will also frequently have a fungal redness between their toes. In addition, the irritation, scratching, and licking/biting that the dog practices can open the way to bacterial infection which can easily be combatted with neomycin sulfate (*Panalog®*, etc.). The fungus, however, must be treated with a fungicide from your veterinarian. Additionally, these symptoms may result from thyroid function insufficiency of a genetic or acquired nature. Flea bite allergy can mimic hypothyroidism stemming from other causes. Have your veterinarian check

thyroid hormone levels and treat dog and premises for fleas.

Fly-bite dermatitis—This is a problem of special interest to owners of German Shepherd Dogs or other breeds with erect ears. White dogs are especially vulnerable to this southern or summer environmental disease. Flies generally buzz around and alight on the highest point of any target, which in your dog's case is the ears. There is also a great percentage of radiant heat loss from the head, which may attract mosquitos and other insects. If allowed to continue biting, flies will eventually destroy the ear tips. There is no good excuse for this condition to exist since prevention is usually a snap. See Chapter 10.

Skin

The word *integument* encompasses not only skin, but epithelial tissue of the feet, hair, nose (bulb), nails, conjunctiva, and the mucous membranes of the digestive, respiratory, and urogenital tracts. All these are contiguous and continuous. Most disorders of the integument involve parasitic or traumatic damage. Next most common are disorders due to hormonal upsets or insufficiencies, such as hyperestrinism, hypothyroidism (supposedly rare in the Shepherd Dog), pituitary tumor, and perhaps defects in other endocrine tissue. Tumors are covered in greater detail later, but may include warts, papillomas, sebaceous cysts, and other types.

Umbilical hernia—Many German Shepherd puppies have umbilical hernias, as the umbilicus for some reason fails to close early and fully. In the fetus and whelping pup the condition occurs where the umbilical cord connects the puppy's system to that of its dam. I have seen many cases of minor hernias, with lumps up to about an inch in diameter at an age of eight to ten weeks. Most were a bit smaller, and could easily be pushed back into the abdomen until the pups were close to ten weeks old. Gradually it becomes more difficult to do this since, as the puppy grows, the hole becomes much smaller than the lump.

Because umbilical hernias differ among breeds, some people who have had experience with those cases (including veterinarians) often rush into surgery. However, I have found that hernias in the German Shepherd Dog often close with the mass inside, and those which remain outside the hole but within the muscle wall become fibrous and tough, and present no problem whatever. Leave them alone if they follow this usual course during the pup's first six months. If the lump is extremely large, i.e., over two inches in diameter, you may want to consider surgery.

Whether the German Shepherd's umbilical hernia is hereditary, or acquired from the dam's hard yank on the placenta and cord has not yet been determined. My own experience leads me to suspect the latter, having seen no familial pattern in the many cases I've observed, and having noted the difference in appearance of the hernia as compared to those of other breeds. If hereditary, it would likely be recessive.

Snow nose—A condition frequently found in white dogs is a somewhat temporary loss of black pigment from the bulb of the nose, usually in a center strip. It has been blamed on mild frostbite, but I am convinced this is not the cause. I suspect that this so-called snow nose is a hormone-related reaction to sunlight, similar to the way length of days affects a female's estrus cycle. I have seen it mostly in lighter-colored dogs, dogs with liver genes whether heterozygous or homozygous, in white Shepherds, and other breeds.

Musculo-Skeletal System

Systemic lupus erythematosus (SLE)—Systemic lupus erythematosus is often mistaken for rheumatoid arthritis (RA). It is very similar to human SLE which is better known as "lupus." Most affected dogs are between two and eight years of age, and some 75 percent are female. Symptoms vary so much that it can be confused with almost a dozen other diseases, and therefore, diagnosis is frequently made by the process of elimination. It is a multi-system disorder with symptoms of considerable pain in the joints, listlessness, diarrhea, loss of appetite, anemia, and many others. SLE is an autoimmune disorder meaning it is a defect in the immune defense system which causes the body's defenses to be directed at its own cells as well as invading microbes and chemical agents.

Hip dysplasia—Orthopedics is the branch of medical science dealing with the true movement of the animal as determined by the bones, joints, and related muscles. The major orthopedic problem in the German Shepherd Dog is hip dysplasia (HD); less severe ones include panosteitis, ununited anconeal process, and spinal column deformities. Most of these are covered in great detail in my 1981 book published by Alpine Publications, Inc.

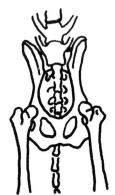

A "normal" joint—allowing for free, easy and non-painful movement.

A dysplastic joint. Note not only the abnormality of the femur heads, but also the almost complete lack of any cup-shape to hold the heads. One can easily imagine the pain suffered by an animal working, running or walking with this continual grating.

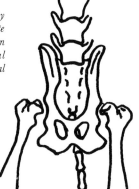

The word *dysplasia* means 'bad form' or 'abnormal formation'. A genetic disorder with highly variable expression, HD is dependent on environmental forces because of its polygenic nature. The nice, deep, congruent fit of the femoral head into the hip socket does not develop as it should in dysplastic dogs, and the hip becomes unstable, abnormal, and painful. Definitive diagnosis is made only by radiographic analysis. The information from a good radiograph, especially when evaluated by the Orthopedic Foundation for Animals (OFA), will help you decide whether or not to use a dog for breeding.

Because of the popularity of the German Shepherd Dog, word has spread that this is "the breed with that hip disease." Logic should, but doesn't always, tell us that if anything is common in a large number of breeds, it will be seen most often in those with the highest populations. Actually, there are over a dozen breeds with a higher incidence of hip dysplasia, but don't let that fact keep you from rigorous breeding control measures.

If you already have a dysplastic dog, you can treat him with pain killers during the most active growth stage (4 to 10 months). When the pup is older, you can have a piece of the pectineus muscle removed, or take other measures recommended by your veterinarian and/or my book on dysplasia.

Osteochondrosis—Osteochondrosis is a catch-all word for any number of cartilage and joint defects. More and more evidence points to some common basis underlying all manifestations, including HD, though certainly not all the genes affect all the joints.

Ununited Anconeal Process (UAP) is the most prevalent elbow joint disorder seen in German Shepherd Dogs. A small piece of bone breaks loose in the elbow joint and causes inflammation and pain which result in a gait in which the dog swings his legs in an arc, best seen as he approaches. It is best repaired surgically when the dog is near skeletal maturity, around ten to twelve months. Such a dog should not be bred.

Other orthopedic disorders in the elbow and other joints are found in the breed, but at lower incidences. Too much calcium and a too high caloric value to the food appear to be the main contributing causes of these other disorders.

Panosteitis—Once known as strictly a German Shepherd Dog disease, "pano" results in intermittent lameness in mostly the large, fast-growing breeds between the ages of seven to eighteen months. It can remain in one long bone of one limb for anywhere from two days to two months, and can appear in another long bone in the same or another limb at the same time, or after the first has healed. Panosteitis is self-limiting, which means the dog will grow out of it, although much consternation is caused by the apparent tendency for it to appear the day after show entries close, and disappear after the shows are over for the season. I predict that someday a viral cause will be found, with a genetic predisposition for it.

A disease sometimes confused with panosteitis is hypertrophic osteodystrophy (HOD), which is primarily found in 3- to 5-month-old setters and Doberman Pinchers. If the bottom end of the leg bone is swollen and sore, it may be HOD; if the center of the shaft is the place where pain is evident when pinched, it is most likely pano.

Spinal disorders—German Shepherd Dogs are frequently diagnosed as having an arthritic condition known as *spondylosis deformans*. Easily detected by radiography, this disorder tends to immobilize sections of the spine by bone proliferation on the

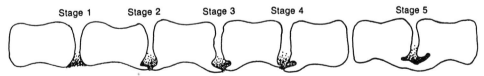

Composite sketch showing various stages of spondylosis deformans.
The arch, transverse processes ("wings"), cord, and other structures are not shown, for the sake of simplicity.
Stage
1: Opacity developing indicates osteophytes (bony growth) beginning.
2: Actual bone protuberances extended toward each other. This is the most common type found in German Shepherd Dogs.
3: Most frequently seen form, all age groups and all breeds. Most common in Dachshunds and Boxers.
4: The bridge is nearing completion.
5: Most severe. Not seen in German Shepherd Dogs.

ventral surfaces of adjacent vertebrae, forming a solid bridge across the disk. Several such bridges have the effect of fixing the spine much as welding the links of a chain together forms an inflexible rod. Although the disorder is not fatal, or even paralyzing, when seen in conjunction with other problems such as HD or myelopathy, it can debilitate a dog rather quickly.

PART 2—INTERNAL ORGANS

Respiratory System: Lungs

The German Shepherd Dog does not suffer from respiratory ailments to any significantly higher degree than do other breeds, but problems are frequent enough. Respiratory failure in dogs can be caused by any one of innumerable conditions; some are controllable, some are not.

Parasites—Lung flukes are varieties of flatworms; one species is quite endemic to the Great Lakes area and another is common in San Francisco's Chinatown. Either will cause shortness of breath, rapid exhaustion, and coughing. Treatment is not very effective, but newer drugs are being developed all the time. The same is true with Fox lungworm and the trachea worm. All of the above can progress to the point of pneumonia, a potentially fatal situation. Roundworm larvae migration throughout the body can also cause some lung damage, but since it is so easy to treat for roundworms, it is seldom serious. Adult heartworms, especially when killed, block capillaries serving the lungs, with pneumonia the biggest danger to a patient undergoing heartworm treatment.

Microorganisms—A number of viruses are responsible for a high percentage of respiratory ailments, the best known being distemper, parainfluenza, adenovirus (also called CAV and infectious hepatitis), and parvovirus. Bacteria and fungi have also been known to cause pneumonia and bronchitis. "Kennel cough," a term used to cover a number of respiratory problems, is probably caused by a combination of microorganisms. It can best be prevented by providing plenty of ventilation and avoiding overcrowded kennels. Antibiotics and other drugs help, but several weeks may be required for complete recovery.

Emphysema is a non-specific condition in which air passages in the lungs become blocked with mucus; air is trapped, bronchioles collapse, and the

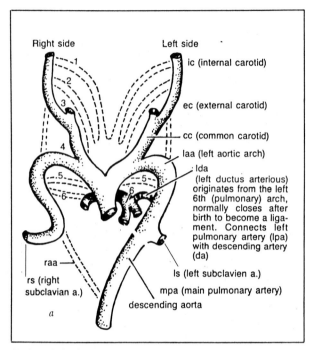

Embryonic development, normal heart, vessels only (atria and ventricles not shown). Dotted lines show embryonic arches and vessels which disappear by or shortly after birth.

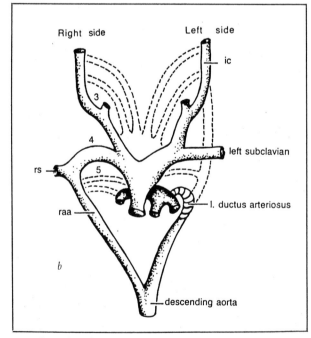

PRAA: Embryonic abnormal development; right arch persists instead of ceasing to function. The left 4th arch becomes merely the beginning of the left subclavian. The left da, remains connected to the right aortic arch (raa) and the descending aorta, forming a closed ring around the esophagus. The heart and vessels grow, but the ring remains small.

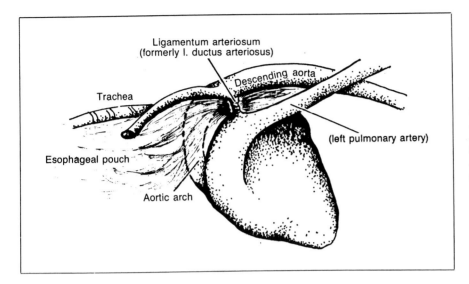

Another view of PRAA, showing structure at ligament, pulmonary artery, and aorta. Esophagus is greatly dilated, having been stretched by solid food accumulation which could not pass quickly to the stomach; it loses strength and ability to recover.

dog suffocates. Several years ago I was handling a handsome, seemingly healthy German Shepherd Dog for a client. A few days before his first show he dropped dead during a leisurely stroll on-leash. The autopsy indicated emphysema, but failed to identify what caused it. Depending on whether the underlying cause can be found, it may or may not be treatable.

Cardiovascular System: Heart

As in humans, heart disease in the canine can be hereditary, congenital, or acquired. Heartworm is an example of acquired disease; a discussion of some of the hereditary diseases follows.

Persistent right aortic arch (PRAA)—This heart defect is twelve times more common in the German Shepherd Dog than in all other dogs combined. PRAA is characterized by the growth of the right aortic arch into the permanent aorta. Since the left arch is supposed to do that, the result is less room for the esophagus. As the heart continues to grow after whelping, there is less and less room for the esophagus and for the solid food that is supposed to pass through it to the stomach. It's like the tight collar some fishermen put on cormorants to prevent them from swallowing the fish. As the pup is weaned and tries to swallow, food goes down only as far as the stricture, causing the pup to vomit within a few minutes. It's a progressively worsening situation, and the affected pup remains tiny while his littermates grow normally. The starved one almost never lives beyond eight weeks, usually dying around five or six weeks of age. Surgery is

very tricky and has a very low rate of success. It is best to put the PRAA pup down before it succumbs to malnourishment.

Sometimes PDA is seen in conjunction with PRAA, and therefore cancel each other's effect. However, the dog still carries the genes and can pass one to each of its future offspring.

Patent ductus arteriosus (PDA)—This defect has been identified in the German Shepherd, though it is more common in Collies, Poodles, and Pomeranians. PDA involves a branch of the heart that, in normal development, closes to become a ligament. In the defective dog, that branch remains open (patent), allowing a back-flow of blood to the heart.

Valvular heart disease—Aortic valvular/semilunar valvular endocarditis (inflammation of these valves) has been called an almost exclusively German Shepherd Dog disease. If your dog seems to cough only at night, or starts coughing very early in the morning, consider valvular heart disease and have your veterinarian check it out.

The occurrence of aortic stenosis is highest in German Shepherd Dogs, Boxers, and Newfoundlands. This congenital lesion refers to a constriction of the aorta and causes these symptoms: lack of stamina, poor growth, and being "out of breath."

There are a number of other non-breed specific vascular and cardiac problems, and it is common for them to appear as a by-product of or in association with those diseases to which the German Shepherd is most prone.

Directions for submitting samples for bleeding disorders— coagulation assays

1. The purposes of this service are to identify affected and carrier dogs so the breeder and veterinarian can be guided in making decisions about breeding. Dogs with inherited bleeding disorders ideally should be withheld from breeding.

2. If a dog is certified normal, its national breed club or registry will be notified. If affected, results are kept confidential and sent directly to the owner and his veterinarian.

3. Draw and prepare blood as follows:
Use one part 3.8 percent trisodium citrate to nine parts whole blood (1:10 dilution). Take the blood sample in a *plastic* syringe into which you have placed 0.4 ml of the anticoagulant. Draw the blood by *clean* venipuncture through the anticoagulant up to a final volume of 4 ml. Mix well and transfer to *plastic* test tube for immediate centrifugation. Centrifuge at 2500-3500 rpms for 15 minutes. Make sure plastic tubes are free from dust and cardboard particles before use.

For small breeds and pups, take less blood but adjust coagulant volume to maintain 1:9 ration (0.2 ml citrate up to 2 ml blood/citrate mixture, etc).

Aspirate off the supernatant citrated plasma with a plastic or siliconized pipette, or a small plastic syringe such as a tuberculin syringe. Place the plasma into a small plastic tube and freeze at 20 degrees C (-4 degrees F.), or lower if possible. Ship the samples to us in dry ice within two weeks after drawing, preferably within one week. The samples must not thaw en route. Ship by air freight, air express, air priority, Greyhound package express, or the U.S. Postal Service's 24-hour guaranteed service, the last two being the most economical. Use plenty of dry ice (10-20 lbs.) in case they get lost for a while. Ship in an insulated, styrofoam type container. Wrap tubes to prevent them from breakage during shipment. Some airlines and other carriers have special regulations and labels for dry ice shipments; please check with them before shipping.

Label package:

''Call upon arrival for immediate pick-up: (518) 457-2663 days, 765-2436 nights.''

Make this label obvious.

Please ship samples early in the week to avoid weekend traffic and receiving problems. Please phone ahead to notify receiver of shipment. Identify contents as ''blood sample.''

4. Do not test bitches in heat, or lactating or pregnant bitches. Pups of large breeds can be tested at eight weeks, but small breed pups should be at least ten or twelve weeks old when tested. Do not test unhealthy animals or animals on any type of medication (except Caracide), or that have been vaccinated within the previous fourteen days. Fasting is not necessary.

5. If the veterinarian does not have coagulant and tubes, contact the testing lab for free test kits. Indicate how many dogs you plan on testing.

6. Include a five-generation pedigree, or as complete a pedigree as possible, so it can be determined if the test dog is related to families known to be affected. Be sure to identify breed, and give registration numbers where known.

7. There is no charge for test or test kits. Ship to: Dr. W. Jean Dodds, Division of Laboratories and Research, New York State Dept. of Health, Empire State Plaza, Albany, New York 12201.

Hemophilia A—Two genetic canine bleeding problems are as commonly found in German Shepherds as in other breeds, or more so.

This disorder also known as classic hemophilia or Factor-VIII hemophilia, is sex-linked, and recessive; passed from dam to sons. So-called bleeders often are discovered at teething time.

Von Willebrand's Disease—The second bleeding disorder is VWD, also known as vascular hemophilia and pseudohemophilia. There are two modes of inheritance; the type of most interest to German Shepherd Dog breeders is an incompletely dominant trait with several modifying genes acting on it, mostly to suppress its effects.

The observance of VWD in Shepherds is stress-related. There is a built-in excitability in German Shepherds predisposing most of them to stress-induced symptoms of one disease or another. Typical symptoms include blood in the urine, excessive bleeding upon surgery, and extra-long seasons in bitches. Diagnosis is by blood analysis, and assays are currently being run at a number of veterinary schools as well as the New York State Department of Health in Albany.

The reason not much progress has been made in eradicating this disease is two-fold: too many uninformed or incompetent people are breeding dogs, and the GSD Club of America has so far shown an abysmal lack of initiative. About 20 percent of Shepherds, perhaps higher in some linebred families, have VWD, and since it is detectable through blood analysis, there's no excuse for ignoring the problem.

Digestive Tract Disorders

Esophagus—Congenital esophageal achalasia is also known by many other names such as cardiospasm, mega-esophagus, dilated esophagus, and

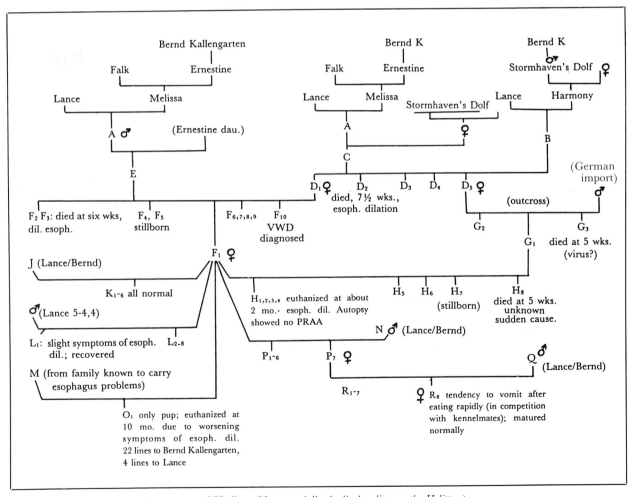

Pedigree Study of Esophageal Dilation in a GSD line. (Note especially the linebreeding on the H litter.)

ectasia. The disorder appears to be caused by a simple autosomal recessive in German Shepherds. While only about one percent of the dog population may be involved, mortality rate is fairly high. Even when PRAA has been ruled out as the cause, I believe the percentage in German Shepherds is quite a bit higher than the reported one percent.

Symptoms include slow or halted growth, weight loss, dehydration, water in the lungs, and persistent and progressively worse vomiting of food minutes after swallowing. The disorder usually is detected at or slightly after the commencement of weaning. As food slightly stretches the esophagus on the way down, an affected pup's muscles apparently fail to contract enough to prevent the food bolus from simply staying in a pouch just in front of the entrance to the stomach. In time, the muscles become weaker and even less able to squeeze the food ball, and even liquid food remains in a hanging pouch forward of the stomach entrance and below it. As with PRAA, the pup becomes emaciated and listless, often dying of starvation. In fact, the two conditions may be indistinguishable without autopsy. The accompanying pedigree study gives food for thought.

Congenital pyloric stenosis is a similar disorder but is mostly found in Boxers and other short-faced breeds; it is very rare in the German Shepherd. Spasm of the pyloric sphincter in excitable dogs, especially toys and miniatures, is also uncommon in the Shepherd Dog. There may be several other causes of esophageal dilation, affecting various breeds to different extents. However, German Shepherds have over thirteen times the incidence (of esophageal disorders) of all other breeds combined, though PRAA may be part of this statistic.

Vomiting and gastritis—Vomiting comes easily to dogs. Grass eating and subsequent vomiting give rise to all sorts of explanations, the most popular being that the dog was sick and ate the grass to help him throw up. Actually, *excess* grass is more likely the reason for the reflex action. Dogs eat grass because they like the taste of it, just as with the case of garbage.

Gastritis, an inflammation of the stomach lining, can be caused by the ingestion of too much grass, garbage, or indigestible materials. It can also be caused by viral or bacterial invasion, but much more common, especially in pups, is the presence of endoparasites: tapeworms, roundworms, hook-worms, whipworms, and coccidia. Actually, tapeworms or roundworms can fill up the belly to the extent that they back up and cause vomiting from sheer bulk. The initial treatment for gastritis or vomiting may be withholding food and administering *Kaopectate®* every four hours.

Torsion—Commonly called bloat, sometimes described as gastric dilation/volvulus, this is a terrifying and frequently fatal disorder that German Shepherds and many other deep-chested dogs experience. A twisting of the entrance and exit to the stomach traps the food and gas, and as the stomach swells, the twist is more unlikely to be relieved without veterinary help. Great strides in surgical treatment have been made, but the key to reducing the high mortality is still *time*. Recognize the symptoms and get the dog to a veterinary surgeon, preferably an emergency or trauma-oriented hospital.

Simple dilation (swelling due to gas) may not be serious as long as the dog is able to pass food into the duodenum, but it has been estimated that 80 percent of all dogs that experience simple dilation will someday also have torsion.

Symptoms of torsion include a swollen, turgid abdomen; the sluggish action of the dog; his white, frothy, unsuccessful attempts at vomiting; and perhaps his scratching in the dirt to make a cool hole in which to lie down. Also, the spleen will feel like a hard lump. The spleen is normally wrapped around some of the stomach and therefore splenic torsion accompanies gastric torsion. When this happens, the return of the blood that flows through the spleen is shut off causing shock, the immediate killer.

The first thing your vet is likely to do is attempt to push a tube down the throat into the stomach so the gas pressure can be relieved. If he cannot get past the twisted part of the alimentary canal, he may opt for immediate surgery so he can untwist the organs.

One emergency veterinary service in the Detroit area uses a different kind of lavage tube in their treatment of acute torsion. The large diameter, stiff, black polyethylene pipe has a smaller, flexible tube inserted into it. This smaller tube is for warm water so that the stomach contents can be flushed out of the larger one for about fifteen minutes. In either case, once the dog has been stabilized, decisions can be made about whether to operate, or untwist a stomach or spleen still in volvulus.

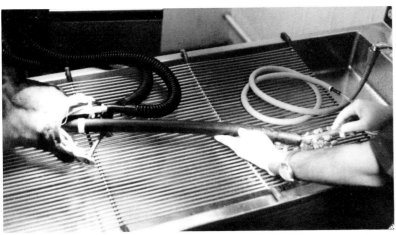

Torsion. Inserting smaller tube in preparation for lavage. Note connection to faucet. Photo courtesy Mark W. Lanier, DVM, director, Veterinary Emergency Service, Inc. Photo originally appeared in VM/SAC, May 1981.

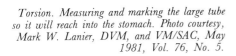

Torsion. Measuring and marking the large tube so it will reach into the stomach. Photo courtesy, Mark W. Lanier, DVM, and VM/SAC, May 1981, Vol. 76, No. 5.

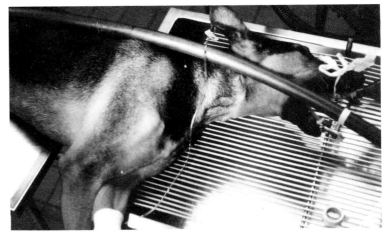

Follow-up surgical techniques are numerous, but the one with the most success in preventing future torsion is a tube gastrostomy. In this procedure, a rubber or vinyl tube is put into the stomach through the abdominal wall, and in a week the stomach wall at that point becomes attached with scar tissue to the peritoneum and abdominal wall. The tube is then pulled out. The surgical opening seals off in a few days, and since the stomach is fused to the abdominal wall, it is prevented from again twisting out of position.

Intussusception—In young pups (and other animals including humans) the intestine can invaginate (one part slips inside another). The condition, also referred to as "telescoping intestines," occurs in adults, too, but not as frequently. Most common causes include worms, obstruction by indigestible materials, garbage, or toxic substances. The German Shepherd seems to experience a high inci-

dence of this disorder and I believe there is a genetic propensity, a familial trait, in certain bloodlines.

Diarrhea and soft stool—Diarrhea can be a symptom of any number of disorders from cancer to overeating, but is most often associated with disease or parasitism of the small intestine. Diarrhea or loose stool is quite common in the German Shepherd Dog, even when no physiological disease has been identified. However, since this is not a normal condition, the owner should make a sincere attempt to find and attack the cause.

Some of the causative factors in true diarrhea are: pancreatic insufficiency, chemical or mechanical irritation of intestinal linings, parasites, micro-organisms, and a psychosomatic condition related to the "high-strung," emotional make-up of the German Shepherd Dog. Foods which can cause loose stool include milk (if suddenly introduced into the diet), liver, fats, and those with a high-fiber content. However, simple overeating is perhaps the most frequent culprit in adults.

Soft to runny stools may be an indication of a general inflammation of the stomach and intestines known as eosinophilic gastroenteritis. It is treated symptomatically with something to coat the lining, plus perhaps a steroid and *Kaopectate®*, until the dog "heals itself." Many veterinarians administer *Pepto-Bismol®*, also.

In the case of young puppies with watery stool or repeated diarrhea, *rush* to your veterinary clinic with the pup and the stool samples. Most of the time the cause of diarrhea in a young puppy is serious, such as parvo or coccidiosis, perhaps with hookworm as well.

Toxic gut syndrome (TGS)—This disorder has recently been identified as a specific syndrome, with some similarities to other disorders such as intestinal volvulus, which may have been blamed for death when TGS was the real villain. The German Shepherd Dog has a higher number of blood cells per unit of blood than do most other breeds, with 50 to 60 percent compared with 40 to 45 percent. When such a dog becomes dehydrated, thickened and/or lessened blood supply to the small intestine increases growth of bacteria which are always present there. These *Clostridium* and *E. coli* bacteria produce such quantities of toxins that the dog is unable to get rid of them fast enough, and death by poisoning occurs.

By the time owners see symptoms such as discomfort when the abdomen is touched, attempts to vomit, and excessive salivation, it is probably too late. Prevention may be accomplished through dietary means (feeding *Lactobacillus* acidophilis, yogurt, or cultured buttermilk), or by the same toxoid vaccine that is given to lambs to prevent *Clostridium perfringens* types C and D. As research is done on this recently defined syndrome, more will become known as to the best treatment.

Other problems—Ulcers have been diagnosed too frequently in German Shepherds and may be related to pancreatic problems or other causes: it's difficult to tell, when several conditions exist at once, whether one is the cause or effect of another.

Necrotic bowel syndrome, a disorder of unknown cause, is diagnosed usually on autopsy, when part of the intestine is found to be dead and rotting away. This condition may be synonymous with or overlap intussusception or other diseases. It takes a small toll, mostly among heavily linebred German Shepherd Dogs.

Eosinophilic ulcerative colitis—This syndrome is most common in Cocker Spaniels and German Shepherd Dogs. If your pup or adult has intermittent to constant diarrhea, with or without blood, this disease may be the cause. Initial treatment may include corticosteroids, antibiotics, and antispasmodics to see if the symptoms can be halted.

Irritable colon—Also known as spastic colon, this disorder with mucus in or on the surface of soft or frequent stools may be the result of stress. The best cure is prevention—breed stable temperaments and build confidence in puppies.

Anal glands—Occasionally, anal sacs may become infected, and the dog may scoot along on the ground, rubbing his rump in an effort to relieve the itch. This won't help, but you can easily "express" these glands. Lift the tail high with almost enough effort to lift the dog's rear off the table or floor, and very firmly pinch the sphincter including the sacs. Be sure to use a couple of layers of paper towel or some cotton to keep the liquid from squirting across the room or on you. Most dogs do not need attention nearly as much as owners think they do.

Perianal fistulas—Known by a number of names, these abnormal passages between two surfaces or an opening to the exterior, in the area of the anus, is a condition seen mostly in German Shepherds. While sometimes congenital, the disorder is sometimes caused by an injury or an abscess. Symptoms include frequent licking or biting at the "vent," and a bad odor and pus may also be seen. If untreated, ulceration will develop.

Good results have been reported with cryotherapy, freezing with liquid nitrogen or nitrous oxide. Since some veterinarians prefer to use familiar surgical procedures rather than cryosurgery, ask for a second opinion if you aren't sure, especially at a veterinary college clinic.

Polyps—Rectal polyps are little round or teardrop shaped red to purplish balls. Sometimes they are clustered like tiny grapes, and are found very close to the anal opening or further inside the rectum. They should be surgically removed, since they rupture easily and are a potential site for infection.

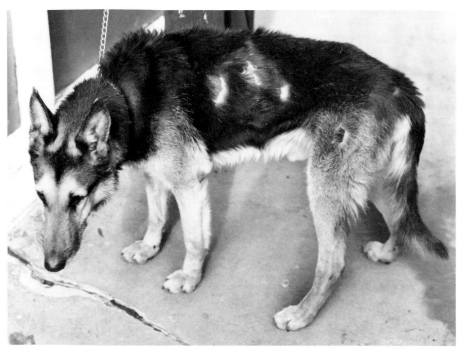

Pancreatitis. Clinical or subclinical (signs not as obvious) pancreatic insufficiency can be treated by feeding Viokase, a brand of whole raw pancreas made by A.H. Robins in powder or tablet form, contributing the amylase and protease enzymes the affected dog might not be able to manufacture himself. Pancreatic conditions are frequently misdiagnosed and frequently ''over-diagnosed'', but many non-specific diarrheal disorders are also improved by enzyme supplements. Photo by A.H. Robins Co.

A drop of bright red blood recurring on the end of stools is a sign that you should have the dog examined for polyps.

The Pancreas

The pancreas is a rather long, V-shaped gland which aids the digestion of food. Located near the stomach, it produces enzymes, bicarbonate, and hormones; the first two are delivered to the intestine, the third is secreted into the bloodstream. One major enzyme, amylase, breaks down the long starch macromolecules, while others break down fats and proteins.

Clinical pancreatitis—The word *clinical* may be used to mean "obvious," at least to a veterinarian with the training and equipment. Most causes of this disorder are of unknown origin. Adult clinical pancreatitis is not tremendously common in the German Shepherd Dog, but when it does occur it is usually the middle-aged, obese bitch on a fatty diet that has it. Chronic pancreatitis symptoms include emaciation, dull dry coat, and high appetite with poor digestion as seen by fatty, loose stools containing undigested starches. Treatment is accomplished mainly by correcting the diet.

Pancreatic atrophy—German Shepherd Dogs have a predisposition to pancreatic atrophy, also known as juvenile atrophy, and certain bloodlines have been much more associated with it than others. For years I have referred to it as subclinical pancreatitis, because people who are not familiar with familial and breed tendencies are likely to miss the subtle signs. The disease usually starts before the dog is one year old, though many are three before symptoms are noticed. When lack of "drive," less coat lustre, coprophagia or poor weight are seen, have the stool examined by your veterinarian for abnormal fat level and absence or low level of the trypsin enzyme.

If the problem is discovered before it becomes severe and chronic, dosage with *Viokase®*, a brand of powdered raw pancreas added to the food, usually produces good results. (By the way, *Viokase®* is also good for non-specific diarrhea.) I believe there is a strong possibility that subclinical pancreatitis can worsen with neglect into an acute attack by enzymes on the pancreatic and surrounding tissues themselves, and that this condition may be the cause of many instances of diagnosed perforated ulcers.

Urogenital System

Prostatitis—The prostate gland, situated behind the bladder, sometimes gets inflamed. Bacteria may be the direct cause, in which case the dog will respond favorably to antibiotics if administered early on. If not, surgery may have to be performed. Prevention (in humans, at least) may be a matter of diet: zinc, in sunflower seeds, oysters or other zinc-rich foods or tablets. Dog foods generally contain adequate zinc, but it wouldn't hurt if you gave your dog some of your herring or roasted pumpkin seeds once in awhile.

Urinary stones—Stones or calculi can be found in various organs such as gall bladder, kidney, urethra, and urinary bladder. Cystine calculi are found fairly often in male German Shepherd Dogs, and since it is a hereditary disorder, dogs that test positive for cystinuria, or whose progeny are positive, should not be bred. Some dogs urinate more frequently, show a tinge of blood in the urine and evidence pain when pressed at the bladder. Antibiotics are give to fight secondary infection, but direct treatment may involve drugs to dissolve the stones, surgery, or ultrasound which pulverizes the deposits so they can exit with the urine. Prevention of recurrence is a prescription diet.

Kidney diseases—Inherited or congenital renal (kidney) diseases are known to affect German Shepherd Dogs and several other breeds. While there is no specific cure, good diet and plenty of water are the best preventatives. "End-stage kidney disease" is a name given to a collection of similar lesions with a variety of causes. Part of the syndrome, which you may read about, is called renal cortical hypoplasia; it has been proven to be hereditary in several breeds so far, and is also probably so in the German Shepherd Dog.

Endocrine System

The endocrine system is composed of a number of ductless glands and portions of various organs which regulate metabolism and other chemical and physiological actions. True endocrine glands are the pituitary, thyroid, parathyroids, and adrenals. Other glands have endocrine tissue dispersed among other types of tissue; examples are the testicles, ovaries, and pancreas. There are also endocrine functions in the placenta, liver, kidney,

Pituitary Dwarfism. All three dogs are littermates; two of them have a pituitary gland malfunction, with the expression of the gene modified slightly by other factors to give differences in the affected dogs. They look like pups I have seen which were so malnourished that I wonder if starvation stimulated the pituitary to slow growth in order to preserve life as long as possible. The opposite (overnutrition) is thought to be possibly to blame for skeletal problems, too, maybe again through the pituitary. A disorder similar to or identical with pituitary dwarfism has been described in Yorkshire Terriers. Photo courtesy Dr. Erik Andresen, Royal Veterinary and Agricultural University, Copenhagen.

and mucosa of the stomach and duodenum although no endocrine tissues are apparent. A characteristic of endocrine tissue is the production of chemicals (hormones) which affect other body systems such as glands, organs, and nerves.

Pituitary—Also known in medical circles as the hypophysis, the pituitary is located underneath the brain. The neural part of the pituitary gland produces three hormones: oxytocin sold under the tradename *Pitocin®* , vasopressin, and the third major hormone is an anti-diuretic. The outer part produces even more hormones which affect growth, gonad activity, and other glands.

The German Shepherd Dog has been called "the ancestral type," one of the "most normal," and so on with regard to body size and shape. But those breeds with pushed-in faces, dwarf legs, and other so-called desirable abnormalities have obvious defects in the gland.

Occasionally a dog will develop a tumor on the pituitary; for all practical purposes, it is inoperable. Symptoms include gross edema, protruding eyes, joint soreness, personality change due to pain, and changes in other organ functions. While there may be a genetic component responsible, I believe this, like most tumors, is due mostly to environmental causes.

Pituitary dwarfism—This disease of unknown inheritance mode is quite rare, but obviously present in the breed. I believe it is the result of recessive genes acting in the homozygous state. Since the pituitary directs the functions of other glands as well as regulates growth, the dogs with this disease are not only stunted, but of precarious health. Most of the poor health may be a result of reduced thyroid activity, so dosing with Thyroxine can help a dwarf live a fairly normal life.

Adrenals—These small glands sitting on top of the kidneys produce several hormones involved in sex function, metabolism, and the nervous system. The outer portion of the gland is called the cortex. Cortisone is a synthetic steroid which duplicates naturally-produced adrenal cortex hormone, and shows that hormone's use in combatting inflammation, shock, and allergies. Epinephrine (*Adrenaline®*) and norepinephrine are administered when the adrenals don't make enough themselves.

Thyroids—Although these glands aren't very often defective, when they do malfunction, the result can be hair loss, infertility, and other problems. Since these symptoms can be attributed to other disorders, have a blood test run before jumping into treatment. A gradual decrease in thyroid function is to be expected in aging dogs and can result in a loss of fertility, poor coat, puffy belly, muscle weakness, lowered appetite and metabolism, or mental sluggishness. Flea-bite allergic reaction can either mimic or cause low-grade hypothyroidism.

Parathyroids—Tiny spherical or ovoid bodies near the thyroids, but quite independent of their larger neighbors, the parathyroids almost never cause a problem unless the thyroids are damaged or removed. Tetany (fever, stiff limbs, locked jaws) is more often a symptom of some other disorder, but the parathyroids or a calcium imbalance could be the cause.

Pancreas—In addition to its involvement with the digestive system, this gland also is involved with the endocrine system due to its secretion of insulin. Diabetes is caused by a lack of this hormone, and is far from unknown in the breed. Symptoms include increased thirst and urination, cracked pads, and dry skin. The treatment for dogs is similar to that for humans and regular medication (oral or injected) may be needed.

Nervous System Disorders

Nervous tissue responds to stimuli by carrying an electro-chemical current from a nerve ending to the brain. From there the current goes to a motor nerve and an ending in a muscle. Disorders are revealed as a loss of balance, vomiting, paralysis, or in other manifestations.

Myositis—An apparently hereditary condition known as eosinophilic myositis is seen most often in German Shepherds and Weimaraners. Discussed earlier in this chapter, this disorder is marked by swelling of the face.

Polymyositis—Weakness in the legs, occasionally in the rear legs only, and partial paralysis brought on by exertion, may be symptomatic of this neuromuscular defect found mostly in German Shepherds. Polymyositis should be considered if one or two limbs tend to slide out from under the dog and gait is considerably shortened. No treatment is satisfactory.

Myasthenia gravis—This is a congenital disorder in terriers, but in German Shepherd Dogs and other large breeds, it is generally acquired around two years of age. Actually, it may be a hereditary weakness or autoimmune disorder that is suppressed until after puppyhood, and it may be brought on by fever or administration of certain antibiotics.

Severe limb weakness, difficulty in breathing, megaesophagus, and other symptoms may be present in the afflicted dog. It is also sometimes associated with tumors of the thymus, and since this organ atrophies with age, old dogs may exhibit signs of myasthenia gravis without having the actual disease itself. Unless a cause is found, there is little hope of any effective treatment.

Coonhound paralysis—Known in some texts as acute idiopathic polyradiculoneuritis, this disorder of the nervous system is found in Coonhounds and German Shepherd Dogs with enough frequency that you should be on the lookout for it. Once thought to be transmitted only by the bite of a raccoon, it also appears in England where there are no raccoons.

At the onset, a progressive weakness begins in the hind legs, with many owners reporting contact with a wild animal a week or two previously. The

A type of peripheral nerve disease (other than in brain or spinal cord) referred to as giant axonal neuropathy can mimic the paresis of GSD Myelopathy or hip dysplasia or trauma to the cord. Fairly rare so first suspect HD if your dog exhibits hindquarter weakness/paralysis. Photo courtesy Dr. Ian Duncan, Montreal General Hospital, and W.B. Saunders, Philadelphia, publisher of the February, 1980 Veterinary Clinics of North America book in which it originally appeared.

severely affected dog may die from respiratory muscle failure, but most dogs recover in weeks or months with good nursing care and physical therapy. This may include lifting and moving the dog due to his general muscle weakness, and enduring his lack of bladder control.

Although the specific cause of the disorder is not known, immunity does not result from exposure, so a typical viral cause may not be at the bottom of this frightening condition. However, I still believe that one day a virus agent *will* be discovered.

Vestibular disease—The ear is made up of outer, middle, and inner sections. The animal's sense of balance originates in the inner ear. In its vestibule are three canals or loops, containing a gelatinous material with crystals and hairlike cilia. The brain responds to changes in orientation through the pressure put on these ingredients. If something goes wrong with the nerve leading from the cilia to the brain, the dog may not know which end is up, almost literally.

Congenital vestibular disease is seen most in German Shepherd Dogs, Dobermans, and Beagles from birth to three months of age. Affected pups may circle to one direction, use a wall for support, or fall over at random. Improvement should be apparent by three or four months, as the inner ear system develops. Occasionally treatment with antibiotics helps accelerate recovery but this is not to be expected because most cases are not acquired.

Hypoxia—Sometimes during whelping a pup doesn't get as much oxygen as he should; this oxygen deprivation is called hypoxia and symptoms can resemble those of vestibular disease. Varying degrees of brain damage can result from hypoxia, the most common being a "slow learner" syndrome. Usually the condition improves somewhat, but it is important that you help a bitch whelp especially-large puppies to prevent hypoxia.

Spinal cord—Many cases of spinal and related nerve damage are due to sudden trauma, but some can result from encroachment of bone or tumors into the space occupied by the cord. Since nervous tissue does not regenerate, such conditions result in partial or complete paralysis.

GSD myelopathy is the first disorder that comes to mind when German Shepherd Dogs and spinal lesions are spoken of together. Peculiar to Shepherds, the first symptoms are usually seen at about

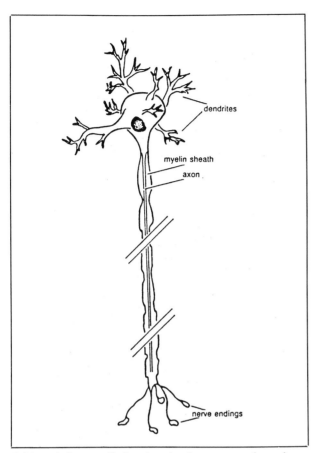

Fairly typical nerve cell. Length and endings vary greatly, and some have no myelin "insulation."

eight years of age and have a duration of five to six months at most. Initially, the dog does not seem to realize what position his rear legs are in; soon he will begin to drag his toenails and the top part of his paws, and may tremble as if palsied. Eventually, he will be unable to get up on all four legs, and by this time most owners will have decided upon euthanasia.

Similar symptoms may be brought on by nerve cell degeneration normally associated with age. However, with this disorder the rapidly progressive nature of GSD myelopathy is not seen. Neoplasms also cause the dog to display symptoms similar to those of GSD myelopathy. These tumors on the spinal cord, neuroepitheliomas, have a special predilection for German Shepherd Dogs from six months to maturity at three years of age.

Spondylosis deformans is common to many large breeds due to their bone proliferation. The ventral surfaces of the bodies of two adjacent vertebrae become bridged from one to the other, as though links of a chain were welded together. Many dogs

with this condition go on for years without sufficient discomfort to warrant medication. A lack of back flexibility during gaiting and dragging of the toenails will probably be the outward signs.

Epilepsy—German Shepherd Dogs, Keeshonden, Poodles, and other breeds are subject to inherited seizures, with Shepherds and the Tervuren showing the highest incidence. Epileptic seizures are brought on by some sort of brain damage, whether hereditary or acquired through head injury, poisoning, or whatever.

Seizures are classified as either *petite mal* or *grand mal*. Petite mal seizures may be as brief as half a second and may never even be noticed. Shepherds are especially prone to clusters of small attacks, from two or three up to a couple of dozen in the space of a day or two, followed by a rest period of about a month. Pre-seizure signs typically seen are excessive barking for about half an hour, restlessness, and a lack of interest in food during such activity.

My first exposure to a grand mal seizure was very unnerving. I was seated at my kitchen table when a visiting client's German Shepherd Dog began whining and moaning. I glanced over to see him staring wide-eyed to one side, apparently at nothing more than a closed cabinet door. Suddenly he started blinking, looked frightened to death, and took off running, moaning all the while, and crashed into the cabinets at the other end of the kitchen. He then rushed wildly in my direction, scattering chairs and scaring the socks off me. I found myself standing on top of the table before the dog collapsed on his side and I realized what this was all about! Lying on his side, the dog then lost control of his bladder and bowels, his teeth chattered, eyes blinked, and mouth salivated. In a few minutes he grew quieter and soon regained consciousness and stood up. Other than panting from exertion, his only post-seizure reaction was a shameful expression when he became aware of his feces and urine on the floor, and anxious humans bending over him.

That dog didn't give any warning, though I've since witnessed others that did. A large number of conditions can trigger an epileptic episode besides the psychological ones such as anxiety and excitement. Ticking clocks, rhythmic thumping of car tires, unexpected or loud noises such as barking, handclapping, gunfire, etc., are sometimes involved. However, most seizures seem to be visually induced: flickering light or even what seems to us to be steady light from fluorescent lamps may induce an episode. Driving past utility poles or in and out of tree shadows, looking through a screen door or at a striped or checkerboard pattern can also do it. Many episodes are traceable to the dog's sleeping under or near a television set, and an article by Thomas Fisher in *Modern Veterinary Practice*, April 1981, indicates that seizures may be more easily brought on by such radiation when the dog's eyes are closed!

In the German Shepherd Dog, epilepsy is mainly a polygenic trait. It is familial, so siblings of an affected dog can be expected to show signs, too,

Immediately after falling—clonic extension of jaws and kicking motion of legs.

Clonic clenching of jaws, slight twitch in front legs, and characteristic spreading of toes of hind legs.

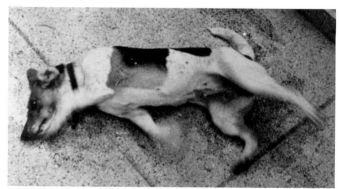

"Running" or "swimming" phase of "automatic stage".

Beginning of recovery phase, starting at the front and progressing to the rear.

Recovery. Note stringy saliva.

Epilepsy. A dog of Horak's Breed specially developed for research into epileptic disorders, is shown in the half dozen stages typical in most grand mal seizures. Photos courtesy Z. Martinek & F. Horak, Prague, Czechoslovakia. Thanks to research/dog fancier/educator Tom Fisher, Horseheads, N.Y.

though not all will. The best advice is to not breed epileptics and their close relatives. In most cases the individual's life can be prolonged with proper medication, but I have concluded that the situation progressively worsens and euthanasia is the eventual end. If you have an epileptic Shepherd Dog, avoid triggering stimuli, follow your veterinarian's medication regimen, neuter the dog, then enjoy him or her as long as you can. Non-genetic epilepsy can be controlled with drugs.

Paroxysmal rage reaction (PRR)—What may be just a variation of classical congenital epilepsy has been called PRR, the word paroxysm referring to a seizure or outburst of emotions from a burst of brain wave activity. PRR has been seen most in German Shepherd Dogs, some spaniels and retrievers, Saints, and Bernese Mountain Dogs. As in classical epilepsy, symptoms first appear in most dogs between adolescence and two years of age. So far, 80 percent have been males. Typically, the afflicted dog starts snapping for no apparent reason, his pupils dilate, eyes are out of focus, and he may growl, attack, and bite indiscriminately, even at his owner. The only ''treatment'' is euthanasia.

PART 3—CONTAGIONS AND POISONS

Contagious Diseases

Infectious disease is usually caused by a virus or bacterium, but another class of microorganism midway between these two is the group collectively known as rickettsia. In addition, fungi can cause infections.

Bacterial diseases include brucellosis, leptospirosis, staph and strep infections, and others. Viral diseases include parvo, distemper, infectious hepatitis (CAV), parainfluenza, a number of herpes varieties, and probably a whole bagful of yet-to-be-discovered types. Spotted fever from ticks is a rickettsial disease.

Distemper—Canine distemper is the most common cause of brain and spinal cord disease, and once contracted is very difficult to treat successfully. Very few dog fanciers of today have actually witnessed distemper thanks to the development of vaccines. Prevention is essential, as is the realization of the fact that there is no such thing as permanent immunity.

Canine Adenovirus Type I—(CAV-1): This virus is the cause of infectious canine hepatitis (ICH) and formerly was best known by the vaccine's name, hepatitis, and in combination with distemper and leptospirosis, as DHL. The virus has more recently been found to cause not only liver inflammation (the meaning of the word hepatitis) but also respiratory and other systems' epithelial cells, and in other, ''endothelial'' cells such as found in blood various organs, and lymph nodes. The uvea and cornea of the eye can be affected; the condition commonly known as ''blue eye'' is a result of the infection described as anterior uveitis and corneal edema. With much care, a pup can regain use of one or both eyes, but the prognosis generally is very poor. The use of CAV-2 vaccine instead of CAV-1 vaccine apparently eliminates the danger of ''blue eye'' resulting from the vaccination itself. It is believed that the virus from contact with an infection source (or sometimes from the CAV-1 vaccination) causes the endothethial cells in the cornea to react when challenged by releasing antigen, which is followed by immune complexes forming in the aqueous portion of the eye. Macrophanges and neutrophils then phagocytize those complexes, but causing cell damage at the same time, which in turn allows fluid accumulation in the corneal tissue. (See Chapter 2 for discussion on pigments and Tyndall scattering for an explanation of the blue color). This desease is very contagious, though not very widespread. Incubation takes from two to nine days, compared to four to six days for distemper and as long as two weeks for parvo. Serums, antibiotics, vitamin B complex, and relaxants are helpful, along with a low fat, digestible diet. About two-thirds of the victims recover.

Rabies—Rabies is a frightening, fatal viral disease which is transmitted by animals that seem to be immune to it, and by others that bite during the infective stage before they die of it. Heavily salivating dogs, without a verifiable vaccine record, and that bite people or other animals must be brought to the veterinarian for observation. There is no cure. Suspected animals are confined till tests can confirm the presence of rabies virus.

Respiratory viral diseases—A number of viruses cause respiratory problems in dogs, and though the individual diseases may be distinguishable, many are collectively known as ''kennel cough.'' Other diseases may enter the body by way of the respiratory system and may or may not cause irritation there as they pass through on their way to another particular site. Parvo seems to be highly fatal when seen in combination with other viral and bacterial conditions in the respiratory tract. If your dog is boarded often or lives in a kennel with several other dogs and not as much air movement as is found outdoors, make sure he is regularly vaccinated against all such diseases.

Herpes—There are many organisms in the family called herpes, the most common in dogs being the puppy killer at ages of around two weeks or less. Herpes seems to be present in most dogs most of the time, but some pups are more susceptible or under more stress which lowers their

---

HERE TODAY, WHO KNOWS TOMORROW?

Viruses have a tendency to mutate. Canine parvovirus, for example, which appeared around 1977 seems to be a mutant of feline panleukopenia virus. Every couple of years humans are subjected to one or more new strains of flu virus which may be resistant to a vaccine made from a strain that previously swept the country.

The decade of the 1940s saw such a new virus afflicting dogs in the northern United States. Whitney reported on its symptoms and breed susceptibility, noting that the dogs that seemingly recovered showed clinical signs of brain tissue inflammation after a couple of additional weeks. This encephalitis was found very often in dogs of excitable breeds, with German Shepherd Dogs having the highest incidence, and those individuals that veterinarians considered high-strung were most often correctly predicted to contract the encephalitis symptoms after the throat symptoms (gagging) had subsided. That particular disease seems to have died out, but may simply have mutated to another form that is now known by another name.

---

resistance. New puppies that are not given adequate drying, heat, and nursing opportunity right after delivery are most at risk. Once the disease has been noticed in a litter, few survive. Prevention is the only remedy.

Parvo—One of the newest diseases on the scene, canine parvovirus (CPV), is a slightly modified or mutant version of feline panleukopenia. This disease which strikes mostly at pups, sick and old dogs, is characterized by light tan-colored, very watery stools, often excreted with explosive force. They may also be grayish in color and mistaken for coccidiosis. Vomitus may show the same color, and both may be heavily spotted or lightly streaked with blood. The onset of parvo is more sudden and violent than hookworm, which has somewhat similar stool symptoms. Loss of appetite, fever, and sudden death, usually within 48 hours, also indicate the presence of parvo, but it might be a good idea to have a section of intestine sent to a pathology lab for confirmation.

At times, there seems to be a 100 percent mortality rate with parvo; at other times a very low percentage of deaths is reported. This discrepancy may be due to the deaths being caused by other organisms in combination with parvo—another virus or a bacterium may act synergistically with the parvo virus. It is known that hookworm's effects will be greatly multiplied in the dog with parvo, so it is important to keep dogs free of parasites as well as vaccinated. There is no real cure in sight, but *prompt* treatment of symptoms may save your dog from death due to complications—contact your veterinarian *at once* when puppies have bad diarrhea.

The primary mode of parvovirus infection is by ingestion of stools or stool-contaminated grass. If the dog merely walks through a contaminated area and later licks his feet, he may contract the infection. For this reason many veterinary facilities regularly use a 1:30 dilution of chlorine bleach to wash the floors. If you maintain several dogs, you, too, would benefit by following their example.

Dogs that have been vaccinated will need annual boosters, especially if they are stressed by work or show circuits. How early one can immunize pups depends on when the mother's antibodies they received at birth and nursing begin to "wear off." A blood test (on the dam) called a "titer" may tell when it's most likely to work, but even then, parvo may spread before the pup's system has a chance to build up its own antibodies.

Pseudorabies—This viral disease resembling rabies can be spread to swine and cattle by canine carriers. Once infected, the animals become paralyzed and thus worthless for market. The principal danger of pseudorabies to dogs is the propensity of farmers to shoot stray dogs before they get near his pigs or cows. In his mind, he is protecting his investment, especially if there has been a report of the disease in the area.

Leptospirosis—"Lepto" is a disease caused by spiral bacteria. It is not extremely widespread, but is highly contagious, and is contracted when a dog tastes or sniffs grass contaminated with an infected dog's urine. Thus, it can and does spread rapidly at dog shows, making it essential that your show dogs be protected by vaccination at least every six months. There are two varieties of leptospirosis, one with a mortality rate of around 50 percent, but vaccines list both types on the package. Symptoms include chills, fever, vomiting, muscle pain, and sometimes diarrhea, and the incubation period is from one to two weeks. Recovered dogs can be carriers for long periods.

Brucellosis—Canine brucellosis, often abbreviated "c.b.," has received much attention in dog magazines in recent years. So far, I've only had a couple of second-hand reports, neither one well-documented, of brucellosis in purebred, show-stock German Shepherd Dogs. You can often get a false positive reading on the blood test, and by the time the second and third tests show normal, the rumor may spread. The incidence is highest among Beagles, most of which are raised and kept six or more to a pen, which may or may not have anything to do with this #1 position. Yet stud dog owners still overreact and demand c.b. tests on all bitches flown or brought in for stud. Have you ever found one such owner to claim his stud dog has weekly c.b. tests? Talk about sex discrimination!

Canine erlichiosis—This is a disease to which the German Shepherd Dog is especially susceptible. Erlichiosis is caused by a tiny viruslike organism of the rickettsia family and transmission is by tick bite. Once infected, the blood cell count drops considerably, and the dog hemorrhages internally and loses weight. Most dogs do not recover. During tick season, watch for the symptoms of fever, excessive

nasal and eye watering, reduced activity, and loss of appetite. A hard lump in the abdomen, indicating a swollen spleen, may also be noticed. Ask your vet about treatment with Diamperone.

Mycoses (fungus diseases)—Various fungal diseases affect dogs. Histoplasmosis, for example, is endemic to the valleys of the Ohio and Mississippi rivers. Blastomycosis is now quite common across the whole country, though it seems to have originated in the Midwest.

Other fungi bother dogs to some extent. Ringworm produces red circles or discs. Interdigital pyoderma is a problem quite common to German Shepherd Dogs. It refers to any number of inflammatory bacterial conditions between the toes. This disorder is often misdiagnosed as strictly a fungus problem because it is often accompanied by a fungus growth, either because the dog's resistance is low or he has been treated for a week or two with topical antibiotics to combat the bacteria. A fungal infection in the outer ear is often accompanied by red spots between the toes, so use the ear medicine to also wash those areas.

Poisons and Toxicologic Problems

The insatiable curiosity of young puppies often exposes them to toxins. Indigestible materials can cause intestinal obstructions which lead to bacterial growth, toxins, and necrosis. Adult dogs also are not immune: I remember a lady who had a terrific stud dog whose favorite toy was an old shoe sole. One day the dog got sick and died; on autopsy, the shoe sole was found inside, blocking the food, setting up bacterial growth, and releasing toxic substances into the blood.

Deadly animals—There are two toad species in the US which can be deadly to dogs: *Bufo alvarius* and *Bufo marinus*. The latter, also known as the Marine Toad or the Giant Toad (15 cm from chin to vent), is the more dangerous and is found in the Rio Grande Valley and south, plus Hawaii and areas around Miami, Florida. The one in Hawaii is less potent than the mainland subspecies, with mortality rates in untreated dogs of 5 percent and nearly 100 percent, respectively. *Bufo alvarius*, the Colorado River Toad, is found in our southwestern states and gets as large as a grapefruit. Most dogs recover within an hour of biting one of these.

Other toads are usually quite repulsive to dogs, since they taste bad and cause salivation. But there are exceptions. Dr. Karen Munekiyo, a Hawaii veterinarian, relates the story of a dog that became intoxicated after mouthing toads, repeatedly setting out to find and "get high" on *Bufo marinus.* The dog developed a tolerance to the bufotoxin, but like an alcoholic on booze, became emaciated. The problem was solved by preventing him from finding toads, and eventually his weight and condition returned to normal as long as he was forced to "stay on the wagon."

In the Southwest, care should be taken to prevent your dog from being bitten by either of the US's two poisonous lizards: the Gila Monster and the Mexican Beaded Lizard. Of course, snake bites are sources of toxins, and the four major types of poisonous snakes should be known by the owner whose dog may venture into snake country. Teach your dog to avoid *all* snakes, as even large non-poisonous varieties can cause severe infections from puncture wounds. In addition, certain ticks secrete their own toxins that produce "tick fever."

Hypervitaminosis—While vitamin supplementation is generally helpful and safe, it *is* possible to overdose with some, especially vitamins A and D. Vitamin toxicity can be avoided if supplements are handled with common sense (see Chapter 8).

Other poisons—Foreign chemicals (those not normally in the system) which commonly cause poisonings in dogs fall into these categories:

- Rodent poisons
- Slug bait and insecticides
- Heavy metal ions
- Herbicides and fungicides
- Paint
- Gasoline
- Solvents
- Pesticides
- Crabgrass killer
- Rat poisons
- Engine coolant /antifreeze
- Poisonous plants
- Animal toxins
- Drugs
- Miscellaneous (garbage, mostly)

Heavy metals include lead and arsenic compounds found in paints, wire insulation, solder, putty, crabgrass controls, roach and ant poisons, and other insecticides. Chlorinated hydrocarbons include chlordane and lindane, ingredients in mange dips. Too frequent dipping may allow too much to be absorbed by the skin's lipid (fat) layer. Carbaryl (as in Sevin dust) and other carbamates should be used knowledgeably. For example, the dog wearing a flea collar and on a heartworm regimen should not be allowed to walk on a kennel run treated to kill hookworm eggs. Similarly, dogs recently fed dichlorvos (*Task®*, *Atgard®*) should be kept away from other organophosphates such as malathion, diazinon, or parathion found in garden or flea spray.

A handsome dog with correct proportions, but incorrectly posed. Note sloping back, overextended left metatarsus, and the right hock consequently on the ground.

Drugs from the owners' medicine cabinets may even be dangerous. For example, aspirin in large doses for prolonged periods is toxic, especially to immature dogs whose enzyme production is not able to detoxify some chemicals. When using sulfa, be sure to provide plenty of water for your dog since these drugs can be toxic and damaging to his kidneys. Misuse of tranquilizers, wormers, and other drugs is common and dangerous in old or debilitated dogs.

Plants—Most dangerous plants don't taste good, or are out of reach, but there are some others that you should know about. Certain toadstools can damage the liver; cyanide is in leaves of peach, cherry, laurel, and flax; a blue-green algae in some stagnant pools can be fatal. Other potentially dangerous house and outdoor ornamentals include:

Amaryllis	Foxglove	Nightshade family
Autumn crocus	Fritillaria	Oleander
Baptisia	Glory lily	Pencil tree
Black-eyed Susan	Goldenchain	Poinciana
Bleeding heart	Horsechestnuts	Poinsettia
Bloodroot	(incl. Buckeyes)	Pokeweed
Bluebonnet	Hyacinth	Poppy
Boxhedge	Hydrangea	Precatory beans
Caladium	Iris	Privet
Candelabra cactus	Jerusalem cherry	Rhododendron
Castor beans	Jessamine	Rhubarb leaves
Chinaberry tree	Jimsonweed	Snowdrop
Christmas rose	(Thornapple)	Spurges
Crown-of-thorns	Lantana	(Euphorbia)
Daffodil	Larkspur	Star of Bethlehem
Daphne	Laurel	Tansy
Delphinium	Lily of the valley	Tobacco (Nicotine)
Dumbcane	Lobelia	Tulips, other
Eggplant leaves	Lupine	bulb plants
English ivy	Mistletoe	Virginia creeper
Euonymous	Monkshood	Wisteria
	Nettle	Yew

Treatment—A phrase from the field of ecology really says it all: "The solution to pollution is dilution." If you wash a dog that has fallen into a dangerous material, you will greatly reduce the danger, and the same is true for bathing the eyes, feet, or mouth with running water. If the dog has ingested a potential poison, to induce vomiting try an emetic from your medicine cabinet such as syrup of ipecac. Don't let him vomit highly volatile solvents such as gasoline, or the vapors may collect in his lungs and compound the problem. The best general rule after you've flushed off or out as much

Persistently swollen vulva, indicative of hyperestrinism, probably caused by tumors on the ovaries.

as you can, is to get the dog to the veterinarian, having called ahead and described the poison.

PART 4

Cancer and Other Neoplasms

The word *neoplasm*, literally translated 'new growth', includes tumors and cancers. A tumor is any swelling or lump characterized by excessive multiplication of cells. They are abnormal in their quantity and in proportion to cells of other tissues around them. When a tumor continues to grow, cuts off or interferes with life processes, or sends out cells to colonize elsewhere (metastasize), it is called a cancer. While most tumors are benign, cancerous ones are malignant and the word *cancer* refers to the *condition* of such neoplastic malignancy, rather than to a particular site or type.

Sometimes the word *tumor* is used to include harmless cysts, and while some cysts are indeed tumors, technically not all of them are. Basically, a cyst is a pocket or sac of loose material of non-cellular nature. It may be the result of a gland plugging up or of the body's encapsulating reaction to physical insult such as a shotgun pellet or larva.

Heredity and non-genetic factors in combination cause neoplasms. Cancer is the leading cause of death in German Shepherd Dogs as it is in other breeds. Mammary tumors are more frequently found in the German Shepherd than is any other single type. Breast tumors are almost completely avoided if a bitch is spayed before her first heat; if the operation is performed after she's mature (at about 2½ years) there seems to be no such protective effect.

When one mammary tumor is found, the standard surgical practice is to remove *all* the mammary glands, since it is likely there are errant cells in each of them. Chemotherapy is sometimes suggested, but since in German Shepherds, the usual life expectancy after surgery is less than nine months, the decision is necessarily based on cost, emotional attachment, the dog's age, and other factors.

Pituitary gland tumors have been mentioned earlier. Most common symptoms are those of Cushing's disease (obesity, weakness), diabetes insipidus (diuretic deficiency), and generalized edema (excess fluid in the tissues).

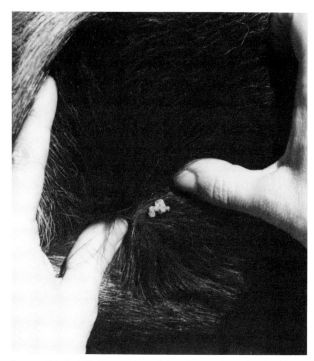

Impacted hair follicles can cause lumps just under or in the skin. The thick, cheesey material can usually be expressed (squeezed out) with the thumbs, and picked up with tissue paper. No further treatment is needed, as a rule, but you may have to squeeze it one or two more times.

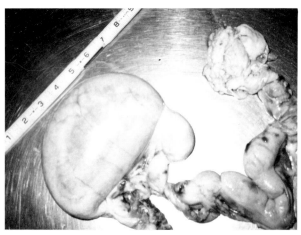

Cystic ovaries.

Ovarian cysts, often called cystic ovaries, are difficult to diagnose early. However, prognosis is usually good, as this type of cancer is slow-growing and does not readily metasticize. As a preventative, spaying is quite successful as a rule. If your bitch has abnormal heat cycles, enlarged vulva, greasy skin, reproductive tract infections, mummified puppies, stillbirths, or resorbed fetuses, suspect an ovarian tumor.

A few skin tumors are seen in German Shepherds, more in white dogs than others. Clogged sebaceous glands are often mistaken for or classified as tumors, but if you can squeeze out the thick, yellowish-white material of a fatty consistency, it is the former. If you are unable to remove the material by expressing the cyst between your thumbnails, it may or may not be a tumor and it must be examined by your veterinarian.

Old dogs seem to develop many wartlike tumors. These are almost always benign and of no concern unless they bleed frequently or change quickly. Most of these are on the muzzle around the whiskers, some are next to nails, and a few can be found almost anywhere on the skin.

The German Shepherd Dog has a fairly high relative incidence of bone cancer, which is probably the worst form when it comes to metastasizing, early in its development. Even with amputation and chemotherapy, most dogs survive less than a year, but without treatment, life expectancy is much shorter.

Cancer is the number one killer of dogs, when all types and breeds are considered.

13

THE GERIATRIC GERMAN SHEPHERD DOG

This chapter by
Charles H. Young, D.V.M.

Growing old is a gradual biological process resulting in a deterioration of body tissues and cells. It is irreversible and inescapable, and the mechanism whereby cells deteriorate and ultimately die is still a profound mystery.

There are three generally recognized theories of aging. The genetic theory proposes that there are aging genes which act as biological clocks. These genes are programmed within the cell and will only allow the cell to divide so many times; when the last division occurs, the cell dies. The second theory states that abnormal deleterious products accumulate in the tissues and wear them out. The third theory says that the cells undergo changes (mutations) which alter their activity and lead to their death.

Being born, we die;
our end is the consequence of our beginning.
—Manilius

During their lifetime dogs pass through three phases: growth, maturation, and deterioration. The growth phase begins at birth and lasts about two years. During this time cells divide and mature and the animal reaches adulthood. The maturation phase is the adult phase and lasts until the dog is about seven years old. The deterioration phase lasts from seven years of age until death. It is this last phase that will be addressed in this chapter.

THE AGING PROCESS

Over the years, the average life span of dogs has gradually increased to thirteen. Although dogs seldom live beyond their eighteenth birthday some have been known to attain the ripe old age of twenty-seven. In general, small and medium breeds outlive large breeds, and females outlive males. Small breeds are considered old at fourteen years, and large breeds at twelve. One pet survey involving dogs seventeen years of age or older showed for every one large dog there were twelve small dogs still alive.

There are certain biological events that seem to be universal to the aging process, regardless of size or sex. There is a decrease in muscle mass, an increase in body fats and a change in their distribution. Organs such as the kidneys and liver gradually deteriorate which inevitably results in a slow-down in their function. Cells lose some volume of water and solids with age. Metabolic rate slows down, and blood pressure increases. The mineral content of bones decreases creating a condition called osteoporosis.

MAINTAINING THE AGING DOG

The primary way to protect the health of an older pet is to immunize against infectious diseases. The most common vaccinations are for distemper, hepatitis, leptospirosis, parainfluenza, parovirus,

Ch. Ulk v. Wikingerblut, owned by R. and M. Roberts. Photo courtesy Mary Southcott

THE SEASON FOR OLD FRIENDS

In my green youth spring beauties bloomed,
Violets jeweled my life with friendly faces.
Each promised purpled constancy
And each I clasped and cherished.

Years, clustered, ripened in my summer's sun,
Bade me dream of wine to share.
Friendships warmed in lengthening days
While butterflies, spiralling, ascending, danced.

Now fallen acorns wait for leaf burial;
Now wither white rays and golden heart
Of pearly everlasting, false to its name.
Trees rust in cold, damp nights
To mirror my own autumn oxidation.
The harvest falls to foxes
And purple verities are dun and done with.

Strange, in the grimness of winter's glare,
Hope ripens orange on persimmon trees
Whose bitter fruit begins to shrink,
To soften, yes, to die.
But mystery unfolds as just before release
It is transformed to total sweetness.

Hold on, my heart, relinquish not
What through the seasons love has bought.
Old dogs are dearer than the rest;
Old wine is good, old friends are best.

F. L. Lanting

coronavirus, and rabies. The immune system of the old dog is depressed, leaving him more susceptible to these viral illnesses. Therefore, the most important thing an owner can do for his or her pet is to vaccinate annually.

Beyond vaccination, the purpose of good geriatric care is twofold: to maintain a good state of health and to increase the life of the pet. The basis of this program begins in the veterinarian's office with a thorough examination including a complete blood count (CBC), urinalysis, stool check, heartworm test, heart check, and musculoskeletal examination. The urinalysis could detect diabetes, or bladder or kidney infections. The stool check could reveal the presence of any of several types of worms which are more dangerous to the old dog. Listening to the heart could determine the existence of defective heart valves called murmurs. A musculoskeletal exam could reveal hernias and skin abnormalities such as hot spots and tumors. A look at the eyes could show cataracts (cloudiness of lens). By examining the ears, mites and outer and middle ear infections may be detected. Caught early many of these problems can be easily treated by the veterinarian with no long-term effects on the pet. Left untreated some of the problems become expensive, time consuming, and can even be fatal.

Once the old pet has passed his physical exam, the owner needs to be aware of other factors which contribute to longevity and good health. Dogs are like people: they need exercise, good nutrition, and a relatively stress-free environment in order to prosper.

Exercise

Most older dogs will not want to exercise, but activity is vital to good health. Exercise maintains muscle tone, aids weight control, increases metabolic rate, improves circulation and respiration, and strengthens bones against osteoporosis. In osteoporosis there is loss of calcium in bones not exercised. When bones are exercised, blood calcium is deposited in them making them stronger and denser. Physical exercise also improves digestion and elimination thereby overcoming flatulence (passing gas).

Nutrition

Good nutrition and proper weight are essential to good health. When dogs reach the age of seven or eight, a slower metabolism plus a more sedentary life can cause serious weight gains. Obesity is also influenced by breed characteristics, temperament, and hormonal irregularities, but no matter what the cause, fat dogs usually have more physical ailments and a shorter life span than their normal-weight counterparts. In addition, surgery is less predictable and more hazardous for the obese dog.

To prevent weight gain the daily caloric intake should be reduced by as much as 20 percent if necessary. In scientific experiments reducing the daily intake in rats delayed the onset of major diseases while overfeeding the young accelerated maturity and shortened life. On the other hand, overeating in the mature animal invited diabetes and heart, kidney, and liver disorders. Likewise, research scientists state that man can increase his life span by reducing his daily caloric intake. In short, there is a direct relationship between nutrition and aging, and the overweight dog does not live as long as his leaner counterpart.

"The lines are fallen unto me in pleasant places; yea, I have a goodly heritage." Psalm 16:6. Martha Kerner and friend, Covy-Tucker Hill's Lucy Locket, two beautiful girls with "goodly heritages."
Photo courtesy Maison du Chien Kennel.

Overweight dogs should be put on a sound nutritional program. They must lose weight while receiving an adequate diet which includes vitamins and minerals. There are dog foods designed specifically for overweight, older dogs. You may get these on prescription from your veterinarian, or your veterinarian can set up a special dietary program for your pet. Vitamins are very important since the aging dog's body does not absorb them as efficiently as does a young dog's. Vitamins also play an important role in your dog's immune system.

With age there is a gradual decrease in the immune system response which protects an animal against disease-causing agents such as viruses and bacteria. This natural decline is accentuated by poor nutrition. Vitamin E, iodine, vitamin B_6, vitamin A, and vitamin C are necessary for the immune system to work. Without these nutrients the animal is more likely to fall prey to agents causing various diseases. The immune system also gives protection from tumor cells. Vitamin supplements given on a daily basis decrease the likelihood of cancer forming in later life. Scientific research has demonstrated that the immune system can be stimulated by oral adminstration of vitamin E. When given to young and old mice this vitamin enables the immune system to form antibodies against infectious diseases.

Your pet's recommended daily intake for vitamin E is 0.51U/lb. of body weight. However, during times of stress and increased unsaturated fat intake the above dosage is doubled. To assure that your pet is getting the proper nutrition a quality geriatric supplement that contains adequate vitamin E is recommended. Remember, never supplement your pet's diet without first discussing it with your veterinarian.

No doubt the topic of vitamin supplementation will continue to be somewhat controversial in research circles. At present, one thing can be said with certainty: The addition of vitamins to the daily diet improves overall health and immunity on a short-and long-term basis.

Stress

Older dogs are at a disadvantage when it comes to stressful events. Any insult or stress lowers the immune system response, and since the immune system of the old dog is already depressed, he is even more susceptible to illness. Because of this, old dogs require extra protection from the environment. One recommendation is to keep an older dog warm and dry during the winter months to protect him from diseases such as pneumonia. Older dogs hear and see less and move more slowly; consequently, they are more apt to be hit by an automobile, so confinement in old age could be a lifesaver. Early treatment of injuries and medical problems such as worms will reduce stress.

Care of Other Systems

Reproductive—Fifty to sixty percent of ten-year-old intact bitches develop mammary gland tumors. If a bitch is spayed before her first heat cycle, her chances of developing such tumors are about zero. Spaying before 2½ years will also reduce the incidence of mammary tumors.

Teeth and mouth—The most common dental problems in the old dog are wearing of the teeth, tumors, and periodontal disease. Wearing of the teeth is a normal aging process; one-third of the tooth could be worn down by the age of ten years. Any outgrowth or elevation of tissue may be indicative of tumors or hyperplasia and should be seen by a veterinarian.

Periodontal disease is the primary cause of tooth loss. It is the most common disease affecting your pet; 90% of all dogs over the age of five years are affected. It can be generally defined as inflammation or ulceration of the gums around the tooth, or gum disease. In periodontal disease there is a wearing away of the bony socket (alveolus) which secures the tooth. This causes looseness and subsequent tooth loss.

The onset of peridontal or gum disease rarely occurs suddenly, but usually develops over a 3-to 5-year period before symptoms become obvious. Gum disease begins by the invasion of plaque, a soft material in the groove between the tooth and the gum line. Dental tarter (calculus) is an accumulation of mineral salts, bacteria, and food particles on the teeth. At first this material called plaque is soft, but with the passage of time it thickens and hardens forming tarter. As the tarter build-up continues, it preses on and between the gums and causes inflammation and recession of the gum line. This invasion causes swelling which in turn is more likely to trap *more* food within the groove. As the process continues, bacteria multiply and destroy the

gum tissues. The gum line then recedes toward the tooth root with the final outcome being gum disease and loosened teeth.

Periodontal disease can be recognized by bad breath and inflamed gums. Gums are usually ulcerated and recessed, teeth are loosened, and tartar is visible on the teeth. Diseased teeth and gums can contribute to even more serious problems such as constipation, vomiting, and loss of appetite. In addition, veterinarians generally agree that certain heart, kidney and liver diseases are caused by diseased teeth and gums.

A good periodontal disease prevention program requires work by the owner and the veterinarian. The owner can clean the teeth with a soft toothbrush or cloth wrapped around the index finger. Most old dogs will not tolerate toothpaste so it should not be used. Instead brush the teeth with equal parts of baking soda and salt. Start training a dog at an early age to accept this dental care. Older dogs may be difficult to train but the owner should give it a try.

Diet can play an important role in keeping the oral cavity healthy. Dogs on a diet of soft foods tend to accumulate tartar more rapidly than those fed dry dog biscuits and other hard or coarse-textured

Modern version of "His Master's Voice"?

"Just a little off the sides, please."   *Photo courtesy New Skete Monastery, Cambridge, N.Y.*

foods that are somewhat abrasive and help self-clean the teeth. Chewing toys such as nylon or rawhide bones also help to clean the teeth and gums. For some pets these suggestions may be ineffective or impossible to implement; therefore, annual or semi-annual visits to a veterinarian for an oral check up and possible cleaning is recommended.

Musculoskeletal—This system is composed of numerous separate bones which are bound together by ligaments, tendons and muscles. These ligaments join two bone ends together in a joint (i.e., elbow). Bones are composed of an outer dense protein-mineral portion called the cortex, and an inner soft portion called the marrow cavity. The ends of bones are capped by a protective layer called cartilage which function to prevent excess wear and tear when the articulating surfaces rub against each other. As dogs enter their geriatric years, pathophysiological changes occur in bones (osteoporosis) and in joints (osteoarthritis).

Osteoporosis takes place where the cortex of long bones becomes thinner, more dense, and brittle. There are many reasons for this, but for our purposes it is due to two processes. The first is that bone-forming cells (osteoblasts) become insufficient

and less active and thereby lay down less bone. The second reason is that bone mineralization is decreased due in part to a negative calcium balance, or calcium deficiency. This mineral deficit may be caused in part by inadequate intake and/or poor intestinal absorption of calcium.

In humans osteoporosis is most common in postmenopausal women. At that time in their lives, estrogens are deficient and can no longer inhibit parathormone, a hormone which reabsorbs calcium from bones. Research has shown that oral supplementation of estrogens may slow the development of osteoporosis but oral calcium and vitamin D supplementation alone did not help.

Osteoarthritis is characterized by a progressive disintegration of joint cartilage. Because joints move, they are worn over time. This is why the disease is generally seen in older pets, especially overweight dogs and large breeds. Arthritis can affect one or more joints and can be localized or generalized. It is the most common problem of the musculoskeletal system in the aging dog.

X rays taken of the dog's stiff joints may show *spondylosis* (new bone formation about intervertebral joints) in German Shepherds, and destruction and remodeling of joint surfaces in all dogs. Treatment consists of relieving the joint pain and aspirin given at 5 grains per 30 pounds 2 to 3 times per day is very helpful, but may cause bleeding if continued. Anti-inflammatory drugs are very beneficial, but should only be used for short periods of time and must be prescribed by a veterinarian.

Renal—The kidneys are a complex filter system with a primary function of eliminating waste products from the blood. They are programmed to handle a lot more work than the body requires; therefore, the old dog can lose the function of one kidney and three-quarters of the other one without any adverse effect to the dog. However, in most old dogs the kidneys are the weakest link of all the organ systems and are usually the first to fail. Because this is true, chronic renal disease will occur to some degree in all old dogs.

The symptoms of kidney problems are variable but start with the aging dog being depressed, unresponsive, and anorexic. He may not show any obvious pain other than slight discomfort when pressed on each side of the spine behind the last ribs (in the kidney area). As the condition progresses, the old dog will urinate more frequently and thirst will increase. By this time the urine contains blood although it may appear normal to the eye; as bleeding increases the urine will become slightly red or coffee-colored.

As the kidneys become more impaired there will be a dramatic change in the dog's disposition. He now has uremia, a toxic condition caused by the kidneys' inability to eliminate toxic nitrogen waste products. He is very depressed, vomits, and has diarrhea. Uremia is very serious, requires the veterinarian's attention and may require hospitalization.

One of the most common renal inflammatory diseases is interstitial nephritis called simple nephritis. It has been diagnosed in three-quarters of dogs eight years of age or older. This condition is caused by viruses and bacteria and is a gradual, progressive disease that runs a slow course. Symptoms are weakness in the legs, vomiting, poor appetite, depression, bad breath, and increased thirst. As the condition worsens, the pet may lie down, convulse, and die. A physical examination including blood and urine tests are used to diagnose the condition.

Because the kidneys are failing, the aged pet should be allowed to urinate several times a day and possibly during the night. He needs adequate water because water helps prevent kidney failure. To reduce the unwanted waste products which must

Rocco vom Busecker Schloss SchH III, at over 10 years of age.

Ch. Linnloch Brigadier at 10 years of age.

Photo courtesy Dorothy Linn.

RONDEAU
ON THE DEATH OF A DOG

They whimper in their darkness and their pain,
But oh, so softly that one has to strain
To hear. The life that Folly whispered low
Would stay (and how we wished that it were so!)
Ebbs out, although we grasp for it—in vain.

Steady the flow, invisible the stain
Their life-blood leaves on those who here remain.
Unwilling to desert us as they go,
    They whimper in their darkness.

We pity pets who painfully are slain,
Or even gently enter Death's domain,
But human-folk will feel Fate's cruelest blow,
For, long after they lay their friends below,
And sorrow weighs them down like iron chain,
    They whimper in their darkness.

be eliminated by the kidneys, specially prepared commercial diets such as *Hill's K/D®* may be purchased, or the owner may prepare his pet's diet with moderate quantities of quality proteins along with vitamin and mineral supplements. With proper medication and diet, many kidney patients can live a reasonably long and normal life.

Urinary incontinence is loss of voluntary control of urination. The cause of the weak bladder may be the absence of the female hormone, estrogen, a condition resulting from spaying of a young bitch. Incontinence shows up in later life, and is treated successfully with estrogens.

Cardiovascular—Heart disease occurs frequently in the geriatric patient. Even though clinical signs may not be recognizable, pathologists have found that three-quarters of all geriatric dogs have heart lesions. Since heart disease is common in all old dogs there are certain early symptoms for which to look: (1) Easy tiring or shortness of breath especially after moderate exercise, and (2) coughing at night or after exercise or excitement. If the condition worsens, the abdomen and legs may swell with fluids and the dog may even faint after exercise or excitement.

As the heart ages, certain physiological changes take place. First, fatty infiltration of the heart muscle occurs, especially if the dog is overweight. Second, chronic valvular disease, in which the valves of the heart become thickened, occurs almost universally in geriatric dogs.

As aging progresses the heart begins to weaken, increasing the work load of the heart, and decreasing the circulating blood to the body organs. The kidneys and liver cannot filter and detoxify the blood as they once did, and eventually, some part of the body will fail and the dog will die. Consequently, early treatment of a failing heart will prevent the geriatric dog from an early death.

Treatment should enhance the heart's ability to pump blood and decrease the excessive body fluid build-up. Most dogs are successfully treated with digitalis, diuretics, rest, diet, or any combination of these. If a pet is overweight, his weight can be reduced by feeding low sodium foods. The objective of this diet is to decrease the cardiac work load by reducing the body's congestion, and feeding low sodium foods is of the utmost importance because a decrease in sodium lowers the work load of the heart. Hill's low sodium prescription diet is a valuable treatment for heart disease in dogs.

BEHAVIORAL CHANGES

Many behavioral characteristics and problems of the old dog are a result of normal physical changes or diseases. The old dog is naturally less active, but at times he may be uncharacteristically aggressive or fearful. He may bark more, urinate more, or lose his housetraining altogether. Most of these behavioral changes are physically linked but some are reactions to social situations.

The old dog may be less active and agile because of such degenerative diseases as arthritis and reduced hearing and eyesight. He is therefore less sure of himself and may react with fear since he has lost physical strength, agility, sight, and hearing. He sleeps more, but his rest does not refresh

his body so he awakes tired and depressed. He may sleep more by day and be restless at night. Because of fatigue, poor eyesight and hearing, and possible senility, he may seem indifferent to many activities.

Uncharacteristic aggression may be caused by brain tumors, but is more likely to be musculoskeletal disease. A dog with hip dysplasia would possibly bite when touched on a painful hip. Another dog with a cervical intervertebral disk protrusion would snap if patted on the head. Drugs can relieve the pain associated with musculoskeletal diseases, and discipline can overcome the habit of aggression.

It is understandable that a deaf dog would be unresponsive to sounds, but sometimes deaf dogs bark excessively. Why they bark is unknown, but discipline can eradicate this obnoxious habit. A

Rocco vom Busecker Schloss SchH III, FH, KKL, "a" (lifetime). An outstanding example of his famous kennel's attention to both utility and beauty of form. Impressive and large, good withers, very good angulation fore and aft, easy ground-covering gait. 10 years old in this 1980 photo courtesy of owner L. Schautt.

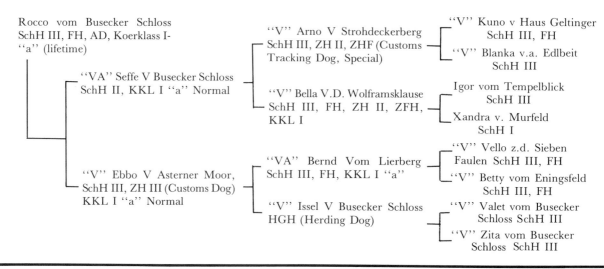

blind pet may be able to successfully navigate in familiar surroundings, but would run into things in a strange place, and exhibit fear or aggression when unsure of strange people or surroundings.

Loss of "housetraining" could be a result of incontinence which is easily treated, but it could also be caused by heart and kidney disease. The pet may drink and urinate more frequently, and therefore make more trips outside, even at night. He cannot be left inside for long periods of time because he can no longer hold the urine.

Some elderly dogs are greedy, especially if they are diabetic. The brain cells which control the appetite of the diabetic dog do not receive adequate glucose and therefore he appears to be constantly hungry. The owner must realize that the dog *thinks* he is hungry but is not.

Changes in the environment such as hospitalization or moving to a new home upset the geratic dog. He may respond poorly to new members or pets in the family. At these times, the dog may require extra attention and understanding and even discipline.

During hospitalization the geriatric dog may refuse to eat or urinate. He may bark excessively, or gnaw on the cage or himself. Therefore, when the old dog goes to the hospital, take a familiar object such as bedding or possibly food with him. Visit him frequently since he misses social contact. If possible, treat him at home. A move to a new home would be facilitated by keeping the same food, bedding, and routine, and providing extra attention.

A new pet in the family may elicit several responses; the old dog may ignore the new pet, resent it, or play with it. A visitor may cause fear or aggression in the old dog. A new member in the family or even a death may evoke obnoxious behavior such as loss of housetraining, barking, or fighting.

EUTHANASIA

Euthanasia is a Greek word meaning "easy death." Basically euthanasia involves an overdose of a sedative which causes unconsciousness and then death when the heart and lungs cease to function. All dog owners probably hope their friends will peacefully die in their sleep; however, that is not usually the case. The final choice of euthanasia belongs to the owner although a veterinarian's advice should be sought because some conditions

(such as incontinence) are treatable and with a little extra care, a pet can live comfortably for a longer time.

Some conditions such as terminal cancer or broken spine speak for themselves: euthanasia is necessary. An illness or disease which is painful and progressively debilitating would require euthanasia at some point. In animals, pain is not always obvious; for example, an owner might not recognize the arched back of a pet as a symptom of a painful kidney stone. This fact underscores the importance of regular veterinary checkups where such symptoms will probably be caught in time. For many pets pain can be easily and inexpensively treated. Arthritis pain can be alleviated with aspirin or steroids.

In arriving at his decision, the owner will want to consider another point—cost. Some treatments are simply too expensive to perform, especially on the aged dog. Another factor is the amount of time required to care for the pet. Some people who work or have small children to care for do not have time to treat a pet several times daily or make weekly trips to the veterinarian.

When euthanasia has been decided upon, several other decisions must be made. Does the owner wish to witness the euthanasia? Most do not, including many veterinarians who are also very attached to their pets. However, some of those who do watch euthanasia come away impressed with the ease with which death comes and are thereby relieved.

Another decision is what to do with the body. The veterinarian can prepare the body for burial by the owner or may dispose of the body. Cremation is an alternative which some veterinarians provide for an additional fee.

How to tell the family is another responsibility. Honesty is the most effective choice, and children should be truthfully informed. They deserve to know the truth and after an initial outburst, will usually accept the necessary death quicker than many adults. In addition, experiencing the death of a pet could help them adjust to the passing of a friend or member of the family. Older people who decide on euthanasia may need extra encouragement or attention since they frequently have become very attached to the pet.

Euthanasia is a kindness to a pet whose health has deteriorated to the point of much pain and no pleasure.

Senior citizen. 1970 Grand Victor Ch. Hollamor's Judd pictured in 1977. Owned by Sandi and Bob Card.   *Morrissette photo.*

14

BREEDING

When I was a member of the Constitution & By-laws Revision Committee of the German Shepherd Dog Club of Toledo, we compared the concern of responsible breeders with canine overpopulation to the wording in our official document. Patterned after suggested examples of the AKC and the GSD Club of America, our document originally stated that one of the objects of the club was to promote the breeding of German Shepherd Dogs. Our committee changed that to read, "Section 2. The objectives of the Club shall be: (a) to encourage and promote *the improvement* of the German Shepherd Dog breed…" (italics added). After a few years we noticed that our lead had been followed by a number of other clubs, including national breed clubs—in some cases the wording was identical.

BREEDER RESPONSIBILITIES

Any owner of a decent stud dog gets service requests for numerous inferior bitches, and if he can muster his resolve and scruples, he'll turn them down for the good of the breed and to prevent more low-quality dogs from appearing on the scene. By so doing, he'll also protect his dog's reputation and contribute to the promotion of more responsible breeders.

When we get letters or phone calls from owners of bitches to be bred, we ask first about OFA certification or to see the X-ray picture of the bitch's hips. Without one or the other we will not accept them for breeding. If the bitch has normal hips or will be radiographed before breeding and we will be able to see the film, further questions are asked regard-ing temperament, physical description, etc. Other stud dog owners may have a slightly different set of questions or ask them in a different order. Unfortunately, too many have no questions other than, "How fast can you get the stud fee to me?"

Why breed dogs? The most obvious answer is to produce more dogs, hopefully of as high quality as the parents. Unfortunately this seldom happens, with most of the pups being less desirable than either parent, a few being of equal quality, and a very few that are better. This fact necessitates that each breeder use only the best possible individuals. Our goal should be to produce better dogs, but in so doing we will inevitably produce average or mediocre dogs in greater numbers. We breeders are always hoping to find that magic "click" that gives the five-champion litter, or the right combination that yields a large percentage of offspring that are better than the parents. This is why some of us breed dogs…what is *your* reason?

Who Should Breed Dogs?

Not all people who raise puppies deserve the hard-earned title of breeder. This term should carry an aura of professionalism, and the person holding it should be responsible which means having compassion for individual dogs, respect for the breed as well as its Creator and founders, and a desire to excel. The breeder should be well-read, observant, and knowledgeable in the areas of anatomy, genetics, psychology, and kinetics. In addition, he needs a *thorough* knowledge of the standard of his breed and to that end this book is primarily based upon the Standard of the German Shepherd Dog. Attendance at dog shows will apply this book learning to visual experience, especially if the observer compares his breed to others. He must be impartial and immune to "kennel blindness," tactful with owners of undesirable breeding prospects, and truthful with potential buyers. He should be willing to start all over again rather than breed his only dog if it is not worthy, and willing to admit to his own error as well as to his dog's faults. It sounds rather Kiplingesque, but if you can rise to this description, you'll be a breeder, my friend.

Which Dogs Should Be Bred?

Perhaps a better way of stating this would be to ask which dogs should *not* be bred. The first to be excluded should be those with serious polygenic disorders. Hip dysplasia in its more severe forms is one example. Extreme or serious temperament problems are also in this class, as are gross structural deficiencies. Simple recessive or dominant traits should be guarded against as well, but their combinations may be more sharply visible in offspring than are those of polygenic origin.

One early cardinal rule is: *Never double up on faults.* Single-gene problems can often be overcome by the next generation in some of the offspring, but multigenic traits are harder to eradicate. If both the sire and dam have turned-out feet, or grade 2 dysplasia, or light eyes, or swayback, or long coat, the chances are somewhere between moderate and

100 percent that the entire litter will have those same problems. The number of affected pups depends on the mode of inheritance (dominant or recessive, single or many genes, etc.) and not only will the first generation be involved, but so will succeeding generations. So...if your dam has a particular fault that you don't want in the offspring, you must make every effort to ascertain that the stud to be used does not exhibit that same fault or carry it in his background.

A second rule to follow in choosing breeding partners is: *Don't try to compensate one fault with its opposite.* If one partner has a roach back, breeding it to a dog with a swayback will not produce all level-backed offspring. That's an extreme example, but it illustrates the principle that Mother used to preach: "Two wrongs can't make a right." *Each partner ideally should be free of the faults you wish to avoid in the pups, but make sure that at least one* does not exhibit them nor do they run in his family.

Third, a rule of thumb that is admittedly unscientific, but which I've used to keep me somewhat on track, can be expressed as: "Three strikes and you're out." All dogs have faults, but the more that are combined in any one dog, the harder it will be for that dog to produce a winner or low-fault offspring. If a potential breed dog has one moderate fault, it may be forgiven. Even if it has two, the other partner's good points may be enough to allow the combination. But if there are three moderately

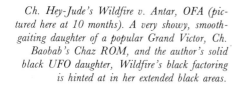

Ch. Hey-Jude's Wildfire v. Antar, OFA (pictured here at 10 months). A very showy, smooth-gaiting daughter of a popular Grand Victor, Ch. Baobab's Chaz ROM, and the author's solid black UFO daughter, Wildfire's black factoring is hinted at in her extended black areas.

1981 Grand victrix, Ch. Anton's Jenne. Sister to the 1979 Gr. Vx, this extremely-angulated sable Zeus daughter had been Select in 1980, Canadian Siegerin in 1979 and 1980, and Canadian Grand Victrix in 1980. A daughter of Jenne's by a Zeus son took Best Canadian Bred from the puppy class over champions and Select dogs at the Sieger show in Toronto in 1980. Bred by Alice Zygmont, owned by Al and Rose Pellatt of British Columbia, Canada. Photo courtesy Pellatt.

serious faults, that dog should definitely not be used as a breeding animal. The faults I have in mind are *slight* softness in temperament, faulty gait, and *mild* hip dysplasia. A relative increase in severity in one or two of these categories might be equivalent to all three being present. Likewise, a passel of minor faults can add up to be as annoying and difficult to overcome as one or two more serious ones.

To return to the original question of which dogs should be bred, a breeder, by knowing which dogs should *not* be bred (at least to each other) will be better equipped to decide which dogs *are* good candidates for perpetuating and improving the breed. This process, along with an understanding of the Standard, plus an "eye" for beauty, harmony, and proportion, will practically guarantee a professional breeder.

When to Breed

Let me preface this section by emphasizing that not all bitches or dogs need be bred, not even all good ones. It is not necessary for every dog to become a parent and there are a number of advantages to spaying females and neutering males. In fact, spayed bitches are possibly the best housepets, but more about that later when we get into the subject of birth control.

At what age should a dog be bred? No matter what the subject, extremism is seldom a good idea. With this in mind, it may not be best to breed a very young or a very old bitch, though she may be able to conceive any time from ten or twelve months to ten or twelve years. Some German Shepherds have their first season as early as eight months of age and some of these are able to become

pregnant at that time. Many people who *believe* they speak with authority make a big deal out of not breeding a bitch until her second or third season and cite "emotional maturity" as their main reason for this theory. However, I suspect that more often than not a bitch that will be a good mother will be one regardless of when conception takes place. The bitch some may call emotionally immature is probably somewhat less than the ideal mother, as described by von Stephanitz, at *any* age. I have probably bred more bitches on their first season than have 95 percent of those who would disagree with me. Therefore, my advice is if you feel your bitch is too "immature emotionally," don't breed her...*ever*.

On the other hand, the older a bitch gets, the harder a litter can be on her. Although she will probably have her seasons throughout her lifetime, simple matters such as hearing, running stamina, resistance to disease, and general condition are all in natural decline and the pregnancy/delivery/lactation routine will be doubly stressful for the older bitch. The oldest pregnant bitch I've ever had was ten years old. She was accidentally bred, though it was fully intentional on *her* part. She developed an infection and we had to have her spayed before that litter reached term, but I've seen a number of normal deliveries from 9-year-old dams. The condition of the individual is the primary factor, but the older the bitch the greater the risk.

Start breeding when you're confident the bitch will OFA-certify (hips) and stop breeding her when it adversely affects, or is contraindicated by her health.

Is she ready?—Determining the proper timing is not simple, but there are a few guidelines that should make the decision of when to breed easier. If the bitch owner does not know for sure what day the bitch started dropping blood, watch her actions with the stud (put them together *only* after they've been introduced with a fence barrier between them); if she flags, breed them as long as the stud isn't scheduled in the next run. You could also feel the vulva to see if the turgidity is decreasing and it is getting softer; of course, having had her in your care for a few days is best for you to ascertain this change. Don't rely on the color of the discharge, as some will show fairly bright red all through the acceptance period, and others will change from bright to pale or colorless discharge long before the end of estrus. Use willingness to stand only as an *indicator*, not a definite sign, as some bitches don't want to breed but on one single day, some not at all; others are not interested even on the day their systems are most hospitable to penetration of the ova. If the bitch doesn't become playful and entice the male, have them play running games; if she knows to fetch, perhaps chasing a ball will arouse the male, since the art of love in canines is mostly pursuit. If the male is experienced and eager but the bitch is not, hold her so he can attempt entry without being snapped at or avoided, but do this only after giving them time to run and play together. Lack of immediate interest is not a sure sign that they are not ready.

Vaginal smears as an indication of readiness are not reliable for the average stud or brood bitch owner, as accuracy depends largely on repeated daily tests to determine the *change* in shape of epithelial cells, not just the fact that those shapes are abnormal. Few breeders have the desire or finances to make daily visits to the veterinarian's office, or to invest in the equipment and chemicals necessary for the staining and microscopic analysis of the cells scraped or swabbed from the bitch's upper vaginal area. However, if you decide to try it, your veterinarian can show you the cytology routine.

Blood tests can indicate the day on which luteinizing hormone reaches the maximum level in the blood, but as you will read in the chapter on reproduction and gestation, this peak serum LH level can be reached anywhere from a couple of days before acceptance (estrus) to a few days after the bitch first stands for stud. And, since it takes one to four more days after that peak for ovulation to occur, the LH level won't tell you exactly when it will happen.

There is no foolproof way to choose the very best day to breed your bitch, but I would recommend the thirteenth or fourteenth day after first dropping of blood (excluding false starts) if that day is known, or my second choice would be the second or third day the bitch is willing. Otherwise, breed them the first day she'll stand, and then every second day thereafter until she is no longer interested.

HOW TO BREED DOGS

Preparation

A variation of Murphy's Law states that if you spend a small fortune shipping a bitch cross-country for three or four ties, plus pay an enormous non-refundable stud fee, then pay for full-page advertisements, your bitch will not take. The "Law" continues as your neighbor's pet shop refugee that has been kept locked in a pen guarded by Pinkerton's for three weeks becomes impregnated by a wandering Cockapoo that squeezed through a 3-inch gap under the chain-link fence and engaged in a five minute rendezvous.

To decrease the risk of failure, several steps can be taken by the brood bitch owner. The bitch should be examined by a veterinarian for worms, fleas, and signs of viral disease, and be brought up-to-date on her booster shots. A gynecological exam is recommended since it may reveal the presence of vaginal infection or obstructions; either could prevent conception.

Vaginal Infection

If a cotton swab on a stick applicator is inserted a couple of inches into the vagina, and a smear put onto a microscope slide, the presence of an abnormal number of leukocytes (white blood cells) may indicate an infection. But the breeder can also make a fairly accurate diagnosis by noticing staining of the hair around the vulva. This stain is usually beige or pus-colored in a sort of halo or ring, and the hairs will appear to be pasted together with the thick liquid secretion. Also, the bitch may engage in abnormally frequent or constant cleaning of the area. Such an infection may require repeated weeks of treatment or it may clear up by itself. One recommended regimen is to give oral antibiotics for about seven days and douche daily or twice-daily, as described below.

It isn't difficult to douche a bitch, and fourteen visits to the veterinarian in one week is out of the question. A 12 cc syringe with about 6 inches of flexible clear vinyl tubing, and a jar of *Furacin®* are all that are needed. With the plunger in the full down position, insert the tubing into the *Furacin* and withdraw 12 cc by pulling up on the plunger. Gently insert the tubing into the vulva and, with a twisting motion, further into the vagina. If it seems to bottom out after only a couple of inches, you may have run into a little shallow pocket on either side of the urethral opening (see below) and will have to back it up a fraction of an inch and try a slightly different angle. The initial penetration should be mostly upward, but the vagina curves over after a short distance and levels off somewhat. The tubing should be positioned far enough in so the end is past that bend or most of the *Furacin* will appear to come right out when the plunger is depressed. The liquid is its own lubricant, so petroleum jelly is not needed in this procedure.

Whether the bitch is standing or lying down is a matter of your preference. My wife had no problem with one bitch that wanted to lie down for the douche, but I had to have the same bitch stand in order to get the tubing far enough in. Sitting on a low stool, I put one leg under the bitch and more or less supported and restrained her by slightly raising my knee to her abdomen. I tucked her tail under one arm to keep it out of my way, and used one hand to guide the tip of the tubing into the vulva, twisting the syringe a little with the other hand. When the tubing was in far enough, I depressed the plunger with a moderately rapid motion. I then put the bitch on a down-stay command to give the *Furacin* a chance to spread a little further and prevent leakage. I don't think there would have been a greater loss if the bitch started walking around immediately, though keeping her in one place for a few minutes does keep the minor dribbling confined to one area. Don't allow her to urinate right away—she should have taken care of this *before* the douching.

Equipment clean-up is simple: rinse in tap water, then dry and store in a clean paper sack. Bacteria won't grow without moisture and a host. Don't clean the equipment with soap, detergent, or clean-

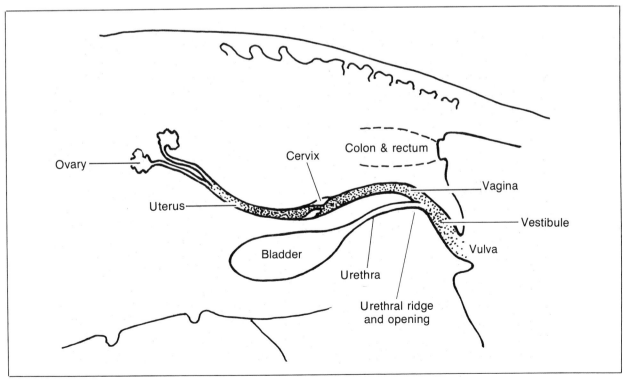

Urogenital structure of the female dog.

Ch. Amber's Flair ROM. No. 1 producing dam in Working Group 1980 (Kennel Review). Dam of Well-spring's H and I litters. Flair was a daughter of Zeus of Fran-Jo and is linebred 3,4-3,3 on F-litter Arbywood. Highest living ROM dam in the early '80's. Born July, 1974.

Photo courtesy owners Rosalind and Franklyn Schaefer.

ing solutions because you may want to use the same pieces for artificial insemination at a later time, and traces of such chemicals can be spermicidal.

Vaginal Obstruction

One of the concerns in stud dog management is the possible presence of one or two constrictions in the bitch's lower genitalia which may prevent penile penetration or delivery of pups. Such a constriction is often called a "ring," (not to be confused with the normal structure in the male called a vaginal ring through which testicles descend around the time of birth). If there are two constrictions, the first one is found at the very beginning of the vulva and can be felt by inserting the finger into the vulva up to a couple of centimeters at most. Dr. Witter of Columbus, Ohio, who has possibly seen more "rings" than most other veterinarians, says the obstructions he's seen are immediately at the entrance of the vulva and that maybe 50 percent of the bitches brought to him for this complaint also have the second constriction further in. If there *are* any with only the deeper ring at the vaginovestibular junction, he hasn't seen them and feels that it may not interfere with breeding. He performs immediate surgery on the vulva ring and allows

insemination right away, as the bitch in question usually has to be bred and flown back to the owner within forty-eight hours.

This first ring is not analogous to the hymen sometimes found in virgin human females, and is not considered a normal structure in the canine. No comprehensive published scientific work has yet been done on the subject of rings, but Dr. George Christensen unfortunately refers to a "vestige" of a hymen sometimes being found at the second, deeper location. In evolutionary jargon, the word *vestige* refers to an organ or structure once useful in an *earlier* stage of development of a species. In humans, such structures as the appendix, the tailbone, even the little toe and tonsils are sometimes called vestiges, or "left-over" organs, once needed by lower beings (which evolutionists concluded were our ancestors). However, some of these structures have been found to be useful after all, and the value or need of others simply has not yet been understood.

Dr. Leon Whitney, author of *How to Breed Dogs*, has also reported on a cordlike web obstruction at the entrance to the vagina, obviously not the first ring discussed earlier. This is additional testimony that a second ring can be present without one in the first position. This obstruction can sometimes be broken with a finger, or by the dog's swelling penis if he can get past it, but sometimes one will have to be snipped with blunt-tipped scissors.

Just what constitutes a true ring is a matter of controversy. Many veterinarians and breeders report feeling a single constriction about two inches in, and predict surgery will be necessary to allow breeding. But it is my hypothesis that in most, if not all, cases of deep constrictions, the abnormality is neurological, not anatomical. That is, the tightness is at the end of the vestibule and is of a sphincter nature which can be relaxed with hormonal or other stimuli. As examples, I cite two cases in which surgery was contemplated: one bitch belonging to a veterinarian was examined by another veterinarian on her way to a stud service. Both agreed the constriction would probably prevent a tie if not partial insertion itself, as the opening was extremely small. (Normally the diameter of a German Shepherd vaginovestibular junction is about 2 cm, or just under an inch, and the distance from the lower tip of the vulva is about 2 to 2½ inches.) Yet, the next day the bitch was bred naturally without trouble, and artificial insemination was unnecessary. The other bitch was one of mine, and had almost as tight an apparent constriction, again about 2½ inches in. I had the equipment for artificial insemination ready and although my veterinarian had been fairly sure it would not be possible, on her tenth day this maiden bitch was bred naturally by an inexperienced stud before I could get out to the kennel to help.

FEMALE GENITAL SYSTEM

We can conveniently divide the reproductive anatomy of the bitch into four sections: vulva, vagina, uterus, and ovaries. Since this chapter deals with the "how to" of breeding, emphasis will be placed on the first two; the latter two will be discussed in another chapter.

Vulva

The external genitalia we call the vulva is visible though partly hidden by hair, tail, and thighs, and much more noticeable when the bitch is in season, is pregnant, or has hyperestrinism. It is comprised of three parts: the vestibule, clitoris, and labia. The vestibule is a sort of chamber which is closed unless something is pushed into it. The cleft is about 1½ inches (3 or 4 cm) during the time between the bitch's seasons. At the further end of the vestibule, on a raised ridge between two shallow depressions, is the urethral opening, through which urine is passed from the bladder.

Vagina

The urethral ridge is continuous with the vaginovestibular junction which forms the beginning of the vagina, a highly dilatable muscular canal extending to the uterus. The vagina has many longitudinal ridges or folds which allow expansion during intromission and delivery, but its diameter is probably less than 2 cm (3/4 inch) at other times. At the far end of the vagina is the cervix which extends into the vagina in such a manner as to form a nearly vertical canal into the uterus. Except during mating and delivery, this canal is sealed with a mucous plug which helps prevent migration of microorganisms into the uterus. Sometimes the plug fails, and a vaginal infection can develop into the much more serious uterine infection.

The distance from vulva to cervix is 15 cm or more (roughly 6 inches) which is close to the length of the erect penis of the stud. Therefore, during the tie, the tip of the penis lies against the cervix so that ejaculation forces the seminal fluid directly into the uterus. The quantity of ejaculate is usually 6 to 15 cc's which quickly fills the tiny pocket under the cervix before being forced through the equally tiny cervical canal. (See below.)

Uterus and Ovaries

The word *cervix* means neck, and refers to a necking or narrowing of the tissues at that point. It forms

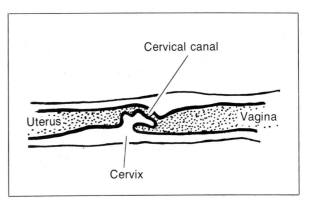

Structure of the vagina and cervix in the female dog.

the end of the vagina and, conversely, the beginning of the uterus. As the function of the vulva is to provide exit for urine and menstrual blood as well as point of entry for breeding, and the function of the vagina is to receive the penis, the function of the uterus is to serve as a route for eggs from the ovaries and a holding place for the fetuses. Thus, we will examine the uterus and ovaries in our later discussion of fertilization and gestation.

MALE GENITALIA

The genital organs of the male canine, as in most mammals, consist of an external scrotum containing two testicles and epididymides, vessels, an internal prostate (not prostrate!) gland, and a penis with its associated tissues. At this point I will emphasize the mechanics of breeding, concentrating on the latter organs. The rest will be discussed in the section on reproduction.

The Prostate

An egg-shaped gland containing muscle fibers, about the size of a walnut, and wrapped around the urethra and the neck of the bladder, the prostate gland is probably essential for successful breeding. This is because the volume of fluid containing the sperm is thought to be too small, without prostatic fluid, to be pushed through the urethra during ejaculation. The secretion of the prostate

dilutes the highly concentrated seminal fluid thereby giving more volume to the ejaculate.

The first fluid to be emitted during coitus is believed to be prostatic in origin and is alkaline in pH, thus it flushes out the urethra and neutralizes the acidity of residual urine. The urethra is of much greater inside diameter than the vas deferens, and thus carries the greater volume added by the prostate at a similarly great speed to the end of the penis during ejaculation. At times other than mating, a very slow secretion of prostatic fluid (perhaps about 1 cc per hour) is normal in the adult German Shepherd Dog. It provides a positive outward flow, tends to keep foreign microorganisms from entering, and to keep the urethra open and available for greater demands.

The Penis

This organ of copulation is, in the canine, only partially external. Much of it is not surrounded by integument (skin and associated tissues) but is attached to the wall of the abdomen and hence covered only on its ventral and lateral surfaces. Only a small portion projects forward free of the body. The non-erect penis in the German Shepherd Dog measures about eight inches, but the forward half expands and lengthens considerably during mating. Three divisions of this organ have been considered:

Rebel Canyon's Artful Dodger, 1970's. A healthy, sound, handsome advertisement for the merits of outcrossing as well as Axel/OsnabruckerLand blending. They are in both sides of the pedigree, but no closer than the 5th, 6th, and 7th generations, which is considered essentially outcross breeding by most. His maternal grandsire was Bodo v. Lierberg, and he had lines to Dolf-Bernd-Watzer, Ulk, Troll, Ceasar Malmannshielde, Ingo Wunschelrute, and other valuable ancestors.
Photo courtesy of owners Audrey and Richard Clark.

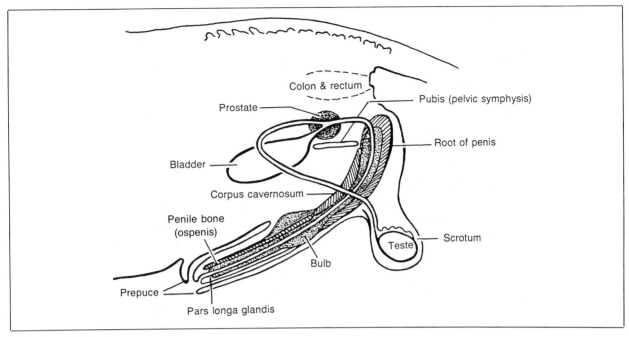

Male Urogenital Structures.

The *root* which extends almost vertically from above and behind the pelvic symphysis, just below the anus, to below the pelvic bone where it levels off slightly.

The body or *corpus* which is continuous with the root and curves more toward the horizontal.

The *glans*. This third part is of most interest to the breeder, as it is the site of erection. It contains a bone known as the os penis, a structure shared by some wild species but by only one other domestic species: the tomcat. In the German Shepherd, this penile bone is about four inches (10 cm) long, its base arising where the body of the penis meets the glans. It is supported by the corpus cavernosum which stiffens during erection, and its other end is a cartilage tip that supports and protects the urethral opening. (See above.)

The Prepuce

This tubular sheath is a structure analogous to a human foreskin. Its interior surface extends as far back as the bulb, and its exterior surface is skin and hair. Some people get all upset if some of the red penis shows, and this concern has resulted in some unnecessary surgery, I'm sure. In my experience exercising the dog caused the prepuce to again cover the red *pars longa glandis* tip. So, if your dog exhibits such a tendency (quite common in puppies), trot him around on-leash for a minute

or have him chase and retrieve a ball or other toy. (See also *balanitis*.)

Erection and the Tie

Briefly, the mode of erection and copulation starts with the bitch in season emitting hormone-induced odors which stimulate in turn the nervous and endocrine systems of the male. When this happens, muscles at the base of the root and at the corpus/glans junction squeeze some veins nearly shut, but not their corresponding arteries which lie outside those muscle rings. This means more blood enters than leaves the two major porous portions of the glans, the bulb and the pars longa glandis (long part), and it becomes larger and turgid. Any contact with the penis at this time, especially with the vulva, will cause a more rapid thrusting motion.

After insertion, the extra stimulation from the tight vagina and possibly pressure against the cervix increases muscular contraction, further enlarging the bulb so that it cannot then be withdrawn past the vaginovestibular area, which does not stretch much until whelping. It is believed that a sphincter muscle in the female's vestibule also contracts some, contributing to this phenomenon known as "the tie." During the time the male exercises his pelvic thrusting motion, after intromission and full erection, his muscles along the urethra from the prostate to the glans rhythmically contract, pump-

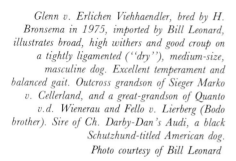

Glenn v. Erlichen Viehhaendler, bred by H. Bronsema in 1975, imported by Bill Leonard, illustrates broad, high withers and good croup on a tightly ligamented ("dry"), medium-size, masculine dog. Excellent temperament and balanced gait. Outcross grandson of Sieger Marko v. Cellerland, and a great-grandson of Quanto v.d. Wienerau and Fello v. Lierberg (Bodo brother). Sire of Ch. Darby-Dan's Audi, a black Schutzhund-titled American dog. Photo courtesy of Bill Leonard

ing fluid into the uterus if a tie has been made. If he has missed the vulva and hit your supporting knee, or if you have tried to guide his penis to the vulva, he may easily be triggered into much more rapid thrusting and ejaculation, including full expansion of the bulb. A good bit of the seminal fluid may thus be lost, but the bulb will shrink to normal fairly quickly if you get the dog walking and his mind off the breeding for a few moments. This fact points up the function provided by the bitch's vestibular muscle contraction: prolonging bulb erection and full ejaculation. If the dog is mounted and thrusting but remains untied, he'll soon dismount and the erection will subside because that stimulation is not present. In the case of a tie, the breeding typically takes twenty minutes for both the female's vestibule sphincter and the male's extrinsic penile muscles to relax enough so that the penis falls out, but the tie may last from as little as ten minutes to nearly an hour.

If you are assisting the procedure, you may wish to help the dog "turn." If his penis has entered to the right of her tail, it would be better if he got off to the right, but it's no big deal if he doesn't. When the dog gets his front feet on the ground, he will have to lean to one side and lift one rear leg, fireplug style. This initiates the turning action where you can help. Generally, if he has any problem at all, it'll be in getting his leg all the way over her, finding himself hung up with his stifle or hock on her croup, not quite able to drag his toes over. After all, at this point the stud is nearly exhausted

after his great psycho-physical exertion. Help the leg over with one hand while you steady your three-legged Lothario with the other.

Now look at the tails. If both are on the same side you'll probably need to reposition one since it's more comfortable if there's one tail curved to each side of the union. The dogs will probably want to walk around, and some inexperienced males will even act as if they want to remount even though still tied. Allow them some tension, for it stimulates completion of the ejaculation in the later pumping stage, but don't let one drag the other around the room. Hold the one that wants to do most of the walking and dragging. Occasionally you'll find a bitch that seems to want to sit down, so tap her upward on the belly and tell her to stand-stay. When the tie period is nearly at an end, both dogs, especially the male, get very itchy and restless— this is a sign they will soon separate.

When the bulb of the penis has lost some of its turgidity and swelling, and the vaginal sphincter relaxes enough, the penis will fall out, and you can let go and try to straighten up again. The stud will generally stand straddle-legged for a few seconds as if he can't walk while the swelling subsides, then he'll lick himself. The bitch will clean herself immediately and may show considerable interest in the male's plight.

That's about all there is to assisting in a normal tie. Some folks recommend putting the bitch in a crate to keep her from urinating right away, but based on a knowledge of the bitch's anatomy and on the absence of any evidence that urinating or running free is detrimental to the success of the breeding, I wouldn't worry about it.

Non-tie Insemination—Incomplete Coitus

It is possible to fertilize the ova of the bitch without accomplishing a tie, but the odds are against it. One way is the natural non-tie breeding, the other is the instrumental (artificial) insemination.

A male of a very small breed may not penetrate far enough for the bulb of the glans to reach past the vaginovestibular border of a large bitch or may fall out immediately after commencing ejaculation, and before much sperm has travelled down the vas and urethra. An inexperienced or poorly handled male may reach full erection before intromission and the engorged bulb then prevents full penetration and a tie. This has often been referred to as an "outside tie," a misnomer because the pars longa section ahead of the bulb is held in only as long as the stud has his pelvis rotated forward. As soon as he relaxes or the bitch takes a step forward, he falls back and out, possibly losing most of the sperm. Even what sperm has been collected in the vagina has little chance of reaching the eggs, as the cervix is a formidable obstacle in the canine. Likewise, unless the tube used in artificial insemination is long enough to butt against the cervix so sperm can be forced into the uterus, this method may also be ineffective. Even in some normal, natural inseminations, a very small percentage of the spermatozoa may reach the area of the ova. It has been estimated that a single good tie releases around 10 million sperm cells; obviously not all reach the fallopian tubes. However, all this is not to say that it is impossible for such less-than-perfect ties to result in conception—there are many, many litters born as a result of halfway measures.

Artificial Insemination

There are several reasons to use artificial insemination with dogs. A bitch we once tried to breed to one of our stud dogs had pulled a rear leg muscle a couple of days before the breeding was to take place and refused to put weight on that limb. The male was very heavy and I could not fully support both him and the bitch even with her abdomen on my knee, which would be an unsatisfactory and uncomfortable position for her anyway. In another instance, one of our studs had a spinal injury that made it impossible for him to support his great weight on his rear legs and the bitch. He was therefore bred artificially, with success every time. Apart from injury, the fact is that some bitches are uncooperative due to inexperience or bad former experiences, and some studs are not all that interested in every bitch on every day, at least not enough to go through the whole procedure. Sometimes a male is promised to three or more bitches that then proceed to ovulate at the same time. When this happens the stud owner may be tempted to split the ejaculate, extend (and consequently dilute) it with saline or nitrofurazone solutions, and artificially service all the bitches. This is accepted practice in cattle, and may eventually become more common in dogs. Rising air freight costs and more available frozen semen also make a convincing case for artificial insemination.

Another important consideration when deciding on A.I. is that disease can be prevented. Studs are not in as much danger of contracting brucellosis if they have no physical contact with the bitch, though suspect bitches should not be bred anyway, and there is more worry than reality about brucellosis in German Shepherd Dogs. Countries and states with long quarantines as measures to prevent rabies cannot presently use foreign studs and consequently breeders must rely on a more limited gene pool. As frozen semen and artificial insemination become more popular, sperm can be held in a bank until such time as officials are sure the donor is not rabid, then can be thawed and used to impregnate local bitches.

Regulations—In the United States, registration of purebred dogs other than racing Greyhounds, gundogs, and a few others, is largely under the control of the American Kennel Club. Although litters had been produced in English Setters (sired by the famed hunting dog Johnny Crockett) and track Greyhounds by the use of frozen semen, it was not until 1981 that the AKC added its comments to the regulations regarding the subject. The May 1981 issue of AKC's official publication, *Purebred Dogs/ American Kennel Gazette,* carried the supplementation that spelled out how records were to be kept, how and when the AKC must be notified of the use of frozen stored semen, location of storage facilities, inspection rights, and penalties. A key phrase in these 1981 regulations is almost identical to one that already appeared in Chapter 3-A of the *Rules Applying to Registration and Dog Shows*: If there is "any possibility ... of doubt as to the parentage," the person who fails to preclude this may be suspended from all AKC privileges, including registering his dogs.

Collection—The equipment needed for artificial insemination includes a collection device, a syringe, and a tube to carry the semen from syringe to cervix. See this chapter's earlier section on equipment used for douching. I use a 12 cc hypodermic syringe (without needle), its 24 cc container or a suitable substitute, and a piece of tubing about 9 or 10 inches long. All must be sterilized in boiling water for at least twenty minutes to minimize bacterial introduction. Do not use detergents in or after the boiling water bath.

I recommend *not* using the syringe as a collector since it is open at the bottom and has a very small top opening when the plunger is removed. Because of this configuration it is very difficult to avoid losing semen or introducing air when replacing the plunger. Most large syringes come in a large plastic tube which is also sterilized inside, and this makes an excellent collection instrument since the top end is flared and the bottom end is closed. Also, its volume capacity is about double that of the syringe.

Some males will attain an erection and ejaculate easily upon manual manipulation, but most will need the presence of a female in heat to get them excited. The best location for collection is one where the stud is comfortable—indoors, and with as few distractions as possible, including people. I recommend tying the bitch to a post or a doorknob and using her to tease the male. Standing over the rear of the dog, reach from one side with one hand holding the collection vial in place and from the other side reach with the hand to be used in stimulating an erection. Starting about three inches back on the prepuce, draw the skin back in short strokes. Erection may start immediately, and when it does, move your hand further back and encircle the base with thumb and fingers, still massaging in a back-and-forth motion but with shorter strokes and a firmer grip. Be ready to grasp him behind the bulb when it enlarges, so keep your grip well back on the penis. When the dog starts his rapid thrusting motion, place the collector mouth over

the tip of the protruding penis, and hang on! The bulb should be visible by now, and if you are shaken loose, the erection may subside almost immediately. You may have to hold onto the dog with the insides of your elbows pressed against his flanks in order to prevent losing your grip or holding the collector. It'll be a little tricky at first to keep the collection tube in place, but the first few drops, maybe even the first couple of cc's, contain little or no sperm, so missing that small volume is no catastrophe.

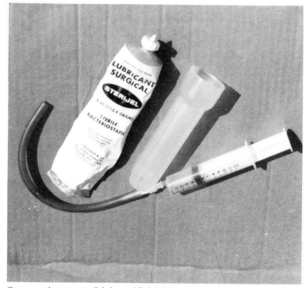

Some equipment useful in artificial insemination.

As ejaculation proceeds and the collection tube is in place, look to see if the end of the pars longa is swelling inside the tube, if so, back it off a little to prevent it from lodging there, but be sure to keep the tip inside the wide opening. The dog will slow his thrusting about the time the second fluid fraction is being secreted, and this is the part, probably amounting to 3 or 4 cc's, that contains almost all the sperm. Gradually the dog will become still, but keep that tight grip on the base of the penis, as this simulates the constriction the vaginal sphincters would produce and mimics a tie. A large third fraction, being mostly prostatic fluid, is pumped out in the following several minutes. The total volume depends mostly on how often this dog has been used in the past few days, how much teasing a "ripe" bitch has done, and how long you hold the penis firmly behind the bulb. A good minimum to aim for is 7 cc's, which should be enough to include almost all the sperm. A larger volume is desirable to insure adequate pressure in the vagina to help force more fluid into the uterus on the other side of the cervix.

Insemination—Place the container of seminal fluid into a holder and put the stud into a crate to keep him from interfering. Some people recommend keeping the syringe in the hand or an insulated holder to prevent ''cold shock,'' claiming this can damage sperm. But since sperm can be preserved by freezing and dies after being held at body temperature for too long, I wouldn't worry about it being at room temperature while you prepare for insemination. Indeed, high temperature is the enemy of sperm vitality, not low temperature. You'll notice that your male's testicles will hang low during hot days and be drawn closer to the body when cold, such as after swimming in cold water. This may indicate that to play it safe and keep your stud dog's fertility at a high level, he should enjoy air-conditioned comfort during those hot summer days.

But back to the insemination procedure. Using the syringe to which the piece of tubing is attached, insert the tubing into the container and withdraw the plunger, thus drawing the fluid up into the syringe with a minimum of air. A variety of tubing types can be used, from the very small diameter rather stiff catheter, to a slightly thicker yet still semi-rigid foot-long clear pipette, to a larger diameter (1 cm) rubber or flexible plastic tubing. The thinner, stiffer types present the danger of accidental puncture of the vaginal wall, so I prefer the presumably safer and more comfortable flexible vinyl medical tubing available at the drug store. Another advantage to this type is that it can be easily looped around to fit, with syringe attached, into a pocket-sized plastic bag or paper towel for ease in transporting it to the stud's location if he doesn't happen to be yours.

With the syringe filled, you are now ready to inseminate. I prefer to have the bitch in a standing position and have described the procedure earlier under the heading of vaginal infections. The only differences here would be that the tubing should probably be longer to assure reaching the cervix, and the equipment should be sterilized in the absence of a bactericide such as *Furacin®*. You may also wish to put a little lubricant such as clean petroleum jelly or *Steri-gel®* on the tubing, but be sure that what you use is not spermicidal.

When you have inserted the tubing past the vestibule and urethral ridge, it should travel another few inches before reaching the cervix. You should be able to feel it when the tubing stops, but if you don't think it's in far enough, back it off an inch, twist the syringe and tubing about 180 degrees, and gently push up and forward again. Then slowly and steadily, push the plunger. If there is more fluid left in the collector, place the tubing into it again and repeat the procedure with minimum handling of the tubing while you re-insert it into the vagina.

Some veterinarians have recommended having an assistant hold the bitch high in the rear during artificial insemination or for at least five minutes afterwards, but I don't feel there is any advantage to this. First, if the tubing is long enough it should deliver a considerable number of sperm cells into the uterus with sufficient pressure. Second, the vagina curves over in the beginning of an S-shape and gravity, if it were much of a factor, would tend to trap the fluid as much as or more than it would tend to allow it to escape. Third, the diameter of the vagina is very small, perhaps completely closed, when nothing is in it, and this organ would tend to keep some if not most of the fluid remaining in a sort of vaginal pouch. Besides, the sperm that has already passed the cervix before the bitch is lifted has the best chance of fertilizing the eggs. So, instead of the uncomfortable and probably unnecessary pose of holding a bitch nearly upside-down for long minutes, I believe putting her in a small crate after natural *or* artificial insemination is adequate and preferred. She will lie down and wait to urinate if she is so constrained for fifteen minutes or so, even though it may not be entirely necessary. The urine exits well posterior to the sperm. In short, think natural, even though the breeding may be otherwise, and your chances for success will be good.

CAUSES OF BREEDING DIFFICULTIES

The would-be breeder may encounter, besides vaginal or vulva rings, other obstacles to mating or fertilization. First we'll consider those problems relating to the act of copulation, or mating. These may be either genetic or environmental: chemical, hormonal, physical, or emotional.

1980 Sieger Axel v.d. Hainsterbach, SchH-III, immediately after winning the title in the Wester football stadium in Bremen. Axel's pigmentation and topline are obvious here.
Photo courtesy Jack Oliver.

Food

Nutrition is not likely to be bad enough to affect the desire or ability to hormonally produce sexual attractiveness, since nearly all breeders are careful feeders. A commercially-prepared food should be adequate, but remember that worms in the intestine interfere with assimilation of foodstuffs.

It has been observed that many a disinterested stud's libido will perk up after a meal. With this in mind, it might be a good idea to give your stud dog a light meal before turning the ready bitch into his run. Additionally, longer-range beneficial effects have been seen regarding libido when liver is added to the diet of a stud dog. Nutritionist Dr. D.R. Collins (*The Collins Guide to Nutrition*), believes this may be due to the high level of unidentified fractions in liver in addition to the many vitamins inherent in it.

Timing

It may be possible that the dogs are introduced too late in the bitch's cycle when the balance of progesterone to estradiol has shifted too much toward the former. An experienced stud will not even investigate after a sniff or two, while a younger stud may make feeble attempts to mount though his heart isn't in it, and he too will soon turn away. On the other hand, a flirtatious bitch may coax a dog into action. An introduction too early in the cycle is also possible, but is seldom cause for lack of interest or the failure to mate.

Size

A bitch grossly larger or significantly smaller than the male may be the cause of an inability to mate. A small bitch can be placed on a platform with her rear feet on the edge, but give them a chance to play first so the male won't be distracted by whatever you use. Likewise, a couple of inches of plywood sheets may be helpful to a shorter male if the bitch is backed up close to it. Neither device will be easy, since the male will tend to want to place his rear feet where hers are, or even past them, during the thrusting motions. At any rate, seldom will a short male be used as a stud for a very tall bitch.

Distractions

A male can easily lose interest if he finds himself in a strange environment; he may be concerned about whose territory he is straying into, whether other males are in the vicinity, strange noises, smells, and other stimuli. Therefore, it is almost always best to bring the bitch to the male. Even on his home territory strangers may distract the stud, so their visits should be kept to a minimum or at least they should be very quiet and slow to move. If assistants are needed, they should try not to talk and should be brought in only at the time of need, such as to steady the bitch's head at arm's length while the stud is mounting, or after the tie. The stranger, and indeed perhaps even the stud owner, might have to purposely avoid eye contact with the stud during the foreplay and mounting stages.

Abnormalities

Physical obstructions to mating are not always female problems, though abnormalities in the genitalia of the male German Shepherd Dog are rare. If you can't find any other reason why your pair can't mate, check to see if the male has any great excess of penile soft tissue extending beyond the penile bone that could be doubled over when attempts are made at intromission. Also, check the prepuce as its opening may be too small due to a congenital fault or to an infection. On rare occasions a tumor on a testicle will affect hormone activity and desire, though this is almost always restricted to unilateral cryptorchids (so-called monorchidism). All these possibilities are so rare that unless there is an obvious physical deformity or disease, one should suspect a psychological problem.

Psychology

Distractions present the most common psychological barriers to mating; however, others do exist. Some males have been overly punished in their youth for exhibiting desire to mount something other than bitches in season. Some females are so shy or afraid of strange dogs that they will lie on their sides or backs when advances are made or even as soon as the male approaches. Others are fussy about which dog they'll stand for, preferring a dog they know well, such as a kennelmate. More often, though, bitches will roam, if allowed to, until they find the most aggressive male. In very few cases, a fiercely aggressive female will intimidate any dog that comes near her, male or female, season or no. Some males will have had a bad experience with a female in season, and this may spoil future attempts. If a bitch has to be tranquilized or muzzled in order to accomplish a breeding, it may be a good idea to weigh these temperament faults against her genetic qualities before proceeding with the mating.

False Starts

Many bitches will show the signs of beginning a heat cycle (dropping blood and a swelling vulva), then stop before true estrus (ovulation). Another

start may occur from several days to several weeks later. I co-owned one Michigan bitch that had dropped blood for a few days, so we arranged to send her to a stud in Oklahoma. She was there over a week and the only thing that happened was that she stopped bleeding shortly after arrival. Neither dog nor bitch had any sexual interest beyond curiosity at first meeting, but I persuaded my friend to keep her there for awhile. A month later the breeder had to go out of town for a couple of weeks, so we had the bitch shipped back. Several days after returning to Michigan the bitch was in season again, and she pulled this little trick a couple more times in later seasons. Whitney had at least one bitch that frequently had false starts, and from his reports and my own experience and observation, I estimate that false starts are generally over in less than a week and the bitch begins her season in earnest about a month after the false alarm, the range appearing to be three to six weeks.

Bad Timing

Even if a tie is successfully effected, the breeding might not "take," (breeders' jargon for saying that the bitch did not become pregnant). The so-called outside tie is a possible cause, though some breeders have been successful or lucky in obtaining litters without a regular tie having been made. So perhaps in many cases it's a matter of timing, or some undetected infection, rather than whether or not the tie is good, that produces the inability to conceive.

If you have ruled out infection, the most common reason a bitch owner is disappointed by temporary sterility is that the bitch may have been mated too early or too late in her acceptance period. The situation of being late is all too common, with bitch owners reporting to the stud owner, "I really don't know when she started, because she was outside most of the time, and I just noticed blood when I brought her into the house last Tuesday." It frequently turns out that the bitch has gone past her prime time, and actual metestrus (the subsiding of estrus) has begun with its resultant inhospitable environment for sperm. Even at this stage many bitches will still stand for the stud, but they often do so without great interest, just mild willingness.

It is also possible that the one and only tie was made too early. While it appears from latest research that sperm are not killed off until the bitch's endocrine system declares metestrus in six days or so, it may be that they lose potency in less than that time. Perhaps early in estrus the chemical environment is harsher than it becomes in a couple of days as ovulation day approaches. Sperm may find a more welcome environment (as regards potency, not necessarily motility) if they are introduced some two or three days after the first day of acceptance. Whitney found the thirteenth or fourteenth day after bleeding commenced was best, and claimed that not one bitch ever sent to his studs failed to conceive. His practice was to breed the bitch every other day following the thirteenth or fourteenth until she refused to stand, unless the stud was needed to service other bitches. So some of them only got one tie, and others got many.

Inadequate Semen Volume

One tie is usually sufficient, if the timing is right, but it should last longer than just a couple of minutes or not enough sperm will be deposited far enough in the female's tract to be effective. The only way to insure a lot of sperm cells where the eggs are, is to insure a lot of sperm cells *everywhere* in the uterus and tubes.

Frequency is related to the above; a daily service may reduce the concentration of sperm. This isn't always the case, as many stud dogs have been used every day for long periods when many bitches were shipped at about the same time, but the danger is still there. If you *can* spare the stud, let him breed the bitch or bitches every thirty-six or forty-eight hours so his system can recover and build up a greater volume of fluids and sperm. Otherwise, schedule a one- or two-day rest for every three consecutive days he is used at stud.

Some males, when bred after a period of sexual inactivity, may have a low potency on the first affair due to insufficient sperm count. A second breeding a day or two later usually gives a much higher count. It has also been shown that high temperature, whether fever or ambient, can adversely affect sperm production. Therefore, males living in extremely hot climates with little or no ability to cool off may be less spermatogenic as a result. It might be a good idea to keep stud dogs in air-conditioned buildings during 100-degree F. heat waves if they are to be bred.

Poor Health

General well-being is required to some degree, as poor health, whether it be from a great parasite load, or infection, can "turn off" either of the breeding pair. An abundance of exercise is usually not needed to insure conception, as lazy, pampered pets can be as prolific as the athletes of the canine club.

Infection in the bitch is possibly the major health reason for inability to conceive or carry fetuses to term. In spite of all the requirements in ads regard-

American and Canadian Ch. Olrac's Catawba, CD. around 1981. One of the top winners in the early 1980's Owners: Walter and Louise Leistner; Fran Foster. Photo courtesy L. Leistner.

ing negative titers, brucellosis is not a significant factor in German Shepherd Dogs with the possible exception of a few feral individuals. However, other bacteria are fairly common, and vaginitis can spread to the uterus, which is much more serious. A few stud owners require a vaginal culture report, but males almost never get infections from bitches.

Most uterine diseases such as pyometra are very dangerous and may be triggered by hormones as a contributing factor. Prostatitis in the male can cause sterility, but penile infections seldom interfere with conception unless they cause a vaginal infection. One exception is when there is a significant presence of pus cells in the semen. Successful treatment can be effected simply by strenuous exercise for a week or more. If that doesn't eradicate the pus cells, your veterinarian may prescribe antibiotics; then use both approaches concurrently.

A physical check-up prior to breeding is obviously important to the success of your venture, but don't wait until the bitch is in season to evaluate her condition and take steps to prepare her. This examination should include weight evaluation as obesity is also a health-related factor in sterility, more often in females than in males. Also, hypothyroidism has been known to reduce sex drive.

Testicle Abnormality

In rare instances, an underdeveloped or atrophied testicle may be the result of a tumor on the opposite testicle, even if the latter is retained in the body rather than descended into the scrotum (see cryptorchidism). Injuries seldom cause sterility unless *both* testicles or vas deferentes are damaged. Also rare is the case of insufficient production of the male hormone, testosterone. Prostatitis, bladder infection, and severe balanitis can spread back to the testicles and cause sterility, but distemper is rarely a cause of testicular-related infertility thanks to common emphasis on vaccination.

CRYPTORCHIDISM

The most common congenital anomaly of the scrotum and testicles is the apparent absence of one or both gonads. I use the word "apparent" because the missing testicle(s) may actually be present inside the body cavity of the dog. The Greek *kryptos* means hidden, secret, or covered, and the Greek *orchi-* is a combining form referring to the testicles.

The condition is therefore called cryptorchidism and the dog so afflicted is called a cryptorchid. If one testicle is retained, he is a unilateral (one-sided) cryptorchid and if both, a bilateral cryptorchid. A word commonly applied to the former is *monorchid* but this is a misnomer, as monorchidism would mean the presence of only one testicle *anywhere* in the body, not just in the scrotum. True monorchids are quite rare, as are anorchids (males with no testicles), and either condition can be verified only be extensive surgery.

A dog whose testicles have been removed is called a castrate, and generally he has no (or greatly reduced) response to sexual stimuli, while a sterile bilateral cryptorchid may have normal sex urge, and a unilateral cryptorchid is usually both virile and fertile.

AKC Rules

The American Kennel Club requires every dog competing in shows under its jurisdiction to have two normal testicles in the scrotum. Judges must examine the scrotum, and usually a quick pass of the hand between the thighs will let them know if one is too spongy, hard, or abnormally small, indicating the possibility of disease or chicanery. In some countries testicle abnormalities are more severely penalized and in some places less is demanded of the judge than is the case in the United States.

Examining the Pups

A tube called the vaginal process runs from the parietal peritoneum (the inner lining of the abdomen) to the scrotum which it encloses. Inside this tube are the spermatic cord, artery, vein, nerves, vas deferens, and the cremaster muscle. It is the function of this muscle to pull the testicle closer to the body in cold environs, and to allow the scrotum to hang lower in warmer conditions. In puppies under eight weeks of age, the cremaster muscle also may function to keep the testicles in the tubes but still outside the vaginal ring, instead of allowing them to descend all the way to the scrotum. This could well be Nature's way of protecting them during siblings' rough-housing. Perhaps a defect in this muscle is responsible for the fairly common "elevator testicle" in certain German Shepherd family lines: in this phenomenon, one goes up, comes down, and goes back up again. Usually this is outgrown rather early, but I knew of one pup that still exhibited this condition at the age of five months.

People who can't find the testicles in young puppies may be holding the little shoelace-tuggers in the wrong position. The testicles should descend before birth, but are so small and mobile they may be nearly impossible to find on a wriggling pup that doesn't want to be constrained. But if you cradle the pup's upper body in your two hands or in the bend of your arm and let his bottom half hang, you should be able to feel the tiny gonads, especially if two fingers are run down the prepuce, one on each side of the penile sheath, toward the scrotum. In some pups, they will have to be pushed into the scrotum this way in order to be noticed.

Some folks panic when only one can be found; they run to the veterinarian for some magic shot of hormone to make the other appear. While the synthetic hormone APL (anterior pituitary-like) has had some success in humans, its efficacy is highly doubtful in dogs. First, it definitely is of no benefit once the testicle has grown too large to squeeze through the vaginal ring, and therefore the need would have to be discovered at the time of birth, which is all but impossible even if one has the most sensitive fingers in the world. Then, if the other testicle *does* appear in the scrotum, it's not necessarily due to the APL. Two other reasons could be given: the testicle was going to drop anyway, or it was in the inguinal canal outside of the abdominal wall and held up by a tight cremaster which loosened as the pup aged. (There is no evidence that APL works as a relaxant on the cremaster.) Even if APL were a successful way to induce testicles to drop, the pup's genetic makeup would remain the same and he would pass the defect along to many of his offspring. As a responsible breeder you would find a pet (non-breeding) home for him.

Inheritance

In Germany for a short while, unilateral cryptorchids were eligible for showing and breeding, as the fault seemed to have no effect on utility or beauty. By 1930, the SV prohibited not only showing but registration as well! The German Shepherd Dog Club of America's 1943 breed Standard disqualified dogs with one or both testicles missing, though the 1929 Standard didn't address the issue

at all. By 1956 the AKC applied the disqualification to *all* breeds. Even today some feel that cryptorchidism is an imported or German bloodline problem, forgetting that *all* our Shepherds derived from Germany, and not knowing that the SV really led the way in prohibiting the fault.

The most recent studies on the subject of missing or hidden testicles indicate that there can be several genetic causes. Retractile testicles, a feature of the dog with an overactive or short cremaster, may be due to a genetic determinant quite different from that which causes classic unilateral cryptorchidism. Bilateral cryptorchidism may also be genetically slightly different, since both are usually found in almost the same ovarian position as they are in the early fetal life of normal males. It seems that this phenomenon may be caused by two or more genes, and such may be the case in unilateral cases too, although there is reliable data to suggest the possibility of a simple Mendelian recessive in the case of classic unilateral cryptorchidism. If two normal phenotype dogs actually carry the recessive, on an average one might expect 25 percent of the litter to show the condition. But since perhaps half a litter is female, the average would only be 12.5 percent and with such breedings that produce one-testicle dogs not being often repeated, it's difficult to find meaningful statistics.

According to one researcher, it is the right testicle which is most often retained, being the more cranial (more toward the head) of the two in the early embryonic stage. In Angora goats, it is also the right testicle which is commonly retained, though this is not hard evidence that all species have the same genetic cause for the same effect. Different genes may even be involved in different breeds of dogs; for example, the gene that causes black in poodles, Labs, and other breeds is a different gene than that which causes black in Shepherds.

Similarly, the right ovary of females and the right kidney in both sexes are further forward than the left organs. In the normal male, the left testicle in the scrotum is usually carried slightly higher and behind the right one. The retained testicle in unilaterally affected dogs is usually found near the bladder or at the entrance to the inguinal canal on the inside of the abdominal wall, as if it had been arrested on its way to join its mate.

As mentioned, unilateral cryptorchidism often seems as if it were a simple, recessive, one-gene

Mendelian trait, though it probably is not. If the problem of unilateral cryptorchidism were indeed simply recessive, the occurrence of bilateral cryptorchids would have to be explained by the action of other, modifying genes, and many geneticists today

Waiting for his playmate to return. Photo courtesy Marcia Hadley

do not find that idea appealing. But for the purpose of explanation, let's use it as an example. If the pup inherits one gene for the trait from one parent and one normal allele from the other parent, he will not show the disorder but will be a carrier. If the normal gene is represented by the capital letter C, and the defective gene is identified by the lowercase c, his genetic constitution on that chromosome is Cc. On the other hand, if a dog is a cryptorchid, his genetic constitution at that locus on that chromosome is cc (two defective genes). If this dog is bred to a bitch that also inherited two such genes,

(she is also a cc), all of their offspring will either be cryptorchids like the sire or homozygous carriers like their dam. It is possible that a testicle found in the scrotum of some males from such a union may later retract and be trapped inside the peritoneum. In some breeds this happens fairly frequently, and some believe it is caused by the same set of genes that cause more typical cryptorchidism.

In addition, some breeds with brachiocephalic skulls have a much greater than 25 percent incidence when supposed normals (actually carriers) are bred. Knowing what we do about such breeds and their pituitary defects, would it not be reasonable to say that *maybe* the German Shepherd Dog, as well as other breeds and species, has in its population a very slight hereditary pituitary defect that acts on the development of the cord and other structures in the genital system?

I believe that cryptorchidism is genetic, that it is in some way recessive, and that there is some sort of connection between bilateral cryptorchids and unilateral ones. Perhaps there is also a connection with the pituitary and floating testicles. At any rate, the unilateral condition at least is so widespread in German Shepherd Dog families that an all-out effort to combat it would take our minds and efforts away from more serious disorders which would consequently increase.

Since cryptorchidism is sex-limited (only affected males, not carrier females, show it) it is likely to persist at about the same prevalence in the breed for a long, long time. In Germany, where registration is denied cryptorchids and sanctions are made against their parents, over half of the VA dogs in a 20-year period sired cryptorchids and hence were carriers. In England, the prevalence is higher, and in the US it is probably only slightly, if at all, lower.

Effects on the Dog

It is typical for retained testicles to give a dog a sour or miserable personality, and the condition also seems to be associated with a high percentage of testicular cancers or tumors on the retained gonad. For both reasons, many veterinarians recommend castration even if the testicles are undescended. A third possible effect is cryptorchidism's reported connection with early fetal death of females in litters with affected males, with these females either resorbed or, in some cases, mummified. The gene or genes may be semi-lethal ones which are only sometimes expressed in the death of the female embryo, and which sometimes cause the surviving bitch pups to be sterile if they are homozygous (cc).

Ethics

Veterinarians are sometimes asked to surgically correct cryptorchidism by moving the testicle(s) down into the scrotum, but this is an extremely difficult and delicate operation with very little chance of success because of the length of the spermatic cord, the effect on attached tissues and blood vessels, and other technical reasons. An easier alternative is to implant a synthetic testicle—glass, silicone, or whatever—and veterinarians are quite often asked to do this. However, nine times out of ten the owner's motives are questionable at best. Usually he wants the surgery so his dog can compete in shows, or so he can fool owners of bitches into paying for stud service from what is supposedly a normal dog.

"What do you mean, fox trot? This is interpretive dancing!"   *Photo courtesy Tom and Sharon McGann*

15

GENETICS

BASICS OF GENETICS

Chemical Basis of Genes and Chromosomes

Even if you have never taken a course in chemistry, you probably know that a certain configuration of hydrogen and oxygen atoms in a molecule results in the compound known as water (H_2O), while another combination gives hydrogen peroxide (H_2O_2). When three or more types of atoms are joined together into molecules in all their different ratios, positions, etc., a more complex structure results. Carbon, hydrogen, and oxygen atoms, for example, are arranged in innumerable ways to form a vast variety of carbohydrates, fats, and, with the addition of nitrogen atoms, proteins.

One classification of carbohydrates is the sugar structure. Although sugars include many compounds, they are all somewhat similar in their C-H-O linkage. Deoxyribose sugar makes up part of deoxyribonucleic acid (DNA) along with other molecular structures containing nitrogen and phosphorus. The DNA molecule looks like a spirally-twisted rubber ladder with the rungs alternatingly representing phosphate groups, purines, and other collections. DNA is of interest here since it is the substance of the little unit called the gene. Even smaller units called mutational sites are, in essence, mini-genes, and there may be up to several hundred of them in one location (in one gene). These mini-genes may explain why no two nose prints are alike, even though the physical *shape* of the nose may be controlled by one or a few genes.

The coiled genes lie on or compose the larger structures called chromosomes, strands of protein-like material found in every cell. When cells divide, chromosome pairs may become visible (though often with great difficulty are they recognized), most of them resembling a box of irregular staples spilled on the floor. One of these chromosomes is shaped like the letter X and obviously is known as the X chromosome. If there is a pair of X chromosomes, the animal is female, but if there is only one and the other is a Y chromosome, the mammal is a male. Each chromosome has a partner, being twins in the respect that they are shaped about the same (except for the X and Y pair), yet these partners may have dissimilar genes on them. Since chromosomes exist in pairs, so do the genes which make them up. This is an important fact which you should fix in your mind so as to understand later comments.

The figure following illustrates the ladder of DNA, here untwisted for clarity. Each leg is made of alternating sugar groups and phosphate groups and each rung is composed of two types of protein-base molecules. There are four types of protein bases present in each DNA macromolecule, each one capable of forming a rung with only one other base, but allowing for many possible arrangements of the four base pairs of the system. Cytosine normally makes a connection only with guanine, and adenine joins only with thymine. The shortest DNA strand (gene) in man contains over 1,650 A-T,G-C combinations, so you can imagine the practically endless variations possible when all the genes are considered.

DNA "LADDER"

DNA "ladder," actually spiralled, but untwisted here for simplicity.

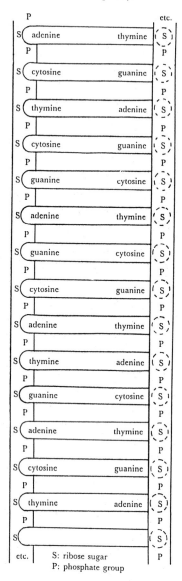

S: ribose sugar
P: phosphate group

Rungs are amino acids, with guanine always attached to cytosine, and adenine to thymine, each attached to a sugar complex which in turn is bound to a phosphate group.

RNA copies the patterns and transferes the copy to new cells including sperm and ova which then carry on the code in the subsequent generation. The complementary copies are made when the ladder splits down the middle during meiosis. DNA is the "chemical" (actually a string of chemical structures) that genes are made of, and chromosomes are strings of genes.

When the strand of DNA splits, each part simultaneously replicates, laying down an identical half-

strand. RNA, an oxidized form of DNA with uracil replacing cytosine, is synthesized on the surface of the DNA molecule/gene. There it acts on the amino acids provided by the animal's digestion, and recombines them in a variety of ways. These recombinations dictate that bone tissue be made, that the color black be followed by yellow as hair protein grows out of follicles, that the brain and personality develop in a certain way, etc.

It would be an oversimplification, and erroneous, to say that one DNA strand (gene) determines one characteristic, such as length of ears. Although I *will* use such simplification for convenience's sake, remember that actually *all* the genes in an individual may have some effect on each of the others, even though their influence sometimes is remote. Differences between dogs may be caused by one of the bases on a rung being replaced (unlikely), or the sequence of rungs changing (very likely), or even half a rung being lost. These chemical forces are felt far away in other parts of that gene, in the other genes which that chromosome contains, and perhaps even in separate chromosomes. This is known as the "total genotype" theory or concept.

Another school of thought holds that each chromosome is completely independent, and that genes on one do not exert known influence on genes in the others. The more I study dogs, the less I am attracted to that alternative theory. However, it does appear to be true that the further apart two genes lie, the less influence they have on each other. Conversely, the nearest-neighbor concept holds that the greatest mutual effect may be between two adjacent genes.

A characteristic governed entirely by one gene pair is called a simple Mendelian trait, and those traits determined by a large number of genes are known as multifactorial or polygenic.

Location and Strength of Genes

We conceive of chromosomes as collections of genes up and down their lengths. Each gene has a specific location (locus) on its chromosome, and these loci are given arbitrary letter designations, with the letter sometimes standing for a key word in the condition's name or description. In referring to dominance/recessiveness, the letter chosen is often the initial of the *dominant* trait.

Two or more gene pairs may work on a specific characteristic, and may be positioned on different parts of a chromosome, or a single pair may be involved, with one gene at a certain locus on one chromosome, the other gene (perhaps identical, perhaps opposite in effect) occupying the corresponding locus on the other chromosome in that pair. In the case where they are different yet occupy corresponding loci (same position) on the two chromosomes, one gene may exert a domineering effect over the other. The condition is known as being *heterozygous* if the genes are different; *homozygous* if they are identical, or call for basically the same trait.

We say that genes on one chromosome often stay together, because we have observed that certain characteristics seem to be inherited in bunches. Such is the case when one pup in the litter looks and acts just like one parent and another pup is just like the other parent. A dog that resembles one parent or ancestor has many genes in common with that individual. Often, however, genes formerly found on one chromosome may become attached to another when the chromosomes split and divide, or may end up on an entirely different end of the same chromosome.

Dr. C. C. Little, whose book on color genetics was first printed in 1957, proposed a "map" of genes affecting coat colors which included letter designations for about a dozen loci, and symbols for the types of genes that could exist there. I'll refer back to this map later, but introduce it here as an illustration of the idea.

PIGMENT

What is it that makes for color in the dog? What we know as light is actually an extremely narrow slice of a seemingly limitless spectrum of electro-magnetic energy in the form of pulsating waves. Visible light ranges from relatively long-wavelength red to shorter-wavelength violet. Various components of atmosphere, liquids, and translucent solids refract (bend) the different frequencies of light by different angles. Therefore, when you look at a sunset, the less-refracted red light reaches you while much of the blue is scattered to the sides. You look up and see this blue, while the red component continues on to be seen as sunset by those living far to the east of you. This phenomenon, known as Tyndall scattering, also explains the blue haze in smoke-filled rooms and the bluish cloudiness in your old dog's eyes. The same condition of turbid materials in new puppies' eyes dissipates in time to allow the normal brown-yellow colors of the melanin pigment in the German Shepherd Dog's eyes to become evident.

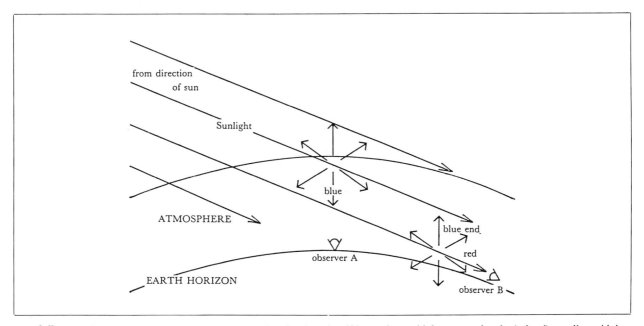

Tyndall scattering. *Sunlight passing through he atmosphere is refracted as if by a prism, with longer-wavelengths (red end) traveling with least amount of directional change, and shorter-wavelengths (blue end) being refracted (bent) the most. Observer A sees more blue light by looking up, through relatively thin layer of atmosphere; observer B sees more red light in the sunset by looking through much more air, dust, and moisture. The more the pollution or moisture such as clouds, the redder the sunset. Same story for orange moon low on horizon. Particulate matter in irises of eyes, or turbid fluid in the humors or lens, can give a blue appearance this way, with no blue pigments being present.*

White light is not a color, but a combination of the colors in the visible spectrum; a white object reflects all those colors equally and still mixed. So, when speaking of pigments, white is again not a color, but in this case is the absence of color. Therefore, the white hairs of a dog reflects ''white'' light partly from the surfaces of the hairs and partly from the surfaces *in* the hair (the air spaces and interfaces in the medullae of the hairs). Some tissues are naturally white or nearly so: unpigmented fat, milk, bone, muscle, nerve, and connective tissue.

Most black, brown, and yellow colorations are due to the presence of melanin-class pigments. The word *melanin* is derived from the Greek word for black, and is commonly used to refer to the two or three known chemicals similar to each other which produce the above color families. It can be said that there are only two colors in the haircoat of the canine: black and yellow, all others being variations of those. Eumelanin gives the black and dark brown colors, phaeomelanin gives the light brown and yellow ones. Certain genes affect the expression of these two so that the dark melanin may appear as black or be diluted to blue or changed to a chocolate-brown, and the various shades of *gelbe* may exist as yellow, tan, light to darker brown, cream, etc. These genes can be referred to as modifier genes.

As the coat grows out, melanocytes manufacture melanin which then passes into the cortex of the hairs, becoming keratinized along with the cytoplasm of the hair cell as it grows up from the root through the skin. Deposited in certain patterns, these melanins along with differences in body form help a German Shepherd Dog identify other members of his breed. That red-brown tipped burnt appearance of the coat that we see sometimes, especially noticeable in black dogs, is a result of sun bleaching the melanin in the hair to some extent, but perhaps more by a partially otherwise hidden recessive modifier gene for dilution or lighter-than-normal pigment.

One of those modifiers of black pigment was mentioned earlier as an example in the allele map. Now, if the gene we call B is present, eumelanin will show up as black, but if B is absent and only b is present, that ''same'' melanin will be expressed as brown. That is, the saddle and other areas which normally may be black in the German Shepherd (or several other breeds) will be liver-brown instead.

ADDITIONAL VOCABULARY OF GENETICS

Dihybrid -   heterozygous in two pairs of alleles at once, as in the parents of ''Isabella'' Doberman Pinschers: DdBb.

Epistatic -   the nature of a gene which enables it to mask other genes which are not alleles to it.

Hypostatic -   that which is obscured by an epistatic gene. For example, a solid black German Shepherd Dog may carry chinchilla genes at the C locus (c^{ch}) which, since they only operate on tan pigment, are not visible in that black individual. c^{ch} is hypostatic to e^b or e^b with a^t.

Lethal gene -   a factor which tends to interfere with life functions in the individual at any time between conception and old age, but more often before or around the time of birth.

Modifier -   a gene with usually minor effect on the expression of another, more obviously active gene. The effect can be considerable if several modifiers act together.

The causative gene will have no noticeable effect on the tan parts of the dog since another gene affects the phaeomelanin which controls these tan parts while the eumelanin affects the nose and saddle.

A hair bulb can manufacture more than one type of melanin, and can alternate production in such a way that some hairs, such as most of those on a sable dog, are dark-tipped, followed by a lighter midpiece and an even lighter base (or perhaps a dark base). There may be two shades of yellow, one reddish and the other cream, on one shaft. Sometimes the phaeomelanin is concentrated in the tip and the eumelanin in the base, though not often. The banding or alternating between dark and light sections results in a beautiful variety of colorations in the breed, especially around the neck, withers, and shoulders.

COLOR GENETICS

The loci we will consider as pertaining to coat color genetics in the German Shepherd Dog are given in the allele map on the following page. In order to help you remember which genes perform which tasks, you can use the following memory bridge. A stands for the *a*gouti series of alleles, or for the *p*attern of coat *a*ll over the body. B is where the gene determining *b*lack or *b*rown lies; C could be for *c*oncentration of *c*olor or melanin; D is for *d*ensity of *d*ilution; E is for *e*xtension; S is for one or more types of white *s*potting.

Agouti (A) Series: Pattern

Agouti is a term borrowed from genetics studies on that type of rat. It refers to the banded-hair coloration or pattern seen in Elkhounds, wolves, and sable German Shepherds, but can also be seen in varying amounts in the neck, shoulder, tail, croup and border markings in saddle-marked dogs. At locus A the German Shepherd Dog has a pair of genes, one on each of the chromosome pair, which determine the major markings we call pattern. This pair may have two of the same or two different alleles. (Alleles, you remember, are alternative genes in a series, and only one can occupy a particular space on the single chromosome.) Some genes have several potential alleles or varieties; some have but one.

A^y, sable—The *y* can be thought of as referring to the yellow pigment which can dominate the appearance of the tan-sable dog. Depending on other genes, the underlying yellow (or tan) can be so overshadowed or light that the dog has a grey appearance. Such a dog is a result of other genes interacting with A^y, especially those that determine the length of the black bands. The word *sable* comes from the French word for black, and sable German Shepherds have many hairs tipped with black. In other breeds, where a more dominant allele for self-color (solid) exists, the sable or yellow pattern is a^y (subcase a). For example, the black Lab is A^s while the yellow Lab is a^y. Dr. Little proposed

separate major genes for tan-sable and gray-sable, but actually the color lying under the black tips is due to other genes. A sable is a sable.

Black-and-tans—Also given the abbreviated description, "B&T," these dogs can be divided into two groups: saddle-marked, and bicolor. While the British geneticist and German Shepherd fancier, Dr. Malcolm Willis, has done an admirable job compiling statistics and photographs pertaining to color pedigrees, Great Britain's quarantine system and fewer German Shepherds have apparently kept him from encountering as many colors and oddities as have I and some others in the United States.

One of his conclusions with which I concur is that there is not one but *two* alleles for black-and-tan. One tends to produce the bicolor pattern found in B&T Cockers, Dobes, Rottweilers, Coonhounds, and a few others. The other allele gives the saddle pattern, in which the tan may be extensively spread over belly, legs, neck, and face, or only partly expressed. Genes on other loci or chromosomes affect the "salt-and-pepper" appearance of cream (*gelbe*) and silver-grey (*grau*) markings in or bordering the saddle and other black areas in the saddle-marked dog.

a^s, saddle—The saddle pattern gene is next in order of dominance below A^y. The use of subcase shows it is not as strong in its influence over pattern as the sable gene, but it is dominant over other alleles in the series. The saddle pattern has been the most popular in the past fifty years. Whether, as the Germans describe it, the base color is black and the tan portions are the markings, or the base color is brown/tan and the saddle, muzzle, and head markings are the areas of added pigmentation. It's like arguing about the color of a zebra.

a^t, bicolor—"Tan points" is a way to remember the shorthand symbol for this pattern in a basically black dog with small tan points or patches on cheeks, eyebrows, boots, characteristic chest markings, and a small area around the anus and underside of the tail. This is the pattern seen in Rottweilers, B&T Coonhounds, and many others.

Since all B&T German Shepherds at birth appear nearly all-black, it is probably impossible to tell with surety whether a given newborn pup is a saddle or a bicolor variety. However, if both parents are bicolors, it's a safe bet to assume the marked pups are bicolors. To distinguish between these and

A possible allele "map" for the German Shepherd Dog's coat colors.

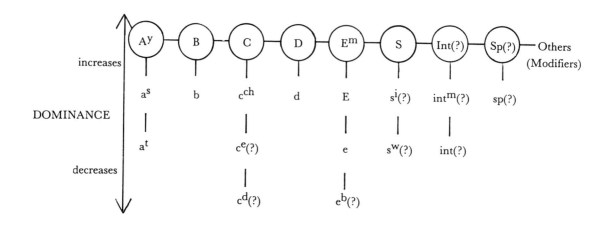

In this simplified figure, the horizontal chain represents a chromosome or part of a chromosome, and the individual spheres are the loci of genes affecting coat color and pattern. The gene designated A^y is shown in the A locus, though any one of the ones below it (a^s or a^t) could be there instead. Likewise with the other loci. Question marks are used to indicate that these may not exist as genes at all. To date it isn't possible to magnify genes large enough to actually see details, so we must deduce much of what we theorize from other facts which *are* able to be seen.

Capital letters are used when a trait is believed to be dominant or "stronger" than the other genes which could occupy that same locus. The world *allele* is used to refer to a *form* of a specific gene. For example, B and b are the two possible alleles which could exist at the B locus in the color chromosome. One calls for black pigment in the saddle, the other calls for brown in the same place. If both members of the pair are B, the saddle (and/or other dark areas) would be black; if both were b, it would be brown or liver-colored. If the cell had one of each (Bb), the dominant one (higher on the map) would prevail, and the color there would be black.

The concept that genes operate in pairs is true in all cases but one. The exception to this paired existence occurs in gametes , or reproductive (sex) cells: sperm in the male, ova in the femle. Each of these cells has only *half* the usual number of chromosomes, 39 instead of 78 in the case of the canine. When these two types of cells meet in conception, the result is again 78 for all the new individual's cells except those sex cells formed approximately at the same time the fertilized egg divides for the sixth time.

Long versus normal-length hair is said to be a simple Mendelian trait in the German Shepherd Dog. If the parents had normal-length coats but many of the resultant litter were long-coated, then they carried what we refer to as a recessive gene for that trait. They also each had a dominant gene for normal-length coat, and this half of the gene pair took precedence when genetic orders were given regarding the length of their *own* hairs. In some of the offspring of these parents, the recessives got together, and in the absence of the dominant short-coat genes (which brother and sister may have received), produced long-coated dogs.

Other traits are not so simple, since genes frequently act in concert in what we call polygenic traits. Even those we call simple are not entirely so, but enough so the result can be predicted with high accuracy. In these simpler traits especially, the amount of masking or dominance one gene has over the other may be incomplete; you may be able to look at the phenotype (individual's appearance) and fairly accurately guess as to his genotype (genetic constitution, what he *carries* as recessive).

Both the forces of nature and the whims of man can cause relationships between genes to change, and when the genes themselves seem to have been changed, the results are called *mutations*. Most mutations die, are sterile, or have no dominance and thus are swallowed up or lost in the normal population. The greater the mutation change, the less likely it is to survive. I have a hypothesis that the first dog (ancestor of wolf, dog, jackal, etc.) started with more alleles than we now see in any of them, and many dominant ones were lost in the dog to enable him to survive in a changing world. This played a greater part in diversification than did mutations, since different genes were lost in different parts of the globe over which the canine was dispersed.

solid black pups, look at the anus—if there is any color there, the dog is not a solid black.

The bicolor allele is recessive to the saddle-pattern. But if both parents have at least one of these bicolor alleles (a^sa^t or a^ta^t) some of the pups could well be bicolors.

Solid black—It was once widely thought that the solid black dog resulted from an allele on the A locus, recessive to all the others so far mentioned, and that a double dose of this allele was needed. It is now fairly evident that the solid black pattern is determined by the interaction of genes at two different loci. For the sake of convenience, Willis assigned the principal gene for solid black to the E series (extension of dark pigment) though it may be at yet another locus. He postulated that the solid black dog can be thought of as a homozygous bicolor (a^ta^t) with the added influence of an E locus gene which is discussed more fully later.

Incomplete dominance—In the A series, incomplete dominance of one A series allele over a lower one is often, though not always, visible to the experienced eye. A heterozygous A^ya^s sable (the genes in the pattern pair not identical) will have a shadow of a saddle with slightly more dark-tipped hairs than the homozygous A^yA^y sable has in the areas commonly marked black in the saddle dog. If the sable has a hypostatic gene (at the E locus) for solid black, such a dog is usually considerably darker in overall appearance than are his lighter grey or golden sable relatives. Karilea's Cito, Dipadon's Dasher, Von Eck's Mark, and other sables that carried the black factor and were capable of producing solid blacks had this dark look. I believe most very dark sables carry the bicolor recessive and/or the black factor at the E locus as well.

Likewise, a saddle-marked dog that produces blacks will usually have an extensive amount of black covering more of his body than do most of his littermate saddle dogs that do not carry the black/bicolor factors. Incidently, I use such qualifying words as *usually* and *probably*, because there are very few dogmatic positions in breeding canines that cannot be modified with reliable exceptions. One such was our von Salix's Heather, a typically saddle-marked bitch sired by Select Ch Caralon's Hein v d Lockenheim CD out of a bitch of good but not especially dark pigmentation. Heather

really fooled us by producing a black pup when bred to the dark sable Hein son, Ch Karilea's Cito, for she just didn't look the part. Hein gave Heather the black factor(s) but she kept his secret until she whelped our P litter.

While a black factor can often be guessed at in a^s dogs by virtue of a larger saddle and extended black down the legs, hocks, and head, the bicolor (a^t) dog does not have much room left for black to encroach upon tan as a result of a gene at the E locus, so it may be harder to guess at one or two "black genes" being present in a homozygous bicolor dog. Further, the a^s dog with the a^t recessive (a^sa^t) may give much the same impression as a homozygous a^sa^s that has the extension series alleles for solid black. When you think of all the pattern and extension combinations possible in B&T dogs, you begin to understand the variety that can exist in amount of black pigment over the body, and why it would be difficult to guess at genotype. We can conclude that the gene for saddle pattern (a^s) is incompletely dominant over the gene for bicolor (a^t) and heterozygous dogs (a^sa^t) may show a range of extension or cover of black color over the dorsal and lateral portions of their bodies.

We will return to the subject of the black dog when we discuss the E locus. For now, let's look at only the A series in an attempt to clarify the riddle of inheritance. Remembering that genes affecting one characteristic usually operate in pairs, we'll consider some practical facts of breeding pertaining to coat color. Since beginners are often confused as to what will happen if they breed a certain bitch to a certain dog, let's put some dogs together on paper and see what we get.

The homozygous sable, with both A series genes being A^y, is bred to the homozygous B&T saddle, a^sa^s. Regardless of other factors such as depth or distribution of pigment, the A^yA^y X a^sa^s cross will give a litter of 100 percent sable phenotype, though possibly not as distinct as the one parent's, and all the pups will carry the a^s as a recessive. Let's take it as an algebraic exercise and multiply A^yA^y by a^sa^s. The first A^y combined with the first a^s will give a pup with the A^ya^s genetic constitution. The same thing happens when the second A^y from one parent pairs with the first a^s of the other, and again when either A^y pairs with the second a^s. Mathematically, the equation is:
$$(A^yA^y) \text{ X } (a^sa^s) = (A^ya^s) + (A^ya^s) + (A^ya^s) +$$

(A^ya^s). Another way to represent the same breeding is by the use of a device known as the Punnett square.

In the following illustration is found the combinations of one allele from one parent, across the top, and one from the other parent, along the side. The zygotes (fertilized eggs) and hence those potential offspring have the genotype indicated in the small square where the gamete symbols intersect. The mathematical probabilities become more likely to occur in the predicted proportions if enough breedings are made and enough offspring are obtained.

Dam

	a^s	a^s
A^y	A^ya^s	A^ya^s
A^y	A^ya^s	A^ya^s

(Sire, on the left side for both A^y rows)

Two more examples of breedings and resultant pups follow. Two heterozygous sables will produce 25 percent homozygous, 50 percent heterozygous sables, and 25 percent saddle-marked dogs.

Dam
(Sable with bicolor recessive)

	A^y	a^t
A^y	A^yA^y	A^ya^t
a^s	A^ya^s	a^sa^t

Sire
(Sable with saddle recessive)

If the two types represented by the right half of the square were bred, one might expect the result shown below. Some of the a^ta^t offspring may be

Dam

	a^s	a^t
A^y	A^ya^s	A^ya^t
a^t	a^sa^t	a^ta^t

Sire

black, if they also carry at least one e^b allele, according to Willis.

It should be noted when I say approximately 25 percent of a litter is of one genetic makeup or about 50 percent is of another, that these are mathematical odds, not a sure thing. If you repeated a breeding ten times, the accuracy of your prediction would be better, although each of the separate litters may vary a good bit with regard to percentages.

Extension Series: E Locus

This is a controversial and insufficiently studied gene locus in the German Shepherd Dog as well as in several other breeds. It is said to affect distribution or extension of dark pigment such as mask (dark muzzle and head) and brindle markings, as well as the extension of dark pigment to other parts of the haircoat such as the chest and the black/tan border areas on B&T dogs. There is almost no doubt that the genes at E interact strongly with those alleles at A and thereby affect the pattern of tan and black markings.

The usual listing of alleles in the E series in order of diminishing dominance is: E^m, E, e, to which some of us add e^b at the end, though this gene for solid black may actually appear at another locus. Based on available data and for convenience's sake, I list it as the most recessive allele in this series. The most dominant could be either E^m (mask) or E (extension), which is why both are capitalized here.

While the mask is most obvious on the muzzle, it can extend to the forehead, though the black is broken up by other genes calling for tan markings. In some other breeds, the mask is more or less limited to the forehead and around the eyes.

Recessive to E^m and E is the allele e, which in the double or homozygous state (ee) produces a solid red, tan, or "fawn" color. Although common in Great Danes, Boxers, and other breeds, it is quite rare in the German Shepherd Dog, and its full expression may depend on an interaction between ee and A^yA^y. The "no black" factor at the E locus (ee) does not allow the sable pattern to appear, so maybe it could be called a "no black tipping" or "no black banding" factor, epistatic to A^y. In heterozygous dogs (only one e, the other E or E^m), the lack of black may be limited to the face, where very little dark pigment exists in many dogs. Such a dog may show a limited or mixed tan-and-black saddle. "Fawn" has been produced out of heavily-covered (a^t?) parents and out of two white parents. Some are as brightly colored as "orange" Pomeranians, others may be faded and incorrectly identified liver-and-tan dogs.

Dr. Malcolm B. Willis, geneticist at the University of Newcastle-Upon-Tyne, England, states that the e allele was at a fairly high frequency in Britain during the 1950s and '60s, with ee popping up in many dogs such as the "pale golden sables" (not really sables at all) descended from the great champion Avon Prince of Alumvale. They had the a^s genotype and very early in life actually had the saddle markings, but lost their saddles during puppyhood and adolescence, so that by adulthood they appeared sable or uniformly colored. I agree that the problem with the e allele is that many dogs carrying it are very attractive and flashy, and therefore in demand as breeding partners. But such animals should only be bred to dogs of strong pigmentation. The combination of ee with the weakest genes on the C series is probably what yields the dingy-white dog, but more about that later.

e^b and the solid black dog—The last in the series for extension of dark pigment is believed to be the e^b allele, which is required to be present (Willis says in double dose) along with a pair of a^t alleles at the other loci, to give a solid black dog. The presence of this recessive e^b gene can be verified in marked dogs only by progeny testing; if both a^s (saddle) parents have the bicolor recessive (a^t) and Ee^b as well, there might be a solid black pup in the litter, with $a^t a^t e^b e^b$ as his partial color map.

Wolves and their close relatives have, over the eons of separation, lost the A alleles for saddle markings (a^s) and apparently for bicolor pattern, too, yet black wolves do exist. They have a somewhat agouti look to some parts of their lower coats, but this seems to be the undercoat showing through a somewhat open topcoat. Now, if what we said earlier about $a^t a^t$ plus $e^b e^b$ being necessary to form solid black is true, why aren't there any bicolor wolves? Maybe the recessive black in wolves is on another locus or has a different relationship to the A locus. Perhaps what we think of as sable in wolves is really agouti, A^w (the w standing for

Occasionally, a white parent will produce buff-colored pups. There were two in this litter. Dam is white and Sire is black.

wolf or *wild*,) and e^b reacts with that as it does with a^t in the domesticated German Shepherd Dog. Apparently, only hybrid crosses between variously colored wolves and German Shepherds could give the answer. I have examined the coats of wolves, coyotes, and sable Shepherds, and can't really pin down sharp distinctions. In northern Alabama, contrary to claims of extinction and the limited maps found in field guides, we still have the sable or agouti red wolf (*Canis niger rufus*) being trapped, with occasionally a black specimen (*Canis niger niger*) being taken.

Regardless of how we explain the black wolf with no bicolors in the population, the theory that bicolor genes and solid black are related is still workable and helpful in studying color inheritance. Two saddle-marked dogs occasionally have produced saddles, bicolors, and blacks in the same litter. The last Punnett square we looked at shows the genetic constitution of such parents and their statistically representative off-spring. The ratio expected in this breeding would be 12:3:1 (12 saddles to 3 bicolors to 1 black), but remember that many breedings and puppies would have to be counted in order to make the results and statistics fairly equal all the time.

In the next illustration, the E could just as easily be e^b in which case the pups presently designated $a^t a^t EE$ and $a^t a^t E e^b$ bicolors would then be solid blacks, with the ratiio of bicolor to black averaging 0:4 if both parents had $e^b e^b$, and 2:2 if one were $E e^b$ and the other were $e^b e^b$. Although one compilation of data shows more bicolors than blacks in the U.S. up to 1972, I have never seen more blacks than bicolors, especially since then, and the reason is that the $e^b e^b$ condition is now being more slected for than are EE and $E e^b$. Black is more popular now, and the dog that produces blacks will get more stud services than one that throws more bicolors.

Dam: $a^s a^t E e^b$

Combinations contributed by dam:

Sire: $a^s a^t E e^b$ — Combinations of A and E locus genes contributed by sire

	$a^s E$	$a^s e^b$	$a^t E$	$a^t e^b$
$a^s E$	saddle $a^s a^s EE$	dark (?) sad. $a^s a^s E e^b$	ext. sad. $a^s a^t EE$	dark, ext. sad. $a^s a^t E e^b$
$a^s e^b$	saddle $a^s a^s E e^b$	saddle $a^s a^s e^b e^b$	ext. sad. $a^s a^t E e^b$	ext. sad. $a^s a^t e^b e^b$
$a^t E$	ext. sad. $a^s a^t EE$	ext. sad. $a^s a^t E e^b$	bicolor $a^t a^t EE$	bicolor (ext.?) $a^t a^t E e^b$
$a^t e^b$	dark, ext. sad. $a^s a^t E e^b$	ext. sad. $a^s a^t e^b e^b$	bicolor $a^t a^t E e^b$	solid black $a^t a^t e^b e^b$

If we assume the only color difference between the sire and dam to be the A^y/a^s (sable/saddle) one, the expected average ratio in the offspring would be 4:2:1:1 (8 sables, 4 saddles, 2 bicolors, and 2 blacks). The actual ratio in that litter was 3:5:0:1 (or 3:4:1:1 if one dark pup that left early was really a bicolor). This litter illustrates several points. One is that the average statistics may not be closely approximated unless a large number of puppies are produced in a few or several litters; second, one

Heather: $a^t E e^b$

Combinations contributed by dam:

Ch. Cito $A^y a^t e^b e^b$ — Combinations of A & E locus genes from sire

	$a^s E$	$a^t E$	$a^s e^b$	$a^t e^b$
$A^y e^b$	sable $A^y a^s E e^b$	sable $A^y a^t E e^b$	sable $A^y a^s e^b e^b$	sable $A^y a^t e^b e^b$
$A^y e^b$	sable $A^y a^s E e^b$	sable $A^y a^t E e^b$	sable $A^y a^s e^b e^b$	sable $A^y a^t e^b e^b$
$a^t e^b$	saddle $a^s a^t E e^b$	bicolor $a^t a^t E e^b$	sad. $a^s a^t e^b e^b$	black $a^t a^t e^b e^b$
$a^t e^b$	sad. $a^s a^t E e^b$	bicolor $a^t a^t E e^b$	sad. $a^s a^t e^b e^b$	black $a^t a^t e^b e^b$

can't be too pat in predicting genotype on the basis of phenotype; third, that there is something more than just one gene locus that produces solid black.

The Black/Brown Series, B Locus

In the German Shepherd Dog breed, only two alleles exist for the B locus. BB or Bb will produce black pigment, but bb will affect the production of eumelanin granules in such a way (more diffuse, different shapes, etc.) that instead of black, they show brown. *This* brown is not the same *braun* as appears on the tan parts, but rather is found where black is normally found in a BB or Bb dog, such as the saddle, nose, eyerims, etc. It is variously referred to as liver, chocolate, or seal-brown, depending on the custom in whatever breed or species is being discussed. German Shepherd Dog fanciers use the term *liver* most of the time.

Black is dominant over liver (B is stronger than b), but most dogs I've seen that carry the liver recessive have a lot of reddish coloration in the neck and croup areas, and much mixed in the saddle as well. Most do not have black on their faces. These genes on the B locus affect only the dark pigment (the eumelanin) not the yellow phaeomelanin pigment. In the case of sables, the phaeomelanin's effect is seen not only on feet, belly, and tan markings, but over the entire dog, but this yellow/tan pigment is overlaid by the darker eumelanin in the tips of the hairs. Sometimes, whether due to the ribbing or to rows of bundles of hairs, sables may have a slightly striped appearance; however, this should not be mistaken for brindling.

The German Shepherd Dog with liver nose and saddle is fairly rare, but other than appearing lighter the liver-and-tans can be as good looking as B&Ts. One very attractive liver-and-tan bicolor male was whelped in a litter of B&Ts. His sire was a B&T bicolor whom I wouldn't have suspected of carrying the liver gene, so was another example of how a dog can hide his genotype. Of course, the dam had to carry the recessive, too, but as with the sire, I don't remember anything unusual about her; she appeared to be a fairly normal though not deeply pigmented B&T saddle-marked bitch.

The liver gene can appear in any coat pattern whether sable, saddle, or bicolor, as B/b is independent of the A (pattern) locus. It is fully visible in the homozygous state, bb. If the liver-and-tan bicolor mentioned above were to be bred to another of the same pattern and color, and if each had the e^be^b alleles on the E locus, they might produce a small percentage of $a^ta^tbbe^be^b$ dogs that would be solid liver. Unless intentionally bred for, this is unlikely to happen as most breeders are quick to hide their "mistakes," not realizing it is a simple Mendelian trait and easier to control than polygenic traits. Pups with disqualifying faults are harder to sell, so such dogs or their parents don't often get bred.

I don't think I've ever seen a homozygous liver sable, unless it was one of those I mistook for fawn, but the condition can happen, and would produce a less-distinct contrast of overlay to the tan ground color. Much of the appearance would depend on what genes are at the C, E, A, and perhaps other, unidentified loci.

There have been reports that b may be a lethal or semi-lethal gene, but the presence of bb has not been shown to be lethal in other breeds and I don't believe it has any such deleterious effect on viability in the German Shepherd Dog either. The liver dogs I've seen are as healthy as other, "normally-colored" dogs are.

Density/Dilution Series, D Locus

The genes at the D locus can be either D which directs a jet-black expression of the melanin, or d which dilutes that expression to "blue," or one of each. Most of the German Shepherd Dogs you are likely to see will be homozygous for D or will at least be heterozygous, with Dd genotype and jet-black or nearly so on their saddles, noses, etc. Some years ago I was given an opportunity to view a litter sired by a handsome young dog that a few years later became Grand Victor. The dam's lines were similar to the sire's, so these pups were linebred on a couple of animals still widely used as the basis for many a kennel's lines. All of the pups had the typical black saddle pattern but in two of them the saddles and markings were blue; the genotype was probably $a^sa^sBBCCddE^m$. While the blue color is really a slate grey, it is a recognized color in several breeds. However, the German Shepherd Dog official AKC Standard describes it as a serious fault. Such a dog will be disqualified, though, because the Standard requires a black nose. The breeder of the above litter had never come across this and was perplexed as to what to do with the affected pups. I tried to persuade her to find nice pet homes

for them since they had absolutely beautiful movement and personalities.

A solid blue dog is the same as a solid black one with regard to the interdependence of e^be^b with a^ta^t, and with regard also to the B and possibly C locus alleles, but instead of the dominant D being present, the dog is homozygous for the dilute-density alleles, dd. Before the Standard was revised to disqualify dogs with other than black noses, there was a top-quality dog, Ch Hoobin's Gray Boy, owned by Langdon Skarda. Quoting one of his former handlers who is now a multi-group judge, "He is the first and only blue to have finished. He is the only one to have an all-breed BIS. He had perfect hips, his nose was black* and he was really ... more like a charcoal grey. No tan. He had dark, dark eyes ... nothing but black-and-tan dogs in the first six generations of his pedigree."

The double presence of d can occur in sables, saddles, bicolors, or solid-colored dogs. The dd dogs will have bluish (dark grey) eyerims, pads, and noses. While to my knowledge it hasn't happened yet, a dog could be dihybrid for both bb and dd. Have you ever seen a dog of another breed that was homozygous for *both* liver and blue, one whose partial genotype was bbdd? Of course you have— the ghostly silver Weimeraner. It *could* happen in the German Shepherd Dog breed, as the genes are all present in the population, and if it did occur it could be a solid-color dog ($a^ta^tbbdde^be^b$), a saddle (a^sbbddE), a bicolor (a^ta^tbbddE), or a sable (A^ybbddE).

When newborn, the blues really stand out, as if dipped in silver paint. As they mature, it becomes slate gray, and may get almost dark enough to pass for black until a normal-colored dog is seen nearby. The nose is darker than the dark portion of the coat. The D or d allele has no effect on phaeomelanin in the tan parts.

---

*Not having seen this dog myself, I cannot confirm this. If the color were indistinguishable from that of other dogs' noses, it would indeed be surprising. This lady also claimed that most blue-and-tans would appear black-and-tan by six months of age. She may have been referring to dogs with a blue dilution recessive (heterozygous Dd) which was not completely masked in the soft puppy coat but does become covered by the D allele when the harsher topcoat develops.

Mid-way Summary: Interactions

Before going further, take another look at the allele map on page 240; there are influences or interactions to consider. Suppose the A^y gene says, "All right, crew, give me some melanin and I'll distribute it over the surface of this dog, but mainly in the tips of the hairs." Another gene, a modifier, responds, "Only where I allow you to do so, A^y! I've been helping to color wolves and other dogs for thousands of years and there are certain areas such as behind the base of the ears, on the belly, and elsewhere that I may refuse to allow darkening." Perhaps another modifier gene elsewhere pipes up and says, "Don't forget, when I'm around, you both have to leave an area on the chest and the tip of the tail white—totally unpigmented!"

The chorus continues: If B is present, it specifies that the dark pigment the other genes have been talking about must be black. But if bb is there instead, they require that the dark pigment be brown instead of black, calling it chocolate or liver. D demands that any black used by the E, A, and B alleles be a true, intense black, but if D is absent, his diminutive cousins, dd, have some fun by making sure the dark parts are a dark blue-grey, not black. Their dilution powers cause the nose as well as dark hair to have that slate-colored tinge. They are joined by E, E^m, e, or e^b who contend as to the extension of black or dark pigment to a mask or not, and influence on what percentage of the body that pigment will be used. E alleles appear to act more as advisors to the A series.

Phantom 2-3 weeks old.

The blue dilute factor. One pup in this litter was "silver" at birth. The blue darkened to a gray, then slate, then close to normal black, though easily distinguished when a real B & T was nearby. "Phantom" was of ideal structure, but the color disqualifies for AKC shows.

Phantom at 2 months.

Phantom at 6 months.

Ch. Von Eck's Mark. An example of the solid black factor (from his sire, black Ch. Caralon's Phantom of Lebarland) "showing through" the sable coat pattern. Mark was the lightest of his litter, with others appearing almost bi-color. All had the "tarheels" (black on hocks and below) and black "pencil marks" (lines on toes), additional evidence of a black hypostatic gene. Mark's dam got her sable coloration from Frigga of Siverlane or Von Nassau's Ophelia, or both.   *Photo courtesy breeder/owner Judith Ecklund.*

The Concentration Series, C Locus

C alleles control the color or concentration of the tan parts of the Shepherd Dog. Newborn B&T (a^sa^s, a^sa^t, or a^ta^tE) whelps often appear all-black until close examination reveals some silvery or tan coloring on lower legs, cheeks, eyebrows, and around the anus, often only at the vent in the case of the darker pups. The tan areas will gradually increase at the expense of the black, with the process tapering off and nearly stopping at maturity. The silvery grey paws will also turn tan, so don't worry if you see that grey in newborns. As the pup grows, the tan creeps up the forelegs to meet the widening chest and neck markings, and up from the hindlegs to the haunches. Eventually, the pup that had a tiny bit of tan on brows, cheeks, and feet becomes a much lighter dog with a saddle halfway down the ribs and just barely covering the hip bones.

Bicolor dogs or saddle dogs with dark recessive modifiers such as a^t and e^b in single doses do not usually change as much. Sable puppies generally start off a little lighter at birth than the shade they later develop, but much influence comes from genes at the E and C locations on the chromosomes, and the delayed development of topcoat. A sable with

a black hypostatic gene (e^b) or a bicolor recessive (a^t) or one of each may be darker at birth than a littermate without such modifiers, other factors being equal, and remain dark throughout his lifetime. A strange paradox has been reported: Dr. Michael Fox has observed that wolves start out darker at birth and get lighter for a while.

There may be three or more alleles which vie for position on the C locus. Although Willis calls C locus the *albino* series because the most recessive can produce a sort of white, given certain genes at other loci, I prefer not to use the term since it may confuse those who associate it with pink-eyed rabbits and mice. The most dominant of the series is C, which directs normal concentration of the phaeomelanin pigment granules in the red-tan-yellow portion of the coat.

Full expression of color is seen in homozygous CC dogs, with modifiers probably making the difference between rust-red and a medium, "average" tan shade. There may be very little difference, perhaps indistinguishable, in phenotype between CC and heterozygous Cc^{ch} or another combination. Recessive to C is the allele c^{ch}, named after the chinchilla because of the lightening effect it has on the tan points or yellow area. I remember being startled by the sight of a German Shepherd Dog at an obedience trial in Canada that had the bicolor pattern, but whose tan was almost white. My first thought was that this was a black-and-white Shepherd. My next thought was that it was a Malamute or Husky cross; but upon closer examination it was found to be a purebred German Shepherd Dog, and questioning revealed some white dogs in its immediate ancestry. This dog probably had a double dose of some recessive paling genes at the C locus, perhaps c^{ch} and/or c^e (extreme). The c^{ch} allele reportedly does not work on the black pigment a dog has, and that "B&W" dog supported this hypothesis. The chinchilla gene may be described as directing *less* pigment by controlling the number and size of phaeomelanin granules in the hairs.

Black-and-tan saddle or bicolor German Shepherd Dogs with somewhat faded points or considerably lighter hair on the inside of the legs may have a chinchilla recessive making itself partially visible (Cc^{ch}). The lighter those portions are, the more likely is the presence of such an allele, and homozygous $c^{ch}c^{ch}$ dogs that have received a chinchilla gene from *each* parent may be very light cream or nearly white at those locations. Careless breeding can thus yield black-and-cream or black-and-silver dogs with dark saddles but poor pigment elsewhere. Yet there is at least one reputable breeder/obedience trainer intentionally selecting for black-and-silver dogs. (Incidentally, many people, when they say black and silver, are referring to those dogs that have a lot of silvery grey mixed in on the neck, belly, and other areas, which may be caused by genes at other loci.) Since many of my dogs have those flashy markings, I always answer "yes" when people call and ask if I have black-and-silvers.

In sables, c^{ch} would tend to give a very pale grey, light golden, or sooty-cream appearance, depending on interactions with other genes. If the dog is $A^yc^{ch}c^{ch}$ or has $eec^{ch}c^{ch}$, it is probably an off-white dog. This color is as much deprecated by breeders of clear whites as by breeders of colored Shepherds. In the off-white dog, the A^y gene may

The white German Shepherd Dog. Registerable with AKC, but not eligible for entry to the conformation ring. Two types appear to be in existence: one, a clear white such as this dog, the other a dingy white with hint of buff or cream-tan along the back, around ears, and elsewhere. This may or may not be a matter of simply different locations on the genetic spectrum. It is believed that the off-whites are more closely related to our faded sables, though sable is a dominant pattern and white is a recessive trait; perhaps this means that different loci are responsible. Owners of white GSDs often are members of the WGSDCI and hold their own, non-AKC, shows. This photo of Sherry's Magnificent Mongo, one of the leading winners in that low-population group, was supplied by owner S. Kirchway. Note black eye rims, lips, and nose; no trace of albinism, which latter is extremely rare.

White German Shepherd Dog Club International 1987 Annual Specialty Best of Breed. Both parents of this dog were out of black and tan lines.

be masked by (hypostatic to) the double c^{ch}, and if the dog also has ee at the E locus, the dark pigment will be prevented in a similar way that the chinchilla gene prevents the tan pigment. The e allele is involved in the pale golden "sables" reported by a number of observers, these dogs being actually B&T in genotype and born with a black and yellow-gold-tan a^s or even a^t constitution and appearance, yet losing the black by adulthood. Therefore, when you breed a sable with e to a dog with c^{ch}, you *may* wind up with off-white offspring.

Breeding to a solid black would not necessarily cover the effect of c^{ch} in the progeny, for, as I have shown, c^{ch} does not act on the black pigment and a solid black dog could easily be $c^{ch}c^{ch}$ in genetic constitution with no way of your knowing without progeny testing. Also, the common claim that breeding to a sable every few generations will insure good pigment is unscientific although not totally without basis. But keep in mind that some of the sables you might choose to use may carry the chinchilla gene themselves. So, generally speaking, if you have an otherwise excellent animal with a lack of strong pigmentation in the tan areas, it would be advisable to breed it only to dogs of good pigment which you feel do *not* carry the c^{ch} recessive themselves. Otherwise, there may be very little color difference between your stock and the "bargains" found in the classified section of the newspaper.

It may be that an allele at the C locus makes the difference between a gray sable and a tan sable, if it acts on the color of the undercoat or the base of the black-tipped hairs.

There may also exist at the C locus an allele which yields *extreme* dilution of the tan pigment, which seemingly is in evidence in a number of breeds that appear white. Little gives it the designation c^e, but Willis attributes the same lack of color to the chinchilla gene. Remember that there are two distinctly different types of white German Shepherds, one with a slightly dingy shadow of color, and the other a clean, clear white. The one with the faint yellowish tinge especially along the mid-dorsal line of the back is *possibly* a sable with one or two of the recessive alleles, c^{ch} or c^e (or one of each), as well as a modifier for "no black" at the E locus. The white Shepherd is discussed below.

Albinism—An albino is a white mutant probably resulting from the recombination of recessive genes which dictate that *no* melanin is to be produced. The only color present in the albino comes from Tyndall scattering in eyes, or, more frequently, red or pink from the blood's color showing through the eyes or skin. Albinos are extremely rare in most breeds, including the German Shepherd Dog. Several years ago there were only fifty to seventy albino dogs in America, and most of them were Pekingese. I do not agree with the classification of ''partial albinism'' as a heterozygous cause of partial loss of pigment such as that seen in snow nose.

The White German Shepherd Dog

No more volatile issue exists among Shepherd fanciers than that of the white dog, with prejudices and misconceptions on both sides of the fence. Because von Stephanitz and some of his colleagues believed that dogs with paling coloration were not as healthy or of as good temperament as darker dogs, the SV gradually imposed greater restrictions on awarding titles, then breeding, then by about 1960 decided to ban registration of whites. The GSDCofA followed this lead in the 1960s, and in the 1968 version of the Standard the AKC changed the working from ''White dogs are not desirable and are to be disqualified if showing albino characteristics,'' to, ''A white dog ... must be disqualified.''

Where did the white come from and why was it banned? Let's address the question of banning first. Max von Stephanitz was probably as well versed in practical genetics as any professor or breeder of his day, but genetics was then in its infancy whereas today it has at least reached adolescence. Von Stephanitz thought of *all* white manifestations as being due to the same genetic factors (except perhaps age-greying muzzles), but over the years, scientific exploration has revealed chromosome locations, interactions, and alleles on each locus which can produce white. Therefore, a white dog of one breed may not necessarily produce all white pups if mated to a white dog of another breed, whose coat color is a result of genes on a different locus. Nevertheless, von Stephanitz said, ''White is only permitted for herdsman's dogs and their relatives, the Old German dogs of Eastern and Northern Germany. In shaggy-haired dogs white is not only ugly, but also prohibited, since it is a sign of heavy loss of pigments and therefore a falling-off of the constitutional hardness, a danger for breeding.'' He also said, ''White occurs in nature only as a protective coloring in cold snowy areas, or else as a sign of degeneration.'' Yet, a few paragraphs later in his last edition he said, ''... our German Shepherd Dogs have never been bred with special regard to coloring, which for a working dog is a matter of quite secondary consideration.''

In the past decade we have given our national club's highest awards to dogs of very poor pigmentation. In fact, some of the champions are nearly as light as the maligned off-whites purposely bred

Liver-and-tan homozygous pups with a B & T littermate. Parents were brother and sister, each carrying the recessive liver (brown) dilute factor. Eye colors in the L & T dogs were all light, indicating the genes are close together and have a high affinity for each other. This also indicates how inbreeding can be used to bring recessive traits ''into the open.'' All pups were healthy and large.

*Gen-Eve's Padrino v. Salix, CDX, OFA.
"Bronx", a Manhattan son co-owned by the author with
Janet and Dick Rowe.
"Bronx" 3½ months old.*

by some people. Though many feel the off-whites are structurally and temperamentally unsound, there is no scientific evidence of genetic linkage in the breed. The genes for poor temperament or proportions are not side-by-side with the genes for white (c^{ch}, c^e, e, s^w, etc.) or faded tan, and hence do not automatically accompany them when chromosomes split to be divided up in sperm and egg cells and later recombined in chance fashion during fertilization. This does not mean there is *no* connection between faded or off-white dogs and poor quality. On the contrary, if any single characteristic such as white color is specifically and preferentially bred for, it is at the expense of the whole dog.

Organized "White Shepherd" breeders are just as opposed, on an aesthetic basis, to the off-white dogs. In the early 1960s when the rift between breeders of whites and breeders of the darker German Shepherds was widening, the White German Shepherd Dog Club was organized in Sacramento, and their Standard which was largely copied from the 1943 AKC Standard, called for "purity of color ... dogs showing albino characteristics are to be disqualified." Under the heading of faults was included the phrase *buff discoloration*. The present club, known as the White German Shepherd Dog Club International, strives to produce clear white dogs with black eyerims, noses, and pads, dark eyes, and a temperament suitable for work and compan-

ionship. From now on in this discussion, unless specifically indicated to the contrary, I will leave the off-white dog and consider only the genetics, origin, and development of the clear white A^y (or a^s or a^t) CC dog with black nose and eyerims.

It seems reasonable to assume either that the E locus alleles are bigger or more chemically active and powerful than A, B, C, and D loci alleles, or that there are other modifying genes still undiscovered, which are pressed into service to help e suppress either the light or dark forms of melanin pigment in the hair. This seems to me to be a plausible explanation for the extremely faded sable appearance of some dingy white German Shepherd Dogs. Undoubtedly both types of whites are the results of alleles at more than one locus interacting to deny pigment to the medullae of the hairs. The white appearance is due to air spaces and colorless cytoplasm refracting and reflecting the incident light, just as flaked lye, shaved ice, and powdered glass all look white until stirred into water where the air is purged from between the particles. Of course, the A locus alleles may just as easily be a^t or a^s if the c^{ch}, c^e, and/or e genes with possible outside help from other modifiers are as influential as I have hypothesized. The various theories would only be proven or disproven by suitable test breedings to dogs of known genotype.

Now let us return to the question of where these white dogs came from. The white dog has been in the breed since the earliest days, and even before. White wolves are still found in the Arctic and occasionally further south. As mentioned at the beginning of this book, the strains contributing to the breed included the "Old German" shepherd dog which was derived in turn from crosses between the large herdsman's dog and the smaller versions of the Bronze Age dog which had also become useful to the shepherd. Later, descendants of the Old German dog developed into the Bearded Collie, Old English Sheepdog, and a similar shaggy variety found in the Southern Germany states of Wurttemberg, Swabia, and Upper Bavaria. All of these had many specimens that were partly or mostly white, and some that were all white. The central and northern states had long-coated white dogs somewhat similar to the Great Pyrenees, and smaller ones known as "sheep poodles" or "shepherd poodles," while to the southeast the Kuvasz had been developing in another direction. It comes as a surprise to most people that the Kuvasz, that large white Hungarian shepherd's dog with Tibetan ancestral roots, is an intermediate form between the other large white Hungarian-Russian herd guardian, the Komondor, and smaller varieties like the Puli and dogs more similar to the present German Shepherd Dog. The Kuvasz is a remarkably close relative of the German Shepherd Dog, and undoubtedly contributed, from the fifteenth to the late nineteenth centuries, some genes to the white German Shepherd Dog and to our darker varieties, especially those with heavy ears and large, bulky frames. The Turkish Akbash is another Kuvasz/Shepherd type.

Further south in what is now Yugoslavia, the Serbs used many dogs of almost identical build to our modern German Shepherd Dog. Many of these Serbian shepherds' dogs were pure white, and size increased a little as their range extended southward through Bulgaria to Macedonia. They all had the easy, loping gait of shepherd dogs and most had the smooth coarse hair of today's German Shepherd; some were long-coated just as they are today.

Much further to the north, in what is now Poland, shepherds migrated westward and introduced the Negretti breed of sheep to the neighboring German states, including Brunswick. They also brought with their flocks a shaggy-haired, frequently white working dog whose gene pool surely was sampled by the evolving sheep-tending dogs

of Germany. In the other direction, over the Caucasus Mountains were found great white dogs, some with wolf-grey masks, of typical shepherd dog build although more powerful, heavy, and with a slightly thicker coat. These, too, were used to guard sheep, but rather than contributing much form and color to the German Shepherd Dog they probably developed separately and in a parallel manner from the same base stock that supplied the Kuvasz, the Brunswick, and other ancestors and relatives of what would become the German Shepherd Dog. The Kurds valued them highly in that area where Turkey, Iran, and Caucasia meet.

Other countries bordering on or near Germany also had white dogs, and in most cases they were large, heavy herdsman's types useful for scaring off wolves and bears, and driving the flocks. Italy's Campagna and Abruzzi districts had such dogs, as did various sections of Spain. The ancient writer, Columella, stated that white dogs were preferred for the herds, so they could easily be seen at night and be distinguished from wolves by sheep and shepherd alike. In the Pyrenees Mountains between Spain and France, the great white dog developed from ancestors that crossed Europe one to two thousand years BC and left the Kurdistan shepherd dog cousin behind. A little of the Pyrenees dog may have found its way into the German Shepherd Dog breed in the eighteenth and nineteenth centuries when specimens were commonly exported into many European countries to satisfy the desires of the wealthy, but here again it may be primarily a dog of separate development.

There is a rare Arctic breed, the Chinook, which is nearly indistinguishable from a white German Shepherd Dog, though lighter in build than most of our too-heavy show dogs.

The logical conclusion, therefore, is that the recessive white color in German Shepherd Dogs has been handed down primarily from the large, "rude" herdsman's dogs rather than through the lithe, graceful shepherds' dogs whose main job was to keep sheep from straying into cultivated fields on the way from one pasture to another. To some, this "impurity of ancestry" is enough to warrant discrimination. But the clear white German Shepherd has inherited *only* the color, not the heavy ears, more ponderous gait, or course skull of the driving dogs and herd protectors, so this prejudice doesn't make sense. The charges of poor quality can just as easily be levied against breeders of colored dogs, and the only fair basis for disagreement would be that they deliberately do not breed to the Standard (yet they *do* have their own). I don't think the argument will ever be amicably settled, but at least the two factions could make an attempt at reconciliation. It seems to me that their energy would be better spent addressing such real problems as poor structure and abominable temperament that are ever-present in the breed regardless of color. Meanwhile, to avoid some of the antagonism, the WGSDCI should try to establish separate variety or breed status in rare-breed clubs.

As to which gene is responsible for the clear white variety of German Shepherd Dog, there isn't even agreement as to which locus or how many genes are involved. Some have proposed a recessive allele on the A locus beneath sable, saddle, bicolor, and even black, but this view is no longer held by most geneticists. Others have given it a position in the series which could exist at the S (spotting) locus. Still others have relegated it to a place on the C locus listing, below c^{ch} and c^e, if that latter exists. There is evidence that two blacks can produce a white. Perhaps the clear white German Shepherd Dog is $a^t a^t c^d c^d e^b e^b$ if both parents are solid black $a^t a^t Cc^d e^b e^b$. But if the c^d allele is epistatic to the "strong" genes at the A locus such as a^s and A^y, would there be white dogs out of sable parents? No genetic research has been done along these lines, or to determine if e^b or e is needed to complement the tendency of c^d to produce white, nor if white

Ch. Von Mibach's Flint, C.D. A son of the popular Bernd son Ch. Rex Edlu-Mibach, this medium-sized dog was one of the few fine American sables NOT descended from the K-litter Waldesruh. His coloration came from his dam's sire, the great showman Ch. Tannenwald's Igor, ROM, who was a grandson of Sieger Volker and of Atlas v. Elfenhain; through his dam came more of the R-litter genes. Flint had a tough yet friendly, outgoing temperament, balanced and fluid gait, and may have inherited his sire's black recessives, guessing from his rich sabling. Shown here with handler Ken Raynor who handled many Igor descendants, and judge Ernie Loeb awarding BOB at the Atlanta GSDC, 1975.

Photo courtesy L. Ryske.

Bronx- 6 months old.

Sire of the L & T pups shown in other photo. As is the case in many recessives, you can see the "shadow" of the trait showing through in the hetrozygous dog. Note that the orange-brown coloration extends over the neck and withers and croup, mixing with the black of the saddle to varying degrees. The sire and dam were similar in pigmentation, and produced normal B & T as well as Liver (brown)-and-tan pups.

can exist in the presence of such "strong" alleles as E and E^m. Willis reported no experience in white dogs of this type, and Whitney felt these clear whites were representative of a separate genetic factor, not the same as those which produce spotting *or* the extremely light cream. He proposed no locus designation, but his experience allows for considering an allele on the A locus, perhaps a^{wh}, recessive to a^t. One could just as easily assign it another location, and/or say it is operable only in the presence or absence of alleles on other loci.

Dr. Little believed that $c^{ch}c^{ch}$ plus ee in the A^yA^y dogs produced whites, but as we have seen, that's probably only true for the off-whites. Clear whites have reportedly been produced out of combi-

nations of sable, black, and B&T dogs as well as out of blacks and other white dogs, so the presence of the A^y allele is apparently not necessary. I agree with Willis that a separate allele probably is responsible for white, and further postulate that some sort of combination such as c^dc^d with ee, ee^b, e^be^b, or perhaps a recessive on the S locus is necessary. It has been shown that a strongly pigmented black is the result of the action of the "weakest," most recessive allele of the A series, a^t, acting with the most recessive allele of the E series, which is probably e^b. Further, it seems that *two* of each of these "weak" genes are needed to produce that "strong" color. This leads me to suspect that the dog would be a different color if only one E allele were e^b and the other were e, E, or E^m. Likewise, an even "weaker" color, clear white, might require double c^d genes *and* double recessive genes at another locus, as for example, $e^b e^b$. It may follow that the *more* recessive or hypostatic a trait is, the more it requires a *combination* of "weaker" alleles rather than rely on genes at only one locus to produce that effect.

Willis states, "... when two blacks are mated together only blacks will ensue," basing his hypothesis only on breeding records from breeders who had already rigorously excluded whites from their programs, or who started with animals which came from such exclusionist kennels. Let me propose that a black dog can carry a hidden factor on a locus other than the E locus which, when combined with another such hidden factor in its mate,

is able to produce a homozygous condition in which the double c^d (or whatever allele at whatever locus) is hypostatic to the $e^b e^b$. That is, the presence of what we conveniently call $c^d c^d$ is powerful enough to negate the $a^t a^t e^b e^b$ combination which would otherwise demand solid black coloration. The same would be true for saddle and/or sable parents.

Wherever the white gene is to be found, we do know that it is recessive or hypostatic and that it has been in the German Shepherd Dog breed and its progenitors as long as any other color genes. Before white dogs were excluded, they won prizes in shows on this side of the Atlantic in the 1920s and were used for breeding in Germany. A holdover from medieval times, white was associated with royalty.

"Bronx" at under one year of age.

Note how the black recedes and tan extends as a saddle-marked dog matures. Also, pups go through "the uglies" often times before regaining their original promise.

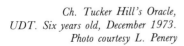

Ch. Tucker Hill's Oracle, UDT. Six years old, December 1973. Photo courtesy L. Penery

Mrs. Dodge and some of her German Shepherd Dogs.

Using dogs from the French province of Alsace which borders Germany's Wurttemberg, the royal family of the Hapsburgs developed a strain of white German Shepherd Dogs. Thus the preference by some white Shepherd breeders to call their dogs Alsatians as if they were a separate breed. (Incidentally, another strain was almost established when for a time an all-white canine corps was formed in the mountains of Germany between World War I and World War II.) The Hapsburg dogs, both white and conventionally colored, must have impressed an American lady who frequented the court in the early days of this century, as she brought some fine dogs back to the US, including the 1912 Tending Champion Luchs Hagmann and Fee v Boll, a full sister to the top field trial champion of 1912, Deborah v Sehningen. One of the results of combining these sheeptending strains and Horand lines was her Stonihurst Edmund, the first known white German Shepherd Dog registered in the United States. This lady was Miss Anne Tracy who is best known as one of the two founders, in 1913, of the German Shepherd Dog Club of America.

That the passage of the white gene (or combination of genes) is inextricably intertwined with the ancestral roots of our greatest early foundation stock cannot be denied. The dog that signalled a new direction in type, and whose choice as 1925 Sieger was a defensive measure against the growing influence of amateurs breeding German Shepherd Dogs, was Klodo v Boxberg. He may have transmitted white, bred as he was on Munko, Roland, Hettel, and others known or suspected to carry the factor. At least one of Klodo's sons, Reipel, sired whites in the US but this could have come through Flora Berkemeyer. Klodo's sire, a dog of great beauty but not as strong in temperament as was desired, was the 1920 Sieger Erich von Grafenwerth. Erich was purchased by the wealthy Mrs. Dodge to become one of the cornerstones of the Giralda Kennels lines which produced a number of white dogs. Erich's sire, Alex v Westfalenheim, was of even more questionable temperament, a trait probably inherited mostly from the black Roland, on whom he was linebred. Erich's dam was also linebred Roland.

Alex's sire, 1909 Sieger Hettel Uckermark, and Hettel's dam Gretel were both linebred on Beowulf and the Krone family, the latter being another source of several whites including some of the ancestors of those at the court of Kaiser Wilhelm. It seems likely that Hettel's sire, Roland v Starkenburg, transmitted this recessive from Beowulf, son of Thekla v d Krone, though it could as easily have been derived through Hector v Schwaben, Pollux/Prima, and Horand v Grafrath, SZ-1. With the lines going at least this far back we find a great deal of inbreeding but less information on coat color because of the greater emphasis in those days on utility than on appearance. If we look in the direction of the modern bloodlines, we find the white genes still being carried by respected families and individuals such as Quell v Fredeholz, Ilex of Longworth, Orex v Liebestraum, the Klodo son, Ch Geier v Blasienberg, and Grand Victor Ch Alert of Mi-Noah's. These are mentioned not to suggest that others of their descendants carry white, but only to show that the colored dogs and the white dogs may differ only in that respect (pigment), and that *structure and temperament are unrelated to color.*

There are only about 500 members of the WGSDCI, which comprises Canadian breeders and owners as well as those who had been members of the WGSDC and the WGSCofA. Yet their negligible influence on colored German Shepherd Dogs and the fact that less than 4 percent of registered German Shepherds in North America are whites, are ignored by those who choose to revile this small group of people for breeding a color that is unacceptable to a slightly larger group. To end this discussion, I offer the opinions of some highly respected people. Milo Denlinger, author of the early edition of *The Complete German Shepherd* has said that a good Shepherd cannot be a bad color. Goldecker and Hart, in *This Is The German Shepherd*, agree that the danger of paling color does not come through the dark-eyed, dark-nosed, white dog.

Other Loci

The intensity gene, Int locus—Some researchers have proposed another gene series at yet another locus, which influences the paling of the phaeomelanin-containing areas of the coat. There may be a dominant gene in many family lines which reduces the intensity or richness of the tan portions toward a dingy white. For practical purposes, one can ignore the question as to whether or not there is such an allele series as Int. Simply follow the general rule of breeding to darker dogs if you want to increase your chances of getting darker pups. If you still get light-colored dogs, blame it on the dominant cream gene.

The spotting series, S locus—The S locus was proposed by Little to determine the type and amount of white spotting and, conversely, restrict the distribution of pigmentation over the surface of the haircoat. In most breeds, the dominant allele is represented by S for *s*elf-color or a tendency toward solidly-colored (no white) but not necessarily all one color, depending on genes at A and other loci. The symbol s^i refers to Irish spotting, the type of white marking found on Basenjis, Beagles, Bernese Mountain Dogs, Boston Terriers, Boxers, and Bullogs. This factor is so common that to continue alphabetizing the Irish-spotting breeds would take too much room on these pages.

The amount of spotting can vary widely, as for example in Beagles where the white markings range from nearly none to around 80 percent of the surface. Whether the same kind of heavy Irish spotting is a factor in the German Shepherd Dog is disputed. The single case reported by Pfaffenberger may be the result of an extraordinarily high number

of mini-genes, plus modifiers on other loci, which came together in the same dog. A white blaze on chest and occasionally a white tail tip are almost trademarks in certain American linebreeding, especially in combination with other characteristics inherited from one or two big winners of the 1960s. The dogs most inbred or linebred on them seemed to have the largest amounts of white on the chest.

The inheritance of such small, localized white marks seems to be produced not by the C or E alleles, but by modifying determiners (less powerful genes at other loci). Little called them "plus modifiers" and "minus modifiers," and said that the more of these that were present, the more white would appear. For convenience, they have been recorded as S and s^i on the allele map on page 240.

Whitney preferred to believe that all types or degrees of white were recessive to "no white," but admitted the many modifying factors involved. Dr. Frederick Hutt, in *Genetics For Dog Breeders*, has expressed reservations about claims for all the alleles at the S locus, desiring to see more evidence that S, s^i, s^p, and s^w are really responsible for all the variation. He rhetorically asks if some number of other genes at other loci might not just as well account for the range seen in white spotting; I feel his is the best position of the subject.

The Standard does not discriminate against white spotting; a little white on neck, chest, belly, toes, and tail-tip is allowed. But many breeders *do* discriminate. Don't let the more important problems take a back seat to your concern over the white spotting factor.

Color Oddities

Recessives often can be brought out by combining them into homozygous individuals, but they can also lie hidden for many generations. Besides livers, blues, and whites, some of the early odd colors may still be carried by a few German Shepherd Dogs. As late as 1932 von Stephanitz listed red merle, blue merle, silver piebald on black background, and brindle or tiger-striped dogs along with the "wolf color" (sable), solid black, and the two B&T manifestations, saddle and bicolor, as being the descriptions required for proper identification of color when entering dogs into the SV stud book. There were a number of merle dogs in use around 1900 and for some years afterward, and these genes may have been introduced by the extremely popular Collie in the previous century. Von Stephanitz had nothing against the color, but he didn't like the trend toward prettiness and away from utility that he noted in the Collie, and preferred not to use the merle in standardizing the German Shepherd Dog.

Brindling has been mentioned as a remote possibility on the E locus in Shepherds. It may actually be caused by the interaction of various genes on different loci. Brindle dogs vary in shade or expression from Irish Wolfhounds that appear almost clear sandy-cream to Scottish Terriers and Boston Terriers whose dark brindle seems almost absolutely black. The gene probably has been completely lost in the German Shepherd Dog.

There are a few more color irregularities, if one wishes to apply that description to the less common variations of color. Among the wide variety of minor departures from the norm are the solid black dogs with very, very small amounts of tan markings but not really tan points. In the early days of the breed there was more variety, of course, and the tenth dog to be entered into the records of the SV had considerable flecked or speckled markings on his legs. However, Beowulf may have been a "solid black" genetically speaking, being $a^t a^t e^b e^b$ just like his grandson, Roland v Starkenburg, the dog that has been heralded by other writers as being the first black.

I believe Roland was not the mutant some claim he was, rather that Beowulf and Roland shared the same A and E locus alleles, with Beowulf having in addition some gene or genes at other loci which

Ch. Arelee's Pardon My Dust "Duster". OFA normal. An ideal head on a magnificent dog with rich pigmentation.

were partially epistatic to the $a^t a^t e^b e^b$ combination, some factor which lowered the strength of that combination sufficiently so that some of the tan markings could be expressed, however feebly, by the latent C genes. We may call such factors *plus* or *minus* modifiers, as we do in the case of the white spotting genes, but to avoid that confusion, permit me to propose another symbol, Sp (non-speckling) for the dominant negative expression and sp for the recessive positive influence of speckling. Even if future research proves the condition to be the result of several genes together, the trait will have been named.

In the late 1960s and early 1970s, a kennel in the Midwest advertised some genetic blacks at stud that had tan hairs between the toes and very little tan around the pasterns and metatarsus, much less than in a bicolor, and not in the bicolor's distinctive pattern, either. When bred to other $a^t a^t e^b e^b$ blacks, the results were always homozygous blacks, some with as much or less tan than the parents. I believed them to be blacks, and still do, of the type that Beowulf represented at the dawn of the breed; the color still appears among today's black dogs.

There are undoubtedly other genes affecting coat color which have not been thoroughly researched. One interesting effect is the slightly faded or brownish undercoat of many black-and-tan dogs.

It is quite rare for markings in the German Shepherd Dog to not be symmetrical. Kaiserberg's Ruler of Hey Jude.

In the adult, it can be completely masked by the black saddle hairs, but can be spotted in the puppies before the adult topcoat develops. In the natal nest, as soon as the whelps have dried off, one pup may have a more intense black than the one next to it. As they grow, the difference is still apparent when two or more are placed side-by-side, facing the same direction. The dogs with the brownish or less black puppy coat will have that same relative characteristic in their adult undercoats, visible only on closer inspection and grooming with a comb. They will also generally be lighter in color in the tan-point areas than their littermates, and a larger percentage of their bodies will become tan as they mature, with smaller saddles and usually lighter nails. Whether this is due to alleles at E or some interaction is not known at this time. It is recommended that such a dog be bred only to a mate of darker pigmentation, as it appears to me that two such animals bred to each other will produce rather poor pigment in all offspring, compared to their darker littermates.

This condition is not likely to be caused by a recessive dilution factor at the B or D loci, nor can the blame be placed entirely on the C locus, since we believe that the chinchilla or extreme-dilute-tan genes have their effect only on the tan portions, not on the saddle. Hence, my suggestion of the involvement of another locus or an interaction of modifiers. Perhaps it's the influence of the intensity gene proposed by N.A. Iljin, author of *Genetics and the Breeding of Dogs*, 1932.

INHERITANCE OF OTHER CHARACTERISTICS

While not as extensively researched as color genetics, other inherited traits are of equal or greater importance to the breeder. Polygenic traits can be broadly classified as more or less dominant or recessive, but it must be remembered that such traits are exhibited along a wide range of expression, and the dominance is seldom clear-cut. Remember that the more genes that are involved in a trait, the less effect any single gene has on the ultimate phenotype. Multifactorial traits are usually seen in a great continuous variation. (The word *multifactorial* is usually used when stressing the input of non-genetic, environmental factors.)

As with color inheritance theories, those expressed in this section are based on valid and repeated observations, and the generalizations and hypotheses which follow are not based on isolated examples, yet in some cases not enough research has been done to warrant a dogmatic, near 100 percent positive statement.

General Characteristics

The paragraph on *General Appearance* in the Standard describes a dog longer than tall, well-balanced regarding front and rear angulation, and alert. Some combination or interaction of genes in the German Shepherd produces an excitable behavior reflected in the Standard's words: *alert, direct, full of life, agile*; and in the negative, *nervous* and *anxious*. The facet of character described by the above words may be recessive to a sluggish, phlegmatic disposition, and the two types of genes may recombine in the grandchildren of a cross between the two types. I don't believe there is enough evidence either way to classify excitability as dominant or recessive in the Shepherd, but it is probably characteristic and selected for.

A trait which is difficult to attribute to one or a few specific genes is the dog's reaction to other dogs. Whitney generalized that German Shepherds seem to avoid a fight whenever possible. However, early selection for herding ability has stamped the German Shepherd Dog with a very strong protective or at least watchful nature concerning whatever he regards as his or his master's property or territory. A similar expression of behavior is what the Russian investigator, Krushinsky, called "passive defense reaction" which others may call cowardice, as opposed to "active defense reaction" found in the feisty terrier breeds, Doberman Pinschers, and a few others that react in anger instead of withdrawal. This may be due to a different set of interacting genes, although insufficient research prevents a firm conclusion.

Another trait which may have a separate genetic cause is shyness—a behavior found in wild animals. When Krushinsky combined the shyness of wolves with the excitability of German Shepherds and other breeds, the result in the offspring was extreme shyness. When the Shepherds were bred to a native, less excitable Russian breed, the progeny were *usually* shy. Undoubtedly some "wolf-shyness" or wild shyness still exists in the Shepherd breed as a somewhat dominant trait, and we should continue to select against it even though the shyness/boldness factor may be highly complex and multifactorial.

One hypothesis is that shyness is an incompletely dominant tendency and therefore can be bred out to some extent by breeding those dogs that exhibit the more recessive, non-shy characteristics. However, care must be taken to prevent the development of a strain of deadheads. Although that's not likely to happen, a general rule to follow is: Don't double up on shyness, or "soft" character. Breed an otherwise good specimen to a mate with unquestionable courage and character (even if it is mostly a result of training), and cull the less-confident progeny out of your breeding program. It may take a couple of generations to correct soft temperament, and regardless of how long you try, you may continue to get an occasional "flakey" dog.

An apparently different characteristic is gun-shyness or, as E.S. Humphrey and L. Warner, authors of *Working Dogs*, Johns Hopkins publisher, referred to it, "auditory oversensitiveness." They suggest a polygenic cause, and indicate it to be not dominant in nature. This means that such "nervous reactions … to strange sounds and sights," as deplored in the Standard, may be hard to breed out to a low enough level to be satisfactory.

The Standard calls for "a certain aloofness" which can be identified with a little practice. It is certainly not typical of a Golden Retriever which is probably the happiest, most eager breed of all, but neither is the German Shepherd Dog likely to hide in the farthest corner or bark furiously at the escorted visitor to the kennel, unless this behavior has been encouraged. Breeders must work to retain that aloofness which is a manifestation of natural possessiveness and protectiveness, not to be confused with shyness or softness.

The Head

"The head is … strong … not fine, and in proportion," according to the Standard. The Polish researcher, Marchlewski, found that the relatively narrow skull of the Shepherd is dominant over the broad skull of some other breeds, and seldom will you see a German Shepherd with a head so broad as to be coarse. The over-all noble, intelligent look has long been selected for, and genes for grossly different shapes just do not seem to be present in the breed.

Ears—Humphrey and Warner, who extensively studied Shepherds in the 1930s, found erect ear carriage to be dominant over faulty carriage, but the *extent* of dominance seems to be influenced by other genetic factors. In fact, several genes are probably involved, as ear carriage variations are numerous, even within one litter raised under the same environmental conditions.

The veterinarian, breeder, and practical geneticist, Dr. Leon Whitney, found in crossing various breeds that lop-ear carriage was dominant over the erect ear. But remember, he was looking at crossbreeds, not strains within the German Shepherd as did Humphrey and Warner. I have seen many Shepherd-Dobe crossbreeds with hanging ears but I have also seen a few with one or two ears nearly erect, or up however weakly, so I would postulate the lop-ears (natural carriage in Dobes) is incompletely dominant, that it has partial penetrance in crossbreeds.

The genes for ear carriage in the German Shepherd Dog may be different from those in other breeds. I have seen Shepherds with semi-erect ears produce whole litters of puppies with completely normal ear sets. This might indicate semi-erect ears recessive to erect ears without negating the possibility of erect ears being recessive to hanging ears, as found in other breeds. Marchlewski also found that in purebred German Shepherds, the correct ear carriage was dominant over poor ear carriage. This means we've been breeding too many recessives to each other, as there has been a larger number of weak ears in recent generations.

Eyes—As dark an eye as possible is recommended by the Standard, and the dark brown eye admittedly contributes to a pleasing expression and therefore a favorable impression. Two or three shades are common to the breed; they range from the preferred and dominant dark brown eye to the yellow (actually light brown) eye. Since the light eye is recessive, it will probably be in the breed longer than you or I. However, it appears the majority of dogs being shown today have either the dark or the intermediate shade, which latter might suggest many with a Yy constitution, Y representing the dark eye and y the light eye. The recessive y allele in such a heterozygous dog may give the same kind of partially hidden, partially revealed trait as the B&T pattern often does in a heterozygous sable.

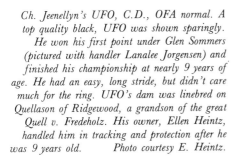

Ch. Jeenellyn's UFO, C.D., OFA normal. A top quality black, UFO was shown sparingly. He won his first point under Glen Sommers (pictured with handler Lanalee Jorgensen) and finished his championship at nearly 9 years of age. He had an easy, long stride, but didn't care much for the ring. UFO's dam was linebred on Quellason of Ridgewood, a grandson of the great Quell v. Fredeholz. His owner, Ellen Heintz, handled him in tracking and protection after he was 9 years old.   Photo courtesy E. Heintz.

One thing that makes it difficult to guess at the genetics by looking into a dog's eyes is the possibility of modifiers acting on the Y and y genes, but it seems more probable that the background coloring around the eye throws one off; a solid black dog's eyes might not look as dark as the same shade would on a lighter-colored face. Even if the two dogs are placed side-by-side, you may still have an optical illusion.

Whitney discovered that Bloodhounds with yellow eyes were also always liver-and-tan colored dogs, but I've not seen enough liver Shepherds to make such a generalization for the breed. Other than a possible linkage with the liver (bb) genes, there doesn't seem to be any connection with coat color. I have observed many dogs with relatively little black in the coat (light sables and small-saddle B&Ts) having the darker eyes, but I've also found the obverse to be as true. Possibly the high percentage of dark dogs with dark eyes found in the show ring is due to both characteristics being selected for separately by the breeder, rather than eye color being linked with coat color. Or it could be that the two traits are governed by genes on opposite ends of the same chromosome and that there is some crossing-over or translocation involved. (Crossing-over involves genes on the same chromosome.) This translocation refers to the chromosomes sticking to each other in such a manner during division of the sex cells that the bottom half of chromosome #1 gets

attached to the top half of #2, and the bottom of #2 ends up with the top of #1. Light eye is not a problem of any significance in the breed, but knowing it to be a recessive will enable you to handle it in your own breeding program.

Teeth—The 1968 revision of the Standard reads, ''Any missing teeth other than first premolars is a serious fault.'' Indeed, Humphrey and Warner found full dentition to be dominant over missing teeth, and theorized the involvement of more than one gene. Yet the doubling up of recessives has produced many a German Shepherd Dog with missing teeth.

An overshot mouth is definitely inherited. The beautiful Ch Ravenhaus Noah was overshot and passed the trait on to many of his descendants. While there may not be enough research as yet to determine the mode of inheritance, or whether it is due to the upper jaw being too long or the lower jaw too short, as a long-time breeder I feel the latter is the case. In my own experience and in observed breedings of others, I have seen evidence that the defect occurs because the lower jaw, which often grows at a different rate, fails to catch up with the upper jaw. Most investigators agree that overbite is a recessive trait, probably with modifying factors, which is to say it is polygenic.

In fewer cases, the arrested growth of the upper jaw allows the lower teeth to exceed the point of a scissors bite, thereby producing a level bite. It sometimes occurs in litters whelped by bitches that have produced overbites. It has been my untested opinion, recently confirmed by other breeder/geneticists, that a level bite is caused by at least some of the same genes that cause overbite and possibly even an undershot mouth; namely, a disruption in the normal growth rate of the lower jaw.

In a level bite, the four center incisors on the top meet, edge-to-edge, with their four opposing ones on the bottom. The incisors next to the canine teeth are seldom involved. Often, the two center bottom incisors are level with the top ones, but the next two are normal (scissors). I make it a practice not to consider this a truly level bite when judging in the ring, though I *do* take notice of the condition. I believe many such bites are caused by other genetic factors calling for an overcrowding of an already-narrow jaw.

The Neck

The only statement in the Standard that could be taken as a reference to dewlap is the line, ''The neck is ... without loose folds of skin.'' Marchlewski in 1930 reported dewlap to be clearly dominant, but the type of dewlap seen in Bloodhounds and other breeds probably is genetically different from what we see in the German Shepherd Dog. I believe our breed's minor throatiness in those big-boned, full-coated, loose dogs with probable upland heritage represents a polygenic trait.

The Back

A relatively long neck is called for, as is a fairly long body in general. The preference for a short loin on a long dog may seem to be at odds with the genetics producing length, but is not impossible to achieve. The long appearance can be achieved by shorter legs, deeper chest, longer vertebrae, or a combination of these. But if we breed for a long dog by selecting for longer vertebrae, we should also be sure to breed for good shoulder layback and broad thighs under a long croup, or the length will all be in the true back (that portion between the withers and the croup), which is undesirable.

If the exhibitor and breeder wants the impression of a short loin on a dog with a long back and considerable rear angulation, it would best be accomplished by plenty of roadwork and adequate feeding after the dog reaches maturity.

Legs

Leg length inheritance has been studied by Whitney, Iljin, Stockard, and others, all concluding that a short leg length was at least imperfectly dominant over a normal length. While most of the breeds studied had much greater leg length differences between individuals, I have observed something like this to be true in a limited number of breedings of especially-low-stationed German Shepherd Dogs.

Shoulder

The shoulder layback, or slope of the scapula, may be related to the lengths of the individual vertebrae, but probably is much more influenced by the nature and attachment locations of the muscles. The scapula is always attached via those muscles and ligaments to the same set of cervical and thoracic vertebrae, but the exact method and insertions have not been sufficiently studied to blame an upright shoulder on differences in muscle fiber types or any other factor. Genetic research

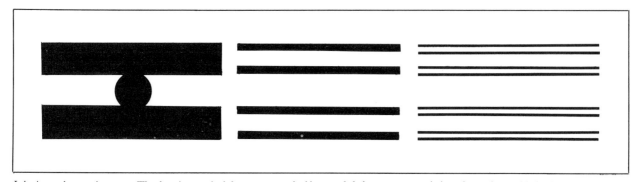

Inheritance by crossing-over. The drawing on the left represents a double-stranded chromosome consisting of two chromatids held together by a centromere, which has been omitted in the other drawings. In the center sketch, each chromatid is seen as consisting of two chromonemata, and in the representation on the right, each chromonema is shown as composed of two strands of DNA (deoxyribonucleic acid).

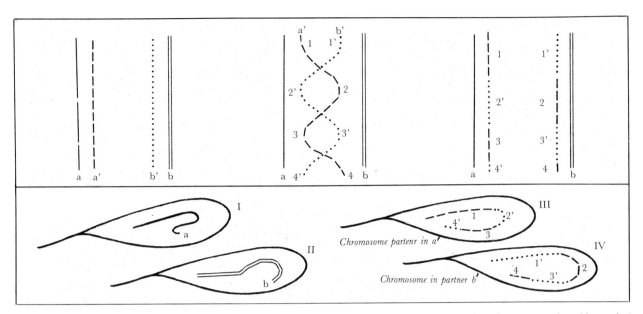

Inheritance by crossing-over. In the top half of this drawing, the sketch at left represents two chromosomes in a chromosome pair, with a and a' being one set of "sister" chromatids in one of those chromosomes, and b and b' are "sisters" in the other. In the center sketch, a' and b' (non-sisters) intertwine in a process called synapsis, a fusion of the two which is responsible for transmitting mixed characteristics (white color from short-coated white sire plus long coat from black, long-coated dam, for example). The example here is spermatogenesis meiosis. At the first phase in meiosis, these non-sisters break apart, but in a new combination of parts, as indicated in the sketch on the right. Some of the characteristics which were carried on a' are now attached to fragments of b', and vice versa.

In the bottom half of the drawing, sperm cells are shown to contain different chromatids each. I and II contain strands a and b, with the same combinations of traits passed on by the sire, but III and IV have the new combinations of re-arranged traits, and the pups which result from the union of such sperm with ova are likely not to resemble the sire of the pups. The greater the variety in the litter, the more crossing-over is likely to have occurred.

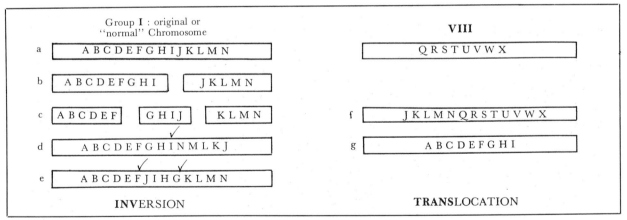

Inheritance by Translocation. While crossing-over involves homologous pairs of chromosomes (the gene loci are in the same order on each, with A next to B, etc.), translocation involves non-homologous pairs. Suppose you have a single chromosome with "normal" gene locus order (group I type, shown on upper left as a, which breaks during cell division either singly (b) or doubly (c). If the right part of b flips end-over-end and reattaches, it results in the new gene locus order shown in d; this is called terminal inversion, and instead of the trait controlled by J being next to (and therefore greatly influenced by) locus I, J is now on the end and locus N has a much greater effect of locus I, since it is now side-by-side with it and the chemical forces are much stronger between the two than they were when further apart. Central inversion is shown in e. Check marks indicate locations of greatest change between parent and offspring, perhaps even enough to be called a mutation.. If, however, the "broken" part of b attaches to another chromosome (we'll call it a Group VIII chromosome) which contains a different set of traits (genes), then a true translocation has taken place, with a new type of chromosome and considerably changed phenotype likely. Gene locus N, formerly intimate with only M, is now also intimate with gene locus Q, and in an entirely different neighborhood. (see f.) Each gene is on a chromosome with a different number of loci than it had "been used to" before.

My appreciation to biologist, scholar, and dog fancier Tom Fisher for the assistance given me in the field of genetics, such as the information and preliminary sketches for the above figures on Crossing-over and Translocation.

indicates that layback appears to be a polygenic trait.

If it is true that most "correct" traits are at least slightly dominant, then breeders must be selecting for upright fronts, judging from the large poportion of faulty assemblies seen today. One explanation is that these breeders think they're only selecting for high withers, not realizing that the highest withers are obtained by locating them right behind the ears.

Rear Angulation

The inheritance of rear angulation is much more complicated. Before going further, let me redefine what is meant by angulation: it does *not* refer to the slope of the topline. It refers to the *sweep* or bend of the stifle area, the angle made by the departure of the *line* or direction of the lower thigh from that of the upper thigh. Very little difference is seen if this area is straight, as in a Chow Chow.

Genes are found in pairs, remember, and as few as three pairs of genes operating on a given trait can give sixty-four possible combinations. Although rear angulation is a polygenic trait, it need not be governed by a great number of genes, just several, to provide us with many variations. Rear angulation is produced by relative lengths of thigh and lower leg, the slope of the pelvis or croup, and perhaps other conditions, and each of these may be determined by several genes or combinations.

Rear angulation appears to be partially independent of the genes affecting length-to-height proportions or spinal length. Some writers have reported extreme (sometimes called "good" or "considerable") angulation to be dominant over a straight-stifle look, but I have been unable to confirm this opinion. I hold to the hypothesis that correct structure tends to be dominant, and that with the least amount of human selection, this correctness will be seen to approximate that seen in the wild. Most wolves, jackals, and related wild dogs have much less variation in rear angles than do their German Shepherd cousins.

Since the German Shepherd Dog is closer to the wild form than is, for example, the Chihuahua or Boxer, we must have been purposely selecting characteristics further and further from the wolf/wild dog type by concentrating on recessives and mutations. The wolf has enough rear angulation and balance with its shoulder layback to enable it

to outperform most of our show-type German Shepherds in endurance, agility, and other utilitarian qualities, and we should be changing our strategy back to selecting for the "natural" structure of moderate angulation in order to prevent the problems which accompany such diversion.

The theory of general dominance of correct structure presupposes that moderate angulation is more correct than either the straight stifle *or* extreme rears, and general crossbreeding (or outcross breeding if within one breed) would tend to bring the particular dog population toward the center. If two dogs described as too straight in the hindquarters are bred, extreme puppies are possible but not probable; a greater number of extremely angulated offspring are produced by dogs of moderate angulation because they carry more genes for that end of the range than do the ones lacking rear angulation. Eko-Lan's Morgan and Paladen, both excellent dogs of moderate angulation, produced many extreme dogs in regard to the bend of stifle.

Gait Inheritance

Extreme rear angulation is usually accompanied by loose ligaments, sloppy hock action, and an overall imbalance due to less angulation in front. Thus the dog bred for extreme rear angulation may easily be a poor mover both coming and going. Gait is a matter of inheriting the right (or wrong) polygenic traits on *both* ends of the dog, but possibly is more affected by the genes determining the rear. Gait is also affected by the length of the spinal column, especially between the withers and the pelvis, as well as by muscle tone, ligaments, length of limbs, angulation, balance, and orthopedic disorders, all polygenic. All are inheritable, but the mode of inheritance of each is not always fully understood.

Another hazard exists in the dog bred for a long back: a loose middle which at certain speeds bounces up and down like a balloon filled with water. While not the only cause of poor backs, an inherited propensity for loose musculature and loose ligaments combined with a long back can have a devastating effect on side-gait.

The condition of gait known as "out at the elbows" is marked by the dog's front legs not moving in a straight line. The elbows move in and out and the forelegs swing forward in a side-winding arc. One cause is UAP (ununited anconeal process), but it is not the only culprit. The pinched-at-the-elbows look which usually is accompanied by "east-west" feet, seems to be recessive to more normal chest width and depth, but remember the variation that can exist with polygenic traits.

Feet

It appears that the correct compact foot form is dominant over the hare foot and the paper foot, and short toes (the final phalanges) dominant over long toes. I believe that each of the characteristics that go into the appearance of feet is controlled by one pair of genes, and that the combination of traits plus environment gives a variation in phenotype that reveals polygenic conditions in complexity. If, for example, a dog were simultaneously heterozygous for short toes and heterozygous for weak foot ligaments, his feet may have a different appearance than those of another dog with the same gene combination because of other genes' interaction or a difference in their environments.

Let us consider for the sake of illustration that a splayed, paper-foot condition is the result of recessives. If the symbol S is used for dominant short toes, and s for recessive long toes, and if further we give compact feet the symbol C and splay feet the designation c, let's see what might happen if we put them together in different ways. A dog that is dihybrid may have SsCc and have a moderate paper foot. Another dog that is homozygous for normal short toes but is also homozygous for weak foot ligaments may have the genotype SScc. Yet these dogs may have the same apparent phenotype to the average observer. If you breed two dogs that are Ss, you can expect about 25 percent long-toed dogs, 50 percent close to normal, and 25 percent short-toed. It may not be too risky to breed a dog with less than ideal toe length (ss or Ss) to one with slightly splayed feet (possibly Cc), but I personally wouldn't want to. Each condition or genotype is undesirable in a different way, and the resulting litter may not be large enough to yield any pups with the combination of good qualities from each gene locus. I would think long and hard before using a dog with poor feet in my breeding program, yet would rather have a dog with long but compact toes than one with shorter but splayed toes.

Complicating the analysis is the possibility that splay foot may be a polygenic trait, as most loose-ligament conditions seem to be. But, in my opinion, the number of such genes is probably very low if not actually Mendelian. This conclusion is based on simple observation of many, many cases of linebred dogs I have owned or handled. The front feet show the genotype possibilities and variation much more than do the rear feet, so in choosing breeding partners, look closely at the front feet of the dogs in question as well as those of their parents, if possible. If ligaments are weak in the feet, be sure to check hocks and back, too, as it appears there may be some linkage or commonality of genes controlling ligament condition over the whole body.

Pasterns

My guess is that the correct pastern—strong, springy, and about 25 degrees from the vertical—is both polygenic and generally dominant over a greater (weaker) angle, and that a relatively small number of genes are involved. It may be that the genes for a stiffer, terrier-type upright pastern have for the most part been lost from the German Shepherd's gene pool by early selection for endurance in sheep-tending dogs.

The weak 35- and 40-degree pasterns in abundance today are probably the result of linebreeding on individuals of that phenotype or carrying the recessive polygenic factors. Besides heredity there are many other contributors to poor pasterns: nutrition, exercise, and footing; one or two of these may affect the feet at well. Another one, perhaps rare, is a specific disease which shows up in completely flat pasterns, the entire "hand" being flat on the ground. I've known of this in other breeds, and have heard several accurate reports of it in the German Shepherd Dog. A survey by the Internal & Anatomical Defects (Genetics) Committee of GSDCA implicated too-high a protein level in weaning and very young pups, leading to this condition known as carpal subluxation.

If the footing during rapid growth has been normal ground or well-varied, I would strongly suspect a genetic cause for bad pasterns, and point the owners to the pedigree, recommending they check out the dog's relatives to gain more evidence. Although there is a tendency for many people to blame environment, I've found that almost all cases of poor pasterns have not been traceable to poor footing, but to heredity, the exception being true carpal subluxation.

Dewclaws and Extra Toes

Dewclaw is a term rightly applied only to the nail and toe of the first digit of the *hind*paw, not the front paw where such a digit is always present and considered normal. The true dewclaw is carried so high on the hock that it is really a metatarsal digit rather than a phalange or toe. In most breeds, dewclaws are not appreciated, but also not severally criticized. Dewclaws are occasionally seen in German Shepherd Dogs, but most of these dogs are out of parents of either very poor quality, or recent import bloodlines.

The condition could be caused by two or more types of genes, on two different loci, perhaps even two separate chromosome pairs. A number of studies on the inheritance of dewclaws give conflicting results. Whitney explained that in some dogs, the dewclaw is present beneath the skin and other tissues and does not protrude enough to be seen. There could be a gene pair for dewclaws and another pair for hiding/not hiding.

Polydactyly, the condition of having extra toes, is sometimes applied to the presence of dewclaws, though I think it should be recognized as a separate entity; it is more correctly used when extra toes are found in the normal footpad location. It has been reported that polydactyly is a recessive trait in Collies, but is expressed in other breeds and in humans via dominant genes. Different genes may be involved in some breeds than in others. I've seen many cases in cats and other mammals, but none in the Shepherd to date.

Tail

A long and bushy tail, useful in maintaining balance when herding sheep at a gallop, and helpful in presenting an attractive picture in the show ring, is required by the Standard to at least reach the hock. When a low stationed or very angulated dog is in a show pose, the last inch or more may actually lie on the floor.

There does not seem to be sufficient research data to warrant a strong conclusion on the inheritance of tail length in the German Shepherd Dog, and this is possibly because there are practically no factors now carried in the breed for anything other than a rather long tail. However, there are conflicting data on tail length inheritance within many other breeds and breed crosses. Wolves and Arctic dogs have shorter tails, a probable dominant trait lost in the Shepherd breed when only the more recessive longer tails were selected for by breeders. I have found that palpating the tail to count the number of vertebrae is highly inaccurate, but I know that most Shepherd Dogs have twenty to twenty-two tail bones. The length of each vertebra and the amount of legginess the dog has will also contribute to the appearance of tail length or shortness.

The question of how much hair constitutes "bushy" is subjective, and some variation will occur in dogs of normal coat length. One very short-coated brood bitch we owned had what my wife described as a "ratty" tail, not very bushy at all, yet she produced dogs with both short coats and slightly longer, normal haircoats, the latter always having a bushy tail to match their coats. The intermediate, normal length may be dominant, with minus modifiers affecting the length of the hairs of the tail as they do the rest of the haircoat. It follows that long-coated dogs have thicker, even bushier tails.

A slight hook to one side is very definitely a hereditary trait, probably recessive and caused by very few genes and perhaps only one locus. There may be one locus for each of two or three types of hooks, with modifier genes and environment accounting for the small amount or variation seen. Or, there may be one locus with several alleles that could occupy it, as in coat color pattern. The Standard intimates that a hook is not very unusual and not vigorously selected against, and there does not seem to be any need to concern ourselves with it at this point.

SUMMARY

Several genetic factors have been reviewed in the preceding paragraphs, using the Standard as guide. In some cases, little or no scientific study has been applied to the phenomena discussed, and in these instances I have offered my opinions based on many years of observation. Remember that statements on inheritance may sometimes be based on limited data, and the more reliable the information the better the chance of accuracy. If you have documented evidence refuting some of the data I have presented I would appreciate hearing from you. Breeders are as rich a resource as veterinary schools, sometimes more so.

16

REPRODUCTION

If mating is the mechanics of breeding, reproduction is its genetic counterpart. The breeding process, then, is the means of getting the sperm and the ovum together—or more accurately merging one set of genes with another. At this point, a short review of these mechanics will help the understanding of the larger subject of reproduction.

The pituitary gland, also known as the hypophysis, is a sort of biological time-clock partially surrounded by the brain. This control center produces hormones and stimulates other glands to do the same. One of its responsibilities is to make the ovaries grow follicles and produce estrogens and other hormones. These hormonal changes eventually result in ovulation and release of chemical stimulants which attract the males.

Upstream from the cervix, the uterus curves toward the belly wall for about four inches (10 cm), lying atop the bladder, then splits into two branches known as "horns." These continue on for some five or six inches (13 to 15 cm) to end as oviducts or Fallopian tubes, partly wrapped around the ovaries where eggs are produced. These eggs are released into the Fallopian tubes where they meet sperm wiggling to the rendezvous, and when a sperm cell enters the ovum, the fertilized egg attaches to the wall of the uterus to begin the new individual life.

FEMALE REPRODUCTIVE SYSTEM

Ovary Function

As it has been used in the discussion of hair, the word *follicle* here also means a type of sac where something grows or develops. In this case it is the ovum or egg cell, which contributes the dam's genetic code to the union. At birth a bitch puppy has around 7,000,000 follicles in her ovaries but by the time she is old enough for her first breeding, that number will have dropped to about 350,000. At five years of age, the typical bitch may have only 30,000, and in the last years of her life but a few hundred. Certain unidentified hormones are apparently responsible for the replacement or protection of these follicles, and said hormones are no longer produced by the maturing female. This fact is confirmed by my observation that bitches that are never bred until, for example, five years old, seldom conceive, or if they do, produce only one or two pups. Conversely, bitches that have had many litters will have as large a number at five years of age as they did as youngsters. The interaction of glands in the endocrine system may be the key to understanding this if it is as common as I believe it to be.

In addition to follicle production, the ovaries manufacture a substance known as estradiol, a female sex hormone, which is in a fluid surrounding each ovum in its follicle. Estradiol affects the bitch's odor, giving her an increasingly attractive (to the stud) aroma as she approaches ovulation. As ovulation begins the follicles migrate to the outer edge of the ovary and burst open, one by one, releasing the ova into the surrounding tissues. This process is nearly completed in approximately twenty-four hours; very few unruptured follicles are present forty-eight hours after estrus begins. The ova enter the serpentine Fallopian tube which zigzags around the ovary, while the emptied follicles begin to fill up with cell masses called luteal bodies. When the luteal hormone, progesterone, surpasses the amount of follicular hormone, the bitch's odor changes, the stud is no longer enamored, and the bitch also loses interest in mating. This change usually takes place in very few, perhaps half-a-dozen, days.

Conception

As the eggs enter the Fallopian tubes, they may encounter free-swimming sperm. Since these tubes are a long way from the sperms' point of entry (the cervix), a word about how they get there is appropriate at this point.

The sperm are propelled by flagellate action in random directions until they enter the ova. They are propelled by the pumping action of the male's organs which can force semen all the way up the narrow-diameter uterus through the Fallopian tubes and into the capsule surrounding the ovary. Some fluid may actually be forced into the abdominal cavity of the bitch, if the volume is great enough and the tie of long enough duration. Peristaltic action in the bitch also moves the seminal fluid toward the ovaries. This is in response to the backward pull on the vagina exerted by the bulb of the male's erected penis during the tie, and as the dog and bitch turn away from each other following ejaculation and dismounting. If the bitch is bred late in her cycle, or if the volume of seminal fluid is not great, the ova may travel down the Fallopian tubes and some distance down the horns of the uterus before meeting sperm. However, the vast majority of ova are found in the oviducts during the entire period of estrus and into metestrus.

It appears that a swarm of hundreds of sperm cells is required to produce the chemical changes resulting in the thick wall of the ovum being receptive to entry by one of them. As soon as one sperm penetrates, the egg rejects all others, probably in response to another chemical or enzyme change. Indeed, if two or more sperm do manage to enter while the wall is weakened, only one survives. Very soon after entry, the egg throws off what is called a "polar cell" containing half of its chromosomes so the sperm's thirty-nine chromosomes pair up with the ovum's remaining thirty-nine chromosomes. Each finds its proper partner and an entirely new life has begun.

Hence different passions more or less inflame,
As strong or weak, the organs of the frame.
                                    —Alexander Pope

The word *estrus*, also spelled oestrus, is derived from the Greek for the near-insanity or excitement produced by the sting of a gadfly. Its most common synonym in our context is "heat," and in male deer and some other animals its corresponding phenomenon is called the "rut." The female canine, as do most other species, prepares for reproduction by periodically entering the estrual cycle during which she can conceive.

Some bitches, especially of certain breeds, have only one cycle each year, while others come into heat every four or five months. Generally, though, cycles seem to tend to occur at slightly more than every six months but are adjusted to twice a year by environmental conditions. The amount of light has an effect, probably via the optic nerve which terminates in the brain very close to the pituitary gland. (This fact enables egg farmers to get more production from their chickens by turning the lights on an hour or two before sunrise, and leaving them on for awhile after sunset.) Bitches shipped from overcast northern cities to the "Sun Belt" usually start their heats earlier than expected. Conversely, bitches shipped from the South to the North can experience delay with their cycles. As an example, we shipped a bitch to Seattle which has about the least incidence of sunshine of medium-to-large United States cities, and found she would not stand for stud until her nineteenth day, whereas she had always before been ready on her tenth day. One scientific study gave the acceptance range (estrus) as three to twenty-one days, which means that it is conceivable *some* bitches might still stand for stud up to forty days after bleeding starts. So, don't end confinement too soon. Three weeks should be a safe minimum, though.

Most German Shepherd bitches in the Northern Hemisphere start a season around the end of December, with variation depending on exactly where they live. As the days get longer toward the summer solstice, what might otherwise be a 7- or 8-month cycle is accelerated, and the bitch may be in season 6 months from the previous time. Bitches

Gin v. Lierberg, SchH-III, KK1"a". Bred by Karl Klug, Muelheim, Germany. One of the truly great dogs of all time. The contrast with some of today's winners is obvious and points to the need for a return to earlier values. The B (Bodo, Bernd, etc.), D (Dolf, etc.), F (Fello, etc.), and G litters vom Lierberg have the same pedigree.

```
                                                    ┌── Lex v. Drei-Kinder Haus
                            ┌─ Vello zu den Sieben-Faulen ─┤
                            │                       └── Grille z.d. Sieben-Faulen
B, D, F, and G litters vom Lierberg ──┤
                            │                       ┌── Arko v. Riedersknapp
                            └─ Betty vom Eningsfeld ─┤
                                                    └── Delfi v. Kleistweg
```

kept indoors most of the time tend to be in season at widely varied times and frequencies, but a kennel full of such animals can be adjusted by putting them out in the natural sunlight for a few months.

The presence of another female may also influence the onset of a bitch's season. For years breeders have been saying that coming into heat seemed somehow contagious; that when one bitch started, she influenced the others to begin. Indeed, recent scientific evidence indicates that there may be something to this; pheromones secreted by one bitch probably are responsible for triggering hormonal changes in others living in close proximity.

The reproductive cycle can be divided into four phases, the half-year resting phase being known as *anestrus* (no estrus). The first week to ten days of bleeding is called *proestrus* (before estrus), then comes the true *estrus* or acceptance period of heat, followed by *metestrus* during which the uterus returns to normal, whether or not a period of pregnancy is included. Since estrus means frenzy or sexual excitement in the female, it should be used only to refer to the acceptance period, but when most people talk about their bitches coming into season or being in heat, they usually are referring to both the bleeding *and* acceptance periods, or just the start of bleeding rather than standing heat (true estrus) itself.

Other authorities prefer to exclude anestrus and classify four periods of the cycle as follows.

Phase 1—Internal changes include congestion or enlargement of the vagina and uterus, and the shrinking and disappearing of old luteal bodies under the influence of follicle-stimulating hormone (FSH) produced by the pituitary. Externally, the vulva swells slightly though it remains firm, and the bitch becomes more playful or restless. This period lasts about five days and is generally missed by most dog owners. However, if you know that a bitch will usually "blow" her undercoat two months before starting, and her topcoat about one month before dropping blood, you will be more likely to be ready to notice these other subtle signs.

Phase 2—Proestrus is the time period from the first day of dropping blood to the first day the bitch will accept service. At this time, estrogen, or estrone, made by the ovary under orders from the pituitary, causes the vulva to swell and the uterus to slough off a lining of cells and begin a bloody discharge. As the follicles approach the surface of the ovary, estrogen production decreases and progesterone production begins. This hormone, late in this stage, results in a softening of the tissues of the vulva. The shape of cells shed from the uterine wall changes from long and narrow to more squarish and irregular with sharp corners. By daily staining a smear on a glass slide and examining the cells under a microscope, your veterinarian may get some idea of how close to ovulation your bitch is or when she starts. But even with frequent

examinations this method is less than accurate partly because few veterinarians are very experienced in it, so the breeder usually relies more on the experienced stud and the bitch's reaction to him. (Other tests are even less reliable than the cell examination.)

The duration of bleeding is not always the same as the duration of proestrus, for some bitches will bleed all the way through and past the acceptance period; others stop before they will stand for a stud. The *average* length of proestrus may actually be as short as seven or nine days, in spite of innumerable reports that the *typical* time *from first spotting* to stud acceptance is eleven or twelve days. Older bitches tend to stand earlier than younger or maiden bitches, though that doesn't mean ovulation necessarily starts earlier. Very few bitches extend the average by first standing later than the twelfth day after bleeding starts. The first spotting is bright red, often profuse, and toward the end it gets a little

Ch. Bel Vista's Joey Baby ROM. Combining the "talented genes" of some of the greatest U.S. dogs including Hein, Lance, Mike, and Hessian's dogs, Joey Baby had a far-reaching, close-to-the-ground gait that was impossible to fault, even with slow-motion cinematography. He was always an alert, vibrant showman.
Photo by C. and J. Poepping, owners.

lighter, turning pink, brown, or cream-colored. During proestrus the bitch is playful but still not willing to mate.

Phase 3—True estrus (standing heat, or the acceptance period) begins when the bitch is first willing to be serviced by the stud. As already pointed out, it is a mistake to wait until bleeding stops to first introduce the bitch to the stud. Another wrong impression is that as soon is the bitch is willing to stand she is ready to conceive. She is not. The reason a few bitches become pregnant after a solitary breeding around the first day of estrus is that the sperm can survive in her system for about two to six days. In essence this means that the sperm are able to "wait" for the bitch to ovulate.

One of the signs a bitch is ready to stand for stud is a lifting of the tail called *flagging*, accompanied by her turning and presenting her rear to the male, while submissively lowering her head. She will usually play in a coquettish manner, then when she has aroused the male, will stand and lift her tail up and to one side, lifting her vulva as well. Unless she continues to raise the vulva this way when the male mounts her, he may have difficulty gaining entrance. To see if she seems ready to introduce to the stud, you can stimulate flagging by petting or scratching the croup at this time, but don't wait for this sign if you want to be safe.

Near the beginning of estrus, the pituitary gland which has been secreting FSH (follicle-stimulating hormone) begins to produce LH (luteinizing hormone); this directs the follicles to release their ova and begin filling up with luteal cells. This timing of egg release called *ovulation* has been controversial although it need not be. Besides getting a good hint from the cytology (cell smear) exam, you can pretty well rely on ovulation starting when the bitch's vulva suddenly becomes noticeably softer under the influence of the luteinizing hormone. This will occur several days after she first accepts stud service and is generally the thirteenth or fourteenth day after the first dropping of blood. With an average bitch, it has long been believed that if mating takes place on the fourteenth day, the resultant litter will have the largest number of pups possible. However, recently there have been indications that with some bitches, the ninth day seems to be best.

While it appears that ovulation most often takes place on the sixth day of acceptance, the commencement of the acceptance period can vary. Whitney found that ovulation most often occurred on the sixth day of acceptance, but many German Shepherd bitches are not receptive for a period of six or more days and later scientific studies on ovulation are more accurate. If you are allowed only one breeding opportunity or tie, it's possibly better to shoot for the fourth day of acceptance rather than wait for the sixth. Therefore, for best results count nine to fourteen days from initial spotting rather than depend on acceptance time. However, in some cases this countdown can be complicated by "false starts"; the bitch will bleed for a few days not really starting estrus for another two to six weeks. Also, many bitches clean themselves so well, that the first day or more go unnoticed. Of course, the ideal situation is to have the stud on hand from the first day to the last.

When to breed the bitch also depends a lot on the owner of the stud. If the stud owner makes only one or two days available to you, try to schedule as close as possible to the thirteenth and fourteenth day after proestrus begins, opting for days *before* in preference to days after. Otherwise, your bitch may be unwilling or the stud no longer interested since ovulation may have passed.

If there is no problem with availability, you can mate the dogs every other day starting with the first day of acceptance and continuing until the dogs themselves decide to quit. Alternate-day service is recommended by those who believe the stud needs to rest while his body manufactures more sperm and seminal/prostatic fluids. I have found that the first ejaculation tends to have much more fluid volume than subsequent ones if the male has been teased for a sufficient time, while some have seen fewer sperm in the first ejaculation of a male that has not been used for some time. These two observations are not contradictory, however. Many owners of popular stud dogs mate them to bitches daily if they are much in demand and each bitch is given only one service. This is especially the case when many bitches arrive around the same time and the stud owner is desirous of getting as many stud fees as possible.

Estrus usually ends suddenly, with the bitch becoming "nasty" and uncooperative, and the stud soon learns that even if she stands she won't flag her tail or lift her vulva, and that attractive aroma has been replaced by a less exciting one. This may be as late as the twenty-first day after proestrus begins, so keep a bitch unavailable to all dogs, except the one she is to mate with, for three weeks following first dropping of blood.

The color of the blood may not be typical on a bitch's first season, but in any case it will generally be a lot lighter during estrus (if it is present at all) than during proestrus. A cytology exam at the time of ovulation will show cells appearing more rounded on the corners, returning to normal as ovulation passes. In addition, there are more white blood cells (leukocytes) perhaps indicating the preparation to fight any infection which may otherwise endanger the pregnancy or the bitch's less-protected tissues during this time of stress.

Bitches' peak seasons are in early winter and early summer, with fewer starting estrus in the off-months, yet some will be found ovulating at any given time of the year.

Phase 4—Metestrus, the period of repair or return to dormancy in the ovaries and uterus, is marked histologically by the presence of "mature" luteal bodies and the beginning of a new ovarian cycle. If the bitch has been successfully mated during estrus, this phase includes the period of pregnancy known as gestation.

THE MALE REPRODUCTIVE SYSTEM

Fertilization or conception occurs when a sperm cell enters an egg cell and the resultant combination begins its mitosis (cell division and growth). Production of sperm actually begins in the pituitary gland, so named because it was once believed that it secreted phlegm (pituita) into the nose. While not essential to the individual's life, this gland is one of the most important in the entire body since it has great influence on the gonads (sex glands). In the male, one of the hormones it produces causes the testicles to descend in the fetal or newborn pup. The pituitary also seems to control the proper functioning (sperm and hormone production) of the testicles. Testosterone, produced by the testicles under pituitary influence, gives the male his masculine appearance ("secondary sex characteristics" mentioned in the Standard) and his sex drive. But if synthetic testosterone is injected, the testicles will quit making it themselves and degenerate, possibly resulting in sterility although the masculine appearance may even be heightened. The testicles also

produce small amounts of the female sex hormone, progesterone. The pituitary hormone that stimulates sperm production (FSH) is chemically the same as that which stimulates follicle development in the female's gonads.

Sperm production takes place in the twisted canals of the testicles called seminiferous tubules. As the sex cells develop, they form tails or flagella, and they migrate to the epididymis (plural: epididymides) for storage. The head of a spermatozoon or sperm cell has about the same diameter as does a red blood cell in its widest dimension; about 2500 of them lined up side-by-side would measure approximately one inch.

The epididymis is a thick, elongated, soft-collagen mass lying on the surface of the testicle. It contains a convoluted tube that is continuous with the vas deferens, its straighter counterpart which exits the scrotum. The epididymis' smooth muscle fibers very slowly move sperm along this coiled route while the sex cells complete their process of maturing. Meanwhile, it secretes a fluid which helps lubricate this passage and which becomes part of the semen, providing nutriment to the sperm as well.

The vas deferens, along with arteries, veins, nerves, lymph vessels, and connective tissue, all make up the spermatic cord which passes through the inguinal (vaginal) ring to enter the abdominal cavity. The function of the vas deferens is to transport sperm by way of rhythmic contraction, to the prostate gland, an egg-shaped structure which varies in size depending on the age and size of the dog, but is approximately two inches wide in the German Shepherd. When pathologically enlarged, it may be three inches in diameter. Although the vas deferens is only the thickness of a lightweight string, many sperm can be transported in high concentration and at considerable speed through this section.

When the dog ejaculates, the great quantity of prostatic fluid being discharged may create a slight suction, assisting the movement of the contents of the epididymides and vas deferens into the reservoir of the prostate. Pumping action of the muscles around the prostate and root of the penis keep the flow going for several minutes. The other parts of the male genitalia have already been discussed along with the mechanics of breeding, so before following the progress of the fertilized ovum during

von Salix's Krissie, OFA. This floating beauty, a Ch. Rex Edlu-Mibach daughter and a Lance granddaughter, produced some very good offspring with excellent shoulders and gait, including Ch. Hey-Jude's S-Capade von Salix, OFA.

that period known as pregnancy or gestation, let's take a look at sperm life in the uterus.

Sperm Longevity

The length of time sperm remain potent in the bitch's reproductive tract is influenced by a number of things, least of all any input by the spermatozoa themselves—for the most part, the bitch's system decides. When estrus ends (and metestrus begins) sperm are rapidly killed off. Time alone is not a significant factor with reference to the season's duration. Nor is temperature a factor in the relatively short time the sperm spend at body heat; the effect it has on them in the case of cryptorchids *is* a function of time/temperature, with the latter half of that factor reliant on the gonads staying within the body cavity of the affected male.

By potency, I mean the ability to penetrate and fertilize the ovum. Motility refers to the ability to wriggle and move about, but motility can continue after potency ceases, with fertile "life" being about half of motile life. In the rare bitch whose true estrus lasts as long as eleven days, motile sperm have still been found. Calculating their potent life as 50 percent of that, it is possible for sperm to exist in sufficient numbers and potency to fertilize ova for at least five days. Generally, bitches remain in estrus less than eight days, and if they are bred in the first couple of days of acceptance, the chances of the sperm lasting long enough to find ova to fertilize are good. However, practical experience reveals

that bitches bred on the first day of standing heat do not have a satisfactorily high rate of becoming pregnant. Perhaps someday a study comparing longevity of sperm compared to unsuccessful breedings (even though ties were early) will provide answers to this dilemma.

REVIEW

Before discussing gestation, let's review the steps leading up to the growth of those new lives.

Hormones initiate proestrus, a variable period of some three to seventeen days, averaging eight or nine days, during which the bitch drops blood and her organs prepare for copulation. FSH causes the ovaries' follicles to develop and come to the surface. Usually about three days before peaking (Day 0), luteinizing hormone level in the blood exhibits a slight episodic surge, then decreases to a normal resting level called "baseline" until about twenty-four hours before Day 0's peak level. At that time, the LH level rises significantly to reach the maximum and in about 1 ½ days on average it is back at baseline. While quite variable among individuals, ovulation usually takes place around forty-eight hours after this peak. Most follicles have burst by the end of the fourth day, with 77 percent between 24 and 72 hours. Since LH serum peaks range from a couple of days *before* the first day of estrus to three or four days *after* the first acceptance, behavior by the bitch is not accurate in determining time of ovulation. Also, since the LH peak precedes the follicles' bursting by anywhere from one to four days, blood tests are not very reliable either. Hence, the use of approximations and averages in making these generalizations.

Following ovulation, the luteal bodies form in the emptied follicles and the ova move into the Fallopian tube. There they start slowly moving down the winding paths of the oviducts where they meet the swarms of sperm and become penetrated before continuing their journey by peristaltic movement toward the uterus.

Division of cells from the one fertilized ovum (cleavage) does not take place until metestrus. For some time the eggs travel up and down the horns and body of the uterus, passing each other and changing places. Gradually they become spaced (as if each contains a repelling magnet) in the horns and attach to the walls of the uterus where they undergo subsequent development known as pregnancy.

PREGNANCY

Growth and Development

Embryology—The fertilized egg divides to form two cells, those divide to four, and so on, the process continuing throughout life. At different stages of this multiplication-by-division, groups of cells become specialized. While the sex of the individual is determined as soon as the sperm enters the egg, it is not structurally distinguishable until much later in fetal life. An intermediate cell mass in the future urogenital system has been formed by progressive specialization steps and continues the procedure by dividing into separate regions: urinary and genital. The excretory system is at one point a combination of intestinal and urinary tissues, which is later separated by a wall that forms between the parts and allows them to develop into two different types of tissue. On one of the ducts entering this excretory structure in the fetal canine, a bud forms and grows into what will be the kidney and its associated tissues. Fish and amphibians' specialization ends soon after this point, while the process continues in amniotes (reptiles, birds, and mammals).

As the end of the fetal intestine becomes the rectum and anus, and is separated from the urogenital cavity, gonads develop from the same intermediate cell mass mentioned above, but from a different section than the urinary one. If the dog is a male, these will eventually move into a scrotum, but if it is a female, they remain near the kidneys and the phallus area becomes part of the vulva instead of developing into a penis.

The same sort of specialization and differentiation take part in all other parts of the fetus at various times and appear in different stages of development at time of birth. Some of these processes, such as ossification of cartilage, continue until the animal is fully adult, but the majority are completed near the time of whelping to the time when the puppy's eyes open.

Most of the fetal growth and development takes place in the last two weeks of gestation. While this is the most obvious time of growth, it is not the most rapid, as the number of cells is very quickly doubling at the beginning of gestation, and it is then that the speed of growth is greatest. A 50 percent increase in the size of a 10-ounce fetus shortly before birth is more dramatic and noticeable than a 1000 percent increase when there are only a few cells involved.

Palpation—With a great deal of practice and skill, a veterinarian or breeder can feel the fetuses in the uterus as soon as twenty-two days after conception. Actually what is felt could be ten times the bulk of the fetus itself at the early stage, being mostly swollen uterine tissue, amniotic fluid, and placenta. In the fourth and fifth weeks, you can put your hand in a U-shape up as far as you can into the abdomen from below the standing bitch, then pinch your fingers and thumb toward each other to feel for lumps. At this stage it is easy to mistake fecal lumps for fetal lumps, so don't be discouraged if you are unable to tell for sure what you're feeling. After five weeks have passed since ovulation, you may not be able to palpate the fetuses this way because of the increase in volume of support tissues and fluid, but by then the bitch should have shown a filled-out loin and deeper abdomen. By the time the pups are kicking and wiggling in the last week of gestation, you may be able to feel the difference between heads and rears by placing your hands on the resting, reclining bitch's loins.

Another way of palpating fetuses especially in a good-sized breed such as a German Shepherd, is to let the bitch lie on her side while you slip your fingers between her abdomen and the floor, your thumb on top. By moving your hand from side to side and squeezing in various places, you may be able to feel the lumps. In early stages, twenty-two to twenty-eight days, the lumps may be just a little above the floor of the abdomen, but in some bitches they will be carried in the upper part of the horns which curve away from the belly, above the bladder and toward the kidneys. These bitches are said to hide their pregnancy by carrying the pups almost entirely under the ribs until the last two to four weeks. Some fetuses are found in the joined part of the uterus near the cervix, but should be as easy to palpate as others if the bladder has been recently emptied. Your bitch may tense up and make palpation difficult, but if you keep a steady upward pressure, she'll tire of keeping her abdominal muscles contracted, and will soon relax them.

Three weeks after conception, the lump of a German Shepherd Dog fetus will be about ½-inch in diameter. At four weeks it may be about 1¼ inches across, and by the end of the fifth week it will have reached about 1¾ inches (between 4 and 5 cm). By now the shape will be more like an egg or a football as the pup's form becomes more of a factor in relation to the other tissues and fluids in the lump, perhaps 2½ inches long at this stage.

Effect on the uterus—The uterus was once perhaps about 8 or 9 inches (20 to 23 cm) long but eventually will reach a length of about 3½ feet (115 cm) in this breed. It also greatly increases in diameter, especially at the nodules containing the fetuses. In so growing, the uterus often changes position somewhat in relation to the intestines and other soft abdominal tissue. At about five weeks into gestation the intestines have been slightly displaced downward and outward, and a smooth, rounded contour is the normal appearance. In the last two weeks of gestation, the abdomen will be obviously distended and the dip in the loin between last rib and haunches will briefly disappear only to reappear as the weight pulls the abdomen downward. During the last week to two weeks, the weight of the fetuses pulls the uterus below much of the small intestines, and "the load has dropped," to use the common lingo. The bulge starts not at the backbone now, but halfway down the side of the loins.

Early signs—The pregnant bitch will give many very subtle signs, most of which can easily be missed. Changes in weight gain, abdominal shape, and loins have been mentioned as fairly late signs. An increased appetite is sometimes seen earlier, but as often as not isn't noticed until at least halfway through the 2-month gestation period. One sign I have noticed in most bitches is that they will become more affectionate, beginning about three weeks into pregnancy and increasing slightly in intensity in the next few weeks. Of course, it could be the variable response some bitches have to signs from their humans which reflect more concern and tenderness, but I truly think there is a change in the bitch regardless of the breeder's disposition at this time. Of course false pregnancies can mimic the real thing right up to the end, including nest building.

Late signs—One of my co-owners in a distant city could not contain her curiosity about whether our bitch was pregnant, so with the help of a friend who was an X ray technician at a (human) hospital, we sneaked the bitch into the radiology lab late one night and took a picture. I believe the bitch was about five weeks along at the time, and rear parts of nine little skeletons were visible on the film. The count was surprisingly accurate, as ten pups were delivered a few weeks later. (By the way, there is no danger in radiographing growing fetuses.)

By five weeks, six in some, you should be able to see an enlargement of the abdomen and the nipples should also be a little larger and softer than before. If there is some dirt on them, it can easily be crumbled off by rolling the nipple between your fingers. At six weeks there will be a little swelling of the mammary glands, which you'll notice if you've been accustomed to examining your bitch daily.

Morning sickness in the third and fourth weeks has been reported, but none of our bitches have ever shown this symptom. It is said to last a few days at most, with minor vomiting and lack of appetite. Loss of appetite is normal in the final week, but if you feed more frequently, the bitch will probably appreciate several small meals a day.

Almost anyone can see that a bitch is pregnant some two or three weeks before the due date, even if she will only deliver one or two pups. There are occasional exceptions, such as an overweight bitch having a small litter, but generally a very small number of pups that are born in one litter will each weigh more than the individuals in a larger-number litter. Add the considerable volume of amniotic fluid and the placenta, which together weigh about the same as the pup they envelope, and you can see why even a litter of one or two pups may be almost as easily noticed as a multiple-fetus litter a couple of weeks before whelping.

The last two weeks may also be marked by more frequent urination, occasionally by constipation or more frequent defecation as well as increasing restlessness and, in some bitches, a change in preference of sleeping quarters. During the final week or so, you should be able to feel and see the pups moving. To feel them, have the bitch lie on her side and totally relax. Keep her from tensing up by speaking to her and petting her head while you gently lay one hand on her flank just behind the last rib. Spread your fingers and keep your hand still. Soon, with the bitch relaxed, the pups may start their exercises: leg kicks, back arches, head rolls, even push-ups. It's a wonderful sensation that I hope each of my readers will experience someday.

The last week is one of increased restlessness. Timing of nest-building varies, but most bitches will start scratching around in leaves or newspapers three days before the due date. Some will dig a hole in the dirt beneath your spouse's favorite ornamental shrub. The closer the bitch gets to the onset of labor, the more active her nest-building. Just before birth, perhaps as much as ten to twenty hours, she may be extremely fervent in tearing up the newspapers with her teeth as well as with her nails. She may go off her feed temporarily in these last days, will almost certainly shed some belly hair, especially around the nipples, and appear generally worried.

Length of gestation—Pregnancy lasts from conception to whenever it ends. That's not a very specific statement but there are many variables such as fetal death, abortion, and resorption that affect the duration of pregnancy. Hormone aberrations may shorten or lengthen the term, and more research on this is slowly but continually yielding new information. Even with normal pregnancies, the term may vary from bitch to bitch. But in answer to the question, "How long does pregnancy last?" I must first refute the whelping calendars perennially published by pet supply companies and writers who have, I believe, merely copied from what they felt were authoritative sources. But old erroneous data that is not rechecked will still be erroneous. In our own experience, 61½ days is the actual average gestation period in the German

Shepherd Dog, and I suspect this is true in all other breeds of *Canis* as well, especially *Canis familiaris*. The innumerable charts notwithstanding, we found that the commonly-accepted 63-day figure is misleading. After compiling data on our own bitches over the years, I was delighted to find that Dr. Leon Whitney, probably the most experienced and astute dog breeder of all time, (produced 12,000 puppies) had already arrived at the same conclusion back around 1940, some half-dozen years before I had my first dog breeding experience, and some thirty years before I had noticed the discrepancy between the charts and my own bitches' gestation periods.

In 1913 the meticulous SV calculated the average gestation period in German Shepherd Dogs to be 61.6 days, and in a smaller number of litters in 1915 to be 62 days. Eighty percent of the litters arrived from the fifty-ninth to the sixty-fourth days and eight percent between the fifty-fifth and the fifty-eighth. Some 40 percent, nearly half, were born on either day 61 or day 62. The SV figures could be just a tiny bit larger for better accuracy, as the percentages of very late deliveries appear in some cases to be possible errors due to later, unobserved copulation closer to ovulation not being recorded

Ch. Feli v.d. Funfzig Eichen, CDX, TD (1966-1976) owned by Bob Emerson, she was sold to Harry Broderson who then put her obedience titles on her. Bred to Ch. Korporal of Waldesruh, she produced Can. Ch. Glucklich v.d. Funfzig Eichen, a top stud in Canada. Daughter of Ch. Oskar v. Busecker Schloss, a Valet grandson; her dam was distantly linebred on R-OsnabruckerLand.
Photo courtesy Bob and Carlee Emerson.

while earlier ties were, and were thus believed responsible for the litters.

Whitney found sixty-one days to be correct and typical. Perhaps one reason for my half-day figure is that my bitches were mostly bred in the afternoon, after work, and delivered in the wee hours of the morning. Or perhaps Whitney simply rounded off the figure. I would recommend that, since ovulation may be closer to the last day of acceptance than to the first, the breeder calculate sixty-one days from either the last tie permitted by the bitch or from the day before that to determine the probable delivery date.

The 63-day figure was probably arrived at by counting from the first day of acceptance, or the average first tie. We have already seen that a bitch will stand from a few to several days before ovulating, and that conception cannot take place until ovulation, but that sperm may live two or three days, lying in wait for the release of ova. Counting from the actual estimated date of ovulation, or from the date of the tie (breeding) made after ovulation, then sixty-one days will be the figure arrived at in most cases. Gestation begins at *conception*, attachment, or cleavage, not the first successful mating.

There are individual, probably hereditary, differences in gestation periods, some bitches consistently carrying pups for a longer or shorter duration than the average, but I don't know of any study that shows whether their female offspring or siblings had the same characteristic. Some people believe that large litters are carried a shorter length of time, but I have not seen that at all. Our bitches simply had smaller individual pups when the litter was large, without affecting length of gestation.

It is not unusual for pregnancy to be as short as fifty-eight days or as long as sixty-six days, but the wider the discrepancy, the more likely it is that problems will occur. Puppies delivered too early may be incompletely formed, with defects including but not limited to midline closures such as cleft lip or palate, involuted tufts of hair in the center of the forehead and top of the skull or along the centerline of the croup, and incomplete, soft, pink pads and nose leather, although these could also be caused by other factors as easily as premature birth. More extreme cases may be hard to distinguish from partially resorbed pups, but once you've seen an incompletely formed pup and know

that the gestation period was short, you'll probably have a good idea of what happened.

On the other hand, pups carried too long may die, but the risk seems much less than with too short a period. Many bitches have delivered healthy, strong pups well past the 61- or 63-day "limit," but nervous owners often worry their veterinarians into giving a shot of oxytocin to initiate rhythmic contractions of the uterine muscles. Many of these cases may well be a result of miscalculation due to sperm longevity. Still others may be delayed deliveries with other normal reasons unknown to us at present.

Prenatal age: It had been thought that the small disparity in apparent ages of the newborns sometimes seen at birth may be caused by different times of conception for each—that, either because ova are released over a period of a couple of days or for some other reason, not all of them are penetrated by sperm on the same date. However, research has indicated that this is not the case. As we know, sperm will last up to a week after copulation, unless it occurs so late in the acceptance period that the end of estrus (and of sperm life) arrives earlier. Also, the processes of implantation (attachment to the walls of the uterine horns) and cleavage (division and development of embryonic cells) are what actually mark the beginning. Therefore, it is now believed, and I concur, that a few of the fertilized ova may attach and begin dividing some time after the majority have already had their starts. This is one plausible explanation for some puppies being born in a so-called premature condition while their littermates are obviously as fully developed as they could be.

Bitches can easily whelp mixed litters, with some pups sired by one dog, and others having one (or more) different fathers. However, I know of no published report showing different days of breeding by different studs resulting in a litter of various prenatal ages. I think time of copulation and fertilization have very little effect on delivery date compared to the time of implantation of most of the ova. I further think that there is a short time of hospitable acceptance by ova, during which fertilization takes place. Otherwise we would not have the many instances of mixed litters resulting from copulation with different studs one or more days apart—the first come would be the first served, with no eggs left over for the next sire in the next day or two. If "runts" happen more often in bitches that have had ties a few days apart than in those that have only one tie or one on two consecutive days, it may give weight to the former hypothesis—that of different times of fertilization resulting in different age pups at birth. But no evidence at present points in that direction. It now appears that *possibly* those fetuses that were implanted later than the others were "washed out" with the delivery of the older, full-term pups. The hormone activity of the first group in concert with that of the birth will be enough to cause onset of labor, and when that starts, *all* of the pups will be expelled, regardless of age *in utero*.

Since labor appears to be brought on by direction of the *pups'* endocrine systems, not the bitch's, it will begin when the earlier-attached eggs, now grown into full-term fetuses, determine it. There's an old saying, "The pups choose the day, the bitch chooses the hour," that bears remembering. The whole litter will be born at one whelping, with rare exceptions due to abnormal cycles or other reasons. So, how does the breeder come to the conclusion that this delayed attachment/cleavage has happened in a small part of the litter? He observes the day the pups' eyes begin to open, when the slits first appear, suddenly giving that glimmer of reflected light. In many years of observation this has occurred with great regularity on the tenth day after birth, so anything else is considered abnormal. Therefore, if you have a litter with some of the pups' eyes opening on the tenth day and other littermates' eyes opening on the twelfth day, you might logically conclude that something caused a delay in their development. As I have stated, it probably is a result of the latter group having been delayed in implantation and cleavage, in this case two days after the first group attached. There may be breed and familial differences—we had a Shiba Inu pup (full term) whose eyes didn't open till the seventeenth day, and they were immediately clear, sparkling black.

Puppies that have had a shorter gestation period than normal, whose premature arrival time has been determined by older littermates and the bitch's reaction, are generally less vigorous at first, maybe less quick to learn compared to the others. Not all premature pups show the same signs and although they are usually physically weaker and domineered by their stronger littermates, I doubt that prema-turity causes mental retardation. The amount of oxygen or the deprivation of oxygen at birth has a far greater effect on intelligence or mental vitality than does length of gestation, as it appears the central nervous system develops quite early in fetal life. However, one must not underrate the potential effect of being delivered early.

Litter size—It has been repeatedly stated that the number of pups in a litter is largely determined by the bitch, although the timing of the mating has the next greatest effect. A low concentration of sperm or volume of semen will more often result in no pregnancy than in a small number of pups. Yet there will always be those who credit the stud with large litters. Give credit where it is due—the bitch should wear the laurels, not the stud.

Genetics determines the number of follicles that will mature and release eggs in the bitch but within the entire population there is always a trend toward the norm. Thus, a bitch that always produced an above-average size litter will have daughters that will mostly produce slightly fewer numbers, trending toward the average for the breed. Likewise, a bitch that usually has only two or three pups will have daughters that tend to produce one or two more than their dam. The fluctuations from one extreme to the other don't happen very often, but whenever there is a characteristic at the extreme end of a range whether it be intelligence, size, litter size, or whatever, there is always that natural force acting to pull succeeding generations toward the norm.

The number of pups in litters whelped by moderately young bitches is strongly related to the size of the breed or the individual bitch. This is especially true after the first litter which does not usually reflect the bitch's or the breed's potential. Toy breeds have fewer pups than do giant breeds. Large-breed bitches, especially setters and pointers, come close to the giant breeds in prolificacy where some 22- and 23-pup litters have been born to Saint Bernards and Foxhounds. Irish Setters frequently have fifteen to seventeen as do Bloodhounds, and in numerous breeds including the German Shepherd Dog, a dozen pups is fairly commonplace. One of our bitches regularly had ten to twelve whelps, and one litter produced when she was about seven years of age had thirteen pups.

While a litter of ten or thirteen is not unusual in the German Shepherd Dog, the average is somewhat less, about six to eight. Statistics compiled in 1925 in Germany showed the average number of pups in a litter to be slightly over seven. Earlier figures from the SV showed that 80 percent of all litters contained from 5 to 10 puppies, with an average of 7.5 per litter. A full third of all litters gave seven or eight pups, with litter size ranging from one to fifteen pups. Humphrey and Warner also found an average of 7.6 while the SV figure at that time (in the 1930s) was 7.3 per litter. The 1972 British registrations of litters sired by champions showed an average of just under six, probably because many pups were never registered due to culling, stillbirth, or other reasons. Litter sizes of 1, 2, 3, 4, 5, 6, and 9 pups each represented about 8 to 10 percent of the total, while 12 percent had 7 pups and nearly 12 percent had 8 pups per litter. Percentages dropped rapidly from 5.7 percent of the litters having 10 pups to 0.5 percent for 13-pup litters. But as I said, all these figures may be more accurate if adjusted upwards to account for some not registered.

As to the effect of the bitch's age on litter size, there is various information available. As far as I can tell from my own observations, a bitch whose first breeding is arranged later than usual, for instance around five or six years old, is quite likely to have a small number of whelps if any at all. The ones she does have will be normal size in most instances (around 14 to 22 ounces in weight). Such a bitch is prone to "miss" attempts at succeeding litters, or to continue having smaller than average litters. Some writers have claimed that prolificacy of bitches declines after they are six or seven years old. I have not seen this to be true, but have not bred enough old bitches, or gathered data from enough people who have, to know if my experience was typical. Incidentally, the AKC requires special evidence such as an affidavit before they will register a litter out of a bitch that is over twelve years old, though I saw a photo and story in the *Gazette* of an Afghan Hound bitch that was still producing at thirteen years of age.

If the bitch is bred in her first season, she will tend to have fewer pups in that particular litter than she will have in her second and subsequent litters. Something in her reproductive system apparently isn't "cranked up" yet. It may be a relative immaturity of the ovaries, but I believe it is due to the immaturity of the whole endocrine system; the hor-

Ch. Rex Edlu-Mibach Select 3.

mones aren't circulating as efficiently as they will as the bitch becomes more mature. It does appear that bitches that have had a litter before three to four years of age seldom have age-related difficulty becoming pregnant later, even if there are a few years between the first litter and the next. However, this observation is based on limited data.

Sex ratio—As we know, the 78 chromosomes in the nucleus of almost every type of cell are in pairs, with each pair being made up of two equal, identical partners (under the microscope, not identical as to alleles). At least, this is true of 38 of the pairs called autosomes, the 39th pair is the exception and is composed of highly unequal partners called sex chromosomes. During growth, cells split into two in a process called meiosis in the sex cells. When this happens, chromosomes can be stained and their shapes seen under a microscope. Most are shaped somewhat like staples or the letter U or V, but the sex-determining chromosomes are different. In the female's body cells, the 39th pair are both X-shaped chromosomes (called metacentric) and are appropriately called X chromosomes. In the cells of males, one of these chromosomes is X but the other half of the pair is very much smaller, and unlike its partner. It is called the Y chromosome.

When the cells responsible for producing ova and sperm divide in meiosis, each resulting ovum has two of the X chromosomes until at a certain point it throws off the polar cell, and is left with only 39 half-pairs, with one chromosome being the X chromosome. Meanwhile, the gonads in the male, produce sperm cells with 39 half-pairs, the 39th chromosome in this case being *either* X or Y, with a 50 percent chance of either being present in any given spermatozoon. Thus, when sperm begins its journey after ejaculation, half have the potential of producing a female embryo by combining their X with the X in the ovum, and the other half have the ability to produce a male by adding a Y to the X already in the ovum it meets and enters.

There have been many theories presented as to why more males than females are conceived and born. Since there is abundant evidence that more male embryos exist at the beginning of egg implantation and growth, possibly those sperm cells with Y chromosomes have more ability to penetrate the cell wall of the ovum, or have a greater chemical affinity for the ovum's membrane or the cytoplasm beneath it. Perhaps the motility of Y sperm is greater than that of X-carrying sperm, allowing for more frequent contact with the ova. However, I doubt that motility of Y sperm means that they will reach the ova *before* their X brothers do because the first and often the only tie occurs in all too many cases before ovulation for that to be the reason. Another possibility is that more X sperm die off in the uterine environment, at least enough of them to significantly lower the ratio below 50 percent; this would allow the Y sperm to be more populous and thus have more chances to penetrate the ova. There are a number of people who believe that fertilization takes place at different times: who hold to the idea that early-cycle mating produces more females, while mating closer to or after ovulation yields significantly more males. I suppose the hypothesis is that X-chromosome sperm are hardier than Y, and are more potent a few days after a first-day tie, and therefore more prepared for ovulation when it occurs. There is really no great compilation of data to support most of these concepts, or to entirely disprove them.

The fact that the pH (acidity/alkalinity) of semen is different from the pH of much of the bitch's reproductive tract (especially the vagina where it is believed urine has made it quite acidic), has led many folks to think that they can determine the sex of the puppies by douching the vagina before mating. By using a mild acid such as lactic acid, boric acid, or vinegar, or a mild base such as sodium bicarbonate, the resulting environment is supposed to inhibit either the Y sperm or the X sperm. Hundreds of experimental douchings showed that such a step was not effective, probably because douche solutions do not get very far into the system unless they are under high pressure to force the chemical past the cervix and dilate the uterus. One scientific study not only showed the process to be ineffective, but also proved it was quite dangerous.

During gestation, especially in the first few days, more males die than females, a phenomenon found not only in dogs, but in most species. This reduces the male/female ratio so much that by birth the ratio is about 108 males to 100 females. Natural selection in favor of the female continues throughout life, until in old age females greatly outnumber males.

Finally, some recent research indicates that the number of males produced at conception or birth can be influenced by the level of fat in the diet. Low levels are associated with fewer males, either by affecting sperm or increasing resorption of the male fetuses.

Order of birth—A point of interest which naturally follows the above discussion is that of placement of males and females in the uterus. Most of our litters have been born with most of the males arriving before the females. Indeed, one of our very prolific bitches always whelped *all* her males first, then all the females, with only a couple of exceptions when one male was "saved" for later in the delivery, following a couple of the females. This bitch followed this routine every time she whelped a litter, and was never bred to the same male twice. All the studs used on her were from widely different lines except for one that was a son of a male we had previously used.

While fertilized eggs pass each other before implantation, once attached, the fetuses do not change position during gestation, nor during birth. (This rarity sometimes happens in the pig, when one piglet from further up the horn gets whelped before the one which was ahead of it.) The horns also tend to alternate in expelling pups, with the one containing the greater number expelling the first whelp (if there's an odd number). It doesn't run like clockwork, but the tendency is obvious: if the latest pup came from the left horn, the next will probably come from the right. Some 75 to 80 percent of the pups will follow this order that is more true for small litters than for large ones. But even in litters of about nine, a good three-quarters will follow the alternating delivery rule.

An experiment in Holland to determine the position of canine fetuses and compare data with that previously collected on other species gave some additional interesting information. A little more than half the pups in the study were born head-first, but about 44 percent were delivered hind-end first; it seemed a little strange to me because my experience has been a greater majority, maybe two-thirds, presented head first. Whether it has to do with the fact that the Dutch study involved Beagles and my observations were mostly in German Shepherd Dogs, I cannot say, but I doubt it. The small sampling (only fourteen bitches and seventy-three pups) may be important, even though that program was carefully organized. My observations involved a couple of hundred Shepherd pups and fewer brood bitches, but I did not keep written records regarding manner of presentation, so I have had to rely on memory to arrive at my conclusions. At the time the Beagle fetuses were marked for later identification in a surgical operation called laparotomy, half of them were in a posterior position. They were marked around their fiftieth day of gestation which indicates there is a definite tendency to turn into head-first position before birth. In dogs, the position at delivery doesn't matter much except when a pup whose sac has broken gets his leg caught over the dam's pelvic bone or vaginal sphincter and has to be eased out with the help of your greased finger.

Incidentally, the time between pups was also noted in the above study, and it varied from 2 minutes to 13½ hours, some of the longer times probably due to the emotional stress of having to whelp in unfamiliar surroundings. A third of the pups were born within 30 minutes of the preceding one, ⅔ within an hour, 71 percent in 1½ hours, and 88 percent within 2 hours of their immediate predecessors. It has been my experience that in most cases two will be born within a few minutes

of each other, probably from opposite horns. Sometimes three come close together, before the bitch rests, though this happens with much less frequency. I did not keep records of whether the bitch had a longer rest after the first pup in an odd-number litter or after the first of an even-number litter, but it may well be that the odd-number litters produce this phenomenon, with the first pup coming from the fuller horn, then a pause before two come close together, one from each side.

BIRTH CONTROL

Sterilization

As in humans, the surest way to prevent unwanted pregnancy is sterilization by surgery. The term *neutering* is technically incorrect, because an adult male that is rendered infertile retains his male secondary sex characteristics such as larger body size, broader head, and deeper bark. The same is true with an adult female that has been spayed. On the other hand, if a male pup is castrated early in life, no testosterone is produced and maleness does not develop, nor does he become very feminine in appearance; he is truly "neuter." Removal of the pituitary which controls the development of the testicles can also give this effect. Females that are spayed early likewise can appear neither male nor female except for underdeveloped or juvenile external genitalia. However, if the ovariohysterectomy (removal of ovaries and uterus) is performed after the first estrual cycle, the bitch will appear as feminine as she was before the operation.

Castration after maturity has been reached may leave a dog with normal sex drive but more tractable than otherwise might be the case. If sterilization is the only reason for neutering, vasectomy is usually chosen as it is a simpler and safer procedure than total castration. With vasectomy a length of vas deferens is removed on each side so that sperm will not be able to reach the urethra. The procedure can be performed on immature dogs without ill effect, and mating will seem as normal as the dog's appearance, but without danger of impregnation.

Tubal ligation is a similar operation performed on females. The procedure involves tieing of the Fallopian tubes to prevent migration of ova to the uterus and thereby keeping sperm from reaching them. This procedure is not generally performed except experimentally because it won't prevent the bitch from going through her seasons; it only prevents pregnancy. Therefore, for females, spaying is usually chosen.

Spaying is technically called ovariohysterectomy and has many advantages: the bitch will not have uterine infections, ovarian cysts, unwanted pregnancies, or heat seasons. She'll not bleed on your carpeting twice a year, or require isolation, she'll shed less, have less chance of developing breast cancer, will be more likely to stay near home, and will generally make an excellent companion—some say an ideal one. Spaying is recommended before the first estrual cycle by some veterinarians, but most of those I've worked with prefer to wait until after that, when the organs are larger and a little easier to find. They also feel that waiting until after the first season gives the bitch more of a chance to properly and fully mature under the direction and interaction of her hormonal system. I think the elimination of mammary cancer risk is worth spaying before first estrus.

Objections to and beliefs about spaying, castrating, or vasectomy are without much logical basis. In fact, the sterilized animal does *not* automatically get fat as a result, weight gain being a consequence of owner indulgence and lack of exercise that have no real connection to the operation. Nor does the bitch need a litter to develop her emotions, "drop her chest," fill her out, or to fulfill any other superstitious, groundless excuse. Furthermore, the next time someone tells you he's breeding his pet because it'll be educational for the kids, invite him to go to the pound with his kids so they can see the other end of the experience. There unwanted offspring and grandchildren of bred pets are put to death in a futile fight against overpopulation.

To continue: the male does *not* need a "girlfriend" to keep him satisfied—as a matter of fact, fewer problems are encountered when a dog never mates or meets a female in season than when he has had a few escapades. The normal male that has been given the most rudimentary training will never give sex a thought if no females in season get near him. Mounting of legs, children, etc., is a sign of confusion engendered by a lack of correction when the young pup was learning about dominance and play.

Finally, if an owner can't help but anthropomorphize about the poor male being embarrassed by his lack of family jewels, choose vasectomy. The natural carriage of the tail generally shields the scrotum from view anyway, and one would really have to be searching to notice the absence.

Isolation

After sterilization, the most used method of birth control in dogs is abstinence. This requires putting the bitch in a lock-up for twenty-one days, only allowing her the freedom of the house if the kids are trained not to leave the doors open or let her run, and keeping her on a leash when she is walked through the neighborhood. I strongly advise avoiding these neighborhood strolls as the maddening aroma can carry for nearly a mile under certain conditions without your broadcasting it further and more insistently.

A persistent problem with confinement of either sex is that of escape. The slimmest of openings between post and gate can become the fabled Northwest Passage to the joys and treasures of the Orient as far as the roaming male is concerned. Therefore, make sure the floor is concrete, that there are double safety locks on gates, and sturdy fencing, preferably a chain-link and covered run. Also, don't allow even an adolescent male puppy in the same area, as some young males can be surprisingly precocious.

Devices

There is at least one device on the market which fits into the vagina in such a way as to allow normal urination and seasonal bleeding, but prevents intromission by the male. Because of its construction and the curved shape of the bitch's vagina, it supposedly cannot fall out and must be inserted and removed by a veterinarian, or by you if properly instructed. Watch for infections if you do it yourself.

Chemical control—Pregnancy prevention by chemical means includes the use of odor masks and hormones. The most widely used may be *Ovaban®*, a trademarked contraceptive which acts on the pituitary to interfere with the production of FSH. This pill can be given prior to the expected start of an estrual period to postpone onset. It may also be effective in postponing standing heat if given within a couple of days after a bitch starts dropping blood. The postponement usually lasts only two or three months, sometimes longer, and it should not be used for more than a couple of heats or there may be increased risk of pyometra (uterine infection). Before *Ovaban* was developed, progesterone was administered to some bitches to prevent the cycle, but it caused pyometra in too many cases. I personally am not in favor of using the ''Pill'' either in dogs or humans because of possible adverse reactions and risks. Too little is known about its long-term effects and it is too easy to convince oneself to use it a little more often than is recommended.

Another contraceptive with the brand name *Cheque*® seems relatively safe if used for a maximum of two years at a time. Longer usage may have a permanent effect on fertility. *Cheque* acts on the LH-manufacturing ability of the pituitary and its interference with normal hormone activity sooner or later will produce unpleasant side effects in many bitches.

Chlorophyll and other odor masking preparations are the least effective methods of birth control. If a male gets really close and she encourages him, he's liable to jump the fence in spite of the tablets you've stuffed down her throat.

Immunology

Some recent scientific research may hold great promise for not only individual birth control, but population control as well. Scientists are now close to discovering a ''shot'' that will act on the bitch's immune response system and make her allergic to and reject her own ova. It may develop that humane societies, animal shelters, and veterinary clinics will someday be able to process hundreds of bitches and finally help solve the pet population problem. Incidentally, the Morris Animal Foundation is in the vanguard of this work.

Abortion

Another birth control measure sometimes taken is abortion, the process in which the bitch is caused to reject the fetuses or in which the unborn pups are surgically taken from her. At times a mongrel or other dog will jump the fence and satisfy his and your bitch's urges while leaving a big problem on your doorstep. If the bitch were never to be bred again because of age or quality, you can have an

Canadian Grand Victrix Ch. Bero's Just Lovely. OFA-normal. Shown here with West Coast handler Carroll Overby and judge Jack Ogren, who is the first American to be given SV judging privileges. Owner: L. Fischer. Photo courtesy of Bonnie Smith.

ovariohysterectomy done, removing the ovaries and the uterus along with its puppy embryos. But abortion can also be accomplished by chemical or synthetic hormone means. If given early enough, specific injections or pills may cause the bitch to start another season right away, flushing out the fertilized eggs with the epithelial cells of the uterine lining. If an estrogen is administered within a week of the liaison, the eggs will be prevented from attaching to the wall of the uterus; however, pyometra and uterine infection must be guarded against with estrogen. The bitch may come into season again a few weeks later.

Douches have been suggested as after-the-fact contraceptives, but unless they are given with high pressure which is very dangerous, they are ineffective in reaching the furthest sperm or fertilized eggs.

One Last Word

Some time ago a GSD club newsletter ran a column by an anonymous author known as Uncle Hairy, who was to dog fanciers what Ann Landers and Dear Abby are to human fanciers. Uncle Hairy claimed to have discovered the perfect birth control device or system. It was completely effective, non-polluting, without medical side effects, reversible (bitch could be bred the next season), non-surgical, applicable to both males and females, non-chemical, had an indefinite storage life, could be "installed" or removed in seconds without veterinary assistance, was reusable and economical, did not cause infections or interfere with urination or secretions, did not need to be scrubbed or autoclaved for sterilization, and had other uses! Uncle Hairy further informed his readers that the device came in different colors and sizes, but usually was brown, about six feet long, and made of leather with a metal clasp or snap at one end that attached to the bitch's collar.

1977 Grand Victor Ch. Langenau's Watson. Not an ideal head because of a tendency toward coarseness, but more masculine than the average in his day.   Morrissette photo.

17

WHELPING

CARE AND FEEDING OF THE PREGNANT BITCH

There are some bitches that can take care of litters all by themselves, but you can cut your losses if you help the bitch in the areas of whelping quarters, conditioning, special food needs, and medication. One of our bitches whelped a litter when I was out of town and my wife was busy readying our house for sale. The litter was whelped in an open dog house with no assistance, yet it contained five healthy pups. Another bitch that I leased to breed to one of our stud dogs had herself been born in a snowdrift and survived. I don't recommend either set of conditions for whelping, for we're not trying to improve the breed by proving the "survival of the fittest" maxim.

Most often it doesn't pay to ignore the many dangers surrounding pregnancy and whelping. As an example, we went to see how a litter turned out which was sired by one of our dogs and found that the owner of the bitch, a garbage collection contractor, had her housed outside no more than seventy-five yards from where he parked his trucks. Too late we learned that her pups had been so badly eaten up with maggots that only one finally survived, and then only when it was taken away from the bitch and raised by a Miniature Poodle foster mother.

Housing

For most of the gestation period, the bitch will do fine in her regular quarters, but as her pregnancy advances, she should be protected from high ambient temperatures. If it's a very hot summer, air-conditioning will take most of the discomfort away with the humidity, and a setting of 80 degrees F. will be plenty comfortable as well as economical. If you keep her in the house and prefer a lower setting, she'll probably enjoy it, but it's not necessary. However, when she whelps, the newborn pups will need a hot environment at first, so the bitch could well get used to napping in the slightly warmer whelping box during the last week or so.

Winter outdoor temperatures are no problem, as German Shepherds prefer the cold, but do bring her in during the last week. If you don't already have a humidifier, buy one; it'll keep the mucous membranes from drying out and cracking in the heater-dried air in your house. It will also prevent colds and infections of the mucous linings, prevent static, and help keep the coat clean and the hair from flying all over the place.

The whelping box—The whelping box or that location where the bitch is to have her pups should be in a draft-free place preferably adjacent to where the pups will later be exercised or paper-trained. Choose a location where foot traffic will be at a minimum, but don't worry about noises other than those with which the bitch is not familiar. Noise won't bother the babies. Controlled sunlight is beneficial if convenient, but a dry draft-free corner in the basement or family room will be fine.

The size of the box or alcove should be such that the bitch can stretch out on her side along at least one of its dimensions, so lay her down in this position and measure her from hocks to nose, or simply plan an enclosure about four feet wide in one direction. The other floor dimension can be four to six feet long, but keep in mind that if the space is too large, the crawling pups may get isolated from each other and the dam. While a 4-foot by 4-foot or 4-foot by 5-foot enclosure may be close to ideal, we've whelped many a litter in a modified coal bin that was a bit smaller than 4 by 4.

The walls should be non-porous, so paint concrete or wood with enamel, a two-part epoxy or urethane, or cover it with another smooth, non-porous material. Vinyl flooring works well if adhered to the wall with a strong adhesive. The floor must also be non-porous but shouldn't be so slick that puppies can't get traction, nor so rough and abrasive that navels and abdomens will be scraped. Cushioned vinyl roll goods (sheet flooring) is ideal for this, and can be grouted where it meets the walls to prevent debris and germs from

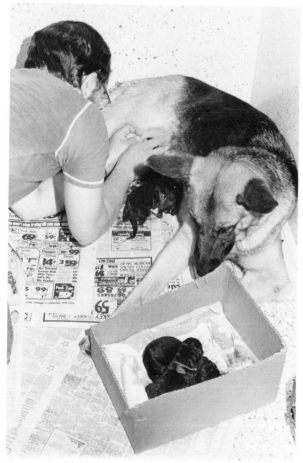

Scene: the whelping box at New Skete Monastery. Note impervious walls and floor, with hygienic newspapers for footing. Some new pups are being given help in finding a nipple shortly after whelping; others are in a "holding pattern" awaiting delivery of littermates.

getting in those cracks—use a silicone tub sealant and run a bead along the base of the walls so that when you press the flooring down it will fill up the seam between wall and floor. Adhesives for both floor and any sheeting you put on the walls should not be the type of panel adhesive that contains eye- and nose-irritants unless you prepare the box months ahead of time to give the fumes a chance to dissipate. Read the label and take a few good sniffs of the flooring adhesive you intend to buy before you bring it home.

The ideal whelping box has three sides high enough to contain 4- to 6-week-old pups, with the fourth side made so that the height can be adjusted up and down. I've found that fastening 1-inch by 2-inch molding strips on two of the walls enables me to add or subtract 4-inch epoxy-coated boards to adjust the height as needed to contain pups, but allow the dam to get in and out at will. Some people construct elaborate, hinged boxes and have relied on a lot of hardware to enable the box to be stored or moved. Your own abilities, needs, and imagination will be your guides. An ingenious, easy, and clean "box" is a 5-foot diameter rigid plastic wading pool made for toddlers. However you construct the box, forget about the so-called protective rail around the inside perimeter that some folks insist on. We've *never* had a puppy crushed by the dam.

Food

Feeding the pregnant bitch need not be materially different than at other times, with some few exceptions. Naturally, she'll eat more, but probably only greatly increase her intake in the last two or three weeks. Don't try to fatten her up early in her pregnancy or you may find the pups to be abnormally small at birth, or the bitch may have difficulty whelping. You'll come across some recommendations in other books or articles that she be given calcium tablets, but she'll get enough calcium in her increased food consumption alone, so save those pills. If you wish, you may gradually switch her over in her fourth to sixth week to a higher biological value diet such as a puppy chow so the stool bulk won't be as high. Alternative rations might include mixing her regular dog food 50:50 on a dry basis with a *balanced* canned food, or using something like *Stress Diet*® made by Hill's. We've simply increased the volume of the regular high protein, high fat diet we feed year-round with good results. If constipation occurs, feed her a chunk of liver every day, as long as it doesn't loosen her stool too much. Several smaller meals rather than once-a-day feeding may also be beneficial, especially if she defecates more often.

It has been mentioned that fat level in the pregnant bitch's diet may affect the sex ratio of litters born, but whether or not this is true, extra fat is cheap insurance, and can improve stool, coat, and energy in the pregnant bitch if used judiciously, with perhaps a daily vitamin tablet. Vitamin supplements may not be necessary, but there is some evidence that vitamin C is useful in stressful situations. Since late pregnancy and lactation fall into this category and are probably as stressful as injury repair and disease resistance, vitamin C supplementation will likely not be harmful and may truly be beneficial at this time. Ask your vet what he/she thinks an effective and safe level is.

Medication

There have been and undoubtedly will continue to be warnings that certain medications and other substances should not be given to pregnant bitches. The arguments will probably continue, because in most cases it is impossible to determine whether such materials had any effect, or if the condition of the bitch would've been the same without it. For example, the warnings against dewormers are probably overdone; any healthy bitch, pregnant or not, should be able to handle a *proper dosage* of worm-killing toxins. In reality, rather than posing any danger, dewormers are nearly essential for maximum safety of the pups as well as protection for the bitch. During gestation, hormones cause release of encysted hookworm and roundworm larvae that have lain dormant in the bitch's body tissues. Upon release they migrate through her body, some get into her blood and intestines, while others enter the placentas and infect the fetuses. After whelping, they continue to develop in both the pups and the dam. Therefore, it is quite important to lower the worm burden in pregnant bitches. We have used *Vermiplex*®, *Nemex*®, and *Task*® dewormers on pregnant bitches at every stage with never any adverse effect.

The same is true with insecticides used externally for parasite control. Fleas can safely be combated by the use of carbaryl, fenthion or one of several other approved preparations. However, care should be exercised in exposing a pregnant bitch to weed killers, spray insecticides, and the like. Also, be careful not to double up on certain cholinesterase inhibitors such as may be present in both dewormers and flea killers. Of course, it is always best to ask your veterinarian's advice before using both types together or singly in combination with tranquilizers or anesthesia. Some veterinarians recommend that the owners of bitches that may need a Caesarian operation remove the flea collar a few days before the scheduled date.

The safety of antibiotics is questionable during gestation. Since they have been suspected as causative agents in sterility, I would hesitate using them on a pregnant bitch, or for a long time on any of my dogs. Antibiotics have also been claimed to be a possible factor in what is known as the "fading puppy syndrome," wherein newborn puppies mysteriously die without obvious reason. Although another cause (or causes) may be more likely, I prefer not to take the chance unless the health of the bitch is really in danger.

I believe hormones and synthetic steroids are potentially very dangerous if given to bitches during pregnancy; cleft-palate is one steroid-caused birth defect. Cortisone and similar steroids can also facilitate spontaneous bleeding, which is more perilous during whelping and surgical convalescence than at other times.

The question of whether to vaccinate during pregnancy is a controversial one, with many authorities stating that no vaccine of any sort should be given during this time. Others who have routinely vaccinated bitches for distemper, hepatitis (CAV-2), leptospirosis, and other diseases have reported no problems despite years of such practice. Still others do not hesitate to give killed virus vaccines, but will not administer modified live virus. Some will not give either vaccines or drugs, especially steroids, during the first third of the gestation period, but do not hesitate during the final trimester. I prefer the last approach mentioned, simply because of my experience with a cleft-palate litter, and my knowledge that abortions and other problems usually have their roots in something that happened early in the gestation period.

Exercise

Physical conditioning should be a year-round, lifelong concern of the dog owner, but too many of us feel that if we just turn the dogs out into the back yard, they'll get enough exercise. Wrong. Unless the dog has a frisky playmate, he'll probably get bored and go to sleep. Since late pregnancy and the period after whelping (post-parturition) are stressful, demanding times, the brood bitch ideally should be kept in great condition long before even being bred. This attention to vitality need not diminish during pregnancy, although the wise breeder will take his cues from the bitch in the last two or three weeks.

Some fantastic "superbitch" stories have been told, such as the one about the hound that dropped a puppy while hunting with a pack, took a few minutes to clean the whelp, then picked it up and headed out again to rejoin the pack. However, most bitches will look for ways to be more comfortable, will move a little slower, will stop jumping from the stair landing, and will naturally be a little less rambunctious when playing with her dogfriends, especially as the delivery date draws nearer when the load gets heavy. While rough treatment during this period is not recommended, it is surprising what the bitch can endure and still not abort. One day we were driving our new 1973 Volkswagen van up a grade, with a bitch in her eighth week lying in the back on the platform above the engine compartment. After stopping at an intersection we lurched forward in low gear, but since the rear window had not closed properly, our big, round bitch rolled out and landed on the road. About a week later she whelped a large, perfectly normal litter. Needless to say, on future trips we not only slammed the lid, but locked it, too.

PREGNANCY DIFFICULTIES

False Pregnancy

Often, when a bitch is mated but does not conceive, her whole body and emotional make-up acts as if she had. Weight gain, enlargement of nipples and mammary glands, and other typical physical signs of pregnancy are fully convincing in most cases, mildly so in others. Some bitches will produce a milk or similar fluid, some make a nest, and a few will actually evidence laborlike discomfort at the end.

A minority of veterinarians and breeders believe phantom pregnancies are a result of a temporary or permanent sterility and abnormal hormone activity, but others say pseudopregnancies are quite common and to be expected. Whitney even claims that bitches that *don't* either become pregnant or have a false pregnancy upon being mated were sterile at that particular time. Some say that many bitches have false pregnancies in spite of not having been mated, though in at least some of these reported cases the bitch may have mated without the owner's knowledge.

When I was in high school, a chum of mine had two bitches but only one would come in season and be bred. However, as the bred bitch swelled up, so did the "virgin" bitch, and when the first one had her puppies, the other would lactate and help raise the litter. Since it was my first experience with false pregnancies, I didn't take notes or practice scientific observation, and neither did my friend, so some important details may have been lost in the shadow of memory. The second bitch may have had abnormal, light-discharge heats that went unnoticed by the humans as well as the male dogs on the farm. Or she may have been mated, but unable to conceive or bring a litter to term. We'll never know for sure. At any rate, many bitches that experience false pregnancy will conceive when bred during a subsequent season.

Resorption

In some pregnancies, especially those of old bitches, the fetuses are resorbed. This is a process by which fetal life ceases and the death evidently triggers a reaction in the bitch's system that results in enzyme attack and dissolution of the fetus or fetuses. It may be that hormones released by the living fetuses direct or stimulate the proper, normal care the dam's body gives them, and in the absence of, or change in those stimuli, the bitch's system may react by disintegrating and dissolving the fetuses.

The time of fetal death seems to determine what happened. If early in gestation, the fetus may disappear as if it never existed, its lysed constituents being carried away by the bitch's circulatory and excretory systems. If much later, the fetus may be only partly digested by whelping time, and if very late, the pup will be stillborn. I believe many so-called false pregnancies are actually real ones in which a number of fetuses die, causing a resorption reaction which takes not only the dead fetuses but the live ones as well. It may be a matter of what proportion of the litter is dead versus alive, the time of death, or the age of the bitch which primarily affects the completeness of resorption and how readily it begins. If a fetus dies shortly before whelping, it apparently does not trigger the same type of reaction, thus my feeling that there is something in the pup's own endocrine system that, in concert with that of the dam, governs resorption, just as it seems to determine when labor is to begin.

A synthetic sex hormone, Stilbestrol, seems to have a beneficial effect in preventing resorption, so if you have an older bitch (or even a younger one) that has had several false pregnancies or resorptions, your veterinarian may prescribe a few milligrams injected every few days in an attempt to carry a litter to term.

Resorption used to be slightly more common, I believe, in the days before the discovery of vaccines. Illness, especially a light case of some disease, tends to cause a pregnant bitch to resorb her fetuses if they are somewhat less than forty days old, and if a bitch contracted distemper and survived, it was usually at the expense of the pups she was carrying (Nature's way of preserving the stronger by letting the weaker succumb). Some bitches thus became naturally immune to distemper this way, though vaccines have greatly reduced such occurrences.

Mummy Puppies

Almost nothing has been written for the general dog public on the subject of mummified fetuses, and not much has appeared in the professional journals, either. Despite this apparent lack of treatment of the subject, mummy puppies have always occurred from time to time, and will probably continue to do so in the breed.

Mummy puppies usually give the impression that they have reached full development before becoming partially dehydrated and encapsulated. Quite possibly the enzyme resorption mechanism fails when the fetus doesn't stimulate labor or abortion.

Ch. Kern Delta's Exakta, ROM. This fantastic bitch followed in the footsteps of her sire, Quell v. Fredeholz, whom she resembled physically. Starting her career at 16 months of age, she was BIS at a large Miami Specialty over champions (on her first try!), then within the next month, she won three more majors including two five-point shows with BOB or better. She finished at Chicago International at 17 months of age. One of 1956's top BOB/BOS winners, she was in the top three contending for the Grand Victrix title the next year. Breeders: J. and N. Henley; Owner: Helen Hess.

My personal experience with mummified puppies involved a bitch we leased to a couple who, as it turned out, gave their dogs very little care. Our bitch was returned in terrible shape after whelping a poor, small litter—three or four, of which one or two died or were stillborn. After this experience the bitch in question never produced another litter for us, and I sold her to a lady who had her bred twice, unsuccessfully. After the second breeding the bitch had to have a Caesarean operation when no labor began, and a single mummified puppy was found, dried up and small but complete. It is remotely possible that the pup was conceived on the first of the two breedings and had been preserved until taken by C-section at the end of the second and this time, false, pregnancy. If so, it may have interfered with conception the second time. Another conjecture is that it may have been formed on the second breeding and been preserved quickly.

WHELPING

The word *whelp* when used as a verb means to give birth, to bring forth a puppy naturally. Used as a noun, it refers to the newborn or very young pup, rarely the older offspring. *Parturition* is a technical term roughly meaning ''birth'' or whelping, but more generally, it means separation of full-term pups from the body of the bitch.

Whelping actually starts with the preparation of the brood bitch, the choice of stud, and other aspects of breeding dealt with in other chapters. Once you have done your genetics homework and have completed your breeding on paper, you will want to make sure the bitch is in top health and condition before and after conception. Especially important are proper diet and frequent stool checks for worms. Have your bitch wormed before mating and again several days before her due date if necessary. If she has been on a heartworm preventative, ask your veterinarian if he thinks medication should be suspended for awhile until the possibility of hook or roundworm can be checked, as that medication can inhibit such worms from laying eggs and revealing their presence.

Supplies to Have on Hand

Wash some rags of different colors and cut them into strips about ½-inch wide and 8 or 10 inches

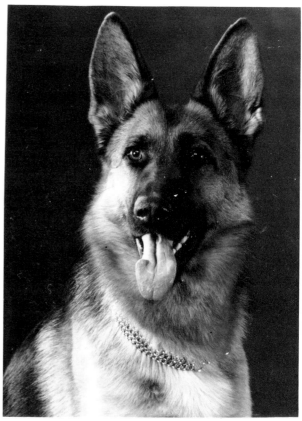

A beautiful bitch - strong yet feminine. Quinte vom Burg Reichenstein SchH I ''a''. 1986 Sieger show: Jugendklasse Siegerin (SG-I). Owner: Jane Steffenhagen

long, with 3 strips each of half a dozen colors. (Yarn will do as well.) Put them on a table next to the whelping box, along with scissors, a dispenser of dental floss or a spool of thread, a baby scale, and a pile of real diapers or clean, absorbent rags. Prepare weight charts similar to that shown in Figure 18-1 and have a pencil or pen handy. Both a heat lamp and a heating pad would be helpful, but the lamp alone will be sufficient. It need not be an infrared heat lamp, simply a 100- or 150-watt bulb in a reflector will do.

By now you've been saving newspapers all year for this well-planned event, and have a considerable stack on hand. Discard the slick Sunday supplement magazines and inserts, and layer the whelping box about ten pages thick. Locate a cot or put a couch nearby, but don't let her get up on it— she's supposed to be getting used to the box.

I cannot stress too strongly the advantages of newspapers: clean, disposable, non-irritating, adequate friction for traction, economical, insulative, and convenient. The ink is even said to be slightly antiseptic. Other materials such as straw, cedar shavings, carpeting, rags, or quilts, can cause a variety of problems. Straw often harbors fungus and other irritants, and is unbelievably hard to clean up and dispose of. Cloth bedding holds moisture, promotes germ growth, and can suffocate newborn pups. In addition, a report circulated in 1980 and 1981 club newsletters involved the use of indoor-outdoor carpeting which many breeders unwittingly use to cover the floor of their whelping boxes. One woman heard her puppies, that were only a few days old, crying, and ran to see that the bitch had urinated on the carpeting during the night and the new pups had been pushing themselves around searching for her. The reason for the distressful cries was that the pups had been badly burned by the ammonia and the chemicals produced by the reaction of the urine with the residues of the carpet-cleaning substances. A couple of pups with severe abdomen burns died, another lost the tip of his nose, and others suffered burns to their foot pads. In response to this story I again must stress the use of newspapers.

Labor

Whelping can be considered to begin about three days before the actual delivery. Whitney found that if abortion occurred earlier than three days before delivery, his bitches ignored the fetuses, but if they arrived within those three days (of the 61st day), they cleaned and mothered them. Perhaps it is prolactin or another hormone that makes the bitch feel like a mother and look for a place to deliver. I've not seen any earnest nest-building much before those last three days.

Make sure your veterinarian or an alternate will be available night or day around the expected due-date in case you run into trouble during labor. Two or three days before D-day the load should noticeably drop, and the belly hang in such a manner that the loin seems sunken by contrast. If this doesn't occur by the expected date of delivery, the bitch may have a false pregnancy, in which case you should contact your veterinarian during regular office hours.

In the few days before labor begins your bitch will be doing a lot of panting and may attempt to build nests behind the shrubbery or in the compost pile. Don't scold her for this, but rather distract her with a game or a walk on-leash, or take her to the whelping box to rest with you. The nest-building usually increases to a point where she almost seems obsessed with the idea; this most frequently develops within twenty-four hours of whelping. When it reaches the "frantic" stage (this will vary from one bitch to the next), whelping is anywhere from a few minutes to a few hours away. At this stage many bitches act as if they can't shred the newspapers fast enough, as if they are behind a terribly important deadline. Incidentally, you won't be helping any if you shred the papers ahead of time for her; in fact, it may be beneficial to her emotional and physical comfort to do it herself. And don't bother to straighten the mess until after the pups start arriving. Then you can again insure that the floor is covered.

"Labor Day"! You're sitting on your cot answering a 5-inch thick stack of letters, each requesting that you reserve one of the choice show-quality pups for ... what was that noise? A grunt! You jump into the box, but the bitch is simply lying there panting. You realize that she had been restless and trying to find a comfortable position just a little while ago, so that must have been a contraction! Don't get excited—some bitches do a lot of grunting and pushing before puppies start arriving, and others pop out two or three without a sound while you're answering the phone in the next room. With some, you have to keep looking every few minutes, so if you have other things to do, make sure to pass the whelping box often. If you decide to go to sleep (most litters are born at night) set your alarm clock to wake you every two hours. If nothing has happened, you can go back to dreamland before you're fully awake. A 7- to 15-watt nightlight over the whelping box is good to have, not only for now, but later for the bitch's sake.

Activity in the adrenal glands and possibly other organs of the fetuses trigger the commencement of labor contractions and probably also the nest-building impulse two to four days earlier. This has been fairly well understood since the mid-'70s. The adrenal glands of the fetus may influence placenta production of estrogens which in turn accelerate production of prostaglandins, substances affecting both pain perception and muscle contraction, especially in the uterus. As to time mentioned above, we've found that most of our bitches deliver beginning in the middle of the night or just before dawn, after they've had a chance to relax in a quiet, non-threatening, non-distracting environment. Also estrogen levels are usually higher at night and suppressed during the day.

Delivery

Sometimes the sac of fluid in which the puppy is encased will break half an hour before delivery, other times it will remain intact until sac and placenta are fully out and the dam starts tugging at it. If after losing her first sac of amniotic fluid, she goes more than thirty minutes without labor, call your veterinarian and report this danger signal.

If the bitch loses *blood* before the first pup is born or labor starts, the placenta probably has broken loose. If the bitch does not immediately deliver that pup, she may require an operation to remove the litter. *This is an emergency situation.* If the pup that has lost the placental connection *does* survive, it may have some temporary if not permanent brain damage. Sometimes instead of, or along with, the heavy loss of blood, a dark green discharge of fluid is noticed. Again, the major danger sign is if you see a great quantity, and *before* the first pup.

Puppies will emerge head first or bottom end first, either of which is normal. In the rare case of one foreleg and one rear leg emerging at the same time, you can easily push one of them back into the vagina. If the bitch has difficulty expelling the pup, you should lend assistance since the longer it goes without oxygen, the more likelihood of brain damage. This is not to condone panic and jerking the head off in an attempt to get the pup out in less than five seconds. The pup is still getting nourishment and blood-oxygen through the placenta at this point, although this source is in the process of being shut off.

As the pup appears, grasp the protruding head (or both hind legs) with one of the clean diapers, and gently pull as the bitch pushes. If you have to pull harder, pull on the skin as much as possible, to avoid damaging a joint. The skin will help spread out the tension over a greater area. Praise the bitch for pushing because, even if it doesn't affect her contractions, she'll get the idea she's doing something that pleases you. You may also need to encourage a first-time whelper or a bitch of slightly soft temperament, as she may not get the hang of caring for that wet little black rat right away. Also, try to remember to make a mental note of the time

the pup arrives so you can put it into your records later.

Most bitches will have the situation well under control all during the procedure—if one does not, she should probably not be bred again, Grand Victrix or no. (Von Stephanitz ranked being a good mother as the number one characteristic of a desirable bitch.) As a rule, the bitch will first pull at the umbilical cord and sac, and start eating these and the placenta, while lapping up as much of the fluid as possible. She'll take care of all but a few ounces of the liquid, and it's advisable to let her do so. By throwing out the placenta you may also be throwing away nutrients necessary for lactation or other functions. The fluid may be greenish due to bile in fetal excretions, or slightly bloody; both are normal. Don't be alarmed if she appears to be rough in handling the whelp, as vigorous tugging on the cord may help prevent excessive bleeding and may stimulate deep breathing to fill the lungs.

When the cord has been chewed off with her molars, the bitch may direct her attention to cleaning herself and her nest. This is an ideal time to give the inside of the pup's mouth a quick wipe to remove any phlegm that may be present, wipe off the nose, and vigorously rub the puppy dry with a fresh cloth diaper or towel. Some people use a bulb syringe to clear the mouth and throat. By now (a minute or less after delivery started) the pup should have emitted some noise or given some indication of breathing and started nursing. I've seen pups start nursing before they were fully out of the vagina!

If the new mother will allow it, and is busy cleaning up or delivering the next whelp, place the previous, towelled pup on a diaper-covered heating pad set on low or medium, that is placed about three feet under a heat lamp or a little closer if a regular light bulb is used. A weather thermometer on the floor of the whelping box can be a guide to the distance you should use; the area should be comfortably warm, around 90 degrees F., to facilitate drying. At this point, warmth is the most important need of the whelp.

When the bitch finishes cleaning up, put the pup to a teat so it can start nursing as soon as possible. This is beneficial to the dam as it promotes contractions, and good for the whelp since it gets additional warmth and energy into its system. Direct the heat lamp toward the feeding station while the

H LITTER Pup: GREEN COLLAR Sex: MALE Birth Wt.: 16 OZ Birth Order: 1 NICK NAME: BULLDOZER

DAY	1	2	3	4	5	6	1 wk.	8	9	10	11	12	13	2 wk.	Comments:
	(OZ.) 17	16	18	22	23	24	27	32	34	35	37	40	44	48	SMALL WHITE BLAZE ON CHEST
DAY	15	16	17	18	19	20	3 wk.	22	23	24	25	26	27	4 wk.	
	50	52	54	60	59	64	70	70	81	88	84	90	90	99	WORMED ON DAY 20 1ST TO BARK IN A.M
DAY	29	30	31	32	33	34	5 wk	36	37	38	39	40	41	6 wk.	
	—	100	(LBS +OZ) 6,9	7⁴	8⁰	7⁷	8⁵	9⁰	9⁸	10⁴	10⁴	11¹	11¹²	12²	
DAY	43	44	45	46	47	48	7 wk.	50	51	52	53	54	55	8 wk.	
	13¹³	13⁰	13¹³	14⁰	14⁴	14¹⁵	15¹	15⁵	15¹⁰	16²	16⁸	17³	17¹²	18¹²	

Pup: RED COLLAR Sex: MALE Birth Wt.: 20 OZ Birth Order: 2

DAY	1	2	3	4	5	6	1 wk.	8	9	10	11	12	13	2 wk.	Comments:
	(OZ.) 20	20	22	24	24	27	28	32	32	36	37	41	44	48	
DAY	15	16	17	18	19	20	3 wk.	22	23	24	25	26	27	4 wk.	
	49	52	51	55	61	61	69	71	72	80	78	85	83	89	WORMED LITTER DAY 20, NEMEX
DAY	29	30	31	32	33	34	5 wk	36	37	38	39	40	41	6 wk.	
	—	88	(LBS OZ.) 6,1	6¹⁴	7⁴	7⁰	8²	8¹⁰	9⁰	9¹⁰	9¹⁴	10⁷	10¹³	11⁹	
DAY	43	44	45	46	47	48	7 wk.	50	51	52	53	54	55	8 wk.	
	11¹⁴	12⁸	13²	13⁴	13¹⁴	14⁸	14⁹	14⁸	15⁶	15⁸	16⁵	17⁴	17⁵	18⁴	

Daily weight record kept next to whelping box. Helpful in spotting trouble such as worms etc., which is shown in little or no weight gain.

1952 Grand Victor Ch. Ingo Wunschelrute, owned and imported by Margrit Fischer, as was the '52 Grand Victrix.
Photo courtesy M. Schuetzler

pup is nursing, and then back to the heating pad area, which should be a near corner of the box so the puppies will be warm and safely out of the way while siblings are arriving. After all puppies have been dried and fed, you can remove the pad (if you still have the lamp), and in a few days the temperature of the room can be lowered to approximately 80 degrees F. as long as there is no draft or cold surface in contact with the puppies. When they are over three weeks of age, they will gradually prefer cooler and cooler sleeping accommodations.

Identification—Between deliveries the pups will usually nurse, but if the bitch is moving about or a pup is full and has fallen asleep, it is a convenient time for you to check the palate, cord, vent and other features to see if all is normal; weigh the pup, and record the markings, and the time whelped. Also record the color of the collar you choose, which brings us back to those brightly colored rags you washed last week. In well-planned breedings, it is not unusual to have considerable uniformity, and if it's a large litter, you may have trouble quickly identifying a particular pup. At Willow Wood, we tie a ribbon around the neck of the first pup while the second one is still wet, marking on the weight chart the color of the ribbon, the sex, and other notes on ''M-1'' or ''S-1'' or whatever letter we had chosen for the litter names (we use the German custom of following the alphabet). If the second is the same sex as the first, it gets the next color ribbon on the table, and so we have ''red male,'' ''green

male,'' ''red female,'' and so on, written on the weight chart next to the numbers representing their order of birth. Customarily the last male and female don't get collars unless or until another pup of the same sex arrives. If we run out of colors and have a lot of one sex, we tie two ribbons together; thus, ''red-green male'' may be written next to ''D-8.'' If you have a litter of sables, black-and-tans, and blacks, you obviously won't need as many ribbons as in a litter of all apparently identical puppies, but it's easy to cut ribbons off later as they lose their identification value. Tie the collar tight enough to enable you to slip your little finger underneath. Too loose, and the pup's arms will get caught during the pushing motions he makes when nursing. Also, cut off excess ends.

As to your supply of floss or thread—it's there ''just in case.'' If there is excessive bleeding or if the bitch neglects chewing off the cord, tie it with a really tight knot two inches (5 cm) or less from the navel, then another knot a couple of millimeters closer to the belly. Snip off the unwanted cord and extra thread close enough so there's no thread for the bitch to nibble on and pull loose.

Whether gnawed off naturally or tied and cut, there will be a little blood on the diapers and newspapers for a day or two. But the remnant of umbilical cord, despite the mother's frequent washings, will dry up and fall off in two or three days. Make sure your utensils are clean but don't bother sterilizing the thread, scissors, and other materials unless you also plan to sterilize the bitch's mouth (a temporary home for a multitude of microorganisms), and everything else in the box including the puppies.

When Help Is Needed

If labor ceases before all the pups have been delivered, and there is an interval of more than three hours, you may want to give the bitch an injection of oxytocin (0.1 cc or less) obtained from your veterinarian. Or you may prefer to take her to his office. If you choose the latter carry her in, don't walk her anywhere between your car and the examining table which has been disinfected. If anxiety, nervous restlessness, or extreme fatigue is noticed, I would definitely take steps to stimulate resumption of labor, and if an injection doesn't work, I would consult the veterinarian about a possible C-section. However, these are not hard and fast rules but are offered as guidelines. As an example we had one experienced bitch in good condition that often took twelve to twenty hours to deliver her large litters. On one occasion she started having puppies around 6 or 7 P.M., quit at midnight after seven whelps, played with them, cleaned them, rearranged them, then decided to go to sleep. My wife, who was in attendance, thought the bitch would start again in two or three hours, so she went upstairs to bed. Eight hours later she went down to the whelping box and told the bitch, "If you don't finish your litter, I'm going to call the vet," then turned toward the stairs. As soon as she put her foot on the first step she heard a grunt behind her—the bitch was starting again, and in less than three hours delivered her remaining six pups. She and those six had apparently decided to sleep through the night. If there are only a couple of pups left, oxytocin (*Pitocin®*) is okay, but I wouldn't give it when several are left to whelp.

If difficulty arises in a normal delivery while a pup is visible in the vulva, you probably can help. If you have some new disposable vinyl gloves, put one on and rub some petroleum jelly or *Furacin* on a couple of fingers, then reach inside the vagina and feel for the cause of the hang-up. Sterile hands are second-best, but don't waste too much time scrubbing up; time may be more important than absolutely sterile fingers. A large puppy's front legs can be pulled out next to its head if you can feel its elbows and shoulders. The rest of the pup's body will then easily pass. Often, the rear will be presented first, and if you see the tail and hindquarters but not the legs, reach in and ease the legs out, or they'll make it very difficult on the bitch. Pups that are breech-born will probably have to be pulled a bit to get the head out. As before, use a diaper for better grip, and pull evenly on the upper body, allowing the skin to transmit most of the tension over the pup's body. Rarely will front legs be presented before the head, but if they are, reach in and reposition the head, which may be lodged behind the pelvic bone or twisted to one side or "raised" in relation to its front legs.

Dystocia—Sometimes the bitch seems to run out of steam before the whole litter has been delivered, perhaps as a result of a large pup that was especially hard to whelp. Whatever the cause, difficulty in labor is called *dystocia*. It is most common in old or overweight bitches that have not had enough exercise. Mechanical blockage such as an especially large pup or an abnormal presentation is not as common as uterine inertia, the lack of sufficient muscular contraction to push the fetus out. Inertia can be caused by a general run-down condition or a large pup that has stretched and strained uterine-wall muscles, or by emotional drain or trauma. This latter can include fear and worry which is why in the wild, bitches go off to a quiet, isolated spot to have their pups. Nutrition imbalance, such as a calcium deficiency caused either by feeding too *much* calcium supplements or too much meat in place of a balanced diet, is a common cause of inertia. Your veterinarian may try calcium injections or a very small dose of *Pitocin®* (oxytocin) if he's sure inertia (not a blockage) is the reason for the dystocia. If you can't get to a veterinarian in a few hours, hook two fingers inside the vulva and pull steadily; this often stimulates the bitch to contract. By the way, any time it is necessary to insert fingers or non-sterile objects into the vagina, it is a good idea to coat them first with *Furacin*.

Caesarean delivery—If inertia of the uterus cannot be overcome with finger tension, drugs, or repositioning of the fetuses, the bitch may have to be opened up and the pups surgically removed. Because Julius Caesar reportedly arrived this way, an operation involving cutting open the abdominal wall and uterus is known as a *Caesarean section* or

C-section. It differs from birth not only in the mode of delivery, but also in the effect on the endocrine system of the bitch. Often, C-section puppies have to be tube- or bottle-fed or given to a foster mother when the natural mother does not lactate or has no interest in nursing the pups; sometimes even her interest in cleaning them is non-existent. It may be that the same signals from the fetuses' endocrine glands, and answers from those of the bitch that triggered uterine contractions, also order the flow of milk and affect the mothering instinct. Perhaps there is another explanation why some bitches are able and willing to nurse after a C-section and others are not.

Caesarean section is not especially risky unless the pups have been dead for some time (a common causative factor for labor not starting), or the uterus has ruptured and peritonitis has set in, or if an infection has started late in the pregnancy. However, it is standard practice in all surgical operations to inject an antibiotic and follow up with tablets or capsules, and as I have already indicated, antibiotics have been suspected as causing adverse effects on nursing puppies (though they'd be in greater danger without them). To be safe, be prepared with a tube feeding kit.

It used to be thought that once a woman had a Caesarean, she would never be able to have natural childbirth again, because of the weakness and inelasticity of scar tissue. But in fairly recent years, thanks to improved surgical techniques, this has changed. Canines, however, are constructed a little differently, and therefore the decision to have a second C-section is more determined by the reason for the first one than by the fact that the C-section had been performed before. For example, if the bitch has a narrow pelvis due to an old fracture she may need another Caesarean, in which case you might consider ovariohysterectomy at the same time.

WHELPING THE WRONG WAY

Potential problems exist, but they occur mainly when the human midwife interferes with nature. As an illustration, I recount the mis-adventures of a friend who apparently believed that, "If some is good, more is better," since he tended to go over board on many instances. To say he sought much advice and heeded none would be correct—actually, he took 10 percent from one advisor, 10 percent from the next, until he was running in ten different directions at once. His first litter of Borzoi would've been whelped on a quilt had he not asked for my help, and was at last persuaded to use newspapers. The bitch had signs of hookworm infestation several days before whelping, but he decided not to worm her at that time. I outlined our methods, lent him our scales and other paraphernalia, and told him to call us when the first pup arrived.

In spite of my efforts to calm him on the big day, he became increasingly anxious, almost frantic, while the bitch was as cool as a cucumber. He insisted on getting in the bitch's way to clean up the nest, and kept worrying that she would crush her babies or hurt them in some other way. His impatience reached a zenith when he decided to cut the umbilical cord on the third pup just seconds after it was whelped, instead of waiting for the bitch to chew it to the proper length and crush the tissues, which promotes clotting and stops the flow. Result: blood spurted a yard away as soon as the scissors snipped the cord. By the time he managed to pinch it shut while I tracked down some dental floss to tie the cord, enough blood had been lost to really put him into a frenzy.

A week or more later, he mentioned that the pups still had very little energy and the dam was always panting, which I took to be a result of the anemia and the postponement of worming them. It turned out he still had the thermostat set on 90 degrees F., although it was summertime in humid Toledo, and it took some convincing that they would all feel better with more normal room temperatures since they were not chilled or orphaned. I nearly had to use a flashlight to find the pups, since he had read somewhere that new puppies should be kept in a dark, quiet corner, and consequently had covered the ceiling lamp with newspapers, and curtained off the whelping box with heavy blankets! In addition, the poor fellow was almost thrown out of a couple of veterinarians' offices because he had shopped for advice on whether or not to worm the puppies, and used the advice of one as an argument against that of the next.

Fortunately, this tale had a happy ending, as the pups survived, but more in spite of his efforts than because of them.

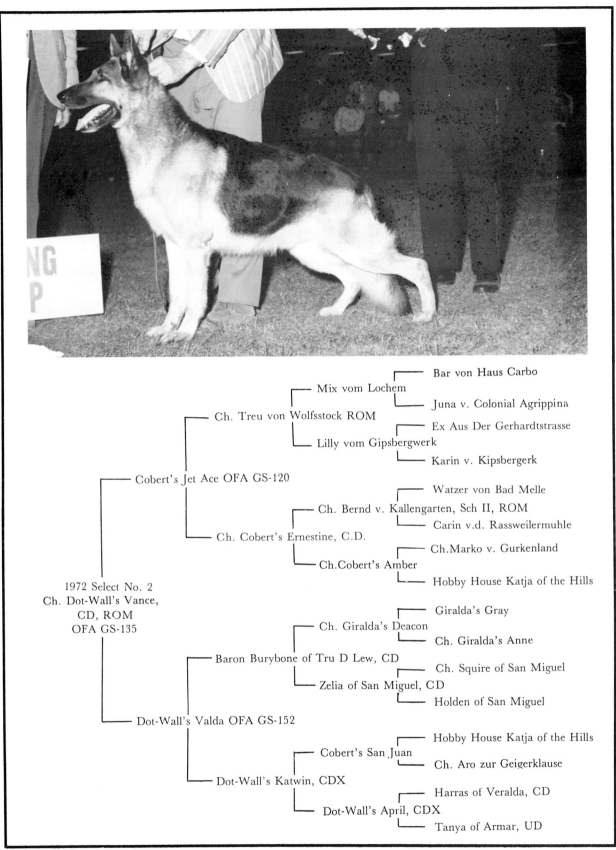

1972 Select No. 2 Ch. Dot-Walls Vance, CD, ROM. Vance produced good balance, gait, and angulation, plus some level bites.
1st in Working Group, Boardwalk K.C.   *Photo by Gilbert courtesy of owner Dorothe Graham.*

Culling

Are any of the pups deformed in any way? Do any refuse to nurse or repeatedly fall off the nipple without getting any food despite warming and glucose therapy? Is there one that doesn't gain weight at the same general rate as the others in the first few days? Are there any runts of nine or ten ounces or less, while the littermates are fourteen ounces and up? If the answer to any of these questions is yes, then you may have to cull the litter this week, possibly right after birth. The abnormality may be an obvious thing such as a bloody stump instead of a nice long tail, but whatever it is, it often proves out that such a pup has something else wrong with him as well—something not immediately noticeable, but troublesome later. In the case of any deformity, it's best to put the pups to a quick end. Don't argue with yourself; don't relate stories of that great champion you heard of that was raised with the help of tube feeding and infant surgery; put the bad ones down right away.

How? Methods range all the way from the violent such as placing the pup in a hole out back and shooting it, or drowning it under a brick in a bucket, to a trip to the veterinarian where death comes by an injection into the heart. You and your veterinarian should discuss the alternatives ahead of time, so you will know what method should be used if it becomes necessary. Some have recommended ether in a fairly air-tight container, but ether is extremely dangerous, volatile and explosive under certain conditions, and most states or cities now have strict regulations governing its sale and use. Again, ask your vet for advice. Whatever method you choose, don't let the dam see you do it. Shuffle her pups around and when she's not looking, pass the bad one behind you to an assistant who can then sneak it out of the room. Or, have the bitch taken out for a walk while you remove the pup.

When breeders speak of culling newborn pups, they usually mean killing the unwanted pups, even though they may use such euphemisms as "put down" or "put to sleep." This is the sense in which I have been using the term in the above paragraphs, but culling also means selling some as pets, without registration papers, or in some other way separating those undesirable individuals from the breeding program or the breed's gene pool. Regardless of what you do with the culls, they should be separated from the others at birth if need be, and again before adulthood, around seven or eight months old, perhaps after a preliminary hip X ray. Dr Braxton Sawyer once told me that he culled his hounds three times: at birth, at six weeks, and at six months. We cull at birth if necessary, then again at seven or eight weeks if the litter has had its hips palpated by the Bardens technique, then again after a wedge radiograph is taken before adulthood. Thanks to the screening affect of palpation, we earlier had done away with the need to have any destroyed or operated on after the second evaluation. And thanks to a history of knowing generations of ancestors later in our breeding program. we no longer found it necessary to kill any after palpation results were seen.

The old German custom of culling for the sake of the bitch, allowing a maximum of five or six whelps on her, was partly based on a lack of nutritious commercial or home-formulated food for young pups, combined with the practice of late or natural weaning of puppies. In 1975, an SV liaison official for the German Shepherd Dog Club of America informed me that this practice was still required there, but in his opinion it wasn't necessarily the best idea for Germans *or* Americans. Apparently other Germans agree as there is a growing feeling that the custom is outdated. Many of us have raised litters of ten to thirteen healthy whelps without resorting to bottle or tube feeding or the assistance of an *amme* (foster mother).

The Germans reportedly seldom destroy any extra puppies in spite of the six-maximum rule. For them it must not be difficult to find a foster mother to share the responsibility of nursing some of the brood, but it is surprising to me that they can be easily located; I once tried in vain to find even one of any large enough breed or mixture, in a city of half a million. Part of the difficulty may be that success depends to a degree on the coinciding of whelping dates, as problems of rejection can occur more easily the further apart the ages are, or the greater the delay in transferring pups. Also, some bitches are more wary than others and will not accept a stranger in the nest. But German breeders probably have an easier time finding *ammes* since they are in greater touch with each other than we in America are, and news of breedings is available to and through breed wardens. The power and authority of the national breed club, the SV, is also a factor.

Contrast this with American regional or local clubs which are notoriously beset with power politics and jealousies to the point that the majority of owners and a large percentage of breeders do not hold membership in any club.

Several years ago I conducted a survey on the topic of culling litters at birth, and responses from random breeders covered the gamut from sensible to sentimental. Although I received no reply from any European breeders, none of the American breeders, including a couple of transplanted Germans, destroyed puppies simply to control the size of the litter. One lady indignantly declared that culling should be left to God alone, apparently forgetting that He already practices it by permitting natural selection to take place in the wild. The weak are eaten, the clumsy fall off cliffs, and the feeble-minded perish. The fittest not only survive as individuals, they are also able to contribute more to the genetic pool of the species through reproducing over a longer period of time than can the misfits. This is why hip dysplasia is not a problem in wolves. Raise wolves for fifty years without culling litters, allowing the weaker members to breed instead of being killed by other animals, and all kinds of ailments not now apparent in wild wolves will appear, including dysplasia.

The true breeder strives to better the breed. Ideally, he will see not only a responsibility, but a mandate. He places stewardship above sportsmanship, and at times must sacrifice the individual for the sake of the breed. With 10,000 cats and dogs born every *hour* in the US, and approaching 100,000,000 a year, some would say that we should stop breeding altogether. But the city pounds and animal shelters would still be taking in 20,000,000 unwanted pets annually (and putting 75 percent of them to death), for they are largely produced by

Ch. Howard's Retrace, a lovely bitch pictured here in an early match , went on to win some nice specialty awards and become the dam of Caralon's Thor of Howard and other fine dogs. Linebred on Lance 3-3,4. Owner/breeder: H. Snodgrass. Photo by Lucas

mongrels and strays allowed to run loose. Still, a significant proportion are out of purebred stock that should have been sterilized or culled before they were old enough for procreation. Only the very best should be bred, and those sold as pets ideally should be vasectomized or spayed, or at least sold without papers to people who can be relied upon not to let their dogs run at large or be bred. In short, the question for each breeder should not be, "Should I cull my litters?"; rather, we should be asking ourselves, "Which ones should I cull?"

Saving the Stillborn Puppies

Sooner or later every breeder encounters the problem of whelps that don't start breathing or exhibit other life signs. If the pup is wiggling but can't seem to breathe, after wiping out his mouth cradle him in both hands, one behind the other, enveloping the thighs, hips, and abdomen with one hand, and the thorax, shoulders, and head with the other, and with one finger keep his mouth open. Keeping your hands together as if grasping a golf club, lift the pup as high as your head and swing your arms and hands in a pendulum motion downward, stopping fairly suddenly at a point just below your knees; the puppy's carefully supported head will be the lowest part of him at that end of the swing. The centrifugal force of one or two such swings will generally force out any phlegm you couldn't reach and which was preventing respiration.

If breathing doesn't start after repeated attempts, try mouth-to-mouth resuscitation. Holding the pup's head down, enclose his mouth and nose with your mouth. Try to suck out any of the clear fluid that may be in the lungs or bronchial tubes. Then take a breath of fresh air and blow up the lungs with enough force to move the rib cage and diaphragm to a normal extent, but not so vigorously as to overextend and damage the tissues. Remove the pup from your mouth and gently squeeze on his abdomen and chest so the air you've given him escapes. If there's considerable fluid, suck it out before again blowing into his lungs. The rhythm

of blowing and squeezing should be somewhat faster than the normal rate of respiration. Keep it up until the pup starts breathing on his own. It would be advisable to step into the next room to do this, so the bitch doesn't get worried and interfere.

If there are no signs of life at all, go through the same steps anyway. It may be a true stillbirth, but then again it might not, and thus can be saved. Many whelps have no detectable heartbeat, but it is a waste of time to search for one, for its absence is meaningless. The heart may have stopped only seconds earlier, or be too faint for you to hear or feel, and even a stopped heart can often be started again. While the warm, "stillborn" pups whelped in your presence are worth some work, the ones that have arrived when you were not around and are already cold, are beyond help. In rare cases one might be revived, but there's too much likelihood of brain damage due to hypoxia.

In addition to the above steps, you can also stimulate circulation by external heart massage. With your thumb on one side and two or three fingers on the other, pinch the chest rhythmically at the point about two or three ribs behind the elbow and upper arm, and about one-third of the way up from the breastbone. Depress the chest about ¼-inch (6 mm) and immediately release, pumping about two cycles per second. During any life-saving attempt, body heat should be protected as much as possible. If any life signs develop, or the puppy does not cool off too much, continue as long as practicable, without neglecting the needs of the dam or her next whelp.

You should get some results in five minutes, which is sure to seem an eternity, so look at the clock. If the pup gets cold and doesn't respond by then, give up on it and concentrate on the others. Remove dead pups and culls when the bitch is busy in labor or her attention is otherwise directed away from them. She can't count and will not know the difference between three and five as long as she doesn't see the removal or smell the pup in an adjoining room. However, this isn't likely to be a problem, as very young animals have much less odor than adults.

18

PEDIATRICS—
THE FIRST THREE WEEKS

Now that your nestful of future champions has arrived, once they have been washed, inspected, dried, and fed by the mother, you must be prepared to take over some of the responsibilities and work in raising them. Since major advances in puppy development usually take place at certain intervals, the subject of pediatric care in this book is addressed over two chapters. However, there is no hard and fast "time-table" of development, and dates and times mentioned in these chapters can vary from litter to litter and individual to individual.

CARE OF THE DAM

After the completion of whelping, the rest of the first day is spent in caring occasionally for the dam. Be sure she has water nearby, and has been taken out on-leash after every two or three pups (many deliver in pairs a few minutes between the two). Then take her out again sometime after the last one. Other than that, and a little snack when she'll eat it, she'll not need much attention but plenty of rest.

Many new breeders feel more secure taking the bitch to the veterinarian for an injection of oxytocin to be sure that any retained fetus or placenta is expelled by extra-strong uterine contractions. I don't like this idea. For one thing, it causes considerable anxiety if you separate the bitch from the pups. For another, it will be a great inconvenience to you if you have to take the pups, and it may be dangerous to the whelps if the outside temperature of the air is low. Also, the trip exposes the dam and her pups to many germs not found at home. However, if I really felt oxytocin were needed, I'd get the recom-

mended amount, bring it home and administer it myself. With experience, a breeder can tell when a bitch has been emptied of her pups and placentas, and must elect not to give her any unnatural stimulant. The bitch can also be examined sometime in the first day after whelping; her uterus palpated to find out if there are any procrastinators, and her milk checked to make sure it's normal. But this too can be done by you at home. Some veterinarians will give or suggest the almost universal antibiotic shot, too, so discuss it with him.

SONNET FOR THE WHELPING BOX

Like fat, black bumblebees, mumbling, murm'ring,
Blind creatures crawl within the confines of
A corner of our home. I dearly love
The drone of puppies learning how to sing.
Expert musicians barely one day old,
They hum in harmony, with patient mother
Their favorite audience. They push each other,
Competing strongly for the milk, as bold
Gladiators in Roman rings once fought,
And then when they are filled with milk, and warm,
They gather in one friendly, drowsy swarm,
Too young to dream of balls or sticks they'd caught,
But twitching just the same, as if they guessed
Their futures while still in their natal nest.

Fred L. Lanting

Food for the bitch should be chosen with care, having both a high biological value as well as a higher energy level than that of a maintenance diet. Lactating bitches generally need about 300 percent of the calories they needed before becoming pregnant. Whole boiled eggs, cottage cheese, and a little liver can be added to a good, high-digestibility commercial ration whether dry or canned. Also be sure the bitch is getting adequate fat and water. Liver, fat, and extra eating may cause loose stools, but as long as it doesn't get so bad that it looks as if the food isn't being absorbed, some softness is to be expected following a litter.

Actually, the bitch's fecal matter will probably cause the novice breeder to worry. It will be black, tarry, loose, and stringy because it is composed of digested blood and placental tissues. This appearance will last a couple of days, the stool becoming more normal-looking about the same time the bitch starts looking a little cleaner. In addition, vaginal discharges may range from greenish-yellow to blood-tinged, but should not be excessively bloody as this would indicate hemorrhaging. Finally, the dam's urine may contain mucus and may be either pink or brown, staining her hocks and the inside surfaces of the thighs for a few days to a couple of weeks. If she and the weather permit, hosing her off is a simple and quick way to clean her. If you wish to wash her more, use very dilute pure soap water on a clean rag and rinse her well.

Post-partum Problems

Mastitis is an inflammation of the nipples or mammary glands, usually limited to the first month and caused by a scratch-induced infection. An abscess can lead to a generalized septic condition, fever, and lack of appetite, which infection can be transmitted to pups. Prevention is largely a matter of clipping the little white hooks off the puppies' front nails by the time they are about one-week-old, and trimming them if necessary ten days later.

Metritis is a uterine infection which sometimes follows an abnormal labor or delivery by one to three days. Sometimes it involves a retained fetus or placenta, though a dead pup may become mummified without resulting in uncontrolled infection. Vaginal infections occurring at other times than pregnancy and whelping can also cause metritis, as noted elsewhere. Whenever it happens,

veterinary care is urgently needed. Both metritis and mastitis require antibiotic therapy.

Psychological factors can interfere with normal care of newborn puppies as well as affect the bitch's personality. Shy or stable bitches can be easily upset by the presence of strangers, or much noise of unknown origin. First-time mothers may not know what to do with the first pup, and pampered house pets may be more interested in getting attention than giving it. Bitches trained for guard duty may be distracted if they suspect strangers are in the house, and may leave off caring for pups to go back on duty. Insecurity due to not being introduced to the whelping box early enough, or to too many noisy strangers around can cause even the normally stable bitch to want to move her litter elsewhere in the first few days. Persuade her not to pick up her babies by the heads and carry them around, but don't holler at her—just say "No" gently and put the pup back, then tell her to lie down.

THE PUPS

Meanwhile, back in the nest, a swarm of humming puppies are making soft demands for love. This love is initially expressed in terms of warmth and nourishment, in that order. Therefore, when you are able to persuade the dam to leave the pups, turn the heat lamp on to maintain a temperature of 90 degrees F., and push all the pups together into a pile before you leave the room. If, when you return the bitch to the nest, there is a pup that has managed to separate himself, give that one first place in line at the milk wagon. The first week or so is the period of least resistance to that worst enemy of new puppies—chilling—with the risk decreasing daily as they approach three weeks of age. Adult dogs and pups over the age of three weeks have a normal body temperature of about 101 to 102 degrees F. (38 degrees C.), and while some claim 95 degrees F. (35 degrees C.) is normal for new pups, chilling is dangerous especially if other factors such as being all alone, dehydration, worm larvae, or lack of milk, are also present. By the way, don't rely on whether or not a pup shivers to tell you if it's too cold, as the shiver reflex apparently doesn't develop until the pup is one-week-old.

Some practices to follow during the first three weeks can be started right away. Handle the pups

Ch. Arelee's Pardon My Dust. Owners: P. and J. Root. Breeders: R. and B. Eshom; Handler K. Tank. A magnificent animal, his only fault being some throatiness (dewlap).

often right from the second day when the dam has rested, including the weighing procedure. Stimulate the development of their senses of balance by holding them vertically, then horizontally, rotating them and rocking them back and forth a little. It has been said that the tactile receptors in the sensory nervous system can be stimulated and the pups' development perhaps accelerated by rubbing or briskly petting them, gently squeezing and separating toes, moving limbs, etc. After ten days try flashing a light into their faces so their visual receptors can also be stimulated. You may want to do this a couple of times a day until you see some definite response.

You will notice a few things on the first day that will continue for several days or weeks, but little that will remain until maturity. Most changes will be gradual, with dates and times in this chapter usually being only approximate, varying from litter to litter, and sometimes between siblings.

The Umbilicus

The umbilical cord should quickly dry up and drop off in two or three days. You can snip off the fully-dry part earlier if you have to do so because of excessive length, but one to three inches of excess is not abnormal, and if there's not much variation in siblings, you can assume the bitch knew what she was doing.

If the umbilicus is raw, bleeding steadily, or infected, rush the pup to the veterinarian, as this is very serious, and sepsis can rapidly spread throughout its body. Pups at this age quickly die under such adverse circumstances. But compare all the pups so you don't go rushing off because of normal redness or slight bleeding.

Dewclaws

If dewclaws are found, they should be cut off between three and five days of age. I prefer to have the veterinarian do this job, as I've not yet had any experience in snipping them off and am afraid I'd not get enough of the joint, in which case the nail could grow back or a lump with part of the digit may remain on the outside. Remember, don't take the first digit off the *front* leg, for that's not a true dewclaw; they are found only on rear legs. The only time one of my bitches produced pups with dewclaws was in the case of a co-owned bitch bred to a recent German import. I didn't keep any of the pups, nor were they born in my home, so I didn't follow that litter very closely.

Sleep

New pups sleep about 90 percent of the time, with the other 10 percent being devoted to eating. A tendency to remain in the fetal position while sleeping is evident until three to five days of age, then the pup stretches out into a position known as *extensor dominance*. This is erroneously taken by many breeders to mean that the pups are hot and seeking to be cooled off—not so. It is merely a reaction to neurological development and involves the motor nerves' messages to the limb muscles; it is not a coordination with the sensory nerves. To arrive at such a conclusion is potentially dangerous because newborns and those up to three weeks of age need ambient temperatures of 80 to 85 degrees F. at first, even in the dam's presence and piled together. One reason it takes awhile for normal adult body temperature to be attained by the pup may be that the liver, which is one of the last soft

organs to fully develop, has very little stored glycogen to offer the muscles. Glycogen and, later, other carbohydrates are used for contraction of muscle fibers, generating heat as they are metabolized. It takes some time for adequate reserve capacity to be built up, so the young pup must feed often and be kept warm in order to stay alive and healthy. Therefore, if the neonate doesn't have contact with his dam or a couple of littermates, even a room at 70 degrees F. may quickly deplete his reserves if he remains in that environment too long. After his liver is developed and he can walk around, his system can handle a lower temperature. Incidentally, if an individual puppy continues to sleep in the fetal position beyond the fourth day of life, whether he is separated or with the others, be suspicious of an abnormality and watch him carefully.

Activated sleep—Normal sleeping puppies will twitch: a leg, then the face, then another leg, etc., several times a minute. Sleep activation apparently is nature's way of testing and developing the motor neurons. The pups will do this while lying on their sides or against the dam's belly or over each other, often with their heads extended. Yawning is one

Ch. Raps vom Piastendamm.

Photo courtesy Julius Due

sign of waking, but they can immediately fall fast asleep again. In fact, they will be about two weeks of age before they go through a drowsy stage between wakefulness and sleep. About this same time, the body twitches and facial tremors that have been present since day one will become less noticeable. They are usually gone by four weeks, and are soon replaced by dream movements, in which the brain replays some of the day's experiences, especially the most recent or exciting ones. Most normal pups in the first week or two will not cry, though some will "talk" and make clucking sounds, adding "umph" sounds while nursing. Experience will enable you to pick out, even at an age of a few days and weeks, those pups that will be more vocal in adulthood. Heartbeat in new puppies may seem high to you, perhaps twice as fast as in resting adults. After the first-day rate of around 160 beats per minute, it jumps to around 225 to 220 for a week, decreasing to a little under 200 at three to four weeks of age. There is variation among individuals, and it is hard to count them without a good stethoscope, or if the pup is active or twitching in his sleep.

Nursing

Healthy pups will be vigorous nursers. Pay special attention to those that aren't. At first, nursing positions and motions will be a little less polished and expert than they will be in a week or more. The pup will swing his head from side to side, batting the nipple with his muzzle before zeroing in on it. If you try to help by guiding his head with your finger, you'll only get him to turn toward your finger, which resistance he feels and naturally seeks. You can help by supporting him by his rib cage behind his front legs, and letting him "wipe" his face on the dam's belly until he finds and latches onto the nipple.

Noises while nursing will vary, but most early sounds are like humming, and older pups will talk to their milk with sounds resembling whimpers. Gulping noises will be accompanied by pushing motions like alternate-arm breaststroke swimming; unlike the treading motions of kittens, puppies push more to the sides. This gives them exercise and a little breathing room, but probably serves most to stimulate the mammary glands.

When the puppies are a few days old you should notice occasions when they suddenly are still and quiet, their tails straight up and quivering, as they almost silently gulp down the milk at great speed. Pushing motions will have ceased, for the bitch unwittingly will have opened the flood gates. Then in a minute or less, and just as suddenly, she'll close them to the usual or slower rate. You'll know when this happens because the pups will let go, complain, and thrash about searching for a teat that "works." When they resign themselves to working for their supper again, they'll resume the foot-pushing and head-jerking. When they get less than they want, they'll frequently tug harder as if to rip the nipple from its moorings.

Weight

The second day in a puppy's life can often bring a weight reduction of twenty-five to thirty grams (about an ounce) without being abnormal, but thereafter it should steadily gain, typically some 10 percent daily for awhile. The pups should be weighed at the same time each day, and the ones that have not increased as much from the previous day should be fed first. If one is consistently lagging behind the others or not gaining at all, there is obviously something wrong. If small doses of *Karo*® and tube feeding don't give satisfactory results, there may be a birth defect that warrants culling, even if your decision has been delayed a week or more. While the numerical values were not scientific, I found an estimate in some of my old notes that three-quarters of such defective pups die within the first two or three days on their own, and over 95 percent have died before two weeks passed. I was later to find out that these figures were quite close to statistics from veterinary schools. If high puppy mortality is a recurring problem in your kennel, and you don't find the answer in a careful study of the bitch's health, and the sanitation conditions in the pup's environs, an autopsy would certainly be in order.

During the first week, pups seem to grow while you are looking at them, and will just about double in eight or nine days. Of course, there will be some variation, depending on their birth weights and the number of whelps in the litter. For instance, a litter of three or four pups is going to have much heftier individuals at birth than will a litter of a dozen, and the larger ones in a small litter will grow with a smaller daily or weekly percentage gain for awhile. The litter of twelve, if receiving adequate

While seven or eight is average, it is common for German Shepherds to whelp about a dozen. This patient bitch is nursing eleven pups! Photo courtesy Char Andres and Pamela Lukaszewski.

knowledge to add to my prediction if the bitch pup looks like the sire or a larger female in the pedigree. Over the years our 21-ounce (600 g) pups have not turned out to be significantly larger than our 14-ounce (400 g) pups from litters of similar size. Puppies will generally follow the growth pattern represented by the curve in Figure 18-2 during their first eight weeks. After this many will be sold so you'll not be able to keep an accurate record of development. There is more danger in too steep a climb on the curve than in falling slightly behind it, as overweight pups are more prone to orthopedic difficulties if genetically predisposed.

WEIGHT CHART

Males				Females		
Small	Medium	Large	Age	Small	Medium	Large
10 oz.	13 oz.	17 oz.	Birth	8 oz.	10 oz.	15 ozs.
20 oz.	24 oz.	36 ozs.	1 wk.	1 lb.	20 ozs.	32 ozs.
40 oz.	3 lbs	4½ lbs.	2 wks.	2 lbs.	44 ozs.	3½ lbs.
5 lbs.	6	8	3	3	4 lbs.	5
7	8	10	4	5	6½	7
9	10½	13	5	7	8½	10
11	13	15	6	9	11	13
13	15	18	7	11	13	15
16	18	21	8	14	16	18
18	21	23	9	16	18	20
20	23	25	10	18	20	22
25	30	35	3 Mos.	22	26	31
35	40	47	4	30	35	42
45	50	60	5	37	45	52
55	60	65	6	43	51	58
58	67	75	7	45	53	60
61	71	81	8	47	55	62
63	72	82	9	50	56	63
64	73	83	10	50	57	64
65	75	85	11	51	58	65
66	76	86	1 Yr.	52	60	67
68	78	88	2	53	62	68
69	79	89	3	54	63	69
70	80	90	4	55	65	70

Fig. 18-1. Weight chart based on weights of litters over a period of twenty years. Marie Leary's chart.

food, will gain a little faster in proportion to their birth weights, and will tend to catch up to their bigger counterparts by the time they are two- or three-months-old. Given equal nutrition, genetics determines size and growth rate differences between members of different litters.

Nor can you be certain the largest pup at birth, even if all seem normal, will be the weight leader at maturity, though there is a bit of a tendency to stay roughly in the same order within the same sex. In every one of our litters we have females that outweigh some of the males at birth by one to several ounces, but the males usually pass them by four to six weeks of age. One 12-ounce male in a litter of 10 pups (the rest all weighed 16 ounces or more) eventually became the largest when fully grown: 95 pounds at 1½ years. Marie Leary had created a chart based on litters over a 20-year period that shows that this male would've been under 80 pounds at maturity. Her statistical averages were no doubt correct, but I have found her predictions to be less accurate than guesses based on the sire's weight if the pup in question is a male, and the dam's weight if the pup is a female.

In predicting a pup's future adult weight it helps to know his ancestors, and sometimes I'll use this

Nervous System Development

Various portions of the anatomy develop at different times, often due to their dependency on the nervous system. At about the tenth day of life the eyes will begin to open. At first you'll notice only

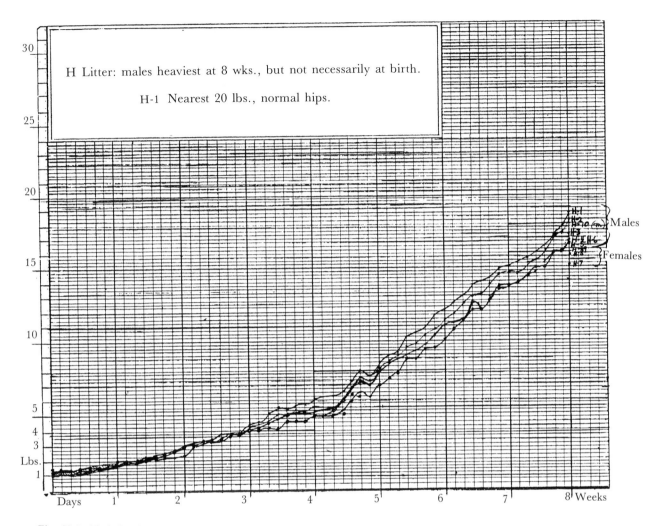

Fig. 18-2. Typical weight gain curve, over-middle size at adulthood.

a glint of reflected light, but the eyes will open a little wider each day. The color is a light, cloudy blue-gray which gradually darkens until the true color develops after a month. The pups can't see yet, but in another ten days they will be focusing and identifying familiar objects. The visual system seems to be complete by the age of four weeks, and recognition of mother, other dogs, and familiar humans develops between three and five weeks as the retina, optic nerve, and central nervous system continue to mature.

Meanwhile, other senses are in various stages of development. Those of heat and touch are somewhat functional at birth, and the ability to distinguish the dam's scent, or at least an adult-dog scent follows almost immediately. Ears become functional between twelve and seventeen days and by fourteen to eighteen days the brain recognizes signals from the ears. By twenty to twenty-five days the

pups have fairly good sound orientation. It's both fun and funny to experience them waking to such stimuli as hand claps with a sudden bark, lifting of heads, or wiggling. If your noisy presence is associated with dinner time, they'll lurch to their feet and bump around the whelping box like the dodge'em cars at the amusement park.

The swallowing reflex is initiated in the neonate by nursing or other application of liquid to the mouth and throat; a slight pressure on the tongue seems to work, too. The lick-swallow reflex, wherein a dog will swallow if you make him lick his nose, starts about at age three weeks, and is later used by the breeder to make sure the dog has swallowed the pill placed on the back of his tongue.

A sense of balance (vestibular sense) has been present since before birth, but the motor nerves won't catch up to the sensory nerves until later. By one week the typical pup is fairly able to hold his head in a horizontal position and by three weeks a greatly improved ability to orient his body will be apparent.

At one week, pups' motor nerves to the pelvic limbs have matured to the point where they can lift their hind ends to defecate, and can move about more easily. By ten days they should be standing (and falling and rolling over), and will walk with amazing facility only a few days later. Perambulation should be steady by three weeks and they'll run fairly competently by four weeks. For some time during this learning period the pups will often run backwards in circles upon waking and getting excited, like some of those wind-up toys that change direction when they hit the wall or a chair leg. Trotting and galloping require more locomotion control and even greater maturity of the motor nerves, especially to the rear part of the dog; these come about between four and seven weeks of age. Therefore, it's difficult to start evaluating gait before the age of seven or eight weeks. Some litters will show motor precocity and earlier or later development of perambulation skills may be due to handling, or may be chiefly genetic. One of our litters seemed a little more advanced than others: all eleven were walking around with considerable ease and sureness at sixteen days of age. Since they were born at a co-owner's house, I had not seen them between nine and sixteen days of age and haven't a clue as to the reason for this development.

In a litter we had early in our breeding program, we had one pup that repeatedly climbed the basement stairs to the kitchen while his littermates at three weeks of age were still trying to keep their balance as they stumbled, tumbled, and staggered around the room. Again, I can offer no opinion for this precocity, but guess at mostly a genetic reason for differences.

Although you won't "see" the nervous system growth, you *will* witness tremendous physical growth during the first two weeks. Some of the pups may need new collars during this time. However, if you can still fit your finger beneath one without much effort, you probably should wait, since collars are more likely to be too loose and a foot or foreleg can get caught in one and make locomotion and nursing more difficult. Their nails may be growing too, and these you can easily clip with your own nail clippers.

Weaning

Some time between two and four weeks you will begin the process known as weaning: making the puppies dependent on nourishment from sources other than their dam. Weaning should not be done by abruptly separating the pups from their mother, as this would cause psychological problems and would also be physically hard on the dam since she needs to have her milk production *gradually* reduced.

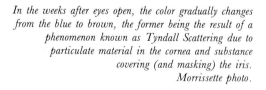

In the weeks after eyes open, the color gradually changes from the blue to brown, the former being the result of a phenomenon known as Tyndall Scattering due to particulate material in the cornea and substance covering (and masking) the iris. Morrissette photo.

Factors which will assist you in determining when to start and how fast to proceed include the number of pups in the litter, the health, age, and temperament of the dam, and whether you wish to get the bitch back into show condition quickly. With a small litter you may wish to allow the old, ''natural'' method, in which the dam determines when she's had enough of fang and claw, and the pups discover her dinner pan and learn what the grown-up world of food is all about. Unfortunately, this can be at about five or six weeks, and with twice her own weight in puppies hanging on her, milk production is unlikely to keep them satisfied. In the wild, canids masticate, swallow, partly digest, then regurgitate food in the nest for the pups. This is more likely to happen with a high-meat diet rather than with a primarily grain-based diet that comprises most commercial dog foods.

A variety of approaches can be used to wean the puppies, but timing and choice of diet should be taken into account. As an experiment, we began weaning one litter at nine days of age, just before their eyes began to open, and long before they could stand and walk. We used commercial strained baby foods, finding beef and lamb gave more enthusiastic responses than chicken or eggs. A finger was dipped into the jar and a dab of the food pushed onto the back of each puppy's tongue. The instinct to suck on anything in the mouth activated the swallowing reflex and at the same time the taste of meat registered: ''Wow!'' After that first taste, the pup went after the food like a Hawaiian politician after poi. The little rascals nearly skinned our fingers with their vigorous sucking and swallowing, and before long each pup had finished off half a jar of meat before his appetite seemed to be slaked. When we put them at the dam's nipples, however, they gladly found room for dessert.

If you prefer to wean your puppies at a later age, you can skip the finger-feeding step and go directly to pan feeding. Some breeders mix baby cereal with milk, and warm some finely ground meat in it. Rice has a higher protein level than some other grains, and you can buy a high-protein cereal blend as well. At first the consistency should be on the thin side and feeding should be timed so the dam has been away from the pups for a few hours in order to make sure they're hungry. After the feeding, bring in the dam so she can nurse them and clean them up. You can help with a warm, damp washcloth if you wish,

since feeding puppies can create quite a mess. To promote weaning, gradually increase the time delay between feeding and bringing in the dam. Coupled with her own reluctance to be clawed and the puppies' partial satiation, this will accelerate weaning.

It is also possible to successfully bypass the special puppy food stage and go directly to adult rations, provided you use a high-protein, very digestible food. This method is also cheaper and less work. Soak some dry food in a slurry of a little hot water and ground meat, raw or cooked, until it is soggy enough to be squashed with a fork, and loose enough not to be gummy or it will stick to the roofs of their mouths. Add a little melted or finely chopped fat (low-cost hamburger will supply this) and maybe a tiny bit of liver every few days. At first all this could be mixed in a blender then simply smashed with the fork when they get used to chewing their food. Initially the consistency should be that of a good milk shake: thick yet still liquid gruel.

As to the feeding dish—we have found pie pans to be just the right size for very young pups, and a larger food pan for weaning older pups. Make sure the rim of the pan is not so high as to press against their throats when they swallow.

As the puppies grow older and get fewer bitch's milk ''chasers,'' cut back on the proportion of meat to meal, so eventually meat replaces no more than 20 percent of the dry food by weight. As they get more and more solid food, even though it's soft, it becomes increasingly more important that they learn to drink water, so their total intake of food won't be too concentrated. Some of our litters didn't want much to do with water until age four weeks, but others started lapping it up earlier. The older the pup, the more he'll enjoy drinking water (and jumping and playing in it).

Roundworms

It has been our experience that in most litters roundworms show an effect during the third week, but in some cases they are evident earlier. If pups have a belly full, they will cough, gag and throw up a worm or two, or pass some in the feces. If pups are not so heavily infested, they will appear bloated after a solid-food meal. Another indication may be a weight stabilization or even a decrease near the end or middle of the third week. If, at an age under six to eight weeks, you notice a levelling off and the pups are not gaining their customary 10 percent a day (or whatever has been normal) you can be almost 100 percent sure they have roundworms.

Another method of detection is the microscopic examination. If you are not set up and experienced enough to do it yourself, take stool samples to your veterinarian for confirmation of your weight-watching. Take tiny samples from each pile, especially any loose stool, and save them in a cool, covered container. Add morning and evening samples for three to five days, and stir or mash them together, then take it to the veterinarian. The reason for all this collecting is that worms seem to lay eggs in "streams," and one stool sample may have none at all, while the next one from the same pup may be full of eggs.

Piperazine® is an old, relatively safe and moderately effective anthelmintic (wormer) for roundworms in puppies under four or five weeks of age. However, anthelmintics developed in later years have proven reliable, safe, and easy, so check with your veterinarian. I have recently switched to *Nemex®* , a wormer effective against canine roundworms and hookworms. It is pleasant-tasting and effective, as compared to the *piperazine*, which tastes so bad that the pups gag and try to spit it out. For their second worming, which may be ten to fourteen days later, you may want to use something stronger or different in its application. If you use something other than *piperazine*, you may not see those scary piles of wriggling "spaghetti," as some wormers dissolve the worms instead. In a couple of days after worming, weight gain should return to normal.

POSSIBLE PROBLEMS IN THE FIRST THREE WEEKS

While some deaths and other difficulties are genetically controlled or otherwise out of the breeder's power to prevent, many are avoidable if the midwife/pediatrician is knowledgeable and careful. Generally speaking, if you pay heed to the subjects of genetics, nutrition, sanitation, disease prevention, and management, you'll increase your chances for a normal, healthy, successful litter growing to adulthood.

Start with the bitch, for a healthy female will make for a healthy litter in most instances. Some drugs or excessive vitamin A administered during pregnancy have been identified as causing cleft palate, reduced litter size, mummified fetuses, and nervous system disorders, as well as eye, ear, and heart defects in the pups. Exposure to too much carbaryl (*Sevin®* is a tradename) insecticide may produce deformities in intestines and abdominal-thoracic fissures; other insecticides may cause skeletal deformities in pups if the pregnant bitch has been exposed to very high levels. Be sensible in your use of these, and your dam will likely be safe.

Like ducks in a row, writer after writer has followed the old line about a bitch sensing something wrong with a sick or abnormal pup, and pushing it away to die. Hogwash! The people who originated this may have had only one or two litters which were not watched with an inquiring eye, and others who have parroted this old wives' tale perhaps were less diligent or observant to be original and accurate. The bitch doesn't *know* the pup is unfit and intentionally push it away so the breeder can later find it isolated from the rest. In fact, bitches have been known to wash and try to care for stillborn pups, which should've been totally rejected according to this popular belief. And if I have seen a dam draw dead pups to herself, certainly others should have seen it happen, too. The truth is that the bitch doesn't intentionally neglect cold pups, she is probably simply busy with the others and doesn't want to leave them for the one. It's the pup himself that doesn't have the strength, maturity, or sense of heat to enable him to crawl and find the dam. He cries and in response she reaches over and licks him or turns him over to establish "here I am" as well as prepare to clean him and stimulate his urination and defecation. However, for whatever reason, the pup rolls over (and usually away) while the healthier pups respond properly to her warmth and vigorously scramble toward her for food and massage. In short, it's a failure of the pup to respond that separates him, *not* any special insight on the bitch's part. Our tendency to anthropomorphize leads us into some strange though understandable errors.

Statistics are of interest, though the amount of deviation from such figures greatly depends upon breed, experience, and environmental factors. On an all-breed basis, the average losses from birth to age of weaning run between 10 and 30 percent. Of these pups, some 70 to 80 percent die in the first two weeks. Inbreeding has also been associated with

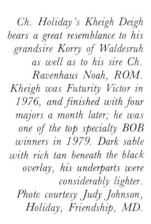

Ch. Holiday's Kheigh Deigh bears a great resemblance to his grandsire Korry of Waldesruh as well as to his sire Ch. Ravenhaus Noah, ROM. Kheigh was Futurity Victor in 1976, and finished with four majors a month later; he was one of the top specialty BOB winners in 1979. Dark sable with rich tan beneath the black overlay, his underparts were considerably lighter. Photo courtesy Judy Johnson, Holiday, Friendship, MD.

increased neonatal mortality and decreased vigor in individual pups, statistically, which is to say there are exceptions. Losses during the first day or first few hours can be categorized as *stillbirth* and *other*, with many causes for stillbirth, most of which are never discovered. Although a study of mixed breeds in England over a 5-year period had stillbirths accounting for less than 5 percent of deaths in the *first eight weeks*, other data indicate almost half of *first-day* losses are stillborn pups with no signs of life, yet no obvious causes of death. Less than 3 percent are mummy pups, some of which are never seen with others being detected and surgically removed at a later time. Another very small percent are malformed and incapable of living. Some 10 to 15 percent may be accident victims, though the bitch is almost as likely to step on and kill a pup during the coming days as on the first day. Perhaps 20 percent or more of first-day losses can be attributed to difficult labor; this percentage would obviously be lower if only easy whelpers were bred. A rare pup loss is due to cannibalism by an overwrought bitch or by overeagerness in removing the fetal membranes including the umbilical cord, with consequent transgression into the abdomen.

During the first week, the combination of the dam's carelessness and failure to lactate account for the greatest losses, and the latter may be partly due to the breeder's carelessness in the area of sanitation and prevention of infection. Statistically speaking, the less common causes of death in that first week include cleft palates which are probably found in less than 3 percent. Such pups either are euthanized on the second day or die soon after from aspiration pneumonia due to the milk they suck going through the nasal passages into the lungs. Exposure to heat or cold, almost always chilling, is a big killer of pups from the first to the sixth week of life, mostly in the beginning, killing anywhere from 10 to 65 percent, depending on kennel management practices. Chilling also exacerbates disease causes of death. Finally, about 10 percent of pups are simply found dead and the cause never discovered.

As time elapses worm eggs hatch and larvae develop, and as maternal antibodies wear off, pups become more susceptible to death by parasites and disease from the fourth and fifth weeks on into adulthood. The value of a good kennel management program is obvious when you take into account the combination of chilling and parasite/disease losses.

Hypoxia

Hypoxia, the medical word for a state of inadequate oxygen, can result from prolonged delivery whether due to the dam being tired or in poor condition, or to a difficult-to-expel extra-large pup. It can also be caused by the pup being too long in the sac after the placenta has been released (the bitch doesn't know what to do), or by the pinching of the umbilical cord between the puppy and the dam's pelvic bones during a difficult delivery. An initial respiration effort is also very important, as a lack of oxygen can yield a "slow" puppy, or even a sick one, depending on the extent of brain damage.

As the pup is whelped, the umbilical cord remains attached to the "life support system" of the mother. Soon the placenta releases from the uterine wall and the cord is crushed and severed by the bitch's teeth. By that time, the pup's head should be out of the sac and he should be making an effort to breathe. If born rear-end first and with a slow delivery, there may be a greater danger of aspiration of placental fluids, and fluid in the lungs or any other hindrance to full air sac expansion can have long-term bad effects. If there's any wheezing or gurgling, or weakness in breathing, swing the pup head-down while you hold the mouth open with a finger, or suck out the fluids from the puppy's pharynx. Don't waste time fumbling with tubes or aspirators—use your mouth.

Nursing Problems

As mentioned before, some bitches seemingly have no interest in mothering and should not be bred again. These should be identifiable before the first breeding as temperamentally unsound, but there may be a rare one that passes initial evaluation, yet fails the future tests of whelping and mothering. Some nervous bitches can be encouraged or trained to stretch out on their sides so that more teats are available; even calm bitches will sometimes lie on the sternum and hide the nipples. In general, good, secure whelping quarters should take care of the normal dam's psychological needs.

Infections will sometimes interfere with milk production or a bitch's willingness to nurse. In addition, premature pups or those that have been chilled or deprived of oxygen may not have a good sucking instinct.

Supplemental Feeding

Supplemental feeding of a commercially prepared bitch's milk substitute such as *Esbilac®*

is sometimes needed when an especially large litter is too much for a bitch to handle and a foster mother is not available, or when certain pups are too immature or weak because of chilling to fight for their fair share, or in the rare case of being orphaned. Also, the bitch may not be interested in nursing if the pups were delivered by C-section; she may not produce milk and colostrum, or she may have toxic milk infection. Three hand-feeding techniques can be used, the choice depending on a number of factors such as how much of the needs must be supplied by hand.

The eyedropper technique is used primarily for toy breeds and kittens, but other than for emergency or minor addition of sugar, this is not feasible for German Shepherd Dogs. For one thing it would take too much time to get appreciable amounts into them, and there is a chance some of the liquid could get into the bronchial tubes and drown the pup.

Bottle feeding—The bottle with nipple works a little better for large breeds, but most nipples are too hard and too big. Doll baby bottles may be the right size, but the nipples are still too hard, so cut an X into the top with a razor blade and the formula will come out easier. A method for softening natural rubber nipples involves boiling them long and often. This produces a softening called reversion, but in the process the nipple becomes sticky and hard to use. If you must try bottle feeding, use the kind with a collapsing liner to reduce the chances of colic, and ask for bottles and nipples used for premature human babies. Again, you may have to enlarge the holes with a razor cut or a red-hot needle or thin nail.

One advantage to bottle feeding over tube feeding is that it satisfies the urge to suck which, if denied, may cause lesions by pups sucking on each other. Also, suckling pups often gain weight a little better than tube-fed ones, but they do need to be burped to lessen the discomfort of gas bubbles.

Tube feeding—Tube feeding, also known as gavage, is faster, easier, introduces less air (if any), and delivers a known quantity before the liquid can cool off. In half an hour a whole litter can be fed, whereas bottle feeding can take that long for only a couple of pups, and your customer may not be cooperative—with gavage he has no choice.

The formula should be mixed at a few degrees above 100 degrees F., then fed when it cools down

Ch. Caralon's Phantom of Lebarland. This great son of Caralon's Hein was the most popular black stud used by fanciers in the U.S. and Canada. Photo courtesy Caralon Kennel.

to the normal body temperature of the bitch (around 98 to 102 degrees F.). A flexible vinyl tube the size of a #10 French catheter, available at most drug stores and any hospital supply outlet, needn't be longer than eight or ten inches. Buy a syringe of between 20 and 40cc capacity and make sure it fits the tube before leaving the store. Your syringe may be marked graduated in milliliters (ml) which are roughly equivalent to cubic centimeters (cc).

Your veterinarian can help you choose specific formulas for dehydrated, hypoglycemic, or otherwise sick puppies, but for simple supplementation purposes, mix up some *Esbilac®* or equivalent as directed, or use a 50/50 blend of cow's milk and canned evaporated milk. One cc of solution for every four ounces of the pup's body weight is a good

volume to aim for. If there is a possibility some of the pups have been chilled slightly, add one or two teaspoons of honey or corn syrup per cup of formula. However, if you are *sure* the pup has been adversely chilled, you need to bring him up to normal temperature before giving him formula, since visceral paralysis sets in when body temperature is below 94 degrees F., and formula cannot then be assimilated. Instead, give such a pup a sugar-water feeding first, to treat the hypoglycemia; a 50/50 mix of 5 percent glucose and lactated Ringer's solution followed in the next feeding by 10 percent glucose (one tablespoon honey or syrup in 9 or 10 tablespoons water is close enough in a pinch) every 20 minutes should serve two purposes: replace water and furnish metabolic energy for heat.

Again, make sure the solution is at 100 degrees F. if the pup has been chilled, though it's not as critical to maintain that temperature in the unlikely event that dehydration is the only symptom (this is a rare occurrence later in puppyhood, and caused by other things). Hold the puppy under the heat lamp when feeding.

Lay the pup on his side and place the tube on him in a position representing his alimentary canal, with the end at the region of the last rib, which is over the stomach. Note where the tube is over the mouth, and mark this with colored nail polish or a bit of electrical tape, for you won't be able to see the end when it is swallowed by the puppy.

Attach the tube to the syringe and with the tube's far end in the warm formula, withdraw the plunger to suck the milk substitute into the syringe. As you pass the tube over the tongue and down the throat, look for the swallowing reflex. Most first-time attempts are too hesitant rather than too forceful. However, if the pup chokes or gags when the tube is about an inch into the throat, you may be tickling the top of his windpipe, so back off and try again. Touching the middle back of the tongue should elicit the swallowing reflex, and make the procedure easier.

When the end of the tube enters the stomach the mark will be at or near the nose. The tube may have "bottomed out" before that, which means it has probably hit the curved wall of the opposite side of the stomach. In either case the tube is in the stomach and you can now slowly depress the plunger to administer the amount desired; this is determined by trial and error, with a weight gain of ½ to 2 ounces daily being the goal during the first week (less the first couple of days, more toward the last). If you continue to tube-feed, your weight gain goal will increase to three or four ounces per day by two weeks of age. However, weaning to solid gruel will reduce or eliminate the need for gavage by that time.

A warning: If you administer too much too fast, it can back up in the esophagus and run out the mouth, and some may even be aspirated into the bronchial tubes. That risk is small, though, and if you remember that there are about 30cc to an ounce, it would appear that ½-ounce or less at a time, given 6 or 8 times a day, will provide sufficient calories and nutrition for the newborn. To start with, give between 10 and 15 ccs at a feeding.

Go from pup to pup with the same tube, without worrying about sterilizing the tube. They all have the same germs in common, and you'll not introduce any that weren't already in the nest. With a large syringe, you can feed a few puppies before refilling, and if you keep the formula in a warmed ceramic container, such as a teapot, it'll stay hot enough to finish the tribe's meal. Feed less if you are merely supplementing the bitch's supply; more if the pups were orphaned. In the former case, as few as one to three feedings a day will do, but in the latter case, a half-dozen feedings should be the minimum. Allow a couple of hours or more between feedings or after nursing; an already-full stomach doesn't need more food.

Chronic overfeeding can cause soft, greenish stool instead of the normal yellow-brown, firm feces. A general rule in nutrition is: The more that is consumed, the less efficient is the digestion. The body tries to get rid of excess food quickly, passing it along faster than nutrients and water can be absorbed through the intestinal walls. The obvious result is loose stools. Use weight gain as your guide, with one ounce per day a pretty good minimum to set for your pups. They should increase about 5 to 10 percent in weight every day for the first week or two, but don't be dismayed if tube-fed pups don't double in the usual nine days. They won't.

By the time the pups are ten to fourteen days old, the windpipe may have grown enough that the feeding tube can accidentally enter it, especially if you purchased a #8 size instead of the recommended #10. Therefore, orphans or supplementally-fed puppies should be weaned earlier than normal. This can be accomplished by gradually alternating strained baby food and tube-fed formula. The pup will probably enjoy this compromise and will help him quickly make the adjustment to solid food. However, don't mix meat and milk for gavage since it is very difficult to clean the equipment and prevent it from clogging up the tube. Use your little finger dipped in strained baby food (meat) as soon as you can get a response.

Hypothermia

The leading preventable cause of death in neonates is chilling, technically known as *hypo* (less) *thermia* (heat). To help prevent chilling, keep the whelping box hot, and make sure all puppies get a chance to nurse, especially the first day. Although a new whelp can go a full twenty-four hours without food, the combination of insufficient milk intake and lowered body temperature can result in convulsions and death, especially in a small or weak puppy. If a pup seems unable or unwilling to suck, or if the skin is comparatively slack and non-elastic when tugged, feed a few full eyedroppers of *Karo*® or other syrup. By administering this source of glucose you will be furnishing an immediate dose of calories that will produce heat through metabolism. You may also want to begin tube feeding right away.

Lest the warnings about cold temperatures frighten the novice unnecessarily, let me repeat that a bitch I once obtained for breeding had been born in a northern Wisconsin snowdrift and suffered no ill effects. She grew into a perfect example of the health and sturdiness admired by von Stephanitz, and undoubtedly had sufficient milk and body heat supplied by her dam during the time it took the owners to find them and bring them into the house. The strength inherent in the breed is amazing, especially in outcrosses, and it behooves us as breeders to maintain that strength at the highest level. This is why many advise ruthlessly culling litters and refusing to breed deficient adults. If a non-suckling puppy fails to *quickly* respond to your efforts, it may be better for the breed to let it go, and best for the pup to *help* it go.

Many references cite ''normal'' rectal body temperatures as being 94 to 99 degrees F. between birth and one week of age, and 97 to 100 degrees F. during the second and third week. However, some of us maintain that just because a large majority have a certain condition or trait, that doesn't make it normal. I recommend that puppies whose dam is outside relieving herself be treated like orphan pups in the interim, with room or box temperature at 90 degrees F. from birth through the first or second day; 85 to 90 degrees F. till four days old; 80 to 85 degrees F. till one week; and 80 degrees F. till eyes open and pups begin to walk around. Less emphasis needs to be given to ambient temperatures after three weeks, since by then the pups are actively running around. If pups tend to be huddled, or the dam stays with them, slightly lower temperatures can be allowed. For the bitch's comfort, turn off the heat lamp when the pups are

nursing unless there's a history of chilling or poor nursing.

When puppies under three weeks of age are separated from the pile of siblings and the mother's body heat, they rapidly lose their own heat, with the ability to stay about 10 degrees above room temperatures for awhile. Therefore, a whelping box temperature of 90 degrees F. is close to ideal for healthy pups in the first days of life. But sick or chilled pups may lose more heat and require additional external heat at a higher level. After gradually warming a chilled pup by holding it against your skin under your shirt, keep him in an environment of 95 degrees F. until he improves. In addition, 85 to 90 percent relative humidity is beneficial in preventing dehydration in immature or cold-traumatized pups while they're being warmed; 50 percent minimum relative humidity is suggested for normal pups. Indoor humidity is best controlled by the use of a room humidifier, and you would do well to have one in the whelping room. Humidity gauges can be found in gift shops, discount stores, and the like.

Pups may survive up to twelve hours of considerable hypothermia while others may die in spite of your best resuscitative efforts. As an example of survival, one of our bitches whelped what appeared to be a stillborn pup while I was on an out-of-town trip—it had no life signs at all. While she was busy whelping her next one, my wife slipped the dead one away and put it outside on the brick patio so she could get right back to helping with the delivery of the rest of the litter. After the dam settled down for a breather, Jeanne went outside to dispose of the pup. This was Toledo, Ohio on a cool night, and when she stepped outside, she heard a mewing sound—the pup was alive and active, having crawled clear across the patio. This pup, a miracle of vitality, grew to be a normal adult, against all odds of even surviving the first few hours.

A warning on the use of extra heat is necessary here, since too much heat without compensating fluid intake can dehydrate pups. To prevent *hyper*thermia, the heat lamp should not be left on overnight or when you are away from home if it is possible you may be delayed in returning, unless the litter is orphaned and has no other source of heat such as a dam or a hot room. The heating pad, if you used one, should have been removed the first day, otherwise it could be damaged and its heating elements exposed by scratching or chewing. If it gets folded over on itself, the heat could become dangerously excessive.

Fading Puppy Syndrome

This is not one cause of death, but several mysterious ones which are gradually being identified through research. Most of the new puppies that succumb are apparently perfectly normal at birth. But then the pup loses weight or fails to gain any, becomes weak, and loses the urge to nurse. It fades away and dies, leaving the owner very puzzled and often distraught. Most "fading puppies" can be saved by following procedures for chilled pups and gavage, but occasionally one will simply be found dead without warning.

Foster Mothers

The Germans call her *Amme*, which can be translated as 'wet-nurse' or 'foster mother'—one given the task and privilege of nursing and caring for part of a litter. If someday you find yourself with an overly large litter or a pack of orphaned pups, you may find yourself looking for an *amme*. Try to find a bitch in good health regardless of breed, that has had a false pregnancy or a small litter, thus having sufficient milk to share. Early weaning or supplemental gavage (tube feeding) can do as well if a ready bitch isn't found or if it isn't feasible to use the one that has been located. However, if you are fortunate enough to find a bitch that can relieve you of some work, be careful how you introduce her to the pups. And best not introduce her to the dam at all, as most will have their killer instincts aroused; try for separate households.

Reactions to another dam's helpless whelps can range from instant mothering to curiosity to rejection or fear, and even to an urge to kill. Perhaps the safest method is to take as much milk from the proposed *amme* as you can, and coat the babies' hair with it, especially around the base of the tail and the belly. If *amme* has some pups already in her nest, rub the newcomers and natural pups together on all surfaces before allowing the bitch back into the room on a short leash. Have her lie on her side and upon presenting them to her, hold her muzzle in your hand and let her sniff and lick them as another person places them at her teats. Watch to see if she acts differently toward the new ones than she does

toward her own, if she has any. If she attempts to nip them, squeeze her muzzle and say "No!" Try again several times, praising her for any other action whether neutral or mothering. Gradually she should allow them to nurse, wash them, and even fall asleep while they feed.

Happy mother? Yes, but they aren't hers. When the real mother went out to "potty", Otti jumped into the whelping box. Always the professional mother, she had a need to possess and care for puppies, no matter whose.

If you stay in the box with her and heap praise on her every time she returns to the box or does the slightest thing correctly or acceptably, you'll reinforce the connection between caring for the pups and getting rewarded. Soon, in a few hours or a day, the puppies may themselves be her reward or her pride and joy.

If you add the excess or orphan pups to a bitch that already has one or a few pups of her own, the transition seems to be easier if the pups' ages are close and if the new pups are only a couple of days old. It has been reported that it is harder to get a bitch to accept older ones, but I can't attest to that as a fact. We had one bitch, the world's best mother, that seemed to want to adopt every young pup she saw, spotting them at great distances and dragging me over to them so she could inspect, wash, and herd them. Pups up to about 8-weeks-old and even some of other breeds were favorite objects of her mother love. A photo herein shows Otti in a nest of 9-day-old pups not her own, and although it had been a year since her own previous litter she was eager to get into the box, allowed the pups to make vain attempts at nursing, and gave them all a thorough bath before we coaxed her away so their natural mother could be returned to the nest.

Immature (Premature) Pups

As previously mentioned, the time of eye-opening is possibly the key sign for determination of prematurity. If eyes don't open until the thirteenth day, I think it possible that those pups were delivered two or three days before they would've been ready. Other signs of prematurity I have seen or have had reported to me by reliable sources include poor muscle tone (pups are flaccid and limp compared to others), tendency toward breathing abnormalities, low blood sugar, poor kidney and liver function, increased susceptibility to infections, pneumonia, undersized and weak, hemorrhage, and/or chilling. In addition, premature pups are usually smaller and lighter in weight, and there have been reports that many of them are lighter in color, duller in coat, have hair of rougher texture, or a combination of these. Others have reported apparently lower general health and vigor for some duration in time.

As a rule, premature pups are seldom vigorous nursers. Autopsies reveal liver weight is less than 1½ times brain weight, while normal newborn pups' livers are twice the size of their brains. Glycogen, a major source of energy, is mainly found in the liver, but newborns have a very small store of it which is rapidly depleted. Since glycogen is constantly replaced through the dam's milk, a non-nursing pup will be hypoglycemic by the second day.

Midline closure defects are apparent in some pups that seem to have been delivered before their time; sometimes the skin on the forehead doesn't knit or close well, leaving either a thin bald streak or a wavy line like a scar, or perhaps a folding of the scalp so that some hairs become ingrown and form cysts as the dog grows. Often, this type of defect will leave a line of white hairs, similar to the way white hairs will appear over scar tissue from an injury or over the site of an injection. Enough premature pups have dusty-dull hair with a hint of grey-brown to make me also wonder if there is a connection with the system's ability to organize melanin granules.

Disease

In addition to carelessness of the dam, chilling, dehydration, and low blood sugar, diseases also cause neonatal deaths. Although disease-related deaths are more common after six weeks of age, there are some that should be addressed in this chapter on the first three weeks.

Toxic milk syndrome—Toxic milk syndrome is manifested in a bloated appearance in a puppy up to about two weeks of age. It can be brought on by metritis in the dam, infection of her uterus, or rarely by toxic substances from other sources getting into the milk. Infected pups cry a lot, strain as if to defecate, and get red and swollen at the anus. They must be tube-fed and kept from the bitch's milk while she is being treated. This does not mean that they must be separated from the bitch herself, and a solution is to make a sweater or jacket for her so she can be with the pups without nursing them. If you notice bloating following feedings, but the pups are over two-weeks-old, they may have roundworms instead. In addition, if pups are allowed to nurse on the bitch's vulva there is a slight chance of their contracting an infection from the postpartum bitch which can give symptoms in the puppy identical to those of toxic milk syndrome.

Septicemia—Septicemia, a bacterial infection with any number of causative organisms, can also cause abdominal bloating, crying, rapid breathing, and weakness in pups in one to forty days of age. Preventive steps include assuring adequate sanitation and ventilation, as the germs love dark, wet, stagnant-air locales.

Umbilical cord infections—Umbilical cord infections in the first three or four days can be caused by streptococcus and other bacteria in pups that are born in and crawl around in filthy environments. The swollen abdomen may or may not be accompanied by a red navel and/or a cyanotic-blue color to the skin in the groin. Weakness and crying are again additional symptoms. Sanitary practices combined with a non-abrasive surface in the whelping box will prevent umbilical cord infections that must be treated both surgically and with antibiotics.

Herpes viremia—Herpes viremia, caused by a herpes* virus, is a major cause of death in pups between five days and three weeks, and may take two weeks to spread through the litter. Death from kidney and liver failure usually occurs within eighteen hours from symptoms which include constant crying, shallow and rapid breathing, loss of appetite and coordination, and a soft, yellowish-green stool with no particular odor. (The stool symptom can be easily missed if the bitch is cleaning her pups to make them defecate.)

Treatment includes elevating the environmental temperature, thus creating a sort of artificial fever since fever is one of nature's ways of fighting virus organisms. One hundred degrees F. for three or more hours is a recommended ambient temperature, followed by 90 to 95 degrees F. for another 24 hours, in combination with frequently giving the pups glucose solution and formula to prevent dehydration. Herpes thrives between 91 and 98.6 degrees F. (33 to 37 degrees C) and chilled pups are especially susceptible. At 100 or 101 degrees F. the virus stops replicating, so the object is to get the pup's body temperature up to that which is considered normal in the adult, about 101 to 102 degrees F. After three weeks of age, the pup's body temperature is usually high enough to prevent herpes growth. However, because damage to kidneys may not produce symptoms until as late as ten months of age, perhaps the pups that show the crying symptom associated with hemorrhage and necrosis should be euthanized right away.

A recently reported experimental treatment for active herpes infection involves the use of a Parke-Davis preparation designed for human herpes encephalitis. Twice-daily shots of ½ cc of Vira-A subcutaneously for five days has saved more than one bunch of puppies. Ask your veterinarian about it.

This virus can remain latent for many months and be reactivated by stress or an immunosuppressive agent such as a shot of cortisone or similar steroid. Pups seem to get the virus through the saliva of their infected dam, though a few may contract it in the birth canal or even in the uterus before birth. If you have a kennel in which two or more bitches are producing litters and one loses a litter to herpes, what should you do to save the next litter? Besides the usual step of cleaning everything with a dilute bleach solution (as with parvo or other viral infections), you may find success by having your veterinarian inject them with serum obtained from the bitch that lost the litter. You may also succeed by keeping them in the high-temperature environment mentioned above.

Other diseases—Other major causes of early death are heavy hookworm or coccidia infestation, especially the combination of the two. Coccidiosis often flares up when pups are stressed by sudden weaning, change in environment, worming, or vaccinations. This might mean that the protozoa, like mange mites in dogs and pneumonia germs in humans, are present most of the time, but "take over" in pups only when the resistance is lowered by some other force. Most coccidiosis cases occur after the age of three weeks, but it can be seen earlier if the dam was heavily infested with worms which were then passed to the pups *in utero*.

Diarrhea and belly rash—Although not technically diseases, either of these can be cause for concern. Diarrhea in the pup under three weeks of age can easily be the result of cows' milk given as supplemental or substitutional food. Such milk contains a partially indigestible saturated fat which is tolerated better by some pups than by others. Also, the lactose in cows' milk causes excess stomach acid production which inactivates enzymes made by the system. Also, not all pups are as able to produce lactase and galactase, enzymes needed to break down milk sugars. Overfeeding by gavage can be a cause of diarrhea in a pup of this age. Past three weeks, diarrhea is more likely due to parasites if the amount of food is normal.

Belly rash, also called *urine rash*, is a rather harmless condition marked by abdominal red spots with pustule centers which later scab over. It is caused by bacteria which multiply in the moist environment between a sleeping or nursing pup's belly and the floor. Although the origin of the moisture, usually urine, is not important, you can prevent this most of the time simply by regularly picking up the urine-wet papers and left-over food

---

*Herpes actually refers to a class of several viruses, so you may encounter the word used in the context of a human disease, or a disease in other animals. One of this class will not produce the same disease as will another.

messes. Rub some neomycin sulfate (*Panalog®*) on the pustules once or twice a day, and if the crust is loose, pick it off first. The rash will go away with sanitation, ointment, and/or patience until the pups are old enough to run around and find dry, cool places to sleep.

Eye infections—Infected eyes sometimes occur in the first week or just after, before the time they are due to open. One or both will be found to be swollen and tender, and the lid of the affected eye will have to be pried open, the pus expressed, and some ophthalmic ointment prescribed by your veterinarian applied. Administration is best done from the container, a tin tube with a long and narrow, almost needlelike nozzle with a smooth tip that will not scratch the cornea. The eyeball can recede an amazing distance into the skull, so don't be afraid to push that nozzle tip well into the area beneath the lid, in the hole the pus came out of. Squeeze some of the ointment out to flush the region clean, and do this three or four times the first day, and perhaps twice a day thereafter for a few days until the lid opens further and normal drainage is apparent. Use cotton swabs to wipe the eye and face around the lesion.

"Swimmers"

An infrequent, puzzling phenomenon is the litter in which many, if not all, of the whelps become strangely deformed sometime in the first two weeks of life. A flattening of the thorax and abdomen, top to bottom, becomes evident about a week after birth from some unknown cause. It happens most often in the dwarf (chondrodystrophic) breeds but has been seen in the German Shepherd Dog and other breeds. Instead of the thorax developing normally into a progressively deeper tube from the prosternum/neck area to the diaphragm, it forms more of a flattened cylinder with the height from floor to spine about the same all the way back to the loins, and perhaps even lower midway down the back. The forechest, instead of dropping from the prosternum to the last sternal vertebra, may even be concave, and as time goes on the puppy becomes even more pancake-shaped.

As the ribs bow out, the heart and other organs may be pushed into the pleural cavity and displace or decrease the air volume of the lungs; as a result, pups become lethargic, lacking in energy and strength. By the third to fourth week, when normal pups would be running around, affected pups have not yet learned to push themselves up into a standing position. If the extended limbs, especially front legs, are moved at all, it is with a paddling motion to the sides, hence the disorder is called "Swimming-Puppy Syndrome." "Swimmers" have very poor circulation, respiration, and ability to swallow food or keep milk in their stomachs, and as they are old enough to wean, are very slow when eating from pans. Stifles may be rotated underneath the belly,

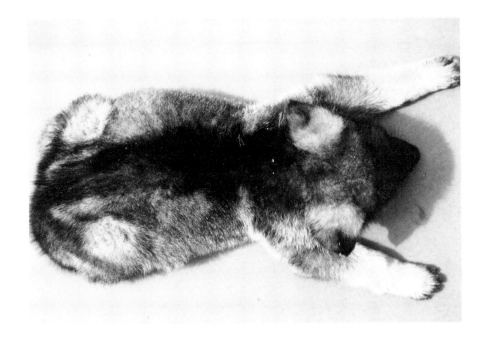

German Shepherd "Swimmer" pup. Note extended forelimbs and retracted hindlimbs.
Photo courtesy Dr. J.E. Harkness, Penn State Univ.

patellas are often luxated, and other orthopedic or osteochondral defects may be noted. Many die from inhalation pneumonia (from inspiring regurgitated milk) or other forms of respiratory failure.

If swimmers are not given some sort of therapy, there is a less-than-even chance they will survive to eight weeks. Those that do manage to live, only begin to walk at or after this age. A 1981 *Veterinary Medicine/Small Animal Clinician* report on a litter of Shepherd pups, five out of six of whom were swimmers, mentions one pup that started walking by nine-weeks-old, but by six months was still unsteady and slightly undersized (female, 40 pounds). Because she tired rapidly, even after only moderate exercise, she was euthanatized. Autopsy showed that her vertebra/rib joints were enlarged, but internal organs seemed normal in appearance. Based on this sort of evidence it's possible to conclude that there might be another cause for the weakness other than ventro-dorsal compression.

Many factors have been accused of contributing to the syndrome, both environmental and some of unknown genetic origin. For awhile, most people blamed slippery floors, but I've raised all my litters on smooth, impervious flooring covered with newspaper and have never had a swimmer in my own operation. The VM/SAC report mentioned above involved excellent footing in the whelping/nursing box: clean, dry, rough-surfaced indoor/outdoor carpeting. Until this report, it was generally believed that such a floor would prevent swimmers from developing.

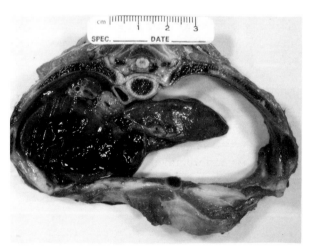

Cross-section of "Swimmer", at about the ninth thoracic vertebra. Left lung is compressed and heart is displaced into left plural (lung) space. Photo courtesy Dr. Harkness.

Some Dachshund breeders told me they were fairly successful in correcting the syndrome by putting each of the pups in a sling for at least part of each day. This practice encouraged them to make contact with the floor with their pads. Some tied hobbles to the front legs to keep them under the body and the elbows close together. This, they felt, prevented the front legs from becoming spread-eagled. Dish-shaped nests of straw have also been suggested, but not only does that present the danger of filthy conditions, it isn't practical. A modification of the idea has also been proposed: put the whole whelping/nursing area into a sling thus making the "floor" more like a hammock with the canvas or vinyl suspended at the corners and edges and lower in the center. I doubt the efficacy of any of these, but, as sailors used to say, "Any port in a storm."

Other therapy which may be beneficial, although tiresome and time-demanding of the breeder, includes massage (passive exercise), administration of vitamin E (with selenium added* if they're not getting solid food yet), taping hobbles to prevent splaying, and suspension in warm water. The last-named is probably the most promising if either active or passive movement can be induced. Thus, swimming (the *real* kind, in water) may help correct the swimming syndrome. Whirlpool baths are beneficial for partially-paralyzed or weak adults such as those suffering from coonhound paralysis, but of course the waves in such a tub would overwhelm a 3- to 6-week-old puppy. Therefore, hold him in your hand or a sling, with support to keep his head up out of the water, and let him paddle for a while in warm water (probably around 75 to 80 degrees F. to prevent chilling), but take him out and dry him thoroughly if he tires. As many of these sessions as you can manage should help the pup to develop coordination, muscle development, and better circulation while putting much less weight on his body. Your hand or makeshift sling plus the buoyancy of the water will take the weight off the chest. Finger manipulation of his limbs would be a good idea, too, while he's in the water, but also when he's out.

---

*Let your vet decide, as it's easy to overdose selenium, which is then toxic.

19

PEDIATRICS—
FOUR TO TWELVE WEEKS

While the first three weeks primarily involve the transition from helplessness to full sense and motor development, the second three weeks continue some of the same processes, but the emphasis shifts to two major areas: health and training.

The breeder who is able to pay careful attention to his charges during their early days will lay a good foundation.
—von Stephanitz

WEEKS FOUR THROUGH SIX

Endoparasites

Hookworm may be found in pups under twenty-five days if the dam had not been adequately wormed or if she did not have sufficient resistance or immunity, but most cases occur after three weeks of age. Because hookworm is usually contracted by walking in stools or soil contaminated by previously-affected dogs, puppies from wormed dams generally aren't bothered much before they are allowed to run around the back yard for a couple of weeks. Whipworms appear even later, if at all, and roundworms can be seen any time from about three weeks on to maturity. Tapeworm is seldom a problem in the young puppy unless there has been a really bad flea problem in his environment.

Coccidiosis can afflict a litter at almost any age, but most often after the twenty-fifth day, when the pups are more likely to be stressed by weaning,

worms, new experiences, and more exposure to the world. I've seen it in pups as old as five months, when it is less serious, although most of our affected litters have been between five and seven weeks. If it strikes earlier, you may have practiced inadequate sanitation or worm control. Flies have been suspected as carriers, but chickens, pigeons, and other birds are more likely to be the secondary hosts.

Coccidia causes feces that are runny, mushy, grayish or grey-tan in color as if the puppies had been eating clay, chalk, and liver as their total diet. If not immediately treated, you will see specks of fresh blood in the messes. Of course, sloppy, bloody stools can also indicate hook, whip, or even roundworms, but the gray color and an unmistakable odor are strong evidences of coccidia. It's the most revolting odor you will encounter in raising dogs: powerful and acrid, smelling a little like blood but mostly like nothing else you've ever experienced. Coccidiosis can be a killer of young puppies and can weaken and lower the resistance of older ones.

Treatment for coccidiosis is twofold: try to kill the protozoa, and treat the dog for the bacterial infections which result when the intestinal lining becomes raw and inflamed. I would administer a wormer, too, regardless of eggs present. Ask your vet for the latest medication which will actually kill the protozoa. Antibiotics are used for the secondary infection; tetracycline used to be prescribed, but it can discolor teeth. Nitrofurazone is still widely used, but most veterinarians recommend the combination of one or more sulfa drugs such as sulfa methoxidine, sulfa guanidine, or triple sulfa.

We have made it a practice to keep a supply of sulfa tablets on hand ever since discovering that section of Murphy's Law which states that coccidiosis will strike approximately five minutes after the veterinarian's office closes on Friday afternoon for a long weekend.

Most antibiotics must be administered for five to ten days, but once a puppy has fought off these protozoa with the help of such drugs, and has healed from the secondary infection, he usually has acquired immunity. Some may have to be treated again, but perhaps for a different strain the second time. It doesn't matter to the owner, nor to the veterinarian, which species of coccidia is present except as a point of academic interest, for they are all treated the same. If you have a microscope or are present when your veterinarian makes a diagnosis of coccidiosis, you will see oocysts, small spherical egglike forms, much smaller than roundworm eggs. Adults seldom have any problem with coccidia, but may be transmitters of the disease. In addition, many breeders report that once your kennel has had coccidiosis, you'll have it with every litter. In fact, we had coccidiosis recur with every litter born in our Toledo basement after one litter had come down with it. This may have been due to spores lurking in the cracks in the concrete and wooden walls where they meet the floor.

It has been reported that coccidia have an immunosuppressant effect, which means that when viruses or other disease organisms are present, they become more dangerous, interfering in some way with the puppy's immune system. There may be actually more of this effect in the reverse direction, the coccidia making the pup more vulnerable to the attack of the virus and bacteria. As an example, one of our co-owned bitches whelped a litter of nine very nice pups. The co-owner left the litter with a veterinarian while he went on a vacation trip, and when he returned, several had died and more were dying. The veterinarian was inexperienced in matters of pediatrics and had not properly treated the litter until it was too late, and a combination of hookworm and coccidiosis had killed the pups. Of the nine, only two were saved with much care and worry. By the time I was called, most of the litter had already died, and I could do nothing but help him in caring for the remainder, and in finding another veterinarian for his dogs. The two that survived were a little smaller than their parents, but grew into healthy, strong adults.

Juvenile Vulva

Some of your female pups may have a somewhat recessed vulva, almost turned in on itself. This is known as juvenile vulva, and some veterinarians will recommend surgery, especially if you intend on breeding the bitch. Don't rush to follow this advice. I've never seen any problems in breeding bitches that had this anomaly as youngsters, nor have I known of any to have whelping difficulties. I've seen a lot of pups with this condition grow up and produce litters with no surgical assistance. Most or all of the recessed nature is outgrown as the pup nears her mature size.

Umbilical Hernia

Possibly a result of the dam's vigorous tugging at the umbilical cord, a lump at the navel is occasionally found. See Chapter 12 for a detailed discussion of umbilical hernias. This, too, seldom calls for surgery, so don't panic and don't automatically agree to it.

Early Training

Memory development—It has often been reported that puppies have no memory until after about three weeks of age, and if so, the daily handling of pups under that age recommended by many dog psychologists may be of greatest benefit to the handler and the dam. I disagree. Regardless of whether this is true, it is extremely important to their behavioral development for puppies to be handled every day, the danger of understressing being much greater than that of overstressing them, given fairly normal kennel conditions. The pups should be thoroughly exposed to noises, strangers, other new experiences, and free play with siblings and dam.

With our many litters at Willow Wood, we made it a practice to handle pups many times daily, and let them get used to our odors, voices and touches. Whether or not they're "learning," there is a possibility of something akin to imprinting at work. This process is seen in fowl and some other species in which the newly hatched or whelped baby assumes the first living thing it sees to be a parent or sibling and follows it around. Dogs aren't as fully developed at birth, but recognition, association, or memory do not instantaneously appear on a specific day. We have seen many evidences of learning considerably before twenty-one days of age.

The noted veterinarian and author, R. W. Kirk, gives the following procedures to be used on puppies between three-weeks-old and the time they are sold. Stimulate auditory receptors with noises of all kinds; provide obstacles for pups to climb over and around, things for them to chase and catch, and stairs to learn to negotiate; introduce them to varied environments and visitors, including children; and begin grooming in order to teach them to hold still. There is no reason why one shouldn't use some of these procedures before three weeks, but they become especially valuable afterwards.

These second twenty-five days are the period of pre-socialization, in which puppies establish an order of dominance, learn the difference between themselves as dogs and other animals and humans, and how to relate to each. They can be reliably tested for temperament differences at seven weeks of age by holding them close to your face, making a vibrating noise with your lips, and observing their reactions. During this time period housebreaking can be stepped up and pups can otherwise be prepared for sale. We prefer to sell at three or four months, unless the buyer is knowledgeable in raising and training puppies.

This second phase of pediatrics is marked by much play, which is nature's way of teaching the pups the skills of combat, pursuit, and escape. Play also has value in later adult life, as such activity between puppies is the primary means of establishing dominance and interpersonal relationships. Pups that play rough may be less likely to be fighters as adults.

WEEKS SEVEN THROUGH TWELVE

Our canine companions need so-called basic training before we can expect them to reliably perform the more intricate maneuvers of the obedience ring, or exhibit the courage of a guard, or the reliability and patience of a guide dog. It seems that everyone has their own idea of when training starts, but after raising hundreds of dogs, we've found that the earliest phase of preparing a dog for life and work with humans and other animals begins almost immediately after birth. Von Stephanitz called it ''upbringing''; I like to call the first lessons ''manners.''

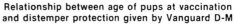

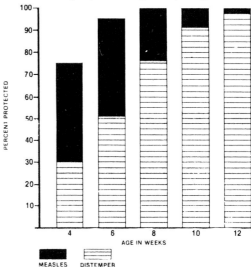

Most of the protection against distemper in a four-week old pup vaccinated with Vanguard D-M comes from the modified live measles virus portion, and that most of the protection such a combination of measles/distemper vaccines gives to the older pup comes from the distemper virus portion. Maternal antibodies, mostly obtained through nursing, may prevent MLV distemper vaccine alone from producing immunity, but measles virus stimulates a pup's own immunity regardless of circulating distemper antibody levels. Norden recommends the first vaccination with D-M at 6-8 weeks. Then distemper vaccine itself at 14-16 weeks. To protect against parainfluenza, they recommended two doses of DA2P or similar vaccine containing the ''P'', three to four weeks apart, then if both of these were given early, revaccination at four months of age or slightly more. This is especially important if Parvo (CPV) is part of the vaccine, such as DA2PL + CPV. The distemper and Parvo viruses are the most commonly encountered and most lethal, so your vaccination schedule should be based on these two.

Chart courtesy Norden Labs, Inc.

Association (Memory)

I use the term *association* rather than memory because the latter connotes some reasoning ability or ability to recall at will without specific stimulus. Ask a person to remember something that happened last Sunday, and his brain will scan and play back that day's specific events. If the dog has any such voluntary recall ability at all, he has it only on a very rudimentary level—a non-reasoning animal must be given a specific stimulus in order for it to respond. This is called association. Example: the words *go for a walk* or the jingle of a choke collar evoke in the brain an association with the stored sensations of previous walks on-leash.

In the area of training, dogs learn mostly by sound. The sense of hearing obviously is depended on by both dog and trainer when the animal is old enough to start formal training, but the question often is asked, "How young does it start?" In our experience, newborn pups do not react to loud sharp noises such as hearty hand-clapping until about ten days of age. This key age is a major milestone in the pups' life, with a number of changes beginning then: eyes start to open, sense of hearing rather suddenly comes about, and interest in food other than the dam's milk begins.

Generally, between ten and fourteen days the suckling becomes the infant, and responds to noise. As the pup approaches three weeks, he shows evidence of associating—remembering what sounds accompany or precede the food dish, for example. To me, this period of ten to twenty days of age marks the beginning of real trainability for it is then that we teach our pups to respond to the hand clap which announces our entry into the room, and to our voices as well. Since food or handling is always associated with these loud noises, the pups born in our house never recoil from such sounds. I believe such early exposure can help prevent gun-shyness from developing, even though that tendency is primarily an inherited trait.

Shyness

It is difficult to come up with a strict definition of shyness, but one that I think comes close to the mark is this: "Your dog is shy, mine is suspicious of strangers; yours has a hereditary temperament fault while mine was not socialized properly by his breeders; your stock produces spooky dogs, but my occasional reserved pup is a result of my being out of town during its critical period of socialization." While this sort of statement is given tongue-in-cheek, it *is* pretty true that many will excuse behavior in their own dogs that they would be quick to condemn in others'. This can be attributed mostly to kennel-blindness, but may be true in part because the owner is familiar with the background and experience of *his* dog but not of his *neighbor's* dog.

Timidity is often used as a synonym for shyness but I believe the terms are slightly different. A *timid* gundog or hound will typically roll over, dribble urine, wag his tail, grin, and exhibit other signs of submission. The extremely *shy* Shepherd Dog (or other breed) will go to any extent to avoid human contact by tucking his tail to his belly and running away. The mouth will usually be tightly closed and the dog will control his bladder unless caught by the human. I see submission-timidity as more a sign of domesticity, while avoidance-shyness concerning humans as a wild trait. This distinction needs to be clear since it is important that we

Gen Eve's Padrino Von Salix CDX, OFA "Bronx" and the wee ballerinas.

Ch. Caralon's Thor von Howard. OFA-normal. This bicolor son of Ch. Phantom v. Lebarland and the "Pacific Coast Victrix" Ch. Howard's Retrace is distantly linebred on Bernd and Nordraak, with lines to Lance and Gengis as well.
Owner: C.L. MacDowell
Photo courtesy MacDowell

retain some degree of suspicion, reserve, and aloofness which are related to the avoidance trait in the German Shepherd breed, so the dog will have the sharpness and excitability so necessary to training for biting, guard, and other work which we expect Shepherds to perform. A breeding program which is designed to eliminate *all* shyness may also eliminate the sensitivity needed in some of the work the German Shepherd Dog will be required to do.

The wolf-related shyness is at least part of the reason German Shepherd Dogs have become known as "one-family dogs." If a pup is not given much human contact between four and twelve weeks of age, he probably will develop a much greater fear of strangers than he otherwise would. An abundance of genes directing shyness *will be accentuated* by such an environment since, like other polygenic characteristics, shy temperament is expressed in a continuous gradation, and is greatly influenced by environment. The genetically very shy dog may be only minimally helped by intensive socializing during the period from one to three months. The moderately affected dog may come through this period without very noticeable personality defects only to develop shyness about the age of four or five months. I've had a couple of dogs that were perfectly normal at three months when I got them, but in the next couple of months developed a mild shyness that took up to a year of age to disappear as maturity approached.

Shy dogs that have not been given maximum exposure to new stimuli, including humans, during that 4- to 12-week-old period, tend to form strong attachments with the individuals or families with whom they *did* have regular contact. These dogs generally do not change, but there are enough improved dogs produced by extremely patient people to prove that changes *can* be effected with hard work. Therefore, I strongly recommend stressing your puppies frequently and increasingly from the age of three weeks on. Take them out onto the lawn, or even in the snow if the sun is shining on their dark coats. Subject them to something new every day, or several times a day if you can. Never present them with anything frightening, but always give them a challenge, even if it's only a grasshopper or a dried leaf. Puppies should be encouraged and assisted to search, investigate and satisfy an ever-growing curiosity. The safety of the pack will help them feel secure, but pups should also be introduced alone to new people and environments.

After your puppy has been vaccinated and protected from parvo, distemper, and other viruses he may be exposed to, take him with you everywhere you can. Introduce him to everybody and everything, and while you are thus building his ability to handle these controlled stresses, you are spreading good will for the breed (that is, if he has relieved himself before leaving home). Be sure your pup hears a variety of noises, sees all sorts of sights,

1952 Grand Victrix Ch. Afra v. Heilholtkamp

and meets a lot of people, especially children. I've seen many a puppy grow up in an adult human world only to be almost terrified when they have their first encounter with a toddler or small child. In short, the more you expose your pup to the world while he is between four weeks and four months, the less will be the chance of his exhibiting shyness.

Shyness has a polygenic basis which is so greatly shaped by early experience that many consider it an almost entirely environmentally determined trait. I have raised too many German Shepherd Dog puppies to agree with such a conclusion. However, near-miracles can be yours if you patiently socialize the shy dog, with greatest success if you start early. Shy dogs can even be trained for obedience competition and other work even if they never develop a happy, independent, confident attitude. The principle to apply with such a dog is the same as for the blind guide or Shutzhund candidate: ALWAYS WIN. Never let the dog be defeated by the unknown, the unfamiliar, or the downright frightening; rather let him know you are backing him up in his investigations. If he is too timid to exercise his curiosity, bring him along as *you* do the investigation, then praise him when he finds out that shadowy object is just a bush or some other harmless thing. Use your imagination to provide

other types of opportunities for your pup to overcome his own fear of his world.

Discipline

It is an easy transition from early response to voices into learning the word *No,* especially when it is accompanied by unpleasant action such as restraint or squeezing the pup's muzzle. This latter technique will be the most valuable trick you'll ever learn in the field of training methods. It's the same technique used by the dam when she wants to discipline them or just show them who's boss. She will bite them on the head or muzzle, hard enough to make them whimper or yelp.

Reprove your child with your left hand, and draw him closer with your right hand
—the Talmud

You must take the dam's place if you wish your pups to learn more than just to stop nursing. We have found the first problem, and thus the first lesson, involves biting the face. Puppies love to try out their dental needles on each other, your hands, and your shoes and cuffs. Hold them up close to your face and they entertain themselves by biting at your hair, ears, and nose. Given the terrible, largely undeserved reputation of German Shepherds being "mean" dogs that attack children and helpless old ladies, it becomes extremely important that *your* dog learns how to conduct himself when face to face with a rough, careless child.

To teach a dog not to do something, grasp him firmly by the muzzle between his eyes and nose, and squeeze. Make sure the tongue is not sticking out, then really bear down hard until the dog whimpers. You are doing no damage at all, so don't be afraid to use maximum pressure, especially on larger, older pups. Insufficient force is as good as none. A cry or whimper doesn't mean the dog is suffering, but indicates surrender and submission. Combine the sternly-voiced admonition, "No!" with the squeezing, and later on the word alone will be sufficient. In any training, the command (or signal) given along with the physical action teaches the meaning of the word while you show the dog the difference between good and bad behavior.

A larger dog may require the use of both hands to keep the mouth closed and exert sufficient force to get his attention, cause enough discomfort, and assure an escape-proof grip. This is especially true when the trainer is a woman or child with small hands. If the dog is strong enough to shake his head loose, one hand can be used to grasp an ear, but it is rare that this step is necessary. Start your discipline early in life since it's easier to teach the tiny 3-week-old the meaning of *No* than it is to struggle with a 70-pound mischievous miscreant.

If you have already trained a German Shepherd, you will have discovered that a dog of this breed is smart enough to learn quickly, but also smart enough to test you again to see if whatever he did was really connected with the correction. It's as if he's saying to himself, "Is that really what he meant? I'll try it again to find out." Usually a German Shepherd Dog has to be told something *twice*. Therefore, when whimper follows correction, release your hold, praise the dog, present the temptation again, and be ready for another immediate correction. Squeezing the muzzle is a sign of authority and dominance easily understood by such hierarchal animals as dogs, and the pup will generally respond by sticking out its tongue as a sign of submission. It may just lick its own nose

or try to lick your hands. It is best that the licking be done at the same location as the biting, or nearby. If the pup licks your nose when you present it again, it has learned two lessons: (1) not to bite faces, and (2) the human is higher in authority.

With large active litters all learning these lessons at the same time, my nose could get too sore, so I would hold each pup up to my ear and say, "Give me a kiss." If it responded with a bite, we'd go through the steps again until it licked my ear. Learning that phrase also has proven to be of value, for many a time we've given babies and toddlers their first introduction to a large dog that would kiss on command. This has helped many children overcome a needless fear of dogs instilled in them by parents who have a terrible habit of saying, "Don't do that, he'll *bite* you," without the slightest realization that they're driving a wedge between child and dog. This activity is also good for the dog since it reinforces the dog's habits—the more he kisses, the less the chance of biting.

Before going further, let's review the heart of your basic training manual. The following are the steps that should be followed, with no lapse of time at all between them. Immediacy is very important for effective training.

Step 1. Make the correction *firmly*; too mild is worse than none at all.

Step 2. Follow the correction with *praise* immediately. The dog must realize right away that you still love him, and that the absence of wrongdoing is right action in itself and brings commendation. Petting and saying, "Good dog" is enough, but do it with feeling.

Step 3. Present the same temptation to the dog and be ready to repeat steps 1 and 2 if he yields.

When re-exposing puppies to temptation, you must remember that repetition reinforces the learning process, but the effect is diminished if there's a time lapse between events. If it's face-biting, thrust your noses back together again right away, scratching behind the pup's ears, or petting him at the same time. If it's chewing furniture, put it back in his path. Better yet, do your muzzle-squeezing while the rung or corner or whatever *is still in his mouth*, holding firmly so he whimpers for a good two or three seconds. The taste and feel of the article being chewed will become associated with pain and discomfort. If you quickly thereafter distract the pup with a toy or rawhide, praise and pet him while you do so.

"Do not call to a dog with a whip in your hand"
—proverb, Lesotho, South Africa

Reinforcement—Reinforcement is another concept in learning/training. If a dog does something you like and you give him a reward such as a tidbit or strokes on his back, you do so in the hope that the reward will positively reinforce the action making it easier for it to happen again. Reinforcement can also be negative, with an undesirable action by the dog being inhibited because he associates it with something unpleasant. Immediacy of the reinforcement is almost a necessity for association and thus good results. Intensity is another important factor in training: if your admonishment is weak and the pup interprets your correction or spanking as a love-tap or a minor interruption, you and your trainee both lose. If your praise is ridiculously lavish, especially with a puppy or with a dog that has been mistreated or mistrained, it'll work better and faster than a softly spoken, "Good dog."

At the heart of every learning experience are these twin motivators of positive and negative reinforcement. The dog should find that doing right brings pleasure and that doing wrong results in discomfort. Even though a reward may be only the *hope* of positive reinforcement, let's use that word and add another motto to hang in the kennel: REWARD AND PUNISHMENT. Be sure that the punishment is not abuse. As a matter of fact, the word *punishment* so often indicates cruelty that a more appropriate word would be *correction*. In the same vein, a modification of that motto would be: (The promise of) REWARD and (the threat of) PUNISHMENT. It'll have just as much effect as long as the dog knows your definitions of the terms. You can inflict pain without damage if you squeeze a pup's muzzle, and you can make a dog very uncomfortable if you tighten up on the choke collar or step on his rear toes if he tries to climb on you, but never carry the correction further than necessary.

Many novices fail to *combine* love with correction; they love their dogs, but they don't show it as the *same time* with the correction. The longer the interval between the two, the more likely the pup is going to develop into a cringing, unhappy adult that acts as if he expects to be kicked at any moment. Expressing love is to often neglected because the people involved don't understand the nature of love. A wise parent corrects the child out of love, not hate or anger. In the same manner, puppies grow into

"You play with the baby, dear: I'll keep watch out for wolves and polar bears."
Photo courtesy Mary Schuetzler

better dogs if love is communicated to them during correction.

Love me, love my dog.
—Latin proverb.

These steps, *Correction, Praise,* and *Temptation,* in that order, can be applied throughout the dog's life to any circumstance. There is no truth in the saying that you can't teach an old dog new tricks. New circumstances may demand new lessons, and the German Shepherd Dog is certainly up to learning them at any age. Another motto to carry with you whenever you wish to correct your dog (or child) is this: FIRMNESS WITH LOVE. One is incomplete and ineffective without the other.

Individual Variance

It must be said that each trainer is an individual, as is each dog, and the training tips may have to be suitably adjusted. While I do give specific examples, training instructions mainly have a conditional value. Some dogs are by nature phlegmatic, others hyperactive, but almost without exception, German Shepherd Dogs have an innate desire to please, which is the key to a dog's education and the master's satisfaction. Understanding the impulses of the dog's soul and the personality variances between individuals will help you successfully train your dog. Therefore, I recommend that you read good books on dog psychology such as those written by Whitney, Pfaffenberger, and Fox.

If you are shopping for a dog, first determine what you will be using him for, then look for the characteristics necessary to fulfill your objectives. The buyer should not only analyze the nature of the dog to be trained, but also his own temperament and willingness to learn. He must always strive to improve himself in the areas of patience as well as technique, for this combination, as I've said, is the basis of all training: firmness with love.

If you are raising puppies to sell, you will make your customers' training efforts easier and more effective if you look for each pup's different talents which can be molded to fit his future vocation. The

pup that enjoys tug-of-war games might best be sold to a police department or a Schutzhund enthusiast. The ebullient, active one would be best for a buyer who plans to train for obedience trials or some daily work, and the quiet pup would go perhaps to a retired couple looking for a companion. By getting to know each pup, you will increase the chances of placing them in suitable environments. Also, when you sell a pup the buyer should be given advice on how to conduct his dog's continuing education to further enhance the chances of success.

Exposure to Unfamiliar Surroundings.

In training your dog the single most important ingredient to strive for is confidence, and the next, perhaps equally vital, is obedience. Even the companion dog in a very secure environment needs to be confident, not flighty or easily shaken. This is even more important for the future guard or protection dog, but preferably each member of the German Shepherd breed would be willing to protect his friend/owner.

Fear is normally not part of a pup's make-up from birth to approximately four weeks of age. But perhaps partly from the dam's discipline, partly from the extremely rapid expansion of their bewildering universe, puppies may show signs of fear around the age of six to sixteen weeks. Although the age of onset varies widely with individuals and is somewhat influenced by the amount of exposure they have to new, strange situations, inheritance plays the biggest part. The more genes for excitable and shy temperaments they have inherited, the greater the effect of isolation. Generally, puppies raised outdoors with a large field of view have a better chance of avoiding most of the fear circumstances encountered by those raised in a basement or kennel building for the first couple of months. Therefore, when they are finally exposed to new situations, these react with fear.

A 1961 study by Freedman, King, and Elliot found that beginning around seven weeks of age, pups that were brought up in an open field where they could not see people were hesitant when introduced to a stranger in an enclosed area. Even though the observer was passive, those pups that were not introduced to strangers until they were three months old had an immediate fear response and never developed a willingness to approach strangers on their own. Dr. J.P. Scott of Bar

Harbor discovered great similarities to wild species among 14-week-old pups that exhibited strong fear and avoidance responses when first exposed to humans.

Just as exercise promotes physical strength, and gradual or controlled exposure to weak antigens results in immunity, exposure to strange events and objects encourages the development of confidence in the dog. But the exposure must also be controlled and planned so as to avoid presenting too stressful a situation. Each experience must be only *slightly* more of a challenge than the previous one, or the pup will be overwhelmed and the trainer will be forced to take many backward steps to start all over again. And this time the risks of failure will be greater.

Puppies should be taken outside as soon as possible after they start walking, so they can gradually expand their world. If this is done often enough and for long enough periods before the age of fear development, one may be able to almost totally guarantee the development of confidence to the fullest extent allowed by the dog's genes. Begin with the ground. Puppies first exposed to a footing other than newspaper or carpet are so fascinated by the grass, dirt, and gravel that it first seems that they will never look up beyond their noses. But very soon the world balloons out to include leaves and twigs, then a garden hose, the stairs, then bushes. Eventually they notice some of the things around them are moving! It's a wonderful time for puppies, and a wonderful time for owners to present new experiences to build up their confidence and thus mold the character described in the breed Standard.

Every dog is a lion at home.
— E. Tilney, 1568

I don't recommend introducing new dogs or cats to puppies of this age because of the danger of disease due to the decrease in maternal antibody titers. New people are only slightly safer, so until the pups are vaccinated and have had a few days' chance to develop their own immune response, limit their confidence training to objects on your own sheltered property, if possible, not a lawn or area accessible to roving neighborhood dogs. An excep-

tion can occasionally be made if the visitor is one who has not had recent contact with dogs, or at least dogs from other than a strictly guarded environment. Dragging branches so they can attack the twigs, tossing plastic milk bottles around, clanking chains, and dropping things should be done purposely with an eye on how the individual pups respond.

If your pup shows some trepidation about a distant bush, rock, or person, pick him up and carry him to the object of his suspicion. The main sense of the canine, the prime means of understanding and communicating with the world, is the sense of smell. Vision is poor at any age and probably much poorer at very early ages when what *is* seen is not understood until it is also smelled and examined up close. The young pup must be introduced to this new world in such a manner that he becomes convinced that the strange and unusual are harmless and without danger to him. This is best done by allowing him to examine these things by scent as well as sight.

While you are approaching the strange new object, pet your puppy, hold him close to your face, and talk softly to him. He must associate the unknown with pleasant things in order to avoid or overcome fear, and the most pleasant thing in his life at this point is probably you. If he struggles, stop and wait a few seconds, then proceed. Soon he will realize there is no danger and next time he can be brought faster to the object of his fear; he may even approach it on his own. Pups of bold nature as well as the more reticent need your help to build confidence.

An excellent time to teach confidence is at night. You will quickly learn how to encourage your young dog to investigate things in the dark if you remember this principle: EASY DOES IT. Don't rush up to the unknown object; go at the speed at which your dog is willing to proceed. He will feel more secure if he is on a leash and heeling, if you have already taught him leash work. Even if you haven't, you should either take him up to the object on-leash or carry him. The loose dog may investigate only so far and then run away, and since you don't want him building a habit of retreating don't give him the opportunity to do it the *first* time. Besides, the leash or your touch means security to him, so make him feel secure.

The larger world outside your own property can be explored once the dog has been vaccinated. If a strange dog is brought to your home, your own pup will likely bark at it, showing much confidence in his own territory. This is especially true if such strangers have not been introduced in the past. However, if you were to take your pup from his familiar surroundings to someone else's property to meet that same dog, chances are he would act submissive, even somewhat unsure of himself. Puppies that are boisterous when with their kennel-mates, behave in very much the opposite way when individually taken from among them and presented to the new, older arrival. If the visitor is a miniature breed, your puppy may at first mistake it for another pup or an inferior, but almost assuredly will quickly find out otherwise. The first time we took three puppies to a fun match they carried on as if they wanted to eat up all the dogs that came near their crates. But on-leash we had to drag them past snoozing Setters, disinterested Dachshunds, and peripatetic Poodles. However, by the end of the match they had learned enough about those other strange creatures and settled down to the point that one of them won the all-breed competition, and at an age under the actual minimum for the show! Training a pup how to ignore or get along with other animals may be a fairly easy and rapid procedure if you use a little patience, persistence,

and experience. That combines two of the principles you've learned so far: *Firmness With Love,* and *Easy Does It.*

Dogs bark loudly at their master's door.
—Babylonian Talmud, about 400 A.D.

Besides other dogs, there are multitudes of new experiences in the "outside world." Traffic is one of these, be it pedestrian or mechanical. It is important that the dog learn to heel in such environments so he will be under control and at the same time feel safe and confident. So be confident yourself—it's contagious. Expect your dog to be at your left side; even better, demand it. And don't allow any lagging or forging ahead, though you need not insist upon precision drilling—that will come later, when you are preparing for competition. For now, concentrate on keeping him from getting underfoot, and on building up his confidence. You can do this by: (1) talking to him almost constantly during the greatest stress, (2) praising him lavishly, (3) giving him directions to follow (heel, sit, etc.) that are easy enough but demand his attention, and (4) *gradually* presenting more and more difficult situations for him to cope with, always with you at his side.

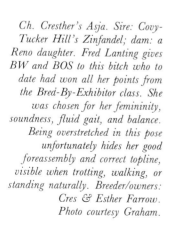

Ch. Cresther's Asja. Sire: Covy-Tucker Hill's Zinfandel; dam: a Reno daughter. Fred Lanting gives BW and BOS to this bitch who to date had won all her points from the Bred-By-Exhibitor class. She was chosen for her femininity, soundness, fluid gait, and balance. Being overstretched in this pose unfortunately hides her good foreassembly and correct topline, visible when trotting, walking, or standing naturally. Breeder/owners: Cres & Esther Farrow. Photo courtesy Graham.

Socializing

Much (*too* much, probably) has been written in dog club newsletters, psychology books, and magazines about the "critical socialization period" and the dangers of emotionally traumatizing 8-week-old puppies. Almost all of these writings have been based on theories and observations of Dr. C.J. Pfaffenberger and Dr. Michael Fox, but a lot of them have been too dogmatic and exclusive of many exceptions. Regard their warnings only as generalizations, not carved-in-granite ultimate truths. In our litters we have not seen adverse effects on pups when we have subjected them to the types of changes Fox says are hazardous at the age of eight weeks. These have included hip palpation, fasting, long trips in a crate, worming, anesthesia, moving to new homes, and other stimulating, tiring, exciting, or unhappy occurrences. Many times people draw conclusions from experience with some breeds or families and apply them erroneously to all.

Pfaffenberger, in his study of guide dog qualities, found an initial "critical period" to be the first three weeks of a puppy's life in which only the necessities of survival were important. This was followed by a month-long period through the age of seven weeks in which relationships with others, especially other dogs, was found to have life-long effects on puppies' temperaments and behavior. As a matter of presumed fact, all environmental stimuli were believed to be most important during this second phase. Even though memory may not fully develop until after three weeks, Pfaffenberger's statement that environment has *no effect* on the puppy's personality until it is twenty-one days old is an exaggeration I have seen parroted in print by so-called experts who sound as if they have never raised so much as a single litter.

My belief is that if a pup is taken from its dam and littermates before seven weeks of age, he may not ever adjust to being a dog. Therefore, we make it a rule to sell no pup under eight weeks unless both of two conditions are met: (1) the buyer must have successfully raised a puppy before, preferably a large breed, and (2) the pup must be going into a home with other dogs, preferably young and playful.

Human Interaction

Socialization with humans should begin between three and five weeks and continue through three or four months. It may be a good idea to expose the pup to some visitors who are not particularly interested in dogs so you can teach him that he need not fawn over every new human. Von Stephanitz urged us to have strangers reject the advances of a curious, friendly pup by shoving it away. If the strangers don't do it, surely *you* must, since real life will occasionally present non-dog people to your pup.

Often, a pup from a large breeding kennel or a commercial "puppy farm" will have a considerable avoidance response. These dogs may have been socialized early until weaned and vaccinated, but then isolated from varied human contact during the latter part of the socialization period. This is known as "kennel shyness" and unfortunately, it is almost never "curable," although it is controllable, with some improvement trained into the dog. There may be breed, family, and sex variations as well. I have known of many German Shepherd Dogs, almost all females, that have developed a shyness similar to the above, after or around the age of twelve weeks, even though they had been and were still in the process of being socialized. Most of them came out of it by the time they were ten to twelve months old, and often the change coincided with the completion of the first estrus.

Over the years, we have discovered a pretty sure way to identify the pups that will later be bold versus those that will develop into withdrawn or fearful individuals. Pick up one pup at a time, making sure he doesn't feel that you will drop him, then note his reaction to being held close to your face. Give him positive points if he wags his tail, joyfully bites or licks your face, or wiggles and squirms to get loose so he can go after your shoelaces or his siblings. Negative points would be given to the pup that acts tense or remains still and disinterested. Worse is the pup that blinks, pulls his head back, or quietly looks away (avoidance) when you make a strange noise in his face. At seven weeks, this is nearly a foolproof way to separate the genetic cowards from the bold, aggressive pups. The test can also be performed at five weeks, or at eight or nine weeks but the resultant prediction seems less accurate.

If you are planning to donate a dog to a guide dog school, there are certain aspects of his training and socialization which are very important. The candidate must be removed from his littermates and dam by about twelve weeks of age, for beyond that age he forms too strong a dependence on the dominance of the older or stronger-willed pup, and will probably fail most of the tests in school.

Personality Dominance

It is both fun and educational to watch the hierarchy develop in a litter. This order of dominance almost always has the largest male at the top, with a noticeable authority gap between him and the next pup, though you will no doubt encounter exceptions—*we* have. The further down the line you follow the progression, the less distinction there is between individuals because all are too busy following the "top dog" instead of the one directly above him. This is even noticeable at birth, where the strongest pup usually gets the biggest rear teats to nurse on. If you sold the number 1 ("alpha") male, the next in command would take over.

Among females, the bossiest little gal is not always the biggest, but is almost always noisier and feistier than the others. Between males and females the hierarchal structure is less ordered, with little "bossing" of the opposite sex. When a female puppy gets the better of a smaller male in a wrestling match, it doesn't appear to be at all permanent—the male may come right back a few moments later and best her. The most dominant pups generally become the boldest in regard to relationships with humans.

Leash Work

Some dogs never see a leash until they're nearly grown, others are introduced to leash and collar almost as soon as they can walk without falling all over themselves. Whether one time or method is better than another will depend on what you want to accomplish. If you hope to get into obedience competition training or fun matches at an early date, you may wish to buy a few small nylon choke collars of different sizes so they can be changed as the pup grows.

Start by letting him drag a fairly heavy leash around while you and he play games on the lawn. When he gets used to that, graduate to letting him lead you around while you hold the leash up and keep just enough tension on it so he knows you're still with him while he explores benches, hydrants, and bushes. The next step is teaching him to come to you. Don't drag or pull him toward you, but put a little tension on the leash while you stand still and call him. He'll fight it at first, rolling over, yelping, freezing, etc., but be patient and praise him, especially when he comes toward you and thus receives two reinforcements at once: a more comfortable leash and more praise.

If you're planning on a show career, let him lead out and gently pull you, with the only corrections being in direction and in teaching him to keep his head up (nose off the ground) while trotting. Later, teach him to stay somewhere in the vicinity of your left side if you haven't already done this off-lead. I carry the food pans in my left hand and by doing so encourage young, off-leash pups to keep on that side. Pups will try to put obstacles between you in hopes of breaking the restraining connection (the leash), so give them plenty of chance to learn. Make the pup come around the tree and walk on *your* side of it.

With the pup you hope to groom for obedience work, you'll want to emphasize different gaits, not just trotting, and include more changes of direction. The number and types of obstacles should be gradually increased. The heel exercise groundwork can be laid early, but precision work is best delayed in preference to enjoyment. Tracking work, which involves tension on a long leash, can be started as early as you like.

In the early stages of leash training, some pups will scream and thrash about as if they're being eaten by an ogre, others will act whipped and stand motionless, and still others will quickly take to the leash. Let the wild one lead you where *he* wants to go, and pet the tense one while you keep a slight pull on the leash. In other words, let the puppy associate something pleasurable with the feel of the leash.

Housebreaking

I cannot resist yet another motto: PREVENT ONLY THE *FIRST* MISTAKE. With some dogs, it will be a matter of teaching them *where* to go rather than teaching them *not* to go. If you follow a few simple rules and have a little luck as well, your dog may fall into that classification.

Puppies raised outdoors are more easily trained to refrain from relieving themselves in the house, but if a pup has had access only to concrete surfaces, it will be difficult to teach him not to soil the basement or garage floors. So avoid leaving such a pup alone in these areas, at least at times when he may be stimulated to urinate or defecate.

Rule #1: Take the pup outside as soon as he wakens, and don't come back indoors until he urinates, defecates, or both. The younger the dog, the more important this regimen will be, and the more frequently you'll be taking him out. In the political world there's a maxim regarding the price of liberty being eternal vigilance. This can also be applied to housebreaking: if you desire the freedom from cleaning up after your pup in the house, keep an eye on him at all times. As he gets older he'll be able to wait longer, but when very young, he'll need to go after every nap. Build the habit with him, and he'll learn to go to the door when the urge strikes.

Rule #2: Take the pup out after eating or drinking. I've found that within five to fifteen minutes of drinking water, younger puppies will have to urinate. Many pups and even adults will have to defecate a few minutes after eating, though not if they've already had a bowel movement in the last few hours.

Rule #3: Take the pup out after play or exercise. Be especially watchful for signs of play reaching a peak, for that means another urge is making itself known to the pup's consciousness. Regularity of exercise is known to promote regularity of bowel movement, so you can apply this rule to prevent discomfort later in the dog's life.

Rule #4: Take the pup out before retiring to bed. He should be given a last-minute opportunity to void his bladder before settling down for the night. If he hasn't had a late drink, and the rest of the night is quiet, he shouldn't need to go out again until morning. During sleep, metabolism slows, brain waves change pattern and frequency, and blood pressure and other body functions change.

"But I don't WANT to be leash-trained!" Hercules von Salix at five months.

If you have to get up in the middle of the night and you wake the puppy in doing so, take him from his crate and let him go outside. You've disrupted that pattern and restarted his activity.

Rule #5: Take the pup out to the same spot in the yard each time (or to the gutter if you're a cliff-dweller in the concrete jungle). You will positively reinforce the habit or impression that it is okay to go there, where the scent from previous leavings linger. Likewise, the habit of *not* doing his business in the house will be strengthened. He will associate the biological urge to excrete with the psychological urge to do it in a certain approved area. The same association route will teach him such proper behavior as whining, fetching his leash, standing at the door, etc.

Housebreaking hints—I didn't want to make every recommendation a rule, so am adding these as mere hints. The above rules require positive action on your part which will result in a positive response on the part of the dog. Sometimes you will need to use negative reinforcement, but if so, remember the requirements: immediacy of correction, praise, and renewed opportunity. If you catch a young puppy in the act of squatting or striking that characteristic pose, grab him quickly by the scuff of the neck and lift him off the floor. If he's too big to lift that way, you've started housebreaking too late! Reaching under him to give maximum support will only get you a wet hand as well as a wet floor, but lifting by the skin at the back of the neck usually stops the flow because picking him up this way immediately changes his posture: his legs hang down close together and tend to inhibit continuing urination or defecation. Make sure he hears you say "No!" while he's in the pose or process, or better yet, while he's only thinking about it. As you carry him to the door, switch from the "No!" command to the word *outside* and then as you place him on the grass, say, "Outside. Good boy!" Be patient and give him time to finish.

Do not bring your hand down to slap the dog or even use the muzzle-squeeze while he's urinating. Releasing urine and squatting low are also means of showing submission, so you don't want the dog to associate correction and your expression of dominance with his urination, or the effect will be to teach him to urinate every time you correct him for something. Also forget the advice to slap him with a newspaper; it would only set your efforts back.

Never "stick his nose in it" despite that old advice. It would suffice to point at the puddle or mess, shame him verbally, then put him outside with "Good boy!" added as you put him on the grass. Confinement to a crate indoors when you can't be there watching him is an excellent way to insure housebreaking, but if you are or have been paper-training him, don't put paper in the crate.

When your pup has progressed to the point at which he *seems* to be housebroken, but you aren't really sure enough to grant him free access to the entire house while you are sleeping, you might want to do what man has done for almost as long as he has been associated with the dog: Tie him up. Between the confinement of the crate and free run of the house, the pup can be tied to a leg of a table or bed or anywhere else you want him to stay. You can also secure the dog in one spot by tying the rope to an object like the wooden dumbbell used in obedience work, then putting that object in an adjoining room with the door closed over the rope. Use a nylon rope, since polypropylene will kink and cotton clothesline rope is too easily severed by sharp puppy teeth. If in the morning you find the end wet, you can scold him to prevent it the following night. Keep chairs out of reach until the pup has outgrown or has been trained/corrected from chewing on rungs and getting tangled up. A rope length of about three feet will give enough freedom of movement yet keep him in one small area and thus help prevent him from soiling his sleeping quarters.

Special Problems

Chewing—Keeping chewables out of the pup's reach is the best way to teach him not to be destructive. Prevention is still better than a cure, but methods of correction must also be in your training kit. I have successfully used one of the more drastic but effective measures suggested by Bill Koehler, author of *The Koehler Method of Dog Training,* Howell Book Publishers, to correct a bad chewing habit when the dog could not be caught at the moment of destruction. Briefly, it involves taping the muzzle shut with the chewed article crosswise behind the teeth so it cannot be spit out or swallowed, and allowing time to replace the positive association of the taste with the negative discomfort.

Furniture—The best way for a pup to learn not to do something is for you to make sure that he never does it the *first* time; this is true for manners, housebreaking, and many other topics. If *you* prevent the first infraction, the dog will prevent the others. But it's not entirely too late for the dog

---

It is bad to let a dog taste leather.
—Demosthenes, 330 B.C.

---

owner who comes home to find the setter on the settee or the poodle on the pillows. There are steps one can take to correct bad habits; the number and variety are limited only by the imagination.

A neat trick I read about early in my dog breeding days worked pretty well for a couple of house dogs, one which grew up without instruction in manners because both of us worked outside the home. This trick involves the strategic placement of mousetraps. Place two on each cushion of every easy chair and the couch, then carefully lay one sheet of newspaper over each pair. When the dog gets on one of these, the noise and flutter will serve too purposes: (1) startle the dog while providing a correction itself, and (2) give the owner in another room a chance to make an immediate application of the reinforcement of correction. You can put those mousetraps to good use on chairs next to the food table, on garbage can lids, and other places that are out-of-bounds to your dog.

Barking—The biggest problem between neighbors and dogs (after that of the dog running at large), is the noise. First the dogs make the noise, then the neighbors make noise at each other, then if the problem is not resolved, the sounds of sirens and the judges' gavels are heard in the land.

The dog that barks at mailmen and other uniformed people has learned that when the intruder approaches his territory, and he barks, the intruder leaves. Although the first bark may have been a "Hello" or a question, the dog soon makes the association that it is his barking which drives the mailman away. His "belief" is reinforced each time the mailman leaves.

Barking is to be encouraged at certain times and can be tolerated at others, but these are usually dur-

ing the day. When your dog barks because a car pulls into your driveway or someone is at your door, you will want to reinforce this. But if he barks at everyone who saunters down the sidewalk, or at every distant sound, he must be corrected. Since this habit is usually formed during puppyhood, the natural correction is the muzzle squeeze and scolding.

Unfortunately, the habit is also likely to *start* at night, when you are least inclined to do more than yell at the dogs through the open window. Unfortunately, that just won't cut it. Sleepy or not, you must teach your dogs to be very discriminating in their evening activity, and when the dog(s) starts barking at some unseen cat or bird or each other, you will have to jump into your slippers and robe, rush outside yelling, "No!" and head for the kennel on the double. Your command should be loud enough for the dogs to hear it before they see your shadowy image streaking across the yard, but soft enough to be less disturbing to the neighbors than is the barking. Keep yelling "No!" throughout the muzzle-squeezing episode. If you squeeze hard enough and start the yelling and running while the barking is in progress, you may be lucky enough to teach this lesson in one night and perhaps as few as three trips. If there are several pups or if you can't recognize the voice of the barker, chastise all of them. Of course, the adults should probably be excluded, but even the pups who did *not* bark will associate the noise with the muzzle-squeeze pain and the command "No!"

I have made the midnight run many a night in unbelievably cold Toledo weather, where the kennels were down a steep hill about fifty yards from the house, and our bedroom was on the second floor at the opposite end. After each dog and each litter had learned the lesson, all that was required was to turn the yard light on and/or give a word from the window. On rare occasions, there was some good reason for them to bark, but I could recognize an urgency in their tone, and they wouldn't stop at a word anyway. I believe dogs can know when they're right or wrong, and when there is an exceptional incident warranting the breaking of a rule.

Begging—The dog that has to be continually pushed away from the table has not been properly taught. If it's not such a big deal at your house,

British champion bitch with the topline found in too many German lines lately. Von Stephanitz called this form a "hyena dog."

you might tolerate an inquisitive glance when you are serving or eating something aromatic at your table. But if the dog reaches his nose over the edge of the table, give it a quick, sharp tap with a couple of fingers, and he'll understand. Of course, it's best to teach the dog from puppyhood to lie on a long-down until your supper is finished.

Dinner etiquette—It is natural for many pups to growl over dinner, especially if it involves meat or a nice fresh knuckle bone. But when an eighty-pound male adult exhibits his year-old habit of menacing whomever he considers to be potential bone thieves, and possibly carries out his threat by snapping at a child, you no longer have a pet— you have a dangerous, uncontrolled beast. The opposite of wild is domesticated, which means "to be at home" or "in the house," and implies doing so at peace with humans and other animals.

Give your youngster a piece of meat or a carefully selected bone with scraps still on it, or something else he will eat or gnaw on with gusto, then take it away from him, with your hand very much in view and accessible to his teeth. Giving it back shows him he has nothing to worry about, and taking it demonstrates your authority over him; both are lessons of value. At least partly cover the morsel so when he lunges for the food, his teeth will meet you instead. Of course, this is not acceptable and

he must be corrected if he doesn't immediately recognize his error. A very young puppy that has not yet learned to temper his grip is more likely to bite the hand, while a slightly older one will probably be surprised or embarrassed to find he has chomped on your hand instead of the morsel.

You may wish to give your pup a second chance before correction, but if he does it again, the muzzle-squeezing technique combined with a stern "No!" will change his habit. Make him wait, with your fist near his mouth, before opening your hand. Allow him to resume his chewing while you pet him and say "Good dog" (unless he growls again). Touch his food, his nose, lips, etc., with your fingers while he finishes.

Feeding tidbits—Dogs often snap at treats because they've been conditioned by nervous people to expect the food to be dropped before it reaches the mouth. Thus the cycle: the dog tries harder and moves faster, which scares the feeder and makes him jerk his hand away or drop the treat, or both. Try holding the tidbit enclosed in your hand. If the dog grabs for it and his teeth meet your knuckles and fingers, tell him gently but firmly, "No," and encourage him to nuzzle your fingers open, but with his nose, not his teeth. Gradually expose more and more of successive tidbits so the dog will eventually take treats gingerly from anyone. Teach your children and friends to do this the same way you do, and not to pull their hands back or drop the treats.

"Piddling"—The tendency of a puppy to urinate when excited or frightened can be exasperating, especially if the pup is old enough that you've expected him to have outgrown the annoyance. I have found this to be an inherited tendency. But correcting the problem of dribbling puppies is a matter of the trainer teaching himself patience above all else, for the pup's incontinence increases in proportion to the handler's agitation. Be cool and calm, not overbearing or obviously concerned.

There are a couple of reasons why a pup loses full control of his or her urethral sphincters; one is fear. The timid, nervous puppy should be praised, never harshly scolded. When you approach him, do so with a friendly tone of voice, softly repeating such words as "Good boy," "Here, puppy," and using his name. At the first indication that he will squat or roll over, if he crouches, suddenly walks wide in the rear, or actually starts dribbling, turn around and run playfully in the other direction while you continue to call him and clap your hands. This first principle is: KEEP HIM MOVING. It is very hard for even a shy animal to urinate while he is running or walking. The second principle is: DIVERT HIS ATTENTION. Turn the introduction or approach into a game which the pup will not associate with fear or with the urge to urinate.

Some puppies are not really shy but are so easily excited at the approach of a favorite human that they will "leak" from a few drops to a big puddle. Use the same two principles of motion and diversion that you would with a shy dog, but you can add an even more effective principle: IGNORE HIM. When you come home, make it a point to totally ignore the pup, even if he stands on his head. When he calms down to the point where *he* ignores *you*, or takes your presence for granted, then you can begin talking to him and playing with him. I advise people with such excitable dogs to putter around the kennel or yard in view of the pup, but not looking at him at first. Gradually work your way closer to the gate and if he is calm enough, open it and let him near you as you continue to walk around. If you notice that he takes time out to urinate normally, wait till he finishes, tell him

he's a good pup, and *then* start playing with him. If he doesn't empty his bladder, he may not have enough left to produce the urge, but may still have enough to dribble. Take him for a walk, but by all means do so with great calm and deliberation, and don't even talk to or look at him at first. If he's indoors, get him outside before you communicate with him. Be patient, and you'll find these techniques will help a pup outgrow piddling.

Females are more likely to lose some urine when excited. Many young bitches will tend to squat if you reach down to pet them even if you've been present for awhile and they've been moving around. If there are other puppies competing for your recognition, such a bitch may squat and dribble when she gets her individual attention. Here's where a quick reaction time comes in handy. Suddenly thrust an arm under her belly and lift her into an arched-back standing position. Have your arm against her stifles, as far back as you can, and don't worry about pressure on the bladder. For females, this position is not conducive to urinating. *If* you speak to her, be sure you don't use either a scolding or excited tone of voice. It would be better not to say anything, and perhaps not make much eye contact at first, but simply release her after a few seconds and move away or turn your attention to something else. Your rapid reflexes and the mild confusion/diversion resulting from an unexpected position and support will do two things at once: change the pup's behavioral or psychological pattern, and interfere with either the physiological or positional response.

The urination-submission reaction is not found so much in the German Shepherd Dog, but is more common in some sporting breeds. I believe there is a difference between this response and the others mentioned above, though some may argue that it is a matter of degree. With this reaction, the pup, or even an adult in some extreme cases, will turn over onto his back or side and urinate slightly when approached. He generally will also "smile," lick at the air, and feebly wag the tail.

Biting during play—Dogs don't have hands with opposing thumbs and prehensile fingers, so they use their mouths to grasp and hold. The way the dam shows authority and trains her whelps is by clamping her teeth on their muzzles or heads. I recently observed a pack of timber wolves at play and before long could identify the "alpha" female (the male was absent at the time) and several of the others in order of dominance. Besides using other body language such as bowing with tail and ears down, or assertion with tail and ears up, they gave evidence of the hierarchy by their biting methods. The more dominant wolf would bite from the top, grabbing the other on the back of the neck or loin. When more than one "attacked" a member further down in the hierarchy, the subservient one lay with belly exposed and paws up. She (or he) would also exhibit some biting action, but mostly light snapping at the air. Soon she would be allowed up so she could resume chasing and being chased.

When a dog bites another dog in play, he can tell how much pressure to apply by the reaction he elicits in the other. If the second dog yelps louder or cries, or snaps back with greater force as if to say, "Hey, that was too hard!" the first will ease up. In the same way, the puppy learns that he can get away with just so much pressure when he bites your fingers, and none at all when your nose is involved. You need to apply the same process of

effective, gentle correction to teach a dog that he must use much less of his power when playing with little children than he would with their father. He probably already has learned that he can use more of his strength on kennelmates than he would on you.

Children can cooperate if they're old enough to understand what you're trying to teach the dog, but with very young ones you'll have to watch their reaction to the dog's use of his teeth. If the bites seem to hurt the child a little, lightly squeeze the muzzle and put the two back together again. If the dog's teeth get too close to the kid's face when they're play-fighting, use that same correction. The pup should have learned by then that biting at faces is serious and will bring correction. If the dog has already been taught that muzzle-squeezing is the automatic result of wrongdoing, all you need do is hold the mouth shut while you look into his eyes and quietly, seriously say, "No." Pressure need not be applied in later stages of training if it was adequately used in the initial stages of basic train-

Multiple Best in Show winner, 1974 Select, Am. & Can. Ch. Ro-San's El Sabre of Charay, CD, OFA. This large impressive, heterozygous sable son of Elwillo's Rand is shown here by Fran Foster under judge Dennis Grivas.
Owner, Rose Levandowski

ing. The *threat* of punishment is sufficient, if the dog knows what the ''punishment'' entails.

GRADUATION DAY

If you have been successful in teaching your dog to keep off furniture, and to let you know when he has to go out; if he's outgrown chewing on things that don't belong in his tummy or toy collection; and if you have encouraged him to bark or growl at suspicious noises, then (to continue the Kipling parody) you have a German Shepherd Dog, my

son! A dog of this breed is at his best when he serves man as protector as well as companion and coworker.

This is the end of basic training for young puppies, and, very nearly, the end of this book. You may now wish to study some good obedience manuals to further the training which will be your dog's development through adolescence and adulthood.

Enjoy your dog. Remember, he is not only a representative of a great breed, he is an individual—your friend.

Ch. Oskar vom Busecker Schloss. Line bred 3-3 on Sieger Arno v. Haus Gersie, and with lines to Jonny v.d. Riedperle and Donar v.d. Firnskuppe, this dog exhibited the masculinity, soundness, and working dog qualities the Busecker Schloss lines are famous for.

Photo courtesy Norton of Kent.

20

TROUBLE-SHOOTING GUIDE TO YOUR DOG'S HEALTH

HOW TO USE THE GUIDE

This guide is separated into sections based on where symptoms of disease are most likely to be seen: in the stool, coat, etc. Look for the section, then the symptom, then by process of elimination, narrow the possibilities to one or two disorders you feel are closest to what you see in the dog. Then refer to the chapter(s) dealing specifically with your possibilities to determine what to discuss with your veterinarian. Remember that the symptoms listed are merely *possibilities*, *not* diagnoses.

Symptom	**GENERAL APPEARANCE**	*Possible Diagnoses*
Bloated abdomen		• Torsion/volvulus (adult).
		• Overeating/drinking (adult & pups).
		• Worms (pups).
with swollen legs		• Edema of heart disease (adult).
Atrophy (wasting away)		• Old age.
		• Inactivity.
		• Coonhound paralysis.
		• Hyperestrinism.
		• Secondary change to heart disease.
		• Esophageal dilation (pups).
Lumps		• Tumors (benign or cancerous).
		• Cysts.
hard, swollen spleen		• Erlichiosis; splenic torsion.
Swelling		
on face, muzzle		• Insect or spider bites.
goiterlike throat		• Venomous snake bite.

Symptom	**BEHAVIOR**	*Possible Diagnoses*
Biting, scratching, licking		• Normal cleaning exercises.
		• Fleas or other insect bites.
		• Stings.
		• Mange (see "Skin: Hot spots").

Mostly on flanks	• Whipworm or tapeworm.
	• Impacted thorns, stickers, briars, etc.
	• Anal sac impaction.
Mostly on feet, pasterns with cracked calluses on foot pads or elbows	• Atopic autoimmune disorder.
	• Chemically/mechanically irritated skin.
Around genitals	• Vaginal/penile infection.
	• Perianal fistula.
Between toes	• Fungus; interdigital pyoderma.

Scooting rear along ground	• Anal gland impaction; tapeworms.

Loss of appetite	• Fatigue; very hot weather.
	• Gastrointestinal upset: poisoning, torsion.
	• Hypervitaminosis.
	• Erlichiosis.

Incoordination	• Distemper; spinal tumor or other central nervous system disorder; GSD myelopathy; vestibular disease; eye disorders.
With shaking/convulsions	• Poisoning; leptospirosis; Coonhound Paralysis.

Fever	• A multitude of possibilities, the list would be so long as to be meaningless.

"But, Mom, the door was open, so we just thought..." Photo courtesy Sharon Peterson & Laurie Van Steenis

COAT AND SKIN

Dog owners should become accustomed to examining the dog's integument (outer covering including hair, pads, nose, mouth) and regular grooming is one way to insure such inspection. But it helps to know what you're looking for and experi-ence will make you more sensitive to various con-ditions. Eventually you should be able to find ticks, cysts, scabs, and other imperfections simply by petting a dog.

Symptom	*Possible Diagnoses*
Hair loss Widespread &/or general	• Normal shedding reaction to weather changes, insufficient brushing. • Allergies (may develop late in life). • Vitamin A deficiency (rare unless secondary to pancreas insufficiency). • Lack of outdoor living. • Toxic or corrosive chemical contact (feel and smell the coat). • Estrogen imbalance: too much may stimulate hair loss in late-stage pregnancy, too little may result from spaying too young showing up later in life as a thin haircoat.
with calluses & swollen elbows	• Friction—lying down in such a way as to rub hair from elbows & hocks or right side of neck where the obedience collar rubs.
After surgery	• Tranquilizer- or anesthesia-induced; could also be stress-related.
Around croup and thighs	• Flea-bite sensitivity & consequent biting & scratching. Hair loss often accompanied by red marks, flea excreta, inflammation on chest under elbows.
On belly & around vulva	• Normal during pregnancy during whelping date.
Around eyes, cheeks, bottoms of ears, elbows, back	• Mange (see "Skin: Hot spots.").
On chest in combination with excess activity, nervousness, weight loss	• Hyperthyroidism (very rare in GSDs).
Brittle hair, sparse coat (often associated with darkened, thickened skin)	• Hypothyroidism (not very common in GSDs).
Loss in patches or circles also dry, greasy, or foul-smelling	• Ringworm or other fungal diseases. • Seborrhea (rare in GSDs); ovarian cysts; hyper-estrinism.
Around genitals in males	• Cryptorchidism; estrogen imbalance.
On torso in combination with skin lesions &/or capillary bleeding	• Medication reaction; abnormal adrenal glands.

Poor coat
   Widespread &/or general
- Insufficient brushing; heart disease; protein deprivation (rare unless as a result of parasitic infestation).

   Non-glossy
- Diet deficient in fatty acids & oils, in combination with too-frequent bathing.

   Brittleness
- Too much dry heat either from being indoors in winter or overexposure to sun's rays.

   Open coat (hairs curled up at ends or standing away from body
- Internal parasites.

Bumps under the skin
   Anywhere on body
   On abdomen
   On chin, lips/muzzle, chest, and near the feet
- Infected hair follicle; impacted thorn or briar; sebaceous cysts; tumors; cancers; hematomas.
- Umbilical hernia.
- Papillomas.

Inflammation
   General red, itchy skin
      with discharge of eyes, nose, throat; nibbling at nails, licking at paws, rubbing muzzle or chin on carpeting
- Flea-bite dermatitis; insecticide irritation.
- Allergies.

   Red ring up to 2″ diameter with hair loss within ring
- Ringworm.

   Red patches usually on the neck and back
- "Hot spots"; may be due to demodectic mange flare-up.

   Red spots with a yellow center on hairless parts of belly in pups
- Impetigo.

   Redness (in adolescent pups)
- Demodectic mange.

Sores
   General
- Impacted thorn or other foreign body, if not removed could cause an abscess.

   On elbows, hocks, stifles
   On toes, wrists, hocks
- Calluses.
- Lick granuloma.

Pad problems
   Redness
- Irritation from salted surfaces in winter; fresh (non-neutralized or acid-washed) concrete; running on abrasive surfaces.

   Hard & cracked
- Diabetes; "hard-pad distemper" virus; hypothyroidism.

The author judging at the FCI-Asian Show, Tokyo 1987 with translator. Steward/Secretary in background; German judges (seated) observing. Note the nice big ring size.

STOOL

Stool examination is possibly the best way an owner can keep an eye on the general health of his dog. For one thing, the odor can tell you much; if it is different from what it has been, try to determine if it smells like blood (usually coccidiosis in pups, worms in adults), or if it simply smells like something the dog has eaten.

Pick the stools apart: is there a lot of grass, straw, hair, sand, insect wings, or beetle shells? Is corn present in large pieces and amounts? Is there any mucus or excess water? Overeating of liver may cause temporary looseness but most stools of a healthy German Shepherd Dog should have *some* form. Color mostly depends on the color of the dog's food and artificially-red meals sometimes mask blood in the stool.

If you have a microscope and do your own stool flotations for worm analysis, also look for undigested starches, fats, pieces of cellulose, and debris. If your regular dog food has been changed by the manufacturer, the dog's appetite or health may be affected. If the dog food is the same but one dog's stool has changed, it may mean that that dog has a health problem.

Symptom	Possible Diagnoses
Loose stool & diarrhea	• Distemper. • Heatstroke (most frequent at dog shows & after working hard. • Emotional stress, especially in "high strung" dogs away from their usual location. • Giardia, a protozoan disease. • Different drinking water (seldom). • Perianal fistula.
With coughing, gagging, & distended belly in pups	• Roundworms.
Very runny, sometimes bloody, with open, dull coat	• Hookworms.
Runny, grey or tan with mucus & a terrible, acrid odor	• Coccidiosis.
Sudden onset, usually bloody, tan, or grayish-tan	• Parvo virus; corona virus; or similar mutants.
Pasty & pale with a fatty consistency	• Adenovirus; pancreatitis.
With vomiting	• Consumption of spoiled food, garbage.
Watery & with nervous system disorders	• Poisoning with insecticides, chemicals or other toxic material.
Stool relatively unchanged, but with excess water and a sour smell	• Overeating.
Foamy consistency	• Bacterial disease such as leptospirosis.
Containing blood	• Advanced kidney disease. • Fungus disease such as histoplasmosis. This type of problem is seen most often in specific areas of the country: Mississippi River valley, Ohio River valley, St. Lawrence River area, Great Lakes area, and around the Appalachians. It can also be contracted in places where many birds roost or around chicken coops.

Constipation or obstruction	• Consumption of bone chips or bone meal; lack of exercise; voluntary retention due to emotional stress (fear of making a mistake) or being kept too long in a crate beyond the dog's normal elimination time. • Perianal fistula.
Small, very dense stool	• Diet may be too low in bulk & too high in high-BV foods (eggs, cottage cheese, meat).
Straining to produce a watery stool in low volume	• Consumption of non-digestibles other than bone.
Drumlike tautness of the abdomen, attempts at vomiting, straining that yields a little watery stool of bad odor	• Enlarged prostate gland; tumors; intussusception; twisted intestines.

Blood in stool (see also "Loose stool & diarrhea")	
With diarrhea (in pups)	• Hookworm.
With poor coat (in adults)	• Hookworm.
With diarrhea (in adults)	• Parvo virus.
With bright specks & considerable streaks	• Roundworm.
Bright red color	• Injury to or disease of the anus or rectum.
with itching	• Polyps or other anorectal disease.
Dark red or almost black color	• Upper digestive system bleeding
brighter dark red color	• Lower digestive system bleeding.
Dark, tarry color, often also runny or stringy	• Normal condition in a bitch that has recently whelped a litter and eaten the placenta.

Flatus (gas) (see also "Loose stool & diarrhea")	• Overeating; consumption of rotten food; consumption of a lot of meat or milk or other foods that commonly cause this problem in humans (cabbage, beans, etc.). • Intestinal worms.
Coprophagy (stool eating) Dog eats *his own* stools Dog eats *others'* stools	• Pancreatic problems. • There does not seem to be any one "cause" for this symptom. Some see it as the result of boredom. I have seen it as the end result of play, especially in winter when frozen stools are tossed in the air, then chewed, then eaten. Cat and rabbit stools awaken this interest in most dogs.

Can. O.T. Ch. Antigua Al-hama vom Tanzhaus, UD 1967-1979. This big red dog, linebred on Bernd, and a grandson of Ulk and Vox Wikingerblut, made friends for himself and the breed everywhere he went, delighting schoolyard and drive-in theatre playground users by his obviously great love of climbing ladders. In competition he usually lost points when the crowd's applause stimulated him to do "extra credit" routines not asked for by the judge, though at one trial he managed to stay in control long enough to earn a score of 199½, one half point behind the 1968 U.S. Obedience Victrix, whom he sometimes trained with.
Photo by owner/author.

EYES

Symptoms	Possible Diagnoses
Cloudy, gradually developing	• Inherited corneal dystrophy. • Scratches; ulcers; other causes of inflammation; distemper (rare). • Coccidioidomycosis, a fungal disorder seen mainly in the Southwest. • Vitamin A deficiency (rare); vitamin B_2 deficiency. • Cataracts (various types): juvenile developmental cataracts; diabetic cataracts; senile cataracts. • Trauma due to a puncture or non-puncture wound.
With frequent nose licking	• Failure of tear ducts or glands to lubricate the eyeball.
With light bluish film	• "Blue-eye"; adenovirus (infectious canine hepatitis) or its vaccine CAV-1.
With bluish-grey haze in middle-aged or old dogs	• Nuclear sclerosis.
With slightly pink color	• Pannus (fairly common to GSDs).
With light, cream-of-tomato-soup color to the retina & milky appearance to the fluid around the lens	• Lipemia, a blood disease rare in GSDs.
With an increase in tear production	• Heartworm microfilaria.
With inflammation of the iris & associated tissues	• Tonsillitis; general infection; coccidioidomycosis, blastomycosis, etc.
Redness	• Conjunctivitis.
With tearing or weeping	• Irritation by a foreign object. • Allergies; purpura; kidney disease in the advanced stages; viral disease; erlichiosis.
With discharge of pus	• Fungal disorders such as coccidioidomycosis, blastomycosis. • Infection: nose & throat or bacterial infections in the blood such as septicemia.
With yellowish mucus discharge	• Hookworm infestation (severe).
Blindness	• PRA (retinal atrophy) if nightblindness is seen first. • Cryptococcosis or blastomycosis. • Glaucoma (rare in GSDs) • Chronic pancreatitis. • Pituitary tumor with optic nerve atrophy.
Poor vision (sudden onset) with blinking &/or confusion	• CNS disruption such as an imminent epileptic event.
Yellowish tinge to the white of the eye	• Liver malfunction or disease.
Very pale pink lids	• Anemia. Check also for vaginal or uterine infection, or hookworm as they are also causes of anemia.

Swelling around eyes Sudden onset	• Eosinophilic myositis. • Insect bite or sting.
Inflammation of eyelid	• Demodectic or sarcoptic mange.
Nictitating membrane flicking over the eye; pupils contracted	• Tetanus. Other signs to look for: retraction of eyeballs and lips, and difficulty swallowing and opening the mouth.
Nystagmus (eyeball oscillation)	• Normal in blind individuals. • Retinal detachment; congenital opacity of the cornea; inner ear disease.
Nictitating membrane protruding over the eyeball	• Rabies; Horner's Syndrome (a CNS disorder); eosinophilic myositis; irritation.
Dilated pupils	• Imminent epileptic seizure; other CNS disorder; cryptococcosis; rabies; distemper; PRA or other retinal disease; poisoning; poor assimilation of vitamin A; intestinal blockage with resultant bacterial sepsis.

EARS

Problems with the outer ears are almost never indicative of a generalized condition, hence are not usually used to diagnose disease at a different site. However, one exception is the bitch with leathery, swollen, cracked skin lining the insides of her ear shells, and a leathery, semi-bald texture to the outer sides. These symptoms I now attribute to hormonal upset which could involve cystic ovaries or a hormonal production change in the ovaries or thyroid.

Symptom	*Possible Diagnoses*
Deafness	• Normal from age nine. • Trauma: eardrum puncture, nearby explosion, etc. • Distemper or other infections. • Prolonged use of sulfa or other drugs.
Ear tips eaten away or pebbly feel to the surface or rash-type appearance	• Fly-bite dermatitis.
Unpleasant odor with excessive, dark wax build-up	• Fungus.
Excessive shaking of head	• Earmites; presence of water or other foreign material (seed, insect, etc.).
Fluid-filled pouch in the pinna	• Hematoma; seratoma.

Symptom **GAIT AND ACTIVITY** *Possible Diagnoses*	
Foreleg lameness	• Trauma: sprains, pulled muscles & tendons. • Nails too long.
And throwing elbows outward while gaiting	• Ununited anconeal process, appears around 3 months of age & progressively worsens.
With pain mostly in the *middle* of the leg shaft	• Panosteitis, appears suddenly between 5 months and 1½ years of age.

With pain at *bottom* end of long bones; often accompanied by diarrhea, splayed feet & swollen wrists	• HOD (rare in GSDs), appears between 2½ and 5½ months.
With stiffness in the shoulder after rest, or worsens after exercise	• Osteochondritis dissecans, appears around 4 to 7 months of age in males.

Rear limb lameness	• Trauma: sprains, pulled muscles &/or tendons; HOD: pano; HD.
	• Arthritis (in older dogs).
With kidney disease, thyroid disease, or over- or under-abundance of minerals	• Metabolic bone disease.
With pain or arising, climbing, jumping, or running; or walking with a short stride with knees & lower legs close together	• Hip dysplasia in a 5- to 10-month-old.
	• GSD myelopathy in older dogs.
	• Coonhound paralysis has similar symptoms.
With instability of knee & different temperature of knee upon touch	• Ruptured cruciate ligaments.
In old dogs: stiff gait & inability to jump	• Spondylosis deformans.
Partial or complete paralysis of rear limbs	• GSD myelopathy.

Lethargy	• Intestinal worms or coccidia in pups.
	• Heart disease or heartworm.
	• von Willebrand's Disease (VWD).
	• Mineral imbalance such as hypokalemia.
	• Head trauma; toxins; poisons; ticks.
	• Orthopedic problems; leptospirosis; infected teeth or gums; parvovirus, corona or other viruses; erlichiosis or other bacterial diseases; pyometra - an often fatal uterine infection.
With chronic gastric upset	• Gastritis.
With excessive thirst	• Kidney disease.
With distended abdomen, white-foamy vomit, lying in cool, shaded dirt	• Gastric torsion - EMERGENCY!
With partial paralysis	• Coonhound paralysis; myasthenia gravis.
With inside of lips & eyelids paler than normal with shivering	• Anemia.
	• Shock - EMERGENCY!
After being wet to the skin	• Hypothermia.
With fever & discharge from nose & eyes	• Early stage of distemper.
With vomiting	• Liver disease.
In pups under 2 weeks old, with deep breathing & lack of interest in nursing	• Fading puppy syndrome.
In pups with liver disease or chilling, exhaustion, intestinal upset. In adults after long hours of hard work without occasional high energy foods	• Hypoglycemia (low blood sugar).

Excessive thirst	• Normal behavior for puppies.
	• Kidney disease.
	• Diabetes.
	• Recent ingestion of salt or salty foods.

Symptom	**DIGESTIVE SYSTEM**	*Possible Diagnoses*

Vomiting
- This is a fairly common occurrence in the dog; it can be either innocuous or a sign of serious trouble. Continued vomiting should be reported to your veterinarian.
- Excessive intake of grass; overeating in puppies; roundworms or tapeworms in pups; simple motion sickness in pups; poisoning; trauma such as being hit by a car; in pups given their first solid food.

With other allergy indications
- Allergic reaction.

With white, foamy mucus & retching
- Gastric torsion.

With retching & possible production of feces in vomitus
- Digestive tract obstruction.

With diarrhea
- Corona virus.

With high fever
- Parvo virus.

With continued retching after vomiting
- G.I. tract irritants: spoiled food, aspirin, chemicals, poisons, bone chips, etc.

In noise-sensitive or nervous dogs
- Emotional stress.

Blood in vomitus
- Ingestion of physical object or chemical irritant; ulcers; lung disease.

If no other cause can be found consider
- Kidney failure; liver damage; diabetes.

During mid-pregnancy
- Morning sickness.

Bad breath
- Infected teeth; tartar build up; infections in other systems or gums or lips.
- Ingestion of spoiled food; change in diet (especially to canned food).
- Kidney disease; diabetes; vitamin deficiencies (rare).
- Eating garbage; coprophagy.

Gums: Color change

More red than usual, often tender & swollen
- Poor dental hygiene; tartar build up.

Less red than usual
- Anemia. Check for shock, external bleeding, worms, vaginal infection, abnormal estrus.

Drooling
- Normal in hot weather.
- Foreign object in throat or between teeth.
- Motion sickness; Pavlovian reaction.

With foaming
- Rabies; toad-biting; distemper; torsion.

With blinking, chewing, dilated pupils, nervousness & other symptoms (sometimes vomiting)
- Possible imminent epileptic seizure.

Symptom	**RESPIRATORY SYSTEM**	*Possible Diagnoses*

Symptom	Possible Diagnoses
Milk froth at nostrils in newborns	• Cleft palate.
Coughing	• Inhaled irritant (i.e., smoke); roundworms in pups.
Dry, hacking, non-productive	• Parainfluenza (kennel cough).
Less forceful cough with swallowing	• Tonsil infection.
Wheezing	• Bronchitis; tickling from foreign object (such as hair) in the throat.
Soft sounding, but deep, worsens with exercise	• Heartworm; emphysema (rare).
Blood in sputum	• Blastomycosis; lung flukes; heartworm.
Gagging	• Allergies; foreign body in the throat; trauma to the larynx.
Breathing difficulties/abnormalities	
Labored breathing	• Torsion, shock, blastomycosis.
Shallow breathing	• Broken rib; emphysema (rare); pleurisy.
Heavy panting	• Heatstroke.
Loud breathing with a sound of fluid or mucus accumulation	• Respiratory infection.
Windy, whispering breathing (in dogs that bark excessively)	• Laryngitis.
Long intake of air followed by a gurgling or squishy sound in the lungs	• Pneumonia.
Dry nose	• Fever.
Discharge from nose with accumulated matter in eyes	• Could indicate any number of problems, either respiratory or non-respiratory. Look for other symptoms.
Sneezing	• Allergies; respiratory irritant (i.e., smoke).
With excess mucus	• Systemic disorder.
Loss of nose pigmentation (from frostbite or lack of sunlight)	• Snow-nose: occurs mostly in lighter-pigmented dogs.

CIRCULATORY SYSTEM

It is difficult for most non-veterinarians to diagnose circulatory problems. A stethoscope is only the first step in arriving at a diagnosis and much practice is necessary for proficiency.

Symptom	*Possible Diagnoses*
General edema (fluid accumulation) anywhere on body	• Heart disease.
Easy tiring	• Heart ailments (look for other signs).
Abnormally long bleeding	• Hemophilia; von Willebrand's Disease.

Symptom	**NERVOUS SYSTEM**	*Possible Diagnoses*
Paralysis		• Spinal injury, disc damage; spinal deterioration; spondylosis.
		• German Shepherd Dog myelopathy.
		• Coonhound paralysis.
		• Myasthenia gravis.
With convulsions, frothing, &/or shaky gait		• Poisoning, either chemical or natural toxins such as toads, snakes, insects.
Seizures		• In pups, heavy worm infestation.
		• Poisoning from insecticides, other chemicals.
		• Epilepsy or other brain damage.
		• Hypoglycemia.

Would you dare say "no" to him?
Photo courtesy Patricia Calvert.

Symptom	**URO-GENITAL SYSTEM** *Possible Diagnoses*
Urinary abnormalities	
Frequent urination or inability to control urination	• Kidney disease; pyometra; diabetes.
Piddling	• Normal for some excitable or overly submissive dogs.
Cessation of urine	• Dehydration; circulatory disorder.
Blood in urine	• Normal in estrus.
	• Cystitis.
	• Bladder stones.
	• Prostate gland problems.
Dribbling, straining, frequent attempts	• Abnormal prepuce.
	• Stones in bladder or urethra.
	• Kidney disease.
	• Prostatitis.
Estrus/breeding problems	
Abnormally long or continuous estrus	• Ovarian cysts; bleeding disorder (i.e., hemophilia).
Yellowish discharge from vulva	• Vaginal infection which can prevent fertilization or inhibit breeding desire in males due to "incorrect" odor.
Absence or irregularity of estrus	• Underactive thyroid; insufficient estrogen; hyperestrinism; ovarian cyst or tumor.
Obstruction of penile penetration	• Vaginal rings (not uncommon in GSDs).
Lethargy, depression, poor appetite, excess urination, problems with conception	• Pyometra.
Testicle/penile problems	
Straw-colored discharge from the prepuce	• Low-grade infection called balanitis or balanoposthitis, found in adult males with great regularity. Ignore it if mild.
Inflamed testicles	• Abrasion; contact with lawn chemicals; frostbite.
	• Cystitis; prostatitis.
Protruding tip	• Seldom a real problem - simply cosmetic.
Overgrowth of the prepuce	• Surgery required to open the sheath so erection may be obtained.

Kingland's Empossible Dream, a son of V-1 Roon vom Haus Solms, SchH-II.   *Photo courtesy Mrs. E.H. King.*

INDEX

Looking for something? If the Table of Contents is not specific enough, this index may help. If you don't see the word you want, try a similar word. Kennel names are used when they are more readily recognized than a dog's "first" name. Others, such as "Lance" or "Manhattan" may be more commonly known.

ABOUT THE AUTHOR

Fred Lanting had planned to become a veterinarian, worked in an animal hospital after high school, and started premedical curriculum in college. While teaching sciences and English in New Jersey high schools and college, Fred pursued postgraduate studies in chemistry and physics. After some years he made another career change enabling him to move his human and canine family to the Midwest, where he had the land and facilities to fulfill his dream of breeding and showing dogs. His work with dogs and veterinarians in the ensuing years led him to write *Canine Hip Dysplasia*, published by Alpine Publications in 1981.

Fred enjoys walks in the woods with his dogs, writing poetry, and judging dog shows. Currently, he is a member of the Shaferhund Verein (SV); director of the West Virginia Canine College; and president of the GSDC of Northern Alabama. He and his wife live in Union Grove, Alabama.